D0208928

Currents in Medieval
Japanese History
Essays in Honor of Jeffrey P. Mass

Gordon M. Berger, Andrew Edmund Goble,
Lorraine F. Harrington, G. Cameron Hurst III
Editors

**A Publication of the University of Southern California
East Asian Studies Center**

FIGUEROA
PRESS

CURRENTS IN MEDIEVAL JAPANESE HISTORY
Essays in Honor of Jeffrey P. Mass

Published by
FIGUEROA PRESS
840 Childs Way, 3rd Floor
Los Angeles, CA 90089
Phone: (213) 743-4800
Fax: (213) 743-4804
www.figueroapress.com

Figueroa Press is a division of the USC Bookstore

Produced by Crestec Los Angeles, Inc.

Printed in the United States of America

Library of Congress Cataloguing-in-Publication Data
CURRENTS IN MEDIEVAL JAPANESE HISTORY: Essays in Honor of Jeffrey P. Mass
Includes bibliographical references and index
ISBN-13: 978-1-932800-52-4
ISBN-10: 1-932800-52-2
Library of Congress Control Number: 2009922922

To the family of Jeffrey Mass, as a token of the warmth with which we remember our friend, colleague, and mentor

CONTENTS

ACKNOWLEDGMENTS

This volume has come to fruition as the result of the collective efforts of many people. All deserve our deepest gratitude, but in addition, certain of our collaborators have gone beyond the scope of contributors as authors. Karl Friday oversaw the compilation of the Bibliography. Bruce Batten served as the cartographer and produced the maps in the volume. For the cover, Andrew Goble made the selection, Mikael Adolphson gained permission to reproduce a scene from the *Ippen shōnin eden* scroll owned by Yūgyōji, the temple graciously granted that permission, and Bruce Batten facilitated the mechanics of obtaining and conveying the actual image. Stanley Rosen and Grace Ryu at the East Asian Studies Center at the University of Southern California have made it possible for the volume to appear under the auspices of the Center. We appreciate also the financial assistance provided by the Center. We have been fortunate to benefit from the enthusiasm and high creative standards of Figueroa Press and of Arnie Olds, in the design and production of the book. We also wish to thank the anonymous readers of the manuscript for their thoughtful and constructive criticisms.

Cappy Hurst's editorial colleagues want to make special mention of the great contributions that he has made to the realization of this volume, often in the face of daunting health problems.

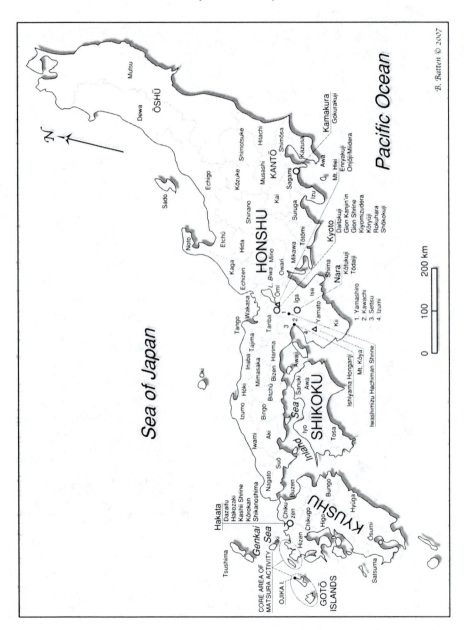

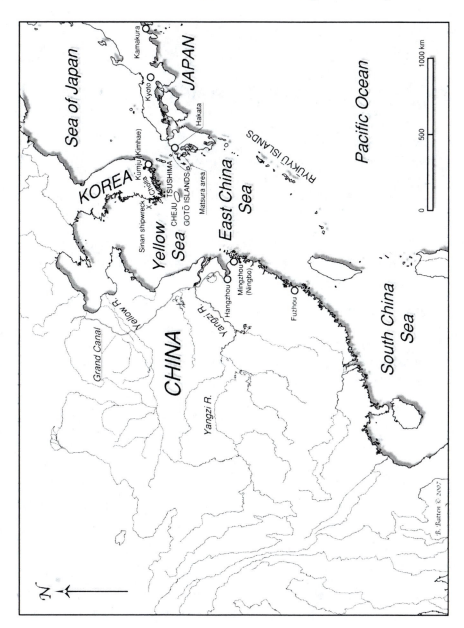

CONTRIBUTORS

Mikael Adolphson (Ph.D. Stanford 1996) is Associate Professor of Japanese History at the University of Alberta.

Bruce L. Batten (Ph.D. Stanford 1989) is Professor of History and Vice President for International Relations at J. F. Oberlin University, Tokyo.

Gordon Berger (Ph.D. Yale 1972) is Emeritus Professor of History at the University of Southern California.

Thomas D. Conlan (Ph.D. Stanford 1998) is Associate Professor of Japanese History and Asian Studies at Bowdoin College.

Karl F. Friday (Ph.D. Stanford 1989) is Professor of History at the University of Georgia.

Andrew Edmund Goble (Ph.D. Stanford 1987) is Associate Professor of History and of Religious Studies at the University of Oregon.

Lorraine F. Harrington (Ph.D. Stanford 1983) is a management consultant in southern California.

G. Cameron Hurst III (Ph.D. Columbia 1972) is Professor of Japanese and Korean Studies and Co-Chairman of East Asian Studies at the University of Pennsylvania.

Thomas Keirstead (Ph.D. Stanford 1989) is Associate Professor of East Asian Studies at the University of Toronto.

Hyungsub Moon (Ph.D. Stanford 2005) is currently Visiting Scholar in the Department of History at Stanford University.

Thomas Nelson (D.Phil. Oxford University 1999) is an undergraduate in the natural sciences at the University of Canterbury in New Zealand.

Joan R. Piggott (Ph.D. Stanford 1987) is Gordon L. MacDonald Professor of History and Director of the Project for Premodern Japan at the University of Southern California.

Ethan Segal (Ph.D. Stanford 2003) is Assistant Professor of History at Michigan State University.

Hitomi Tonomura (Ph.D. Stanford 1986) is Professor of History at the University of Michigan.

ABBREVIATIONS

The following abbreviations are used in the notes. Each work has an entry in the bibliography of primary sources.

BSS	*Burakushi shiryō senshū*
CHSS	*Chūsei hōsei shiryōshū*
CSSS	*Chūsei seiji shakai shisō*
HI	*Heian ibun*
HSS	*Hennen sabetsushi shiryō shūsei*
KI	*Kamakura ibun*
NBI-Ch	*Nanbokuchō ibun Chūgoku Shikoku hen*
NBI-Ka	*Nanbokuchō ibun Kantō hen*
NBI-Ky	*Nanbokuchō ibun Kyūshū hen*
NBI-Tō	*Nanbokuchō ibun Tōhoku hen*
MKS	*Matsuratō kankei shiryōshū*
TMN	*Tamon'in nikki*
Tokitsune	*Tokitsune kyōki*

Throughout this volume, we follow the standard practice of rendering Japanese names in accordance with Japanese custom, with the family name preceding the personal name. For the sake of internal consistency, we have deleted the "no" from all names such as Minamoto no Yoritomo, except where they appear in direct quotation or in published titles. The names of Americans of Japanese ancestry have been cited in conformity with the Western practice of placing the personal name ahead of the family name.

Romanization of Japanese words follows the style of the fourth edition of Kenkyūsha's *New Japanese-English Dictionary*. Exceptions, with macrons omitted, appear in the case of familiar place names, such as Tokyo, Kyoto, Osaka, Kyushu, and Honshu, and narrative usages of words, such as samurai and shogun, which have entered the English lexicon.

Introduction: The Rhythm of the Volume

Shortly after the death of Jeffrey P. Mass in 2001, Stanford University—where he had taught since 1974—hosted a conference of his friends and graduate students in his memory. The papers they presented on that occasion collectively defined the cutting edge of Anglophone historical studies of medieval Japan, and the participants decided to compile their work into a volume that would delineate the state of the field at the moment of the passing of its most prolific and influential figure.

Considerable time has passed since the Stanford conference, and the contents of the volume have also evolved to incorporate the most recent research of the conference participants. It is now finally—and more currently—complete. It aims to be more than simply a tribute to Jeff Mass: it intends to offer fresh views on aspects of the medieval Japanese world that fully reflect Mass's concern for a thorough investigation of the historical record. He himself would never have countenanced a festschrift designed solely to honor him. As in each of the conference volumes that he edited, he would have demanded a very high level of academic rigor. With some trepidation, we as a group of authors hope he would have been pleased at the result.

At the time of his death, Mass was the Yamato Ichihashi Professor of Japanese History at Stanford, and concurrently a Fellow of Hertford College at Oxford University. As such, he was the premier Anglophone scholar of medieval Japanese history, a mantle he inherited from his mentor, John Whitney Hall, upon the latter's death in 1997. A specialist in the legal and institutional history of the Kamakura period (1185–1333), Mass's eminence rested on his reputation for a profound knowledge of the primary sources from the medieval era. Indeed, his passion for documents was legendary: not only his use of them, but also his dogged determination in locating and collecting them. His own collection, now housed at the University of Southern California, represents the most extensive private library of medieval Japanese primary sources outside of Japan. The legacy of this passion lives on within the large cohort of scholars he trained, who today produce much of the Western-language research in Japanese medieval historical studies. Nothing would please him more than a collection of essays meeting his demanding standards that was produced by those he trained. All of the authors in this volume were mentored by him at Stanford or, in the case of Nelson, at Oxford.

Mass produced ten books on medieval Japan, six monographs and four edited collections. He wrote five volumes on the Kamakura period, a goal he set for himself early in his career that pleased him greatly to have met. His views fundamentally reshaped the study of premodern Japanese history outside of Japan, and his work was highly regarded by scholars in Japan. He established the study of original sources—administrative documents, wills, land transfers, diaries, and the like—as the fundamental approach to medieval history, and demonstrated that non-Japanese could in fact master the arcane language in which these sources were written. Focusing on original sources made possible new interpretations, as scholars moved away more boldly from literary evidence and secondary works in Japanese to confront the documents directly. As a result, Mass, his students, and others influenced by his work were able to set aside older interpretations that posited Japan's medieval era as fundamentally analogous to that of the West, and to demonstrate instead that Japanese history had a rhythm and flow of its own.

Mass urged his students to step beyond the confines of existing historical periodization schemes, and never to accept standard interpretations without careful appraisal. Nothing better illustrates his position than that his final book was an explicit critique and recomposition of his first. His earliest monograph, *Warrior Government in Early Medieval Japan: A Study of the Kamakura Bakufu, Shugo, and Jitō* (Yale, 1974) had immediately established him as the premier young scholar in the field, but ultimately, he saw that changing interpretations of the late twelfth century in Japan—many of them the fruits of his own research and that of his students—made that work outdated. *Yoritomo and the Founding of the First Bakufu: The Origins of Dual Government in Japan* was fittingly completed in 1999, on the eight hundredth anniversary of Minamoto Yoritomo's death.

His intellectual reach is reflected in the diversity of the editors' relationships to him. Lorraine Harrington and Andrew Goble are his former students; Gordon Berger, a graduate-school colleague from their days at Yale, shared a career-long interest in Japanese history with him, spanning a millennium between their areas of specialization. I (Hurst) knew him also from our graduate-student days, and over the course of three decades, sent a number of my M.A. students on to Stanford to complete their doctoral work under his supervision.

His professional relationships were inevitably laced with personal concerns as well, and he was especially famous among us for his fierce devotion to his students. Jeff was so proud of all of them, but worried endlessly about their degree progress and then their professional careers and personal well-being. Often he called to regale me with stories of how wonderful the newest doctoral student was, thanking me for sending such a fabulous student to work with him, or seeking my advice on how he should structure letters of recommendation in fairness to two or three of his students applying for the same position. This last matter was a frequent dilemma for him, since most of the younger scholars in the small field of premodern Japanese history had studied with him. The attentiveness and skills that he brought to handling these vexing situations have resulted in an unusually collegial group of scholars in the field, and this volume has been written in reciprocation by many of them with profound feelings of love and appreciation.

He shared life experiences and supported them, as well as his friends, through the various academic and personal vicissitudes life holds for us all. For example, my mother was extremely fond of Jeff, and whenever I visited her in northern California, she expected that we would drive down to Palo Alto to see him. And it was Jeff, more than anyone else, who helped me deal with her death only a year before his own. Our personal relationship was such that when his daughter Karen called on March 30, 2001, to tell me with painful simplicity that "we've lost Dad," I knew immediately that I had lost not only one of my dearest colleagues, but also one of my best friends. The news arrived just as I was preparing to travel to Palo Alto for what Jeff and I both knew would be our final visit, so the sorrow of his loss has, to this day, always been tinged with feelings of guilt for not having made that final trip in time to say goodbye. But again, it has been the wealth of positive memories Jeff left behind for all of us that provides the greatest consolation in managing these difficult emotions.

The essays herein flow through and around several important themes, some familiar, such as issues of central vs. local power, or, phrased differently, the multitiering of power and influence across the political and economic landscapes of medieval Japan, and some less so (such as the diversity of individual experiences, depicted here with startling granularity). Old or new, each theme is subjected here to fresh scrutiny, as Jeff would have required of us. The editors have divided the book into several sections that seem to us to comprise natural groupings, and we have in collaboration with one another written the brief summaries that follow.

SOURCING DOCUMENTS

Thomas Conlan's essay, "Traces of the Past," explores the social and cultural importance of Kamakura documents. Whereas documents are sometimes criticized as an elite form of communication of narrow political importance and thus somehow unrepresentative of society at large, Conlan suggests that such representations are themselves narrow and misleading. He shows that these records had a special significance even during the time when they were written. In arguing that they were thought to represent talismans that physically represented the writer's body, Conlan provides a new way of exploring writing and reading that avoids many of the shibboleths of modern studies of literacy.

Conlan reveals in particular how the aural presence of these records was understood to be the disembodied voice of their author. People capable of fluently and flawlessly reading records, particularly secretariats (*kurōdo*) and imperial messengers, possessed great influence because they transmitted the voice of authority. Even otherwise literate officials would refrain from reading a missive from the sovereign, for they were loath to change his voice. Conlan also describes the fourteenth-century shift regarding these documents, as the physical presence of the paper, rather than its aural presence, ultimately became most important.

FRACTIOUS FLOWS

Given that from the outset of his career, Jeffrey Mass was interested in the rise to power and exercise thereof by Japan's medieval warriors, it is no surprise that many of his students should likewise be concerned with warriors. Indeed, the essays in this section reflect that shared interest. In "What a Difference a Bow Makes," Karl Friday compares the "rules of war" in early medieval Europe and Japan, finding them essentially absent in the latter. In the process he draws some important distinctions between forms of warfare common to early medieval Europe and Japan. Although careful to delineate the features shared by knights and *bushi*, Friday considers the two military orders quite distinct, as the products of very different social conditions. He is concerned here with spelling out especially some of the ways in which the behavior of late Heian *bushi* deviated from that of early medieval European knights. For example, he notes, the Heian warrior had not developed anything as elaborate as a European sense of chivalry, and was thus far less "gentlemanly" than once believed.

Though both knight and *bushi* were concerned with something that may be labeled honor, notions of honorable action might diverge widely. Thus, European ideas of "playing fair," giving quarter to an enemy, protecting non-combatants from injury, declining to capture enemies for ransom, or sparing women, children, and the elderly from harm figured rarely, if at all, in the descriptions of late-Heian warriors found in contemporary documents. Bushi were apparently motivated more by matters of practical political and strategic advantage than by adherence to abstract concepts. Friday argues convincingly that very different social and political realities in Japan—a centralized (if weak) polity, a lower pedigree for most warriors and less well-developed sense of class, a religious world in which there was no single religious authority akin to "the Church," different military technology, and the fact that wars in Europe and Japan were fought largely for different reasons—led early medieval warriors to perform their military duties differently from their European counterparts. Medieval Japan, notes Friday, lacked a strong sense of warfare rules (*jus in bello*), instead favoring practical strategies that emphasized self-interest and political advantage.

If, in an early phase of Japanese historiography, it had been common to equate samurai with knights, fiefs with *shōen*, and feudalism East with feudalism West (what Wayne Farris has described as the Western-analogue theory), another familiar approach has been to exoticize, or "orientalize," the samurai image. Indeed, Hurst identifies a non-cinematic "samurai trilogy" to characterize the phenomenon found commonly among undergraduates who know before any study of medieval Japan about samurai, ninja, and even *sōhei* (the most common term for medieval warriors from Buddhist monasteries). Even students with little other knowledge of Japan are familiar with these three versions of the Japanese warrior—as well as the post-medieval "ronin"—from anime, manga, and the numerous samurai-oriented video games.

In "Benkei's Ancestors," Mikael Adolphson revises some common misperceptions of the Heian monastic warrior. Long before their debuts in the pages of contemporary manga, the *sōhei* appear in literary sources and various scroll paintings wearing cowls and *geta* sandals, and clutching "long-swords" (*naginata*). Adolphson's exploitation of Heian temple records and courtier diaries allows him to accomplish several tasks. First, he lays to rest the long-standing idea that warriors fighting on behalf of their monasteries in late Heian times were somehow responsible for significant change—indeed, decline—in Japanese Buddhism. He demonstrates that a certain level of violence had always been characteristic of the Buddhist orders in Japan, but reminds us as well that the evolutionary origins of the warrior were traceable not simply to armed Buddhist clerics, but to much broader social phenomena.

Most importantly, Adolphson identifies those individuals who might have qualified as the well-known type of *sōhei* called "*akusō*," or "unruly monks." The reader here will be treated to several mini-biographies drawn from the documentary record of militant monks from the tenth through twelfth centuries, featuring Ryōgen, Jojin, Hoyaku, Shinjutsu, and Kakunin among them. (Benkei—the faithful twelfth-century follower of the legendary Yoshitsune—is invoked here only as the warrior monk known best in legends, historical accounts, and contemporary popular culture.) Adolphson finds two sorts of monastic warriors in the documents. Most were low-ranking and unnamed members of the rising provincial warrior class, who sought service to the monasteries as fighters and low-level estate managers. Leading monastic warriors, on the other hand, tended to be drawn from mid-ranked members of the Fujiwara, Taira, and Minamoto lineages, who "regardless of their status as monks, were still mainly aristocratic commanders." They were, then, warriors who made their careers within monasteries rather than monks-turned-warriors. From that perspective, Adolphson explicates the "militarization" of the monasteries as a consequence of the emergence of armed men in the provinces more generally, and their recruitment in the struggles for wealth and resources not only by powerful late Heian courtiers but by temples as well.

In the final essay of those focused on the fighting man, Thomas Nelson presents a valuable case study of a single important warrior family, the first research subject of its kind perhaps since Peter Arnesen's now classic pioneering studies of the Ōuchi in western Honshu. Motivated by what he finds to be a curious lack of interest in *shugo* (provincial constable) families from the early Kamakura period, Nelson provides a penetrating look at the Ōtomo family in northern Kyushu, far from the heartland of leading warrior-house activities in eastern Japan during the thirteenth century. To begin, Nelson directs our attention to the countryside in Bungo province, where Yoritomo had placed several members of the eastern Ōtomo warrior clan, including the founder of the lineage, Yoshinao. Examining the documents of the house during its early years of growth in extensive territories held previously by vassals of the defeated Taira lineage, Nelson uncovers much new data illuminating the overall structure of the clan, and the constitution of both free and un-free subgroups of its vassals. He shows, for example, that the *shugo* in Kyushu were granted far more extensive powers than their counterparts elsewhere, and he suggests that the reason for this anomaly may have been because lands previously held closely by Taira enemies required new, centrally appointed officials such as the Ōtomo, to replace local notables exterminated during the Battle of Dannoura in 1185. Surely, it was advantageous to Yoritomo to have his direct appointees in the area, but bakufu backing also made things easier for strangers in a strange land like the Ōtomo to build power locally.

The sweeping legal authority granted to the Ōtomo allowed them to hear cases involving slave trafficking, and even, on occasion, to prosecute shogunal vassals themselves. They found it advantageous to issue their own legal codes as well, more than a century before other great warrior houses began to do so. Nelson's study of the Ōtomo sheds considerable light on the early days and emerging powers of warrior houses in the Kamakura era, a research topic not heretofore of great interest to scholars who have preferred to focus on the growth of the most important of these entities into major hegemons centuries later. In so doing, he evokes the hope that more scholars may become motivated to turn their attention to the origins of other prominent medieval warrior families, and thereby trace "the rise of the warrior" from new and different local perspectives.

FLUID BODIES

The three papers by Andrew Edmund Goble, Hitomi Tonomura, and Thomas Keirstead take up issues touching on how the body and its relationship to society is understood. Reflecting a nuanced understanding of the broader cultural, religious, and political contexts within which medieval bodies operated, the papers demonstrate that in the medieval era, bodies were not static entities, and further, that interpretive categories and the values and assumptions used by modern scholars tend to impede, rather than facilitate, our understanding of those bodies. The papers provide such disparate examples as: focusing on the fact of bodily display rather than engaging the nuances of perception that the bodies may betoken; applying unsuitable models such as the notion that public and private were binary opposites and thus obscuring female political influence and participation; or reading back into the medieval era later historical ideologies and structures, as with the concept of outcasts and the polluted, assuming the existence of lineal medieval antecedents that in fact did not exist. All three papers offer alternative interpretive stances, highlight the fluidity of bodies in social continuums, and caution against comfortably fixing our understanding of shifting human and cultural landscapes.

In "Images of Illness," Goble examines two illustrated medieval scrolls, the *Scroll of Afflictions* and the *Scroll of Gross Afflictions* (together, the *Scrolls of Afflictions*). The fifty-nine scenes depicted therein illustrate an extensive range of physical and psychological ailments. Going beyond the standard descriptions of and comments on these images provided by scholars in the fields of art history and medical history, Goble uses the scenes as sources for elucidating the contours of medieval perceptions of illness, and for illuminating medieval responses to the presence of the afflicted. Goble informs his interpretations of the images with a wide range of written sources, attention to the religious and cultural milieux in which they were produced, and careful consideration of the medical aspects of the images. In this way, he discerns meaning in the images that is not conveyed by simple description.

Goble's essay takes up in turn the issues of scatology and pathology, afflictions and states of mind, afflictions as spectacle, and afflictions and care. He demonstrates that medieval understandings of, and responses to, afflictions were nuanced rather than monolithic. On the broader issue of illness and society, he calls into question a number of assumptions that scholars have brought to the interpretation of the images. He shows on the one hand that those assumptions have deflected productive engagement of afflictions of both the body and of the mind (the latter admittedly more difficult to track). On the other hand, Goble demonstrates that when looking at the *Scrolls of Afflictions* scholars have often unnecessarily drawn attention to organs of reproduction, rather than more generally appreciating that the body has many parts, any and all of which may be the site of affliction. Indeed, that is the perspective of the *Scrolls of Afflictions* themselves. Failing to appreciate this inclusiveness, Goble argues, has directed attention away from a fuller consideration of what it is bodies may portray or convey, and has obscured the multiple ways in which bodies were apprehended in the medieval era.

In "Court and Bakufu in Her Flesh," Hitomi Tonomura addresses the issue of female participation in the political process. Tonomura argues that narrowly conceived notions of political space that utilize a dichotomy of public and private are inadequate for understanding the medieval aristocratic polity. Instead, Tonomura interprets from a "gray analytical zone," recognizing that the entire aristocracy and its doings constituted an actual political arena at the center, and thus much more than simply the formal structures of bureaucratic organization. Tonomura deploys this analytical stance to investigate how Lady Nijō, an "unattached" woman holding a tenuous position within the imperial sphere, was embedded, literally and figuratively, at the fulcrum of power. From a liminally central position, Nijō was able to exploit her talents and use her acumen to assert herself in the political process.

The essay analyzes Lady Nijō's memoir, *Towazugatari* (Telling without Being Asked), as a carefully constructed narrative that successfully proclaims a discursive authority regarding her experiences in the late Kamakura age. Those experiences were in turn a key component in, and intersection point for, a range of social, sexual, and political relationships which embodied the most crucial disputes over imperial succession in her time. Tonomura first examines the political setting of Nijō's patron, Go-Fukakusa, and then moves to consideration of the position of Nijō's family and personal history in that context. Highlighting Nijō's insecure position amid the libidinal dynamics of court society, she points out that those circumstances also presented opportunities for influence. Finally, selecting three episodes from *Towazugatari*, the essay elucidates how Nijō constructed her involvement in the political process. Lady Nijō's story enables us to see the fundamental inapplicability of the public/private dichotomy as an analytical tool, and to recognize the possibilities for representing women in the context of what is formally a male-dominated political structure.

Thomas Keirstead's essay, "Outcasts before the Law," examines outcasts (*hinin*) and marginal groups in the medieval era, before the creation of legal definitions that later assigned them to a marginal place in society (during the Tokugawa era). Keirstead notes that scholars have attempted to assign the history of early modern and modern discrimination anachronistically back into the premodern past, assuming incorrectly that the modern system of legal discrimination originated in pre-existing medieval "systems" which were simply regularized during the Tokugawa era. Keirstead's essay examines medieval practices without seeing them as precursors for a later period. He thus provides insights into the phenomenon of the fluid production and reproduction of the medieval outcast, as well as into the overall character of the medieval polity.

Keirstead first highlights the fluidity of the medieval outcast order. The order was not stable or rigidly defined, but was characterized by a wide variety of terminology, a bewildering range of occupations and types of people, and a continuous process of production and reproduction. Indeed, the medieval outcast grouping was so large that, far from being the type of marginal social category that it was to become under the Tokugawa order, under varying circumstances it included people from all levels of society. Outcasts were not a specific social group, but became "different" according to a variety of designations, emblematic of the ambiguity that was fundamental to the medieval polity, where people's roles and places in society were not rigidly determined.

The essay then moves on to a consideration of the issue of defilement, a concept seen as integral to the definition of the outcast order in the early modern period. Keirstead finds that in medieval times defilement is not a useful framework for understanding the medieval outcast, since the medieval social topography was one in which there was a symbiotic relationship between cleansing and defilement. Indeed, the power to cleanse, to rid of defilement, was a distinctive manifestation of medieval royal powers. The role of monarchs as "purifiers" established a political principle upon which the medieval court defined its exalted position above the rest, the polluted. In short, outcasts were not peripheral, but central to the medieval order.

LIQUID ASSETS

The three essays comprising part 4 of the volume add considerably to our vision of social, economic, and political trends by approaching these matters from the "periphery." Authors Batten, Segal, and Moon delve into topics that involve foreign relations (both formal and informal, legitimate and illegal), remote locales, fringe occupations, and emerging sources of power. At the same time, each author draws on his understanding of the peripheries to illuminate core underpinnings of the dual polity and the complex social entities it supported. The essays temporally cover the late Heian to early Ashikaga periods, enabling readers to draw connections among the recurring themes, and pushing against the limits of our thinking about the diverse social and economic conditions that influenced political currents.

In his treatise on "An Open and Shut Case? Thoughts on Late Heian Overseas Trade," Bruce Batten utilizes intriguing data on foreign visitors to show that trade volume was low and rather easily controlled or monitored by central authorities until the twelfth century. Thereafter, distinct signs of less-controlled movement became evident in the diaspora of merchants along Hakata Bay, in the Hakozaki area, and into individual *shōen* as well. At the same time, local deputies became slightly more independent from the central authorities in their dealings with foreigners. While minimal, these indicators alert us to larger developments as well, over time and across geographies.

Ethan Segal, in "Awash with Coins: The Spread of Money in Early Medieval Japan," chronicles the expansion of commerce, by presenting specific evidence of the influence of money on the ultimate breakdown of traditional political authority. Using both documentary and archeological evidence, Segal describes not only how the use of coins spread geographically, but also the extent to which money enabled economically depressed local retainers to trade, acquire or borrow against land rights, and even exchange titles normally granted by central authority. He points out that by the end of the Kamakura era, the percentage of land transactions that involved coins grew from 40 percent to 80 percent. Moreover, it proved increasingly difficult for central authorities to control this growth. While payment of land taxes in money may have represented a convenience to absentee land owners, trade in titles and positions served to weaken the retainer relationships the bakufu was always seeking to build with local figures. Ultimately, the nascent commercial economy provided local elites opportunities to move outside traditional practices, and in the process, served as a corrosive influence on central control.

The Batten and Segal essays provide a vivid sense of the fluidity of power relationships in medieval Japan. The authors are not focusing explicitly on shifts in political or economic power, but in their careful examinations of the evolution of foreign relations and trade, they make highly significant contributions to what we know about subtle alterations occurring in the local landscape.

Hyungsub Moon provides fascinating detail about the Matsura family and its cohort, adding a third intriguing view of "the multiplicity of factors that might enter into central-local relationships." The Matsura comprised a league (*tō*) of coastal warriors who controlled much of the Hizen area in northern Kyushu from the twelfth to the fifteenth centuries. Their "property" rights were not limited to the land: their *jitō* authority extended out into the seas abutting their lands as well.

Moon draws from a wide variety of sources—diaries and chronicles as well as Japanese and Korean documents—to chart the evolution of this band from its first appearance on the losing side in the sea battle at Dannoura, to its plunder of Korean tribute-trade boats. The Matsura knit together a network of seamen in a hierarchy based upon personal relationships, not solely kinship, and thus began to illustrate how local interest could become a stronger bond than familial ties. Though the Matsura league does not "fit neatly" into the social categories we have become accustomed to encountering in previous studies, they are a richly documented group who provide a meaningful perspective on how local families moved adroitly between central authority and local interests to establish a significant local presence.

REVISITING INTERPRETIVE STREAMS

Let us again recall that in his final book, Jeffrey Mass essentially refashioned his initial monograph. He felt compelled to undertake this task because of the knowledge uncovered and elucidated by his own research as well as the contributions of other scholars—not least of all his own students—to the burgeoning field of medieval Japanese history. In "Navigating Kamakura History: Perspectives on the Last Work of Jeffrey P. Mass," Joan Piggott provides readers with a detailed examination of the several streams of thought that changed Mass's interpretation of the role and power of the bakufu, its leaders, and its cohorts.

Piggott examines the many new points of fact and interpretation informing Mass's matured perspective on the institutional and political Kamakura landscape. She thereby does students of the period a significant service, and beyond that, illuminates the lasting significance of the dedication and excitement carrying Mass, himself, forward in his engagements with both Yoritomo and his own students. In this multiple set of meanings, this essay is therefore a most fitting conclusion to a volume of groundbreaking work, itself the consequence of the multi-directional curiosity, enduring commitment to others' intellectual and personal growth, and abiding love for deciphering the past that marked the career of the inspiring historian, Jeffrey Mass.

SOURCING DOCUMENTS

Traces of the Past: Documents, Literacy, and Liturgy in Medieval Japan
Thomas D. Conlan

Few today can read the documents of the Kamakura era and of those who can, and who teach in North America, most, if not all, were trained by Jeffrey Mass. His advanced seminar in Japanese sources attracted a select number of students, for to enter one had to be well versed in modern and classical Japanese. The first meeting, held in his office, proved memorable. Jeff, seated at his desk, near where a sketched portrait of Yoritomo looked on approvingly, solemnly read an 1184 Yoritomo edict (*kudashibumi*), from the Jingoji archives, and I, along with my classmate, Rob Eskildsen, took copious notes on the pronunciation.[1] We were then required to read and translate five documents for the next week. For, as Jeff confided, "you cannot fully understand them unless you read them out loud."

I managed to read the documents and translate them, and every week Jeff would correct our pronunciation and discuss our translations. Some passages proved so opaque that we all debated the precise meaning. Jeff was always open to new interpretations, even admitting on occasion errors in his own published translations. This course opened up the world of Kamakura documents, and I remember being enthralled by their content: the endless, complex judicial cases that included references to cormorant fishers and fish tribute, absconding paper makers, nuns on guard duty, or daughters named "Crane Demon."[2] After going to Japan to conduct my dissertation research, my experiences in Kyoto University mirrored those at Stanford, but now we were reading original handwritten documents, rather than published versions. Again, the emphasis was on fluent reading. Much of my graduate training in Japan, it seemed, consisted of learning the art of reading such difficult sources.

Accuracy in reading sources has determined scholarly reputation, particularly in Japan, and explains the seemingly pedantic debates concerning the proper pronunciation of a particular term. Nevertheless, the definitive pronunciation of some terms remains unknown. For example, a directive is called a *migyōsho* by Tokyo scholars, while in Kyoto the same document is invariably read as *mikyōjo*.[3] Because Jeff was trained in Tokyo, he adopted the *migyōsho* reading, and I could see my Kyoto tutors wince when I followed his lead.

I assumed that the necessity of reading documents aloud stemmed from their inherent difficulty. Most were written only in Chinese characters, in the manner of *kanbun,* which profoundly differs from Japanese language structure and pronunciation. In the medieval era, too, basic competence in recognizing Chinese characters was rare. Taira Tsunetaka, writing in the mid-thirteenth century, characterized one gathering of high-ranking nobles as "infantile," while lambasting one courtier for confusing the character for the "eight ministries" of state with a similar one of radically different meaning, resulting in the erroneous rendition of the "eight tigers."[4] The essayist Yoshida Kenkō, writing in the early fourteenth century, preserved an anecdote about a physician who was ridiculed for failing to identify the radical for a Chinese character, a mistake that cast doubt on his competence in medicinal and pharmacological matters.[5]

On the other hand, proficiency in reading, writing, and interpreting texts, especially ones which had come to be seen as repositories of significant cultural wisdom, added much to a person's standing. Yoshida Sadafusa, an able administrator, was immortalized as one of the "Three Fusa," or three masters of calligraphy of the fourteenth century.[6] One of the bases for his reputation lay in his ability to copy out, and presumably understand, obscure texts such as the *Kojiki*, the oldest written history of Japan.[7] Sadafusa's political forecast proved less accurate, for he argued that the Kamakura bakufu was at the height of its powers only a few years before it collapsed.[8] Sadafusa also leaked word of Go-Daigo's plot to overthrow Kamakura in 1331, which caused his emperor to endure arrest and exile. However, Sadafusa's reputation seems not to have suffered, for when Go-Daigo destroyed the bakufu and returned to power in 1333, he promptly reinstated Sadafusa as an adviser.[9]

Documents, and those exhibiting facility reading them, thus enjoyed a social and political significance beyond their literal content. Rather than focus on administrative content per se, this essay will explore how documents served as an important medium. At one level, the act of writing served as a physical link to the individual. In addition to its indisputable legal value, the handwritten document had a talismanic link to its author, and the document itself could stand as a valid representation of his physical body. On another level, documents, themselves a formalization of language, were written to be read flawlessly out loud by qualified individuals. The act of reading a document served to make its contents "real"—less a trace of the author, as one might assume, than of his actual voice. The aural presence of documents thus served as their own truth, requiring the formality of response as if the person writing them were present. Documents, in this sense, functioned as a kind of liturgy, which required exacting precision from the scribe in reproducing the oral sounds, and the messenger, who could take these ritual cues and allow them to be heard as they had been spoken. Hence, considerable influence and prestige accrued to those who were capable of fluently reading documents, particularly the more difficult sources of the court, for only through their pronouncements could the voice of those in authority exist. The most important admonitions, orders or explanations had to be drawn orally from documents, for in order to be real, and realized, they had to be heard.

Oral Arguments, Petitions, and the Increasing Importance of Literacy

In Japan, the act of reading initially entailed the vocalization of written records. Members of the court were most proficient in reading, and during the ninth century, they stopped voicing administrative documents, preferring instead to peruse them in silence.[10] This process remained limited to the confines of court administration. Appeals to the court and contracts of sale continued to be read aloud.

Speaking documents (mōshijō)

One particularly old genre of documents, known quite literally as "spoken documents" or *mōshijō*, functioned as petitions. They represented utterances that were encoded in writing at the time of their creation, and were spoken aloud during all subsequent exchanges. The format is of a direct quotation, for the word "states" (*iwaku* 云), marks the beginning of speech which ends with a final quotation mark, known as *teheri* (者). The first reference to such a document appears quite early in Japanese history, for a bill of sale of slaves.[11] The embedded quote in this *mōshijō* may be translated as "the petition states that these slaves were purchased."[12] After questioning the veracity of these words (*kyojitsu toiseshime*), three people agreed to serve as guarantors, or witnesses for the sale of slaves. The original statement (*mōshijō*) was then embedded in a witness's statement vouching for the transaction, and formalized on 10.21.748.

Other documents reveal that *mōshijō* were generated after an oral statement. Thus, someone described merely as a "woman," presumably a wife or daughter of a certain Hiroyoshi, spoke (*mōshi iwaku*) about a land transfer to district officials, who then created a *mōshijō* that recorded her words, thereby granting them the stamp of authority.[13] *Mōshijō* were written down in the presence of the one who spoke their words, and this person had to be present when others heard its words.

A new term, *taiketsu*, came to describe the actual meeting of aggrieved parties, each armed with documentary statements.[14]

In one of the earliest uses of the term, a 1076 inspection of documents (*monjo no taiketsu*) met with difficulty because one party failed to appear. This reveals that documents themselves had to be explained or described by those contesting land rights.[15] A *taiketsu* required plaintiff and defendant to be physically present. This practice seems to have continued in the early Kamakura era, for the shrine attendants (*shōji*) of Nitta Hachiman Shrine traveled to the capital in order to state their case. Likewise, the Nitta Hachiman document reveals that on the provincial level, a document was then issued on the day that "particulars" concerning a dispute were stated (*shisai o gonjō seshimuru hi*), suggesting again that documents were created through transcribing actually spoken words.[16]

Despite the rise of more formalized institutions of adjudication in the thirteenth century, the notion remained that individuals actually needed to state their cases orally. Written evidence served to formalize statements, but plaintiffs needed to be heard during court proceedings. In some court cases, individuals were summoned for personal meetings, or *taiketsu*, and they also argued their cases at the bakufu court of appeals (*teichū*).[17] Picture scrolls commissioned by Takezaki Suenaga, a Kyushu warrior who traveled to Kamakura just to speak to a bakufu official, provide one of the most vivid examples of such an encounter. Suenaga had an artist depict his official meeting, and he recorded verbatim his debate over the precise meaning of documents describing actions against the Mongol invaders of 1274.[18]

After the Kamakura regime's creation of a comprehensive legal code in 1232 (*Goseibai shikimoku*, or Jōei code), the ability to decipher the language appearing in documents gained importance, despite the continued oral nature of legal defenses. Those unable to read or write seem to have been stigmatized, for the pejorative term "text blindness" (*monmō* 文盲) begins to appear in documents around that time.[19] Some used their illiteracy to justify spurious accusations, but the illiterate proved to be at a disadvantage in most legal cases. They not only lacked an understanding of the law, but they also had to rely on others to present their documents at court. [20] An inability to read became the basis for declaring incompetence among officials. In 1242, the head of the Ise Inner Shrine declared an attendant unable to understand objects of antiquity because he was illiterate, and prevented him from traveling to the capital.[21]

The writing of documents "in one's own hand"

With increasing recourse to Kamakura law and the need to transmit and defend land transactions in court, those who could read and write had an advantage in maintaining their property. Wills proved to be particularly significant for transmitting land rights, most commonly in the form of confirming authority to manage the land. In order to be accepted as valid, these documents had to be written by the land donor.[22] It was much easier to write in the phonetic *kana* syllabaries (*hiragana* and *katakana*) than in *kanbun*, and this partially explains the increase in records written phonetically in Japanese. In one case, a donor had a conveyance prepared in *kanbun* by a scribe, but then added in *hiragana* the comment that "as [proof] for the future, I have written in my own hand on the reverse." He wrote his name in *hiragana* and added his signature.[23] In another example, Kumagai Naotoki attested to the veracity of his testament, which he had written in *hiragana*, with the comment that, "as this is in my own hand, there will be no later doubt."[24] When the donor was incapacitated, a scribe could be relied upon to a limited degree, but some appended statement remained necessary. In one such case, the author declared that "this should be in my own hand, but [I] had trouble seeing and writing proves difficult so I had a scribe record the list [of statues and sutras at Ise's Kōmyōji] and wrote only this postscript (*tetsuki*) in my own hand."[25]

The increasing numbers of documents in the Kamakura era

The Kamakura period (1185–1333) witnessed a marked growth in literacy. Analysis of chronological compendia of Japanese documents reveals roughly how the numbers of surviving sources increased in Japan. The *Heian ibun*, a compilation of documents from the Heian era (794–1185), consists of thirteen volumes and 5,775 documents while the *Kamakura ibun* (1186–1333) comprises forty-six volumes and 35,036 documents.[26] The first thirteen volumes of the *Kamakura ibun* cover only eighty-three years (1185–1268), in contrast with the Heian period, where reaching a similar number of documents required a span of nearly a hundred years. At the same time, although omissions are rife, the final thirteen volumes of the *Kamakura ibun* cover only twenty-eight years (1306–1334), providing ample testimony to the increasing amount of written documentation.

Wills or testaments conveying property, written by provincial landholders, and judicial documents recounting disputes over property account for some of the increased volume of Kamakura documents. For the Heian period, 207 testaments (*yuzurijō*) survive, with over three quarters written after 1123 and fully half written just between 1158 and 1185. The Kamakura period witnessed a tenfold increase in testaments (2,946) written or referred to in judicial documents.[27] Of these, 655 were written phonetically in one or another of the two *kana* syllabaries. The number of wills so written increased dramatically, with as many surviving for the years 1300–1333 as for the years 1185–1300.[28]

Methods of Writing

Some scholars have postulated that the two phonetic scripts used in testaments functioned differently, with the blocky *katakana* used virtually as italics to express utterances such as oaths. Amino Yoshihiko theorized that this distinction explains the use of *katakana* in modern times to convey sounds, while syllables written in cursive *hiragana* are used for standard administrative documents.[29] Unfortunately, this generalization overlooks the fact that the systematic use of one type or another did not terribly concern the denizens of the thirteenth and fourteenth century. Wills were written in both *katakana* and the more common *hiragana*.[30] Some individuals wrote functionally similar documents with both *kana*. Hōjō Shigetoki, for example, wrote one precept in *katakana*, and another in *hiragana*.[31] Some documents even mixed both phonetic forms indiscriminately.[32]

Katakana seems to have been thought the easier to write, for as Kanezawa Sanetoki explained, somewhat defensively in a testament to his son, "as the days pass my illness worsens, and as the years have passed, now my hand shakes, my eyes cannot see but I have written this in my own hand thus."[33] *Katakana* remained a favored means of clarifying Buddhist texts, and one sees that inhabitants of regions located near the great temples, such as Mt. Kōya, tended to use this script more commonly. Generally, however, no systematic rationale fully explains differences in usage for the two syllabaries.

In addition to the absence of any standard or systematic usage of *kana*, no common pronunciation existed for numerous words. Documents written in *kana* reveal important variations in the pronunciation of even the most significant offices or terms. For example, the Mōri of western Japan pronounced the office (*shiki*) of *jitō*, which determined status as a provincial warrior, as *jitō shoku* rather than *jitō shiki*.[34] Such a pronunciation, if offered by a graduate student today, would be deemed erroneous. Likewise, the names of provinces sometimes appear incorrectly. The nun Shinmyō, who was in fact a resident of Bungo province in Kyushu, wrote out the province name as Fuko or perhaps Bugo in one of her wills.[35] For another example, the famous era name Jōei was read by the Fukabori of northern Kyushu as Tei'ei.[36] These differences in pronunciation are obscured, however, because official documents, particularly edicts of *jitō* investiture, were written solely with Chinese characters.

Documents written in *kanbun* possessed more prestige than those in *kana* and avoided vagaries in pronunciation. When Kamakura quoted phonetically written wills in its judicial documents, the *kana* were transcribed into *kanbun* by officials adept at the more difficult style of writing.[37] Writing in *kanbun* had its appeal for petitioners, for it allowed them to conceal that they did not necessarily know the "proper" pronunciation for some place names, important offices, or era names.

Important documents of investiture were sometimes rewritten phonetically so that provincial warriors could read them out loud.[38] Given the large numbers of provincial warriors and their wives, daughters, or mothers represented in documents, a substantial percentage of the population wrote wills, but only the more educated could read or write in *kanbun*. When coupled with variations in dialect, this meant that one could write phonetically, or even recognize, Chinese characters and yet still be unable to pronounce them properly.

The documents of the Aokata family, from the geographically isolated Gotō islands, are unusually well preserved. They contain an original Kamakura bakufu judicial decision and a *hiragana* copy of that decision, which was a record of the messenger's speech.[39] When the Aokata received an important edict, they reproduced it in *kana* so that they could in turn read this record precisely. Concern over the proper reading of a name or term partially explains why the Aokata went to the trouble of reproducing a long court case phonetically. At the same time, replication in *hiragana* suggests that they themselves intended to read this document to relatives, retainers, rivals, and their descendants as well. Long after the Kamakura messenger had departed, the judgment and words of the document would continue to reverberate throughout the Gotō islands.

The act of individually writing a will mattered more than its actual content. Phonetically written wills continued to predominate, but some heroically attempted to write in Chinese, copying a *kanbun* will even though they were illiterate. One such example, written by Mataga Muneie on 1.11.1422, contains minimal *kana*, but the characters are in an unsteady hand, and have a tendency to slope to the right, as was often the case for the texts of an unskilled writer. Mataga Muneie most likely copied a scribe's template to the best of his abilities, but his weakness of hand forced him to explain that: "[I] the writer am illiterate but my lord should not doubt this record's authenticity." Poignantly, he wrote "illiterate" incorrectly.

The personal writing of wills served as legal proof of intent, and was evidence of the "presence" of the individual. Any personal communication seems to have required that the person actually be the one who wrote the words. This meant, in cases of illiteracy, that individuals such as Mataga Muneie copied down records that they otherwise could not understand. Letters were likewise expected to be in the hand of the writer.[40] In addition, documents in a person's hand were considered an extension of the individual's body. For example, the letters of Yamanouchi Tsuneyuki, a warrior who died in battle during the fourteenth century, were cut into small pieces, and stamped with images of either the *Fudō* or *Daikokuten* deities.[41] These documents served as a trace of the deceased, and a means of praying for his salvation, or rebirth. At the same time, the paper might have an image printed on it, thereby making it a talisman that could be, if necessary, ingested to allow the health of a stricken individual to recover.[42]

In sum, documents written in one's own hand possessed a special legal and cultural significance. They served as evidence of the wishes expressed by an individual. They also served as a trace, or talisman, of an individual, as with the letters of the unfortunate Yamanouchi Tsuneyuki. Some documents even functioned as a kind of liturgy, for they allowed messengers to reproduce the actual voices of individuals, and the sound of the voice functioned as a disembodied truth. This meant that those who read the documents possessed an important role as speakers or interpreters of this particular reality.

Documents as Disembodied Voices

The act of voiced reading served to formalize edicts, much as mastery of knowledge today in graduate school is formalized through an oral defense.[43] The significance of hearing the sound mattered more than formalization, for in the case of Kamakura documents, they were thought to constitute the disembodied voices of the writers when heard. The same respect was due these words as to the individual who had had them committed to paper.

Writing, in other words, was not an end unto itself. Rather, the written paper served as the medium for conveying these utterances. The one who read from this medium had to do so flawlessly, for his words constituted disembodied speech of another. It was through hearing that one gained a sense of the truth. Added explanations carried weight equal to the text itself, for voiced words were most "real." Hence, a messenger had to be deeply trusted.

The *Azuma kagami*, a late thirteenth-century compilation of sources that constitutes a history of the Kamakura regime, provides valuable evidence of contemporary behavior, even though on occasion it has not been absolutely accurate in institutional chronology.[44] One memorable episode, drawn here from Minoru Shinoda's translation, illustrates Minamoto Yoritomo's behavior upon his initial receipt, in the fourth month of 1180, of the edict that would legitimate his uprising:

> 27th day. Today the edict (*ryōji*) of Takakura no Miya [Prince Mochihito] was delivered by Minamoto Yukiie to Minamoto Yoritomo at the Hōjō Residence in Izu province. The Military Protector [Yoritomo], wearing ceremonial robes and bowing respectfully toward distant Otokoyama, gave instructions to have the pronouncement opened and read.[45]

Yoritomo's listening to the words voiced by Yukiie demonstrated what was considered typical practice, even though one cannot verify that he actually listened to these documents in this manner. The nature of Yoritomo's reaction suggests that the words voiced by Yukiie, the messenger, were those of the prince who was actually dead by this point, causing Yoritomo to bow to Mochihito's presumed current location at Otokoyama.

Fictional accounts also suggest that the reading of documents, particularly important edicts, occurred commonly, and they provide rich detail regarding the ceremony of having these documents read. The *Genpei jōsuiki*, a fourteenth-century chronicle of the Genpei War (1180–1185), describes how Yoritomo washed his hands, gargled (*ugaishite*), and changed into clean clothes before the messenger Mongaku read to him a document from the retired emperor Go-Shirakawa.[46] In another passage from this tale, Yoritomo dispatched an edict to Miura Yoshimura, who changed into white robes, put on a formal standing cap (*eboshi*), washed his hands and rinsed out his mouth (*kuchi susugi nando shite*). He then had the document from Yoritomo opened and read to all the relatives of the Miura, along with retainers (*rōtō*) and even low-ranking followers (*zōshiki*).[47] The reply, when given, was likewise proffered orally.[48] Thus, the giving and receiving of documents occurred quite literally as a formal conversation that required a purification of hands (which held the document) and mouth (which voiced it), suggesting that the one who read the documents might even be seen as functioning as a kind of shaman who brought back the traces, or speech, of another.

Even more prosaic orders were voiced. For example, Kamakura officials read their edicts out loud to their "housemen" (*gokenin*). A 1305 letter (*shojō*) by Kurasu Kaneo describes how, in the aftermath of a rebellion by Hōjō Tokimura, warriors residing in the capital and Rokuhara council members (*hyōjoshū*) were summoned to hear an edict (*migyōsho*) read (literally, "read and listened to" [*yomikikasare sōrai owannu*]) by the head of the Rokuhara headquarters.[49]

Social superiors read important orders out loud to their subordinates. The practice was quite common, and varied references exist to documents being "read and listened to." The priest Nichiren added the following postscript to his document: "All my disciples and followers should read and listen to this letter. Those who are serious in their resolve should discuss it with one another."[50] Variations in language exist, for one finds references to "have read," or, most commonly, having someone "read and state" (*yomimōsu*) their content.[51] For example, Sahara

Naritsura "read and stated" a retired emperor's edict (*inzen*) at a Kamakura bakufu council.[52] The notion of having documents read out loud for others suggests a shift in consciousness from the Heian to Kamakura periods. For the Heian period, although thirty-three references exist to prayers and documents read at court (*yomimōsu*), during this era no examples exist of documents being read out loud, and only occasional references to documents being "seen."[53]

The rationale for this shift in Kamakura times seems to be that the written words when read had a formality and weight otherwise missing from regular conversation. Nichiren demanded that his followers hear his words, not merely read them silently. Likewise, Hōjō Shigetoki wrote to his son that "to impart my precepts by word of mouth would be inadequate; that is why I have put them into writing. Never show them to a stranger; but in your spare time you should get someone in whom you can have complete trust to read them aloud to you while you listen carefully to every detail."[54] Carl Steenstrup and other commentators have suggested that this message implies that Shigetoki's son was too young to read at the time, but this conclusion seems mistaken.[55] A second letter, written considerably later in life, contains similar sentiments, namely that words when written had a formality and weight that something merely spoken did not:

> While I would like to explain to you by word of mouth how to achieve this [i.e., be a person whom others remember fondly] I am aware that there may be no suitable occasion to do so. For this reason I have put my ideas into writing, in proper form, and here present them to you. When you have nothing else to do, read them carefully. But let no one else see them![56]

In another precept, Shigetoki specified that his son was to "try then to get together in a small group and read them quietly together."[57] He who read the document out loud spoke with Shigetoki's presumed voice. This record had to be kept a secret, for only those worthy of hearing Shigetoki's voice were to be given access to this record. The most trusted individual of all, however, was he who read these precepts, for by sounding them out, he reproduced the voice of Shigetoki, and was obligated to do so precisely and accurately.

The significance of messengers

Messengers possessed the voice of authority when reading documents out loud. Their power doing this proved great, and was enhanced because they not only read documents, but by voicing them, concurrently interpreted them as well. A passage from the *Mineaiki* proves informative, for it reveals how messengers explained, or contextualized, these texts. Accordingly, "On the twenty-fifth day of the eighth month of 1331, at half past the hour of the cock [6 p.m.], a messenger from the protector (*shugo*) [of the province] arrived, unfolded an edict (*migyōsho*) and said 'To the *jitō* and *gokenin* (*onchū*) [of the province]: During the past night of the twenty-third, [the emperor] departed from the palace (*kinri*). Find another time to travel to the capital.'" To this opaque message, the messenger added the following verbal statement, which is quoted directly: "This is the beginning of upheaval in the realm," thereby suggesting that travel to the capital at this time would be construed as an act of political rebellion.[58] Hence, orders could be given, but nuance or context was best expressed verbally by messengers. The distinction allowed for discretion.

Messengers transmitted documents in a way which gave weight to their words, in order to emphasize that they were not mere disseminators of rumor. Above all, they orally conveyed the most important content, which had not been explicitly recorded in documents. This can be gleaned from contemporary writings. One fourteenth-century document declares that "I would be delighted if you could question and listen to the messenger, as I have told him what I have intended to say. Please state the particulars [of your situation] to the messenger."[59] Other documents, such as one written by Kanezawa Sadaaki, are notable for an almost singular lack of content, serving only to vouch for the veracity of a messenger's oral comments. Sadaaki would, for example, write: "As the situation is not yet settled, [I] shall abbreviate this letter. Respectfully."[60] Save for notifying his compatriot of a disturbance, his letter contains almost no information. Most likely, however, the messenger who brought this letter to the priest Meinin would have verbally explained the situation in more detail. This conduct becomes manifest in another document describing the rebellion of Hōjō Tokimura. Here, Sadaaki writes "concerning the unusual circumstances these days (*yo no ue no koto chinji sōrō*) the details of those events will be stated by Shukuen."[61] By writing this missive, Sadaaki did not record any sensitive information, but he ensured that Shukuen's narrative would not be dismissed as unsubstantiated rumor. Messengers, then, orally conveyed sensitive and significant information, which is why they were so important, and why, during the outbreak of a civil war, their capture proved significant.[62]

Messengers possessed discretion as well, not only to explain documents, but at times to withhold information, or threaten to do so. Sadaaki would write of how a messenger was unable to explain the particulars of his promotion, which suggests that these men had the discretion to withhold certain information.[63] Such behavior appears again in the fictionalized *Genpei jōsuiki*, where the priest Mongaku purportedly refuses to convey information to Yoritomo without a prior confirmation of lands.[64]

The speech of emperors

Messengers proved most significant when conveying messages from the court, and the need to enunciate imperial documents explains the particular format of these records. *Rinji*, an imperial order that was issued by a secretariat (*kurōdo*), marked a simplification of the mechanisms for transmitting records that bypassed the older institutions of court bureaucracy. These new documents provided a method of conveying speech by directly quoting the imperial command. The oldest surviving *rinji* from the emperor Go-Reizei dates from 1054 and reads:

It has been ordered as follows. From this night, [you] are to arrive and serve. So [I have received] the personal imperial order (*rinji*). The Captain of the Bodyguards of the Right (*Ukonoe chūjō*) Takatoshi reports this respectfully (*uketamawaru*). 2.12.

Respectfully (*kinjō*): To the head (*zasu*) of Daigo temple (Daigoji).[65]

Go-Reizei's spoken order, "From this night, [you] are to arrive and serve" was transmitted to the *kurōdo*, Takatoshi, who concurrently served as the "Captain of the Bodyguards of the Right." Takatoshi wrote this imperial command, which served as a medium of transmitting it to the head of Daigoji, who in turn was to serve as a protector priest, issuing prayers for the welfare of the imperial body. A messenger took this document and conveyed it to Ningai, the Daigoji priest. The document served as a vehicle to ensure that the words were conveyed as precisely as possible, and that, through a messenger, the imperial voice could be heard.

Secretariats possessed great skill in calligraphy, and their fluid cursive *hiragana* contrasts sharply with the blocky, clear *katakana* style of Kamakura wills and judicial documents. Of all orders and edicts, those from the secretariats possessed the ultimate prestige. They confirmed rights to the land and were faithfully enforced by the bakufu. In sum, orders from the secretariat's office (*kurōdo*) of an emperor were known as *rinji*, and those issued from a retired emperor's office were called *inzen*. Both documentary forms linked the sacerdotal prestige of sovereign authority, or the authority of the lord who rules (*chiten no kimi*), with the mundane minutae of policy. Even though thirteenth-century Japan was judicially fragmented, the exalted nature of these orders remained unquestioned.

Imperial orders constituted the physical manifestation of authority. Through an almost metonymic process, these pieces of paper constituted tangible representation of the state and were awarded the same respect due to its officials. Picture scrolls reveal that when a man received such a document, he did so in his most formal court robes, with his family arrayed around him respectfully.[66] The mystique of these documents proved so great that some families, such as the Iriki, kept their *rinji* and *inzen* in a special box, separated from all other records.[67] In other instances, imperial documents were preserved in brocade bags, and their prestige could be transformed into sacerdotal power. Aso Korenao, for example, perished in battle in 1336, and the brocade bag containing his documents was discovered in a remote valley by a commoner. The bag was then presented to a local *jitō*, who in turn handed the documents over to the Aso shrine because the deity claimed the imperial edict (*rinji*) as a treasure of the gods (*kami no ontakara nari*).[68]

As these documents were thought to represent imperial authority, the voice of the emperor, or the sovereign himself, the act of throwing one of these edicts to the ground was regarded as an "unspeakable and outrageously evil act" demanding the strictest punishment.[69] Such conduct was conceived as the equivalent of striking the person of the emperor. Even in the midst of military campaigns, generals stopped to read or listen to imperial messages as if the emperor were present. Not only would individual generals serving on behalf of the court read imperial edicts (*senji*) aloud with their helmets removed, but even armies advancing against the court would pause and carefully listen to an imperial missive.[70]

For example, in 1221, a messenger carrying Go-Toba's edict (*inzen*) confronted the attacking Kamakura bakufu army. Hōjō Yasutoki, behaving as if he were meeting the sovereign, immediately dismounted and removed his helmet as a sign of respect. He then promptly searched for someone in his army who possessed the requisite knowledge and ability to read this edict accurately, representing the exalted personage who had ordered it produced.[71] According to the *Azuma kagami*, only a miniscule number would have been qualified to read the message flawlessly.[72] This episode is not indicative of Yasutoki's literacy; it was he who created Kamakura's legal code and frequently adjudicated disputes. Rather, it suggests that the ability to read such a document aloud was confined to a handful of "experts," who might transmit the imperial voice with perfection.[73]

Such records functioned as the vehicle for conveying policy, and at the same time, they could only be created and interpreted by experts. Those who wrote these records occupied a privileged position where policy became reality and where orders were codified and articulated. The expertise of *kurōdo* remained unquestioned and indispensable even in times of civil war. Emperors might be deposed and replaced with more pliable successors, but the writers of edicts were firmly embedded within the fabric of government and occupied a privileged position in state and society.

The political power of the imperial secretariat (kurōdo)

Writers of imperial documents flourished as the thirteenth century progressed. Their mastery of the language of power deployed in these documents allowed them to monopolize a vital position at court, even though their nominal rank remained low. Their absence or indisposition could adversely affect the ritual functioning of the state, or imperial processions. For example, on 3.23.1294, Hino Toshimitsu and his fellow secretariat (*kurōdo*) Masatoshi decided to rest and do some drinking, thereby obliging the entire procession of a retired emperor to pause until they returned.[74]

Even the most ambitious emperors relied upon their *kurōdo*. Go-Daigo, who strove to rule as an absolute monarch, nevertheless could not countenance issuing orders without his secretariat. Once, during the turmoil of 1333, Go-Daigo needed to issue edicts while his *kurōdo* Chigusa Sadaaki was directing armies far away. Go-Daigo resorted to the drastic step of writing an imperial edict in his own hand, but then forged his secretary's name on the document to assure its credibility![75] An emperor characterized as a revolutionary determined to forge a new order, Go-Daigo could not imagine supplanting his secretariat.[76] He purportedly stated that *rinji* were like sweat: having once seeped out, they could not be retrieved. *Kurōdo* of the mid-thirteenth century favored this statement as a legitimization of absolutism, and an enduring justification of their own positions as the actual producers. To extend the analogy, while Go-Daigo saw the *rinji* as sweat, the *kurōdo* saw themselves as the pores. [77]

Just as only a select few could write these documents, so, too, only the expert few could properly read them. Qualifications seem to have included not only expertise but also status. Cases where men of insufficient rank or status read the documents resulted in dire consequences for those who had the temerity to peruse the lofty phrases from the most elevated. The *Taiheiki*, a fourteenth-century chronicle, records how a Kamakura scribe was commanded to read an imperial letter from Go-Daigo that denied any participation in an aborted rebellion.[78] When he read: "Let the Sun Goddess be the witness that the imperial heart is not false... suddenly his eyes were blinded, blood dripped from his nose, and he withdrew without reading the rest."[79]

Imperial commands, in short, expressed imperial power, but at the same time, transubstantiated it. Indeed, they were invested with the same authority as the regalia, which earlier narratives described as blinding men who looked upon them.[80] The taboos associated with the imperial body, and their regalia symbols of legitimation, also accrued to *rinji*, *inzen*, and any other documentary forms used exclusively by emperors and members of the imperial family. Nevertheless, giving such ominous warnings to prevent those able to read, but lacking sufficient status to do so, suggests that in actuality, the casual reading of imperial records had become conceivable.

Thrown in the mud: Changing attitudes toward documents

Late in the thirteenth century, the documents themselves served as the basis for legitimacy as much as the spoken word, but an increasingly transparent reliance on these documents alone undermined their prestige. For example, a retired emperor's *inzen* legitimated the transfer of lands according to a map drawn from early in the tenth century, but those who were thereby dispossessed resisted violently in favor of their precedent-based rights.[81] The resisters were declared to be enemies of the court and the gods, but when confronted by the imperial edict, they remained unfazed, assaulted the shrine attendant who carried the *inzen* to them, and threw the document into the mud.[82]

This hitherto unthinkable abusive handling of documents became more common in the late thirteenth century, when a sense that inheritance trumped even imperial edicts was augmented further by the fact that the court was increasingly active in redistributing lands.[83] Some litigants threw an edict into the mud as an expression of their disdain, and by doing so, prevented its words from being spoken. In addition to inviting punishment on those who dared to defile imperial edicts, such affairs led to a focus on the legitimizing force of the document itself, rather than on the act of reciting its contents. Even administrative nobles who did not serve as *kurōdo* attempted to emphasize the sacrosanct nature of their own documents, and asserted that they, too, had the right to demand absolute obedience to an imperial command. Kitabatake Chikafusa, who served as the head (*bettō*) of the imperial police (*kebiishi*), later explained that this office not only had the same policing and judicial powers, but also had the authority to compel absolute obedience to the results of its adjudication that imperial edicts (*rinji*) required.[84] This increased emphasis on the inviolability of the written word also explains why, precisely at this time, some who had their interests ignored resorted to throwing these documents into the mud. Over the course of the fourteenth century, it became progressively more difficult to hear the pronouncements of those in authority.

Conclusion

Documents functioned as a trace of the individual who wrote them, and at the same time, they represented a medium for reproducing the voice of important individuals. Most analysis of literacy sees writing as an end to itself, as individuals progressed from emphasizing sounds, to focusing on the written word. In the Kamakura era, however, individuals capable of writing were not always competent to read all records, particularly those emanating from the court. Imperial records, after all, possessed unsurpassed prestige and power in their own right, for they functioned as talismans and shrine treasures worthy of special preservation precisely because they embodied the voices of Japan's sovereigns.

The act of reading documents out loud in the Kamakura era allowed for the wide dissemination of the voices of emperors and retired emperors, who were otherwise constrained by ritual and social prerogative from talking directly to all but a few. To a degree, the mystique associated with the words of imperial documents explains how the court retained primacy in spite of the institutional and judicial advances of the Kamakura regime.[85] Likewise, the nature of the transmission of these documents meant that imperial messengers and secretariats exercised considerable power, and that their actions during the Kamakura era deserve further scrutiny.

The medium of documents began to change in the Kamakura period, however. The earlier notion that they constituted immutable voices requiring the deference due to their authors began to shift, as the documents themselves came to be emphasized as talismans, having a unique meaning and inviolability. This trend allowed the court to gain power, and led to a civil war from 1333 until 1392, but also witnessed incidents where these talismans were literally and figuratively thrown into the mud. As time passed, the papers themselves mattered as much, if not more, than the voices that they had conveyed.

Jeffrey Mass anticipated the unique importance of these records when writing that documents "are not merely remnants of the past, but also a window to the future. More effectively than other sources they reveal human aspirations and indicate life's options by exposing its constraints. Documents anticipate—and in the process help make us contemporaries."[86] His observation proves accurate and suggestive, for by reading documents out loud, one can still hear the whispers of the distant Kamakura past.

NOTES

1   This represents the first document translated by Jeffrey Mass in *The Kamakura Bakufu: A Study in Documents*, pp. 25–26.

2   For cormorant fishers and disputes over fish levies, see Jeffrey Mass, *The Development of Kamakura Rule 1180–1250*, p. 193; for nuns on guard duty, ibid., p. 271; for paper makers fleeing rapacious warriors (*jitō*), see Mass, *The Kamakura Bakufu*, p. 117; for "Demon Crane," see Gentoku 4 (1332). 4.28 Ama oni tsuru gozen yuzurijō an, in Takeuchi Rizō, ed., *Kamakura ibun* vol. 41, doc. 31743, p. 79. (Hereafter, *KI*, 41:31743).

3   Some documents, most notably wills, are written phonetically, allowing for a reconstruction of how these records were read. Unfortunately, the reason for such an intractable debate is because the diacritic markers that distinguish a "g" from a "k", or a "sh" from a "j" are absent, making it difficult to ascertain the correct reading. For a similar debate concerning "*shigyōjō*" versus "*segyōjō*," see Seno Seiichirō, *Rekishi no kansei*, pp. 124–128.

4   The two characters superficially resemble each other. For the "juvenile" nature of the courtiers, see *Heikoki* Kangen 2 (1244).10.15. For the incompetent courtier, see entry for Kangen 3 (1245).4.14. See also Hayakawa Shōhachi, "Kangen ninen no Iwashimizu Hachimangū shinden oai jiken," p. 268.

5   Donald Keene, trans., *Essays in Idleness*, no. 136, pp. 114–115.

6   Reference to the "later three Fusa" of Go-Daigo's reign (1318–1339) as a direct comparison with the three Fusa of Go-Sanjō's reign (1068–1072) first appears in Zuikei Shūhō's diary, *Gaun nikkenroku batsuyū*, entry for Bunshō 1 (1466).7.12. For a treatment of Go-Sanjō's seminal period as emperor, see G. Cameron Hurst, *Insei:*

Abdicated Sovereigns in the Politics of Late Heian Japan, 1086–1185, esp. pp. 100–124.

7   See Hirata Toshiharu, "Yoshida Sadafusa," p. 343, and Nakamura, "Yoshida Sadafusa," p. 267. The *Kojiki* is written phonetically, using Chinese characters for their sounds rather than their meanings, making it virtually incomprehensible to most readers. Reference to Sadafusa appears on the Shinpukuji text of the *Kojiki*, the oldest surviving copy (dating from 1371–1372) by the priest Ken'yū. See Donald Philippi, tr., *Kojiki*, p. 30.

8   Satō Shin'ichi et al., eds., *Chūsei seiji shakai shisō* (hereafter *CSSS*) 2, pp. 149–154. There has been debate for some time whether this essay dates from 1324 or 1330. More recently, Murai Shōsuke has suggested that it may even be dated to 1321; see his "Yoshida Sadafusa sōjō wa itsu kakareta ka."

9   For Sadafusa's betrayal of Go-Daigo, see Gentoku 3 (1331).2.22 *Kamakura nendaiki, buke nendaiki, Kamakura dai nikki*, p. 64. For further on Sadafusa, see Andrew Edmund Goble, *Kenmu: Go-Daigo's Revolution*, pp.11–13, 44, 66–69, 139.

10   Yoshikawa Shinji, "Shinbun shibun kō."

11   Tempyō 20 (748).10.21 Ōhara mabito kushigami nuhi baibaiken, in *Dainihon komonjo, hennen monjo*, vol. 3, p. 126, Tokyo daigaku shiryō hensanjo Nara jidai komonjo full-text database (accessed April 29, 2007).

12   Here, English conveniently allows for the usage of a verb (states) that accurately conveys this oral exchange.

13   Jōwa 8 (841).8.11 Ōmi no kuni Achi gunji ge, in Takeuchi Rizō, ed., *Heian ibun*, vol. 1, doc. 50, p. 34 (hereafter *HI*, 1:50).

14   *Taiketsu* was characterized by Jeffrey Mass as "a court trial or hearing in which the two sides had to confront one another." Jeffrey P. Mass, *The Kamakura Bakufu: A Study in Documents*, p. 211.

15   Jōho 3 (1076).11.23 Tōji ryō Ise no kuni Daikoku no shōji no ge an (*HI*, 3:1137).

16   Kenkyū 5 (1194).5 Nitta Hachimangū shojira mōshijō (*KI*, 2:727).

17   Shōan 1 (1299).6 Raishin teichū mōshijō dodai (*KI*, 26:20151).

18   Thomas Conlan, *In Little Need of Divine Intervention: Takezaki Suenaga's Scrolls of the Mongol Invasions of Japan*, p. 88.

19   Jōei 1 (1232).9.11 Hōjō Yasutoki shojō (*CSSS*, 1, pp. 40–41; also *KI*, 6:4373). See also Jeffrey P. Mass, *The Development of Kamakura Rule 1180–1250*, pp. 90, 102ff. The oldest reference to illiteracy (*monmō*), dating from the late eleventh or early twelfth century, describes the Middle Counsellor Fujiwara Yoshichika. Matsumura Hiroji, ed., *Ōkagami*, p. 146. This term does not commonly appear in documents and literary sources before the thirteenth century.

20   For the accusations, see Jōei 1 (1232).11.28 Kantō gechijō an (*KI*, 6:4407). Bun'ei 3 (1266).4.9 Kantō gechijō (*KI*, 13:9521), p. 163, contains a passage about a certain illiterate Honbutsu relying on others to present documents in court.

21   See the Ninji 2 (1241).4.26 Arakita Ujitoshi ukebumi (*KI*, 8:5812); Ninji 2 (1241).4.26 Arakita Nobunari ukebumi (*KI*, 8:5813); Ninji 2 (1241).5.2 Arakita Nobunari ukebumi (*KI*, 8:5833); Ninji 2.(1241).5.3 Daijingū kannushi chūshinjō (*KI*, 8:5835); Ninji 2 (1241).5.3 Arakita Ujitoshi ukebumi (*KI*, 8:5836); Ninji 2 (1241).5.9 Arakita Ujitoshi ukebumi (*KI*, 8:5848); Ninji 2 (1241).5.9 Arakita Nobunari ukebumi (*KI*, 8:5849); and Ninji 2 (1241).5.13 Arakita Tsunemoto ukebumi (*KI*, 8:5858).

22   For an example of how the fact that a document was written by the donor proved decisive, even where a seal, or monogram, was otherwise lacking, see Kōan 9 (1286).5.3 Kantō gechijō (*KI*, 21:15888) and, for an English translation, see Mass, *Lordship and Inheritance in Early Medieval Japan*, doc. 115, p. 248.

23   See Mass, *Lordship and Inheritance*, doc. 150, p. 291, and Gentoku 2 (1330).3.18 Chōkai (Yamanouchi Michisuke) yuzurijō (*KI*, 40:30977).

24   See Kōchō 3 (1263).10.8 Kumagai Naotoki okibumi (*KI*, 12:8998). For another example, see the Engyō 4 (1311).3.26 postscript to a will of Shōan 3 (1301).2.5, which states: "As Ebina Saemon no jō Tadatō states that this document is a forgery (*bōsho*), I have written this on the obverse." (*KI*, 31:24264). These records are quite common. For another written in the hand of the donor, which was confirmed by Kamakura, see Genkō 4 (1324).3.29 Ama Ikuwan yuzurijō (*KI, hoi*

4:ho 2034). For a variant transcription of this document, see *Dai Nihon komonjo Yamanouchi Sudō ke monjo*, doc. 33, pp. 39–41.

25   Ama Rennin okibumi an (*KI, hoi* 3:ho 1424).

26   Index volumes of these series were not included in determining the number of volumes of these series.

27   *Kamakura ibun* full-text database, Tokyo daigaku shiryō hensanjo (accessed on December 23, 2006).

28   Thus, the same number of phonetically written wills (203) exist for the period from 1185 to 1280 as from 10.5.1280 until 10.16.1311. Furthermore, while 203 wills were written during the thirty-one years of 1280 until 1311, 248 were written with some kind of phonetic script over the next twenty-two years. *Kamakura ibun* full-text database, Tokyo daigaku shiryō hensanjo (accessed on February 14, 2007).

29   Amino Yoshihiko, "Nihon no moji shakai no tokushitsu o megutte." For an excellent summary of Amino's argument in English, see Henry Smith, "Japaneseness and the History of the Book," p. 510.

30   Amino Yoshihiko has postulated that documents such as wills would be written in *hiragana* because they were not oral records, but in fact his generalization ignores that approximately 5 percent of all surviving wills written phonetically were written in *katakana* (20 out of 407 written between 1185 and 1311). Tokyo daigaku shiryō hensanjo database (accessed December 2006). Many wills written in *katakana* can be found in Kii province (modern day Wakayama), suggesting that considerable regional variation in practice and education existed. See for example, Shōō 3 (1290).11.20 Minamoto Kagetomo denchi kakiuchi yuzurijō and Jōwa 5 (1349) Minamoto Kagetomo, haha Yashame renso denchi yuzurijō (*Wakayama kenshi, chūsei shiryō*, vol. 2, pp. 640-642.) The former document is not included in *KI*.

31   Compare Shigetoki's two precepts, in *CSSS*, 1, pp. 310–346. See also the Taira Shigetoki shōsoku (*KI*, 12:8730) and the Hōjō Shigetoki shōsoku (*KI*, 12:8731). Inconsistencies in practice exist, however, even among relatively close relatives. Shigetoki's nephew Sanetoki preferred writing his similar, if more succinct precepts, in *katakana*. For translations of Shigetoki's letters, see Carl Steenstrup, *Hōjō Shigetoki*.

32   One can see in a 1350 document that Raiyū and Raishin purchased lands, and in their document of sale, they mixed both

syllabaries. Jōwa 6 (1350).3 Raiyū Raishin rensho denchi uriwatashijō (*Wakayama kenshi, chūsei shiryō*, vol. 2, p. 460). For a later example exhibiting a similar amalgamation of *kana*, see Kakitsu 3 (1443).11.6 Tenjinji Kenjiku hatachi uriwatashijō (*Wakayama kenshi, chūsei shiryō*, vol. 2, pp. 540-541).

33   Hōjō Sanetoki kakun, *CSSS*, 1, pp. 348–349.

34   Eiwa 1 (1375) Mōri Motoharu kotogaki utsushi, in Matsuoka Hisato, comp., *Nanbokuchō ibun Chūgoku Shikoku hen*, vol. 5, doc. 4250, p. 76 (hereafter *NBI-Ch*, 5:4250).

35   Shōgen 1 (1259).12.19 Ama Shinmyō yuzurijō (*KI*, 11:8450). I am grateful to Andrew Goble for bringing this document to my attention.

36   Jōei 1 (1232).7.6 Hōjō Yasutoki (?) shojō (*KI*, 6:4339).

37   For a translated example, see Mass, *Lordship and Inheritance*, doc. 59, p. 182; see also document 75, p. 202. For the originals, see En'ō 1 (1239).11.5 Kantō gechijō (*KI*, 8:5496) and Kenchō 8 (1256).7.9 Shōgun ke mandokoro kudashibumi (*KI*, 11:8010).

38   Examples exist of edicts written in Japanese characters (*wa no ji no migyōsho*), which were most likely transcribed copies of an edict that had originally been written in *kanbun*. See Kenchō 4 (1252).6.30 Kantō gechijō an (*KI*, 10:7454). For the text and a photograph of this document, see http://www.hi.u-tokyo.ac.jp/IRIKI/EJTL/ejt50-2.html.

39   Shōwa 4 (1315).6.2 Chinzei gechijō (*KI*, 33:25527) and Shōwa 4 (1315).6.2 Chinzei gechijō an (*KI*, 33:25528). See also Seno Seiichirō, *Zōtei Kamakura bakufu saikyōjōshū ge*, doc. 94, Shōwa 4 (1315).6.2 Chinzei tandai saikyōjō, pp. 194–198 and added (*hoi*) document 6, pp. 342–348. The few Chinese characters used, largely names, were written with phonetic glosses. Thus, the name "Saki no Kazusa no suke Taira no ason" is written in characters, but also with glosses written in *furigana* so as to allow the participant to read the document out loud correctly, and on a few occasions where the character for "year" appears, one sees it glossed as "nen."

40   This becomes evident in the writing of Kanezawa Sadaaki, who apologizes for using a scribe because his eyes are strained. See the (year unknown) intercalary 6.3 Sūkan (Kanezawa Sadaaki) shojō (*KI*, 40:31093). For analysis of this letter, see Kanagawa kenritsu Kanazawa

bunko, ed., *Kanezawa Sadaaki no tegami*, p. 12. This letter most likely dates from 1330.

41   See Minegishi Sumio, "Tainai monjo to inbutsu," in *Hino shishi shiryōshū Takahata fudō tainai monjo*, pp. 181–84. Most of the images (sixty) were of *Fudō*, while eighteen were of *Daitokuten*.

42   See the explanation of Yamanouchi Tsuneyuki's documents in Kodama Kōta, ed., *Hino shishi tsūshi hen jō*, pp. 198–205.

43   Walter Ong, *Orality and Literacy: The Technologizing of the Word* (Routledge, 1982), p. 115.

44   Jeffrey Mass, *Antiquity and Anachronism*, pp. 53–56.

45   *Azuma kagami* Jishō 4 (1180).4.27. This translation is drawn from Shinoda, *The Founding of the Kamakura Shogunate 1180–1185*, p. 150.

46   *Genpei jōsuiki*, vol. 4, maki 19, p. 30. I am grateful to Vyjayanthi Selinger for bringing this to my attention.

47   *Genpei jōsuiki*, vol. 4, maki 20, pp. 54–55.

48   Ibid., p. 56.

49   Kagen 3 (1305).5.16 Kurasu Kaneo shojō (*KI*, 29:22218).

50   Bun'ei 11 (1274).1.14 Nichiren shojō (*KI*, 15:11519), which has been translated as "The Votary of the Lotus Sutra Will Meet Persecution," in the Gosho Translation Committee, ed., *The Writings of Nichiren Daishonin*, pp. 447–449. Likewise, the postscript of this letter (p. 449) mentions how "Toki . . . and the rest of you, gentlemen and priests, should read this letter to one another and listen." Nichiren also uses the phrase "listening to readings" in a Kenji 2 (1276).3.18 Nichiren shojō (*KI*, 16:12266). See also *Minkeiki*, entry for Katei 1 (1235).1.10 for mention of a court document (*senji*) being read and listened to. These references were discovered via the Tokyo daigaku shiryō hensanjo full-text databases (accessed December 2, 2006).

51   For "have read," see the undated Hōjō Shigetoki shōsoku (*KI*, 12:8731) and Bun'ei 1 (1264).4.17 Nichiren shojō (*KI*, 12:9076). For a translation of Shigetoki's letter to his son, Nagatoki, see Steenstrup, *Hōjō Shigetoki*, pp. 143–157. The Nichiren letter has been translated as "The Recitation of the 'Expedient Means' and 'Life Span' Chapters," in *The Writings of Nichiren Daishonin*, pp. 68–72. "Read and state" appears commonly. For a few examples, see the Jōō 3 (1224) Jien

ganmon (*KI*, 5:3202); Katei 2 (1236).3.20 Hōin Shūsei kokubumi (*KI*, 7:4948); Bun'ei 3 (1266).11 Sonshin okibumi an (*KI*, 13:9600); Kenji 3 (1277).11.10 Kantō hyōjō sadamebumi (*KI*, 17:12901); Kōan 7 (1284).9.10 Hōjō Hisatoki shojō (*KI*, 20:15302); and Shōō 4 (1291).5.12 Bō sojō an (*KI*, 23:17614), Tokyo daigaku shiryō hensanjo full-text database (accessed December 2, 2006).

52   Kenji 3 (1277).11.10 Kantō hyōjō sadamebumi (*KI*, 17:12901). This document is an excerpt from the *Kenji sannenki*.

53   According to the Tokyo daigaku shiryō hensanjo kokiroku full text database, thirty-three references to the term *yomimōsu* appear in Heian courtier diaries and twenty-six in Kamakura era diaries. The term 'being read" (*yomare*) appears eleven times in Heian diaries. In Heian documents, no references to documents being read out loud, or for that matter, words such as "illiteracy" appear at all. Examples can be found, however, of court documents (*senji*) being "seen." See Ten'ei 1 (1110).12.10 Tōdaiji sangō chūshin an (*HI*, 4:1738) and Ten'ei 2 (1111).2 Tōdaiji mōshibumi (*HI*, 4:1743).

54   Steenstrup, *Hōjō Shigetoki*, p. 143. See also *CSSS*, 1, p. 310.

55   For Steenstrup's analysis of the age of Shigetoki and his son when this letter was written, see *Hōjō Shigetoki*, n. 11, pp. 284–285.

56   Steenstrup, ibid, p. 162. For the Japanese version, see *CSSS*, 1, p. 322.

57   Steenstrup, *Hōjō Shigetoki*, p. 197, and *CSSS*, 1, p. 346.

58   See the *Mineaiki*, pp. 66–67.

59   *Maeda hon "Gyokudaku hōten" shihai monjo to sono kenkyū*, document 1–30, (year unknown).3.29 Sadakiyo shojō, p. 16. See p. 148 for analysis of these previously unknown documents, many of which were issued by the administrative headquarters (*mandokoro*) of Ashikaga Tadayoshi in 1348.

60   (Year unknown).12.19 Kanezawa Sadaaki shojō (*Kanazawa bunko komonjo*, vol. 2, doc. 410, p. 43.) This document appears not to be included in *KI*.

61   (Year unknown).5.9 Kanezawa Sadaaki shojō (*KI*, 29:22206). See also the (year unknown).12.4 Kanezawa Sadaaki shojō, (*KI*, 29:22207). For another example of messengers "explaining the

particulars in the capital," see the (year unknown).7.1 Kanezawa Sadaaki shojō (*KI*, 28:21883).

62   See William H. McCullough, "*Shōkyūki*: An Account of the Shōkyū War of 1221," p. 207, for the seizure of the imperial messenger, Oshimatsu, for "if he succeeds in making the proclamation known" most warriors "will probably turn" against Kamakura. See also *Azuma kagami* Jōkyū 3 (1221).5.19 (William H. McCullough, trans., "The *Azuma Kagami* Account of the Shōkyū War," p. 105). For one example of the Kōno family turning against Kamakura after the imperial forces had been defeated, see Jōkyū 3 (1221).6.28 Rokuhara gechijō (*KI*, 5:2762). For related Kōno documents, see Mass, *The Kamakura Bakufu*, document 172, p. 182, and Mass, *The Development of Kamakura Rule*, docs. 31–32, pp. 183–184. For more on the Kōno, see *Azuma kagami* Jōkyū 3 (1221).6.28 (McCullough, trans., "The *Azuma Kagami* Account of the Shōkyū War," p. 137).

63   (Year unknown) Third month Kanezawa Sadaaki shojō (*KI*, 30:22911).

64   *Genpei jōsuiki*, vol. 4, maki 19, p. 30.

65   The 1054.2.12 Go-Reizei record appears in the Daigoji records. See *Daigoji monjo mokuroku*, p. 1215. This document and the Tenjō 1 (1131).2.2 Sutoku tennō rinji are the oldest surviving original imperial orders. They do not appear in *Heian ibun*, although the latter record has been transcribed in Satō Shin'ichi, *Komonjogaku nyūmon*, p. 293, doc. 16 and p. 105.

66   For an early analysis, see Gomi Fumihiko, *Chūsei no kotoba to e*. This *Eshi zōshi* scroll has been reproduced in *Haseo sōshi, Eshi zōshi*.

67   I thank Kondō Shigekazu for showing me these Iriki documents in July 1997.

68   Kenmu 5 (1338).6.18 Maki Hidehiro kishōmon utsushi, *Nanbokuchō ibun, Kyūshū hen* (hereafter *NBI-Ky*), 1:1182, pp. 357–358. See also the (year unknown).9.5 Chōhen shojō (*NBI-Ky*, 6:6631) for more on this discovery.

69   Shōō 5 (1292).8 Kakushō mōshijō (*KI*, 23:17994) for a dispute stemming from a virtuous government decree abolishing debt, known as a *tokusei*. Other documents reveal similar disputes. In Sanuki province, where public revenues were earmarked for the imperial

family, the residents of the province disobeyed an imperial edict (*rinji*) in a similar manner. See the Einin 2 (1294).6.23 Fushimi tennō rinji (*KI*, 24:18584).

70   McCullough, "The *Azuma Kagami* Account of the Shōkyū War," p. 123. The *Azuma kagami* entry for Jōkyū 3 (1221).6.8 mentions one man reading an imperial edict (*senji*) aloud with helmet removed.

71   In an apocryphal debate as to what to do if the Retired Emperor himself should resist the Hōjō, who were nominally attacking his evil advisers, Hōjō Yasutoki stated that he would take off his helmet, put down his bow, and with head bowed surrender. See *Baishōron*, p. 41. This text has been translated by Uyenaka, p. 101. This dialogue appears in other sources, too: see Perkins, *The Clear Mirror: A Chronicle of the Japanese Court During the Kamakura Period (1185–1333)*, pp. 51–52. For a study of the topic, see Haruyo Lieteau, "The Yasutoki-Myōe Discussion."

72   On 1221.6.15 a messenger from the court approached the advancing Kamakura army. A search revealed that only one warrior of five thousand could do so. McCullough, "The *Azuma Kagami* Account of the Shōkyū War," entry for 1221.6.15, p. 130, refers to this episode. The variant *Azuma kagami* text transcribed by Ryō Susumu (vol. 4, p. 205) reads one out of fifty warriors as being able to read this document, while the "orthodox" *Azuma kagami* text, translated by McCullough, reads as one of five thousand. See *Azuma kagami* Jōkyū 3 (1221).6.15.

73   Farris mentions this episode in *Heavenly Warriors*, n. 111, p. 434, and equates the ability to read such documents with general literacy. However, examination of a wider range of Kamakura documents reveals varying levels of literacy, and so a more nuanced view of the matter would seem to be in order. For an informative study of many of the modern shibboleths concerning literacy, see M. T. Clanchy, *From Memory to Written Record in England 1066–1307*, particularly pp. 1–21.

74   *Sanemi kyōki* Einin 2 (1294).3.23.

75   For photograph and brief analysis of a handwritten (*jihitsu*) Genkō 3 (1333).3.4 Go-Daigo tennō rinji, see plate 1, *Nihon Rekishi* 2002.6 (no. 649), analysis by Hongō Kazuto. Go-Daigo wrote it after arriving in Izumo following his dramatic escape by fishing boat from

the remote island of Oki where he had been banished in 1332. For more on *rinji*, see Tomita Masahiro, "Chūsei kuge seiji monjo no saikentō," pp. 2–3. For a document relating to the movement of his secretariat, Chigusa Tadaaki, see the Genkō 3 (1333).11 Echigo Suwabe Enkyō kyōdai mōshijō (*KI*, 42:32727), which notes him leading an army on 1333.3.22, and attacking the capital on 1333.4.8.

76   See Goble, *Kenmu: Go-Daigo's Revolution*, especially pp. 29–45; and his "Visions of an Emperor."

77   For a mid-thirteenth-century reference to this phrase, drawing on Chinese texts, see *Yōkōki*, entry for Hōji 1 (1247).4.27, which draws upon a document from Kangen 4 (1246).12.20 (in *KI*, 9:6779, as Fujiwara Tsunetaka kanmon). The document recorded in the *Yōkōki* argues that in fact because *rinji* were inviolate, respect for precedent must be maintained. Go-Daigo had a different view of precedent, but a similar view of the inviolability of *rinji*. According to the Kenmu laws, "*Rinji* issued after Kenmu (1334) cannot be easily changed. If for some reason a *rinji* must be revoked, that clause must be written in a document, and conveyed to the provincial governors and *shugo*. Through this mechanism, *rinji* shall be obeyed." Kenmu shinsei no hō, no. 8, in *CSSS*, 2, pp. 71–72. See also Goble, *Kenmu*, pp. 145–50; and Goble, "Visions of an Emperor," pp. 128–130, 134–137.

78   1324.9.24 Go-Daigo tennō rinji. This document, not included in the *Kamakura ibun*, is translated in its entirety in Goble, *Kenmu: Go-Daigo's Revolution*, pp. 68–69. A convenient published version of the Japanese text may be found in Murata Masashi, *Fūchinroku, Murata Masashi chosakushū*, vol. 7, pp. 57–59. Technically, this document is not a *rinji* but rather a *kokubumi*. It was written and transmitted by one of Go-Daigo's most trusted secretariats, Yoshida Sadafusa, and was personally delivered by Madenokōji Nobufusa.

79   Helen C. McCullough, trans., *The Taiheiki*, p. 26. For a variation, stating that he grew faint, a tumor appeared in his throat, and one week later he died coughing blood, see the *Jingū chōkokanbon* version of the *Taiheiki*, maki 1, "Kokubumi no tsukai tatsu koto," pp. 20–21.

80   See, for example, Tsuchida, trans., *The Tale of the Heike*, vol. 2, "The Death of Noritsune," p. 678. A number of accounts exist about the mysterious properties of the regalia. Smoke emitted from their box when the insane emperor Reizei tried to view them, and the sacred

sword was sheathed as of its own accord. See *Zoku kojidan*, p. 344. The *Fukego*, written by Fujiwara Tadazane (1121–79) attributes this very episode to the emperor Yōzei. See Gotō Akio et al., eds., *Gōdanshō, Chūgaishō, Fukego*, pp. 442, 585.

81   Ōchō 1 (1311).7.7 Fushimi jōkō inzen an (*KI hoi*, 4:ho 1927).

82   For one representative description of the violent attacks, see Engyō 3 (1310).11 Kitano Tenmangūji shikan ra ge an, (*KI hoi*, 4:ho 1903) and Engyō 4 (1311).4 Kitano Tenmangūji shikan ra rensho mōshijō an (*KI hoi*, 4:ho 1913). For resisters characterized as "enemies of the gods," see Ōchō 1 (1311).7.7 Fushimi jōkō inzen an (*KI hoi*, 4:ho 1927). For the throwing of the edict into the mud, see Engyō 3 (1310).11 Kitano Tenmangūji shikan ra ge an (*KI hoi*, 4:ho 1903). This appears to have been a particularly vile offense, variously described as "extremely evil" (*mōaku*) or "an unprecedented and unspeakable outrage" (*kidai no rōzeki gongo dōdan*). See the Engyō 3 (1310).9.20 Kitano Tenmangūji kumonjo Taizen ukebumi an (*KI hoi*, 4:ho 1901) and Engyō 3 (1310).11.4 Fushimi jōkō inzen an (*KI hoi*, 4:ho 1902). Other examples of throwing edicts in the mud may be found in Shōō 5 (1292).8 Kakusō mōshijō (*KI*, 23:17994) and in Mori, *Kamakura jidai no chōbaku kankei*, note 31, p. 417.

83   For more on the late Kamakura rise of a sense of judicial right, see Thomas Conlan, *State of War: The Violent Order of Fourteenth Century Japan*, pp. 194–212.

84   *Shokugenshō*, found most conveniently in Shiroyama Yoshitarō, *Shokugenshō no kisoteki kenkyū*, pp. 240–241. Chikafusa, who twice served in this post, stated that to disobey this was as great a crime as disobeying an imperial edict. This has been noted by Hashimoto Hatsuko, "Chūsei no kebiishi chō kankei monjo ni tsuite," pp. 3–5. For Chikafusa's appointment to this post, see *Kebiishi bunin*, vol. 2, pp. 377, 379, 390–391.

85   Indeed, I remember, in conversation from 1993 or 1994, how Jeff, when pushed as how best to describe the Kamakura era in light of the fact that he perceived the fourteenth century to be transformative, described the age not as the dual polity but as "Heian II."

86   Jeffrey Mass, "Documents, Translation and History," in *Antiquity and Anachronism in Japanese History*, p. 156.

FRACTIOUS FLOWS

What a Difference a Bow Makes: The Rules of War in Early Medieval Japan

Karl Friday

Intriguing similarities—and equally tantalizing differences—in technology and circumstance between the knights of medieval Europe and the *bushi* of medieval Japan beguile observers and beckon comparing eyes. Indeed, both parallels and dissimilitude can be seen even in the names used to identify the two warrior orders. While in Europe knights were members of the *ordo equestris,* or practitioners of chivalry—from the French *chevalier* or "horseman"—in Japan early samurai styled themselves followers of *kyūba no michi*, "the way of **bow** and horse."

Comparisons of the customs and institutions of medieval Japan with those of medieval Europe are as old as scholarship on the former, beginning with the descriptive essays of the first Jesuits in Japan and continuing in the writings of nineteenth-century Western visitors to the islands.[1] Asakawa Kan'ichi, writing in the early decades of the last century, introduced a new level of refinement to such comparative study, offering the first systematic explanations of Japanese institutions couched in the vocabulary of European medievalists.[2] Asakawa's work was premised on his perceptions of an essential similarity between Japanese and Western "feudalism," a belief that was reified by the succeeding generation of historians, to the point at which assertions such as, "there are only two fully proven cases of feudalism, those of Western Europe and of Japan," or "almost every feature of Japanese feudal development duplicated what had happened in Northern France," could pass virtually unchallenged.[3]

By the 1980s, however, historians were becoming increasingly uncomfortable with what one author eventually dubbed the "Western-analog" view of *bushi* development.[4] Led by John W. Hall and Jeffrey P. Mass, scholars began to question the applicability to the Japanese case of hoary constructs like "feudalism," and to use comparative analysis to illuminate the fundamental differences between developments in medieval Japan and Europe.[5]

The military conventions that evolved with the knights and the *bushi* offer fruitful ground for assessment in this vein. For war is, as Michael Walzer has observed, "a social creation."[6] Modern politicians and soldiers sometimes fancy that "war itself" knows no intrinsic limits, and is independent of the moral codes of particular societies. But historians and anthropologists have long understood that war, like other human activities, has no existence apart from the context in which it takes place, and from which it takes its meaning. People decide what war is and is not, and build limits—including ideas about who can fight and how—into the very construct of war itself.

Medieval European theorists distinguished between two kinds of rules of war: those governing the reasons for fighting ("Just War," or *jus ad bellum*) and those governing the way wars are fought ("Just Warfare," or *jus in bello*). The two constructs are logically separable, but in practice a society's definitions of what constitutes Just Warfare are shaped in large measure by its ideas about why wars are—or should be—fought.

The following essay contrasts the world of the samurai with that of European knights, focusing on their rules for war as they emerged during the tenth through the thirteenth centuries, the formative ages for both traditions. It examines the ways that the socio-political climate in which the early *bushi* functioned shaped Japanese customs and beliefs regarding battle ethics, and the reasons these conventions differed so dramatically from European notions of *jus in bello*.

Just Warfare West and East

Much of the battlefield gallantry we now celebrate was more idealized than real, but there is little doubt that codes of war did operate in medieval European warfare, or that these codes provided the framework for later Western ideas about the rules of war. Chivalry was shaped in part by the values and the politics of the church, but it was primarily designed by and for the aristocratic knights who led war, and reflected their sense of themselves as professional fighting men.[7]

The most systematic efforts by the church to restrain war were the Peace of God and Truce of God movements of the tenth and eleventh centuries and the Second Lateran Council of 1139. Collectively, these declarations defined particular days as unacceptable for fighting; insisted that those who, by definition of their social function, have nothing to do with war-making were to be protected from the ravages of war; and attempted to ban the use of missile weapons and siege machines in warfare between Christians. But the real origins of the conventions governing warfare in medieval Europe lay outside the church, in the sharp division between the armed noble and the rest of society brought about by military, social, technological, and economic changes that swept across northwestern Europe during the centuries surrounding the turn of the first millennium. The emerging knightly class inherited and broadened long-established codes of conduct for nobles on the battlefield, giving birth to a body of custom concerned primarily with regulating the profits, and mitigating the rigors, of conflict.[8]

Except in the case of specific disciplinary regulations issued by specific commanders, violations of this body of custom lacked the force of law and were thus not enforceable in any judicial sense. But they became generally accepted—if not universal—through frequent repetition, and because of their innate practical value. The application and observation of such customs of war depended first on their pragmatic advantages, and second on the dictates of honor and reputation.[9]

Although chivalry was a uniquely European construct, scholars have long postulated the existence of similar sorts of gentlemanly norms and conventions underlying the conduct of fighting between the early *bushi* as well. Early medieval battles have often been portrayed as set pieces, following an elaborate choreography determined by rules that made the conduct of the fighting almost as important as the result. Eiko Ikegami's characterization of early medieval warfare as "a complex social ritual of death, honor and calculation," and "actual combats on the medieval battlefield" as "colorful rites of violence, death and honor," is a recent case in point.[10]

But this vision of early medieval warfare owes more to received tradition than to the actual historical record.[11] Historians who have described ritual and formality on early medieval battlefields have done so because they *expected* to find it there, and allowed preconceptions to restrict their views of their sources and preclude alternative interpretations. More recent scholarship, based on closer analysis of the sources, including the most familiar ones, indicates that Heian and Kamakura period warriors were a good deal less gentlemanly in their battlefield antics than was once believed.[12]

Unlike "chivalry," which was at least in part a prescriptive and proscriptive code of conduct, the early medieval Japanese "way of bow and horse" was simply a vocational description. The reasons underlying the gap in perception of military ethics that separated knights from *bushi* can be found in the fundamentally dissimilar socio-political structures of the worlds in which they lived and fought.

Honor and Its Ambits

In medieval Japan and Europe alike, honor and reputation lay at the heart of warriors' self-perception, and provide the context for evaluating warrior adherence to the conventions of war. Honor—or conversely, shame—could reach beyond the warrior himself, and even beyond his lifespan. Knights and *bushi* could prosper through the inherited glory of their ancestors or suffer the stigma of their disgrace. Thus, even a warrior's life could be of less consequence to him than his name and image, and we find in accounts of battles numerous sketches of *bushi* choosing to sacrifice themselves in order to enhance their reputations or those of their families.[13]

The priorities of Norman knights, which placed preservation of honor ahead of defense of family, church, state, or territory, are reflected in a speech imputed to William Marshall in *Histoire de Guillaume le Maréchal*. He begins, "At a time when, to preserve our reputation, to defend ourselves, our wives, our children, our friends and our land, to win honor for the peace of Holy Church which our enemies have broken, to be pardoned for our sins, we support the burden of arms . . . ." Among the qualities germane to a knight's reputation and honor were loyalty to his lord and his kin, sagacity of counsel, largesse to vassals or companions in arms, greatness of spirit, piety, and even courtliness and refinement. But above all, a *chevalier*'s reputation and pride were built upon his military record. As a result, pragmatic self-interest and honorable conduct in battle often overlapped, but did not always coincide perfectly.[14]

A samurai's reputation, honor, and pride were almost tangible entities that took precedence over all other obligations. As a thirteenth-century commentary enumerating the "seven virtues of a warrior" concludes, "To go forth to the field of battle and miss death by a hair; to leave behind one's name for myriad generations; all in all, this is the way."[15] Slights to reputation or honor were often catalysts to bloodshed. Warriors might refuse orders from their superiors, risk the loss of valuable retainers, and even murder men to whom they owed their lives, all for the sake of their reputations.

One must, however, be cautious about making anachronistic or ethnocentric assumptions about the nature of honor or about the sort of battlefield conduct it might be expected to engender. For while concepts of honor and shame were of the most profound importance to the self-perception of the knights and *bushi* alike, a warrior's honor turned on his military reputation, which rested first and foremost on his record of victories. And early medieval Japanese concepts of honor and of honorable conduct in battle appear to have been flexible enough to permit successful warriors to rationalize almost any behavior.[16] Thus, unlike their European counterparts, *bushi* were seldom, if ever, faced with choosing between military advantage and adherence to chivalric norms. Pragmatism, self-interest, and tactical, strategic, or political advantage proved to be much more powerful determinants of early medieval Japanese military conventions than abstractions like honor.

Deception and Guile

One of the most important features of the Western corpus of customs pertaining to behavior in battle was the set of rules governing the onset of hostilities. European lords saw a fundamental need to mark cleanly the transition from a state of peace to one of war. It was a serious matter to claim that someone had begun an attack "without keeping his honor" or "without issuing a challenge." The required interval varied by customary law and specific compacts from a minimum of three days to two weeks or even a month between challenge and opening of hostilities, and tricks designed to observe the technicality, while preventing opponents from learning that a feud had been declared, were similarly held in contempt.

In point of fact, as Matthew Strickland observes, the act of formal challenge filled many functions. It first, of course, sought to establish a fixed time and place for combat, to avoid ambush and surprise attacks, but it also served as a "public assertion of a lord's power and aggressive intent, an act of bravado and intimidation." As such, challenges were not always mere preludes to inevitable battle. They were just as often a deliberate means of *avoiding* conflict, a means to call an enemy's tactical bluff.[17]

Japan, in any case, developed no such conventions. Although *bushi* did sometimes issue challenges and even set times and places for battle, such promises were honored far more often in the breach than in the event. In fact, the preferred stratagem was to catch opponents off-guard, utilizing ambushes, night attacks, and other surprise tactics.[18] The preference for this sort of fighting is reflected in even the most romanticized accounts of early medieval warriors.

Indeed, one of the most striking passages in the *Hōgen monogatari* relates the council of war held by forces of the retired emperor (Sutoku) on the eve of battle. When asked by Fujiwara Yorinaga, the Minister of the Left, how he recommended conducting the coming hostilities, Minamoto Tametomo is purported to have replied:

> According to my experience, there is nothing so advantageous in striking down enemies as a night attack. Let Tametomo go now, while the heavens are not yet light, and press down upon Takamatsu Palace. If we set fire to three sides and secure the fourth, those fleeing the flames will be struck down by arrows, and for those who seek to avoid the arrows, there will be no escape from the flames.

Yorinaga was, however, unpersuaded:

> Tametomo's plan is crude; it lacks wisdom. This is the effect of his youth. Night attacks and such are suitable to private fights involving ten or twenty men, but when the emperor and retired emperor contend for a whole nation, a night attack is unthinkable.[19]

Concerns for matters of propriety in warfare such as Yorinaga expresses in this passage are notably absent from contemporaneous accounts of *bushi* behavior.[20] It is significant that even here the words are placed in the mouth of Yorinaga—a courtier, not a military man—rather than attributed to any warrior. Heian-period audiences considered surprise attacks so normal that an early eleventh-century text could begin a description of the archetypical *bushi*, "the greatest warrior in the land," by informing us that "he was highly skilled in the conduct of battles, *night attacks*, archery duels on horseback, and *ambushes*" (emphasis added).[21]

Among the most famous apologues of early samurai behavior is a story about a conflict between two early tenth-century warriors, Minamoto Mitsuru and Taira Yoshifumi. After gossip carried between the two sparks a quarrel that results in a challenge to combat:

> The two sides exchanged documents, agreeing to meet on the field on a specified day. After this both put their troops in order and prepared to fight. On the agreed-upon day, the two war bands set forth, coming to face each other across the designated field at the hour of the serpent [10:00 AM]. Both were forces of five or six hundred men. While all prepared their hearts, readying to cast aside their bodies and disregard their lives, they planted their shields in rows, facing each other at a distance of about one *chō* [approximately 110 meters].

> Each side then sent forth a warrior to exchange documents. As those warriors returned to their ranks, there began, as was customary, a flurry of arrows. The warriors did not look back or even hurry their horses forward, but returned quietly—thus displaying their bravery. After this, both sides moved their shields closer together and were about to begin shooting, when Yoshifumi called to Mitsuru,

> "To simply set our respective troops discharging arrows at one another does not serve the interest of today's battle. Let only you and I learn of each other's skill. Instead of having our troops engage, how about if only the two of us ride at one another and take our best shots?"

Mitsuru concurs and, after cautioning his men to stay out of the fight, even should he lose, rides out to engage Yoshifumi alone. The two make several passes at one another, but neither is able to score a decisive shot. At length they agree to call the matter a draw and, having settled their quarrel, spend the remainder of their lives amicably.[22]

The behavior of Mitsuru and Yoshifumi in this tale accords well with the eidolon of the received wisdom, and is, in fact, the principal source cited in support of several key tenets thereof. But it contrasts vividly with another account, in the same text, about two other tenth-century warriors, Taira Koremochi and Fujiwara Morotō.[23] A dispute over a piece of land festers, fueled by gossip, until at length a challenge is issued and date and place are decided. As the day of battle approaches, Morotō finds that he is outnumbered nearly three to one and, apparently believing discretion to be the better part of valor, flees instead to a neighboring province. The text that records the tale informs us that "those who spoke between the two warriors pronounced favorably on this."

Koremochi, upon receiving this news, determines things to be safe and demobilizes his men, who have been pestering him to allow them to return to their homes. But shortly thereafter, Morotō, approaching with a sizable force, startles Koremochi and his household from their sleep. Morotō's men surround Koremochi's compound, set fire to the buildings, and shoot down anyone who emerges. When the fire has burned itself out, they search the ashes, "discovering men of high and low rank, children and the like—all told more than eighty persons—burned to death."

En route home, Morotō stops near the home of his brother-in-law, to give his troops a rest. The brother-in-law, identified only as Ōkimi ("the great prince"), sends food and *sake*, on which Morotō's men gorge themselves, until they pass out. Unbeknownst to them, however, Koremochi is not dead. He has escaped by seizing a robe from one of his serving women, and slipping past the attackers under the cover of the smoke.[24]

"Dropping into the depths of a stream to the west, he carefully approached a place far from the bank where reeds and such grew thickly, and clung to the roots of a willow," where he hides until the fighting is over and Morotō's troops have withdrawn. Some of his own troops who have not been in the house find him later, and resupply him with clothing, weapons, and a horse. He explains what has happened, adding that he had chosen not to flee into the mountains at the beginning of the attack because he feared that "this would leave behind the reputation of one who had run away." His men counsel him to wait and reassemble his forces before going after Morotō, whose troops outnumber them five or six to one. But Koremochi shakes off this advice, arguing:

> Had I been burned to death inside my house last night, would my life exist now? I escaped in this manner at great cost, yet I do not live. To show myself to you for even one day is extremely shameful. Therefore, I will not be stingy with this dew-like life. You may assemble an army and fight later. As for myself, I will go [on to attack] alone. . . . No doubt I will send off [only] a single arrow and then die, but to choose otherwise would be a limitless shame for my descendants. . . . Those of you who begrudge your lives need not come with me; I will go alone.

Koremochi and his men then fall upon Morotō's troops, taking them completely by surprise. Drunk and sated, Morotō's side is able to offer only a feeble defense, and is soon utterly destroyed. After taking Morotō's head, Koremochi advances on Morotō's home, which he puts to the torch.

In spite of very similar beginnings, the conflicts between Yoshifumi and Mitsuru and between Morotō and Koremochi proceed in such stark contrast to one another that readers are left wondering if perhaps there could have been two competing ethics of battlefield conduct during the tenth century. But while at least one scholar has concluded that there was in fact a "dichotomy about confrontation" at work among Heian warriors, Ishii Susumu offers a simpler explanation. The confrontation between Yoshifumi and Mitsuru, he observes, would have to have occurred about 150 years before the text that records it was compiled. The text's editorial comment, that "the warriors of old were like this," suggests that the actions portrayed represent an idealized image of earlier *bushi*—creative nostalgia on the part of twelfth-century litterateurs—in the same way that the medieval war tales represent an idealized image of twelfth-century warrior behavior.[25]

Even if one accepts the account of Yoshifumi's duel with Mitsuru at more or less face value, the conclusion that the warriors' conduct therein was exceptional—even unique—seems inescapable. In other sources, the aplomb with which the early samurai engaged in deceit and even treachery is striking. The acceptance of both warrior and non-warrior audiences of this sort of behavior is still more so.

Another incident related in the same text, for example, describes the illustrious Taira Sadamichi's tactics in carrying out an order to hunt down and kill another warrior. Sadamichi first befriends the man and wins his confidence, then rides out of sight to don his armor and prepare himself, and returns minutes later to catch his hapless victim unarmored and riding a spare horse. Sadamichi shoots him before he can even reach his weapons. In yet another tale from that text, a samurai slays the man who killed his father by disguising himself as a servant bearing food, sneaking into the man's room (while he rests in the home of the samurai's lord), and slitting his throat while he sleeps. The *Azuma kagami*, the Kamakura shogunate's own didactic record of its history, recounts how Minamoto Yoritomo had one of his men executed for treason by summoning him to his quarters and entertaining him with food and drink, in the midst of which another of the once-and-future shogun's men, Amano Tōkage, stepped forward with a sword to lop off the unfortunate man's head. In none of these accounts is there any suggestion that this sort of conduct is improper.[26]

A fondness for surprise attacks and ambush was not, of course, by any means unique to Japan. European lords also happily built on tactics of betrayal and deception to secure victory. The 1118–1119 campaigns between Henry I and Louis VI, fought principally in Normandy, for example, demonstrate the repeated use of guile in almost every aspect of warfare, yet few of these acts accrued reproach from the pens of those who chronicled them. On the contrary, knights applauded cunning, guile, and surprise, even in tournaments, and acknowledged them as fundamental and ubiquitous elements of war.[27]

Even so, the Japanese attitude toward this issue stands out. For in Europe, betrayal and deception were acceptable only within limits, restricted by conventions of war that sought to regulate fighting to the mutual benefit of both sides in any struggle. They were legitimate only because of a legalistic sort of loophole that arose from formalized conventions of oaths, truces, declarations and challenges. Knights wishing to exploit surprise and guile, without setting precedents that undermined the conventions, took pains to ensure that their actions violated no specific promises or agreements. And such tactics were successful largely because careless enemies failed to take note of the absence of any such prior agreements. It was not, in other words, low cunning itself that was dishonorable, but the perjury of an oath promising to abstain from such acts.[28]

Japanese custom lacked all such qualifications. Promises and truces were violated with impunity, as Minamoto Yoritomo demonstrated in his campaign against Satake Hideyoshi, in 1184. Finding that Hideyoshi had ensconced himself behind fortifications, Yoritomo used a relative of the Satake, Taira Hirotsune, as an intermediary, to persuade Hideyoshi's father, Yoshimasa, to meet him alone, at the center of a bridge leading to Yoshimasa's home. When Yoshimasa reached the meeting point, however, Hirotsune abruptly cut him down, causing many of Yoshimasa's followers to surrender and others to turn and flee.[29]

In plotting strategy, early medieval Japanese warriors seem, for the most part, to have concerned themselves only with the most efficient means to bring about the desired result, with the ends justifying almost any means. The notion that certain sorts of tactics might be "fair" while others were "unfair" was not only inapposite to such deliberations, it was utterly extraneous to *bushi* culture. The whole concept of "unfair tactics" is, in fact, meaningless to analyses of early samurai warfare, because it simply did not exist at the time, for the principals involved. Japanese warriors just did not think in such terms.

Capture and Surrender

Another key component of medieval European military custom was the body of conventions surrounding the treatment of surrendered enemies. These centered on the somewhat quaint practice of ransoming captured knights back to their families, in exchange for payments in cash or arms, a routine that had precedents in ancient Greek hoplite battle and reappeared in early Frankish warfare, becoming well-established by the mid-eleventh century.

As castles proliferated, wars between knights became dominated by sieges. The tendency to stalemate fostered by castle-based warfare was exacerbated by the small and essentially evenly-matched forces available to the emergent political entities of the eleventh century, with the result that fighting was relatively small in scale. The contraction in both the geographic and logistical scale of operations diminished opportunities for extensive plunder and tribute, necessitating the discovery of other means to make war pay for itself. Moreover, by this period knights primarily faced other Christian knights, which reinforced nascent ideas of brotherhood in a common profession of arms. These factors were further buttressed by the rapidly changing political alliances that characterized the period, by which today's foe could be tomorrow's friend.

The result was the emergence of a convention whereby knights focused on capturing, rather than slaughtering, one another. Knights were not supposed to kill other knights unless it was absolutely necessary. The code of chivalry demanded instead that a beaten enemy be given quarter and that prisoners be treated as gentlemen to be ransomed for sums not beyond their means to pay. Captivity came to be a form of contract, originally established orally on the field but recorded in writing once the battle was over.[30]

Political, social, and technological circumstances in medieval Japan were substantially different from those in Europe, with the result that Japanese warriors developed no comparable canon of ethics and procedures for dealing with prisoners, and no comparable customs of quarter, capture, and ransom. Instead, the fate of a captured *bushi* depended entirely on the particulars of his case. A pair of incidents that followed Minamoto Yoriyoshi's loss to Abe Sadatō at the Battle of Kinomi, in 1057, highlights the degree to which the treatment of prisoners varied with their circumstances.

> Fujiwara Kagesue was the eldest son of Kagemichi. At twenty years of age, he was a man of few words, skilled at mounted archery. During the battle he faced death and returned undaunted. Seven or eight times he galloped into [Sadatō's] lines, killed an enemy leader, and emerged. But his horse stumbled and he was captured. The rebels were moved by his valor, but at length they executed him, because he was a cherished retainer of Yoriyoshi.[31]

> In addition, there was a man of Dewa province, San'i Taira Kunitada. He fought with strength, courage and skill, always defeating many with only a few. Until this time he had never met defeat; people thus called him Taira the Unbeaten (Heifufu) [a revision of his formal sobriquet, Heidaifu]. Yoriyoshi had made him a commander in his vanguard, but his horse fell and the rebels took him captive. Now, this Kunitada was a brother-in-law to the rebel commander Tsunekiyo. For this reason he was set free. The warriors regarded this release as shameful.[32]

The divergence of Japanese from European conventions pertaining to prisoners was the result of differing political, social, and technological circumstances. In point of fact, capture was rare in Japanese warfare. Most prisoners mentioned in the sources were taken into custody as the result of surrender, rather than seizure. One reason for this was probably the nature of the weapons employed by the early *bushi*. Essentially, it is difficult to use a bow and arrow to capture rather than kill, although some attempts to do just this, such as aiming at horses rather than riders, appear to have been made.[33] More fundamentally, European feudal custom sanctioned the right to redress personal grievances through force-of-arms, rendering much of the fighting between

Christian lords akin to a lawsuit pursued through other means. Warfare was a direct means of securing some form of profit, and usually centered on limited, clearly defined objectives. This situation was logically conducive to self-imposed restraints. For when the belligerents could be satisfied by the accomplishment of more limited objectives, there was little reason to destroy an opponent gratuitously, and largesse could readily be seen as a function of enlightened self-interest. Moreover, if the winner achieved his immediate objective by means that brought him the censure of the society around him, he would have realized no long-term profit. The convention of ransom thus simultaneously satisfied the desire of knights for financial gain, their desire for self-preservation, and their concerns for reputation and honor.

The political structure of early medieval Japan, however, made no allowance for the pursuit of private ends through violence. From the perspective of the law—of the state as a corporate entity—recourse to arms was acceptable when and only when sanctioned by the government. The principle that final authority and formal control rested with the central government was a key feature of Japan's military and police system from the late seventh century until well into the fourteenth: the state jealously guarded its exclusive right to sanction the use of force throughout the Heian and Kamakura periods and attempted to do so, albeit with diminishing success, under the Muromachi regime as well.

Central authorities were forced, with increasing frequency, to look the other way during private squabbles between warriors, but they never dignified such activities with the veneer of legal respectability. Until the mid-fourteenth century at least, Japanese law made an unambiguous distinction between lawful military action, in which one (or more) of the parties involved possessed a legal warrant, and unlawful, private fights.

Throughout the Heian period, all major military officers were appointed by the imperial court; all but the most minor criminal problems were first reported upward, and the appropriate action was decided upon and ordered by the Council of State. Any form of military action undertaken without a Warrant of Pursuit and Capture (*tsuibu kanpu*) was subject to punishment.[34]

After the 1180s, many of the court's military police functions were appropriated by the Kamakura shogunate, but the essential premise of central control over the right to violence remained intact. The Kamakura regime's first and most important piece of legislation, the 1232 *Goseibai shikimoku*, was unequivocal on this issue, noting in article three (dealing with constable authority) that:

> No person, even one whose family has been hereditary vassals of the shogun for generations, shall be able to mobilize troops for military service without a current proper investiture of jurisdiction.[35]

The Muromachi regime had similar policies. A 1346 supplement to the shogunate's legal code, the *Kemmu shikimoku*, insisted that:

> To willfully initiate hostilities with attendant loss of life constitutes a crime that cannot easily be tolerated. In the case of offensive warfare, even when the original petition is justified, usurpation of [the shogun's authority in this area] constitutes a crime that will not be tolerated. Still the more so when there is no justification ....Cases of defensive warfare by persons other than the lawful holder of the lands shall constitute the same crime as offensive warfare.[36]

Early *bushi* warfare was, therefore, legitimized only under the rubric of what modern legal terminology would describe as criminal, rather than civil, law. One side in any conflict was, by definition, seen to be acting in the name of the state, while those on the other were cast as rebels or outlaws. In practice, these labels could shift back and forth over the course of a long drawn-out war—such as during the Genpei War of the 1180s, and the Nambokuchō wars of the fourteenth century—but in the end the winners could justify their victory only in terms of law enforcement and defense of the polity. This characterization of the purpose of warfare not only made winning the only real imperative (and thereby justified any actions taken toward that end), but it also defined captured or surrendered enemy warriors as criminals and set the parameters for dealing with them accordingly.

European chivalry was, moreover, a code of conduct for knights—noble warriors—that served to intensify the separation of the knight from the rest of society and, at the same time, to define his obligations to other knights and to other orders. Significantly, the customs that governed ransom applied only to knights and squires, because they were made practical only by mutual recognition of status and the expectation of reciprocity of treatment. A knight could offer quarter to an opponent, because he could expect to receive similar treatment should the roles be reversed, and could gain glory by this display of magnanimity toward a defeated equal. Peasants and other nonknightly soldiers were outsiders to this code, and could not for that very reason be trusted to reciprocate courtesy, and accordingly had no claim themselves to call upon courtesy in combat. Thus infantrymen, archers, miners, and other nonnoble troops neither gave quarter nor received it from knights—even those on their own side.[37]

Early *bushi* had a far less developed sense of group identity and separateness than did their Western counterparts. By the eleventh century, in northern Europe, knights formed the ruling class and nearly all secular rulers were knights. Kings, counts, and other feudal lords all self-consciously identified themselves as *miles*, members of the same *ordo militaris* or *ordo equestris* as their warrior retainers. The awareness of a common bond of knighthood, and concomitant feelings of professional empathy, were enhanced by ecclesiastical efforts to define the role of knighthood in Christian society, and by the institution of the tournament. Tournaments, which brought together knights from different principalities in an artificial and controlled environment that emphasized the social as much as the martial, gave knights on different sides of shifting political alliances and animosities the chance to get to know one another, as well as to display their prowess and win glory and ransoms. This was an ideal setting for fostering display of largesse, for while tempers might flare, and the risk of serious injury or death was always present, the emphasis on profit and prize required the formulation of basic rules, and the essentially nonhostile nature of these war games provided fertile ground for the development and propagation of conventions of war. Tournaments, moreover, gave knights practice in, and incentive to develop, skills at unseating and capturing opponents relatively unharmed.[38]

The Japan of this same period was still ruled by civil authority; its socio-economic hierarchy still culminated in a civil, not a military, nobility; and the idea of a warrior order was still more nascent than real. Warrior leaders, scions of the lower and middle tiers of the court nobility, still looked to the center and to the civil ladder for success, and still saw the profession of arms largely as a means to an end—a foot in the door toward civil rank and office. And *bushi* at all levels in the socio-political hierarchy still identified more strongly with their nonmilitary social peers, than with warriors above or below them in the hierarchy.[39]

A sense of warriors as a separate estate did not begin to emerge until after the first shogunate was in place. The new institution, which was in essence a kind of warriors' union, created the category of shogunal retainer (*gokenin*), as a self-conscious class of individuals with special privileges and responsibilities. It also narrowed the range of social classes from which *bushi* came. Yoritomo consciously helped foster this new sense of warrior identity by holding hunts and archery competitions, which were held in an atmosphere not entirely unlike those of European tournaments.[40]

Thus the different purpose of war, the different weapons employed, and the different view of who they were—and of their responsibilities to one another and to the rest of society—all mitigated against the *bushi* developing customs resembling those of quarter and ransom. Their place and function in the socio-political structure prevented warriors from seeing battle as a game-like activity properly pursued only by a particular order of sportsmen, and also from perceiving prisoners as human booty that could be exchanged for a profit. During the early medieval period, prisoners did not belong to their captors; they belonged instead to the higher authority that had sanctioned the military action in the first place.

Up through the early 1200s the fate of prisoners varied, but largely reflected tenets of criminal law. The central figures of enemy armies—those deemed responsible for the conflict—were sometimes severely punished, but the majority of the warriors on the losing side were usually pardoned.[41] It does appear, however, that treatment of captured or surrendered enemy troops hardened over the course of the thirteenth and fourteenth centuries. During the 1300s, as war became more pervasive, more frequent, and more open-ended, commanders displayed an increased willingness to embrace deserters and turncoats. Warriors, particularly powerful ones, who capitulated or otherwise changed sides before any actual fighting, could expect generous treatment and confirmation by their new lord of all or part of their lands. On the other hand, commanders became much less willing than they might once have been to deal with enemy troops captured in battle, perhaps fearing that pardoned troops would simply return to the fight later. Prisoners were viewed as liabilities. Most were summarily executed. The rest were imprisoned, interrogated, and (in most cases) executed later.[42]

Neutrality and Noncombatants

A fundamental premise underlying modern views on military ethics is the notion that war is, or should be, combat between combatants; that those who cannot or do not fight—women, children, old men, priests, neutral tribes or states, and wounded or captured soldiers—are entitled to some degree of immunity from attack. Indeed, some scholars have argued that rules protecting noncombatants are both natural and nearly universal across time and cultures.[43] But while there may be some universality to the sentiment that war ought to be between warriors and only between warriors, in practice the definitions that separate noncombatants from proper belligerents have been closely bound to time and circumstance.

Noncombatants can be defined in terms of their social function (those who by virtue of their occupation cannot or do not make war) or by their circumstances (those who cannot or are not bearing arms at any given time). European notions of who can and cannot be a morally acceptable target or casualty of military action embraced both definitions, being rooted in the medieval Church's efforts to establish immunity for its property and its personnel, and in knightly condescension, born of pride of class, which dictated that knights should defend rather than harm the weak and innocent.[44] But the socio-political structure of early medieval Japan hindered the emergence of strong imperatives for noncombatant immunity based on either sort of definition, with the predictable result that warrior treatment of those not directly involved in a particular fight was shaped largely by circumstances of the moment.

In contrast to the monolithic dominion of the church in Europe, ecclesiastical authority in Japan was fragmented among a half-dozen or so autonomous institutions representing different schools and sects, and maintaining a consciously controlled religious balance among themselves that one historian terms a "doctrinal multitude." The great temples and shrines, moreover, not only competed with one another for patrons and followers, they also contended for secular power with the elite noble houses of the court and (from the late twelfth century) with the shogunate. By the eleventh century, the larger religious institutions had organized themselves along lines parallel to those of the great court houses. Each had its own private administrative headquarters (*mandokoro*), portfolio of rights and perquisites (*shiki*) over private estates (*shōen*), and head abbot, usually of noble or imperial birth, who represented the institution and served as a channel of communication to the other powers-that-were, or *kenmon* (as Kuroda Toshio dubbed them). Many also maintained sizable private military forces to police their lands, defend the grounds and personnel of the main temple, and enhance their political clout within the capital. Thus, the medieval Japanese religious establishment lacked a unified voice through which to dictate military ethics to warriors, and was insufficiently separate from the secular realm to make compelling claims that its lands and its clergy deserved immunity and shelter from warrior activities.[45]

At the same time, early medieval warriors could scarcely have looked upon all nonwarriors as inferiors in need of mercy and protection. Defined more by craft than by pedigree, and drawn from lower and middle ranks of the court nobility and the upper tiers of rural society, they were servants and officers of the powers-that-were, not a ruling order unto themselves. And their responsibilities were delimited accordingly.

A description recounted in a thirteenth-century Japanese anthology—and paraphrased in part from the ancient Chinese classic, *Spring and Autumn Annals*—observes that "the functions of warriors are: to caution against violence, to suppress weapons, to preserve the great, to determine merit, to soothe the people, to pacify the masses, and to enrich assets."[46] It is noteworthy that while this passage enjoins warriors to serve their rulers by controlling the rest of the population, it says nothing about *defending* or *protecting* the people.

Under normal military circumstances, warriors were seldom prone to worry about largesse or noncombatants. Women, children, and other innocents in the proximity of early medieval battles were usually slaughtered indiscriminately along with the warriors. Raiding, which entailed burning the fields, plundering the houses, and killing the inhabitants of an enemy's lands, was a common tactic. So were sieges of enemy strongholds, which often involved surrounding the compound, setting fire to its buildings, and shooting down any and all occupants who attempted to escape the flames. In at least one case, warriors demolished the houses of a nearby village for use as kindling for the fire! Women who somehow survived raids, sieges and other battles—even women of status, such as the wives and daughters of enemy officers—might be handed over to victorious troops to be robbed of their clothing or raped. Those who wished to avoid this fate sometimes committed suicide.[47]

In the rare instances when *bushi* did take care to distinguish noncombatants, there were specific reasons for doing so. The account of Taira Koremochi's attack on Fujiwara Morotō's home discussed earlier, for example, notes that:

> When fire had been put to all the buildings, Koremochi said, "Lay not a hand on the women, high or low. As for those you might call men, shoot them down as you see them." Standing outside the flames, they shot them all dead.

It is abundantly clear, however, that Koremochi's motive was not mercy or gallantry, but the very practical desire to avoid creating trouble with Morotō's brother-in-law, Ōkimi:

> After the fire had burned out, Koremochi and his troops returned in the twilight. Approaching the gate to Ōkimi's house, Koremochi sent in the message, "We have shown no shame to the wife of Lord Morotō. As she is your younger sister, I have deferentially refrained from any such actions and respectfully present her to you now."

Koremochi's orders safeguarding all the women in the household were necessary to avoid the possibility that Ōkimi's sister might be accidentally or mistakenly harmed.

This appears to have been a wise precaution. A few decades earlier, two of Taira Masakado's commanders captured the wives of two of his principal opponents. When Masakado heard about this, he issued orders that they "not be shamed" but he was too late; some low-ranking troops (*fuhei*) had already assaulted them, stripping one of the wives naked. In apology, Masakado wrote her a poem and presented her with a set of clothing.[48]

On or off the battlefield, early medieval Japanese warriors appear to have held little concern for the lives of others, or for distinctions between warriors and noncombatants. Neither the warriors themselves nor those who chronicled their exploits seem to have attached much impropriety to killing, except under extraordinary circumstances.

A Kamakura-era picture scroll tells of a warrior, named Obusama Saburō, who left standing orders to maintain a steady supply of fresh human heads hanging on the fence surrounding his riding grounds, presumably to intimidate potential enemies. It also says that he had a less than congenial habit of abducting beggars and travelers who passed his gate for use as targets for "chasing archery games" using blunted arrows.[49]

This account is not particularly critical of such customs; instead, it focuses on drawing a contrast between Saburō, the rough-and-tumble provincial *bushi*, and his elder brother, Yoshimi Jirō, who, although also a warrior, is portrayed as enthralled with the culture of the court and the capital. Saburō is said to have been so fully devoted to his warrior calling that he despised such cultural pursuits as reading poetry and playing music as useless.

> "When you face an army [he demanded], do you draw a brush or blow a flute?" ... All the residents of his household, including women and children, were made to follow this path of the warrior; to ride spirited horses, and to love great arrows and strong bows.

In contrast to Jirō, who married the daughter of a capital nobleman, Saburō is said to have believed it to be improper for a warrior to take a beautiful wife, and to have searched the eastern provinces for the ugliest woman he could find, settling at last on a daughter of a provincial landowner named Kumeda Shirō. She was quite a prize, standing over seven feet tall, with a face "on which one saw naught but her nose" and a mouth "drawn up like the character *he* (へ)." Significantly, Jirō was eventually ambushed and killed by bandits so in awe of Saburō's martial reputation that they had earlier let him pass their stronghold unmolested.[50]

Such stories are, of course, most likely apocryphal, but they say a great deal about the light in which their contemporaries viewed early medieval warriors. A famous petition addressed to the court in 988 from the "peasants and district officials" of Owari province, further details the brutality provincial residents ascribed to *bushi*:

> For the sake of their own honor and reputations, they willfully pluck out people's eyes. Arriving at people's homes, they do not dismount from their horses but enter. Retainers on horseback tear down the wooden shade-screens that hang outside homes and carry off tax goods. Those who dare to complain that this is unjust are meted punishment.
>
> ....
>
> [These warriors] are no different from barbarians. They are like wild wolves. They butcher human meat and use it as ornaments for their bodies.[51]

Nevertheless, the medieval *bushi*'s disregard for the lives and property of noncombatants arose from detachment, professionalism, and practicality, rather than savagery or cruelty. Their willingness to kill seems at least in part related to their willingness to die. In an anecdote relating an encounter between Minamoto Yorinobu and a thief who has taken a child hostage, Yorinobu expresses this sentiment dramatically, when he admonishes the child's distraught father, who was also the son of Yorinobu's wet nurse, for losing his composure over the matter:

> Is this a thing to cry about? You must think you have taken on a devil or a deity or some such thing! To cry like a child is a foolish thing. Only one small child—let him be stabbed to death. With this sort of heart does a warrior stand! To think of oneself, to think of wife and children, is to abandon all that is proper to a warrior and his honor. To

> speak of fearing nothing is to speak of thinking naught of
> oneself, of thinking naught of wife and child.[52]

Even more fundamentally, however, *bushi* indifference to the fate of third parties stemmed from a single-minded focus on the ends of their actions, with little attention to the moral character of the means. This in turn was at least partially a consequence of *bushi* tactics and ethics having evolved in an age in which military force was mostly employed either in pursuit of criminals, or in pursuit of criminal activity. Noncombatants were thus viewed as either accomplices to the criminal, or simply as "collateral damage" (to borrow a term from the modern U.S. military).

Catholic moral theology promotes a doctrine known as the law of double effect, which holds that it is permissible to bring about a result knowingly that is a side effect of one's actions, but which would be utterly impermissible to bring about as an end in its own right. In application to war, this principle permits such things as the killing of civilians, when the deaths are incidental to attacks on enemy troops or other primary military targets, but only if the cost is not too great to be otherwise justified by one's objectives.[53] It is likely that a similar sort of principle underlay *bushi* behavior toward noncombatants.

In point of fact, similar considerations promoted similar tactics and behavior in England and Normandy during the same period, where ravaging the enemy's towns and countryside was among the most common, and arguably the most fundamental, manifestation of warfare. One basic form of ravaging was the foraging for supplies, which served the dual purpose of provisioning the invading army and inflicting economic damage on the enemy. The right to and necessity of plunder of this sort, which stemmed from the poor logistic organization of early medieval campaigns, was even recognized in medieval law. But while provisioning one's army was a fundamental concern, commanders went well beyond this in their attacks on the countryside and the peasantry of their enemies, aiming at the temporary dislocation or even the destruction of the enemy's economic resources. Burning crops and vineyards was a principal tactic in both local private warfare and major campaigns. So was the destruction of mills, and the destruction or seizure of ploughs and draft animals to prevent cultivation. Burning of peasant homes and villages, and even the slaying of farmers and husbandmen themselves, were also commonplace. Villages were seldom, if ever, fortified, and thus formed easy targets, such that they became principal objects of attack. This behavior was simply a logical extension of other kinds of economic warfare, a means of disrupting the enemy's labor force.

Ravaging and raiding entail little or no direct contact between opposing troops, but consist instead of assaults on the material and psychological bases of an opponent's lordship. Wanton killing of defenseless peasants, and burning of villages and fields, highlight aspects of knightly behavior that contrast markedly with the conventions of conduct that held for fighting between knights and knightly armies, and sit somewhat uneasily with the ideal of the knight as protector of the weak—a duty that became increasingly explicit as the idea that knighthood constituted a discrete order with both privileges and moral responsibilities solidified. But while modern sensibilities might be offended at the apparent discrepancy between the rules knights applied to combat with one another and those they applied to dealing with the peasantry, the knights themselves did not see a contradiction, because the actions and gestures that made up chivalrous behavior were never intended to be applied to the lesser orders. The church, of course, saw ravaging as a violation of the fundamental interdependence of the three orders, and made criticism implicit from the tenth century, in the legislation of the Peace and Truce of God movements. Yet attacks on unarmed peasants and such did not trouble the knights' sense of honor, for they were breaking regulations not of their own making and, to them, obviously impractical.[54]

Conclusion

To summarize, there is a tempting, superficial resemblance between the military circumstances of early medieval Europe and early medieval Japan—the privatization and professionalization of war-making, the elite status of men-at-arms, and the tactical focus on mounted warriors—but in the final analysis, the divergences between the conditions under which early knights and early samurai lived and fought proved more telling than the similarities. The crucial differences revolved around the fundamentally dissimilar socio-political structures in the two regions.

In Europe, political sovereignty was fragmented and mutable, while religious authority was monolithic. But in Heian and Kamakura Japan, legal and political authority remained centralized, while religious authority was fragmented. In Europe, warriors were the ruling class: not all knights were lords or kings, but all lords and kings were knights. But in Japan, warriors had only limited political power; even warrior leaders were just officers and servants of the *kenmon* powers above them. And in Europe, knights developed a strong sense of identity as members of a special order of their own, distinguishing themselves from the clergy and from the peasantry. But in Japan warrior class identity emerged much later and much more slowly, such that until the thirteenth century, skill at arms was a means to an end, not a profession in and of itself, and *bushi* at most levels of the socio-political hierarchy identified themselves more closely with nonwarrior peers than with *bushi* at other levels of the socio-political hierarchy.

As a result of these factors, war itself had different identities in the two regions. Warfare in early medieval Japan was cast primarily as a function of law enforcement, while warfare in Europe was alternatively the pursuit of a lawsuit by other means, or the pursuit of intrapolity diplomacy by other means.

Thus, the continued existence of a centralized polity in Japan, the low pedigrees and political weakness of even warrior leaders, the weaker identification of the *bushi* as a class, the existence of a civil nobility above them, the absence of tournaments, the diversified religious establishment, and the military technology of Japanese warriors all combined such that war and the ethics of war bore scant resemblance to the European traditions of *jus in bello*.

NOTES

1   Luis Frois's untitled 611-clause treatise, translated into Japanese by Okada Akio as *Nichō bunka hikaku*, was among the first such descriptive essays. The Japanese version of Frois's treatise appears in *Taikōkai jidai sōsho*, vol. 11. In English, see Robin D. Gill, trans., *Topsy-turvy 1585*, Key Biscayne, FL: Paraverse Press, 2004.

2   Asakawa's work is collected in *Land and Society in Medieval Japan*.

3   Rushton Coulborn, ed., *Feudalism in History*, p. 185; Archibald Lewis, *Knights and Samurai: Feudalism in Northern France and Japan*, p. 55. Emphasis on the "striking" resemblance of medieval Japan to medieval Europe persists in survey texts. Edwin Reischauer's assertion (*Japan: The Story of a Nation*, p. 46) that "Japan affords the only close and fully developed parallel to Western feudalism" is a case in point.

4   William Wayne Farris, *Heavenly Warriors: The Evolution of Japan's Military, 500–1300*.

5   Hall's landmark work on this topic was *Government and Local Power in Japan 500–1700: A Study Based on Bizen Province*. For Mass's views, see *Warrior Government in Early Medieval Japan: A Study of the Kamakura Bakufu, Shugo and Jitō; The Development of Kamakura Rule 1180–1250: A History With Documents*; "The Early Bakufu and Feudalism"; "What Can We Not Know About the Kamakura Bakufu?"; *Lordship and Inheritance in Early Medieval Japan: A Study of the Kamakura Sōryō System; Antiquity and Anachronism in Japanese History; Yoritomo and the Founding of the First Bakufu*; and "Family, Law, and Property in Japan, 1200–1350."

6   Michael Walzer, *Just and Unjust Wars: A Moral Argument with Historical Illustrations*, pp. 42–44.

7   Walzer, *Just and Unjust Wars*, p. 35.

8   James Turner Johnson, *Just War Tradition and the Restraint of War*, pp. 123–150; Robert C. Stacey, "The Age of Chivalry," pp. 28–30.

9   Robert C. Stacey, "The Age of Chivalry," pp. 28–30; James Turner Johnson, *Just War Tradition and the Restraint of War*, pp. 123–131; Matthew Strickland, *War and Chivalry: The Conduct and Perception of War in England and Normandy, 1066–1217*, pp. 31–54.

10   Eiko Ikegami, *The Taming of the Samurai: Honorific Individualism and the Making of Modern Japan*, pp. 97, 98; fuller discussions of early medieval warfare appear on pp. 97–103. Other examples of recent scholarship that has portrayed early medieval warfare as ritualized include: Ishii Shirō, "Kassen to tsuibu"; Nishimata Fusō, "Kassen no rūru to manaa," pp. 146–147; Okada Seiichi, "Kassen to girei"; Seki Yukihiko, "'Bu' no kōgen: kōchū to yumiya"; H. Paul Varley, *Warriors of Japan as Portrayed in the War Tales*; Takahashi Masaaki, "Nihon chūsei no sentō: yasen no kijōsha o chūshin ni"; Farris, *Heavenly Warriors*, pp. 8–9, 132–133, 231–233, 237–238, 269–270, 298–300; W. Wayne Farris, "Japan to 1300," pp. 60–62, 66–67. The image of ritual and formalism in early medieval warfare has been virtually reified in popular and textbook accounts. See, for example, Mikiso Hane, *Premodern Japan: A Historical Survey*, pp. 73–74; Stephen R. Turnbull, *The Book of the Samurai: The Warrior Class of Japan*, pp. 19, 22–36; Turnbull, *The Lone Samurai and the Martial Arts*, pp. 14–28; John Newman, *Bushido: The Way of the Warrior*, pp. 13–14, 16–17.

11   Such creative nostalgia found its most eloquent and best-known expression on the pages of the great medieval war tales: *Hōgen monogatari, Heiji monogatari, Heike monogatari*, and *Gikeiki*. Modern literary scholars have demonstrated, however, that much of the compelling detail contained in these narratives was in fact the product of formulaic techniques of oral composition, not remembered history. See Kenneth D. Butler, "The Textual Evolution of the Heike Monogatari"; Butler, "The Heike Monogatari and the Japanese Warrior Ethic."

12   A growing body of scholarship implicitly or explicitly rejects the idea of early samurai warfare as ritualized or formalistic. This includes studies by Kondō Yoshikazu, Kawai Yasushi, Fujimoto Masayuki, Yamamoto Kōji, Gomi Fumihiko, Thomas Conlan, and

myself. In English, see Karl Friday, *Mononofu: The Warrior of Heian Japan*; Friday, "Valorous Butchers: The Art of War During the Golden Age of the Samurai"; *Samurai Warfare and the State in Early Medieval Japan*; Thomas Conlan, *State of War: The Violent Order of Fourteenth-Century Japan*; Conlan, "The Nature of Warfare in Fourteenth-Century Japan: The Record of Nomoto Tomoyuki"; or Conlan, *In Little Need of Divine Intervention*.

13 See, for example, *Mutsuwaki*, pp. 23, 24–26; *Azuma kagami* Jishō 4 (1180).8.26, Genryaku 1 (1184).4.21, Genkyū 2 (1205).6.22, Jōkyū 3 (1221).6.6, Ninji 2 (1241).11.29.

14 Strickland, *War and Chivalry*, pp. 98–131. The passage from *Histoire de Guillaume le Maréchal* is quoted on p. 98.

15 *Kokon chomonjū* 9.12.333.

16 Matthew Strickland observes that, "despite drawing on established concepts, honor [is] ultimately a personal issue . . . governed by the conscience and self-esteem of the individual." Strickland, *War and Chivalry*, pp. 125–131.

17 Strickland, *War and Chivalry*, pp. 42–43; Otto Brunner, *Land and Lordship: Structures of Governance in Medieval Austria*, p. 65. Brunner notes that "The *Summa legum* of Raymond of Wiener Neustadt contended that to kill someone 'without a challenge, without open enmity' (*sine diffidacione et sine manifesta inimicitia*) was just murder."

18 Friday, "Valorous Butchers," p. 8. Out of sixty episodes recounted in various sources for the tenth to twelfth centuries in sufficient detail to permit judgments concerning the order of battle, forty-three involved ambushes or surprise attacks of one form or another.

19 Yamagishi Tokuhei and Takahashi Teiichi, eds., *Hōgen monogatari (Nakaraibon) to kenkyū*, pp. 26–27. Takamatsu Palace was the residence of Emperor Go-Shirakawa.

20 The *Nakaraibon* version of the *Hōgen monogatari*, from which this passage is drawn, is thought to have been compiled shortly before 1318, while the events it relates took place in 1156. Yamagishi and Takahashi, p. 146.

21 *Shin sarugakuki*, p. 138.

22   *Konjaku monogatari shū* 25.3.

23   Recounted in *Konjaku monogatari shū* 25.5.

24   *Azuma kagami* Genryaku 1 (1184).4.21 recounts a similar incident involving a warrior escaping danger disguised as a woman, and even having a friend impersonate him to draw off pursuers.

25   William R. Wilson, "The Way of the Bow and Arrow: The Japanese Warrior in the Konjaku Monogatari," p. 188; Ishii Susumu, *Chūsei bushidan*, p. 117.

26   *Konjaku monogatari shū* 25.10; 25.4; *Azuma kagami* Bunji 1 (1185).6.16.

27   Strickland, *War and Chivalry*, pp. 128–131.

28   Strickland, *War and Chivalry*, pp. 128–131.

29   *Azuma kagami* Jishō 4 (1180).11.4.

30   Strickland, *War and Chivalry*, pp. 133–138; Joseph Ober, "Classical Greek Times," pp. 13–17; Johnson, *Just War Tradition*, p. 126; Stacey, "The Age of Chivalry," pp. 36–38.

31   *Mutsuwaki*, p. 25.

32   *Mutsuwaki*, p. 26.

33   Strickland, *War and Chivalry*, pp. 176–182, raises similar considerations with regard to infantrymen in medieval Europe.

34   Friday, *Hired Swords*, pp. 122–166.

35   *Goseibai shikimoku*, article three, in *CSSS*, 1, pp. 8–9; Ikeuchi Yoshisuke and Satō Shin'ichi, eds., *Chūsei hōsei shiryōshū*, vol. 1, pp. 4–5. (Hereafter *CHSS*, 1, pp. 4–5); also in *Gunsho ruijū* (hereafter *GR*), vol. 17, *buke bu* 1, p. 357.

36   *CHSS*, 2, Muromachi bakufu *tsuika-hō* no. 26. For the Muromachi laws, see also *GR*, vol. 17, *buke bu* 1, 380–406. An alternative translation appears in Kenneth A. Grossberg, *The Laws of the Muromachi Bakufu*, p. 40.

37   Johnson, *Just War Tradition*, pp. 131–150; Strickland, *War and Chivalry*, pp. 16–30, 132–182.

38   R. Allen Brown, *Origins of English Feudalism*, pp. 23–27; Strickland, *War and Chivalry*, pp. 149–153; Johnson, *Just War Tradition*, pp. 131–150; Stacey, "The Age of Chivalry," pp. 36–38.

39   See Friday, *Hired Swords*; and Farris, *Heavenly Warriors*, especially pp. 367–380.

40   Takahashi Masaaki, *Bushi no seiritsu*, pp. 130–134, 144–148, 210–226; Nakazawa Katsuaki, *Chūsei no buryoku to jōkaku*, pp. 99–107; Noguchi Minoru, *Buke no tōryō no jōken: chūsei bushi o minaosu*, pp. 56–64.

41   Kawai Yasushi, "Jishō Jūei no nairan to chiiki shakai," pp. 11–12.

42   Conlan, "The Nature of Warfare," pp. 320–321.

43   Michael Walzer, "Political Action: The Problem of Dirty Hands," pp. 42–43; Thomas Nagel, "War and Massacre"; R.B. Brandt, "Utilitiarianism and the Rules of War"; R. M. Hare "The Rules of War and Moral Reasoning."

44   Johnson, *Just War Tradition*, 131–150. Johnson argues that the protection for noncombatants derived from the chivalric code was of a qualitatively different sort than that defined and enforced by the church, because the two concepts of immunity sprang from different principles or assumptions about the nature of noncombatancy. By canon law, noncombatants had a *right* to be spared the ravages of war because they were not themselves making war, and only relinquished this right when they took up arms or sheltered soldiers. The knights themselves, by contrast, viewed immunity and protection extended to the weak or innocent as a *gift* offered to inferiors. By the end of the fourteenth century, these two very different traditions concerning noncombatancy had merged. Under this fourteenth-century synthesis, the knight owed protection not only to those who rendered him service or who were potentially able to return the favor someday, but to all members of the community of Christendom. And the church now extended its call for immunity to all nonwarriors in the community, not just those who served the church directly.

45   For a fuller description of the role of temples in the socio-political and economic structure of early medieval Japan, see Mikael Adolphson, "Enryakuji: An Old Power in a New Era"; Martin Collcutt, *Five Mountains: The Rinzai Zen Monastic Institution in Medieval Japan*; Joan R Piggott, "Hierarchy and Economics in Early Medieval Todaiji."

46   *Kokon chomonjū* 9, 12:333.

47   See, for example, *Shōmonki*, pp. 99, 117–119; 125–127; *Mutsuwaki*, pp. 27, 31–34; *Chōya gunsai* Kanwa 2 (986).10.20 *Sesshō ke ōsesho*, pp. 179–180; *Konjaku monogatari-shū* 23.13, 25.1, 25.5; [Tengi 4 (1056).4.23] Tōdaiji goshi tō nikki an (*HI*, 3:797); Chōhō 2 (1000).3.2 Kebiishi bettō sen (*HI*, 10:*ho* 7); [Taiji 1 (1126)].10.6 Daizen no kami Sukekiyo shojō (*HI*, 5:2091); Kyūan 2 (1146).7.11 Kawato Naritoshi ra monchū mōshikotoba no ki (*HI*, 6:2583); *Fusō ryakki* Engi 2 (902).9.26, Jōmei 5 (919).5.23; *Nihon kiryaku* Tenryaku 1 (947).2.14; *Chūshūki* Kaho 1 (1094).3.8.

48   *Shōmonki*, pp. 117–119; *Konjaku monogatari-shū*, 25.1. For more on this incident, see Friday, *The First Samurai*, pp. 129–131.

49   *Obusuma no Saburō ekotoba*, p.15; this kidnapping is illustrated on pp. 18–19.

50   *Obusuma no Saburō ekotoba*, pp. 3, 15, 24–26.

51   Eien 2 (988).11.8 Owari no kuni gunshi hyakushō ra no ge (*HI*, 2:339). For a general treatment of the peasant complaints in this famous document, see Charlotte von Verschuer, "Life of Commoners in the Provinces: the *Owari no gebumi* of 988."

52   *Konjaku monogatari shū* 25.11.

53   Nagel, "War and Massacre," pp. 8–13.

54   Strickland, *War and Chivalry*, pp. 258–273; Johnson, *Just War Tradition*, pp. 131–150; Walzer, *Just and Unjust Wars,* pp. 160–162. Strickland reminds us that it is the church's decrees that reveal the extent to which ravaging was a commonplace activity of war. He argues that many of the specific criticisms found in chronicles, such as those of Orderic, indicate that the church's principal wrath was directed not at ravaging per se, but at the ravaging of church properties, and in fact seem to imply that the lands of knights were a legitimate target for their fellow warriors.

Benkei's Ancestors: Monastic Warriors in Heian Japan[1]
Mikael S. Adolphson

In 1985, the mayor of Kyoto decided to assess a new tourist tax on forty of Kyoto's many culturally significant locations. Of these, thirty-six were temples, and it was therefore hardly surprising that monks, abbots, and other representatives of the old capital's religious associations protested against the new levy. Evoking their status as tax-exempt religious organizations, the temples claimed that their cultural assets could not be assessed a public tax. The mayor would not budge, however, and several of the most popular tourist spots, including Kiyomizudera and Ginkakuji, closed their gates in protest, while negotiations continued with the city officials throughout 1986.[2] In the end, the civil authorities prevailed, and Kyoto visitors, who inevitably came to carry the burden, faced admission fees up to twice as high as the previous year.[3]

The conflict recalled images of rampaging monks from the past, and critical articles with such allusions were widely published in the national press. One headline read, "Monk-Warriors [sōhei] Riot against the Old Capital's New Tax." Another article observed that "warrior-monks no longer exist, but when one looks at the dispute surrounding the 'old capital tax,' one realizes that Kyoto is a historical city still tied to its medieval heritage."[4] Although the authors of these articles belong to the realm of popular journalism, their assumptions about warrior-monks have been widely shared among Japanese historians as well. For example, it is common to find historical accounts that confuse strategies of protest employed by influential temples in the late Heian and Kamakura eras with armed attacks.[5] However, contemporary records show that the strategies used during protests involved no military elements, even if they contained rowdy members of the monastic clergies. Later biases and a desire to discredit the most influential temples have provided the fuel for such misleading interpretations.[6]

Another questionable assumption is the tendency to equate the whole spectrum of armed religious forces with stereotypical images of *sōhei* who were trained both to pray and to fight. Thus, the typical monk-warrior—often represented by Benkei (?–1189), the loyal retainer of the legendary Minamoto Yoshitsune—is shown dressed in a white monk's robe and a distinctive hood, armed with a *naginata* (similar to a halberd) and two swords. Even though these images are contained in later narratives, most scholars have neglected to question the validity of applying such characteristics to monastic forces of all ages. In particular, the socio-political origins, role, and military background of armed religious forces in the Heian age (794–1185) remain far more obscure than those of the warrior class. Even the terminology presents challenges, since the term *sōhei* first appears in Japan in a Confucian text of 1715.[7] Although this term does indicate a new perception of armed monks, its importance lies in what its usage says about the eighteenth century, rather than in information it provides about the Heian era.

Coupled with the scholarly aversion to religious institutions and monks with secular and military power in particular, these images have sustained a negative view of such monks, or at best, a general neglect of armed monks as a topic of serious inquiry. Only a handful of Japanese scholars have offered extensive treatments of these religious forces.[8] Moreover, earlier studies have tended to be overwhelmingly institutional, emphasizing one temple over another, and thus failing to explain armed religious forces as a historical phenomenon. By focusing on the human element of armed conflicts involving religious institutions, this essay will offer an analysis of how, why, and when such forces emerged in Heian Japan. As I hope to show, the context of the emergence of monastic warriors had less to do with specific developments within temples and shrines than with the social and political transformations that led to the rise of the warrior class in general.

Of Origins, Hoods, and Evil Monks

Buddhism as introduced and taught in Japan was heavily laden with Chinese and Korean influences. The earliest legal codes of the seventh and eighth centuries explicitly prohibited private monks and regulated the behavior of Buddhist clerics, emphasizing that they must not incite commoners to stage rebellions, despite the absence of any documented evidence that such injunctions were necessitated by local conditions. The regulation of Buddhism included, in other words, the experiences of Chinese rulers from the distant past. There are, for example, records of Buddhist temples keeping arms when the Northern Wei ruler attacked Chang'an in 439.[9] A record in the *Nihongi* also indicates that ordained monks in Japan did not always feel restricted by the precepts:

> Thirty-second year of Empress Suiko's reign [624], fourth month.[10] There was a monk who took an axe and struck his paternal grandfather. Now the Empress, hearing of this, sent for Oho-omi, and gave command, saying:—"The man who has taken the Buddhist vows should be devoted to the Three Precious Treasures, and should cherish devoutly the prohibitions of the Buddhist Law. How can he without compunction be readily guilty of crime? We now hear that there is a monk who has struck his grandfather. Therefore, let all the monks and nuns of the various temples be assembled, and investigation made. Let severe punishment be inflicted on any who are convicted of offences." Hereupon the monks and nuns were all assembled, and an examination held. The wicked monks and nuns were all about to be punished, when Kwallŭk, a Buddhist monk from Paekche, presented a memorial, as follows:—"The Law of the Buddha came from the Western country of Han. Three hundred years later it was handed on to Paekche, since which time barely one hundred years had elapsed, when Our King, hearing that the Emperor of Japan was a

wise man, sent him a tribute of an image of Buddha and
of Buddhist sutras. Since that time, less than one hundred
years have passed, and consequently the monks and nuns
have not yet learned the Buddhist Laws, and readily commit
wickedness. On this account all the monks and nuns are
afraid and do not know what to do. I humbly pray that
with the exception of the wicked all the other monks and
nuns may be pardoned and not punished. That would be
a work of great merit." Accordingly, the Empress granted
[his petition].[11]

Considering the didactic purpose of the *Nihongi* and its
later compilation date, one must obviously be cautious in
accepting all accounts at face value. Yet it is not unreasonable
to conclude that there were monks in the early years of Japanese
Buddhism who engaged in violent activities. In fact, in at least
one case, the imperial court itself appears to have condoned
monks' participation in armed conflicts. Specifically, young
monk novices (*sō shami*) were part of a government army that
put down the rebellion of Emi Oshikatsu (Fujiwara Nakamaro,
706–764) in 764.[12] Although some scholars have taken this entry
to mean that these figures were fighters and the precursors of
"monk-warriors," the record does not even indicate that they
carried weapons.[13] It is thus quite conceivable that they were part
of the army in other capacities, such as performing ceremonies
intended to gain victory for the imperial army.

Most scholars today agree that monasteries adopted the use of
arms in conflict resolution during the Heian age, but it is difficult
to find a consensus beyond that. The most significant problem
lies in the existence of scattered evidence of violence throughout
the entire age, and in determining exactly when such forces may
be seen as having become a regular part of the institutional and
social life of the temples. In short, it is a question of separating
isolated cases of local and individual violence from any general
trend. The important denominator among the instances of
violence by monks from the early Heian age is the local origins
of the conflicts as well as of the combatants themselves. For
example, one source states that monks were performing various

illegal acts in the provinces in 805, resulting in expulsions from their respective temples.[14] A slightly later incident, recorded in the *Nihon sandai jitsuroku*, featured two monk novices:

> Jōgan 16(874).10.19. The high council reported that the monk novices Kyōhō (secular name Kamitsukenu Toyomaro) and Zenpuku (secular name Mizutori Sadae) led more than forty rowdy monks [*ransō*] in Funai-gun in Tanba province. They killed a messenger of the Kangakuin[15] named Himatsuri Matayoshi and dismembered the body. They torched two residences, killing one woman in the fire. The council ordered the Ministry of Punishments to handle the matter, and [the Ministry] sentenced them to death by decapitation. [In a separate incident] a man of Iwami province, Wakaebe Toyomi,[16] quarreled with and killed one person. He was sentenced to death by strangulation. The Emperor ordered that [the punishments for the criminals] be decreased one notch below the death penalty, and [all three] were accordingly exiled to a distant province.[17]

The terms used to identify these rambunctious monks are of some importance. Both *ransō* and *akusō* indicate monks who engaged in a wide range of activities beyond the limitations normally imposed on those who had taken Buddhist vows. Their "evil activities" were not limited to military acts.[18]

Clearly, lawless and violent monks were not new to the Buddhist discourse even at the time of its introduction in Japan. From that perspective, it seems pointless to use these records as "evidence" of a decline of Buddhism, as many scholars have done. What they do suggest, however, is a general trend of difficulties that the capital elites faced in controlling the provinces. Such problems reached a crucial juncture in the early part of the tenth century, as evidenced by the piracy of Fujiwara Sumitomo in the Inland Sea and the uprising of Taira Masakado in the Kantō during the 930s. It is less known, though equally important, that similar lawlessness was manifested among locals who wore monks' robes. In 914, Miyoshi Kiyoyuki, a ranking noble, submitted a twelve-article statement to the imperial court reporting on the situation in the provinces. One of the articles specifically dealt with various evil deeds performed by people in monks' garments. Kiyoyuki first noted that an edict had been issued in 901, ordering that the appropriation of land and withholding of taxes by local men of power be stopped. He continued:

> However, evil monks and billeted guards continue to perform rebellious and extremely malicious deeds. I respectfully submit that among the two or three hundred yearly allotted [monks] and temporary ordinands in various temples, over half are such evil and rebellious fellows. Further, land-holding farmers of various provinces evade tax labor and escape from land and product taxes by cutting their own hair and putting on monks' robes without permission.[19] Such fellows are gradually increasing every year, so that two out of three subjects in the realm now have shaved heads. They all keep wives in their houses, and put smelly meats in their mouths. In appearance, they resemble novices but their hearts are like hunters (who kill for a living). Not to mention more extreme persons who gather to make up gangs of thieves and secretly mint coins on their own. They do not fear Heaven's admonitions and do not look twice at the Buddhist monastic rules.[20]

This memorandum provides compelling evidence that the capital elites faced serious challenges in various parts of the realm even before the Sumitomo and Masakado incidents. Indeed, Kiyoyuki's memorandum is far from the only record reporting trouble involving monks in the tenth century. For example, menial workers at Tōdaiji rioted in 935 until a dispatched imperial police captain stopped them.[21] In 949, some fifty to sixty Tōdaiji monks went to Kyoto to protest the appointment of one Kankyū as head abbot of their temple. Once in the capital, ten of the monks approached the mansion of one of the court nobles to emphasize their concerns, resulting in a brief skirmish in which one person was killed.[22] Ten years later, a conflict between Gion's Kanjin'in (the main temple within the Gion shrine complex) and Kiyomizudera (a branch temple of

Kōfukuji) resulted in skirmishes that forced the imperial court to dispatch imperial police captains to arrest the violators.[23] In 968 there was a serious incident involving supporters of Tōdaiji and Kōfukuji, who fought over a small piece of land (a little more than one *tan*) in Nara, resulting in some fatalities.[24] Undoubtedly, violence involving members of Japan's religious communities became substantially more common and intense from the early tenth century.

Apart from Kiyoyuki's memorandum, perhaps the most persuasive records reflecting this surge of violence are related to the Tendai monk Ryōgen (912–985). Ryōgen was both talented and well connected, and made quite a name for himself in religious debates in the capital. In 937, he was awarded a prestigious function in Kōfukuji's *Yuima* ceremony despite being trained in a different school. We learn from a later chronicle that a number of evil monks from Nara (*nanto akusō*) wearing hoods and carrying staffs tried to stop Ryōgen from participating as he approached the city.[25] Although we do not know exactly what occurred during the confrontation, the description of hooded monks provides some important clues. As noted earlier, they became one of the main symbols for representations of the *sōhei*, but that was not the case in the Heian age. Further information may be found in another source related to Ryōgen. In the seventh month of 970, during his tenure as head abbot of the Tendai sect, he issued a set of twenty-six articles to regulate the behavior of his monks. Among these articles, two address trends that confirm the presence of rowdy monks in the late tenth century. One of them prohibits hooded monks, such as the ones Ryōgen had encountered some three decades earlier, from appearing at Enryakuji:

> It is the practice of a woman to hide one's face so that others cannot see [who you are]. Up until now, that has not been the practice of young boys and men in monks' robes. But in recent years, when lectures are given all day at the Nenbutsu Hall, hooded monks assemble in great numbers in the yard when it begins to turn dark. Groups of dirty fellows then enter into the temple halls, and if they

are told to obey the rules, they start cursing and become exceedingly loud, while they wave their staffs and swords, cutting this way and that way. The masters of ceremonies all leave when they see this, and those who attend have no choice but to return home. Can there be anything worse than to thrive on obstructing the Buddhist Law [as these fellows do]? An order was issued to the Jōgyōdō on the first day of the eighth month of the fourth year of the Kōhō era [967] to stop this kind of behavior.[26] After that, monks who have the [Buddhist] Way in their hearts obeyed, but those who do not have not yet complied. Thus, the regulation is issued again. As for the upcoming lectures and ceremonies of the New Year, the second month, the Fudan Nenbutsu and the internal debates, the performers of the ceremonies and the attendees should all make sure to wear the proper robes. Those who wear inappropriate attire and cover their faces with hoods are strictly forbidden to attend. If there are those who ignore the regulations, the organizers will make sure to report them and quickly submit an appeal, so that they will be punished without leniency.[27]

The appearance of hooded monks with staffs, who were not averse to using their gear, including swords, to act freely despite Buddhist regulations, can thus be confirmed from the mid-tenth century. Perhaps it is not surprising that the hoods in particular have come to stand as the symbol for evil and armed monks. Later sources, especially picture scrolls, unmistakably depict armed men from religious institutions in such hoods. But the use of hoods was not exclusive to armed monks or rebellious activities during the Heian age, as demonstrated in Ryōgen's regulations. The hoods were used to conceal the identity of monks and people in general who wished to attend ceremonies and sneak into places from which they were normally excluded. For example, young nobles and women covering their faces in order to attend exclusive Buddhist rituals occasionally appear in later picture scrolls.[28] Other sources indicate that monastic teachers were able to attend and whisper answers to their disciples during difficult examinations, and that the acolytes, for their part, could get sneak previews of ceremonial procedures by wrapping a piece of cloth around their heads.[29] Hoods could accordingly be used in a variety of situations, despite the later artistic symbolism associating them with armed monks.

In another article, Ryōgen addressed the issue of weapons on Mt. Hiei, by proclaiming that those who carried arms should be detained and forwarded to the imperial court:

> Military equipment is carried by secular warriors, while the sutras are the trade of holy men who have taken the Buddhist vows. Secular scholars may learn about the Buddhist texts, but why should those who have taken the vows use arms? ... We have heard that monks now assemble bands in large gatherings, forgetting the merits and embracing anger. They carry swords going in and out of monk dwellings, while others have bows and arrows attached to their bodies, freely going back and forth into the sacred grounds. To kill and cause injury to other people at will is no different from [being] butchers, and to embrace the behavior of violence is like behaving as drunken elephants. This is a great shame for the entire sect, and a peril for the three Buddhist treasures.[30]

Despite these regulations, Ryōgen has been characterized as an aggressive and wily monk. Yet his tenure as head abbot on Mt. Hiei can only be described as extremely successful, as he managed to restore temple halls and residences that had fallen into disrepair. He also established strong ties with the Fujiwara Regent's line, receiving land donations and accepting nobles as his disciples, while converting smaller temples and shrines, including the prestigious Gionsha, into branches of Enryakuji.[31] But later observers, who saw in his leadership the roots of aggressive and belligerent monks, also criticized his success. In particular, by driving the monks of the rival Enchin-line faction off Mt. Hiei to the nearby Miidera (Onjōji), he earned the reputation among chroniclers in the fourteenth century and in histories written in the Tokugawa era of actually having started the militarization process of the clergy. Such a characterization ignored the fact that his twenty-six articles were addressing and trying to contain a trend that was already underway.[32] And from Ryōgen's standpoint, the separation of the two factions may have appeared as the only logical solution to avoid further confrontations and violence within Enryakuji itself. On the other hand, the institutional separation also isolated the two centers from one another, solidifying factional differences. Indeed, a dispute over the abbotship of Tendai between Enryakuji and Onjōji resulted in protests at Regent Yorimichi's mansion and rumors of an attack on Onjōji in 1038–1039. Contemporary records are few, but a later source, the late twelfth-century *Fusō ryakki,* states that more than three thousand monks descended from Mt. Hiei in 1039, a figure which is highly unlikely and can only be attributed to the later authorship of the source. In either case, Yorimichi responded by closing the gates to his mansion, causing the rowdy protesters, some carrying bows and arrows, to camp outside. A certain Jōsei, who appears to have been the ringleader of the "evil monks," proceeded to detain the Enryakuji clergy's own candidate, Kyōen, as hostage to force a cancellation of Myōson's appointment. The strategy failed, however, and Jōsei was forced to release Kyōen and then defend his actions at the imperial court, while several of his superior monks were punished for not controlling the clergy.[33]

More violent behavior was noted between Onjōji monks and the clergy of Enryakuji in the fourth month of 1040, during a dispute over a separate ordination platform for Onjōji. One source explains that the capital was full of people with bows and arrows, and "violent and evil monks" carrying swords; some also appear to have set certain buildings on fire. While the nobles discussed how to rid Kyoto of these elements, they could only condemn the behavior.[34] Two months later, the court was troubled by another incident involving monks from Enryakuji. Kanjūmaru, a page in the service of Minamoto Sukefusa, was kidnapped by "rowdy Tendai monks." Sukefusa, who seems to have been quite attached to Kanjūmaru, asked the mother where the page was, but ultimately was unable to locate the boy. Sukefusa subsequently learned that Kanjūmaru had become the disciple of a monk on Mt. Hiei. An attempt to bring the page back to Kyoto also failed as Kanjūmaru escaped, before being helped back to the mountain by "rowdy monks." Sukefusa eventually detained the page's mother to force the renegade servant back, but we do not know if this stratagem worked since the sources offer no more details.[35] It is not clear why Kanjūmaru was so important to either side, but it is obvious that the term "rowdy behavior" could be used to describe a wide range of monks' activities, not only armed disruptions.

To what extent did the gradual increase of violence from the tenth and eleventh centuries indicate an incorporation of armed religious forces into the institutional framework (in other words, the "militarization") of temples? To properly interpret the sources, we must place the events above in their historical context. First, as noted earlier, violence by clerics was nothing new, even if there is evidence of more occurrences during the tenth and early eleventh centuries. Second, there is a visible lack of planning, leadership, and professionalism (i.e., the presence of professional warriors) in these incidents; those involved were a far cry from images of the *sōhei*. The skirmishes might best be understood as the result of the discontent or ambitions of smaller groups or individuals within the larger temple complexes.

In other words, to speak of a general "militarization" of religious institutions, in which armed men were used as a means to solve conflicts by temples as a whole in the tenth and eleventh centuries, is both misleading and ahistorical. Moreover, the use of arms was restricted mainly to the local arena. Even if the perpetrators were part of a religious organization, their violent behavior had little to do with the temple itself. Nevertheless, under the prevailing judicial system, religious institutions would be held accountable for the behavior of their monks and servants, even if the institutions did not condone their acts. It is for this reason that both nobles and temple leaders condemned violent monks and tried to contain them. However, the growing presence of armed men in the provinces, combined with increased pressure on land and greater uncertainty within the religious hierarchy during the resurgence of the imperial family, soon led to even more evidence of military pressure being used for conflict resolution.

Aristocratic Monk-Commanders and Temple Warriors

Isolated incidents and minor skirmishes involving religious forces were supplanted by outright attacks by the late eleventh century, and in the Hōgen Disturbance of 1156, the losing faction even recruited a force led by a Kōfukuji monk, marking the first appearance of religious forces in a strictly political dispute. This transformation was gradual, evolving slowly as competition for land and religious status among the leading monasteries took more violent form. Nevertheless, the year 1081 stands out as a sort of watershed in the development of this new level of violence. First, a combined force of armed monks and secular retainers from Enryakuji launched an attack on and burned down parts of Onjōji, marking the first of several destructive actions in the many disputes between the two Tendai centers. A counter-attack by Onjōji monks some days later resulted only in more destruction by the superior Enryakuji forces.[36] Then, following disturbances in a Kōfukuji estate by some local Tōnomine monks in the third month of 1081, Kōfukuji attacked Tōnomine (a branch temple of Enryakuji in Yamato province) in what would be the first of many incendiary assaults.[37] Thus, on two occasions in 1081, forces involving large numbers of monks engaged in premeditated attacks upon another temple. What made it possible to execute such attacks and cause such destruction with this new level of organization and coordination? The answer lies in the emergence of new kinds of leaders within the monasteries who had solid military training, the willingness to use arms to reach their ambitious goals, and the proper status and authority to lead provincial and lower class forces. The records rarely reveal exactly how these attacks were conducted, but a number of monk-commanders from the twelfth century have left ample traces to enable us to get a sense of their social background, political connections, military training, and leadership capabilities.

The Belligerent Monks of Mt. Hiei

Jōjin (1037–1118) was undoubtedly one of the most belligerent monks of Shirakawa's era. He was the son of Fujiwara

Yoshisada, a mid-ranking member of the Northern Fujiwara who served as governor of Bingo province in the 1040s and early 1050s.[38] The family had a history of ambitious officials, but they had met with little success owing to the family's comparatively low status within the Fujiwara. Jōjin took Buddhist vows on Mt. Hiei, perhaps with the hope of escaping the limitations of his family, but even as a cleric, his promotion through the ranks was slow. Despite counting two of Enryakuji's most influential leaders as his teachers, Jōjin reached the level of preceptor (*risshi*) only in 1085, at the age of forty-seven.[39] This belated promotion did, however, allow him to participate in ceremonies attended by important members of the imperial court in the early 1090s. Late in 1095, he was promoted to *gon no shō sōzu* (supernumerary junior prelate) in recognition of his services. In fact, he appears to have been so busy in the capital that he did not return to Enryakuji for four or five years prior to this promotion.[40] But Jōjin began to pay more and more attention to matters on Mt. Hiei the following year, when he became involved in a dispute over the abbotship of Saitō, where his mentors had served as abbots before becoming head abbots at Enryakuji.

The previous Saitō abbot had been selected much to the dismay of Jōjin, which may have contributed to his decision to remain in the capital for several years. Now, with the abbot gone, he saw an opportunity to become head of one of the three sections of Enryakuji and brought armed men with him when he suddenly ascended the mountain to confront his opposition. Battles ensued between the two factions, until the Tendai head abbot, Ninkaku, stepped in to award the prestigious abbotship to Eijun, a non-ranking monk of Jōjin's own cohort. There was more than just religious politics behind this decision. The head abbot was well connected among the capital nobles, a descendant from Michinaga's line and the uncle of chancellor Moromichi. The latter, in particular, disliked Jōjin, whose family in general was not on good terms with the regent's line. In fact, Moromichi's father (Yorimichi) referred to Jōjin as coming from a family "with evilness deeply rooted in their hearts."[41] One can certainly not deny that Jōjin was ambitious, since he fought his opponents at the Saitō section even after the head abbot's decision, causing fatalities on both sides. Interestingly, contemporary diaries call these clashes "battles" (*kassen*), indicating a new level of violence, strategies, and leadership as compared to the skirmishes earlier in the eleventh century. In the end, though, Jōjin could not single-handedly beat the powerful coalition of the opposing faction, the Tendai head and the regent, and he was obliged to concede defeat.

Jōjin returned to the capital, where he resumed his career as a performer of Buddhist rituals. However, when Eijun was succeeded in 1100 by another monk of the same group, Jōjin again objected with the support of warriors on Mt. Hiei, and the appointment was only enforced with some difficulty.[42] Then, head abbot Ninkaku died in the third month of 1102 at the age of fifty-eight, leaving the court with the difficult task of choosing his successor. The seventy-six-year-old Keichō appears to have been selected as a compromise solution. For Jōjin, this was a stroke of good fortune, as Keichō was his maternal relative and the two monks lived close to one another in the capital. In fact, they both participated in a ceremony at Hosshōji sponsored by Retired Emperor Shirakawa in 1103, Keichō as lecturer and Jōjin as reader.[43] When the Saitō abbot died the following year, Jōjin moved again to seize control of the Saitō section. Although his forces were outnumbered, the fighting spread throughout the Enryakuji complex. Several tens of dwellings were destroyed and four or five battles took place before the confrontation was interrupted by heavy rains in the middle of the sixth month of 1104.[44]

A few days later, Jōjin's opponents appealed to the imperial court to exile Jōjin for his misdeeds. Although most nobles felt equally uneasy about Jōjin's opponents, they generally agreed that Jōjin had been responsible for much of the violence.[45] Yet, Jōjin was clearly not the only one capable of leading forces and fighting among the clergies. Fujiwara Munetada, a retainer of Shirakawa, observed:

To assemble more than twenty warriors without reason is strictly prohibited in the law codes. However, the clergy on Mt. Hiei have recently assembled thousands of warriors to battle from dusk to dawn, and there are too many fatalities to count. Mt. Hiei and Kyoto are not far apart and are like one. Thus, even if the mountain monks do not file an appeal, order should be imposed. But there is no such decree, and we are therefore pressured by the clergy's demands, as we are forced to hold a meeting like this for the first time. At this point, there is not much we can do, except to listen to the advice of the emperor.[46]

The court thus seemed to lack the ability or determination to confront the clergy through traditional means and was also unwilling to resort to force. It eventually decided that Jōjin was the principal responsible party, and while the court stopped short of ordering his exile, it stripped him of his rank within the Office of Monastic Affairs. However, these actions failed to calm the waters. When head abbot Keichō climbed Mt. Hiei shortly afterward in the eighth month of 1104, he was accused of having endorsed Jōjin's actions, and driven off the mountain. His dwelling was destroyed in the process, and the clergy also managed to steal his head abbot seal.[47] While the ranking monks of Enryakuji were called to Kyoto to explain their behavior toward the head abbot, supporters and disciples of Jōjin and Keichō struck again, attacking more monk dwellings within the Saitō section, killing some of its members. It was clear from the explanations submitted by Enryakuji that the monastery was now severely divided. Although a large part of the clergy supported the ouster of the head abbot, a separate statement from the Ryōgon'in cloister of the Yokawa section stated that the decision had been made by certain members of the clergy, but was by no means endorsed by all on Mt. Hiei.[48]

The members of the imperial court were now quite frustrated by the aggression of these "rowdy monks," as well as by their own inability to contain the violence. It was not merely the incident at Enryakuji that bothered the courtiers, but also what appeared more broadly to be a growing pattern of encroachments and illegal behavior by monastic communities. Efforts were intensified to stop "evil monks, who carve up the various provinces by calling them branch temples or private estates," and prohibitions were issued against "supporters with arms on Mt. Hiei, as well as monks carrying weapons within Tōdaiji, Kōfukuji, Enryakuji, and Onjōji." Several experienced government warriors, including Minamoto Yoshiie and Yoshitsuna, were additionally ordered to "besiege Mt. Hiei in the east and the west, arrest evil monks, and detain and bring supporters trying to ascend the mountain to Kyoto."[49] But even these measures proved insufficient.

Following Keichō's ouster, the administration of Enryakuji was managed by Hōyaku Zenshi, who had been one of the ringleaders in the coup. He was in every way as belligerent and ambitious as Jōjin, and commonly known as a "rough monk," "extremely skilled in the way of the warrior, [who] led tens of warriors in various battles, engaging in thefts and killings in the Kyoto area."[50] Nothing is known of his origins, but references in contemporary diaries indicate that he was a low-ranking administrator of provincial origin with limited religious training. Be that as it may, once in command on Mt. Hiei, his main concern was to maintain and expand Enryakuji's control of estates and branches. One of his first acts was to send lower-class temple servants and service people of Hiesha, many of them his own personal retainers, to Kamadoyama in Chikuzen (in Kyushu) in order to obstruct the administration of Kōsei, the new abbot there.[51] Kamadoyama shrine was a local branch of Daisenji, in Hōki province, which in turn had been a powerful branch-temple of Enryakuji since the late ninth or early tenth centuries. Shirakawa had appointed Kōsei as administrator of Kamadoyama even though appointment rights belonged to the main temple. Not surprisingly, the appointment of Kōsei, who also was the head of the rival shrine-temple complex of Iwashimizu Hachimangū, was interpreted as a direct threat to Enryakuji, and Hōyaku Zenshi's ouster of Keichō had been in part related to the latter's unwillingness to protest on Enryakuji's behalf. Although Hōyaku Zenshi's troops encountered resistance in Chikuzen, Enryakuji eventually emerged victorious in this dispute late in 1105. By that time, however, Hōyaku himself had been arrested for reasons unknown, and his name then disappears from the sources as suddenly as it had appeared only a few months earlier.[52]

The aging Keichō returned to Mt. Hiei to resume his duties as Tendai head abbot, but found opposition from the clergy too difficult to manage, and he resigned in the second month of 1105. An Onjōji monk named Zōyo was appointed as his successor on 2.14, but he was forced to resign after only one day as head abbot. He was succeeded by Ningen, who, as the son of Fujiwara Morozane and the uncle of Regent Tadazane, appeared to have the right support at court to stabilize matters. However, the scramble for arms could still be heard on Mt. Hiei, and Jōjin finally managed to be appointed abbot of Saitō on 1106.9.30, at the age of sixty-nine. In actuality, Jōjin had now become the most influential man on Mt. Hiei.[53] Even so, he was unable to sustain his position. One of his retainers apparently killed a messenger of Retired Emperor Shirakawa in the second month of 1107, and Shirakawa understandably became enraged. Fingers were soon pointed in the direction of Jōjin, who was taken into custody and interrogated by the imperial police. Although it is not clear if the slaying was carried out with the support of Jōjin (it is hard to imagine that it would have benefited him in any way), he refused to name the person responsible for the crime, and a substitute was eventually forwarded to be punished.[54] Shirakawa was not at all satisfied, however; he had Jōjin banished from the capital home province of Yamashiro on 1108.1.9. Some courtiers appear to have felt relief. Fujiwara Munetada commented from Shirakawa's camp that "Jōjin is a very evil person, and he has been the instigator [of trouble] among the clergy many times, performing exceedingly evil deeds for years. It is for this reason that he is punished like this." Jōjin's long-time adversary, Kankei, who had personally led forces against Jōjin in 1104, was now generously promoted, and received frequent employment in Buddhist rituals in the capital. Kankei's loyalty to the court during these struggles is no surprise, as he was the older brother of another of Shirakawa's trusted retainers (Fujiwara Munemichi).[55]

It is not clear where Jōjin went in exile, but he likely spent most of his time in neighboring Ōmi province, on the eastern side of Mt. Hiei. At some point, the aging monk must have been pardoned, because he was invited back to the capital and even reinstated as a ranking monk of the Office of Monastic Affairs, participating in a ceremony at Hosshōji in Kyoto with Shirakawa in attendance on 1114.2.20. It is difficult to explain exactly why Jōjin was permitted to return to the capital. Perhaps the complete destruction of his faction, coupled with the confiscation of his estate rights, made him weak enough to be tolerated again. Or perhaps the head abbot Zōyo, who was also his cousin, interceded on his behalf. Whatever the reason, he spent his final years in reclusion, and died at eighty-one on 1118.2.25. Even at that point, he was still known as a violent monk, who, as Munetada noted in his diary, "had been involved in several tens of battles on Mt. Hiei."[56]

As the best documented monk-commanders of Enryakuji during the *insei* age, Jōjin and Hōyaku Zenshi provide important clues to the social and political background of monk-commanders during Shirakawa's times. While Jōjin sought prestigious monk titles and was deeply involved in factional politics both on Mt. Hiei and in the capital, Hōyaku was an administrator with ambitions centering on landed assets. Both commanded substantial forces, using them to further their own interests. Most important, the sources reveal that their retainers were recruited from among provincial warriors, which indicates that these forces might better be understood in the context of the warrior class than the monastery itself. Cases from three other powerful monastic complexes—Kōfukuji, Tōdaiji, and Kōyasan—will be helpful in further exploring this issue.

Kōfukuji's Shinjitsu: "Japan's Number One Evil Martial Monk"

Among the belligerent monks of Heian Japan, Shinjitsu (1086–?) must certainly be one of the most recognizable. Two historical sources describe him as "Japan's number one evil martial monk."[57] Shinjitsu has therefore become the ultimate representation of greedy and violent monks, and by extension, of the degeneration of Buddhist institutions and their negative impact on legitimate rulership by court nobles. But such interpretations have fallen prey to predetermined negative views of armed monks, while neglecting to put monks such as Shinjitsu into their proper historical context. An examination of Shinjitsu, his alliances and involvement in various incidents, is thus crucial to obtain a balanced understanding of the role and origins of armed monks in general.

Shinjitsu came from a branch of the Seiwa Genji (Minamoto), a lineage of warrior background. His father (Yoriyasu) and grandfather were both ambitious and aggressive warriors of some stature, who eagerly appropriated land for their own gain. Indeed, Yoriyasu earned himself a reputation as "a well-known warrior troublemaker of the realm."[58] Still, he was not impervious to Buddhism, since he practiced the reading of the Lotus sutra. Shinjitsu appears to have inherited both of these traits from his father, making an unprecedented career as a military leader within the Kōfukuji clergy. We can surmise from his appointment as assistant head administrator of the Fujiwara family temple in 1121 that he was born in 1086, and promoted to head administrator (*jishu*) of Kōfukuji in 1129. This post allowed him to dominate a large portion of the clergy.[59] Yet, Retired Emperor Toba, who took control of the imperial court following the death of Shirakawa that year, patronized the monk Chōen, who also had ambitions to become abbot of Kiyomizudera, a branch temple of Kōfukuji. Several members of the clergy disapproved of Chōen, and about two hundred "evil monks" attacked him on the road, ripped off his monk robe, and inflicted severe wounds to his head. In addition, some of his young disciples were killed, others were seriously injured, and the carts he and his entourage traveled in were destroyed. Chōen was detained by these clergy who opposed him and taken back to Nara, where the Kōfukuji head abbot, Genkaku, persuaded the unruly monks to release him.[60]

Toba responded forcefully, sending government forces to Nara under the command of several renowned warriors, including Mitsunobu, Masashige, and Tameyoshi of the Minamoto; Fujiwara Morimichi; and Taira Masahiro. These measures were undoubtedly the strictest ever taken against one of the elite temples, resulting in serious skirmishes with "evil monks." On one occasion, a confrontation led to the killing of three retainers of the imperial police captain and ten Kōfukuji supporters. Toba's fierce pursuit of these Kōfukuji monks may in large part be explained by his close relations with Chōen, who was supported by one of the retired emperor's consorts.[61] Toba subsequently deposed Genkaku as head abbot, blaming him for not containing the clergy, and stripping him of his official monk rank. The ringleader, Egyō, was exiled to Harima, while more than ten other monks were moved to various provinces. As contemporary observers noted, such punishments and measures against one of the elite temples were unprecedented. Chōen, on the other hand, improved his position, as he gained appointment as abbot of Iwashimizu Hachimangū.[62]

Shinjitsu was not directly involved in this incident, but was pursued and arrested by Minamoto Tameyoshi, who also seems to have been responsible for burning the monk's residence. However, perhaps realizing the monk's innocence, Tameyoshi shielded the besieged Shinjitsu instead of handing him over directly to the authorities, and the monk subsequently slipped away to Regent Tadamichi's mansion for protection. But Tadamichi betrayed Shinjitsu and handed him over to Toba in a strange change of loyalties.[63]

Shinjitsu eventually confessed under pressure to committing crimes during the original attack on Chōen, but Toba limited his punishment to house arrest, realizing that the monk was not part of Egyō's faction and thus not one of the instigators. By the third month of the following year (1130), Shinjitsu was pardoned and allowed to return to Nara.[64] Two years later, Genkaku was also pardoned for his inability to control the clergy and subsequently re-appointed head abbot of Kōfukuji, after which Shinjitsu was once again put at the apex of the administrative hierarchy of the monastery.[65] In 1137, Shinjitsu was promoted to *gon no jōza* (supernumerary preceptor), confirming and further enhancing his status within Kōfukuji. But contrary to what one might expect, it was not Shinjitsu's military prowess that allowed him to rise through the monk ranks, but rather his connections with ranking members of the Fujiwara regent's line. For example, in the eleventh month of 1136, Shinjitsu and his disciple Genjitsu—Shinjitsu's true son—hosted the young Fujiwara Yorinaga (Tadazane's second son, whom he favored over Tadamichi), when he visited Kasuga. Some observers found it inappropriate, however, that two known troublemakers should have the honor of hosting such a illustrious personage. Clearly, the monks were important enough associates of the Fujiwara for Yorinaga to ignore precedents for his pilgrimage. Although highly unusual, it was therefore hardly surprising that Shinjitsu was allowed to handle the affairs of Kōfukuji upon the death of head abbot Genkaku on 1138.9.21.[66]

A new head abbot, named Ryūkaku (1074–1158), was appointed about a month later, but he was quite unpopular with the clergy. Ryūkaku attempted to appease the monks by bringing rice for the clergy from his Suita estate. However, some of Ryūkaku's own followers disagreed with his gesture and forestalled the planned handout. At this point, Shinjitsu headed a force that confronted the spoilers, after which the Kōfukuji monks, with his blessing, simply appropriated the rice.[67] Tensions thus ran high at the temple between the clergy and its leadership, eventually sparking another conflict that caused serious problems and concerns in Kyoto. When a monk named Eiken was killed in the first month of 1139, the clergy, probably under the leadership of Shinjitsu, blamed the death on the head abbot. They attacked and burned his cloister as well as dwellings belonging to some of his deputies. In addition, the Kōfukuji clergy marched toward Kyoto to stage a demonstration (*gōso*) to incline the imperial court toward deposing Ryūkaku. Approaching the capital from the south, the clergy paused on the western shore of the Uji River. The court responded immediately by sending government warriors, led by Taira Tadamori and several Minamoto generals, who fortified the eastern shore in order to prevent the protesters from actually entering the capital. Unable to move forward, the clergy sent an appeal to Regent Tadamichi and returned to Nara. Shinjitsu and another ranking monk, Kan'yo, were held responsible for the affair, but in the end, both were pardoned.[68]

Needless to say, the monks' connections with two of the Fujiwara leaders (Tadazane and Yorinaga) played an important role in securing their pardons. But the original issue was far from resolved. In the eleventh month of 1139, Ryūkaku brought government warriors to Nara in retaliation for the humiliations he and his followers had suffered at the hands of the Kōfukuji clergy. The defending monks managed to fend off Ryūkaku's forces, capturing fifty of his warriors who were subsequently turned over to the imperial police. Despite his involvement in the incident, Shinjitsu was immediately promoted to preceptor (jōza), owing to his Fujiwara connections, while Ryūkaku was replaced as Kōfukuji's chief abbot for his belligerent acts, in favor of a new abbot named Kakuyo (1086–1146).[69] Promoting Shinjitsu, however, did not end the violence at Kōfukuji, for there were also elements of the Kōfukuji clergy opposed to his advancement. Indeed, some "evil monks" from Kōfukuji went to the Kangakuin in order to seek the exile of an important backer of Shinjitsu, Minamoto Tameyoshi. While the court obliged them, the monastery remained mired in internal tensions and brawls, which eventually resulted in the exile of fifteen "evil monks." Shinjitsu, however, was shielded from punishment, because of his connections with Tadazane, although it appeared clear to everyone in the capital that he was actually behind much of the clergy's actions.[70]

With partial control of the Kōfukuji clergy, Shinjitsu set out to expand the influence of his temple (and indeed, himself) in Yamato province. One tenacious obstacle to his ambitions was the Kinpusen temple, which Shinjitsu attacked in the seventh month of 1145. Interestingly, a contemporary account notes that Shinjitsu headed these forces as daishōgun (Great General), indicating his qualities and occupation as a warrior leader.

Nevertheless, he could not subdue Kinpusen, and was forced to retreat after a campaign of two weeks.[71]

Late in 1146, Kakuyo died and was succeeded by Kakusei (1090–1148). Kakusei's tenure as head abbot was abruptly terminated by his death in 1148.5, which resulted in another edict from the Fujiwara chieftain Tadazane, placing Shinjitsu in charge of the administration of Kōfukuji.[72] With the help of his son, Genjitsu, Shinjitsu controlled Kōfukuji completely for three full years, aided by the fact that the position of head abbot remained conveniently vacant. In 1149, he and Genjitsu were accused of a bizarre scheme to steal rocks from the tomb of Emperor Shōmu. Tōdaiji, which acted as manager of the tomb and its environs, complained that father and son had stolen rocks from the tomb to use in the construction of a hall within Kōfukuji. Shinjitsu and Genjitsu responded that they had taken material from a hill known as Nahosan, which housed the tomb of Empress Genshō, and not from Sahosan, where Shōmu's tomb was located. Since the tombs are more than two kilometers apart, it appears likely that Tōdaiji's accusations were well founded. Furthermore, the value of using rocks from Shōmu's tomb provides a motive for Shinjitsu's actions. By the late Heian age, a Shōmu cult had emerged which linked him with both Kannon and the Shōtoku Taishi cult. Rocks from his tomb could be used as relics to enhance the spiritual presence at the new temple hall. Shinjitsu's denial thus appears unpersuasive, although he cleverly exploited the court's unfamiliarity with the area and similarity of the place names to defend himself. Unfortunately for justice, the imperial officials charged with resolving the conflict never visited the actual site, relying instead on statements from the conflicting parties.[73] An examination of the adjoining hills would certainly have indicated if there was any truth to the accusations. Tsunoda Bun'ei speculates that Shinjitsu's forces were so feared that the officials simply chose not to pursue the matter any further.[74] It seems more likely, however, that Shinjitsu survived because of the support of Tadazane and Yorinaga in the capital.

This theory gains additional credibility from subsequent events known as the Hōgen Incident (1156). Once Tadamichi, the estranged son of Tadazane, assumed the Fujiwara chieftaincy, he re-appointed Ryūkaku as the head abbot of Kōfukuji, despite Shinjitsu's vigorous objections. This was clearly a setback for the belligerent monk, but he still remained the most influential monk in Nara. The head abbot's adherents in the monastery were outnumbered by Shinjutsu's backers, while Shinjitsu still retained the support of Tadazane, the scheming Fujiwara chieftain emeritus. It was in fact this alliance that led Shinjitsu to join Tadazane in an attempted coup d'état with Retired Emperor Sutoku against the newly enthroned Go-Shirakawa in 1156. Contemporary sources are unfortunately of little help in revealing the size and composition of Shinjitsu's forces, but they must have been substantial since his allies in the capital decided to wait for his arrival before making their move. According to a later war tale, Fujiwara Yorinaga (Tadazane's favored son) and the disenchanted Minamoto Tameyoshi headed some six hundred warriors in the capital, to which Shinjitsu was to add one thousand warriors from Nara. But as is well known, Go-Shirakawa's forces preempted his enemies by striking first and driving them out of the capital. Shinjitsu and his son failed to arrive in time, but instead joined the defeated Tadazane and his warriors in flight to Nara.[75]

One of the most astonishing aspects of the aftermath of the failed coup was the leniency of the Kōfukuji monks' punishment. To be sure, Shinjitsu and Genjitsu lost their monastic titles, and their confiscated estates were transferred to Kōfukuji. However, where other rebels were banished or executed, the monks escaped with only a blow to their social status and financial foundations.[76] Deciphering the reason for this lenient treatment is crucial for our understanding of the monks' position and also the court's perception of their functions. First, such leniency may have reflected the view that the monks had not been the ringleaders of the uprising, only allies who had responded to the summons of more exalted nobles in Kyoto. And, while Shinjitsu had aligned himself with the wrong side, the court may have elected more lenient punishment since his forces had not engaged in actual fighting.[77]

Second, as Tsunoda suggests, it is possible that the court still feared Shinjitsu's forces to the extent that it avoided the more common punishment of exile to avoid further disturbances and perhaps even armed resistance from the monk's followers.[78] Yet, the basis for imagining such a scenario seems shaky, given the confiscation of his estates. As a Minamoto warrior whose provincial resources were now gone, Shinjitsu lost most of his power. Perhaps the final documented incident in his stormy career can be instructive in understanding the lingering perceptions of his potential influence. The court decided in 1158 to perform a survey of public land in Yamato province, most likely in an attempt to forestall further conversions into private estates by influential estate patrons, such as Kōfukuji and its shrine affiliate, Kasuga. Surprisingly, Shinjitsu was part of the government's high-profile surveying group, together with the governor himself. To say the least, Shinjitsu's appearance in this capacity did not please the clergy currently under the control of his monastic rivals. His residence was assaulted, and Shinjitsu was forced to use his remaining faithful retainers to defend himself. There were tens of fatalities and many injuries on both sides of the lines of battle, and the survey group fled in fear.[79] Shinjitsu's shifting loyalties at this point suggest a great deal about the leniency of his punishment after the abortive coup in 1156. Although aligned with the rebelling and losing faction, Shinjitsu probably managed to escape severe punishment by cooperating with the victors. He surrendered his managerial rights to estates he controlled, and may additionally have promised as part of his settlement to cooperate with the governor in the future. That this cooperation might include surveys to curb the landed interests of Kōfukuji may not have been clear at the time, but such terms provide the most plausible explanation of Shinjitsu's unexpected participation in the survey and the subsequent attack by the clergy.

Were it not for his monk robes and titles within Kōfukuji, it would be easy to characterize Shinjitsu as an overly ambitious warrior, who used his military skills and control over land and retainers to further his interests, much in the manner of his father and many other members of his lineage. Indeed, it seems difficult to describe him as anything but a warrior. From this perspective, his involvement in the futile coup attempt seems not at all exceptional, even though it marks the first time in Japanese history that forces from a temple were called to battle by members of the imperial court. Although there can be no doubt that Shinjitsu fits the stereotypical image of a "monk-warrior" poorly, his case is important, not because he fought as a monk, but because he made his career within Kōfukuji as a warrior-administrator. His life, in other words, speaks clearly of the inseparability of the monastic, noble, and military worlds of late Heian Japan.

Kakunin: Estate Manager

Owing to the vast documentary collection of Tōdaiji, the life and activities of the monk Kakunin are well chronicled. His name first appears in the sources on 1127.11.20, when his service as administrator of Tōdaiji estates earned him the ranking of *gon no tsuina* (assistant temple provost).[80] By 1133, Kakunin had advanced to *gon no jishu* (supernumerary temple head administrator); his primary tasks were protecting and expanding Tōdaiji's possessions in Iga province against the local official class, while extending his own influence both in the estates and within Tōdaiji itself.[81] However, his methods also became increasingly aggressive, and we find him referred to as an "evil monk" for the first time in an edict of 1147.10.2, relating to complaints from Ise province, Iwashimizu, and Kasuga. Then, in 1149, the governor of Iga lodged a complaint against Kakunin, charging that he had joined forces with regional landlords to appropriate harvested rice from a village within the boundaries of the public domain. Unsurprisingly, since Kakunin "could not prove beyond any doubt the rights of Tōdaiji," the dispute ended to the advantage of the local officials.[82]

These activities—the cooperative efforts of regional landlords and Kakunin to take control over a larger portion of the harvests and exclude them from provincial taxation—continued well into the 1150s. In particular, his efforts in the Kuroda estate in Iga appear to have been relentless. In 1158, the provincial officials again accused him of appropriating taxes and trying to steal land from the public domain in collusion with these mid-level landlords. The complaint quotes a statement from timber laborers under Tōdaiji's jurisdiction:

> Last year, the administrator from the main temple, Kakunin, known in the realm as an evil monk of Nara, stated that he was appointed estate manager, sometimes traveling to the estate himself, sometimes sending his representatives—making it unbearable for a long time. He has caused various illegal activities that are unheard of, and we had little choice but to leave our homeland and flee.[83]

Everything in Kakunin's behavior indicates that he treated the temple's assets as his own, and felt entitled to expand his interests in the name of Tōdaiji. It is perhaps not surprising, then, that he would eventually encounter resistance from within Tōdaiji itself. Matters came to a head shortly after the complaint against him in 1158, when another ranking monk named Nōe attempted to re-establish his cloister's control of estates under Kakunin's management. The sources do not reveal how these tensions grew into a more serious dispute and what other issues were contested, but Kakunin was eventually accused of having stolen 194 horses. Kakunin did not receive support from other monks within Tōdaiji, a strong indicator that his main power base and support lay in the estates. Nevertheless, he defended himself adroitly, and managed to retain most of his rights. He was important to Tōdaiji's ranking clergy as an able manager, and an influential member of the temple's administrative corps with extensive knowledge of the procedures of litigation.[84]

Kakunin relied on his local contacts, not on patrons in the capital, to promote his career within Tōdaiji. He was born a Taira and derived much of his personal power and charisma from his family's background within the provincial class of officials.

Pedigree and blood relations were useful to sons of aristocrats, who could usually expect a fast track career as monks with active support from their relatives. But, with Shinjitsu and Kakunin, family connections also helped in securing material support and followers in the provinces. It was not unusual for warriors and monks from the same family to coordinate their efforts to expand their influence. Kakunin involved himself in local estates supported by several followers, many of whom were armed and recruited, not as servants of Tōdaiji, but as retainers of the Taira. Factional politics, blood lineages, and family alliances were salient also within the walls of Japan's monasteries in the late Heian age.

Kakunin's position was further strengthened in the third month of 1159, when a new head abbot named Kanpen was appointed at Tōdaiji. Kanpen must have been on good terms with Kakunin, since the latter was promoted to the highest level (*jōza*) within the temple's executive organ (*sangō*) less than a month later. As a ranking member of the *sangō*, it is hardly surprising that Kakunin's signature appears with increasing frequency in important estate documents of Tōdaiji.[85] Heavily involved in internal administration within Tōdaiji, Kakunin now had even more clout in land matters. Serving as the ranking estate manager of Kuroda-no-shō, Kakunin had judicial rights in the estate, as evidenced by his adjudication in disputes over office fields in 1159 and 1169, but he also continued to appropriate assets for himself. Appeals, accusations, defense statements, and skirmishes were thus all part of the daily management issues. A verdict issued in 1162 by the imperial court provides yet another glimpse of Kakunin's local influence and human resources. The provincial officials stated:

> When this Kakunin was appointed land manager, he began to perform evil deeds. He assembled a band of over three hundred armed men [*gunpei*] and drove away the hamlet manager, Toshikata. Toshikata even fled together with the farmers, because Kakunin tried to kill him. As a result, this district has now been removed from public

taxation. These are evil deeds beyond words. To disobey
generations of imperial decrees and gather armed men to
plan killings reflects the utmost lack of respect for the law
of the imperial court.[86]

Kakunin's aggressive land policies also led to a conflict with
Kōfukuji, which filed an appeal against him in 1161, stating that
he performed various illegal deeds, such as detaining messengers
and stealing oil and rice.[87] The conflict continued for several
years with Kakunin using his regular strategies of a strong local
presence, forcing the subsequent Tōdaiji head abbot, Ken'e, to
submit letters to the Fujiwara chieftain in 1167 and 1168. To
divert the charges, Tōdaiji accused Kōfukuji supporters, headed
by the Kōfukuji monk Kinsai of the Saikondō, of appropriating
taxes from Tōdaiji's Takadono estate by claiming that certain
fields were part of Kōfukuji's private possessions. The Fujiwara
administrative headquarters was unable to reach a decisive verdict
in this dispute, merely stating that taxes should be collected as
before, undoubtedly disappointing both sides. The Kōfukuji
monks felt compelled to take matters into their own hands and
went to the estate to stake their claims to several residences while
harassing representatives from Tōdaiji. Kakunin responded by
going straight to the capital to lodge another complaint, this
time to Retired Emperor Go-Shirakawa, in the fourth month of
1170. Yet he neglected to appear for a trial confrontation when
the court attempted to settle the dispute, preferring instead to
continue to apply pressure directly in the estate.[88] His use of
force and pressure locally, his own status within Tōdaiji, and
manipulation of his contacts and the litigation system in Kyoto
were masterfully combined. He was never punished, despite
accusations from the Kōfukuji clergy that it was Kakunin, and
not Tōdaiji, who was behind the complaint against Kōfukuji.
He remained active into the mid-1170s, without any indication
that he was ousted or punished for his aggressive managerial
strategies.

Kakunin was not only a Taira descendant with significant armed support but also part of the fairly large contingent of mid-ranking nobles with knowledge of the legal procedures of the Heian court, as evidenced by his appearances in Kyoto in various judicial hearings, both to appeal against his opponents and to defend himself against various accusations. Indeed, in its statement of 1170, the Kōfukuji clergy stated, "Kakunin has the appearance of a monk, but in his heart, he is an enemy of the Law."[89] His exploitation of legal procedures, his authority as a ranking Tōdaiji manager and his band of warrior followers made him the most successful monk-commander of the twelfth century. From a social perspective, Kakunin played a role similar to other mid-ranking nobles, who rose through the court rankings as important retainers of the retired emperor or the Fujiwara chieftain by commanding armed forces while serving as aggressive administrators. Kakunin filled the same function for a religious elite, bridging the gap between the temple and the local inhabitants of its estates.

Sōken: The Dress Code Enforcer on Mt. Kōya

The monastic complex on Mt. Kōya struggled to sustain itself during the mid-Heian age, owing to repeated fires and difficulties in securing sufficient funds for repairs and maintenance. Its fortunes improved, however, during the eleventh century, as prominent nobles and then retired emperors began to make regular pilgrimages, with accompanying donations of funds and estates. Kakuban (1095–1143) was particularly successful as a favorite of Retired Emperor Toba and his main consort, Bifukumon'in (1117–1160), leading to the establishment of a powerful and wealthy cloister within Kōyasan, the Daidenpōin. But the granting of estates and titles also earned Kakuban the envy of monks belonging to the main temple, Kongōbuji, resulting in a highly competitive atmosphere between the two centers. The wealth and favored status of the Daidenpōin alienated the Kongōbuji monks, and there is evidence of arms used in a skirmish as early as 1162. Six years later, Kongōbuji monks attacked the Daidenpōin, destroying dwellings and stealing Buddhist artifacts. According to an appeal submitted by the Daidenpōin clergy, the incident began during the annual New Year's ceremonies. The accused ringleader was in fact the master of ceremonies, a ranking Kongōbuji monk named Sōken (?–1183). Sōken was accused of bringing "armed evil-doing fellows with him, entering various halls at the Daidenpōin" on the fourth day of the ceremonies. Apparently, he and his armed followers slashed in every direction as they made their way through the temple, causing the Daidenpōin monks to run for their lives. Once the temple was abandoned, Sōken's group rampaged through the area, stealing a variety of "Buddhist images, sutras and other valuable objects." Tearing down dwellings and repositories, they then took with them relics and food items reserved for the residing monks.[90]

The primary cause of this mayhem was quite simply envy of the lucrative patronage the Daidenpōin enjoyed. When the New Year's ceremonies were about to begin, the Daidenpōin had just gone through a renovation that made it look even more glorious than before. In addition, the Daidenpōin monks decided to wear silk robes instead of the black hemp robes prescribed by Kūkai for the ceremony, further causing envy and anger among the Kongōbuji monks. Following the brawl, monks from both sides were called to Tōji, the Shingon center in Kyoto, to explain themselves. Seventeen monks went to Kyoto, but instead of admonishing them himself, the head abbot handed them over to the Imperial Police, and three of the monks were swiftly exiled for their role in the incident.[91]

Sōken's case took more time, perhaps because he did not fit the typical description of "evil monks" who headed forces of warriors to further their own interests. He came from Kii province, from a village not far from Mt. Kōya, and did not have anything close to the kind of following that a Taira or Minamoto warrior would have. Still, he was most certainly a figure of some local stature, since, according to a later source, he took time to travel back to his home area on several occasions as a monk, spearheading the construction of Buddhist halls and donating sutras to local shrines.[92] There is no extant record showing that

Sōken made fighting and the commanding of armed men his prime vocation. Nevertheless, for his role in the New Year's brouhaha, Sōken was sentenced to exile by Retired Emperor Go-Shirakawa early in the fifth month of 1168. Accompanied by seven guards, Sōken was sent to Satsuma, while his accomplices Genshin and Kakuken were exiled to the islands of Iki and Tsushima respectively.[93] Exile was undoubtedly a severe punishment for anyone with ambitions in late Heian Japan, especially if it was carried out for some time. We know little of Sōken's fate in the wake of his exile, but he was eventually pardoned and allowed to return to Mt. Kōya to resume his duties, and appears to have stayed out of trouble until his death in 1183.

However, the aftermath of the New Year's incident offers an instructive and rare description of how men of arms came to appear within the monastery. Concerned about their safety and position on Mt. Kōya, the Daidenpōin clergy submitted another appeal to Go-Shirakawa in the eighth month of 1168, asking that a prohibition against arms on the mountain be issued. According to the imperial decree issued thereupon:

> To chastise the monks residing at the Daidenpōin, a group of evil monks harbored cruelty and planned a rebellion. They called together the resident administrators of the temple headquarters, mustering and deploying warriors [*bushi*] from nearby provinces and districts. They performed evil deeds day and night, and both young and old now carry arms [on the summit] to defend themselves.[94]

Although the term "evil monks" appears in many court diaries, this important document demonstrates that the men actually involved in armed conflicts within the major monasteries were not monks. Rather, we see a clear division between the ringleaders, who are referred to as "evil monks" and the armed warriors, thus contradicting the stereotypical image of "monk-warriors." At any rate, in responding to the Daidenpōin appeal, Go-Shirakawa issued a decree warning the clergy on Mt. Kōya about misbehaving, promising that anyone who disobeyed the Buddhist precepts would be banished just like Sōken.[95] While tensions between the clergies of Kongōbuji and the Daidenpōin persisted until the latter left the mountain to found their own branch at Negoroji in the thirteenth century, the severe punishments of Sōken and his comrades served to discourage any further resort to violence on Mt. Kōya for decades thereafter.

Conclusion

Records of armed conflicts involving monks in the Heian period can broadly be divided into three subperiods. First, ordained people were involved in isolated incidents of violence in the eighth and ninth centuries, but those were quite localized and had little effect on the capital. Second, as local lawlessness reached new levels beginning in the tenth century, sometimes threatening the court system itself, violence by men in monks' robes increased as well. But these conflicts were not the result of a decline within the Buddhist system per se, since many of the perpetrators took vows, or simply dressed as monks, to escape taxation. Those who participated in violence usually did so without the approval or sanction of the ranking clergy. Yet the threat that increasing outbreaks of violence actually posed to the imperial court should not be underestimated. The warrior challenges to the court's authority by Taira Masakado and Fujiwara Sumitomo in the 930s were quite serious. The capital elites responded by rewarding and promoting warriors to quell these provincial uprisings, adjusting the structures of their own rulership to the threats they posed. Such adjustments clearly prolonged, if not strengthened, the capital's authority, and enabled the court-centered system to grow further, but they also incorporated men of arms into the imperial order. By the late eleventh and twelfth centuries, military means had become so fundamental in applying pressure and strengthening factions in central Japan that dispute resolution by arms became commonplace. This trend is clearly evident in the comparatively high-ranking posts that warrior leaders now secured as retainers and allies of the capital elites. It is this third stage in the development of arms within the monasteries that marks what some scholars have termed a "militarization" of the religious communities in Japan.

The central issue for this essay, however, is less about such trends as about the character of these armed retainers of Buddha. As shown here, they may be divided into two types, depending on their social background. Most undoubtedly stemmed from the provincial warrior class itself, as indicated by the terms (*heishi, bushi,* or *gunpei*) used to describe them in contemporary sources. Most of them remain unidentified in the records, but a few, such as Enryakuji's Hōyaku Zenshi, appear to have made it far enough up the monastic ladder to leave documented impacts. It is unclear whether Kongōbuji's Sōken personally hailed from such a military background, but he certainly came from the same class of local strongmen, as did many of the lower level warrior-managers. But leaders who provided the vital linkage between these provincial warriors and the monastery itself fall into a second category. They were without exception sons of mid-ranking aristocrats with military training or members of the warrior aristocracy, who functioned as "bridging figures" to the secular elites in Kyoto, to use a phrase coined by Jeffrey Mass. Shinjitsu and Kakunin came from the Minamoto and the Taira respectively, while Jōjin was a member of an ambitious, but lower ranking, line of the Fujiwara. Their careers appear quite similar to those of Shinzei (1106–1159) and Fujiwara Narichika (1137–1177), who rose through the ranks as effective commanders under the protection of Go-Shirakawa only to become victims of the very factionalism that they had used to increase their own influence. Regardless of their status as monks, they were in the main principally aristocratic commanders. Hence, it is questionable to insist upon the existence of a separate class of "monk-warriors" in twelfth-century Japan. In the same way that aristocrats could become commanders of military forces while remaining aristocrats, and warriors such as Taira Kiyomori could advance within the traditional court structure, the monk-commanders made their careers as monks through their social status and training. They were not monks who became warriors, but aristocratic warriors who used their skills within the context of monastic and political factionalism.

The militarization of religious institutions in the Heian period had little to do with any "secularization" of these institutions or of Buddhism itself. Rather, it was part of the same important processes that allowed the warrior class to rise to national prominence: the emergence of armed men in the provinces and their enlistment by court leaders in the increasingly intense factional struggles in Kyoto. The nobility in the capital did much to bring these two trends together, as witnessed by the important role played by aristocratic monk-commanders in capital factionalism. In a word, the religious sector went through the same changes that the imperial court and the countryside did. That is, as private means became more crucial in managing assets, military men became more prominent in all circles of society. Some served the imperial family or other court nobles; others served the Buddha and its institutions. It is only in later sources and different contexts, such as literary works and the "old capital" tax dispute in Kyoto in the mid-1980s, that warriors like Benkei and *sōhei* are given a separate identity from the warrior class itself.

NOTES

1   This essay is based on portions of my *The Teeth and Claws of the Buddha: Monastic Warriors and Sōhei in Japanese History*. Thanks to the editors' generosity, I have been able to add several more source quotations in this piece, and as such it is my hope that it will both give a more concise treatment of the central figures fighting for temples in the Heian period and provide additional insights into their behavior. I wish to thank the University of Hawai'i Press for permission to draw upon that work. The treatment of the monk-commanders can be found specifically on pp. 87–105.

2   It was at this time that I first visited Kyoto, only to have my sightseeing plans disrupted by these prestigious temples. At the time, I did not realize the historical implications of the dispute. Ironically, my *The Gates of Power: Monks, Courtiers, and Warriors in Premodern Japan* in a sense defends the temples' right to demonstrate in such a way, albeit in an earlier age.

3   In most cases, the admission fees were raised more than the actual tax, which drew further criticism from the media.

4   Nishi Nobito, "Sōhei, koto shinzei hōkisu"; Okuno Tetsuji, "Sōhei no ran imada owarazu."

5   See, for example, Hioki Shōichi, *Nihon sōhei no kenkyū*; Hirata Toshiharu, *Sōhei to bushi*; Tsuji Zennosuke, "Sōhei no gen'yu," in his *Nihon bukkyō shi: jōsei hen*, pp. 756–824.

6   See Adolphson, *The Gates of Power*, chap. 6.

7   *Kansai hikki*, p. 229; Kuroda Toshio, *Jisha seiryoku*, pp. 31–32.

8   In addition to the aforementioned studies by Tsuji, Hirata, and Hioki, see Katsuno Ryūshin, *Sōhei*; Tsuji Zennosuke, "Sōhei jinnin no katsudō," in his *Nihon bukkyō shi: jōsei hen*, pp. 824–920; Watanabe Morimichi, *Sōhei seisuiki*; Hiraoka Jōkai, "Dōshu, akusō ni tsuite," in his *Nihon jiin shi no kenkyū*, pp. 384–417.

9   Watanabe, *Sōhei seisuiki*, pp. 2–3.

10   Aston has this as the thirty-first year, but maintains the year as 624. See W. G. Aston, *Nihongi: Chronicles of Japan from the Earliest Times to A.D. 697*, p. 152.

11   The quotation is based on Aston's translation, pp. 152–153. See also *Nihon shoki*, pt. 2, pp. 164–165; Ōshima, "Sōhei no hassei ki ni kansuru isshiki ron," p. 31; Hirata, "Nanto hokurei no akusō ni tsuite," p. 262.

12   *Shoku Nihongi* Tenpyō jingo 2 (766).9.6.

13   For those identifying the Nara age as the beginning of armed religious forces, see Tsuji and Watanabe.

14   *Ruijū kokushi* Enryaku 24 (805).1.14; *Nihon kōki*, same date; Hirata, "Nanto hokurei no akusō," p. 262.

15   The Kangakuin was originally founded as a dormitory for Fujiwara sons, but soon became a center for learning. It also came to handle administrative matters, especially those related to any of the Fujiwara-sponsored temples.

16   Professor Tajima Tadashi of Tokyo University's Historiographical Institute has kindly pointed out to me that since no records of a Wakaebe [若枝部] family exist from this age, the man's name is likely Wakazakurabe [若桜部], which may be found on a large number of wooden tablets from the Nara age. I am furthermore indebted to Professor Kondō Shigekazu of the Historiographical Institute for his generous assistance in working on many of the sources used in this essay.

17   *Nihon sandai jitsuroku*, p. 352; Hirata, "Nanto hokurei no akusō," p. 263.

18   Hirata points out that the *Ruijū kokushi* was written in 892, at a time when the *akusō* mainly referred to monks who broke the law and were punished for it. The term thus had no specific linkage to the bearing of arms ("Nanto hokurei no akusō," p. 262).

19   In other words, they did not take the vows and were not acknowledged as monks by the state. The benefit of being a monk in this case was that religious people and estates were generally tax-exempt.

20   *Iken jūnikajō*, p. 127, and *DNS*, 1:4, pp. 604–606; Watanabe, *Sōhei seisuiki*, pp. 24–26; Hirata, "Nanto hokurei no akusō," pp. 262–263. A more extensive translation of this article can be found

in Paul Groner, *Ryōgen and Mt. Hiei: Japanese Tendai in the Tenth Century*, pp. 8–9.

21 *Chōya gunsai*, in *DNS*, 1:6, p. 921; Watanabe, *Sōhei seisuiki*, p. 22.

22 *Nihon kiryaku* Tenryaku 3 (949).1.16; *DNS*, 1:9, p. 324; Watanabe, *Sōhei seisuiki*, p. 23.

23 *Nihon kiryaku* Tentoku 3 (959).3.13 (75): *DNS*, 1:10, p. 539; Watanabe, *Sōhei seisuiki*, p. 23.

24 *Nihon kiryaku* Anna 1 (968).7.15.

25 *Jie daisōjō den*, p. 15; *DNS*, 1:6, p. 147.

26 The Jōgyōdō was the location of the Nenbutsu rituals. For an account of its importance during Ryōgen's age, see Groner, *Ryōgen*, pp. 168, 175–179.

27 *DNS*, 1:13, Tenroku 1 (970).7.16 (p. 213). My translation differs slightly from the one included in Groner's work (*Ryōgen*, pp. xii, 358–359).

28 For an interesting analysis of the usage of hoods in picture scrolls, see Kuroda Hideo, *Sugata to shigusa no chūsei shi: ezu to emaki no fūkei kara*, pp. 30–45. Kuroda argues that figures with hoods in thirteenth- and fourteenth-century picture scrolls were primarily young boys.

29 Katsuno, *Sōhei*, pp. 149–152.

30 *DNS*, 1:13, pp. 213–214; Hirata, "Nanto hokurei no akusō," p. 264; Watanabe Eshin, "'Jie daishi kishō jūnikajō' ni tsuite," in idem, ed., *Gansan jie daishi no kenkyū*, pp. 10–11; Groner, *Ryōgen*, pp. 359–360.

31 Ryōgen's close relationship with Fujiwara Morosuke, whose son became the monk's disciple and later succeeded him as Tendai head abbot, is well documented. See Neil McMullin, "The Enryaku-ji and the Gion-Shrine Temple Complex in the Mid-Heian Period," and Groner's work, which pays much attention to this matter.

32 Hirata, "Nanto hokurei no akusō," p. 264. The source that first puts the blame on Ryōgen is the *Sange yōki yūryaku* [supposedly completed on Ōei 6 (1399).2.21, which contains a section entitled "Shuto bumon no koto" ("Regarding the militarization of the clergy")]. It states: "During the abbotship of Ryōgen, there was a principle that if there is no knowledge, then there will be no proper etiquette above,

and if there are no arms there will be no respect for authority below." Further, "those who lacked talent and intelligence to excel in the teachings were chosen to become part of the armed clergy" (Watanabe, *Sōhei seisuiki*, p. 14; Kuroda, *Jisha seiryoku*, p. 30).

33   Hirata, "Nanto hokurei no akusō," pp. 266–267; *Fusō ryakki* Chōryaku 3 (1039).2.18 (p. 284); *Tendai zasuki*, pp. 54–56.

34   *Shunki* Chōkyū 1 (1040).4.29.

35   *Shunki* Chōkyū 1 (1040).6.6 (p.165); Hirata, "Nanto hokurei no akusō," pp. 265–266.

36   *Suisaki* Eihō 1 (1081).8.18, 9.14, 16, 17, 20, 10.4; *Hyakurenshō* Eihō 1 (1081).6.9, 17, 9.14, 15; *Fusō ryakki* Eihō 1 (1081).6, 1.9; *Tendai zasuki*, pp. 64–65; *Tamefusa kyōki* Eihō 1 (1081).9.14.

37   *Sochiki* Shōryaku 5 (1081).3.9; *Suisaki*, same date; *Kōfukuji ryaku nendaiki* Eihō 1 (1081).3 (p. 141); *Hyakurenshō*, Eihō 1 (1081).3.6.

38   *Sonpi bunmyaku*, vol. 1, p. 313; *Kokushi bunin*, 4: pp. 349–351; Tsunoda Bun'ei, "Jōjin sōzu no yakuwari: Sōhei dan soshikisha toshite no" in his *Ōchō no eizō: Heian jidai shi no kenkyū*, pp. 471–472. Although his analysis of Jōjin's military activities remains less than satisfactory, Tsunoda's chapter is very helpful in its comprehensive treatment of the monk's social background and political connections.

39   The genealogical records indicate that Jōjin was one of his father's principal heirs, perhaps even his oldest son. It is thus puzzling why he became a monk. Perhaps he saw how bright a future awaited a ranking monk in one of Japan's most powerful temples.

40   *Go-Nijō Moromichi ki* Kanji 7 (1093).12.8, Eichō 2 (1096).2.15; *Sōgō bunin*, p. 170; Tsunoda, "Jōjin sōzu," p. 473.

41   *Go-Nijō Moromichi ki* Eichō 1 (1096).2.12, 13; *Shunki* Eishō 7 (1052).7.12.

42   Hirata, "Nanto hokurei no sōhei," pp. 273–274. The details regarding the confrontations of 1100 can be found in the diary of Fujiwara Munetada; more than a year later, he wrote, "A letter arrived from the Tendai head abbot's residence stating as follows: 'What caused the battle that took place at Saitō?' Jōjin brought warriors, and attacked Zōnin's dwelling. But the clergy mobilized and confronted them in a battle. During this time, the mountain [i.e., the temple complex on

Mt. Hiei] was closed, and the situation was thus very troubling." See *Chūyūki* Kōwa 3 (1101).12.3.

43   Tsunoda, "Jōjin sōzu," pp. 475–476.

44   *Chūyūki* Chōji 1 (1104) 6.15, 21. The significance of the addition of the Tōtō clergy should not be underestimated. In particular, it appears that Kankei, who was the head administrator of that section's Sanmai'in, was a highly skilled leader of the clergy in armed confrontations. See Tsunoda, "Jōjin sōzu," p. 476.

45   *Chūyūki* Chōji 1 (1104).6.24; *Denreki* Chōji 1 (1104).6.24–27.

46   *Chūyūki* Chōji 1 (1104).6.24.

47   *Chūyūki* Chōji 1 (1104).6.22–24, 29, .8.13; *Denreki* Chōji 1.7; *Sōgō bunin*, p. 171.

48   *Chūyūki* Chōji 1 (1104).10.14, 21, 26, and 12th month.

49   *Chūyūki* Chōji 1 (1104).10.26.

50   *Chūyūki* Chōji 1 (1104).10.7, 29; Chōji 2 (1105).10.29.

51   *Tendai zasuki*, pp. 72–73; *Chūyūki* Chōji 2 (1105).10.30; *DNS* 3:8, p. 272; Murayama, *Hieizan shi: tatakai to inori no seichi*, p. 167.

52   *Chūyūki* Chōji 2 (1105).10.30.

53   *Chūyūki* Kajō 1(1106).9.30.

54   The idea of "representative justice" in Heian Japan meant not only that elites were expected to punish or hand over criminals in their service, but also that substitutes could be sent into exile or detained in lieu of a favored retainer.

55   *Chūyūki* Kajō 2 (1107).12.30, Tennin 1 (1108).1.9; *DNS*, 3:9, p. 744; *Sonpi bunmyaku*, vol. 1, p. 269; *Sōgō bunin* Kajō 2 (1107).12.28; Tsunoda, "Jōjin sōzu," p. 481. Interestingly, Kankei was a distant relative of Jōjin, as was Munetada, who was consistently critical of Jōjin's behavior in his diary.

56   *Chūyūki* Gen'ei (1118).2.15, 2.20.

57   *Sonpi bunmyaku*, vol. 3, p. 162; *Kōfukuji bettō sangō keizu* (unpublished facsimile at the Historiographical Institute, University of Tokyo), p. 27.

58   *Sonpi Bunmyaku*, vol. 3, p. 162; *Kōfukuji bettō sangō keizu*, p. 27; Tsunoda, "Shōmu tennō haka to Kōfukuji sō Shinjitsu," in his *Ōchō no meian: Heian jidai shi no kenkyū*, vol. 2, pp. 339–340. Further back in the genealogy, Minamoto Yorichika (Shinjitsu's great,

great, great grandfather) had been a governor of Yamato province, but exiled because of an appeal from Kōfukuji. Yorichika's son, Yorifusa, suffered a similar fate, as an Enryakuji protest resulted in his ouster as governor and subsequent exile (Hirata," Nanto hokurei no akusō," p. 282).

59 *Kōfukuji bettō sangō keizu*, p. 27; Tsunoda, "Shōmu tennō," p. 349; Hirata, "Nanto hokurei no sōhei," p. 283.

60 *Chōshunki* Daiji 4 (1129).11.11, *Chūyūki* Daiji 4 (1129).11.11.

61 *Chōshunki* Daiji 4 (1129).11.21; *Chūyūki* Daiji 4 (1129).11.12.

62 *Chōshunki* Daiji 4 (1129).11.24, 28, 30; *Chūyūki* Daiji 4 (1129).11.25, 29; *Kōfukuji bettō shidai*, pp. 13–14.

63 *Chōshunki* Daiji 4 (1129).11.18.

64 *Chōshunki* Daiji 4 (1129).11.18; *Kōfukuji bettō shidai*, p. 15.

65 *Kōfukuji bettō shidai*, p. 15.

66 *Taiki* Hōen 2 (1137).11.7; *Kōfukuji bettō sangō keizu*, 27; *Kōfukuji bettō shidai*, 15; *Kōfukuji ryaku nendaiki*, p. 147.

67 *Kōfukuji bettō shidai*, p. 16.

68 *Kōfukuji bettō shidai*, pp. 16–17; *Nanto daishū jurakuki*, pp. 325–327.

69 *Nanto daishu jurakuki*, p. 326; *Hyakurenshō*, Hōen 5 (1139).11.16, 12.2; *Kōfukuji bettō shidai*, pp. 16–17.

70 *Taiki* Hōji 1 (1142).8.3.

71 *Taiki* Kyūan 1 (1145).7.12, 26, 9.13; *Kōfukuji ryaku nendaiki*, p. 148; *Honchō seiki* Kyūan 1 (1145).7.18.

72 *Kōfukuji sangō bunin*, pp. 706–707; *Kōfukuji sangō keizu*, p. 27; *Kōfukuji bettō shidai*, p. 18.

73 *Honchō seiki* Kyūan 5 (1149).10.30, 11.25.

74 Tsunoda, "Shōmu tennō," pp. 350–351.

75 *Heihanki* Hōgen 1 (1156).7.11; *Hōgen monogatari* (*NKBT*, vol. 31, pp. 85, 125).

76 *Hōgen monogatari*, p. 126; Tsunoda, p. 348.

77 Hirata, "Nanto hokurei no sōhei," p. 287; Tsunoda, "Shōmu tennō," p. 348.

78 Tsunoda, "Shōmu tennō," p. 348.

79   *Heihanki* Hōgen 3 (1158).7.17; *Hōryūji bettō ki*, p. 799.

80   Taiji 2 (1127).11.20 Tōdaiji kumonjo kanjō (*HI*, 5:2112); Hisano Nobuyoshi, "Kakunin kō: Heian makki no Tōdaiji akusō," pp. 3–4.

81   Hisano, "Kakunin kō," pp. 11–12, 14.

82   Kyūan 5 (1149).9.12 Kansenji (*HI*, 6:2676); Hōgen 3 (1158).4 Iga no kuni zaichō kanjinra ge (*HI*, 6:2919).

83   Hōgen 3 (1158).4 Iga no kuni zaichō kanjinra ge (*HI*, 6:2919).

84   Hōgen 3 (1158).9.11 Sō Nōe chinjō an (*HI*, 6:2947, 2948); Hisano, "Kakunin kō," pp. 18–22.

85   Hisano, "Kakunin kō," pp. 26–30; undated Tōdaiji monjo shutsunō nikki (*HI*, 6:2973), Heiji 1 (1159).intercalary 5. Tōdaiji kumonjo kudashibumi an (*HI*, 6:2985), undated Tōdaiji monjo shutsunō nikki (*HI*, 6:2987).

86   Ōhō 2 (1162).5.22 Kansenji (*HI*, 7:3221).

87   Ōhō 1 (1161).6.9 Shoshin hosshi Ken'yo chinjō an (*HI*, 7:3154).

88   Kaō 1 (1169).11.19 Kangakuin mandokoro kudashibumi (*HI*, 7:3520); Kaō 2 (1170).intercalary 4. Kōfukuji Saikondō shūtō ge an (*HI*, 7:3547); Kaō 2 (1170).intercalary 4.15 Sō Kinsai satsumon an (*HI*, 9:4871); Izumiya, *Kōfukuji*, p. 84; Hisano, "Kakunin kō," pp. 31–32.

89   Kaō 2 (1170).intercalary 4 Kōfukuji Saikondō shūtō ge an (*HI*, 7:3547).

90   Nin'an 3 (1168).2 Kii no kuni Daidenpō in sōto ge an (*HI*, 9:4857).

91   *Heihanki* Nin'an 3 (1168).5.3; *Gumaiki* Nin'an 3 (1168).5.3.

92   *Kokawadera engi*, pp. 183–184.

93   Nin'an 3 (1168).5.3 Go-Shirakawa jōkō inzen (*HI*, 9:4859); *Heihanki* Nin'an 3 (1168).5.3.

94   Nin'an 3 (1168).8.2 Kii no kuni Daidenpōin sōto ge an (*HI*, 9:4860).

95   Nin'an 3 (1168).8.9 Go-Shirakawa jōkō inzen an (*HI*, 9:4861).

The Ōtomo Family in Northern Kyushu: Creating Constabular Authority in Early Kamakura Japan
Thomas Nelson

The rise of the *bushi* between the years 1100 and 1600 is the subject of numerous surveys of Japanese history. Indeed, it is an almost universal view that the militarization of Japanese society was the defining phenomenon of the age. With the notable exception of Peter Arnesen's work on Suō province,[1] studies of the early political and institutional history of the Kamakura era have focused on the growth of military government developing in Kamakura, and have discussed provincial vassals, or *gokenin*, in the context of their relationship to the Kamakura regime. However, institutional historians have become increasingly directed toward the *shugo*, or provincial military constables, in examining developments during the first half of the fourteenth century. This shift in scholarly focus anticipates and reflects the dynamics of decentralization characterizing the post-Kamakura age. Likewise, the new focus reflects the fact that the *shugo* themselves, who gave assiduous attention to building their own local fiefdoms, were key figures in those dynamics.[2]

However, the *shugo* were not a new institution in the fourteenth century. They had first been appointed a century and a half earlier, by Minamoto Yoritomo. Given that the *shugo* institution is so fundamental to understanding this era, it is curious that its origins and early development should have received so little attention. For those few historians whose interest may be piqued by the early *shugo*, it is almost always as a mere prelude to an examination of their later role as autonomous regional magnates.

What I propose to do here is to examine the Kamakura-era development of the Ōtomo *shugo* house of Bungo province (in northeastern Kyushu).[3] The Ōtomo command our attention as an institution because they were *shugo* who indeed later became autonomous regional magnates. Moreover, their experience was in many ways quite different from that of *shugo* families elsewhere, including those nearby geographically. The Ōtomo house was not native to Kyushu; it was a Kantō family appointed, almost in the fashion of colonial administrators, to take up and create a *shugo* position in a part of the country to which it had had no prior links. In Bungo, the Ōtomo were outsiders who had to attend both to establishing a local presence, and to creating a family structure that might enable them to survive in their "strange land." Thus, while this case study of the Ōtomo may provide lessons for understanding *shugo* in other regions of Japan, we will pay attention to identifying those (earlier) elements which were particularly germane to the subsequent creation and maintenance of Ōtomo rule.

Through the lens of the Ōtomo case, I will examine a number of topics relating to the *shugo*. First I look at the establishment of the *shugo* constable position in local context. I will take note of the origins of the position and the jurisdictional underpinnings of the post, the *shugo*'s peacekeeping and organizational role, and additional powers held by constables in Kyushu. Then I examine the issues relevant to the Ōtomo expansion of constable authority, as noted in their own legal code. In the second part of this study I will focus more closely on Ōtomo efforts to create a family organization that would undergird their formal powers as constable. The issues demanding our attention in this section include how the Ōtomo extended authority over their domain, what class relationships existed under their control, how the house sought to maintain Ōtomo family unity, and how this preserved the sacerdotal role of the Ōtomo clan head.

Establishing the *Shugo* Institution

The "taibon sankajō" *and the origins of the* shugo

In their first incarnation, the *shugo* were given three primary tasks, tersely summarized in the term *"taibon sankajō,"* or "three great crimes."[4]

To understand why officers of this type were necessary and why they were given these powers, it is necessary to refer to the *kenmon* theory, first formulated by Kuroda Toshio in the 1950s and since described exhaustively in almost all studies of the period. Japan was divided up into power hierarchies (*kenmon*) centered on a leading court aristocrat or temple, which had the authority to defend the legal status of its clients at court from the rapacity of other *kenmon* heads. They were served at a lower level by provincial warriors, who, in return for legal protection, forwarded a proportion of the produce of the lands they administered to the *kenmon* in Kyoto and retained a proportion for themselves. These rights and duties were defined by the term *shiki*. At the lowest level, ordinary cultivators had *"gesaku shiki,"* entitling them to legal protection and the right to retain a certain proportion of the produce of the land in return for cultivating it. This much is common knowledge. What is less well known is that the *kenmon* also enforced a measure of discipline within its hierarchy. From early on, large *kenmon* estates maintained a *samurai dokoro* policing office, while even the smallest piece of land had someone assigned to the duty of prosecuting crimes there (*kendan*).

As long as the scope of law-breaking was limited enough to fall within the management capacities of local *kendan* authority, there was no need for central authorities to intervene in the process of administering local justice. However, once violence occurred on a greater scale (or across local boundaries) such that the local authorities could not control it, a peacekeeping officer would be appointed with the right to override the barriers set in place by the *kenmon*. These officials derived their authority from the very fact that the court was the meeting place of the various *kenmon* heads, and it was the court that appointed them.

This was the political structure inherited by Yoritomo, who was no great administrative innovator. The rights and duties he accorded his *shugo* agents summarized in the *taibon sankajō* had thus long been prefigured in the rights and duties accorded to such figures as *ōryōshi*, *tsuibushi*, and *tsuitōshi*, the officers who had for centuries been commissioned by the central authorities to deal with serious outbreaks of rebellion and lawlessness in the provinces.[5] The role of central authority in dealing with large-scale crime was put succinctly by Kujō Kanezane in 1185 when he was asked by the retired sovereign Go-Shirakawa if the court should give Minamoto Yoshitsune an order empowering him to proceed against Yoritomo:

> Official orders are handed down for the arrest of those who, by committing any of the eight major crimes (*hachigyaku*), have acted against the public authority. If Yoritomo has committed such a crime, then such an order should be issued.[6]

Such "major crimes," specified in the *ritsuryō* legal code, necessitated official intervention in the Heian era in the same way that *taibon* were later placed within the jurisdiction of the Kamakura *shugo*. Similarly, brigands operating beyond the authority of any single regional powerholder were called *kutō* or *kuzoku* in the Heian era and *akutō* during the Kamakura period. Shimomukai Tatsuhiko has compiled an exhaustive list of all the crimes committed by *kutō* and *kuzoku* in the Heian era and categorized them into six classes: the murder of officials and attacks on the public land (*kokuga*), pirate attacks on shipments of rice-rents, brigandage committed by *kenmon* officials, battles between the servants of different *kenmon*, riots instigated by monks, and attacks either by aboriginals in the north or Korean pirates in the west.

Korean pirates and untamed northerners were not, of course, dangers that the Kamakura regime had to face, but control of almost all the other crimes mentioned would now have been transferred to *shugo* jurisdiction. Notably, the majority of the six categories involved crimes by the servants of one *kenmon* against another. These acts could not have been resolved internally and so the intervention of some centrally appointed authority was required. Those who attacked the agents of central authority were likewise classed as major felons.

Given that the jurisdictions of the agents of central authority remained unchanged throughout the late Heian and Kamakura periods, it seems reasonable to draw parallels between *ōryōshi* and the *tsuitōshi* officials and the later *shugo*. Although only rarely drawn by modern scholars, there can be no doubt that the parallels were obvious to many contemporaries. Early *shugo* were often under the impression that they had been appointed *shugo* precisely because their ancestors had held the offices of *ōryōshi* or *tsuitōshi* within the *kokuga*. In their eyes, they were merely performing the same tasks under a different name, as noted in 1209:

> *Kudashibumi* (investitures) appointing *shugo* were drafted. Among the warriors receiving these was Chiba Naritane who states that, since the time of his ancestor, Motonaga, his forebears had been *kebiishi* at the local estate. As a consequence, Chiba Tsunetane had been appointed *shugo* of Shimoosa in Yoritomo's time. Similarly, Miura Yoshimura stated that his grandfather had been dealing with violent crime in Sagami province ever since the Tenji era (1124–1126). Miura Yoshizumi, it was likewise claimed, had exercised police authority in Yoritomo's time. Oyama Tomomasa said that he no longer had the original investiture from Yoritomo, but his ancestors had long ago acted as *ōryōshi* in Shimotsuke province.[7]

We may read this entry as assuming that *shugo* as shogunal appointments were equivalents to the old court-appointed *ōryōshi* and *tsuibushi*, with their role being to deal with crimes beyond the competence of individual *kenmon*. If this was the case, then we may ask how—if at all—did the exercise of *shugo* powers differ in practice from their predecessors?

The peacekeeping and organizational role of the shugo

When the Koremune family first arrived in Satsuma province to represent the interests of the new shogunate there, they did so not as *shugo* but as *kenin bugyō* (official in charge of organizing the vassals). It is possible to see the shogunate as a kind of military *kenmon*, and like all *kenmon*, it required some kind of bureaucratic apparatus for organizing its own clients. In the east it was possible to rely on the clan heads or *sōryō*. In the west, however, such figures had by and large been killed in the wake of the battle of Dannoura in 1185. As a result, and especially in the province of Hizen, they were succeeded as *sōryō* by minor warriors who lacked the prestige requisite to act as agents of shogunal authority. Thus, the role of the *shugo* in directly organizing vassals was especially important in Kyushu. Surviving documents appointing *shugo* are extremely rare, but, as Gomi Katsuo points out, among those that do exist, those in the west refer specifically to the mustering of housemen, while those in the east do not.[8]

It is only when one sees the *shugo* as part of a bureaucracy through which the shogun organized his clients in the same way any other *kenmon* did, that the significance of the rule prohibiting entry of the *shugo*'s agents onto the property of another *kenmon* becomes clear. *Kenmon* were, after all, independent entities and one did not have the right to trespass on the affairs of another. Equally, however, the shogun and the *shugo* had also inherited the duty to prosecute major criminals, which on occasion might mean overriding the rights of other *kenmon*. This prohibition was in evidence if a *jitō* served on the land in question. A *shugo* might serve the shogunate and another *kenmon* simultaneously, but his duties to the shogun were superordinate. The duality of the *shugo's* functions in this respect reflected in the thirty-second article of the Jōei code:

> Entry by the agents of the *shugo* is forbidden. When *akutō* appear, however, they shall immediately be handed over at the offices of the *shugo*. If this is refused, then the *shugo's* agents may be sent in and the *jitō's* agent replaced, or the *jitō shiki* may be seized and an agent of the *shugo* allowed entry.[9]

Additional powers of the Kyushu shugo

The *shugo* first appointed to Kyushu were given a series of additional powers, one of which in particular—the power to stop the human slave trade—has long aroused the attention of historians. The following passage clearly articulates this expanded power:

> The office of the Former General of the Right sends the following orders to Sahyōe no jō Koremune no Tadahisa. You are required to fulfill your duties as *kenin bugyōnin* in the provinces of Satsuma and Ōsumi, to wit: …You are to put an end to the trade in human beings. Repeated government orders have been issued to this effect, but it has come to our attention that the residents of outlying provinces are defying the law. This shall cease. If anyone goes against this ruling, let him be severely punished.[10]

The order is not as surprising as it may at first seem, when one bears in mind that medieval Japan was a slave-owning society, and what historians have traditionally translated as kidnapping might better be referred to as slaving. If slavers were allowed to operate freely in the wake of any serious breakdown in law and order, then they could strip a district of its labor supply. One of the first duties of the military officials sent in to pacify rebellion was, therefore, to stamp out slaving.[11]

The *shugo* in Kyushu also appear to have had the right to adjudicate lawsuits involving shogunal vassals, although the lack of surviving documentation implies that these rights were rarely invoked. According to the Ōtomo house laws:

> The legal decisions of Nakahara Chikayoshi, Ōtomo
> Yoshinao, and Ōtomo Chikahide should not be questioned.
> ... However, in extreme cases, further investigations may
> be carried out especially if the matter involves a temple,
> shrine or shogunal vassal.[12]

In light of the above directive, it is of no surprise that the one
surviving legal verdict issued by the Ōtomo lord does indeed show
him upholding a decision made by Nakahara Chikayoshi.[13]

However, there is further evidence that Kyushu *shugo* might
enjoy broad judicial discretion. That evidence comes from a
case that was adjudicated by the Hizen *shugo* Mutō Sukeyori
in 1222. The case was brought by the shogunal vassal Ishishi
Kiramu, a member of the Matsura-tō of northwestern Kyushu
[see Hyungsub Moon's essay below]. Kiramu claimed to have
been awarded the bulk of his father's lands, but his older brother
Ken, who had assumed that as eldest son he would be the major
heir, was unwilling to accept the validity of the will. Kiramu
accused his older brother of illegally moving on to his land
and harvesting his barley. The older brother countered that the
original chief heir had died and that, as a result, the inheritance
had now passed to him. He had been performing guard duty in
Kyoto when he heard that his father was gravely ill. When he
returned to Matsura, he discovered that Kiramu had pressured
their father to endorse a series of documents that Kiramu had
himself prepared, and which disinherited him as oldest sibling.

The case was not especially complex in terms of the facts,
but it touched on significant issues dealing with bakufu service,
standing as a vassal, and fundamental rights of allocation of
inheritance within warrior families.[14] As Moon indicates below,
this decision was ultimately to have significant implications for
the structure of warrior households in the Kamakura age. We
may assume that the *shugo* adjudicating was not unaware of
the precedent set by his decision, even as the decision reflected
the highest standards of justice for which the Kamakura era is
known.

Kyushu *shugo* were also empowered to put on trial and punish a number of perpetrators of property crimes (*shomuzata*) that did not fall within the jurisdiction of the *shugo* elsewhere in Japan. For example, in 1315, the shogunal vassal Hishijima Tadanori accused a priest of refusing to pay interest on a debt. Initially, Tadanori had referred the matter to Shimazu Tadamune "as he had jurisdiction in these matters as *shugo,*" but later had chosen to go instead to the shogun's military commander on Kyushu, the *tandai*.[15]

Why western *shugo* should have been so favored is not immediately obvious. Surely it was significant that Kyushu had been the final bastion of the Taira, and the local aristocracy was decimated in the aftermath of their defeat. With the local warriors who had once enforced *shomuzata* now eliminated, it perhaps became necessary for the centrally appointed *shugo* to step in to replace them.

The Ōtomo expand the shugo's role: The "Shin goseibai shikimoku" of 1242

In order to carry out their duties to the shogunate, the Ōtomo promulgated two legal codes. The first, issued in 1242, has come to be known as the *Shin (New) goseibai shikimoku*.[16] The second, issued in 1244, goes by the name *Bungo Ōtomo shi no hōrei* (Laws of the Ōtomo in Bungo).[17] Many of the elements in the codes are simply lifted from the shogunate's own Jōei code of 1232, and are in effect a restatement of the *shugo*'s duty to deal with offenders whose activities exceeded the jurisdiction of any individual *kenmon*. However, the Ōtomo codes go further than the shogunate's regulations in describing the precise nature of these crimes and include others that would not have fallen within the jurisdiction of *shugo* outside Kyushu:

> Concerning murder, brigandage, piracy, night attack, theft, wounding, arson and assault, shogunal law clearly states that offenders should be executed, exiled, or have their

property rights seized. Furthermore, there should be no reprieve.[18]

In a number of other instances, the Ōtomo appear to have felt that the original shogunal statute was unenforceable, and thus they altered it slightly. For example, the fifth article of the Ōtomo code reads:

> Rents should be paid without fail every year. If there is an unavoidable lapse, then in accordance with the *shikimoku*, this should be made up over three years. People who do not cooperate shall lose their positions as *jitō*.[19]

This language differs from the shogunal original in that it omits the phrase: "in the case of small quantities of unpaid rent, these should be forwarded forthwith." To expect the *shugo* to concern himself personally with every grain of unpaid rice was unreasonable, and the Ōtomo opted simply to ensure that the bulk was forwarded. As Kasamatsu Hiroshi has demonstrated,[20] the Ōtomo codes also differ from shogunal legislation in their treatment of runaway slaves. The shogunal law applies a ten-year statute of limitations on all runaways. By contrast, the Ōtomo apply this only to the children of abscondees. Adult slaves themselves are never freed from their bond.

Creating a Family Organization

The authority of the shugo *and the spread of Ōtomo territorial control*

For the Ōtomo, the devastation of the local leadership organizations of Kyushu society provided untold opportunities denied to their peers elsewhere in Japan. Not only had the Ōtomo been awarded huge tracts of territory seized from dispossessed enemies, but their status as the chief representatives of the shogunate gave them the opportunity to take over the lands even of many local warriors who had not been executed in the immediate aftermath of the Taira defeat.

The first Kyushu family to have had lands confiscated in this manner appears to have been that of Ōno Yasumoto, who led an unsuccessful rebellion in Bungo at the end of the twelfth century. His confiscated lands were given to Nakahara Chikayoshi and later distributed among various members of the Ōtomo clan. However, the destruction of the Ōno house did not mean the disappearance of the Ōno name. Ōtomo Yoshinao's tenth son, Yoshimoto, inherited the Shimomura *jitō shiki* (stewardship) on the Ōno estate and then passed it on to his own son, who styled himself Ōno Motonao. Henceforth, the Ōno were just another line of Ōtomo collaterals.[21]

Another favored means used by the Ōtomo to gain land rights was to force local families to adopt junior heirs from the Ōtomo clan. Ultimately, the adopted would inherit both the new family's name and their lands. For example, Bekki Koreie had no children of his own and so some time prior to 1285, he adopted Ōtomo Shigehide as his heir. From that time onward, the Bekki were counted as Ōtomo collaterals.

When Ōtomo Chikahide's son, Yoshiyasu, moved to Bungo and established himself at Nozubara in Ōita-gun, he obliged a local warrior, Wasata Tadatsuna, to adopt his newborn son, Tomotsuna. When Tadatsuna died before the child reached majority, members of the household began to foment trouble. Ōtomo domination of the Wasata became visible when Yoshiyasu stepped in to head the household before Tomotsuna inherited. Thereafter, the head of the Wasata house would remain a descendant of Tomotsuna, and Ōtomo control remained unchallenged.[22]

Sometimes, adopted heirs from the Ōtomo did not even trouble to adopt their new family name. Although indirect evidence of this practice exists throughout the Kamakura period, the best documented cases date from the end of the era. In 1329, the head of the Sonezaki *jitō* house in Bungo allowed Tabaru Sadahiro, of the Ōtomo family, to inherit five *chō* of his holding. The documents refer to a parent-child relationship developing between the two men despite their differing family names.

Quite clearly, a decision by local warriors to adopt an Ōtomo heir was not always taken entirely voluntarily. When Hōgan Yukihide of Bingo was prevailed upon to hand over his holdings to the Ōtomo, he made his anger plain:

> Concerning various fields within Aki-no-gō in the province of Bungo, the details of my agreement with the original proprietors, Motosada and Motohide, have already been made plain. However, we have been instructed to commend them to the Iwamasu no Goryō. This is outrageous. As we have received a directive from the shogunate concerning my holdings, there should have been no difficulty in our keeping them. However, we are not in a position to ignore your instructions and are therefore passing the lands over to you in their entirety. These and the seven other land parcels that we made over to you recently, shall be passed to your son, Yoshisato.[23]

Outright purchase was another option for the Ōtomo in their quest to increase their land base at the expense of native proprietors. The following quotation, dated 1259, comes from Shinmyō, the widow of Yoshinao (founder of the Ōtomo line) in her will to her son, Shiga Yoshisato:

> I purchased the *benzaishi shiki* in Kachigatsuru some time ago and have been managing it for a number of years. It happens that you have received the *jitō shiki* to the same area from Hōgen Yukihide of Bingo, so I am bequeathing this office to you as well.[24]

Through these examples, we see the Ōtomo exercising a variety of methods for increasing their lands. Yet, the process by which Ōtomo collaterals replaced the native houses of Kyushu as proprietors required several generations. The question remains of how the Ōtomo made their presence felt in the first decades of their administration. No major figure within the Ōtomo house was then even present in Kyushu. The issue then becomes understanding the origins and role of the men the Ōtomo initially chose to serve them in their new lands to the west.

Free and unfree in the Ōtomo clan

The men who served the Ōtomo may broadly be divided into free and unfree. These are terms having specific meanings in the context of medieval Japan. "Freedom," in the sense of political freedom within a system of representative government, is a translation of *jiyū*, a term that may mean that one is without inhibitions or impediments and is able to embark upon a chosen course of action. The word is not a nineteenth-century neologism, but has a venerable history reflecting the changing nature of Japanese society over the centuries. Certainly, we find "*jiyū*" often in medieval sources, but any of its meanings there are far from positive. As one would expect in a society where service to one's lord was held up as conduct most worthy of admiration, motivations of personal gain were customarily clothed as acts of "loyalty." To be "*jiyū*" meant to be selfish and unmindful of one's social responsibilities. For example, *jiyū* often occurs in the compound phrase "*jiyū rōzeki*," where *rōzeki* is a general term for violent crime.

Jiyū could also imply freedom from the personal ties that bound one individual to another. Thus, medieval warriors of samurai status enjoyed the right of "*kyoshū no jiyū*," or freedom from obligation to any particular lord; that is, they were free to choose whom to follow. Similarly, medieval Japanese peasants, or *hyakushō*, were free in the sense that, once they had paid their dues, they were free to leave and work for a new master. This concept was known in medieval Japanese jurisprudence as "*kyoryū no jiyū*" (freedom of dwelling place).

The notion that some people had "*kyoshū no jiyū*" or "*kyoryū no jiyū*" carries with it the implication that others did not. If some were designated as enjoying the right to choose their master, then others, by implication, were denied that right. This was a distinction that ran through Japanese society, and affected people differently depending on their position within the social hierarchy.

Essentially, two types of people were "unfree" in that they were bound to one particular lord: the *rōdō* at the upper end of the hierarchy and the *genin* at the lower. Their equivalents among the free population were the above-mentioned samurai in the case of the *rōdō*, and *hyakushō* (or *bonge)*, in the case of the *genin*. However, medieval Japanese lacked a term that grouped *rōdō* with *genin* and placed them in contradistinction to samurai and *hyakushō* (i.e., unfree men vs. free men). *Rōdō* would never have tolerated being likened to *genin* slaves. If asked what terms distinguished those of ordinary and base status, a contemporary Japanese would undoubtedly have replied "*ryōmin*" and "*senmin.*" *Ryōmin* were those not forced to perform the most lowly tasks and included the *rōdō*. The *senmin* comprised the *genin* and the outcast *hinin*. The *hinin*, or non-people, inhabited riverbanks and waste-ground, and huddled close to temples for protection eking out a living by performing the basest tasks such as skinning animals and disposing of the dead. These people were not so much at the bottom of the status system as completely outside it.

A type of petition document, the *gunchūjō* (battle service report), is highly instructive in delineating important dimensions of the relationships among warriors and non-warriors, and between "free" and "unfree." As Thomas Conlan has shown, the relationship between medieval warrior and vassal was temporary and shifting:

> A hegemonic lord was obliged to keep his followers content through the magnanimous distribution of rewards. If he failed to offer adequate compensation or his promises were unreliable, then his followers would desert him. In other words, land grants were offered in exchange for service (*chūsetsu)*; no further obligation was entailed. Land was merely a conduit that linked a hegemon's promises and legitimating authority to the interests of independent free-spirited warriors.[25]

Vassals of the Kamakura and Muromachi eras took up arms freely in the hope of material reward, and were not motivated from any abstract but inescapable loyalty. After the fighting was over they would submit *gunchūjō* describing their deeds, and cite witnesses who could confirm their claims. These petitions for reward survive in great numbers.

In a *gunchūjō* submitted in 1336, Bekki Yoritaka, scion of a close Ōtomo collateral line, described the service he and his men had rendered during a recent campaign. Yoritaka is extremely direct in describing his motivations for going into battle, and states boldly at the end of his deposition that his motives have been purely mercenary. Such documents are long and slightly tedious, but interesting in that they show how warriors believed their reward should be precisely calibrated according to the amount of service they had rendered.[26] This document begins typically with an exhaustive account of the claimant's actions while on campaign (here heavily abbreviated), and then continues with a frank request for compensation as a result of the loss of relatives and retainers:

> Last year, on the twelfth day of the twelfth month, we were among the first to join your side at the battle of Sanoyama. We rendered loyal military service.
>
> On the thirteenth day of the same month, we were involved in various engagements around the provincial capital of Izu. We locked swords and performed meritoriously. We took three heads. Fourteen of my *wakatō* ("youngsters") were wounded. On the second day of the first month, in Ōmi province, we rode to Hamade by Ikisu castle. We were in the front line of the attack and performed with merit. We took three heads. Eight of my *wakatō* were wounded.
>
> As related above we fought with loyalty both along the Tokaidō and at the capital. At Hakata, having been given an official order (*migyōsho*) I proceeded to Kusu Castle. The details of my meritorious military service are known. I request a document of acknowledgement (*ikkenjō*) for this, and that these matters be reported to higher authority, so

that I may receive reward, and that my reputation with the
bow be widespread.[27]

Much the same kind of information is contained in a petition
by another Ōtomo collateral line head, Shiga Shōgen. What
is most distinctive about Shiga's deposition is that he did not
perform the reported acts of valor himself. He was not even
involved in the fighting. Instead, being "old and infirm," he had
a deputy (*daikan*) lead his men in his stead. Nevertheless, it was
he who demanded reward:

> On the tenth day of the first month of 1336, I allied myself
> to your cause in the company of my clan head. We were
> engaged in various battles around the capital. Because of
> my advanced age and infirmity, I remained in hiding in
> the vicinity of the capital when the shogun and his family
> moved south. I waited for the shogun's return to the capital
> and was the first to move out to join him. Because of my
> age, I did not go myself, but remained in the Tōji temple.
> Instead, I sent my agent (*daikan*), Matagorō Yasunori and
> others. At Imajigoe on Mt Hie on the fifth day of the sixth
> month they rendered meritorious military service. On the
> eighth day of the same month, they proceeded to the foot
> of the mountain below Saitō and, on the thirteenth and the
> fourteenth, were involved in the battle of Senzokumine.
> On the eighteenth day, they attacked Saitō Minami Nakao.
> On the nineteenth day Yasunori was shot through the head.
> Kodawara Shirō Saemon *nyūdō* and Sabo hyōe *nyūdō*
> conducted an investigation and prepared a statement on
> his deeds. This was seen by Kodawara Rokurō *nyūdō* and
> Toyohigashi Hikoroku *nyūdō*. I request that a document
> of acknowledgement be given to me immediately. I make
> this deposition as proof of my military service and I look
> forward to reward.[28]

These *gunchūjō* illustrate two important facts. The first
gunchūjō shows that Bekki Yoritaka was accompanied not just
by his clansmen, or *ichizoku*, but also by a large, if indeterminate,
number of *wakatō*. In the first two engagements the only ones

wounded were *wakatō*. In the second *gunchūjō* a *daikan* did all of the fighting for the aged Shiga Shōgen.

Daikan (deputies) and *wakatō* ("youngsters") receive little mention in historical writing on medieval Japan, yet they seem to have formed the backbone of warrior bands. They were among those warriors known more generally as the aforementioned *rōdō*, who remain unfortunately removed from the research foci of most medieval historians, and appear in the sources largely as bit players in the larger dramatic activities of their masters.

The *rōdō* comprised a specifically classified group within the larger social hierarchy, but their location was often unclear. They retained the prestige of being warriors, but unlike even the peasant *hyakushō*, they lacked the freedom to choose their master. Though they were in this sense as unfree as the lowly *genin* slave, there is no record of their being bought or sold, as were the *genin*. For most of Japan's medieval age, the shogunate refused to deal with *rōdō* directly, conceiving of them as the bound retainers of its own vassals. As a consequence, they had no more access to the courts than the *genin*. *Rōdō* fell entirely under their lord's jurisdiction legally. Their status is reflected in a shogunal law governing the order of precedence in seating arrangements at trials. *Rōdō* were placed above base *zōnin*, but below free samurai warriors.[29] Further evidence that the *rōdō* were warriors who lacked for samurai status is provided in a discussion of punishment in article thirteen of the Jōei code, dealing with physical assault, which notes "Samurai should have their property seized. Those of *rōdō* status and below should be imprisoned."[30]

As indicated by the *gunchūjō* cited above, *rōdō* who committed acts of bravery were not directly rewarded for them. Instead, rewards went to their lord and any recompense they received came from him. Equally, if a *rōdō* were remiss in his duties, it was his lord who was held responsible. A serious case in point comes from 1188, when a warrior called Yata Tomoie sent a *rōdō* to perform guard duty on his behalf. The *rōdō* was so lax, however, that his master was ultimately punished, by being ordered to repair all of the streets in Kamakura.[31]

Early in the Kamakura era, when the nature of the new military order was still in flux, there are occasional cases of Yoritomo personally commending the *rōdō* of other warriors for especially meritorious conduct. However, the shogunate ultimately realized the danger of interfering in the relationships between its vassals and their bound warriors, as an *Azuma kagami* entry from 1209 makes clear:

> Some long-standing *rōjū* [*rōdō*] from the province of Sagami have made private entreaties to be raised to the status of samurai in recognition of their military service. If these requests are entertained without the permission of their masters, then their descendants will forget their bonds of loyalty and attempt to serve the shogunate directly. This would be to invite disaster in the future.[32]

The shogunate also avoided adjudicating between a free vassal and his bound warrior by issuing laws banning *rōdō* from taking their own masters to court.[33] Simultaneously, the concept that the *rōdō*'s loyalty should be to his master and no other were backed up by edicts banning them from holding court office.[34]

The means by which one became a *rōdō*, and the functions *rōdō* performed within the warrior band, further illustrate significant dimensions of relationships among medieval warriors. The case of the Ōtomo clan yields significant insights on this matter, thanks largely to the rich body of documents collected on this family.

Of the hundreds of *rōdō* who served the Ōtomo, information remains only about the very highest ranking of their number, and even that is sparse. Nonetheless, it reveals much about how a warrior might attain, or be reduced to, *rōdō* status. Three houses served the main branch of the Ōtomo house as *shugodai* (deputy *shugo*), the Kodawara,[35] Furushō, and Saitō. The Kodawara were blood relatives of the Ōtomo, but were not styled *ichizoku*, or clansmen, because their connections ran through the female line. The first Ōtomo to hold the rank of *shugo* was Ōtomo Yoshinao, whose biological father came from the obscure Furushō house of Sagami. Yoritomo seems to have taken an unusually strong personal interest in young Yoshinao; the *Azuma kagami* refers to Yoshinao as beloved above all others by Yoritomo (*muni no chōnin*). It was long suggested that Yoshinao was actually Yoritomo's illegitimate son, but this view no longer finds acceptance. Whatever Yoritomo's interest in the boy may have been, it resulted in Yoshinao's adoption by Nakahara Chikayoshi, scion of a line of court aristocrats. Yoshinao was then made first *shugo* of the provinces of Bungo, Buzen, and Chikugo. His biological mother, Tone Tsubone, remarried after the death of his biological father, and bore a son, Shigeyasu, who later became progenitor of the Kodawara line. The Furushō line of *rōdō* became attached to Ōtomo through Yoshinao as well. The Furushō not only had included Yoshinao's biological father, but his younger brother, Shigeyoshi, who became the head of the Furushō house, in the service of his older brother's clan, the Ōtomo.

As the Furushō example demonstrates, distinctions between *rōdō* and kinsmen, or *ichizoku*, were not always clear. Before their fluorescence after 1336, the Ashikaga clan consisted of some houses such as the Kira, that were so economically independent that they were effectively clans in their own right, while many others were truly collaterals lacking a land base of their own. The latter were dependent for their survival on the economic largesse of the Ashikaga main line (*honke*), whom they served in a variety of functions, much as did the *rōdō*. As the Ashikaga rose to prominence, these landless *ichizoku* began to acquire land-holdings of their own, and subsequently emerged as major local figures (the so-called *shugo-daimyō*) in their own right.

Saitō Kunihira is an example of a warrior who founded a line of *rōdō* in the service of the Ōtomo house, with no biological ties to his masters. His brother, Sanemori, had been a Heishi partisan during the Genpei wars, and had died fighting for their cause. After the Genji victory, Kunihira was promptly arrested, and placed in the custody of a warrior called Kazusa Hirotsune. However, Nakahara Chikayoshi (who, it will be remembered, was a court aristocrat and the adoptive father of Yoshinao, founder of the Ōtomo line), managed to secure Kunihira's release on the grounds that he was a brave and capable warrior. He then gave him over as a *rōdō* to Yoshinao, instilling some of those qualities needed to be a good warrior (since Yoshinao's early life as Yoritomo's pet could have done little to foster such qualities). Kunihira immediately performed as hoped; thanks to him, the effete Yoshinao was able to win the coveted laurels of being the first warrior chief to break into the enemy camp during the 1189 campaign to destroy the Northern Fujiwara.[36]

Rōdō received economic support either indirectly in their lord's residence, or directly by means of a grant of land. A complaint in 1226 illustrates the latter practice.

> The *jitō* should have no control over the fields set aside to fund the reading of sutras (*kookyōden*) that have been declared exempt. It is an act of great wantonness (*jiyū*) on his part that he should *have distributed them among his own* rōdō.[37] (emphasis mine)

Clearly, lords benefited from attracting *rōdō*, who were likely to make far more efficient land administrators than the often fractious *ichizoku* clansmen. Medieval Japan had no system of primogeniture, and lesser heirs were often unwilling to accept the direction of the designated clan-head, or *sōryō*. Thus, using them to manage land was inviting the possibility that they would attempt to turn these lands into private fiefdoms. For most of Japan's medieval age, *rōdō* stood no chance of having any land-holding confirmed by higher authority and so, *faute de mieux*, were obliged to serve as loyal administrators. Only at the end of the Muromachi era, when official sanction meant increasingly little, did the *rōdō* begin to convert the lands assigned to them into private holdings.

The essential reliability of the *rōdō* as land administrators is illustrated by the experience of the Ōta estate in Bingo. After the Jōkyū war of 1221, the *jitō shiki* on the estate passed to an eastern warrior, who nonetheless continued to administer the territory using local agents (*jitōdai*). In time, however, he found it convenient to replace these men with *rōdō* sent out from the east.

Rōdō had two primary roles within the warrior household (*ie*), as warriors and as administrative agents. The members of the Ōtomo warrior band can be found performing both these roles. For example, by the end of the Kamakura period, the Kodawara had been appointed resident deputy provincial governors (*shugodai*) and, during the brief return to direct rule by the court under Go-Daigo, they played an important role in northern Kyushu in suppressing the Kiku-Itoda Rebellion by partisans of the defeated Hōjō.[38] In a separate example dating from 1223, the following rebuttal to a legal accusation (*chinjō*) illustrates the role that *rōdō* frequently played in land management.

> Concerning the post of reeve (*kumon*) for Yamanaka-no-gō, which is under the administration of Yasutsugi. Since olden times, the *jitō* has appointed a *rōdō* to this post. This precedent was set by the former jitō, Mitsuie.[39]

Maintaining the coherence of the Ōtomo clan

The Ōtomo relied on unfree warriors for their day-to-day administration, yet the presence of so many related families in Kyushu meant that, if the Ōtomo could maintain even a semblance of control over them, the prestige and authority of the Ōtomo clan would be enormously enhanced. In theory, the backing of the shogunate meant that the clan head had very real authority over his relatives. Moreover, as the *gunchūjō* battle service report quoted earlier revealed, the first generation of Ōtomo collaterals continued to serve under their *sōryō* until the middle of the fourteenth century.

As has been noted, the degree of independence enjoyed by the various collateral branches of a warrior clan was a function of their economic viability. However, the personalities of the various actors involved were also an important variable in the equation. Among the early Ōtong, it was probably the decisive factor. Neither Yoshinao, the founder of the line, nor his chief heir, Chikahide, can in any way be called strong characters, and both remained very much under the control of the clan matriarch Shinmyō throughout their lives. A number of entries in the *Azuma kagami* give an indication of Yoshinao's personality and his exceedingly "warm" relationship with Yoritomo. The text strongly implies that Yoshinao was actually inside Yoritomo's bedchamber. But at seventeen years of age and being physically weak, it seems unlikely that he could have been acting as bodyguard to the great hegemon.

> Chikayoshi's adoptive son was continually serving in particularly close proximity [to Yoritomo]. One day, Chikayoshi summoned Kunihira and spoke to him thus: "This will be the first time that Yoshinao has gone into battle. You should support him and help him to fight." Kunihira honored this undertaking. Last night, he secretly went to Yoritomo's bedchamber and summoned Yoshinao. They together crossed over to Azukashiyama, and in the course of their attack they killed Satō Saburō Hidekazu (a *rōdō* of Kunihira's close relative) and his son.[40]

Yoshinao's son, Chikahide, seems very much to have been cut from his father's mold. Few sources reveal much about his personality, but what light they do shed is not very flattering. An entry in the *Meigetsuki* from 1228 tells us that Chikahide once attended a drinking party at the home of his friend, Suga Jūrōzaemon. During the proceedings, Chikahide turned to the master of the house and insulted him. Both men drew their swords, and their companions all rose up together and pushed Chikahide out of the house. Chikahide lost his outer cloak and was left in only his underwear (*ōguchi*). As it was broad daylight there were many people watching. His warriors rode with him to stop them staring.[41]

Some of Yoshinao's sons inherited their mother's forceful personality rather than their father's weak one. The second son Yoshihide inherited his father's holdings in Higo province and immediately moved to take up residence there. The main branch of the Ōtomo house by contrast, did not move its base of operations to Kyushu until the time of the third *shugo*, Yoriyasu.

The result was that, despite being *sōryō*, Chikahide was forced to treat his younger brother as an equal, and to sign the following humiliating agreement with him.

> At heart, we are both brothers and love one another deeply. We would not do anything underhanded or deceitful to one another. Moreover, should any grave matter, public or private, arise we would act in concert and support one another. We would not abandon one another. Moreover, if some unpleasantness should arise between us, or we should hear of any such thing, we shall discuss the matter. We should neither mutually give nor receive suspicion. For any untruth that I, Chikahide, should utter may the punishments of the following deities descend upon me for each of the eighty-four thousand hair-holes on my head.[42]

Over this stood the domineering clan matriarch, Shinmyō. She was the mother of most of her husband's children, but he also had a few by women mentioned in the sources simply as "the dancing girls" (*shirabyōshi*). Only one of these offspring, Hidenao, inherited anything. Hidenao was given less extensive holdings than the sons born to Shinmyō in an isolated corner of Chikugo away from the family's main holdings. Left to the mercy of Shinmyō, after their father's death, none of the dancing girls' other children received anything.

Twenty-five years before her death Shinmyō made dispositions of the properties she had received from her husband. Chikahide was given the family holding at Ōtomo-no-gō, enabling him to take over the family surname. The main Ōtomo holding in Bungo province was split up among all the children. Takuma Yoshihide and Shiga Yoshisato each received half of Shiga-no-mura. Yoshihide remained in Higo, however, and took the name Shiga as his surname. Kagenao (also known as Tokikage) was given only one minor holding, at Ichimanda, and founded the Ichimanda line. The youngest son, Yoshimoto, became the chief priest of the Tomari temple on the Ōno estate and received a small amount of land to provide income.[43]

Still, Shinmyō seems to have had too strong a personality to leave her children in peace. After Chikahide died in 1248, bequeathing the bulk of his lands to his own son, Yoriyasu, Shinmyō reasserted her authority. She removed two residence compounds in Ōtomo-no-gō from him, and gave them to her younger children who had no base in the Kanto, so that they would have somewhere to stay while on duty in Kamakura. On other occasions, her desire to interfere was apparently less well-intentioned. For example, Shiga Yoshisato had received the bulk of his holdings on the Ōno estate from her and not from his father, Yoshinao. This was not unreasonable as he had been a minor when his father died. Less easy to explain is the fact that Yoshisato's own children did not receive their holdings from him, but from their grandmother, Shinmyō. Shinmyō's strong personality in its own way held the Ōtomo together.

The sacerdotal powers of the Ōtomo clan chief

With few economic or legal levers over their collaterals, and only the occasional strong personality to engender allegiance, the heads of the Ōtomo clan relied on the spirits to consolidate their control over their men. Yet, conditions were not favorable for the Ōtomo to establish a sacerdotal presence. The Usa family, the chief priests of the Usa Hachiman Shrine, already dominated a key spiritual institution in Kyushu, and were among the very few native families to survive the establishment of the shogunate. The awe in which their office was held seems to have given them a degree of protection such that they were able to maintain a consistently hostile attitude to the shogunate for decades. The Usa Shrine also presided over a network of lesser institutions all over Bungo, the most important of which was the Yusuhara Shrine. There is some evidence that the chief priests of this institution too remained hostile forces, as the chief priest was accused of saying prayers against the shogunate during the Jōkyū war.[44]

With control of the most important shrines denied to them, the Ōtomo concentrated on winning over lesser institutions, particularly the Fukayama Hachiman Shrine on the Ōno estate. The last native chief priest of this shrine, Ōga Yasumoto, may have been forced to commit suicide after being slanderously accused of plotting rebellion.[45] This appears to have left the path open for the Ōtomo to claim the shrine for themselves. The first evidence of direct Ōtomo involvement in shrine affairs comes in 1220, when Yoshinao's signature appears on a document ordering the chief priest to perform a series of ceremonies for the indefinite future.

The spiritual prestige of the Fukayama Hachiman Shrine was soon pressed into service in an attempt to maintain the unity of the Ōtomo clan, when the clan chief insisted that all his relatives, including the virtually independent Takuma, take part in ceremonies there. The Takuma were equally active in using religion to their advantage, making the Wakamiya Hachiman Shrine their own main center of worship.

Buddhist temples were likewise pressed into service, although again the hostility of the Usa Shrine meant that the Ōtomo were forced to work through lesser institutions. Thus, the Ōtomo took over the Tomariji, which had previously served as the spiritual home of the extirpated Ōno clan. Early Ōtomo clan heads habitually stayed there when visiting Kyushu; most Ōtomo collaterals, including the Takuma, held land there; and the temple was one of the burial sites for Yoshinao. Medieval Japanese believed in the concept of *shigai tekitai*, according to which the corpse retained many of the qualities and aspirations its inhabitor exhibited while still alive. The grave of the clan founder may therefore have had a profound spiritual significance for his descendants.[46]

A suitable *ichizoku* was soon chosen to become chief priest of the Tomariji. The first member of the clan to be thus forced into the priesthood was Ōtomo Yoshimoto, who took the priestly name Myōshin. His adoptive son Zenri was likewise ordered to care for the graves of Yoshinao and Shinmyō. Before long, the Tomariji was to prove too small to serve as *ujidera*, or clan temple, to the mighty Ōtomo and the more imposing Shōkōji was built on the Ōno estate.

Before long, all Ōtomo collaterals had adopted temples of their own. The Shiga first adopted the Tomariji after it had been abandoned by the Ōtomo in 1217.[47] They continued building, establishing the Hōjuji on the Ōno estate as their clan's center of worship. In 1375, the Tabaru founded the Senpukuji, and as early as 1316, even the humble Ichimanda were claiming the Chikushioji as their clan temple.[48] Thus, although the religious policies of the Ōtomo reflect an attempt to establish direct links with local deities and temples and to use these as a focus for family ceremonies and family cohesion, by the end of the Kamakura period, this strategy was to prove less and less efficacious as each individual collateral adopted deities and worship centers of its own.

Conclusion

The *shugo* of the Kamakura era may have received relatively little attention from scholars, but certainly in Kyushu they were important figures from the very beginning of the era. All across Japan, the *shugo* inherited their role from the earlier *tsuibushi* and *ōryōshi*, namely to deal with crimes beyond the scope of individual *kenmon*. The *shugo* were also given the duty of organizing the shogunal housemen for duty in Kyoto and Kamakura. In Kyushu, they were given the additional right to try cases involving crimes such as theft and slave trading that, elsewhere in Japan, lay outside the *shugo* jurisdiction. On occasion they are even found trying cases involving shogunal vassals. Indeed so great was the legal competence of the Ōtomo that they needed to draft their own legal code in imitation of the shogunate.

Internally, the Ōtomo house, like all other major clans, reflected the fundamental division in Japanese society between the free and the unfree. The free members of the clan tended to be related to the house head in the male line. Those with significant economic resources of their own were effectively separate clans in their own right. Those without a landed base served the clan chief in a variety of administrative functions. The agricultural lands from which all warriors drew their income were overwhelmingly cultivated by free *hyakushō* (commoners).

The unfree members of the warrior band consisted of two classes, the *rōdō*, who were counterparts to free samurai, and the *genin*, who were counterparts to the free *hyakushō*. What made *rōdō* and *genin* unfree was that they were bound to a master. The freedom to seek greener pastures was known as *kyoshū no jiyū* among warriors and *kyoryū no jiyū* among commoners. The *rōdō* administered their master's lands sometimes even serving as deputy *shugo* (*shugodai*); they fought as his soldiers and even acted as commanders. They usually relied on the *shugo* directly for economic support, but were occasionally assigned lands in their own right. In most cases, they were either distantly related to their lords, often through the female line, or were ex-samurai who had been reduced in status after defeat in war or as punishment for some other infraction.

The *genin* acted as the hewers of wood and drawers of water and performed the basest tasks within the warrior household. Only exceptionally did they engage in agricultural work. They were in most cases born into that estate or descended into it through indebtedness or an inability to pay agricultural rents.

Unfree warriors were reliable servants. After all, they had nowhere else to go. The free warriors within the Ōtomo clan could be a constant source of irritation to the clan head, or *sōryō*. The *sōryō*'s authority relied on the legal backing of the shogunate, but was frequently challenged. This situation was more complex in the case of the Ōtomo because of the personalities of key players. Neither clan founder Yoshinao nor his heir Chikahide, the first two Ōtomo *shugo,* had strong personalities. By contrast, Yoshinao's wife and second son, Yoshihide, were forceful characters. The result was that Chikahide, despite being clan head, was forced to sign a humiliating oath acknowledging his younger brother as an equal, and also had to yield lands to lesser relatives.

In the absence of effective constraints on the actions of economically independent collaterals, the Ōtomo fell back on spiritual suasion. All collaterals took part in religious ceremonies on the Ōno estate. However, even here, the Ōtomo suffered from the hostility of the major religious institutions on the island (who opposed the post-1185 settlement that gave the *shugo* their legitimacy) and, in the later Kamakura era, from the propensity of their collaterals to bolster their independent authority by adopting clan temples and shrines of their own.

NOTES

1   Peter Judd Arnesen, "Suō Province in the Age of Kamakura." For a broader study of this region through the sixteenth century, see Arnesen, *The Medieval Japanese Daimyo: The Ōuchi Family's Rule of Suō and Nagato.*

2   See, for example, Lorraine F. Harrington, "The Regional Outposts of Muromachi Bakufu Rule: The Kantō and Kyushu"; and Thomas Nelson, "Bakufu and Shugo under the Early Ashikaga."

3   I have examined the Ōtomo at greater length in "The Early Shugo to 1390: The Ōtomo Lords of Northern Kyushu."

4   Clearly, their duty was not to commit great crimes—murder and brigandage are specified—but to prevent such misdeeds as well as capture and punish violators. The third task was presumably related to unspecified crimes requiring them to muster guards in the capital. For an extended revision of earlier interpretations of the *taibon sankajō*, see Nitta Ichirō, "Taibon sankajō isetsu—jōshiki no saikentō," passim.

5   For a cogent explication of the early history of such figures, see Karl F. Friday, *Hired Swords: The Rise of Private Warrior Power in Early Japan*, especially pp.122ff.

6   *Gyokuyō* Bunji 1 (1185).10.17. The ground-breaking research on this subject has been done by Shimomukai Tatsuhiko in "Ōchō kokka gunzei kenkyū no kihon shikaku." Shimomukai has broken with the previous scholarly tradition of looking for the precursors to the *shugo* in the provinces and focusing on regional collections of *komonjo* documents. Appreciating that *tsuitōshi* were essentially agents of the central authority, he instead began to look for references to them in the diaries of court aristocrats. The result has been a radical and successful reevaluation of the military command structure in the late Heian period.

7   *Azuma kagami* Jōgen 3 (1209).12.15.

8   Gomi Katsuo, "Kamakura gokenin no ban'yaku kinshi ni tsuite."

9   Ikeuchi Yoshisuke and Satō Shin'ichi, eds., *Chūsei hōsei shiryōshū*, vol. 1, p. 20. (Hereafter *CHSS*, 1, p. 20).

10   Quoted in Satō Shin'ichi, *Komonjogaku nyūmon*, pp. 123–124.

11   This subject has been dealt with at length by Fujiki Hisashi in *Zōhyōtachi no senjō*. Although the book deals with the sixteenth and early seventeenth centuries, Fujiki argues on pp. 73–75 that his findings are also relevant to the early medieval period. For further information on slavery see Thomas Nelson, "Slavery in Medieval Japan."

12   *CHSS*, 1, *tsuikahō* no. 220 (also see *KI*, 9:6383).

13   Shōka 2 (1258).4.5 Ōtomo Yoriyasu kakikudashi an (*KI*, 11:8208; in *Zōho teisei hennen Ōtomo shiryō* 2:282, as Ōtomo Yoriyasu andojō an).

14   Jōō 1 (1222).12.23 Hizen no kuni shugosho kudashibumi an (*Matsura tō kankei shiryōshū* [hereafter *MKS*], 1:37; in *KI*, 5:3032, as Dazaifu shugosho kudashibumi an).

15   Shōwa 4 (1314).5.12 Chinzei gechijō (*KI*, 33:25508; *Chinzei tandai shiryōshū* 1:411).

16   This appears in *CHSS*, 1, as *tsuikahō* nos. 172–198; also see Ninji 3 (1242).1.15 Shin seibai shikimoku (*KI*, 8:5979).

17   This appears in *CHSS*, 1, as *tsuikahō* nos. 217–231; also see Kangen 2 (1244).10.9 Kantō hyōjō kotogaki (*KI*, 9:6383).

18   *CHSS*, 1, *tsuikahō* no. 175 (also see *KI*, 8:5979).

19   *CHSS*, 1, *tsuikahō* no. 176 (also see *KI*, 8:5979).

20   Kasamatsu Hiroshi, "Bakufu no hō to shugo no hō."

21   Ashikari Seiji, "Tōgoku bushidan no tōchaku to hatten," pp. 67–69.

22   See the Ōga genealogy cited in Toyama Mikio, *Daimyō ryōkoku keisei katei no kenkyū*, p. 121, and in Watanabe Sumio, *Bungo Ōtomo shi no kenkyū*, p. 51.

23   Jōō 2 (1223).7.25 Bingo Hōgan Yukihide saribumi (*KI*, 5:3140; *Bungo no kuni Ōno no shō shiryō*, 8; *Zōho teisei hennen Ōtomo shiryō*, 2:92).

24   Shōgen 1 (1259).12.19 Ama Shinmyō yuzurijō (*KI*, 11:8450; *Zōho teisei hennen Ōtomo shiryō*, 2:294).

25   Thomas Conlan, "Largesse and the Limits of Loyalty," p. 42.

26   For further on warriors and their expectations in warfare in the fourteenth century, see Thomas Conlan, *State of War: The Violent Order of Fourteenth-Century Japan*. For issues relating to casualties in battle, which came to be a major basis for claiming rewards, see Andrew Edmund Goble, "War and Injury: The Emergence of Wound Medicine in Medieval Japan."

27   Kenmu 3 (1336).3 Bekki Yoritaka gunchūjō utsushi (*NBI-Ky*, 1:543; *Hennen Ōtomo shiryō* 2:335).

28   Kenmu 4 (1337).3 Shiga Tadayoshi gunchūjō (*NBI-Ky*, 1:906; *Hennen Ōtomo shiryō* 2:340).

29   "Samurai should be seated in the Kyakujinza, *rōdō* in the Hall and *zōnin* in the Courtyard (*ōiwa*). *CHSS*, 1, *tsuikahō* no. 160 (also see *KI*, 8:5785).

30   *CHSS*, 1, p. 9.

31   *Azuma kagami* Bunji 4 (1188).5.20.

32   *Azuma kagami* Jōgen 3 (1209).11.14.

33   *CHSS*, 1, *tsuikahō* no. 265 (also see *KI*, 10:6993).

34   *CHSS*, 1, *tsuikahō* no. 130 (also see *KI*, 8:5535).

35   The correct reading for the name Kodawara is problematic. There is a settlement called Kodawara in Bungo province, but Sagami, the family's original home base, contains a settlement called Odawara, written with the same characters as Kodawara.

36   *Azuma kagami* Bunji 5 (1189). 8.9 and Bunji 6 (1190).1.13. Kunihira appears to have been the victim of an ancient practice in the eastern provinces known as "*shūjin azukeoki.*" Although prisons did exist in medieval Japan, it was far more common for prisoners to be placed in the custody of a vassal. Indeed, one of the ways in which a vassal could serve his lord was to accept such a prisoner. Ishii Susumu has briefly examined this subject, showing that the duties the prisoners might be required to perform included acting as competitors at mounted archery (*yabusame*) contests, helping to build temples and shrines, going into battle and acting as managers (*daikan*) on distant territories. Ishii Susumu, *Chūsei bushidan*, pp. 22–25.

37   1226 (Karoku 2).8.18 Kantō gechijō an (*KI*, 5:3515).

38   For background on this rebellion, see Andrew Edmund Goble, *Kenmu: Go-Daigo's Revolution*, pp. 219–226.

39   Document from Kōyasan monjo, dated Jōō 2 (1223).11.1, cited in Ōae, *Hōkenteki shujūsei seiritsushi kenkyū*, p. 470.

40   *Azuma kagami* Bunji 5 (1189).8.9.

41   *Meigetsuki* 1228.7.12, quoted in Ashikari, p. 93.

42   Karoku 2 (1226).11.6 Takuma Chikahide ukebumi an (*KI*, 5:3542; *Zōho teisei hennen Ōtomo shiryō*, 2:122).

43   See En'ō 2 (1240).4.6 Ama Shinmyō daikanchō (*KI*, 8:5553); En'ō 2 (1240).4.6 Ama Shinmyō shoryō haibunjō (*KI*, 8:5554; in *Bungo no kuni Ōno no shō shiryō*, 13, as Ama Shinmyō sō haibunjō); En'ō 2 (1240).4.6 Ama Shinmyō yuzurijō (*KI*, 8:5555).

44   Toyama Mikio, *Chūsei Kyushu shakaishi no kenkyū*, p. 246

45   *Ibid*, p. 249.

46   For a detailed discussion see Katsumata Shizuo, "Shigai tekitai." On p. 43, he cites the *Azuma kagami* for Jūei 3 (1184).3.28 as an example. Yoritomo says to his prisoner Taira Shigehira, "it was to assuage the wrath of my lord and to remove the shame felt by the corpse of your dead father, that I summoned you to battle at Ishibashiyama." Similarly the records of the Takao Shrine in Chikugo province mention that, when a shogunal vassal of samurai status was insultingly called a commoner (*bonge*), he saw it as an offence to the corpses of his ancestors.

47   The transfer of the Tomariji from the main line of the Ōtomo to collaterals occurred in 1297 when Zenri, the *inshu* and *jitō* of the Tomariji, bequeathed the titles that he had received from his grandmother Shinmyō and adoptive father Ōtomo Yoshimoto, to his elder brother Shiga Yasutomo. He did so because his beri beri had recurred and he was at death's gate. See Einin 5 (1297).8.5 Zenri yuzurijō (*KI*, 26:19426; *Hennen Ōtomo shiryō* 1:657).

48   Toyama Mikio, "Ōtomo shi to Zenshū," p. 11.

FLUID BODIES

Images of Illness: Interpreting the Medieval *Scrolls of Afflictions*

Andrew Edmund Goble

Introduction

In the ninth month of 1549, monks at the Kōryūji temple near Kyoto recited a special prayer on behalf of parishioners. The prayer sought relief from a long list of afflictions from which ordinary people suffered. The afflictions included throat ailments, whitlows, carbuncles, male genital afflictions, buttock sores, insect sores, pustulent sores, "stirrup sores," runny noses, malaria, bloody stools, morning sickness, contagious "corpse transmitted diseases," and winter problems such as great chaps, cracked skin, and coughing illnesses.[1]

The prayer is a rare source, but as we learn from a wide variety of other materials, concern with afflictions was ubiquitous in sixteenth-century Japan.[2] For example, problems for which people sought treatment included head banging, eye injuries, feet stepped on by horses or impaled by nails, falls from horses, snake bites, cat bites, childhood falls, hair loss (men, women, and children), warriors' self-inflicted sword wounds, dislocated hips resulting from falls from ladders, injuries from falls from the second stories of buildings, injuries caused by lightning strikes, diarrhea, food poisoning, malaria, "leprosy," smallpox, syphilis, unwanted pregnancy (abortion), miscarriages, generalized difficulties during pregnancy, bleeding in the final months of pregnancy, and a variety of postpartum problems including unexpelled placenta, delirium, swelling and nausea following a stillbirth, dizziness, chest pains, urination, and sore stomach and bottom.[3] The documentary record likewise contains references to "folk remedies" for infant bedwetting, fish bones stuck in the throat, ringworm, sore teeth, breech birth, lacquer poisoning, hemorrhoids, swellings, and "toad-tongue."[4]

Beyond recording this litany of concerns about illness, the record highlights a point so obvious that it is easily overlooked: life in premodern times was defined by illness rather than by health. Being ill or afflicted, rather than consistently healthy, was the normal expectancy for the living.

Given the central place of illness in human existence, we might expect that historians of Japan would have addressed such a potentially rich area of inquiry into people's lives. Scholarly attention has, however, been sporadic. To be sure, scholars have produced surveys of medical history and general studies on illness.[5] As a result of interest in issues of discrimination, research has been published on perceptions of skin, on attitudes to and treatment of the disadvantaged or disabled, and on issues associated with leprosy.[6] Studies are also available on various causes of death, the treatment of corpses, and funeral practices.[7] Some studies reinterpret literary and artistic material with an awareness of psychological and somatological factors, such as Hotate's study of the folk-story of Sannen Netarō against a possible background of epilepsy, and LaFleur's exploration of the phenomena of "hungry ghosts."[8] Studies in English also include translations on the topics of acupuncture and sexual well-being from the tenth-century *Ishinpō* (Prescriptions from the Heart of Medicine); Hurst's instructive case study of one person's illnesses; some attention to ophthalmology; an obscure survey of obstetrics; and a monograph touching on issues of disease and economic growth.[9]

Despite this list, issues of medicine and society, the impact of illness on people's life decisions, the types of medicines available, even a basic sense of what afflictions people confronted generally, not to mention the specific medical issues attending the normal cycle of women's lives, have received scant attention. It is only very recently that we see studies of medical issues that focus on specialized medical texts and shed light on clinical issues and on the social context of medicine and illness.[10] In the absence of any extensive effort to understand the social implications of epidemic, illness, and affliction more generally, we are sometimes left with observations that may point to an important topic for investigation but which are not otherwise illuminating, or to identifications of ailments that are historically inaccurate and misleading.[11]

Ample opportunity thus exists for an examination of how illness and affliction were perceived, and how people responded to the presence in their midst of those with illness and afflictions. Written sources—medical works, diaries, dictionaries—and their listings do not always directly address these issues of medicine and society, but they do permit us an expanded view of striking visual information provided by two illustrated scrolls identified for convenience here as the *Scrolls of Afflictions*. The first of these scrolls is the *Scroll of Afflictions* (*Yamai no sōshi*; alternatively, "Scroll of Illnesses")[12] produced at the end of the twelfth century, and containing twenty-two scenes. The second, which I identify as the *Scroll of Gross Afflictions* (*Ihon yamai no sōshi*, "Variant Text Scroll of Afflictions"; alternatively, *Kishitsu emaki*, "Scroll of Diseases and Deformities"),[13] is a composite work of seventeen scenes originally produced around the twelfth and thirteenth centuries, and an additional twenty produced in the sixteenth and seventeenth centuries.[14]

Our exploration will commence with a brief introduction to the *Scrolls of Afflictions*, noting some issues of interpretation, and then providing an outline of the material. Second, since attention has been given to the prominence of genitalia in the *Scrolls*, we will look at issues of pathology and scatology. Third, we will examine issues relating to psychological afflictions and states of mind, and some responses to the behavior of people so affected. Fourth, we will look at reactions to affliction, focusing on the notion of affliction as a spectacle. Fifth, moving in a different but related direction, we will take up the topic of afflictions and care. Finally, we will offer some concluding comments.

The *Scrolls of Afflictions*—An Outline

There are a total of fifty-nine scenes in the two scrolls. These appear to have been based on information drawn from the general environs of the city of Kyoto, and drawn from observed or reported experiences, incidents and events that generated comment or gossip at the time.[15] However, whereas many of the scenes in the *Scroll of Afflictions* are accompanied by a textual description, those in the *Scroll of Gross Afflictions* have no accompanying commentary. This provides a certain challenge in trying to interpret or classify the scenes in the *Scrolls*, or indeed in trying to establish what might have motivated their production.[16]

While the *Scrolls* deal with issues of affliction, and a variety of both physical and psychological states are represented, they provide very little guidance to treatment or medicines. It is also not clear that having a "picture" of something might have been of any professional utility for physicians. Accordingly, while the *Scrolls*, as we shall see, do tell us much about illness, and commentary on the scrolls by modern physicians is helpful in identifying from what people might have been suffering and to what those around them may have been reacting,[17] the *Scrolls* do not appear to have been produced in order to serve as a clinical guide for physicians. Similarly, while the scenes obviously represent humans suffering from illness, one of the elements that is a central part of the human condition in Buddhist understanding, there is some consensus that the *Scrolls* were not produced for didactic Buddhist purposes. That is, the *Scrolls* do not fall into the "Six Realms of Existence" (*rokudō*) genre of paintings.[18] In another vein, since quite a number of the scenes deal with suffering, and some provide evidence that the ailing or afflicted might be subject to marginalization, ridicule and the like, some commentators have suggested that not only was the very production of the *Scroll of Afflictions* motivated by a sense of discrimination, but that the *Scrolls* in toto should be primarily seen as evidence of discrimination that has pervaded Japanese society through time.[19] As we shall see, discrimination, and callousness are pervasive in the *Scrolls*, but so, too, are other elements. And, we might exercise some caution in giving credence to perspectives that project onto the medieval interpretations that might derive from a concern to find putative antecedents for later historical issues. As I hope to explore below, the *Scrolls* do not easily admit of uniform and convenient characterization.

Moreover, the scenes themselves provide challenges to understanding, for a simple description of a scene may not satisfactorily address what the scene may convey or reveal. Let me offer an illuminating, and cautionary, example. One scene in the *Scroll of Afflictions* portrays a rooster (*tori*) which is situated in very close proximity to a woman who is leaning toward the rooster. Her face, and thus her eyes (*me*), are in close proximity to the rooster's beak. One art historian has noted that the picture is of a woman who is having her eye pecked by a cock (*tori ni me wo tsutsukaseru onna zu*). Another has noted that "since there is no accompanying text for this strange scene the subject matter is unknown. The figures of a cock pecking at the eye of a woman seated on a mat are isolated against a blank background."[20] However, the *Scroll of Afflictions* deals with afflictions, and while being pecked by a rooster would, no doubt, be unpleasant, it is not an affliction. So, what affliction might we have here? Since the Japanese word for night blindness is *torime* (rooster- or chicken-eye), springing from the belief that roosters could not see in the dark,[21] then what is in fact being portrayed, in the form of a visual pun, is night blindness. Ironically, our scholars have failed to see it. My broader point, then, is that simply describing a scene may not tell us what the scene itself may be portraying.

Being aware of the limitations of description, let us nevertheless provide a brief guide to the *Scrolls*. The following "Outline Index" for each of the two scrolls, the *Scroll of Afflictions* and the *Scroll of Gross Afflictions*, follows the order and numbering assigned by modern scholars. For some of the scenes I have suggested which medical conditions might be depicted. Other possibilities for interpretation or "labeling" are discussed in the body of the essay below. References, for example to Scene 1 in the *Scroll of Afflictions,* will follow the format of A1; similarly G1, identifies Scene 1 in the *Scroll of Gross Afflictions*.

Scenes in the Scroll of Afflictions

A1.   Man and children with black noses.
A2.   Woman with insomnia.
A3.   Man with nervous disorder.
A4.   Man with "toad tongue" (*ranula glottis*).
A5.   Man vomiting excrement.
A6.   Hermaphrodite.
A7.   Man receiving treatment for an eye disorder.
A8.   Man with pyorrhea.
A9.   Man with anal fistula.
A10.   Man with crab lice shaving pubic hair.
A11.   Woman with *cholera nostrus* (*kakuran*).
A12.   Priest with spinal curvature.
A13.   Woman with halitosis.
A14.   Man with lethargy (narcolepsy?).
A15.   Woman with facial macula.
A16.   Albino woman.
A17.   Male dwarf.
A18.   Hunchback mendicant priest.
A19.   Obese woman.
A20.   Man with visions of little Buddhas (brain tumor?).
A21.   Woman with night blindness.
A22.   Man receiving acupuncture treatment.

Scenes in the Scroll of Gross Afflictions

G1.   Woman gnawing at a corpse.
G2.   Dancing priest displaying his erect penis, guided with string, to a crowd.
G3.   Woman with odiferous vaginal discharge.
G4.   Woman with fluid issuing from a distended abdomen (ovarian cyst?).
G5.   Man with a scaly skin disease (hives or pustules?).
G6.   Man with eye ailment being treated by old woman.
G7.   Man with swollen abdomen being massaged (?) by a woman from a shrine.
G8.   Priest about to sever his penis, watched by two priests and a young woman (fixation or delusion?).

G9.   Man pointing to his swollen testicles (*rinbyō?*).

G10. Priest with swollen testicles (elephantiasis?).

G11. Woman with a fever, another woman with skin disease.

G12. Woman suffering from skin disease (measles or smallpox?).

G13. Household scene: recumbent fleshly female, emaciated female, prone emaciated male, child, older man and woman.

G14. Woman being given treatment for abscesses on her back.

G15. Woman with a large facial swelling.

G16. Priest falling into a hearth (epilepsy or dizzy spell?).

G17. Man approaching death, grieving people around him.

G18. Woman with anal fistula and diarrhea.

G19. Woman inserting a bone from a horse-skeleton into her vagina.

G20. Infant being treated with a needle to the abdomen.

G21. Altercation between priests (anger?).

G22. Man dancing around a discarded corpse, observers fleeing.

G23. Bedridden man in a "Chinese" scene.

G24. Crippled (*izari, ashinae*) man who moves with *geta*-clogs attached to his hands.

G25. Priest writing charm on an old woman's chest.

G26. Woman with elephentiasis of the legs.

G27. Man with no mouth, eating through hole in his chest.

G28. Man vomiting while dining.

G29. Priest in a "cripple cart" (*hekisha*) being propelled by children.

G30. Woman with a large swelling on her back being examined by two men.

G31. Child with smallpox (?) being held by a female (mother?).

G32. Woman ripping cloth.

G33. Woman with a disfiguring tumor on the nose.

G34. Man with a tumoral fistula leaking from his side.

G35. Dark-skinned beggar receiving alms from a woman.

G36.   Street scene, includes people begging and a woman exposing her genitalia to an audience.

G37.   Women, one with a dangling suppository (?) between her legs, bathing themselves and a child, a male attendant at a fire, being peeped at by two men.

Pathology and Scatology

One particularly delicate issue regarding perceptions and reactions arises from depictions of "private parts." The depiction of genitals in the *Scroll of Gross Afflictions* has at times been censored, even in the Edo period where illustrations of the genitalia are generously furnished in popular art.[22] In some Edo-era reproductions of the *Scroll of Gross Afflictions* genitalia were obscured by painted-over clothing, while some were apparently not even reproduced.[23] And, continuing this mindset, whereas the *Shinsen yamai no sōshi* (Newly Selected Scroll of Afflictions) of 1850, compiled as a conscious addition to the earlier scrolls, portrays genitals among its sixteen scenes,[24] when it was reproduced in one early twentieth-century collection some of the "offending parts"—one depicting blood-swollen labia, and another depicting a prolapsed uterus—were simply blanked out.[25] As recently as the 1980s and 1990s certain art historians commenting on genitalia in the *Scroll of Gross Afflictions* complained that the depiction of genitals was excessive,[26] that scenes displaying genitals reflected a perverse spirit of exhibitionism or elevated sex-drive,[27] or that a scene (G16) was humorous because it depicted the "flailing genitals" of an unfortunate individual.[28] This concern specifically with "private parts" may suggest much about the perspectives of various editors and commentators on "naughtiness." At the same time, however, such responses ought not deflect our attention away from a more substantive interpretation of the scenes, which might otherwise extend what is known about medieval understandings of affliction.

First, then, before looking further into what may be learned from the scenes of the scrolls, let us see if the moralizing about them holds up under scrutiny. A comparison of what the scenes show to examples of scatological material available in the medieval era places the issue in perspective.

Portrayals of urination are rare,[29] but references to defecation and flatulence are common. The *Uji shūi monogatari* (Collection of Tales from Uji) provides such tales as: the loose-boweled priest Zōga who, upon leaving an imperial audience, gleefully evacuates from a verandah;[30] an ascetic revealed as a fraud when examination of his excreta reveals rice grains;[31] wind-breaking by a court lady that ruins a romantic mood;[32] and the constipated young woman who believes that calendar entries prevent her from defecating.[33] In contrast, laxative misfortune is featured in the illustrated *Fukutomi zōshi* (Scroll of Fukutomi). Assured by a rival that his quest for borborygmic distinction would be aided by ingesting morning glory seeds, Fukutomi expels not the flatulent anal arias he wishes for, but a massive drizzle of diarrhea.[34]

Genitals are also given their due. The hapless Fukutomi, for example, staggers home, bedraggled and in pain, removes his clothes, and sits shivering, his "balls hanging down darkly."[35] Penises were consciously flashed in public,[36] or accidentally displayed in full tumescence to stunned in-laws.[37] Penises or vulvas were investigated to reveal truth, as when genitals that had been powdered or painted were later inspected for proof of infidelity,[38] or when a man was proven innocent of rape when examination of his penis (six inches, "capped") shows that it was not that of the assailant.[39] Certain genitalia might lack sufficient size, as was the case of a man from Ise, whose wife embarrassed him into silence when she noted that despite the well-known reputation the men of Ise enjoyed for great virility, his own member was "unbelievably small and weak," and not even worthy of notice.[40] Other genitals might be notable for their odor, as was the case of a very short man who slept with his face nestled next to his taller wife's pubic region rather than her face, but remarks on her bad breath.[41]

References to sexual activity are likewise common, as in a story of a man who hollowed out and "married" a turnip in order to assuage his uncontrollable lust.[42] Genitals are particularly featured in illustrated tales. The late twelfth-century scroll painting *Koshibagaki zōshi* (Tale of the Brushwood Fence), given as a wedding present to an imperial princess, provides the earliest Japanese visual portrayal of, and indeed reference of any kind to, cunnilingus and fellatio.[43] Another late Heian-period scroll painting, *Yōbutsu kurabe emaki* (Penis Competition), features penises of Beardsleyesque proportions.[44] The early fourteenth-century *Chigo zōshi* (Acolyte Scroll) clearly portrays homosexual anal sex and the use of dildos by males, while the contemporaneous *Fukuro sōshi* (Priest in the Bag) attests to the use of dildos by females.[45]

While these references are somewhat fragmentary, the writings of the scholar Fujiwara Akihira (989–1066) suggest that interest in sexual matters was constant rather than occasional. In his *Unshū shōsoku* (Letters From Izumo Province; also known as *Meigō ōrai*) Akihira notes a country performance of live sex on the stage, which was the literal climax to a one-act play re-creating the first night of a newly-wedded couple.[46] He also alerts us to a brush that is useful for copying Buddhist sutras in order to gain religious merit, but is also indispensable for enhancing heterosexual sexual activity.[47] His *Shinsarugaku ki* (Account of New Monkey Music),[48] which describes the talents, occupations, or appearances of household members, has some memorable references. The original wife of the householder is described as old with straggly hair; her upper and lower teeth have fallen out leaving her looking like a pet monkey, and her left and right breasts droop pendulously like the balls of an ox in summer. The thirteenth daughter has an unattractive body, is smelly, has bad skin, and is ugly. The reprobate, unfilial, braggadocio gambler who is the husband of the fourteenth daughter has one redeeming quality—his immensely thick and gnarly penis, so big that no other woman would marry him, but which turns out to be perfectly compatible with the vagina (not described, but obviously capacious) of the fourteenth daughter. The sixteenth daughter, an entertainer and provider of sexual services,[49] excels in at least two classical positions for intercourse ("upside-down dragon," and "tiger-step"),[50] and is noted for the sublime virtues of her sex organs. Akihira was also the author of *Tettsui den* (Record of an Iron Hammer), the biography of a penis which he wrote under the nom de plume "Dick Large."[51] The text, which includes technical vocabulary for various parts of the male and female genitalia and for a number of positions for intercourse, suggests intimate acquaintance with classical sexological works.

In fact, issues relating to sexual technique, male reproductive vigor, and the health of the reproductive organs were commonly addressed in medical literature. Topics taken up in the *Ishinpō*—positions for intercourse, frequency of copulation according to age, classification of female pudenda, erectile capability, for example—are, not unexpectedly, found in later compilations that draw on it, such as the 1288 *Eisei hiyōshō* (Essentials for Safeguarding Health and Longevity). Works that were intended for a broader population than that of the imperial court likewise take up such issues. For example, the fourteenth-century work *Gotai shinbun shū* (A Collection Treating the Five Portions of the Body) notes a treatment for making penises larger and longer.[52] Another fourteenth-century medical work, Kajiwara Shōzen's (1265–1337)[53] *Ton'ishō* (Book of the Simple Physician) devotes an entire chapter to problems in sexual congress, covering such topics as erectile insufficiency, inadequate penile size, length, or firmness;[54] an oral tradition for lengthening penis size in one day;[55] a folk recipe for a lubricant touted as a wonderful enhancement for sexual intercourse;[56] and a treatment for wide vaginas.[57]

To move now to the *Scrolls of Afflictions*, I would submit that in contrast to the scatological material that can be found in literary and in some visual sources, the genital depictions in the *Scrolls of Afflictions* are neither erotic nor pornographic. While some scenes convey humor, we should regard these body parts in a medical vein, as legitimate topics for depiction, and as parts of an overall composition, rather than in a prurient light.

Indeed, one could hardly illustrate problems of personal hygiene or disorders of urinary and reproductive organs without such illustrations.

There are illustrations such as that of the man with crab lice (A10), who in one hand is holding his penis by the foreskin and shaving his pubic region with a shaving blade held in the other; one clearly depicting the vulva of a woman suffering from a vaginal discharge (G3); and depiction of common testicular problems,[58] such as the swollen testicles of a priest, who is perhaps suffering from *rinbyō*[59] (G9), or those of a lay person who may be suffering from elephantiasis of the scrotum (G10).

Indeed, parts of the body associated with reproduction are not infrequently encountered in visual sources. However, they are incidental to the scenes, rather than a specific focus of them. In one scene depicted in the thirteenth-century *Shokunin uta-awase* (The Tradespeoples' Poetry Competition), the genitals of the naked and forlorn gambler are exposed quite naturally since he has literally lost the clothes off his back.[60] There is similar exposure for males in the Hell of Flaming Rain and Fiery Rocks or the Hell of Flowing Hair Fire in the *Jigoku zōshi* (Scroll of Hell).[61] Moreover, underwear seems to have been a rare item, as suggested in the scene (G13) that includes a man sitting at home with robe akimbo and genitals exposed, or in the depictions of defecation in the *Gaki zōshi* (Scroll of Hungry Ghosts). Scroll paintings depict as a matter of course the breasts of women engaged in manual labor or breast-feeding,[62] and we know that in summer, court women might go topless in their homes or wear transparent upper-body garments. The unclothed body was not an uncommon sight. This is not to say that there would not be displays of the body that could embarrass people: one aristocrat's wife engaged in various forms of odd behavior, such as lounging about with exposed breasts when guests were present.[63]

Given that parts of the body related to reproduction and other bodily functions were observable in the normal course of daily life, it would be a mistake to assume that their appearance in the *Scrolls of Afflictions* implied any special attention to them.

Thus, it is difficult to see humor in the scene (G16; for Sano, an example of insanity) of a priest falling backward onto an open hearth, and particularly to attribute such humor to a sense that the genitals are "flailing." But, Teramoto also notes it as a possible instance of epilepsy,[64] and it is not unlikely that the scene depicts a case akin to one of priests who either fainted suddenly while on a visit to a shrine,[65] or, as a result of a nervous disorder such as apoplexy (*chūfū*), become dizzy, lose their balance, fall into a latrine and die (a spectacle which elicited the wry comment that the unfortunate cleric had fallen from the present world into a Buddhist hell of excrement).[66] Let us note two other scenes.

A scene of a woman displaying her genitals to an audience (G36) has been characterized both as exhibitionism and as an example of insanity. There seems no doubt that the people crowding in front of the woman displaying her vagina are interested in looking. Still, while the woman may indeed be displaying the "holy treasures,"[67] there is little reason in and of itself to believe that it was the consequence of a psychological affliction whereby she would gain sexual gratification from her "exhibitionism." The charge of insanity likewise requires more justification. Moreover, this image is only one part of a larger scene in which beggars are also to be found. Is the presumed affliction to be found in the woman actually hers? Is it in her audience? Is it in the people begging for food? Might it be that the larger affliction depicted is the condition of a society where the unusual and noteworthy includes both display of sexual organs and begging? Alternatively, might the display of sex organs derive from a different perspective entirely?

Audience interest also appears in a scene (G37, Sano classifies this as an instance of old age) depicting four women of various ages and a child bathing, with a man tending a fire, and two men who are standing outside the fenced area peeping at the bathers. The nakedness of those bathing and the visibility of genital organs probably reflects the fact that few people bathe in their clothes. The focus of the scene, and a sense of any affliction, is properly directed at the men doing the peeping. That is, in a culture where nakedness generally was seen as neither inherently erotic nor shameful, we still find voyeurs. And if the men were peeping not at nudity but at what might be the string of a vaginal suppository (these are attested from the beginning of the fourteenth century)[68] dangling from between the thighs of one older woman, they are still engaged in voyeurism, attracted by an unusual object. In this vein, the desire to look is akin to that in the scene (A6) where some males, having been intrigued by a person's gait, sneak in while the person is sleeping, lift the robe (no underwear), and upon seeing the clearly shown male and female genitalia, realize that the person is a hermaphrodite.[69]

Moving to scenes where the anus is involved, it is hard to see coprophiliac intent in the scene of the woman with diarrhea and an anal fistula (G18), or that of a man with an extraordinary clustered fistula (A9, which led people to think that he had two anuses), or that of a woman suffering from *kakuran* (A11). The fistula may have been of interest, and no doubt people suffering hemorrhoids would have been discomfited and unable to see for themselves the site of the problem, which may explain the presence of observers. And the portrayal of suffering of the woman with *kakuran* requires no tortured interpretation. As the commentary notes: "There is an affliction called *kakuran*. In the stomach there is pain like being stabbed; one vomits from the mouth, and leaks diarrhea from the backside. One lies prostrate in convulsions, and it is truly unbearable agony." This is a riveting depiction of an affliction that was immensely painful, frequently recorded, and fully reflective of an environment in which food poisoning, with ensuing potentially fatal diarrhea and attendant bodily dehydration, was always a problem.[70]

In sum, if in the *Scrolls of Afflictions* we discovered *not* that genitals were present, but that they were absent, then *this* would be worthy of remark. To explain their presence by suggesting prurience, libidousness, or exhibitionism is of little help in trying to interpret scenes. None can fairly be seen as examples of the excrement humor that characterizes the *Fukutomi zōshi* or other scatological anecdotes. However, the display of genitals can elicit a variety of responses, which directs us to broader questions of perception and of states of mind.

Afflictions and States of Mind

Medieval Japanese were aware of mental health as well as physical well being. There was an explicit realization that a person's state of mind could have a notable impact on behavior and physical condition. It was also understood that physical or environmental circumstances could affect psychological balance.

The *Scroll of Afflictions* contains two examples that directly address mind-body issues. The first is a scene (A2) of a woman with insomnia, whose "invisible mental suffering" is described as follows: "There was a woman from Kataoka in the Katsuragi district of Yamato province. Even though she was without any specific physical ailment (pain) in any place, even at night she was unable to sleep. Through the night she stayed up, something that was more miserable than anything, so [she] said." That is, in a society in which human bonds and karmic connections were accorded great importance, to be alone without anybody to converse or share experiences with was a source of suffering.

The second example is the scene (A20) of an ailing man (possibly suffering from a brain tumor?) having visions of dwarfs or little Buddhas. "Recently, there was a man who had a chronic illness. When he had an attack of this illness he would see lined up together near his pillow innumerable midget priests no more than six inches (*sun*) tall, wearing paper clothes." While it is not clear precisely what the small figures represented (a means of instilling fear in the afflicted? gods, or demons of the disease?[71]), it was apparent that the person was hallucinating, alone in a world of his own.

Other sources refer to actions proceeding from, or symptoms taken as exhibiting, distressed states of mind. Texts for the *noh* theater deal frequently with madness.[72] *Sakuragawa* (Cherry River), for example, portrays a mother's crazed distress at separation from her child, the recollections and associations that triggered her madness, and the callousness of some who extracted amusement from her plight.[73] Medieval tale collections show awareness that behavior was affected by mental balance. Descriptions include people listlessly abed as a result of "love-sickness,"[74] and grief leading to suicide or thoughts of suicide. In one example of the latter, a son died after being accidentally stabbed by his father, whereupon the father stabbed himself (dying three days later), and then in her grief the mother and widow contemplated killing herself.[75] In *Hatsuse monogatari* (Story of Hatsuse), a person whose strange behavior included being angry and violent when left alone, goes out to the street to glare at and insult passers-by when drunk, and tries to cut off a woman's hair.[76] Medical works also acknowledge the idea of stress. The *Gotai shinbun shū* devotes one chapter to the treatment of fear (*shiokuji*, which also seems to include cowardice), offering the definition that "There are those who are afraid and lose their ability to speak either on the battlefield or in the presence of the elevated. It is said that there are those, usually inferiors, who on such occasions vomit blood."[77] The *Ton'ishō* devotes three chapters to afflictions of *ki* (vital energy), afflictions the root causes of which are understood in both Buddhist and Chinese medicine to lie in emotional upset.[78] Indeed, the connection between emotional and physical well-being seems to have been commonly understood. Disciples of the iconoclastic Zen priest Ikkyū believed that his attacks of diarrhea were directly related to his state of mind.[79]

Notwithstanding these examples, it is fair to say that little attention has been given to the range and types of experiences that might elicit strong emotional responses, which might in turn prompt odd or unusual behaviors. Most generally we might consider famine or warfare as the type of events liable to impact the psyche. More particular events that might elicit strong responses from observers, survivors, or those close to victims, would include such things as thirty-six Zen monks burnt to death in a temple fire, or a young child burnt to death when lightning set a house on fire;[80] children being abducted and having their livers cut out to be used as medicinal ingredients;[81] and the discovery of a child's body in a drained pond.[82] Other examples attest more directly to the impact of loss.

A diarist writing during a famine in 1461 brings to our attention the poignant scene of a mother sitting by the roadside holding a dead baby to her breast, perhaps hoping that it might still be capable of drinking mother's milk.[83] An example from another famine (in 1544) reveals the reverse, the trauma of a ten-year-old child sobbing and wondering what will become of him as he sits next to a fifty-year-old woman (his mother?) who, near death, is described as "merely a passageway for breath."[84] A father whose eldest son and heir was murdered at the age of nineteen is plunged into long-term grief.[85] The emotional impact of the loss of a child is also attested to in the case of a twenty-nine-year-old woman who requested that prayers be said for her at a shrine because she had completely lost her spirit (*honshin*) following the death of her baby the previous spring.[86]

Sometimes psychological trauma could be so great that people responded by taking, or trying to take, their own lives. Our diarist recording the 1461 famine in Kyoto noted that the waters of the Kamo river were dammed up by the multitude of corpses (82,000 people were noted as having died unnatural deaths), and some people went mad from hunger, their insanity prompting them to leap into the waters.[87] We have references to other suicides, too, such as that of a shrine attendant at Kashii shrine around 1200,[88] a priest at Iwashimizu Hachiman shrine in 1254,[89] a child near Gion shrine in 1284,[90] and a shrine servant in 1425.[91] Other cases reveal even more the dramas of life and their impact on mental well-being. We have stories of women drowning themselves because of family circumstances: a courtier's wife and two children drown themselves (the volition of the children may be questionable) when they believe him to be dead;[92] or the case of a woman who was distraught over the belief that her husband had disowned her and her children.[93] An apparent instance of bullying at Daitokuji led one Zen acolyte to commit suicide in 1447.[94] Losing the affections of his long-time homosexual lover was enough to make Kōfukuji priest Aimanmaru take his own life in 1474.[95] Still others took their lives to ease suffering that preyed on their thoughts: the man who, realizing that he would die soon, slit his belly, and died two days later;[96] the fifty-two or fifty-three-year-old man who went to a graveyard, and reciting the *nembutsu*, "tied his head" and committed suicide;[97] or those who weighted themselves down with rocks and drowned themselves in the sea in order to enter paradise.[98]

Other distraught people lashed out at those around them. We can only speculate what lay behind the case of a twenty-two-year-old man who first killed a nineteen-year-old woman and then himself.[99] But in other cases the causes are clearer. Someone possessed by a fox-spirit had gone mad and killed a fourteen-year-old temple page;[100] in a tragic outcome to a broken relationship, the wife of a shrine official left him, and then later drowned their three-year-old child in a well.[101] In another instance, a person went mad, killed a servant and her two children, and then committed suicide; his wife was then crucified in retribution.[102] Money troubles might also lead to disaster. In a striking sequence from the early 1590s we learn that a person from Komori county near Nara killed a gold-dust dealer in Kyoto; a gold-dust dealer threw a person into Kōnoike pond in Nara (probably killing him); someone pressed by lack of money committed suicide; and a person in the money business, beset by debts, killed his wife and children, slit his belly, set their house on fire, and died.[103] And the anger and "rush of blood" unleashed by illicit sexual relations might inspire killings: one enraged husband slew his wife's lover in front of her, bound her, "cut off the privities of his slain rival," placed them in a box which he had her open in front of dinner guests, and then decapitated her as she fainted at the sight.[104]

It is no stretch of the imagination to believe that the authors of the *Scrolls of Afflictions* would have been aware that states of mind could affect behavior of "normal" people, and that unbalanced behavior might be the product of more profound mental disturbance. With this understanding, we are well placed to interpret some further scenes from the *Scroll of Gross Afflictions*.

One of the most arresting scenes is of a woman sitting on the ground, her legs spread wide apart, as she inserts a bone from the nearby skeleton of a horse into her clearly portrayed vagina (G19). The action suggests several interpretations. One is that she is inducing an abortion. However, the few references that we have to abortion prior to the Tokugawa period suggest that it was more common to employ drugs or external pressure rather than the more dangerous method of rummaging around inside the uterus with an object. Another line of interpretation, followed by Sano and Teramoto, is that she is insane, and that she is driven to masturbation by a heightened sex drive. However, if we move beyond the concern with the physical actions that inform these two suggestions, another possibility emerges. Namely, the action is not motivated inherently by concerns related to reproduction or sexuality, but by her reaction to some form of emotional exhaustion or trauma, expressed in repetitive genital manipulation as a form of bodily self-absorption and regression. We have, then, less a portrayal of a wanton sexuality than of someone shattered in her own world, perhaps even trying to stabilize a fragmented sense of self, distanced emotionally from anyone around her, and thus separated from the care and concern that is commonly extended to the afflicted.

This is not the only scene in the *Scroll of Gross Afflictions* where we may better understand the behavior portrayed if we focus less on the action than regard it as a symptom of psychological disturbance. Another scene (G32) depicts a woman ripping or tearing cloth, and with a pile of such items next to her. We may think that she is making bandages, small towels or similar items, although it is hard to see this in itself as an affliction. Rather, what we more likely have is a portrayal of a woman who is alone, self-absorbed, gazing vacantly ahead, and engaged in the repetitive behavior of ripping cloth. We cannot know why—though we may suggest obsession, depression, shock, or even perhaps Alzheimer's disease. But it is clear that she is self-absorbed, and blocking out the surrounding world. Two other scenes portray or suggest cannibalism. In the first scene (G1) we see a thin and disheveled woman gnawing upon a corpse, to the fascination of observers. In the second scene (G22) we see two women running away from a man who is gleefully dancing around another corpse. Yet, we may suggest that these are unusual actions by individuals who seem to be in their own worlds, and are ones, taken in extremis, that reflect some type of psychological imbalance.

These preceding examples are ones in which we have noted that the principals are lost in their own world and struggling (albeit in extreme ways) to cope with the shattering power of trauma, not engaging in actions for the benefit of observers. Other instances of odd behavior, however, seem to reflect a conscious desire to communicate to the audience. For these, our interpretation is greatly helped by considering elements of medieval religious culture.

Our first example is a scene suggesting a desire to engage in deliberate bodily mutilation, a rare act in premodern Japan.[105] In the scene (G8), a priest is threatening to cut off his penis, much to the consternation of those around him. Perhaps his impulse was similar to that of a philandering husband who, realizing that his sexual activity was harming his marital relationship, convinced his wife that he had cut off his penis.[106] Yet the fact that we have a priest portrayed here suggests that we may offer further nuance to such an interpretation. The colloquial Japanese word for "dick" was *mara*,[107] a term taken from the Sanskrit and Buddhist word *mâra* (魔羅), denoting delusion and "illusion." The scene thus provides us with a visual word play (as we have already noted for the scene of night blindness in the *Scroll of Afflictions*, A21) alluding to carnal fixation, a play made even more pronounced when we recall the Buddhist phrase *bonnō ni tachikirenai*, i.e., "one cannot sever oneself from one's delusions." So the scene here is a vivid, humorous, and subtle portrayal of somebody laboring under the mental affliction of attachment to the physical world. He is perhaps unbalanced by his addiction to carnality,[108] one further symptom of which may itself be his public display of his solution to the problem.

Our second example is the scene (G2) of a priest dancing on a raised dais before an audience, guiding his erect penis with a string (noted by Sano as "priest dancing"). The expressions of the audience suggest that the display may have elicited a variety of responses, ranging from amusement to embarrassment. Some no doubt thought the priest a little unsettled or an exhibitionist, perhaps sharing a general perception of unorthodox behavior that was pithily summed up by the essayist Yoshida Kenkō: "If you run through the street, saying that you imitate a lunatic, you are in fact a lunatic."[109] Yet, as with the priest threatening self-mutilation, there is perhaps more to it than this.

Let us note some other examples of sex organs being displayed by people in religious life. The tenth-century monk Zōga, for instance, seems to have used his genitals to make statements about carnal fixations, both his own and those of others. In one story we find that his mentor considered him mad for walking around on a pilgrimage completely nude. Zōga's rationale was that he had given away his clothes in order to symbolize his abandonment of wealth and fame.[110] In another story, it appears that his penis had been the subject of some discussion among court females, yet Zōga regarded his natural endowment, and his impotence in old age, with equanimity. As he noted to a dowager empress: "Why did you insist on having me come? I can't think why. Was it because you'd heard that I've got a big you-know-what? It is bigger than other people's, certainly, but it's all wilted and floppy now, like a bit of silk."[111] A second example involves disciples of Ippen (1239–1289), who in the *Tengū zōshi* (The Goblin Scroll) are criticized for a variety of behaviors. There is some suggestion that female followers enjoyed same-sex relationships, and clear comment that male and female followers alike walked around exposing their genitals to all and sundry.[112] Ippen himself is depicted dispensing his urine into a bamboo tube, reverently held in place by two women seeking this "holy water" as a panacea medicine.[113] Like Zōga, perhaps, Ippen and his followers made conscious ideological comments about body, society, and values.

Thus the scene of the priest displaying and manipulating his erect penis in the *Scroll of Gross Afflictions* may not be any odder than the behavior of religious people that is otherwise attested. Yet we might also concede that those witnessing the display might nevertheless have their own opinions on the matter, and might feel that his state of mind was sufficiently different from the norm that it could be regarded as an affliction. Still, the obvious element of display here leads us to another topic, that of affliction and behavior as spectacles in themselves.

The Spectacle of Afflictions

From at least the Heian era we find evidence that the misfortune of others could be a source of humor, an unusual condition be an object of fascination, or physical impairment be an entertaining spectacle (*misemono*).[114] One early example of this is the "dwarf dance" (*hikiudo mai*) included among other dances in the *Shinsarugaku ki*.[115] The noted aristocratic author Sei Shōnagon describes the time when she and her acquaintances heard of a man's devastating loss of his possessions in a fire. Unable to control their mirth, they conveyed the hilarity of the situation to others.[116] The priest Zenchin's large, discolored, wormy nose featured in *Uji shūi monogatari* could be a source of humor.[117] The diarrhea-induced agonies of Fukutomi likewise provided amusement.[118] In an incident not related to humans, a fascination with the unusual prompted the dispatch of a nine-legged horse (five legs in the front, and four legs in the back) across the country from Awaji province to Kamakura to be inspected by Minamoto Yoritomo, the founder of the Kamakura bakufu. Repelled by the oddness, Yoritomo ordered it sent to the farthest extremity, Sotohama in Mutsu province.[119] In a similar vein we have a vignette about the courtier Hino Suketomo (1290–1332), who found pleasure observing a deformed "crowd of cripples." He found them "unique oddities" worth preserving, but before long "he found them ugly and repulsive." Upon returning home he "realized that his recent fondness for potted plants and the pleasure that he had taken especially in finding curiously twisted specimens was of the same order as his interest in the cripples," and so dug them up and threw them away.[120]

Some scenes in the *Scrolls of Afflictions* underscore this fascination with the different, and suggest a spectrum of both afflictions (congenital, acquired later in life, treatable, or temporary) and responses (sympathy, amusement, or repulsion). The woman watching the man shaving his pubic area (A10) in order to get rid of crab lice seems to find the situation amusing. The attractive woman suffering from halitosis (A13) provided amusement: "Men who caught sight of her were completely smitten; but her breath was so foul that those who drew near quickly ran away holding their noses. Even when she was just in the home those who were near her found the stench unbearable," and those depicted near her appear to be tittering while covering their noses. Situations involving physical difference could also prove fascinating. The man who was alleged to have two anuses (A9, but more likely had grossly swollen hemorrhoids) from which he defecated, the man depicted with no mouth, an unlikely occurrence, it must be said), and the man who vomited excrement (A5, most likely suffering from an intestinal obstruction rather than an imperforate anus), were obvious oddities. The scene of a man receiving treatment for an eye problem (A7) reveals rapt onlookers watching as blood pours into a bowl held by a bemused young lady, and the fact that he might lose his sight (which he did) may have added to the fascination. The women who are in the presence of a man with a nervous disorder (A3) are obviously amused by the fact that the pupils of his eyes "were always rolling around. It was just like the trembling and shuddering of someone who is naked in the severest cold."

Other conditions of the body also provided some fascination, but seem to have elicited concern (and perhaps some distaste) rather than outright amusement. An albino woman (A16) is an object of attention, and is obviously aware that people are

fascinated by her lack of pigmentation, but she does not seem to
be held up to ridicule: "From ancient times until the present this is
something that occasionally appears in the world." A man whose
ambulatory problems are so severe that he has to drag himself
around with wooden clogs attached to his hands rather than his
feet (G24), which may have been not at all uncommon,[121] seems
to be pitied more than targeted. Others with ambulatory problems
enjoyed greater mobility, if not a great deal of independence.
The *Scroll of Gross Afflictions* shows a hunchback priest being
pulled around in a "cripple-cart" by some children, with mixed
reactions on the faces of two bystanders (G29), though the use
of such an item may have been not unfamiliar: the *Nenchū gyōji
emaki* (Scroll of Annual Observances)[122] depicts a hunchback
in a cart being pulled by three children; and the sermon-ballad
Sanshō dayū features the use of a "cripple's dolly" for the
disabled Zushiō.[123] In another case those in contact with an
afflicted individual expressed some sympathy, even as they
found the behavior unsettling. One man depicted in the *Scroll of
Afflictions* (A14) suffered from narcolepsy, and was prone to fall
asleep "even when relaxing for the shortest time," for which he
was pitied, but nonetheless his presence "detracted from a social
gathering."

Responses could also be cruel, particularly when directed
at the physically impaired, or at people whose conditions
were apparently congenital. To understand this, we need do no
more than cite the following commentaries from the *Scroll of
Afflictions*. For the hunchback mendicant priest (A18):

> Recently in the capital there was a mendicant priest whose
> neck bone was frightful and whose hipbones were bent,
> and apart from rolling around his eyeballs he was unable
> to raise his head in any way, and who went walking around
> face down from dawn to dusk.

For the priest with spinal curvature (A12):

> There was a person who was bent and looked like the coil
> of a dragon. This was not the shape that the world at large

would like to see mingling with people, but with head bent down he would walk around the capital begging for food. Anyone who saw him would laugh and ridicule him.

For a dwarf (A17) the commentary notes:

A dwarf sometimes appeared and walked around the capital begging for food. Children would hang around him and laugh at him. Even though he would stare back at them angrily this would only make them laugh harder.

The condition of a body could also be a source of embarrassment or revulsion. The woman depicted with a facial macula (A15) in the *Scroll of Afflictions* reflected the former:

A woman had a macula on her face, and she lamented this from morning till night. A macula is untreatable and something which occurs on people's bodies, but in places where it can't be seen it causes no distress. When it occurs on the face, when associating with people where it is not in the least seemly or suitable to be sporting swellings and the like, then it is truly an affliction.

Repulsion is attested in such examples as the priest who had such a hideously swollen face that he refused to show himself in public;[124] that of Tokugawa Ieyasu who was so discomfited by the syphilis-ravaged nose of his son Hideyasu that he refused to see him in audience;[125] and some people depicted in the thirteenth-century Saint Ippen scroll (*Ippen shōnin eden*) wear masks to cover the swellings on their face that are a mark of "leprosy."[126]

This brings us to the scene (G35) in the *Scroll of Gross Afflictions* that shows a woman giving something (money?) to a man who is literally on the social margins. He seems not to be simply a "beggar." His darkish skin contrasts strikingly with the light skin of the four other people in the scene; the face is swollen around the jaw, and the fingers of one hand seem swollen or disfigured. The facial swelling is reminiscent of the lepers depicted in the *Yūgyō shōnin engi e* (Illustrated Record of Saint Yūgyō).[127] We are also struck by the correlation between the scene and the pen-portrait provided by the Dutchman Reyer Gysbertsz:

> The Lepers, of whom there are many in Japan, are greatly abhorred; and nobody will easily be persuaded to enter into their huts or hovels, which are very miserable and merely slight things of straw put up to keep off the rain at nights, since they go abroad to beg by daylight.[128]

Leprosy (Hansen's disease) was one of the bodily conditions which in the medieval era was subsumed under the term *rai*. In general, that term was applied to conditions where there appears to have been ongoing bodily deformation and deterioration, where there was no particular cure. It struck randomly within the population, and no one knew with certainty what caused it. *Rai* was a terrifying condition.

As a social issue, *rai* elicited both negative and positive responses. The label of *rai* could be used to excoriate and stigmatize people in the most vicious and abusive terms.[129] In oaths and pledges where people would invite punishment should they break their commitment, not only do we find reference to an impressive array of deities and Buddhas who may inflict retribution, we also note that the signers agree to be visited by leprosy.[130] In general, those afflicted with *rai* were feared, shunned, driven from their communities, and marginalized as social outcasts.[131] They were sometimes subject to violent harassment, such as having their dwellings incinerated by gangs.[132] Leprosy was feared, as much for the stigma associated with it as for its clinical manifestations. The horror of leprosy was underscored in one thirteenth-century story where suspicion that a chief priest of a shrine had contracted *rai* was grounds for seeking his removal, and incentive for him to have physicians determine whether or not he had contracted *rai*.[133] However, in contrast to this negative perspective, we also note a response that saw the affliction in a positive light. The most notable example of this is found in the writings of Nichiren, whose religious impulse was to assuage people's fears and provide positive interpretation to suffering in order to foster a mind-set conducive to escape from the cycle of birth and rebirth.[134] In letters dealing with the problems of illness and karma, and in which the problem of *rai* is a central motif, Nichiren argued that *rai* illness is a sure sign that karmic sins had accumulated to a fullness, and were thus about to be expiated.[135] *Rai* sufferers were therefore not to be shunned, but embraced.

As a medical issue, *rai* elicited at least two responses. One was frustration, as suggested by an exasperated physician in 1284 who declared it untreatable.[136] The second response was to see it as a medical challenge requiring clinical investigation and treatment. The most prominent example here involved Kajiwara Shōzen, a Buddhist monk active at Ninshō's Gokurakuji temple in Kamakura. Gokurakuji operated under the religious impulse of the healing Mañjuśrī Buddha,[137] and provided extensive social welfare services. It contained hospital facilities, clinics, a dedicated *rai* clinic, and dispensaries, and treated sick horses as well as people. As a result of his clinical exposure to *rai*, Shōzen included in his *Ton'ishō* the first specialized study of this complex phenomenon. *Rai* came in at least twelve variations; some were curable and some were not; and it was interpreted through different disease etiologies, one of which was the concept of karmic illness.[138]

Shōzen and other physicians appear to have been well aware that perceptions of *rai* and of being labeled as afflicted with karmic illness could be socially disadvantageous; accordingly, they made assiduous efforts to determine whether an illness was or was not *rai*, and if it was whether or not it was karmic in nature. Shōzen determined that only four (later three) of the twelve varieties of *rai* were karmic in nature. In the fourteenth-century *Gotai shinbun shū*, we come across references to a wind-warm disease that is *not raibyō*; and to a white-hot wind that is *not* a karmic disease (*gōbyō*). The appearance of snake sores (*hebikasa*) on feet, hands or nose, which are itchy and cannot be treated with moxibustion, were telltale indicators that "leprosy" (*rai*) has been contracted. [139] Another fourteenth-century source, the pharmacist's handbook titled *Iyaku chōzai koshō* (An Old Work on Compounding Medicines), notes a treatment for horrible sores that have not healed in ten years and which resemble *rai*. [140]

In short, *rai* leprosy elicited multiple responses. One of the visible outcomes of *rai* leprosy was that sufferers often became marginal and impoverished beggars. The label "leper *rai* sufferer" was a powerful one that could be applied capriciously, and equally capriciously not applied when as a clinical matter it could have been. As the last medical example above suggests, we must wonder what skin condition, and at what stage and after how long, might be considered sufficiently bad as to require social distancing. [141] Ten years is, after all, a long time for *any* skin condition to last. Yet, it only "resembled" *rai*.

Indeed, unblemished skin was probably quite rare in medieval Japan, and dermatological problems and ailments were a common sight. Diaries mention such things as: [142] snake-eye whitlow, inflammations caused by lacquer poisoning, fever-related rash associated with catching a cold, ringworm, pemphigus, cut or scratch, white abscesses on the tongue, folliculitis, syphilitic chancres, collapsed nose due to syphilis, genital ulcers, and combinations of genital ulcers with syphilitic chancres. Contemporary dictionaries [143] list such terms as: whitlow on the hand; inflamed and pustulent fingertip; pustulent and swollen carbuncle on fatty parts of the body, such as back and buttocks; non-itching, non-painful swelling; pus; boils; blackening of facial skin; scabs; scars from boils; smallpox; heat rash; weeping then scabby eczemic skin rash associated with fever; a type of dermatitis caused by a suppurative germ; eczemic problem in winter caused by severe cold and excessive perspiration where skin becomes inflamed and very itchy; dry cracked skin; pimple or boil caused by insect bite; pimples; itchy nose; scars; face moles; gum inflammation; cold sores on lips; catfish skin (scrofula), with brownish ash-colored blotches on neck and skin; eczemic forehead and cheeks; mole or birthmark;

a type of wart; warts and dangling warts; hard boils; green-black bruise or purpling of skin due to cold; hard and lumpy skin on foot, finger or palm, where the surface keratin hardens, producing pea-like shapes; shingles-like small boils; head sores; contagious rash on the head; and scabby eruption on the vulva. A late sixteenth-century handbook lists, under "unclean things," "food server with skin-diseased arms"; while under "disgusting things" we find "drool, spitting phlegm, human nature, bloody pus, boils, and leper's vomit."[144]

However, if we look once again at the visual record, we see any number of scenes where those with skin afflictions, far from being avoided, are tended by those around them. One scene from the *Kokawadera engi* (Illustrated Record of Kokawa Temple) depicts a woman suffering a terrible skin affliction, with red blotches all over the body, but in a "sick room" attended by several women who are trying to cure this "difficult affliction."[145] Several scenes in the *Scroll of Gross Afflictions* portray people, most likely family members, providing care to those whose skin or features are disfigured by such things as: a scaly skin disease (G5, hives or pustules?); a woman with eruptions on the skin (G11); another woman, possibly with measles or smallpox (G12); a woman with abscesses on her back (G30); the woman with elephentiasis of the leg (G26); a child with what might be measles or smallpox, being cradled by a woman (G31); and a woman with a repulsively disfiguring nose tumor (G33). Thus, afflictions whose symptoms appeared on the surface of the body were not so unfamiliar or repellent that the sick were automatically shunned; rather, they were tended.

Afflictions and Care

Scholarly comments about how people cared for others are few and far between, and tend to emphasize instances which highlight exclusion and lack of caregiving, as in the case of a woman who was abandoned on a river bank when her illness was far advanced.[146] More generally, the apparent prevalence of lepers and beggars raises some significant social issues. In illustrated scrolls we encounter beggars who are bereft of all but the charity of some religious folk, are poorly dressed, poorly fed, eking out a miserable existence, and generally suffering alone when sick. The Korean traveler Song Hŭigyŏng took special note in 1420 of the large numbers of beggars and sick on the roadside between Hyōgo and Kyoto.[147] The vulnerability of such people is attested by the priest Eishun, who wrote that because of a recent dramatic increase in the number of wolves, the hungry animals ate not only the temple deer, but also the ill among the beggars around the temple.[148] Indisputably, some in society fared badly.

Yet, it is important to recall that, just as the response to affliction was not monolithic or unnuanced, neither was the provision of care. We have considerable evidence that the afflicted did receive hospice attention. It also seems that the instinct of family members (and those in a close community) was to nurse the afflicted and to make efforts to acquire medicines and medical treatment, rather than to shun or abandon them. Indeed, we might make the broader point that, with some clear exceptions, the ailing were not left alone to fend for themselves, but remained within their immediate social community.

While depictions of care and hospice in visual material are infrequent, they are prominent in the *Scroll of Afflictions*. One example is the portrayal of a sick and vomiting person being tended to (set off by a corpse lying under the eaves of a house), which we find in the *Kasuga gongen genki e* (The Miracles of the Kasuga Deity).[149] This is not to suggest simply that we have scenes of people receiving treatment: an infant, held by a woman, being given what appears to be acupuncture treatment by a much older lady (G20); a man with an eye problem being treated by a woman (G6); a woman being given what appears to be moxa treatment in order to collapse a swelling on the back (G14). Rather, we have scenes of people being tended and nursed, as with the scene from the *Scroll of Afflictions* noted earlier of the woman suffering *kakuran*, which shows her being tended by a woman, while another woman prepares food, and children scamper about (A11).

The *Scroll of Gross Afflictions* gives even more prominence to caregiving. One scene (G13) depicts an entire family in various stages of health: a prone and emaciated male lies on a mat half-covered by a sheet or blanket; a thin woman sits on the floor with a bowl of liquid in her hand, close by another woman resting her head on a container; a fleshly and corpulent young woman rests half-covered by a blanket; a wrinkled and aged-looking male sits in conversation with a woman cooking food, whose attention is being sought by a naked infant. Other scenes are equally illustrative. That of a woman suffering what might be an ovarian cyst (G4) is heart-rending: naked and emaciated, she is feebly supporting herself while two streams of liquid pour out from her grossly distended abdominal region into a large metal bowl. But she is not alone; she is tended by three women, one of whom is trying to support her with both hands on one arm, while one of the others is weeping. In another scene (G11), a woman covered by blankets is attended by three people, one of whom appears to be feeling the temperature of her forehead. In another scene (G12), a woman with measles or smallpox (?) is being tended by a man and by a woman who is holding her arm, while another woman is preparing to offer the patient some liquid from a bowl.

These visual sources provide us with snapshots of "care," and allow us to infer that care may have been given for various periods of time. Other sources confirm that the provision of care and medicine to the afflicted was commonplace. Let us look first at the example of the wife of Yamashina Tokitsugu (1507–1579), and then at some more general examples that appear in the diary of his son Tokitsune.

In 1566, Tokitsugu's wife Minami Mukai was laid low by an attack of malaria that took just over nine weeks to run its course.[150] Tokitsugu's forty-one or so diary entries (including almost daily during the eighth month) on Minami Mukai's condition during this period attest that she received continuous care. Indeed, the meticulously careful description itself reflects great care. No doubt the observations of family members were passed on to her attending physician in order to assist his diagnoses and prognostications. Thus, we find references to the onset of an attack, a general note that she had a temperature throughout the day, and that an attack of malaria or the shivering commenced halfway through the night. More often than not, references were rather specific; precisely the time when an attack occurred, the frequency of the episodes, and when they receded. We also find general comments on her condition: running a temperature all day or all night; having a headache; that the attack might be less severe than the previous one, or a light one; that there was no attack "this evening" or during the day; that she was having multiple or single attacks of diarrhea, or was vomiting; that she might be in great pain; that she might be semiconscious and unable to eat; that she might be feeling better and eating again.

We also have information on Minami Mukai's medication. The diary lists the prescriptions from the doctor; occasions when other crude drugs were added to the original prescription; ingredients that were sent from the doctor; and occasions upon which the doctor was going to be away for a few days and so sent a note regarding medicines to which the family was to refer during his absence. The diary also enumerates what items were compounded personally by Tokitsugu for his wife; whether or not the medicines were administered as they had been the previous day; and whether recourse might be had to a reputedly potent ingredient, such as charred cuckoo. Of course there is also record of when the doctor came to examine the patient (usually by pulse diagnosis) and discuss her condition with Tokitsugu. Overall, while we have only minimal reference to which people or how many people were in attendance on her, the information that we do have makes it clear that Minami Mukai was surrounded by people who were prepared to tend to her (and when necessary take time away from their public duties) on an ongoing basis, night and day, for an extended period of time.

When we turn to Tokitsune's diary we readily find that concern for people's medical needs was not restricted to learned professionals like the Yamashina, but was a common phenomenon. People evidently kept detailed records of their condition: a woman's general illness record; the record kept by a man for his cough; a woman's prepartum illness record (*sanzen shorō mokuroku*); and the illness record of a woman who had suffered a miscarriage.[151] They also paid attention to their diet while ill, using lists of permissible and contraindicated foods when afflicted by such things as blocked bladders, phlegm, and indigestion.[152]

It is also clear by this time that physicians themselves were keeping records of illness and treatment, which encompassed both information on the treatment they provided, and on medical matters in the community more broadly (these two elements were not, in practice, too separate). Concern for the ill was shared not just by the immediate family, but also by friends, neighbors, and sometimes by total strangers. In one example, an old nun fell ill during a visit to Kyoto and was taken in and cared for by the rice merchant Mago Saemonnosuke and his family for three weeks until she was well enough to return home. They sought Tokitsune's professional advice, bought medicine for her, fed and housed her, and had Tokitsune make house calls.[153] In another example, the wife of Shin Uemon visited Tokitsune to inform him that the woman next door was already overdue and having a difficult birth, and so they needed some medicine. Tokitsune provided some "quickening medicine" (*hayame gusuri*) to facilitate labor.[154] In another example, Kataoka Han Uemon no jō visited Tokitsune in order to obtain medicine for his older brother's wife as she was nearing birth. After the birth, Tokitsune was asked to provide medicine since the infant was regurgitating breast milk.[155] In another case, a woman in service with the wife of an acquaintance informed Tokitsune that a third woman had had a stillbirth, that the fetus was expelled the previous day, but that she was still suffering. Tokitsune prescribed medicine. He learned the following day that while her delirium had been successfully treated and her urinary and bowel movements restored, she still had a bloated feeling. So Tokitsune prescribed medicine for that, and also for her nausea. He learnt two days later that that she had largely recovered but was urinating profusely.[156] As a final example, the wife of one Sukehachi visited Tokitsune and requested that he come examine her husband. She visited the doctor every second day over the next ten days to obtain medicines to treat his ailments, which included bloody stools, a sore head, cramps, fever, coughing, and a sore stomach.[157]

Some Concluding Comments

The *Scrolls of Afflictions* are rich sources that provide great opportunity to engage a multiplicity of perspectives on such issues as perceptions of states of mind, attitudes towards the afflicted, responses to physical manifestations of some afflictions, humor at others' misfortunes. And, while the *Scrolls of Afflictions* do not appear to have been produced in order to serve as instructional materials for physicians, they do provide a more vivid view of afflictions and those who suffer them than we obtain from prose references or medical works. The *Scrolls of Afflictions* invite study beyond those areas that we have addressed here, but let us note three general points that we may take away from our engagement with these remarkable sources.

First, the *Scrolls of Afflictions* provide an extraordinary window into issues of affliction and society. A wide variety of afflictions are portrayed. Some afflictions are chronic, some acute, some appear congenital, some may be hereditary, some seem life-threatening, some seem uncomfortable but readily treatable. Virtually any part of the body that could be the site of an affliction is represented. Moreover, the *Scrolls of Afflictions* depict not just physical afflictions, but also address psychological afflictions, and do so through depictions of behavior that is the manifestation of those problems. Again, the *Scrolls of Afflictions* portray, with the notable exception of the warrior class, an inclusive range of social types: females and males; infant, adult and aged; lay and religious; aristocrats and commoners. And, while a variety of afflictions are presented in context, they enable us to see a range of responses to those different types of afflictions.

Second, relating to this multiplicity, in answer to a question such as "how did medieval Japanese regard those with afflictions?" it is evident that there was no one response. The actual responses do not invite ready categorization, nor do they provide the basis for an overarching, somewhat uniform conclusion to such a question. Accordingly, it is, and has been, more fruitful to examine the particularity of scenes in order to suggest nuances of interpretation rather than paint with an overly broad brush. We encounter thus a continuum of responses to bodies impacted by a variety of conditions, which bodies bore a variety of relationships to those in proximity to them, which proximity might simply be a physical nearness (or distance), a social and personal proximity, or a social proximity in which there is a psychological and emotional distance. That said, we do notice the frequency with which care and hospice treatment is provided to the afflicted.

Third, with respect to interpreting the images in the *Scrolls of Afflictions*, we have suggested that merely observing the images and providing a description (e.g., "priest about to sever his penis"), or providing a focus ("private parts") that seems not to be originally intended, is not the most productive approach. We have also suggested that when attempting interpretations there is danger of reading back into the medieval era interpretative standpoints that may be anomalous for that era, which of course affects any understanding of what the images are trying to depict or are trying to communicate (issues that we separate from that of the purpose of the production of the images in the first place). As an alternative, we have suggested that, while of course our effort at interpretation may be usefully informed by perspectives that post-date the era of production (a point beyond the trivial truth that we inevitably interpret from another time), it is important that research into these images is accompanied by engagement of other contemporaneous sources (diaries, documents, medical texts, and works of literature), and in particular pays heed to the religious and cultural common senses that were part of medieval society.

NOTES

Various versions of this essay have been presented at the University of Queensland; Washington University in St. Louis; UC Santa Barbara; Montana State University Bozeman; Gonzaga University; Waseda University; the Reischauer Institute at Harvard University; Ryukoku University; and AAS and WCAAS panels. I would particularly like to thank Mr. John Weik of the University of Queensland and Professors Nabeshima Naoki of Ryukoku University and Mark Unno of the University of Oregon for their thoughful feedback.

1   Hattori Toshirō, *Muromachi Azuchi Momoyama jidai igakushi no kenkyū*, pp. 297–302. The afflictions are, respectively, *atahara, hifū, chōsō, yōsa, fugurikaze, shirikasa, mushikasa, umikasa, abumikasa, okori kokochi, kusochi, tsuwari, denshibyō, dai akagari, hibi, gaibyō, hanadari*.

2   As two examples, we have the *Tamon'in nikki* (hereafter *TMN*) of the Kōfukuji physician and priest Eishun (1518–1596; diary 1534–1596) in Nara, and the *Tokitsune kyōki* (hereafter *Tokitsune*) diary of the aristocrat physician Yamashina Tokitsune (1543–1611, diary 1576–1606) detailing his activities in Kyoto and in Nakanoshima Honganji. For useful studies of the latter diary, see Hattori Toshirō, *Muromachi Azuchi Momoyama jidai igakushi no kenkyū*, pp. 104–121 and *Nihon igakushi kenkyū yowa*, pp. 88–103; Hanada Yūkichi, "*Tokitsune kyōki* kō."

3   *Tokitsune* Tenshō 19 (1591).8.15 (4.262); *Tokitsune* Tenshō 16 (1588).10.19, 20, 21, 27 (3.136, 3.137, 3.138); *Tokitsune* Bunroku 4 (1595).8.24 (6.338), six entries through 9.11 (6.346); *Tokitsune* Tenshō 19 (1591).6.14 (4.238); *Tokitsune* Tenshō 14 (1586).8.24 (2.173); *Tokitsune* Keichō 9 (1604).intercalary 8.14 (13.32); *Tokitsune* Tenshō 17 (1589).5.5, 5.6, 5.7, 5.8 (3.217, 3.218, 3.219); *Tokitsune* Tenshō 16 (1588).3.30 (3.47); *Tokitsune* Tenshō 14 (1586).7.24 (2.160), *Tokitsune*

Tenshō 14 (1586).8.29 (2.175), *Tokitsune* Tenshō 17 (1589).10.29
(3.304); *Tokitsune* Tenshō 16 (1588).4.20 (3.56); *TMN* Tenmon 12
(1543).4.9 (1.319) and *TMN* Tenshō 12 (1584).6.13 (3.353); *Tokitsune*
Tenshō 16 (1588).6.24 (3.96); *TMN* Tenshō 20 (1592).6.3, 6.4, 6.5, 6.6
(4.351); *TMN* Eiroku 12 (1569).6.2 (2.132); *TMN* Tenshō 9 (1581).9.9
(3.175), 10.1 (3.179); *Tokitsune* Bunroku 1 (1592).2.3 (5.19); *Tokitsune*
Tenshō 15 (1587).3.21 (2.253); *Tokitsune* Bunroku 4 (1595).12.26
(6.410); *Tokitsune* Tenshō 10 (1582).9.7 (1.296), *Tokitsune* Tenshō
11 (1583).9.25 (2.27–28); *Tokitsune* Bunroku 3 (1594).9.8 (6.141),
Tokitsune Keichō 2 (1597).12.24 (8.144–145), *Tokitsune* Keichō 5
(1600).6.15 (10.171); respectively, *Tokitsune* Tenshō 17 (1589).7.12
(3.148), *Tokitsune* Bunroku 3 (1594).6.29 (6.97); *Tokitsune* Tenshō
15 (1587).1.25 (2.229), *Tokitsune* Tenshō 18 (1590).9.14 (4.107);
Tokitsune Tenshō 15 (1587).4.18, 19, 24 (2.265, 266, 269); respectively,
Tokitsune Tenshō 16 (1588).intercalary 5.18 (3.81), *Tokitsune* Tenshō 17
(1589).7.3 (3.245), *Tokitsune* Tenshō 15 (1587).5.8 (2.274), *Tokitsune*
Keichō 9 (1604).intecalary 8.23 (13.37).

   4   *TMN* Eiroku 11 (1568).5.21 (2.72); *TMN* Tenmon 8 (1539).9.3
(1.230); *TMN* Eiroku 11 (1568).5.21 (2.73); *TMN* Tenmon 8 (1539).8.10
(1.221); *TMN* Eiroku 11 (1568).6.9 (2.76); *TMN* Tenmon 13 (1544).3.6
(1.348); *TMN* Eiroku 10 (1567).2.8 and 2.13 (2.7, 8); *TMN* Eiroku 11
(1568).6.9 (2.76); *TMN* Eiroku 12 (1569).3.1 (2.116).

   5   For the period under consideration here, the most relevant
Japanese works are Hattori Toshirō's *Heian jidai igakushi no
kenkyū*, *Kamakura jidai igakushi no kenkyū*, and *Muromachi Azuchi
Momoyama jidai igakushi no kenkyū*; Shinmura Taku's *Kodai iryō
kanjin sei no kenkyū*, *Nihon iryō shakaishi no kenkyū*, *Shi to yamai
to kango no shakai shi*, and *Oi to kantori no shakaishi*; Maruyama
Yumiko, *Nihon kodai no iryō seido*. For an English translation of an
early survey, see Fujikawa Yū, *Japanese Medicine*; for some brief
articles see Tatsukawa Shōji, "Diseases of Antiquity in Japan"; W. W.
Farris, "Diseases of the Premodern Period in Japan, 500–1600"; Ann
Bowman Jannetta, "Disease Ecologies in East Asia." On other aspects
of medieval illness, see Yokoi Kiyoshi, "Chūsei hito to *yamai*"; and
Fujiwara Yoshiaki, "Chūsei zenki no byōja to kyūzai," in his *Chūseiteki
shii to sono shakai*, pp. 111–143.

   6   See respectively Kuroda Hideo, "Chūsei minshū no hifu
kankaku to kyōfu," in his *Kyōkai no chūsei, shōchō no chūsei*, pp.

233–258; Kōno Katsuyuki, *Shōgaisha no chūsei*; Kanai Kiyomitsu, *Chūsei no raija to sabetsu*.

7   Katsuda Itaru, *Shishatachi no chūsei*; Tatsukawa Shōji, "Shishatachi no chūsei"; Suitō Makoto, *Chūsei no sōsō, bosei: sekitō o zōritsu suru koto*; Jacqueline Stone, "By the Power of One's Nembutsu: Deathbed Practices in Early Medieval Japan."

8   Hotate Michihisa, "Monogusa Tarō kara Sannen Netarō e," in his *Monogatari no chūsei—shinwa, setsuwa, minwa no rekishigaku*, pp. 259–287; William LaFleur, "Hungry Ghosts and Hungry People: Somaticity and Rationality in Medieval Japan."

9   C. H. Hsia, Ilza Veith, and Robert H. Geertsma, *The Essentials of Medicine in Ancient China and Japan, Yasuyori Tamba's Ishimpo*; Howard Levy and Akira Ishihara, trans., *The Tao of Sex: An Annotated Translation of the Twenty-eighth Section of the Essence of Medical Prescriptions (Ishinpō)*; G. Cameron Hurst, "Michinaga's Maladies"; Sakai Shizu, "A History of Opthalmology Before the Opening of Japan"; John F. Weik, "Majima Seigan and the Myōgen-in Tradition: The Origins of Opthalmology in Japan"; Mary Standlee, *The Great Pulse*; William Wayne Farris, *Population, Disease and Land in Japan, 600–900*.

10   See Andrew Edmund Goble, "Kajiwara Shōzen (1265–1337) and the Medical Silk Road: Chinese and Arabic Influences on Medieval Japanese Medicine"; "Medicine and New Knowledge in Medieval Japan: Kajiwara Shōzen (1266–1337) and the *Man'anpō*," (1), (2); "War and Injury: The Emergence of Wound Medicine in Medieval Japan."

11   Michele Marra, *Representations of Power*, p. 62, notes (my emphasis) "the **obsession** of medieval Japanese with death and defilement." On p. 63 we have a reference to pneumonia, which is a more precise identification than the sources allow; and on p. 102 the phrase "sores on the body" (*mi no kasa*) is identified as "syphilis," which is both more precise than the phrase suggests, and seems historically impossible.

12   The most complete reproduction (in black and white) of the *Yamai no sōshi* scroll, and the basis for the numbering of the scenes, is Ienaga Saburō, ed., *Jigoku zōshi, Gaki zōshi, Yamai no sōshi*, in the *Shinshū Nihon emakimono zenshū* series. Fewer scenes, but in a

superior color reproduction, may be found in Komatsu Shigemi, ed., *Gaki zōshi, Jigoku zōshi, Yamai no sōshi, Kuzōshi emaki*, in the Nihon no emaki taisei series.

Studies include Sano Midori, "*Yamai no sōshi* kenkyū" (1), *Kokka*, 1039 (1981), pp. 7–28, and (2), *Kokka*, 1040 (1981), pp. 7–23; these are also included as "*Yamai no sōshi* kenkyū," in Sano Midori, *Fūryū, zōkei, monogatari: Nihon bijutsu no kōzō to yōtai*, pp. 519–602; John Tadao Teramoto, "The *Yamai no Sōshi*: A Critical Reevaluation of Its Importance to Japanese Secular Painting of the Twelfth Century." An analysis of two segments cut from larger items and later pasted onto a decorative folding screen suggests that scenes depicting illness other than those known to us from the *Yamai no sōshi* or other extant scrolls were "in circulation." See Sano Midori, "Monogatari-e dankan nizu."

13   For the *Scroll of Gross Afflictions* (*Ihon yamai no sōshi*), I have relied primarily upon the excellent color reproductions from variant texts found in Nihon ishi gakkai, ed., *Zuroku Nihon iji bunka shiryō shūsei*, vol. 1, pp. 105–142. The numbering of the scenes is based upon the order of the black and white reproductions, referred to as the *Kishitsu emaki*, found in Kyoto Kokuritsu Hakubutsukan, comp., *Tan'yū Shukuzu*, pp. 79–93. The main difference between the order in these two sources is that scene 22 (man dancing around a corpse) is "out of order" in the *Zuroku Nihon iji bunka shiryō shūsei* reproduction, and is found on page 135.

For a fuller description of the scenes, see Teramoto, Appendix C (pp. 306–313); for a guide to the scenes in various texts see ibid., Appendix A, Table 2.1 (p. 292), Tables 5.1 through 5.5 (pp. 295–299).

14   See Hayashi Yoshirō, "Ihon *Yamai no sōshi* no denbon ni tsuite." For reference, following Hayashi, the scenes created in the earlier period, twelfth and thirteenth centuries, are numbers G1, G3, G4, G5 , G9, G13, G14, G15, G20, G22, G24, G25, G26, G27, G30, G33, G34; and those created in the later period, sixteenth and seventeenth centuries, are G2, G6, G7, G8, G10, G11, G12, G16, G17, G18, G19, G21, G23, G28, G29, G31, G32, G35, G36, G37.

15   However, the scenes do not reflect the more fanciful type of stories that were in circulation. As examples of those, we may note the story of a man's fatal encounter with lice (*Kokon chomonjū* 20.696, pp. 523–524); or the two reports of "oddities" (*Gaun nikkenroku batsuyū* Kanshō 1 [1460].6.15). The first report is of a fish discovered in the

Tone River in eastern Japan that had the face of a woman, the body of a carp, legs like a bird, and the mouth of a dragon. The second report was that the wife of a money-lender on Rokujō street in Kyoto was said to have had, from the hips down, the body of a snake.

16   The rich details and nuances of many of the scenes do not facilitate ready categorization, and categorization itself can obscure. Nonetheless, for one effort at categorization, see Sano, "Yamai no sōshi kenkyū," (2), p. 18, where the thirty-seven scenes are divided into three types: i/ illnesses—twenty-nine instances: G3, G4, G5, G6, G7, G9, G10, G11, G12, G13, G14, G15, G17, G18, G20, G23, G24, G25, G26, G27, G28, G29, G30, G31, G32, G33, G34, G35; ii/ insanity—six instances: G2, G8, G16, G21, G22, G36; iii/ old age—three instances: G1, G20, G37 (the listing of G20 here seems to be an error for G19, which on p.17 is placed in the old person category).

17   Fujinami Kōichi, "Emakimono shosai no yamai ni kansuru ishigaku teki kōsatsu"; Hattori Toshirō, *Heian jidai igakushi no kenkyū*, pp. 97–106; and his *"Yamai no zōshi* igakuteki kaisetsu"; Hayashi Yoshirō, "Ihon *Yamai no sōshi* no denbon ni tsuite."

18   See Teramoto, pp. 43–97, 216–219, 284–289.

19   Koyama Satoko, *"Yamai no sōshi* seisaku to Go-Shirakawa hōkō no shisō"; Nishiyama Ryōhei, *"Yamai no sōshi* no rekishigaku."

20   See Sano, *"Yamai no sōshi* kenkyū," (1), p. 12; Teramoto, "The Yamai no sōshi," p. 25.

21   See too John F. Weik, "Majima Seigan and the Myōgen-in Tradition: The Origins of Opthalmology in Japan," p. 4.

22   A useful starting point is Timothy Screech's *Sex and the Floating World*.

23   See *Ihon yamai no sōshi*, in *Zuroku Nihon iji bunka shiryō shūsei*, vol. 1, p. 132 (woman with vaginal discharge), and p. 133 (household scene, cloth over man's genitals).

24   See *Shinsen Yamai no sōshi, Zuroku Nihon iji bunka shiryō shūsei* edition. This text is also online at: www.library.tohoku.ac.jp/med/d-lib/zoushi/ks-1/flowers.html.

25   See *Shinsen yamai no sōshi, Kyōrin sōsho* edition, p. 63 (blood-swollen labia), p. 180 (a swelling protruding from the mouth of the vagina and extending farther than the clitoris). Part of another

scene, depicting intestinal worms emerging from a young woman's anus (p. 178), was also blanked out.

26   Sano, "*Yamai no sōshi* kenkyū," (2), p. 15.

27   Sano notes the depiction of the old woman with a horse bone in her vagina (G19) as an example of excessive sex drive, though she also lists it in the category of "old people." Teramoto views her as insane. Sano looks at the street scene (G36), selects the section where a woman is displaying her genitals, and characterizes the act as "exhibitionism." However, the scene of the priest dancing around and displaying his erect penis to a crowd (G2) is described as a scene of a "dancing priest," and is placed in the category of insanity.

28   Teramoto, p. 172.

29   One remarkable exception, describing a man accidentally drenching his wife (*nyōbō*) through a window, may be found in *Kokon chomonjū* 16.546 (*NKBT*, p. 429).

30   *Uji shūi monogatari* no. 143 (*NKBT*, pp. 337–339; D. E. Mills, *A Collection of Tales from Uji* [12/7], pp. 362–363): About the venerable Zōga's behavior when he visited the dowager empress from the Third Ward.

31   *Uji shūi monogatari* no.145 (*NKBT*, p. 341; Mills, [12/9], pp. 364–365): How a grain-abstaining holy man was shown up.

32   *Uji shūi monogatari* no. 34 (*NKBT*, pp. 121–122; Mills, [3/2], pp. 192–193): How the mistress of Fujiwara Major Counsellor Tadaie broke wind.

33   *Uji shūi monogatari* no. 76 (*NKBT*, pp. 182–183; Mills [5/7], p. 244): How a young woman ordered a calendar simple enough for her to read.

34   *Fukutomi zōshi*, in Komatsu Shigemi, ed., vol. 25 of *Nihon emaki taisei*; and, in Umezu Jirō and Okami Masao, eds., vol. 18 of *Nihon emakimono zenshū*. See also James Ulak, "Fukutomi zōshi: The Genesis and Transmutations of a Medieval Scatological Tale"; and Virginia Skord, "The King of Farts," in *Tales of Tears and Laughter*, pp. 157–167. For another story involving "that trusty medicine for innards in need of encouragement, ground morning-glory seeds," see Royall Tyler, *Japanese Tales*, no. 8, pp. 10–13.

35   Skord, "The King of Farts," p.164.

36   See Tyler, *Japanese Tales*, no. 7, p. 10.

37   *Uji shūi monogatari* no. 14 (*NKBT*, pp. 71–72; Mills, [1/14], pp. 150–151): How Kotōda was startled by his son-in-law.

38   Both of these stories appear in *Shasekishū*. 1: A wife daubs rice powder on her husband's privates, he goes off to meet his lover, and after they have had sex she reapplies her own rice powder. When the husband returns from the tryst the wife, wetting her finger and tasting the powder, notes that whereas there had been salt in her rice powder there was none in what was now applied to his body (*NKBT*, p. 493: 58; Robert E. Morrell, *Sand and Pebbles (Shasekishū): The Tales of Mujū Ichien, A Voice for Pluralism in Kamakura Buddhism*, pp. 209–210); 2: A husband paints a picture of an ox on the wife's privates, she meets her lover, the drawing gets smudged during their sex play, so the lover draws another. After her return the husband notes that the ox that he had painted had been lying down, but that the one she has now is standing up (*NKBT*, p. 493: 58; Morrell, *Sand and Pebbles*, p. 209).

39   *Kokon chomonjū* 16.549 (*NKBT*, pp. 431–433).

40   *Kokon chomonjū* 16.544 (*NKBT*, pp. 427–428). The fuller context is that the husband had, with delight, discovered that one of his wife's female servants was from Tsukushi (Kyushu), whose women were, he noted, reputed to have outstanding sex organs. His wife remarked, as we noted, that perhaps this might not be the case—men from his home province of Ise have a reputation for virility, yet she knew all too well that his own organ was unbelievably small and weak (*hito shirezu chiisaku yowai*).

41   *Kokon chomonjū* 16.548 (*NKBT*, p. 431).

42   Hitomi Tonomura, "Black Hair and Red Trousers," p. 149. The story is from the *Konjaku monogatari*, tale 26–2. As far as I know, this is also the earliest reference we have to male sex aids.

43   *Koshibagaki zōshi*, pp. 24, 48–50. The scroll is based upon a sex scandal involving an imperial shrine princess and a noted roué, which occurred in the year 976.

44   *Yōbutsu kurabe emaki*. The first such scroll is attributed to the priest Toba, and dates from the 1160s. See Hayashi Yoshikazu and Richard Lane, *Higa emaki Koshibagaki zōshi*, pp. 17–18.

45   See Gary Leupp, *Male Colors*, pp. 40–46; Shunroan Shujin (Watanabe Shin'ichirō), *Edo no seiai bunka—Hiyaku higu jiten*, pp.

155–159. The earliest reference to a dildo comes from the year 807.

46   *Unshū shōsoku* (*Meigō ōrai*) a letter of the fourth month, p. 522.

47   *Unshū shōsoku* undated letter, p. 544.

48   For the original wife, see *Shinsarugaku ki*, pp. 135–136; for the thirteenth daughter, pp. 144–145; for the husband of the fourteenth daughter, pp. 145–146; for the sixteenth daughter, pp. 146–147.

49   For more on this topic, see Janet R. Goodwin, *Selling Songs and Smiles: The Sex Trade in Heian and Kamakura Japan*. For the sixteenth daughter, see pp. 16–17.

50   For these, see *Ishinpō*, chap. 28; C. H. Hsia, et al., *The Essentials of Medicine*, pt. 2, p.177; and Ishihara and Levy, *The Tao of Sex*, pp. 48–49 (translating the positions as "the dragon turns over" and "the tiger's tread"). For genital vocabulary, see Hsia, et al., 2, p. 198, and p. 165; Ishihara and Levy, pp. 161–163.

51   This is also briefly discussed in Ivo Smits, "The Way of the Literati: Chinese Learning and Literary Practice in Mid-Heian Japan," p. 121.

52   *Gotai shinbun shū*, chap. 18, 92–B.

53   For information on Shōzen and his background, see Andrew Edmund Goble, "Medicine and New Knowledge in Medieval Japan"; and "Kaziwara Shōzen and the Medical Silk Road."

54   *Ton'ishō*, chap. 45 (Kagaku shoin edition 1986; p. 673, at section XXII, sheets 23, 24). Hereafter cited as *Ton'ishō*, chap. 45 (*KS*, 673; XXII–23, 24). I have used two texts of *Ton'ishō*, the Kagaku Shoin edition of 1986 (based on a text held by Naikaku Bunko), and a second, more legible, unpaginated Naikaku Bunko text (microfilm hard copy held in the Department of the History of Medicine, Oriental Medicine Research Center of the Kitasato Institute). Chapter references are to the latter, page citations to the former.

55   *Ton'ishō*, chap. 45 (*KS*, 673; XXII–24).

56   *Ton'ishō*, chap. 45 (*KS*, 678; XXII–41, 42).

57   *Ton'ishō*, chap. 45 (*KS*, 679; XXII–47).

58   A mid-fourteenth-century pharmacist's handbook notes a treatment for suddenly swollen and red testicles: see Shibata Shōji, ed., *Hōryūji shozō Iyaku chōzai koshō—hakken sareta 14 seiki no kusuri*,

pp. 38, 52. For a reference to the agonies of testicular affliction, see 1280.4.16 Ingō shojō (*KI*, 18:13926).

59   While the term *rinbyō* is these days most commonly applied to gonorrhea, in earlier times it referred to a wider range of genito-urinary disorders.

60   See Iwasaki Kae, *Shokunin uta awase*. Iwasaki nonetheless is drawn to the genitalia of the gambler, and remarks (caption to frontispiece) that "the depiction of the genitals in full view truly is one of the things that indicates the power of the *Shokunin uta awase* to fascinate our eyes."

61   See *Jigoku zōshi* in Komatsu Shigemi, ed., *Gaki zōshi, Jigoku zōshi, Yamai no sōshi, Kuzōshi emaki*, vol. 7 of *Nihon emaki taisei*; Ienaga Saburō, ed., *Jigoku zōshi, Gaki zōshi, Yamai no sōshi*, vol. 7 of *Nihon emakimono zenshū*.

62   See, for example, the nursing woman in the scene (A19) depicting the obese woman in the *Scroll of Afflictions*; the old woman being treated for an abscess on the back, with clothing on the upper body rolled down, appearing in the *Scroll of Gross Afflictions* (G14); the depiction of a breast-feeding mother in the *Kokawadera engi* (Komatsu Shigemi, ed., *Kokawadera engi*, p. 6); or a woman breast-feeding an infant, and another woman whose upper torso and breasts, and legs, are exposed as she washes clothes, which we see in the *Shigisan engi* scroll (Komatsu Shigemi, ed., *Shigisan engi*, pp. 99, 101). The commentator for this scroll feels it necessary to remark on the exposed torso and breasts.

63   See Helen Craig McCullough, *Ōkagami, The Great Mirror*, p. 170. Nakedness was not the only example of inappropriate behavior. She also threw gold dust over the screens at the guests. People "considered her action inappropriate and unwelcome, but they scrambled for the gold dust to keep up appearances."

64   See Teramoto, pp. 309–310.

65   *TMN* Tenshō 14 (1586).8.6 (4.35).

66   *TMN* Tenshō 20 (1592).12.8 (4.378). The author Eishun's reference is to the Hell of Excrement (*funsho jigoku*) which is depicted in the *Jigoku zōshi*: see Komatsu Shigemi, ed., *Gaki zōshi, Jigoku zōshi, Yamai no sōshi, Kuzōshi emaki*; Ienaga Saburō, ed., *Jigoku zōshi, Gaki zōshi, Yamai no sōshi*.

67   This may be an early example of the colloquial use of "*kaichō*," a term originally applied to the annual viewing of a secret image but later used to refer to genital exposure when a woman parts her thighs. We find one example in *Ukiyoburo* (*NKBT*, ed. Nakamura Michio), p. 160, when a woman slips in the bathhouse and exposes herself, her friend immediately saying "*o kaichō Nanmamida [namu Amida] butsu.*"

68   *Ton'ishō*, chap. 29 (*KS*, 456; XIII–145, 146); *Ton'ishō*, chap. 30 (*KS*, 462; XIV–12).

69   Heian sources define a hermaphrodite as a person who was female for the first fifteen days of a month, and male for the other fifteen days. See Hattori Toshirō, "*Yamai no zōshi* igakuteki kaisetsu."

70   For death from *kakuran*, see *Tokitsune* Tenshō 17 (1589).5.22 (3.225). For less severe food poisoning, see *TMN* Eiroku 12 (1569).6.2 (2:132): "Yesterday when I visited Seimei'in I had some noodles; I have had diarrhea all day; the others are all suffering from *kakuran*." The problem seems to have been a common one, for we see Eishun the year before instructing that: "for preventing stored *sōmen* noodles from becoming moldy and rotten, place one bunch of the flowers of the Star Anise (*Illicium anisatum*) tree on them:" *TMN* Eiroku 11 (1568).5.21 (2.72). As it happens, Japanese Star Anise is highly toxic if ingested, and can cause inflammation of the digestive organs, among other problems.

71   See Hotate Michihisa, *Chūsei no ai to jūzoku*, pp. 240–246. Hotate notes a story from the *Konjaku monogatari* (27–30), in which ten six-inch officials are emerging from an "odds basket" (*nuri gome*) and advancing across a pillow. He suggests two points. First, the fact that the little fellows were carrying sticks was intended to double the fear of the patient. We might also observe, however that sticks were at times considered to possess magical properties and were employed to drive off colds and pollution. Second, the heads of the little ones, some shaven and some with unkempt hair (the latter type of hairstyle considered, as a type, to belong to base people) are varied; they should be regarded as small gods (*kami*), but they might also be regarded as representing demons, the disease itself. Hotate is unsure how to interpret the wearing of paper clothes, the mixture of shaven pates and unkempt hair, and the brandishing of sticks. He suggests, tantalizingly, that there is a "hidden deeper meaning" in this picture. Also see Yokoi

Kiyoshi, *Mato to ena*, pp. 154–162, "Yume to utsutsu no *kohosshi* tachi."

72   Hosokawa Ryōichi, *Itsudatsu no Nihon chūsei: kyōki, tōsaku, ma no sekai*, pp. 13–55.

73   See Robert N. Huey, "*Sakuragawa*, Cherry River."

74   Margaret Childs, *Rethinking Sorrow*, in "The Three Monks," pp. 74–75, and in "The Seven Nuns," p. 98.

75   Childs, *Rethinking Sorrow*, pp. 100–101.

76   Margaret Childs, "Didacticism in Medieval Short Stories: *Hatsuse monogatari* and *Akimichi*," pp. 260–261.

77   *Gotai shinbun shū*, chap. 13, 51-A. See also Hattori Toshirō, *Muromachi Azushi Momoyama jidai igakushi no kenkyū*, p. 233.

78   *Ton'ishō*, chaps. 10, 11, 12 (*KS*, 191~237; VI–2~VII–68). For discussion on the issue, see, for example, *Ton'ishō*, chap. 10 (*KS*, 192, 193; VI–10~16).

79   See Sonja Arntzen, *Ikkyū and the Crazy Cloud Anthology*, pp. 175–177, citing the *Kyōunshū* no. 839 and prose introduction: "When Ikkyū was old he contracted the illness of diarrhea. He would recover and then contract it again, two or three times in succession. Everyone said 'it is dangerous.' But when affairs went against his heart, his vital vapors would escape. Yesterday, as chance would have it, he lost about a hundred sticks of ink that he had been saving. He searched but could not find them. As a result, his spirit was not happy, and the diarrhea threatened to start again. All the attendants turned pale."

80   See the diary of Fushimi no miya Sadafusa (1372–1456), *Kanmon gyoki* Ōei 32 (1425).8.17 (1.515), *Kanmon gyoki* Eikō 5 (1433).5.14 (2.111).

81   *Kanmon gyoki* Ōei 32 (1425).3.20 (1.483): "Recently in and around the capital abductors of children are very active, taking them in a variety of ways; it is said that three sick people are responsible, (bakufu official) Inoo Kaga, his wife and another woman. I am unsure whether it is true or not"; 3.22 (1.483): "It has been reported that two children were taken in the lower part of the city, one is returned." *Kanmon gyoki* Eikō 5 (1433).4.4 (2.103) records that "recently children were being abducted in and around the capital from all levels of society. Some were returned, and some were killed. It is rumored that it is because

they are used as an ingredient for medicine for hideous sores (*akusō*)."
See also, Shinmura Taku, *Shi to yamai to kango no shakaishi*, pp.
247–248.

82   *TMN* Tenshō 12 (1584).6.24 (3.357).

83   See the 1460.3.16 passage from the *Hekizan nichiroku* quoted
in H. Paul Varley, *The Ōnin War*, p. 117.

84   *TMN* Tenmon 13 (1544).7.28 (1.356).

85   See Seta Katsuya, "Ichi seinen kizoku no ijō shi—chichi
Yamashina Tokikuni no nikki kara," in his *Rakuchū rakugai no
gunzō—ushinawareta chūsei Kyoto e*, pp. 323–341, dealing with the
impact on Yamashina Tokikuni of the death of his nineteen-year-old
son Sadatoki, murdered by robbers in 1494.

86   *Kanemi kyōki* Tenshō 8 (1580).intercalary 3. 11 (1:209).

87   Jon Carter Covell, *Untangling Zen's Red Thread*, p. 128.

88   Kangen 2 (1244) 10.14 Kugyō sadamebumi (*KI*, 9:6391)
refers to the suicide which occurred in the Shōji era, 1199–1200. We
learn of this death because it prompted a discussion of the polluting
aspects of blood being shed on shrine precincts.

89   *Azuma kagami* Kenchō 6 (1254).5.9.

90   *Kanchūki* Kōan 3 (1284).7.10, 12. A question arose of whether
this was defiling, with the decision that it was not. A similar case from
1280 is also cited in this entry.

91   *Kanmon gyoki* Ōei 31 (1425).8.15 (1.514). This suicide was
noted as being an unusual occurrence.

92   *Taiheiki* (*NKBT*), chap. 33, 3:250–251.

93   Childs, *Rethinking Sorrow*, "The Seven Nuns," pp. 123ff.

94   See the *Kyōunshū* prose introduction to poems nos. 100–108:
"In the autumn of the year 1447, there was a monk at Daitokuji who for
no reason committed suicide. Scandal-loving monks made slanderous
reports to the officials. So, in connection with this calamity, five or
seven of my fellow monks were imprisoned." (Arntzen, *Ikkyū and the
Crazy Cloud Anthology*, p. 103).

95   See Hosokawa Ryōichi, *Itsudatsu no Nihon chūsei: kyōki,
ōsaku, ma no sekai*, pp. 69–75. The depth of such bonds is also
illustrated (though with less tragic results) in the case of Konoe Iehira

(1282–1324), as noted in the *Masu Kagami*: see *Jinnō shōtōki, Masu kagami* (*NKBT*), pp. 425–426; and George W. Perkins, *The Clear Mirror: A Chronicle of the Japanese Court During the Kamakura Period (1185–1333)*, p. 173.

96   *TMN* Tenshō 13 (1585).4.25 (3.416), observing that the person cut his belly on the fourteenth and died on the sixteenth.

97   *TMN* Bunroku 2 (1593).4.16 (4.393–394).

98   Michael Cooper, *They Came to Japan*, p. 323.

99   *TMN* Tenshō 18 (1590).7.2 (4.244).

100   *TMN* Tenmon 13 (1544).6.6 (1.352).

101   *TMN* Tenshō 10 (1582).2.11 (3.202).

102   *TMN* Tenshō 19 (1591).5.10 (4.348).

103   *TMN* Tenshō 19 (1591).6.22, 25, 7.4, 7.23 (4.301, 302, 303, 305). For the broader context of these events, see Kawauchi Masayoshi, "Toyotomi seikenka no toshi Nara ni okotta ichi jiken—*Narakashi, kin shōnin jiken, Nara kashi*.

104   Francois Caron and Joost Schouten, *A True Description of the Mighty Kingdoms of Japan and Siam*, pp. 38–39.

105   On Myōe's religiously motivated self-mutilation, cutting off his ear, see Ryuichi Abe, "Swords, Words and Deformity: On Myōe's Eccentricity."

106   *Kokon chomonjū* 16:547 (*NKBT*, pp. 429–431). In this story the philandering husband only pretended to cut off his penis. In a piece of legerdemain, he substituted the head and neck of a tortoise for his penis, and amid the blood and rough resemblance, convinced his wife that he was more attached to her than to his carnal passions.

107   Not unexpectedly we find the term in the *Tettsui den*, op cit., p. 430. The characters 磨裸 ("grind" and "naked") are glossed as *mara* and used as a rebus for the characters 麻良 or 魔羅 which are more commonly used for "dick." The ubiquity of the term *mara* is attested in medical texts also. The condition of swollen penis (陽腫) is glossed as *mara harete* in the priest Yūrin's medical work, the *Fukudenpō* (traditionally dated to the 1360s): *Fukudenpō*, chap. 10 (*KS*, p. 846).

108   Lust was also seen as the cause of horrible bodily conditions. Eishun notes the case of a shrine servant who died the year after

contracting the ailment "vomiting blood" (*toketsu*), caused by an unquenchable lust for women. He and his wife were driven out of their existing quarters and lodged elsewhere in the shrine precincts; before they could move however, he "vomited blood, and, his whole body seeping blood, he died." *TMN* Tenmon 12 (1543).5.3 (1.327).

109 Donald Keene, trans., *Essays in Idleness: The Tsurezuregusa of Kenkō*, no. 85, at p.72.

110 Michele Marra, *The Aesthetics of Discontent: Politics and Reclusion in Medieval Japanese Literature*, p. 61.

111 *Uji shūi monogatari* no. 143 (*NKBT*, pp. 337–339; Mills, [12/7], pp. 362–363, regarding the venerable Zōga's behavior when he visited the dowager empress from the Third Ward).

112 *Tengu zōshi*, text pp. 56–57 (sheet 18 of original), p. 168 for printed version of text: "*Dannyōkon wo kakusu koto naku, tabemono wo tsukami kui, futō no konomu arisama.*" See also Kuroda Hideo, "*Tengu zōshi* ni okeru Ippen,"in *Sugata to shigusa no chūseishi*, pp. 15–29.

113 *Tengu zōshi*, op cit., text pp. 58–59 (sheet 19 of original): "*yorozu no yamai no kusuri nite sōrō.*" See p.168 for printed version of text. See also Yokoi Kiyoshi, "Nyō kou hitobito to kawaramono no koto," in his *Mato to ena*, pp. 175–182. For a sense of Ippen as a healer, see Sunagawa Hiroshi, "Ishō toshite no Ippen."

114 See Yokota Noriko, "Kinsei toshi shakai to shōgaisha—misemono wo megutte."

115 See *Shinsarugaku ki*, p. 134.

116 *Makura no sōshi*, Ivan Morris, trans., *The Pillow Book of Sei Shōnagon*, no. 168 (pp. 250–251), "One day I was in the apartment."

117 Zenchin's nose was five to six inches long, reddish purple with a pimply surface like a mandarin orange. It was also infested with white worms that could only be removed (temporarily) by boiling the nose in water, treading on it, and extracting them from the pores with tweezers. But it could be a source of humor, as when it splashed down into Zenchin's bowl of rice gruel: *Uji shūi monogatari* no. 27 (*NKBT*, pp. 102–106; Mills, [2/7], pp. 172–175): About the priest with the long nose.

118 See Virginia Skord, "The King of Farts," pp. 162–164.

119 *Azuma kagami* Kenkyū 4 (1193).7.24.

120 See Donald Keene, trans., *Essays in Idleness* no. 154 (pp. 136–137). For further on Suketomo, see Andrew Edmund Goble, *Kenmu: Go-Daigo's Revolution*, pp. 42–43, 83.

121 See *Ippen shōnin eden* (*Nihon no emaki* edition), p. 196, for the scene at Horikawa.

122 *Nenchū gyōji emaki*, in the Takatsukasa text, pp. 109ff., roll 13, "*Saiin onharai no gyoretsu nado.*"

123 See Susan Matisoff, "Holy Horrors," p. 250. Zushiō had become crippled as a result of being enclosed in a basket. On one occasion, since he was unable to stand, a group of children loaded him onto a flat wooden cart (*tsuchi guruma*) and pulled him to his destination.

124 For the story of Gyōga, whose facial features were so radically transformed by progressive swellings that he did not show himself to other priests, see Donald Keene, trans., *Essays*, no. 42 (p. 38).

125 Tatsukawa Shōji, *Nihonjin no byōreki*, pp. 56–60.

126 *Ippen shōnin eden*; *Ippen hijiri e*. See also Shinmura Taku, "Yamai no zuzō hyōgen."

127 *Yūgyō shōnin engi e*, 2d scroll, sect. 5, color pl. 3.

128 Reyer Gysbertsz, "History of the Martyrs who have been killed, or endured fearful and insufferable torments, for the sake of the Roman Catholic Religion in Japan," in Caron and Schouten, *A True Description of the Mighty Kingdoms of Japan and Siam*, pp. 73–88, at p. 78. Also quoted in Michael Cooper, *They Came to Japan*, p. 54. By the time that Gysbertz was writing, the terms "beggar" and "leper" ("*rai* sufferer, *raija*") were interchangeable. Kanai Kiyomitsu, *Chūsei no raija to sabetsu*, pp. 28–29.

129 Ikkyū's vituperative comments about a rival give a sense of the viciousness with which charges or characterizations of leprosy could be leveled. In his *Jikaishū*, Ikkyū describes the death of Sōki, heir of Yōsō, whom Ikkyū detested: Chōroku 2 (1458).3.23.

> He became ill, but it was not an ordinary illness. Little by little his hair and eyebrows fell out, and from the sixth day of the fifth moon, his body began rotting from the hips down. Later pus oozed out from his throat and

blood poured forth so that from the sixth moon he was continually vomiting. His disciples did not recognize leprosy, but when the priests inside the temple and their servants began talking with people outside, some said "This is leprosy." On the twenty-seventh day of the sixth moon, he died and his disciples burned his body to the rear of Daiyu-an (Daitokuji subtemple). Such was against the law since this was an imperial temple (Covell, *Untangling Zen's Red Thread*, pp. 140–141).

For a story of visiting leprosy upon a person who is disliked, see Susan Matisoff, "Holy Horrors," at p. 252.

130 See Kuroda Hideo, *Kyōkai no chūsei, shōchō no chūsei*, pp. 233–258.

131 For some issues here, in addition to the studies of Kanai Kiyomitsu and Fujimoto cited earlier, see Fujino Yutaka, ed., *Rekishi no naka no "raija"*; Kuroda Hideo, "Chūsei minshū no hifu kankaku to kyōfu," in *Kyōkai no chūsei, shōchō no chūsei*, pp. 233–258; Yokota Noriko, "*Monoyoshi* kō—kinsei Kyoto no raija ni tsuite"; and Suzuki Noriko, "Shodai Manase Dōsan no rai igaku."

132 *TMN* Eiroku 10 (1567).8.16 (2.28). For another instance of lodgings near the temple being torched, see *TMN* Eiroku 11 (1568).9.3 (2.87).

133 See *Kokon chomonjū* (*NKBT* text, pp. 240–241. *KT,* pp. 164–165). The *NKBT* text declares that the affliction was determined to be *hakudan* "white sores," a type of ringworm, and not *rai*. The *KT* text notes the affliction being determined was "white *rai*." These two different readings of the term provide us with two diagnoses and opposite social implications. In any event, the point is the concern exhibited by a person who thought that he had contracted "*raibyō*."

134 See Andrew Edmund Goble, "Nichiren Calming Karma: Fear, Sickness and Lotus Unto Death."

135 See, for example, Bun'ei 1 (1264).12.13 Nichiren shojō (*KI*, 12:9194; translated in The Gosho Translation Committee, ed., *The Writings of Nichiren Daishōnin*, no. 10, Encouragement to a Sick Person); [Bun'ei 12 (1275).2?] Nichiren shojō (*KI*, 15:11810; *The Writings of Nichiren Daishōnin*, no. 129, On Prolonging One's Lifespan); [Kenji 1 (1275)].11.3 Nichiren shojō (*KI*, 16:12102; *The*

Writings of Nichiren Daishōnin, no. 76, On Curing Karmic Disease);
Kōan 1 (1278).6.26 Nichiren shojō (*KI*, 17:13095; *The Writings of
Nichiren Daishōnin*, no. 120, The Two Kinds of Illness).

136 Koremune Tomotoshi, in his *Idanshō*. See Minobe Shigekatsu,
ed., *Idanshō*, pp. 190–192.

137 See David Quinter, "The Shingon Ritsu School and the
Mañjuśrī Cult in the Kamakura Period," particularly chaps. 1, 2,
and 5.

138 *Ton'ishō*, chap. 34 (*KS*, 516–534, XVI–1~72).

139 *Gotai shinbun shū*, respectively, chap. 3, 13-A; chap. 12,
47-B; chap. 12, 48-A.

140 Shibata Shōji, ed., *Hōryūji shozō Iyaku chōzai koshō*, (51) at
pp. 36, 51.

141 Didactic literature, which no doubt had a strong role in
influencing perceptions, provides such portraits as:

> "Her hair was standing up, extremely dishevelled like that
> of a demon. Her face, once so refined, was blue in some
> places and yellow in others. Her legs had lost their former
> color and were filthy. Her robes were covered here and
> there with blood, and smelled unbearably repulsive." See
> Rajyashree Pandey, "Women, Sexuality and Enlightenment:
> *Kankyō no tomo*," p. 349.

It is of some note that the author of this story, Keisei, was quite
interested in bodily afflictions, having suffered from a crooked spine
as a result of a childhood accident, and was influenced by the Tendai
notion that contemplation of pollution (e.g., rotting corpses) was an aid
to enlightenment: see Donald Keene, *Seeds in the Heart*, pp. 768–770.
For an engagement of issues related to that latter topic, see Gail Chin,
"The Gender of Buddhist Truth: The Female Corpse in a Group of
Buddhist Paintings"; Fusae Kanda, "Behind the Sensationalism:
Images of a Decaying Corpse in Japanese Buddhist Art."

142 *TMN* Tenshō 12 (1584).6.6 (3.351), *(jaganchō)*; *TMN* Tenmon
13 (1544).3.6 (1.348); *Tokitsune* Tenshō 14 (1586).5.28 (2.141),
(kasahoroshi); *Tokitsune* Tenshō 17 (1589).7.20 (3.254), *(sensō,
senigasa)*; *Tokitsune* Tenshō 16 (1588).9.21 (3.126), *(tobihi)*; *Tokitsune*
Tenshō 14 (1586).10.4 (2.188), *(ayamachi)*; *Tokitsune* Tenshō 17
(1589).5.21 (3.225), *(shita shitogi)*; *Tokitsune* Tenshō 17 (1589).6.20

(3.239), (*natsubushi*); *TMN* Eiroku 12 (1569).5.13 (2.127), (*yokone*); *TMN* Tenshō 3 (1575).3.15 (2.360), 3.28 (2.362), (*rayaku*); *Tokitsune* Tenshō 19 (1591).12.8 (4.309); *Tokitsune* Bunroku 4 (1595).12.26 (6.410), (*rayaku*), (*karakasa, tōkasa*).

143 This partial list is drawn from the *Satsujōshū* of 1454, compiled by the Muromachi bakufu official Inoo Tametomo (d.1458); and the anonymous *Ruijū mojishō* of c.1486. (*tehyōsō*; *tsumaharami*; *katane*; *shiine*; *umishiru*; *kasa*; *kurokasa*; *kasabuta*; *kasatokoro*; *mogasa*; *asemo*; *shimumisō shininsō*; *chōsō*; *hibi*; *akagari*; *mushikasa*; *nikibi*; *hanakayushi*; *seiraku*; *hahakuro hokuro*; *hakusa*; *kuchihibi*; *namazuhada*; *hatake*; *aza*; *kuhiibo*; *fusube, sagarifusube*; *kataikasa*; *urumu*; *ionome*; *chichihakuru*; *kashiragasa*; *shirakubo*; *kasatsubi*.)

144 Edward Putzar, "Inu Makura: The Dog Pillow," at p. 105 and p. 112. The author, physician to Toyotomi Hidetsugu, also wrote a number of medical treatises.

145 *Kokawadera engi shū*, p. 40.

146 See the well-known passage in *Sanetaka kyōki* for Eishō 2 (1505).11.6 (vol. 4b, p. 472), cited in Michele Marra, *Representations of Power*, p. 63. Marra determines the woman's illness to be pneumonia. The entry, however, identifies the illness as *chūfū*, which is usually understood to be apoplexy.

147 See his *Ilbon haengnok*. Murai Shōsuke, trans., *Rōshōdō Nihon gyōroku*, pp. 96–97.

148 *TMN* Eiroku 12 (1569).3.6 (2.117).

149 *Kasuga gongen genki e*, pl. 11, p. 20.

150 See *Tokitsugu kyōki* Eiroku 9 (1566).7.26, 27, 28, 29, 8.2, 8.3, 8.4, 8.5, 8.6, 8.7, 8.8, 8.9, 8.10, 8.11, 8.12, 8.13, 8.14, 8.15, 8.16, 8.17, 8.18, 8.19, 8.20, 8.21, 8.22, 8.24, 8.25, 8.26, 8.27, 8.28, 8.29, intercalary 8.3, int.8.5, int.8.6, int.8.10, int.8.11, int.8.15, int.8.26, int.8.27, 9.3, 9.5. A partial tabulation of the information in the diary may be found in Hattori Toshirō, *Muromachi Azuchi Momoyama jidai igakushi no kenkyū*, pp. 112–113. Mizutani Isaku, "Kokiroku ni mietaru Muromachi jidai no kanja to iryō (2)—*Tokitsugu kyōki* Eiroku kyūnen Minami Mukai tōbyō kiroku kara," provides a wider discussion of many details, and identification of people appearing in the entries.

151 For the illness record (*byōshō mokuroku*) of the wife of Terauchi Touemon no suke, see *Tokitsune* Bunroku 4 (1595).8.16

(6.333); and *Tokitsune* Bunroku 4 (1595).9.27 (6.356). For the record (*mokuroku*) of Mago Hyōe for his severe cough, see *Tokitsune* Keichō 4 (1599).3.5 (9.171); *Tokitsune* Tenshō 18 (1590).7.21, 29 (4.87, 91); and *Tokitsune* Keichō 8 (1604).3.10 (12.48).

152 *Tokitsune* Tenshō 15 (1587).5.12 (2.276); for the wife of Terauchi Touemon no suke, see *Tokitsune* Bunroku 4 (1595).6.4, 30 (6.279, 298). For mention of a list of permitted foods for a woman suffering from a blocked bladder, see *Tokitsune* Keichō 2 (1597).11.6, 11 (8.102, 106). For mention of a list of permitted foods for *chūfū*, phlegm, and indigestion (*mune ni tsukae*), see *Tokitsune* Keichō 10 (1605).8.27 (13.228).

153 *Tokitsune* Tenshō 15 (1587).5.3 (2.272), 5.4, 5.5, 5.7, 5.9, 5.10, 5.11, 5.12, 5.14, 5.16, 5.19, 5.21, 5.22, 5.24, 5.25 (2.281).

154 *Tokitsune* Tenshō 14 (1586).4.8 (2.126).

155 *Tokitsune* Bunroku 4 (1595).6.6, 12, 22 (6.281, 286, 292). For other examples of this request, see *Tokitsune* Tenshō 16 (1588).2.27 (3.33); Tenshō 17 (1589).7.11, 18 (3.320, 3.326); Bunroku 4 (1595).12.15 (6.402); Keichō 4 (1599).int.3.22 (9.199).

156 *Tokitsune* Tenshō 15 (1587).4.18, 19, 24 (2.265, 266, 269).

157 *Tokitsune* Tenshō 15 (1587).4.23, 25, 26, 27, 28, 29, 5.1, 5.3 (2.268, 269, 270, 271, 272).

Court and Bakufu in Her Flesh: Nijō's Contribution to Dual Polity
Hitomi Tonomura

Introduction

How and to what degree did women of premodern Japan participate in political processes? An answer to this question depends on how we understand "political processes" and what it means to "participate" in them. The "political" is typically considered a corollary of the concept "public," and as Jean Bethke Elshtain asserts in her influential book, *Public Man, Private Woman: Women in Social and Political Thought*, it is also closely associated with the male. Deeply entrenched in Western philosophical traditions from Plato to Marx, the concept of public also stands conceptually and analytically distinct from its opposites: private, woman, and domesticity. As Elshtain notes, this dichotomous construct leads to the understanding that women participated in political processes only exceptionally, if at all. She then proposes the subordination or elimination of the notions of "public" and "private" in favor of the integration of the two, while reminding us of the functional benefit of the bifurcated notion of the two spheres: that it has "served to reveal as well as to conceal a multiplicity of human desires, purposes, fantasies, and activities."[1]

When we consider women's participation in political processes in premodern Japan, we typically direct our attention first to the roster of female rulers and quasi-rulers who occupied the space the dichotomous approach would call "public." The list begins with the archaic Queen Himiko of the kingdom of Yamatai in the third century and the six female emperors who reigned for about half of the period between 592 and 770. Hōjō Masako (1156–1225) and Hino Tomiko (1440–1496), though wives and mothers of shoguns, can also be counted as the de facto power in, respectively, the Kamakura and Muromachi warrior governments of their day. The mythological origin-figure Sun Goddess Amaterasu and the quasi-mythological third-century heroic empress Jingū may also fit on the roster. Represented in official documents and records, these women's standing and authority are typically assessed through the epistemology embedded in the system that was, for the most part, gendered male. To many historians, the more their leadership resembled that of men, the more authority they seemed to possess. These female leaders are, in a sense, historiographically trapped in the structure of discourse that validates the political system in its dichotomous configuration.

The political structure of premodern Japan both supports and undermines the dichotomy that the public/private terminology embodies. On the one hand, the imperial bureaucratic offices, staffed predominantly by men, outlined the structure of public and ritual authority. On the other hand, the entire aristocracy was a political arena, where human interests—including sexual, emotional, and aesthetic—were deeply implicated in the distribution of formal authority and power connected to such visible markings as lineage names, office titles, court ranks, and even rights to estate holding. The spectrum of the gray analytical zone would include the space occupied by female title-holders, who worked in the inner quarters of the palace serving emperors and empresses, or ministerial wives, who managed their own household organizations.

This chapter moves away from the narrowly conceived notion of the political and adopts an integrative approach by examining the space that existed, both architecturally and figuratively, outside the official discourse of the bureaucracy and its men. Specifically, we consider women's participation in political processes by relying on the personal writing of one aristocratic woman, Lady Nijō (1258–after 1307). Though she held no official post, court rank, or title, Nijō served Retired Emperor Go-Fukakusa (1243–1304; r. 1246–1259) as his companion from the age of fourteen through twenty-five, when she was expelled from the court. Thereafter, she became an itinerant nun, traveling to Kamakura and elsewhere. Lady Nijō was a poet and author and at the age of forty-nine completed her memoir, *Towazugatari* (Telling without being Asked) after years of reflection. It provides an intimate account of her relationships to men and women who occupied the top tiers of the court space and high and low officials in the provinces.[2]

Nijō was both a participant in and an observer of the sharply competitive political environment of the late Kamakura age. Her memoir offers remarkable insights into the court's operation that are unavailable in conventional court records or the diaries of male courtiers. In Nijō's writing, though she demarcates the formal spaces of male officials (by describing them in their official titles instead of lovers' aliases), the notions of "public" and "private" are infused into one continuous whole. Situated at its center is her body, endowed with the sexual power and textual authority pliable enough to influence crucial political affairs. The mode of political participation Nijō demonstrates in her writing contrasts dramatically with that attributed to the famous women who occupied important positions in the formal political system. Unlike their situations, which can be verified through official chronicles, documents, or others' diaries, Nijō's life story, likely too trivial for another's brush, is practically a creation of her own narrative act. However, in this writing, she insists on projecting a self that, although conscious of her own insignificance, proclaims a potent discursive authority over her experience, crediting herself with sufficient force to reshape the complex and often unpredictable arena of political competition. Excluded from the field of official discourse, Nijō's life and memoir provide us with a sample of participation in political processes that was unabashedly feminine and personal.

We begin our exploration of Nijō's role by elucidating the political setting in which her patron, Go-Fukakusa, found himself and his specific needs and goals. We will then examine Nijō's family, lovers, and life at court as they related to Go-Fukakusa's goals. Finally, we will select three episodes from Nijō's memoir that show her consciously constructed involvement in political processes. Throughout, we will be mindful of the narrative strategy that Nijō employs in constructing her past. It is well to remember that *Towazugatari* hardly represents a day-to-day recording of her life history. Rather, it is a closing statement of the author's life and reflects her perspective on her past at that time. The memoir is an edited and reconstructed version of her life's story that is purposely readjusted through narrative techniques, such as accents, emphases, and elision, as well as chronological misalignment and hidden poetic allusions to classical works. By imposing literary techniques, Nijō as author controls the action and sentiments of Nijō as protagonist and fits the latter's significance to her overall authorial intentions. In this way, the text allows Nijō to participate in political processes at different levels of reality and narrative imagination.[3]

Court and Bakufu in Go-Fukakusa's Time

Go-Fukakusa, Nijō's patron, lived at a time when the traditional authority of the imperial court was forced to maintain a modus vivendi with the relatively new, but increasingly assertive, warrior government, the Kamakura bakufu ("Kantō" or the "East" in contemporary terms). It is this reduced stature of the court and the pull of the political center to Kantō that ultimately shaped Go-Fukakusa's sexual relationship with Nijō and defined the position she would acquire in court. The direction of changes in the evolving court-bakufu relationship likewise gave prominence to Nijō's first, and other significant, lover, Saionji Sanekane, who grew powerful as the imperially designated liaison with the Kantō.

When the warrior government was set up in the 1180s, its goal was to supplement rather than overthrow the authority of the imperial government in Kyoto. Court and bakufu came to operate in tandem in what historians have come to call the dual polity. The relationship between the two political centers was not without tensions. In the Jōkyū uprising of 1221, Retired Emperor Go-Toba (1180–1239; r. 1183–1198) tried by force to diminish if not eliminate the Kantō's prerogatives.[4] Instead, Go-Toba's failure tipped the balance of power heavily toward the Kantō.[5] Nonetheless, the Kantō continued to maintain the structure of a dual polity by promoting smooth communications and areas of common interest between the two centers, while strengthening its authority with respect to the imperial family, in an effort to preempt future troubles.

In the wake of the Jōkyū uprising, three retired emperors who had been implicated were exiled,[6] their supporters were executed, and their lands were confiscated. For the next quarter of a century, the imperial succession was determined in Kamakura, and only members of the imperial family untainted by the plot were tapped to be new emperors. Go-Fukakusa's father, Go-Saga (1220–1272; r. 1242–1246), was enthroned following Go-Horikawa (1212–1234; r. 1221–1232), and Shijō (1231–1242; r. 1232–1242).[7] In addition, in a matter of importance to Go-Fukakusa and Nijō, the Kantō also revamped the diplomatic functions of the Kantō liaison (*Kantō mōshitsugi*), which had only recently been established and which functioned as a tool of the Kantō rather than as anything like a neutral contact between the centers.[8] For good measure, the Kantō also established its own branch office in the capital, headed by the Rokuhara deputies (*Rokuhara tandai*), who were always members of the Hōjō family.

Go-Fukakusa was a child of the post-uprising years. He began his life as a son of an emperor whose position owed itself entirely to the bakufu. Following Go-Saga's abdication in 1246, Go-Fukakusa ascended the throne at the age of four. Almost simultaneously, as part of a "restructuring program," the post of Kantō liaison was reassigned from Kujō Michiie (1193–1252) to Saionji Saneuji (1194–1269),[9] whose descendants were to hold the post as a hereditary preserve until the end of the Kamakura era in 1333. The position greatly empowered the Saionji within the aristocracy, identifying them as Kantō clients at the heart of court politics and deeply involving them in matters of imperial succession.

The year 1249 saw the fateful birth of Go-Fukakusa's younger brother, who later became Emperor Kameyama (1249–1305, r. 1259–1274). Kameyama's arrival marked the beginning of trouble for Go-Fukakusa, inasmuch as Go-Saga seems to have been partial to the younger sibling. In 1258, he made Kameyama crown prince and the following year forced Go-Fukakusa to yield the throne to his brother. Nine years later, the signs of Go-Saga's favoritism again emerged. While the sons of Go-Fukakusa and Kameyama were of equal status by birth (their mothers were both daughters of Saionji Saneuji's younger brother), the former (later Emperor Fushimi) was two years senior to his cousin (later Emperor Go-Uda). The equality of their birth status permitted Go-Saga to ignore criterion of seniority as he had in 1258–1259, and now he designated Go-Uda as the new crown prince.

Since Go-Saga had forced Go-Fukakusa to yield the throne to his younger brother and had further chosen Kameyama's son as crown prince, it may be safely assumed that Go-Saga preferred Kameyama's line to Go-Fukakusa's. However, his death on 1272.2.17 left unsettled the line of future succession. Go-Saga's wife, Ōmiya-in (1225–1292), who had given birth to both Go-Fukakusa and Kameyama, confirmed her late husband's preferences when questioned by the Kantō, but the matter was not one to be resolved simply. Ironically, both Go-Saga and the Kantō leadership had apparently assumed that they would defer to the other's wishes on the future succession, but in the shadow of Go-Saga's passing, neither the Kantō nor the Kantō liaison at court was predisposed to make a recommendation favoring either imperial brother.

Go-Saga's death removed a monumental figure, the undisputed head of the imperial family and the glue holding the aristocracy together. Nijō wrote at length about this pivotal moment, and noted her own presence at the scene, clearly suggesting that Go-Saga's passing would be enormously consequential for her patron and indeed, for herself as well. As a retired emperor and the father of the reigning emperor, the deceased patriarch had been the *chiten no kimi*, the "lord who governs the heavens," for twenty-six years.[12] The issue of succession was also an issue of who would preside as the next *chiten no kimi*, the supreme public representative of the imperial family, who was superior to any other retired emperor. The *chiten no kimi* had the authority to arbitrate on issues of property and position within the imperial family and also presided over the oligopoly of imperials, aristocrats, and religious institutions constituting the vast majority of the country's estate (*shōen*) holders. This supreme position was endowed with specific powers over the earthly domain, such as the authority to adjudicate the disposition of estate holdings either through the investigatory records office (*kirokujo*) or through his advisory council (*in no hyōjōshū*).

The role of *chiten no kimi* increased in importance in Nijō's time because of the transformation in inheritance practices accompanying the division of lineages into splinter lines. The trend toward divided lineages led to a rise in the number of estate-related litigations and, as well, disputes between and within lines over entitlement to the fixed number of court ranks and titles. Increased disputes naturally enhanced the judicial and appointment prerogatives of the *chiten no kimi*. The potential impact of decisions or preferences of the *chiten no kimi* was further magnified by two facts: that the imperial family itself held superior title to a vast number of estates and that the two brothers held separate parcels.[13] The prerogatives of the *chiten no kimi* mattered to the aristocracy because, in the complex and vertically structured patron-client networks of interests invested in the estate holdings, the civil elite held rights to income from and subsidiary title to the constituent estates.[14] In terms of economic benefits, symbolic power, and judicial authority, tensions surrounding the position of *chiten no kimi* could have immense repercussions for the imperial family and the entire aristocratic class.

For a while, Go-Fukakusa's situation looked bleak; there was a very real possibility that he might never become a *chiten no kimi*, which also meant that his line might never become eligible to provide future emperors. In reality, after Go-Saga's death, no *chiten no kimi* presided until 1274, when Kameyama passed the throne to his son Go-Uda and then acquired the title for himself. Following this development, Kameyama also would then have the opportunity to nominate the next crown prince, who would follow his line. Still, Go-Fukakusa was the older brother, and he was unwilling to surrender what he regarded as his birthright. Thus, from 1268, when the future Go-Uda was designated crown prince, Go-Fukakusa competed vigorously to have his own son (the future Emperor Fushimi) designated as the subsequent crown prince.

Nijō's memoir shows that, from the moment she entered the court as Go-Fukakusa's companion, she was aware of the political tensions over the succession. In her nuanced expressions, Nijō charted her position in relation to Go-Fukakusa and key human resources. In the next section we examine who Nijō was and how and why she came to be involved in Go-Fukakusa's affairs, personally and textually.

Nijō's Life at Court

Nijō commenced service to Go-Fukakusa in 1271, but she was not a new figure at court. She had grown up there from the age of four, under the care of Go-Fukakusa himself. Her mother, Shijō Kinshi (?–1259), a daughter of Shijō Takachika (1203–1278), had served Go-Fukakusa as his handmaiden (*dainagon tenji*) "day and night." Kinshi died the year after she had both married Nijō's father, Koga Masatada (1225?–1272), and given birth to Nijō. Children normally lived at their mother's residence, but when Nijō lost her maternal residence, she was entrusted to Go-Fukakusa. According to Go-Fukakusa's recollection, as told by Nijō, this was because of his affection for her mother. Go-Fukakusa had learned the way of sex from Nijō's mother, and he desired Nijō from her infancy as a substitute for Kinshi.

Nijō's memoir begins with a coercive sexual episode in 1271 in which Go-Fukakusa reportedly "handled [Nijō] so mercilessly that [her] thin gown was being badly torn."[15] Immediately after this incident, Nijō was placed in service to Go-Fukakusa, in a new persona. Regrettably for Nijō and her father, the new arrangement gave her no official designation, such as "wife" or even "handmaiden" (*tenji*), like her mother. In this ambiguous status, Nijō came to manage and exploit the opportunities and disappointments that presented themselves to her. We shall try to position Nijō and her writing more precisely by first describing Nijō's field of operation, the context of the web of human relations that shaped the court of her day.

The skeletal structure that operated in the court was a form of Confucian bureaucracy that Japan had adopted in ancient times and continued to modify. It defined each person's social station in terms of rank (such as "junior first") and title (such as "major counselor"). The nomenclature of offices and titles allowed for considerable flexibility, and over time, positions were added to the original structure, such as the offices of the imperial regent, retired emperor, *chiten no kimi*, and, new in the thirteenth century, the Kantō liaison. Sanekane, the Kantō liaison for most of Nijō's adult life, owed his power to this office, to his court rank (senior second rank and up), to titles pertaining to the bureaucracy (beginning with provisional major counselor), and to his multi-generational familial ties to the imperial family.

Sanekane's grandfather, Saneuji, had successfully placed two daughters as imperial wives. One, Ōmiya-in, was the wife of Go-Saga and mother of both Go-Fukakusa and Kameyama. The other, Higashi-Nijō-in (1232–1304), became Go-Fukakusa's wife when he was fourteen and she was twenty-five. Sanekane's sister Kishi (1253–1318, later Imadegawa-in) was Kameyama's wife, and another sister Sōshi (dates unknown), was a mistress of Go-Fukakusa. Sanekane, therefore, had two aunts and a sister who were wives of emperors and a sister who was an imperial mistress. And in the next generation, three of Sanekane's four daughters would also wed emperors.[16] From the standpoint of the imperial family, Go-Fukakusa had Saionji females as mother and as wives, and four of Kameyama's wives were Saionji daughters. Thus blood ran thick between the imperial family and the Saionji.

Nijō's position in this structure was precarious, despite having some advantages. Although she was born to two prestigious lines, neither matched the stature of the Saionji. Though her father had achieved high position (major counselor, senior second rank) at the time of his relatively early death at forty-five, his death left her an orphan only one year after she began serving Go-Fukakusa. Nijō's highest-ranked relative was her maternal grandfather, Shijō Takachika, a major counselor. Takachika gained proximity to the imperial family by providing it with wet nurses,[17] but his greatest asset, and hence Nijō's as well, was his sister, Teishi (1196–1302). Called Lady Kitayama, she was the influential wife of Saionji Saneuji, the mother of Ōmiya-in, and thus the grandmother of Go-Fukakusa and Kameyama. She was also Sanekane's grandmother. Being a granddaughter of Takachika did not necessarily ameliorate Nijō's precarious situation, for he sometimes gave preference to his daughter (that is, Nijō's aunt) over Nijō in apportioning scarce resources.[18] However, having Lady Kitayama as her great aunt did help. Nijō was adopted as a *yūshi* (roughly, a "ward") by Lady Kitayama and Saionji Saneuji. This form of adoption did not integrate the adoptee into the new lineage but it did dispense exclusive social markings associated with the adoptor. In Nijō's case, it meant that she could surpass her own station. She could don "forbidden colors" normally reserved for the exclusive use of the most elevated personages, wear more layers of gown than were specified by the "code," or ride in a superior style of palanquin to which she was not otherwise entitled.

The privileges that allowed Nijō to display herself at the top of the court's visual and symbolic hierarchy did not change the fact that she was without title or rank. She remained far inferior to Lady Kitayama's own daughters. Before her initial sexual union with Go-Fukakusa, her father had hoped that Nijō would be an imperial wife. This meant entering the court as *nyōgo*, a title that referred to a woman who served the emperor in various capacities, including sexual. Such women would advance, after the initial period of sexual relations, to more lofty stations, with titles such as *chūgū, jusangū, kisaki,* or *kōgō,* all of which had a functional meaning of "imperial wife."[19] For Nijō and her father, the situation turned out to be worse than disappointing. Without any title or rank, Nijō effectively remained Go-Fukakusa's personal "servant," whose chores, according to entries in her memoir, consisted of tasks such as: sharing "the pillow" with Go-Fukakusa; massaging him; serving as his messenger to procure women for his other affairs; accompanying him on outings in his palanquin; participating in courtly entertainments by demonstrating her cultural accomplishments, such as playing the lute and composing poetry; serving as a *sake*-pouring hostess to him and other men at banquets; and even sharing her body with other men on demand by Go-Fukakusa. Nijō found some tasks worthy but the last duty, on several occasions, made her truly miserable.

Nijō's situation also provided her no economic security. Women with the titles of imperial wives had corresponding privileges that added not only to their prestige but also to their wealth. One privilege was the receipt of court ranks, such as junior third, similar to those of men, to which economic perquisites were attached. These women also received the designation of "retired" (as *in* or *nyōin*), which granted more institutional resources.[20] As with "retired" emperors who took the "*in*" designation, the female "*in*" nomenclature elevated their status, enhanced the authority of their private administrative offices, and often gave them more economic prerogatives. By contrast, Nijō's memoir mentions only personal gifts. Her years as an itinerant nun, during which she donated memorabilia to temples in order to support her sutra-copying devotional activities, also suggest her penury. In the court, gifts circulated profusely on all occasions, but they came irregularly and were not to be counted upon. Nijō's greatest source of gifts was Sanekane, whom she acknowledged as the sender of many a gown, often ordered for a specific occasion.[21]

Ironically camouflaged by the very weight of prestige expressed in the visible code of clothes, the precarious existence Nijō led at court depended solely on the desires and needs of Go-Fukakusa. He had no obligation to keep her, but instead held the authority to dispose of her on a whim. Nijō was in no position to refuse service to him. However, four other factors worked to Nijō's advantage: Go-Fukakusa's own precarious position in the imperial family; his apparent psychological and sexual dependency on her; her cultural capital (not the least of which was her literary and musical talent); and most of all, her sexual body. Nijō's memoir conveys how she turned these conditions into dynamic resources that allowed her to claim a meaningful role for herself and leave, at least in her mind, an enduring impact on the life and political legacy of her patron, Go-Fukakusa. In hindsight, we can understand perhaps the most important factor in why Go-Fukakusa would not have wanted to welcome Nijō as his proper wife. Had he done so, Nijō's value as a conduit to the Kantō liaison would have been diminished. If she were a proper wife of a retired emperor, Nijō and Sanekane likely would have ceased their relationship. From the start, then, Go-Fukakusa probably had no intention of formalizing Nijō's position.

Three Episodes

Nijō's memoir provides considerable detail regarding the reinstatement of Go-Fukakusa's line through her connection to the Kantō liaison. Indeed, this focal theme of the memoir is punctuated by three episodes of particular note, beginning with Go-Fukakusa's sexual ravaging of her in 1271. As mentioned earlier, this opening scene recounts the launch of Nijō's sexual career at court and simultaneously introduces her prior engagement with a romantic, unnamed lover, who ultimately appears textually as the "Saionji Major Counsellor" and in her private musings as "Dawn Snow."[22] This lengthy account ("Nijō with Two Men") serves as the base upon which Nijō builds a narration of her evolving relationship with Go-Fukakusa in connection to Sanekane, as well as other sexual relations. The second episode ("The Crisis of 1274 and Nijō's Contribution") details Nijō's pregnancy with Sanekane and showcases the process of the childbirth that follows. The entire parturition experience required deceiving Go-Fukakusa. Relying on a subtle but complicated discursive technique, Nijō's text conveys the psychological weight of deceit that implicated Sanekane's moves and ultimately produced results both joyful and lamentable for Nijō. The third episode ("Nijō in Kamakura") follows Nijō's journey to Kamakura in 1289, illuminating along the way the dual polity from the perspective of a woman who, despite being a nun, gained recognition for her cultural resources. Throughout these episodes, we will carefully consider her reflexive stand, which gave order and shape to her past through literary devices, such as highlighting and elision of certain events and thoughts, and which sometimes depended on temporal alteration of actual sequences. The intertextual dialogue she employs to reference certain canonical works also offers depth and hidden clues to her sentiments.

Episode One: Nijō with Two Men

Towazugatari begins in 1271, about two weeks before Go-Fukakusa fulfilled his sexual intent.[23] Nijō introduces herself through a description of the magnificent clothes she wore to celebrate the New Year in Go-Fukakusa's court, furnishing a visual cue to her outwardly privileged status, youthfulness, taste, education, and self-worth, as well as the public character of her life.[24] The reader learns only later that this appearance was due to her "adoption" by Lady Kitayama. Soon, Go-Fukakusa, now twenty-nine years old, with several wives and children, approaches Nijō's father to convey that it is time to submit Nijō to him.[25] Nijō's narrative insists on her lack of comprehension of the continuing conversation.[26] In preparation for the dramatic twist that awaits her, the narrative keeps Nijō in a state of pure innocence regarding Go-Fukakusa's plan. In a remarkable narrative intervention, Nijō-the-author constructs an elaborate subplot involving Sanekane, who is yet unnamed. The segment establishes the foundation for the triangular relationship among Nijō, Go-Fukakusa, and Sanekane that evolves thereafter, and it is therefore worth describing fully the ways in which Nijō "remembered and relived" it.

Upon returning to her room after the New Year's celebration, Nijō finds a letter, a poem, and a set of sumptuous outfits: "an eight-layered robe shaded from deep to light red, a deep maroon under-robe, a light green outer gown, a formal jacket, pleated trouser-skirt, and two- and three-layered small-sleeved robes." The letter states, "On the snows of yesterday, from this spring day onward, my letters as footprints shall leave their mark, on the paths to that long tomorrow."[27] Nijō immediately knows who sent these gifts, but sees no need to disclose his name to the inquisitive reader, effectively suggesting her prior association with the man and a sense of the "private space" that existed between them. The gift, of course, was from Sanekane. As Sanekane well knew, clothing was the most powerful, intimate, and direct medium for the expression of status. It defined the person, male or female, in the public setting of the court. The whole economy of clothes, not only what one wore but also who gave it or with whom it was exchanged, minutely mapped the elite's social space. By sending this gorgeous set of garments, Sanekane not only conveyed his amorous thoughts to Nijō but also projected who Nijō could be, in the public space of the court.[28]

Outwardly surprised to receive this unexpected gift, Nijō feels compelled to return it to the sender. She then notices another note attached to the sleeve of one of the robes:

Tsubasa koso	Unlike the wings of lover birds,
kasanuru koto no	Our sleeves
kanawazuto	May never touch,

| *kite dani nare yo* | Yet wear this plumage |
| *tsuru no kegoromo* | That you may feel my love.[29] |

With the gown, she sends him a poem in response:

Yoso nagara	How could I yield
narete wa yoshiya	Wearing these gowns,
sayogoromo	Though we are far apart?
itodo tamoto no	The sleeves would surely rot
kuchi mo koso sure	From my tears.

And she adds, "Only if your love proves true until that tomorrow . . ."[30]

But the garments, not surprisingly, come back to her with a new poem.

Chigiri okishi	If the love you pledged
kokoro no sue no	Remains unchanged,
kawarazu wa	Then till that tomorrow,
hitori katajike	Lay out the gowns
yoha no sagoromo	And spend the night sleeping with them alone.[31]

To Nijō and the reader, the gift of expensive clothes on this day suggests the man's seriousness in pursuing her, despite, or perhaps because of, the new situation with Go-Fukakusa; it also indicates the sender's social and economic station, good taste, and generosity. According to Iwasa Miyoko, the reiteration in the poems, with slightly different wording, of references to "gowns" (*koromo*), an erotic metaphor for shared flesh, is evidence of a prior exchange of vows, with parental approval, between Nijō and Sanekane, the as-yet-unnamed lover. Furthermore, much later in her narrative, Nijō describes Sanekane as one whom she should "consider her first love" (*niimakura to mo iinubeku*).[32]

Two days later, on the occasion of Go-Saga's visit to Go-Fukakusa's mansion, where all the important people, including Sanekane, were present, Nijō presented herself adorned in this gift. This strategy was obviously meaningful to her, since she made a special point of mentioning it. It has the effect of confirming Nijō's spatial position in court gatherings. She also seeks to display how her relationship to Sanekane was mutual but remained a public secret. The gown immediately drew the attention of her father, who asked if the attractive outfit came from Go-Fukakusa. Nijō writes that, suppressing her pounding heart, she quickly and nonchalantly named Lady Kitayama as the source. While she deftly preserved a secret space from the patriarch's intrusion, at the same time she loudly proclaimed her affiliation with Sanekane through her gowns, which all, including Go-Fukakusa, could witness.[33]

Having established her connection to Sanekane, Nijō's brush now turns to Go-Fukakusa's advances. In line with the convention followed in classical women's writings, Nijō explains male-female relationships in terms of desire, refraining from expressions that may suggest motives tinged with political goals. The memoir presents Go-Fukakusa purely as a ranked man, whose yearning for Nijō is finally about to be consummated. On the fifteenth day of the same month, Nijō's father sent a cart to bring her from Go-Fukakusa's palace to his house. Because Nijō's mother was dead, it was the father who "hosted" Nijō when she was away from her courtly residence.[34]

Upon arrival, the unusually splendid furnishings of the house puzzled Nijō who, in her writing, insists on her ignorance and innocence of what was to come.[35] In the evening, a three-layered white under-robe and deep maroon trousers were laid out for her. Her stepmother brought a lavish short-sleeved gown to be worn over them while her father told her not to go to sleep but to serve the lord well; he said it is good for a lady-in-waiting to do what her lord expected of her without defiance. But Nijō fell asleep.[36] While she was asleep, Go-Fukakusa arrived and, to the call, "Wake her," responded, "It is fine. Let her sleep." Switching from a story-telling mode to her more subjective mode, Nijō describes how she found a man sleeping comfortably beside her. As she tried to get up and leave, Go-Fukakusa stopped her and confessed: "I have been waiting ten and four years since I began desiring you when you were but a child." "I could not hear anything," Nijō says, "but could only weep and sob, until even his sleeves had no dry place left." Go-Fukakusa "continued to plead and comfort me without acting inconsiderately." The night ended with no action, as Nijō resisted Go-Fukakusa's verbal advance. Pretending to be ill, she refused to respond to Go-Fukakusa's morning-after poem as well.[37]

At this point, abruptly, the narrative once again directs us to Sanekane's actions. A different letter arrived around midday, this time from the "unexpected someone." In it, Sanekane swore he "would vanish if the smoke ends up trailing over in another direction." In contrast to her treatment of Go-Fukakusa's poem, Nijō responded immediately: "You may not understand that, confused, underneath the evening smoke my true heart does not waver."[38] What amazes the reader is the speed with which the news traveled in the court circle, and the ability of Sanekane to respond so rapidly to the new situation. It is almost as though the scenario had been established prior to the incident, and the only person who did not (or pretended not to) know about it was Nijō herself. The memoir flaunts Sanekane's extraordinary competence and verve and suggests the efficacy of the communication network and the density and importance of human relations.

The following night, Nijō no longer was able to guard "her true heart that does not waver" for her favored lover. After the sound of the imperial carriage was heard, Go-Fukakusa opened the door in a familiar manner and asked Nijō about her illness. "Having no desire to respond," she simply lay there, whereupon he rested besides her and spoke about this and that. Nijō feared what was to happen, her anxiety compounded by the idea of "letting the smoke trail over into the other direction" after having pledged otherwise. Go-Fukakusa then behaved "so mercilessly that her thin gown is badly torn (*itaku hokorobitekeruniya*) and hardly anything is left" of herself.[39] As the dawn approached, Nijō's dread turned to what people would think of her. "For these undercords that came untied against my will, what rumors shall see my name exposed to misery and shame?"[40] But she felt strange that "I still had enough mind to think." Perhaps in order to win Nijō's empathy, Go-Fukakusa pledged that his tie to her would never end, no matter in what form they were reborn. Even if he could not see her nightly, their hearts would never be separated. Nijō remained unconsoled. The scene that follows, however, complicates our understanding of the situation and of Nijō's evolving mind. As the temple bell announced the dawn, Go-Fukakusa implored Nijō at least to see him off, even if she did not regret his departure. She walked out with him, a thin jacket covering her tear-drenched gown. At this juncture, Nijō comments: "I notice Go-Fukakusa more keenly than usual," describing his clothes, evidence that her gaze was upon his figure. He wore "an ordinary imperial robe, green on the outside and red inside, a light purple robe under it, and stiff trousers gathered at the bottom. I wonder from whom I have learned to feel this way," she concluded.[41]

Through this description of Go-Fukakusa's clothes, the reader understands that Nijō observed Go-Fukakusa differently now, as a sexual being instead of the patron in whose house she was raised, and, in turn, reflects upon herself as a woman transformed, someone who has shed earlier innocence. Importantly, the gaze signifies that she has become a proactive participant in a new formulation of sexual relations, not a mere recipient of sexual advances. The evidence of her gaze now cast upon Go-Fukakusa in a reversed subject-object position suggests to the reader Nijō's grasp of an emerging sense of agency and self-validation.[42] Nijō-the-author transformed Nijō-the-protagonist from an innocent sexual victim to a participant in the maelstrom of court politics. She had no choice but to have the smoke "trail in the other direction" and, by the same token, neither did Sanekane have the wherewithal to prevent it from occurring. As powerful and important as he was, Sanekane, after all, was a minister, not a retired emperor. In status and rank, he was no match for Go-Fukakusa. Once Nijō became Go-Fukakusa's woman, Sanekane's affair with her necessarily and theoretically rested on Go-Fukakusa's benevolence. The sexual culture of the court was such that monogamy was hardly the rule and, judging from the extramatrimonial pregnancies imperial wives experienced, men, including emperors and retired emperors, seemed to have shared each other's wives in an unpredictable manner.[43] Nonetheless, the system of official rank and status that defined the male world also would have marked where men stood in their privileged access to the female body, especially those that circulated in the court. Sanekane's romance with Nijō came to be redefined after Go-Fukakusa imprinted his imperial stamp on her body. Sanekane indeed came to owe Go-Fukakusa a return favor for his indulgence in Nijō's body and person, which were now claimed by Go-Fukakusa.

In the next narrative turn, Nijō was carried off by Go-Fukakusa to his palace, before she could bid farewell to her father, a circumstance she decried. Her father was equally disturbed, for it had become evident to him that Go-Fukakusa had no intention of welcoming his daughter as an official wife. Nijō did not "enter the court" in the manner befitting a future consort, as had Higashi-Nijō-in, Go-Fukakusa's primary wife; there were no palanquins filled with ladies-in-waiting and no male relatives eagerly awaiting her at the palace. In line with these circumstances, when she arrived at court, Nijō noted that Go-Fukakusa instructed everyone that his relationship with her "is to be kept secret" for the time being.[44] The hopeful father had traded his daughter's sexuality for what turned out to be a disappointing payment. Without an official title and the protection and privileges it promised, Nijō had no secure position. Instead, her security in fact derived from her usefulness, which "official" wives could not fulfill. Her resource was her physical and romantic engagement with the generous and influential statesman Sanekane, who held the most powerful connection to Kantō among all the aristocrats. We recall that at this time in 1271, Go-Fukakusa's hope for retaining the primacy of his imperial line had been crushed; Kameyama was reigning and his son was in line to succeed him. Go-Fukakusa had his needs and knew his option: to lean on the authority of the Kantō liaison who, by pressuring Kantō, might reset the course to Go-Fukakusa's advantage.

Was Nijō aware of these connections in 1271? We cannot be certain. But as she "documented" her life years later, she carefully constructed her narrative to highlight Sanekane's authority vis-à-vis Kantō. While in the foregoing exchange of poems and clothes, Nijō hides Sanekane's identity, in the following year, Nijō reintroduces him, this time not as her lover (in which capacity she later refers to him as "Dawn Snow"), but as a statesman whom she calls "Major Counsellor Saionji." The occasion was the visit to Go-Saga's mansion by the Kantō's leading administrators in Kyoto, the two Rokuhara deputies, on the ninth day of the second month of 1272 (Bun'ei 9). Because Go-Saga was gravely ill, Sanekane, Go-Fukakusa, Kameyama, Higashi-Nijō-in, Ōmiya-in, and Nijō herself were all gathered in his suburban mansion. Amid this the two deputies, Hōjō Tokisuke (1248–1272) and Hōjō Yoshimune (1253–1277), paid a sympathy visit and were "received and announced by the Major Counsellor Saionji."[45] By emphasizing Sanekane's political position in the setting shared by the three imperial figures, Nijō's narrative succeeds in situating him as the man in charge of mediating court-bakufu relations and one upon whom Go-Fukakusa would rely. We might note also that Nijō never fails to articulate her own importance by simply being present in these men's company. At this juncture in the memoir, Sanekane emerges as an able administrator, who bridges the imperial institution and the warrior government in his official cloak. The explicit link that Nijō makes of Sanekane to the warrior officials is followed by another passage related to Kantō. "On the fifteenth day, there rose a huge cloud of smoke over the capital. I inquired whose house may have burned down, and was told that it is the house of Hōjō Tokisuke, who was executed."[46] Deftly, Nijō's narrative attention to the matter involving Kamakura turns to the succession problem that loomed immediately after Go-Saga's death "at the age of fifty-three, on the seventeenth day of the second month, Bun'ei 9." She connects this problem to the role of Kantō without mincing words: "Although everyone returned to the capital after participating in the forty-nine days of rites [following Go-Saga's death], administrative issues (*onseimu*) were becoming complicated, and agents were dispatched to Kantō, thereby postponing further prayers."[47]

Nijō's focus on the affairs of the Kamakura officials is a rare straightforward mention of an episode in her court life that was not directly related to the court, its members, and especially to herself. The correct dating of the incident is likely intentional. The accurate representation of a historical incident contrasts with Nijō's other narrative technique, which deliberately misrepresents certain incidents out of the true historical order.[48] The accuracy with which she describes the incident related to the Kantō, but completely unrelated to her personal welfare, thus suggests Nijō's underlying narrative motives: to amplify the relevance of Kantō in the lives of the emperors and aristocrats, to accentuate Sanekane's role in the court community, and to highlight his role as a liaison with Kantō, as well as to remind the reader of her own perspicacity in grasping the significance of political matters and her participatory role in them.

Episode Two: The Crisis of 1274 and Nijō's Contribution

The foregoing description has shown how Nijō sought to transpose the strategic need of Go-Fukakusa and the utility of Sanekane's official role, through her body that was shared by both. Nijō's mediating function literally bore fruit in 1274. It was a moment that Go-Fukakusa had waited for since 1268: designation of his son (later Emperor Fushimi) as the crown prince. In the three years since Nijō reentered the palace, much had happened. Both Nijō's father and Go-Saga had died, and Nijō had given birth to a son by Go-Fukakusa, who was being reared elsewhere. Then Nijō became pregnant by Sanekane and gave birth to a daughter. It was this pregnancy, birth, and the deception Nijō and Sanekane practiced upon Go-Fukakusa (though he knew the truth through a dream) that, in Nijō's elaborate narrative construction, culminated in the much awaited outcome.

In her text, Nijō connects the two seemingly unrelated events, of the birth of her daughter and the royal appointment, by organizing them into a bundled cluster. In order to signify her own role in the positive turn in the greatest problem of Go-Fukakusa's lifetime, Nijō alters the chronology, moving the date of the royal appointment closer to the birth in which Sanekane was deeply involved. The effect is that Sanekane's psychological debt to Go-Fukakusa, stemming from the birth and deception, yielded a favorable compensating result for the hitherto dispirited Go-Fukakusa. Nijō shapes a chronology that offers subtle yet effective textual atmosphere and logic to a string of human feelings.

As Nijō tells it, she became pregnant by Sanekane in the first month of 1274 while Go-Fukakusa was on a month-long religious retreat.[49] By means of a poem that cited his dream, Go-Fukakusa let Nijō know that he knew she would be having sex with Sanekane in his absence. In response, Nijō lied.[50] Despite other tell-tale signs throughout the memoir that Nijō's "extramarital" affair was public knowledge, the text carefully conveys its inappropriateness, perhaps in order to create tension. In this particular instance, the need to conceal the pregnancy from the retired emperor was deemed urgent and heightened the drama in the ensuing narrative progression that hinged on feelings of remorse. Nijō tried to make it appear that the child she was carrying was Go-Fukakusa's. She lied about the date of conception, announcing it to be two months later than was actually the case so as to match the time of Go-Fukakusa's return to the court, and naturally she also moved back the expected delivery date. In so doing, Nijō presented herself as stricken with fear and consternation.

When she entered her sixth month of pregnancy, Go-Fukakusa, believing her to be in her fourth month, planned to send her a maternity sash, a symbol of paternity. Learning that this was to take place on the twelfth day of the sixth month, Sanekane presented her with one of his own a few days before, on the seventh day of the sixth month. Nijō had two maternity sashes, she mused, an ironic condition that vividly illustrated her involvement with the two men. As the time of her delivery approached, Sanekane suggested that she should feign a contagious illness to keep others away. Nijō declared she could not even drink warm water and lay in a dark room buried under covers. Sanekane stayed with her, but announced that he was at a religious retreat at Kasuga shrine (his family shrine), sending a proxy there instead. Nijō recalled the birthing scene with striking poignancy. She describes it in great detail and successfully conveys the depth of Sanekane's involvement in the entire birthing process. To show the minute narrative care Nijō adopts, it is worth summarizing this scene.

> When the time came near, I noticed the absence of ritual purification—no twanging of bows, no priestly prayers. Seeing that I was feeling sadly alone, Sanekane said: "Shouldn't I be holding up your waist? Maybe it's taking so long because I am not doing that. How should I hold you?" I held on to his sleeves and the baby was delivered. Sanekane, pleased, ordered [the one or two servants who were around] "Bring warm rice water. Quickly." Where he learned all this, I do not know, but his knowledge was impressive. He then lit a lamp and looked at the child who had, as I glimpsed, abundant black hair and open eyes. My child naturally was darling to me but Sanekane took her and wrapped her in a white short-sleeved kimono, took a small knife that was near the pillow and cut the umbilical cord, held her, and went out without saying a word. I could not even take another look at her face. I wanted to say, "Please, one more look," but that would have been useless.

Instead, I tried to stop my tears with my sleeves. Sanekane consoled me by saying, "if she lives long enough, you will be able to see her again." But it was difficult for me to forget the face of the baby. Though I knew it was a girl, I didn't even know where she was taken to. The following morning, I sent a message to the palace saying that "I was very ill, and I had a miscarriage. I was able to tell it was a girl."[51]

This remarkable account of the actual delivery, a description of a kind we find nowhere else in medieval literature, focuses on Sanekane's action as well as the mother's emotions. Sanekane assisted Nijō with great tenderness; he physically supported her at the moment of birth, wrapped the baby in a gown, cut the umbilical cord himself, gave Nijō warm water, and took the baby away to be raised in his household.[52] Sanekane thus showed that he knew how to handle not only the delicate situation vis-à-vis Go-Fukakusa, but also the physiological needs of a birthing woman and a newborn. He was deeply involved in both the political and obstetric aspects of this birth.[53] Nijō then lied again to Go-Fukakusa, saying she had had a miscarriage and suggesting the loss of the baby had been of minor importance because the infant had been only a girl. Nijō was fearful as Go-Fukakusa sent much medicine and showed an understanding that "the doctor also says it is common to have a miscarriage when one is ill with a fever."[54]

The section that follows the birth scene is dense with suggestive meanings. In a state of what one might call "postpartum blues," compounded by the removal of her newborn to Sanekane's household, Nijō received the grave news that the son whom she bore Go-Fukakusa the previous year had died on the eighth day of the tenth month. She linked this development, through the workings of karma, to her (and Sanekane's) deception about her latest pregnancy and birth. In this mental state, Nijō longed to abandon this world and begin an itinerant life as a disciple of Buddha.[55] Quickly, the focus of the narrative shifts to the situation of Go-Fukakusa who, out of despair over the state of affairs revolving around the imperial succession, announced, in the fall of the same year as the birth of Nijō's daughter, a decision to renounce the world and enter a monastery. Nijō's expressed desire to follow a religiously inspired itinerant life connects with Go-Fukakusa's statement of his plan to enter a monastery. Nijō and Genkimon-in (1246–1329), a wife of Go-Fukakusa and the mother of his eldest son, were to accompany him, a decision that Nijō found pleasing amid sorrow. Then Kamakura sent a message. Obviously engineered by Sanekane in his official role as Kantō liaison, Go-Fukakusa's son by Genkimon-in was named as the next crown prince (the future Emperor Fushimi), instead of the appointment going to a prince from Kameyama's line. In Nijō's chronology, she must have given birth to Sanekane's daughter sometime around the ninth month, and this positive turn of events would thus have occurred close on the heels of Sanekane's deep involvement in Nijō's pregnancy and brazen deception of Go-Fukakusa. At least, this is how Nijō would like the reader to understand the situation.

Historical records, however, suggest a different chronology. In fact, Go-Fukakusa did not announce his decision to enter the monastery until the fourth month of 1275, that is, the spring after Nijō gave birth,[56] and his son born of Genkimon-in was only ceremonially confirmed as crown prince a further seven months later, in the eleventh month of 1275.[57] Apart from Nijō's version, why did Sanekane help to bring about the shift in favor of Go-Fukakusa? This decision depended on many factors, including the direction of the intralineage conflict Sanekane himself was fighting at any given moment. The division within his lineage began in the generation of Saneuji in the early Kamakura period, as his brother, Sanekatsu (or, Saneo), established the Tōin line. Since Sanekane had assumed the Kantō liaison position and the lineage headship at the age of only twenty as a result of the deaths in quick succession of his father Kintomo (b. 1223) in 1267 and his grandfather Saneuji (b. 1194; Kantō liaison 1246–1269) in 1269, he needed the support of imperial figures to strengthen his own position against the rival Tōin branch.[58]

One weapon of struggle for Sanekane was highly traditional: sending the line's female members to be wives of the imperial sons. In this area, Sanekane's line did not fare well after the resounding success of Ōmiya-in, who became the mother of two emperors. Higashi-Nijō-in, Sanekane's aunt and Go-Fukakusa's wife, had only a daughter (born in 1270). Both Go-Uda and Fushimi were born out of the daughters from the Tōin line. Although Sanekane was an opportunist who had no sustaining loyalty to Kameyama or Go-Fukakusa, it is possible that Sanekane held a grudge against Kameyama at that moment. The reason may have been that his sister, Kishi (1253–1318, from 1268 Imadegawa-in), who had become Kameyama's wife in 1263, received little attention from Kameyama. Kameyama's laxity meant that there was little possibility for the birth of an imperial offspring with direct ties to Sanekane.[59] Kishi would produce no son and would take the tonsure in 1283 at the young age of thirty-two. As for Sanekane, by securing Fushimi's designation as crown prince, he himself took on the position of the chamberlain to the crown prince's household (tōgū no daibu) in 1275.[60]

Whatever the actual political factors involved, Nijō's memoir, by creating a one-frame pastiche of these events through the alteration of their chronology, placed her own affair at the center and as the cause of the significant events taking place in Go-Fukakusa's life and court politics. It is a convincing private explanation that involves Nijō's body and its multiple meanings. Nijō-the-author manipulates dates for Go-Fukakusa's threat to enter the monastery and his change of heart subsequent to Fushimi's designation as crown prince. By doing so, she suggests subtly a causal link between the physiological consequences of the sexual desire that bound "Dawn Snow" to her and the decisive action taken by Sanekane as influential statesman on Go-Fukakusa's behalf. Placement of these events immediately after the birth of Sanekane's daughter, a process in which Sanekane was deeply and practically involved, suggests that Sanekane promoted Go-Fukakusa's line as a way to compensate, politically and spiritually, for his deception of the retired monarch. For Nijō, the death of her son by Go-Fukakusa ended her potential to become an imperial wife or mother. Instead, Nijō represents herself as having contributed to the prosperity of Go-Fukakusa's line by providing Sanekane a strong emotional reason to throw his support behind Go-Fukakusa. The losing figure in this process was Kameyama, who received another blow in 1288, when Fushimi's son was designated the crown prince, ensuring two successive reigns from the Go-Fukakusa side.[61]

Thus, by altering the chronology of critical events, Nijō organizes her contrapuntal treatment of the triangular relationship into sequential clusters around the birth of her child by the Kantō Liaison and its consequences. Nijō endows herself with the power to shape the course of court politics because of physical ties to the courtier who was in close communication with the warrior government.

Episode Three: Nijō in Kamakura

Nijō's relationship to Go-Fukakusa and Sanekane changed after the nomination of Go-Fukakusa's son as crown prince in the eleventh month of 1275. In the eighth month of 1277, Nijō accompanied Go-Fukakusa to Fushimi, along with about half a dozen men. The group included Sanekane as usual, but also another prominent figure, Takatsukasa Kanehira (1228–1294). A member of the Fujiwara regency family, Kanehira had risen in the court hierarchy at a meteoric rate. In 1248, at the age of eleven, he attained the junior second rank and in 1252 became not only the head of the family but also both regent (*sesshō*) and chancellor (*daijōdaijin*). Subsequently, he resigned, reassumed, and was ousted from the regency post. But his connections were good. According to Nijō, "Go-Saga on his deathbed had requested him to look after Go-Fukakusa, and His Majesty always received him warmly."[62] Kanehira was reappointed to the regency post on 1275.10.21, shortly before Go-Fukakusa's son was formally named crown prince on 1275.11.5. In fact, the two appointments seemed to have been proposed at the same time. Envoys from Kamakura entered Kyoto on 1275.10.18 in order to deliberate on "questions of the crown prince, regency appointment, and unlawful seizure of estates."[63] The nearly simultaneous positive turns in the fortunes of Go-Fukakusa and Kanehira may be relevant to what happened to Nijō during the excursion.

Nijō's memoir states that, after the entertainment, everyone retired to sleep. While Nijō was out of her room to meet Sanekane, Kanehira grabbed her gown and indicated his interest in her. Since Kanehira's actions apparently occurred with Go-Fukakusa's connivance (much to Nijō's chagrin), she eventually complied. She found the situation "so mortifying I wanted to die" (*shinubakari kanashiki*), Go-Fukakusa's attitude the following morning "unbearable" (*taegataki*), and the whole episode, which continued for several days, "emptying" (*ukikara nokoru*).[64] From this description, it is difficult to know why Nijō became a victim of Kanehira's lust and why Go-Fukakusa encouraged the tryst. If the reappointment to the regency post and the naming of the crown prince resulted from the two men's mutual support, as some scholars have suggested, did Nijō serve to bind their friendship?[65] Alternatively, was Nijō a compensatory gift to Kanehira who, despite being the regent, in fact had little actual power? In the judicial process, especially in matters of estates, decisions traveled from Kamakura to Saionji Sanekane, then to the "lord who governs the heavens," who then was Kameyama. They bypassed the regent, despite the importance of that title.[66] Whatever the reason, when we consider this incident in combination with another mini-episode described below, we begin to see the evolving circumstances in Nijō's role as a conduit linking Go-Fukakusa's needs to Sanekane's power.

As before, Nijō employs the symbolic language of clothes to convey the memoir's significant meanings. When she was summoned to accompany the group to Fushimi, Nijō implied that she was without an appropriate outfit to wear for the occasion. Sanekane came to the rescue with a timely gift of "an unlined layered gown shaded from yellow to green with an autumn scene embroidered on the sleeves" and "a scarlet jacket, another silk small-sleeved gown, and trousers," and more.[67] Nijō exclaimed how she "was more than usually pleased," a well-placed phrase by the author in anticipation of Go-Fukakusa's shocking gesture that followed.

After a few days of much drinking and merry-making, which included Nijō's servitude to Kanehira, Go-Fukakusa invited cormorant fishermen to perform.[68] When this entertainment was over, he proceeded to grant the fishermen the gown Nijō was wearing, right off her back.[69] The vivid imagery portraying the transfer of the status-defining silk gown to men dressed in drab work clothes pointed to the first-ever instance of Go-Fukakusa's denunciation of the goodwill and mutual appreciation that tied Sanekane and Nijō. By transferring to nameless fishermen Nijō's gown which bore the imprint of Sanekane, Go-Fukakusa rejected symbolically the continuing utility of Nijō's connection to Sanekane. The passage succinctly paints the changing atmosphere that surrounded her and foreshadowed what awaited her.

Indeed, from this juncture, Nijō rarely mentioned Sanekane as her lover "Dawn Snow," and instead became passionately involved with a priest of no political importance, who likely was Go-Fukakusa's half brother, with whom she became pregnant several times. She continued to serve Go-Fukakusa in various ways, such as being a messenger for his liaisons with other women. Her political role seemed greatly diminished, now that Go-Fukakusa had attained his goals. However, in one episode, which is described only ambiguously, Nijō served the interest of Go-Fukakusa by engaging in sex with his brother, Kameyama. The time was the tenth month of 1281, and it was Kameyama, not Go-Fukakusa, who stood on thin ice as far as imperial succession was concerned. Although Kameyama's son, Go-Uda, was the reigning emperor, and Kameyama was therefore the "lord who governs the heavens," his future seemed uncertain. Fushimi, Go-Fukakusa's son, was slated to replace Go-Uda. No decision had been made as to who—a son of Go-Uda or Fushimi—would then follow Fushimi. Perhaps in order to ameliorate the prevailing tension, Go-Fukakusa shared Nijō with Kameyama by having her lie sandwiched between them, an act Nijō abhorred.[70] By 1283, various other incidents had developed to prompt Go-Fukakusa to dismiss her from the palace, purportedly at the insistence of Go-Fukakusa's wife, Higashi-Nijō-in.[71] Although Nijō returned briefly in 1285 at the invitation of Ōmiya-in to participate in the ninetieth birthday celebration of Lady Kitayama, essentially she had become an outsider.[72]

For the next four years there is a hiatus in Nijō's memoir. During this time of narrative silence, much happened in Kyoto that increasingly favored Go-Fukakusa's fortunes. In the ninth month of 1287, administrators from Kantō visited Sanekane's residence frequently and submitted the proposal to enthrone the crown prince as Emperor Fushimi. On 1287.10.21, as Fushimi took the throne, Go-Fukakusa secured his position as the dominant retired emperor, that is, *chiten no kimi*. Furthermore, in 1289.4.11, several months before Go-Fukakusa's son was sent to Kamakura as shogun, Go-Fukakusa's grandson, later emperor Go-Fushimi (1288–1336; r. 1298–1301), was declared crown prince. Kantō liaison Sanekane reaped some benefit from this. Sanekane's daughter, the wife of Fushimi, was made the "official mother" of the future emperor Go-Fushimi, although she was not his biological mother, thus Sanekane managed to acquire an "imperial grandson," perhaps a fitting reward for the favors he had granted to Go-Fukakusa's line.[73] These events provide further context for the next phase of Nijō's memoir.

After the four-year hiatus, Nijō reappears as a traveling nun making her way toward Kamakura. In the new itinerant phase of her life, Nijō describes fresh discoveries and experiences, honors her father and mother and, most significantly, remembers Go-Fukakusa and reestablishes actual and abstract ties with him despite the lingering memory of misery. Over the eighteen years of her sojourn, with one exception, Sanekane was eclipsed from her textual space, now that the prior triangular link had no value to either man. As I have described elsewhere, the memoir is ultimately about Nijō's attachment to Go-Fukakusa, in court and on her travels, regardless of the quality or intensity of that attachment. Nijō frames her text around Go-Fukakusa precisely because Go-Fukakusa himself was immortal. As the "lord who governs the heavens," his name would continue to live in literary creations, official records, and in images and statues. In contrast, Nijō, who held no titles or rank, was a non-entity in the court circle. Were it not for the connection to Go-Fukakusa, whether in person or in discourse, her memoir, her name, and her life would vanish like a morning dew drop on a hot summer day.[74] Comprehending the memoir this way, we find it fitting that Nijō would visit Kamakura on the first leg of her travels as a nun. The incoming shogun in this year was Go-Fukakusa's son, Prince Hisaaki (1276–1328; r. 1289–1308).

Nijō writes her travelogue with a carefully crafted purposelessness. The reader is not told of her itinerary or destination. At times, her literary proclivity takes her to sites known to her through classical works, such as *Ise monogatari*.[75] At other times, Nijō remembers her father or mother by stopping at places with family connections, such as the Atsuta shrine in Owari province, where her father held a governing post.[76] Other places draw her because of their association with famous people. For example, her visit to Izu province takes her to the Mishima shrine to attend a ritual that, she remarks, the "late General Yoritomo" (*Ko-Yoritomo no taishō*) began.[77] Even in these few phrases, it is clear that Nijō was aware of the world beyond the claustrophobic confines of the court, such as the warrior government and some of its history, as well as aspects of the landholding system that supported the economy and human relations of the court and bakufu. We imagine that Nijō, living in the palace, by no means led a life of isolation but instead was exposed to conversations concerning matters of political and economic interest that filled the space in which she circulated.

Early in her travels, Nijō reminds the reader of her identity as a woman of the court by mentioning objects, such as a fan from the capital that she presented to a *yamabushi* (a traveling ascetic) living in a humble but elegant rock cave in Enoshima, in return for the fresh shellfish he offered her. Likewise, she compared and found comfort in the deportment of temple priests at Gokurakuji, which seemed no different from that of priests in the capital.[78] As author, Nijō stresses her pristine cultural upbringing and positions herself as an expert in matters of aesthetics; this became cultural capital that she could draw upon throughout her travels, beginning in Kamakura.

To Nijō, Kamakura was not just the capital of the warrior government. As she gazed at the Tsurugaoka Hachimangū, the protective shrine of the Minamoto and the warrior government, she reminds the reader of herself "having been born into this lineage," through her father, a Koga, one of the sublineages of the Minamoto clan.[79] But clearly, there was more to her views of Kamakura, as her narrative later clarifies. The connection of the warrior government to Go-Fukakusa's prince once again linked Nijō to her previous life with her patron. After an illness that prevented Nijō from moving on to another location, she was invited by Lady Komachi, a distant relative and lady-in-waiting of the shogun, to participate in the Hōjōe festival at Tsurugaoka Hachimangū on the morning of 1289.8.15.[80] The festival scene served as a background to her long and detailed reporting of the status and treatment of imperial princes who became shogun in the warrior capital.[81] Toward the end of the procession, Nijō saw the shogun and his retinue passing, and the shogun stepping out of his palanquin. She was duly impressed, except with the courtier attendants' appearances, which she describes as "despicable (*iyashigena*) and shabby."[82] The shogun, whom Go-Fukakusa's son would replace, was Prince Koreyasu (1264–1326, r. 1266–1289), Go-Saga's grandson, who had succeeded his own father, Prince Munetaka (1242–1274; r. 1252–1266), the sixth shogun and brother of Go-Fukakusa by a different mother.

After a few days, Nijō heard a rumor that something was happening in Kamakura and soon learned that the shogun Koreyasu was being returned to Kyoto. Nijō went to see, and witnessed scenes so pitiable that she was "unable to watch."

The first offensive scene was the shabby state of the palanquin in which the shogun was seated. If this were not bad enough, a proxy for the shogunal regent (*shikken*), then Hōjō Sadatoki (1271–1311), arrived and ordered that the palanquin be carried facing backward in accordance with precedent. This symbolic gesture was a reminder of the shogun's supposedly treacherous intent. Nijō also lamented the behavior of a low-level official, who climbed into the shogun's chamber without removing his sandals, and began tearing down the blinds.[83] Meanwhile, Nijō's eyes moved to the shogun's female attendants, perhaps because she herself had been an attendant for an important person. She notes that they were left in the lurch, wondering where the shogun had gone. Some were crying and leaving the residence. Others with some connections went elsewhere, accompanied by young samurai. Nijō found the spectacle too awful to describe.[84] And the situation got worse. After a five-day stay in Sasuke valley, Prince Koreyasu was to depart for Kyoto. The departure time was set for the hour of the ox, the time of ill fortune, and the weather reflected it. A torrential downpour and stormy winds hit the palanquin, which men merely covered with straw matting. In a narrative mode to authenticate her on-the-scene, eye-witness account, Nijō writes that she could hear him gently blowing his nose and could imagine him sobbing.[85]

Shifting from a position of reporter to that of analyst, Nijō explains who the shoguns were and how they came to serve in this capacity. This passage, which could be called a diatribe, reflects Nijō's thorough knowledge of the political reality that had integrated a high-born civil noble among the inferior warriors into a position that was traditionally military. Apparently struck by this contradiction and with her solidly status- and Kyoto-dominant consciousness, Nijō provides the following points of information. Though called shogun, they did not receive this title as a result of fighting for the realm with their own military might. Prince Munetaka, the previous shogun, was a year older than Go-Fukakusa, but was considered the second prince of Go-Saga because of his mother's humble birth. If Munetaka had reigned as emperor, then his son, Koreyasu, also likely would have succeeded him to the throne. However, Munetaka's mother's status was low, so although he was the oldest, he was sent down to become a shogun. Even so, he remained an imperial family member and was known as Prince Nakatsukasa. The mother of Koreyasu, unlike the mother of Munetaka, came from the Fujiwara regency family. She was a daughter of Takatsukasa Kanetsune (the older brother of the same Takatsukasa Kanehira who in 1277 had engaged in an unwelcome tryst with Nijō). On both the maternal and paternal sides, Koreyasu's impeccable bloodlines could not be questioned.[86]

Nijō, therefore, questions the outrageous manner in which the prince/shogun was handled by people of the military profession, who occupied inferior rank in the social hierarchy. Nijō emphasizes the shogun's imperial blood and the fact that he did not engage in military pursuits to receive the title. Regardless, the fact that he was of imperial stock never changed. Nijō implies that, even carrying the title of shogun, he was of a noble status that should have been viewed with awe. Nijō seems to say that the abusive treatment he received was unthinkable not only for his sake, but also in consideration of the overall worldly and cosmological scheme that placed the emperor, the kind of being who was her patron, at the top.

Nijō seemed to be well aware of the history of the shogunate. As she states, the post of Kamakura shogun was initially granted to a warrior, the founder of the warrior government, Minamoto Yoritomo. After the suspicious deaths of the second and third shoguns (Yoritomo's sons) the post came to be filled not by warriors, but by aristocrats of the capital and imperial sons. No real power or authority was accorded the shogun. He was a puppet of the bakufu, if not a scapegoat. Ever suspicious of possible collusion between rebellious warrior elements and capital aristocrats, or simply fearing the potential authority in the shogunal post, the Hōjō regents appointed them young and powerless. Kujō Yoritsune (r. 1226–1244) became shogun at the age of eight; his son Yoritsugu (r. 1244–1252) at the age of five; Prince Munetaka (Go-Saga's son) at the age of ten; Prince Koreyasu (Prince Munetaka's son) at the age of three; Prince Hisaaki (Go-Fukakusa's son) at the age of thirteen; and finally Prince Morikuni (son of Prince Hisaaki; r.1308–1333) at the age of eight. Of these, all but the last two were expelled by the bakufu in disgrace under an implicit accusation of rebelliousness. The last Kamakura shogun died with all the other warrior officials when the bakufu was destroyed in 1333.[87]

The lamentable episode involving Prince Koreyasu moves seamlessly into a description of what promises to be the celebratory arrival of a new shogun, Hisaaki, the son of Go-Fukakusa by Sanjō Bōshi (Fusako), who holds the court rank of junior second rank.[88] Kamakura was preparing to receive him into a respectably arranged space with officials and women dressed in proper outfits. Lady Komachi served as a mediator for Nijō's involvement in the preparations as "an advisor of taste." When Nijō showed reservations, Lady Komachi assured her that nobody knew who she was. Nijō's narrative carefully presents the entire experience as a spontaneous occurrence that had nothing to do with her identity or connections. But Nijō proved her expertise in cutting, sewing, and assembling gowns. In particular, a set of gowns that had been sent by Higashi-Nijō-in to the wife of an important official called for much reshaping and rearranging; cloth was resewn to place certain motifs in certain locations, different colored robes were layered so that shades were coordinated to run in certain directions, and so on. She described minutely the errors that were made and proudly instructed "how to correct this amusing mistake."[89] It was as though Nijō was in conversation with Higashi-Nijō-in and the culture she represents through the coded language of clothes.

Hōjō Sadatoki, who identified Nijō as "the person from Kyō," called her to assist in preparing the shogun's living room. In the memoir, Nijō expresses displeasure with this task but complies in a half-hearted way. It is unclear why Nijō initially expressed reservations about helping with the gowns and even showed disdain toward assisting with the room arrangement. While Nijō found humor in the erroneous ways the gowns were assembled and eventually showed much enthusiasm for repairing them, she was nearly dismissive of Hōjō Sadatoki's request to oversee the chamber. Perhaps she considered the latter task below her station or outside the range of proper activities for a woman of her background. Perhaps she resisted being ordered by a warrior official instead of someone with a court background, such as Lady Komachi. It is also puzzling to see the attempt, at least textual, to keep her identity concealed. Did she want to conceal it so that officials in Kamakura would be unaware of the presence of one so close to Go-Fukakusa? Was she there of her own accord, or was she in fact sent by Go-Fukakusa or Sanekane to oversee the situation? While we cannot answer these questions, it is clear to us that Nijō was no mere traveler who by chance dropped in to find this important event taking place in Kamakura. Despite her expulsion from court, the political developments that linked court and bakufu remained a part of Nijō's life and concerns.

Nijō was rewarded for her efforts. Hisaaki arrived in a magnificent manner, about which Nijō could not find fault. She describes the size of the procession, including the five-block-long line of cavalry and warriors, the splendor of outfits worn by people of different stations, and the display of horses. The shogun rode in a palanquin, with the blinds rolled up, wearing an embossed robe of green and yellow. Seeing all this, Nijō was saddened as she remembered her days at the court, but nonetheless reasserted her role in managing affairs related to Go-Fukakusa.[90]

Between this incident and the closing scenes in the memoir, a period spanning seventeen years of her life from the age of thirty-two to forty-nine, Nijō traveled widely across the archipelago, visiting various shrines and temples, as well as scenic spots that had been immortalized in canonic literature. During these years, Nijō reencountered Go-Fukakusa twice, and, in response to his queries, essentially declared her perpetual spiritual and sexual faithfulness and devotion to her old patron. Gradually, she lost her former contacts in the capital, such as

Lady Kitayama, Higashi-Nijō-in, Kameyama, and Go-Fukakusa, who died one by one, and she also donated to temples all her material possessions, including a *sayogoromo* that Go-Fukakusa had granted her at their last meeting. Nijō's last glimpse of her patron was both tangible and eternal: she saw Go-Fukakusa's portrait being carried into a mausoleum, and witnessed from a distance the smoke rising as he was cremated. By always associating with Go-Fukakusa, Nijō had succeeded in making herself as immortal as Go-Fukakusa himself.[91]

Conclusion

Nijō's memoir is an account of a life that has been reevaluated and reordered from the perspective of her later years. It selects certain episodes and highlights certain moments, while omitting and reconfiguring others. It is a controlled text and not what one would call a straightforward historical account. Nonetheless, in her selection and accenting of incidents, Nijō offers us a broad spectrum of possibilities for understanding the undocumented aspects of court politics, including women's roles in it. The account she provides is precisely what we do not find in the historical sources written and kept by men in their official or otherwise privileged capacity, and therein lies the greatest value of this work. *Towazugatari* offers information that is acutely personal and suggestive, if not outright honest and expository. Unique in transcribing the highly insecure and obsessively libidinal atmosphere of the court, it reveals the potential contribution of an "unattached" woman situated below the apex of the status ladder and free of the controlling or protective gaze and requirements of ranking parents, but encoded with the cultural training, traits, and taste that characterized the court's bluest blood.

The narrative structure, chronological positioning of the memoir, and episodic images help convey how Nijō contributed to reestablishing her lord's imperial future. Her contribution was channeled through her flesh, deemed desirable both by her lord and by the man with the means to realign the future.

By altering the narrative chronology, Nijō insists on her direct, albeit psychological, contribution to the decisive and positive reversal in the future of the imperial succession. The subtext of this assertion is that because the hierarchy of prestige placed the emperor at the top, men who slept with the "emperor's women" did so by his grace and therefore owed favors to him. The question of whether or not Nijō in reality influenced the political event of succession is immaterial. What matters is her self-perception and assertion that she did. Maximizing the power and authority embodied in her sexuality, fertility, and literary capital, Nijō assumes the position of control in her memoir and claims her own place in a bureaucratic process that formally barred women from participation.

The question of how women could be represented in a male-dominated, formal political structure, both in reality and in discourse, has stimulated much feminist inquiry. In the case of Nijō, precisely because she had no formal titles, she could maximally exploit her personal talent and political acumen to assert her place in the structure and to influence political processes, though admittedly not without regrets and suffering. The story of her participation in court politics shows us the fundamental falsity of the dichotomous concept that distinguishes the public from the private. Nijō's greatest political act was the writing of her memoir. Not only does it redeem and immortalize her literary self and discursive authority, but it also presents a fresh, unbridled, and feminine vision of politics in Japan's medieval times.

NOTES

1   Jean Bethke Elshtain, *Public Man, Private Woman: Women in Social and Political Thought*, p. 203.

2   Works by other aristocrats of her own time do not mention Lady Nijō at all, perhaps signaling her insignificance in the formal prestige-based hierarchy. However, her memoir came to attract the attention of later writers. *Masukagami*, a historical tale of the court in the Kamakura period, written sometime in the first seventy-five years of the Ashikaga period, incorporates eighteen episodes from *Towazugatari*. Tokieda Motoki and Kidō Saizō, eds., *Masukagami*. Also see the translated version by George W. Perkins, *The Clear Mirror: A Chronicle of the Japanese Court During the Kamakura Period (1185–1333)*. The journal of Sanjōnishi Sanetaka, *Sanetaka kyōki*, mentions copying *Towazugatari* at the request of Emperor Go-Tsuchimikado (1442–1500; r. 1464–1500) in entries for 1497. Matsumoto Yasushi, *Towazugatari no kenkyū*, pp. 35, 93–94. A large portion of this chapter, especially the material on Nijō's background and authorial position, is taken from my previously published article, "Coercive Sex at the Medieval Japanese Court: Lady Nijō's Memoir." I thank Kate Wildman Nakai, the editor of the journal, for allowing me to adapt what has already appeared. While the previous article focused on the question of coercive sex in Nijō's life and court, this essay examines her actual and narrative relationships to what we call "the political."

3   In reading *Towazugatari*, I have been influenced by the methods outlined in Mieke Bal, *Lethal Love: Feminist Literary Readings of Biblical Love Stories*.

4   For a survey of court and bakufu through the Jōkyū War, see Jeffrey P. Mass, *The Development of Kamakura Rule 1180–1250: A History with Documents*, pp. 3–58.

5   For a general sense of the rhythms and prerogatives enjoyed by each, with an emphasis on the court side, see G. Cameron Hurst III, "The Kōbu Polity: Court-Bakufu Relations in Kamakura Japan," and Cornelius J. Kiley, "The Imperial Court as a Legal Authority in the Kamakura Age."

6   Those exiled were Go-Toba and his sons, Tsuchimikado (1195–1231, r. 1198–1210), and Juntoku (1197–1242; r. 1210–1221). The bakufu also dethroned the reigning emperor, Chūkyō (1218–1234; r. 1221–1221), Juntoku's four-year-old son, to whom Juntoku had yielded the throne when he became involved in the uprising. Chūkyō had no imperial "name" until the Meiji period when "Chūkyō" was conferred belatedly.

7   Because Shijō died without issue, Tsuchimikado's third son Go-Saga was enthroned.

8   It is clear that the relationship of court and bakufu was an evolving process, and that when the Kantō deemed it necessary, it could act unilaterally and proactively. One clear illustration of this, which also calls into question the overall role of the Kantō liaison (of which more below), emerges from the events surrounding the Mongol invasions, which were contemporaneous with Nijō's time at court. In 1268 the Mongols sent messages, demanding a tributary relationship, to the "King of Japan." When the court decided, independently of the Kantō, to respond to the Mongol overtures, even if negatively, the Kantō rejected the decision and determined to ignore the threat. In the years of preparation and actual invasions in 1274 and 1281, Kantō continued to ignore the court's proposals regarding how to respond, but it maintained the appearance of a proper protocol by funneling communications through the Kantō liaison. Kantō also requisitioned fighters who were not its own vassals in the name of this office. How the liaison office participated in responsibilities other than the communication function remains unclear. Kantō Liaison Saionji Sanekane does not appear among the participants in deliberations at the court at this time. Mori Shigeaki, *Kamakura jidai no chōbaku kankei*, pp. 218–20, 226, 230; Uwayokote Masataka, "Kamakura Muromachi bakufu to chōtei," pp. 107–108; Nam Ki-hak, *Mōko shūrai to Kamakura bakufu*, p. 133; Yamamoto Hiroya, "Kantō mōshitsugi to Kamakura bakufu."

9   Kujō Michiie lost this position because of the deposition of his son, Yoritsune (1218–1256; r. 1226–1244), who was the first aristocratic

shogun after the murder of Sanetomo, the third and last Minamoto shogun, and who later came under suspicion by the bakufu.

10   Ryō Susumu. *Kamakura jidai, jō, Kantō*, p. 89.

11   Misumi Yōichi, ed., *Towazugatari*, pp. 16–19.

12   For a survey of the development of *chiten no kimi* for the early and late Kamakura periods respectively, see Shirai Katsuhiro, "Kamakura-ki kuge seiji kikō no keisei to tenkai: 'Chiten no kimi' no taiseika o megutte"; and Ichizawa Satoshi, "Kamakura kōki kuge shakai no kōzō to 'chiten no kimi'." On Go-Saga's activities as the *chiten* ruler for more than twenty years during his two sons' tenure on the throne, see Mikael S. Adolphson. *The Gates of Power: Monks, Courtiers, and Warriors in Premodern Japan*, pp. 185–239.

13   The estates themselves were held in trust in several blocks by imperial females, but with respect to their disposition, the *chiten no kimi* had a substantial voice.

14   For the longer-term consequences, and the complex disputes over both the tangible and intangible assets of the imperial family, see Andrew Edmund Goble, *Kenmu: Go-Daigo's Revolution*, esp. chaps. 1 and 2; H. Paul Varley, *Imperial Restoration in Medieval Japan*, esp. pp. 52–65.

15   Misumi, *Towazugatari*, p. 10; Tonomura, "Coercive Sex," p. 283.

16   These daughters were wives of emperors Fushimi (1265–1317; r. 1287–1298), Kameyama, and Go-Daigo (1288–1339; r. 1318–1339), but none gave birth to a male offspring.

17   For an introduction to this topic, see Thomas D. Conlan, "Thicker Than Blood: The Social and Political Significance of Wet Nurses in Japan, 950–1330."

18   For example, in a symbolic and graphic gesture, at a social gathering he replaced Nijō as lute player with his daughter, although lute playing was Nijō's expertise. Deeply humiliated, Nijō got up and left. Misumi, *Towazugatari*, pp. 93–95.

19   The Saionji daughters entered the court as *nyōgo*. The titles for imperial wives were complex and their uses and meanings varied over time, because of the absence of solid rules regarding the number of wives or sexual partners. However, only one woman seems to have

served as an emperor's primary wife at a given time, bearing the highest-ranked consort title. A good description of the complicated system of imperial wives in the Heian period, the antecedent for the Kamakura pattern, may be found in William H. McCullough and Helen Craig McCullough, trans., *A Tale of Flowering Fortunes: Annals of Japanese Aristocratic Life in the Heian Period*, pp. 818–822; and William H. McCullough, "The Capital and Its Society," esp. pp. 123–127.

20   As mentioned by Nomura Ikuyo, the institution of *nyōin*, or women's *in* (as opposed to the male emperor's *in*) is just beginning to be understood. More has been written about *nyōin* in the Heian period than for later times, from its origin in the tenth century and transformation in the late twelfth century. Basic questions demand further examination, such as: when, on what qualifications, and for what reason the designation of *in* was granted to an imperial wife and sometimes even to unmarried "fictitious mothers" (*junbo*) of emperors. Nomura Ikuyo, "Nyōin kenkyū no genjō"; also see Takamatsu Momoka, "Nyōin no seiritsu: sono yōin to chii o megutte."

21   For example, as mentioned below in "Episode Three," the gown that Go-Fukakusa knowingly gave away to a fisherman in 1275 was a specially ordered gift from Sanekane, about which Nijō was "more than usually pleased." Misumi, *Towazugatari*, p. 113; the description of the gown is on p. 109.

22   Misumi, *Towazugatari*, pp. 17 and 97, for the first textual appearance of the terms. Nijō used "a secret person" and some other ambiguous terms before using "Dawn Snow" for Sanekane for the first time in 1277.

23   This is an abridged and reshaped version of the description of the same incident in Tonomura, "Coercive Sex," pp. 303–313. I have omitted here what I call "the second reading" of Nijō's expressions that, when analyzed through her intertextual dialogue with canonical literature, reveals another layer of meaning about her sexual prowess that nonetheless supports our present interpretation regarding her political role.

24   She recalls that she was "wearing a seven-layered robe, shaded from light pink to plum red, with a light green outer robe, and a red formal jacket." She then adds, as though searching her memory, "I wore a two-layered small-sleeved under-robe with a brocade pattern of

plum blossoms and Chinese grasses, embroidered with bamboo fences and plum trees." Misumi, *Towazugatari*, p. 3; Karen Brazell, trans., *The Confessions of Lady Nijō*, p. 1. Nijō's luxurious seven-layered gown, forbidden in her time for all but those closest to the center of power, immediately sets her apart from other ladies-in-waiting who typically wore five-layered gowns. Similarly restricted was the red jacket (*akairo no karaginu*), which also marked Nijō as special. The shades of plum red and purple red emphasize that Nijō is a young maiden. According to Shimegi Miyako, Nijō conveys a strong sense of self by using the word "I" (*ware*) at the very beginning of the memoir, unlike other female authors who would do so only at a later point. Shimegi also notes Nijō's use of phrases that indicate the present moment, such as "this morning" (*kesa*), "today" (*kyō*), and "this evening" (*koyoi*), through which she constructs a "historical present." This technique, combined with the frequent use of "I" (*ware* or *ware nagara*), provides the sense of immediacy that allows her to appear to be reliving the past years later. See Shimegi's explanation of "first-person narration" in Nishizawa Masashi and Shimegi Miyako, *Towazugatari*, pp. 424–426. I thank Aileen Gatten for sharpening my sense for clothes-related codes. The permissible number of layers in gowns worn by palace women became stabilized in the late eleventh century when, on special public occasions, five layers became the norm for all but the most prestigious. See Tsuda Daisuke, "'Kazuginu' seido no seiritsu: Shashi kinsei to yūsoku kojitsu." I thank Nakai Maki for calling my attention to this article.

25   "Let 'the wild goose of the fields' come to me this spring (*Tanomu no kari mo wagakata ni yo*)" Go-Fukakusa says. Misumi, *Towazugatari*, p. 3. The translation is from Brazell, *The Confessions of Lady Nijō*, pp. 1–2. The phrase, from *Ise monogatari*, refers to a situation in which a man, through the "wild goose" metaphor, wins a daughter because her mother strongly approves the arrangement regardless of the father's wishes. It allows Go-Fukakusa to imply that Nijō is ready to be given to him at this time in accordance with her mother's wish, that his request is legitimate, and that the father has no say in the matter. *Ise monogatari*, *dan* 10, in Takeoka Masao, *Ise monogatari zenhyōshaku*, p. 264, with the various interpretations of the passage on pp. 264–283. In the story, the mother is an aspiring Fujiwara and the father is of lesser birth. The wild goose (the daughter) is crying out to be with the noble upon whom she can depend.

26 "When my father received the 'three times the nine cups' (*ku-san*) of *sake* from my lord, it looked as though my lord whispered something to him, but I had no way of knowing what was said." Misumi, *Towazugatari*, p. 3.

27 Misumi, *Towazugatari*, p. 4. I thank Esperanza Ramirez-Christensen for her invaluable assistance in rendering this passage and many of the poems below into English.

28 For extensive information on all aspects of clothes figuring in *Towazugatari*, see the appendix, "Fukusō kankeigo yōran," in Misumi, *Towazugatari*, pp. 320–341. Aristocratic women who did not serve at court only rarely mention clothes in their diaries. For example, the author of *Kagero nikki*, who lived at home, mentions clothes only once or twice. Iwasa Miyoko, *Kyūtei ni ikiru: tennō to nyōbō to*, pp. 130–131.

29 Misumi, *Towazugatari*, p. 4. The translation of the poem is from Brazell, *The Confessions of Lady Nijō*, p. 2.

30 Misumi, *Towazugatari*, p. 4. The translation of the poem is by Esperanza Ramirez-Christensen. Scholars have interpreted it in various ways.

31 Misumi, *Towazugatari*, p. 4. Translation provided by Esperanza Ramirez-Christensen. The terms shift from *kegoromo* (plumage) to *sayogoromo* (night clothes) to *sagoromo* (gown). In the medieval period *sayogoromo* typically meant "night clothes," with or without sexual connotations. Anne Walthall has pointed out to me that with the development of a more sharply defined concept of adultery in the Tokugawa period, *sayogoromo* became a metaphor for adultery. See *Nihon kokugo daijiten*, vol. 5, p. 149, for examples. Along this line, see Go-Fukakusa's much later poem in which he employs "someone else's sleeves of *sayogoromo*" to hint at Nijō's liaison with Sanekane. Misumi, *Towazugatari*, pp. 45–46.

32 Iwasa Miyoko, *Kyūtei joryū bungaku dokkai kō: chūseihen*, pp. 347–353; on the meaning of *sayogoromo* per se, see pp. 343–347. Misumi, *Towazugatari*, p. 122.

33 Misumi, *Towazugatari*, p. 4.

34 As mentioned above, court ladies normally considered their mother's residence as their "home," to return to when they needed respite from court duties. For Nijō the absence of a maternal home was

a disadvantage. The sexual encounter with Go-Fukakusa takes place at her father's house, which may in actuality have been his new wife's residence. After the death of her father, Nijō seems to go to her wet nurse's house when in need of privacy.

35   When she asks the reason, her father explains that the lord is coming tonight because of a certain directional taboo, and that Nijō is to serve him. "But what directional taboo?" Nijō asks. The people of the house all laugh, commenting on her naiveté. In her room as well, there are new furnishings. "Here too?" she asks, but everyone in this stepmother's household smiles and tells her nothing. Misumi, *Towazugatari*, p. 5.

36   "I had no way of knowing why he was giving me this admonition," Nijō states. "It was a bit annoying, so I leaned against the brazier and fell asleep." Misumi, *Towazugatari*, p. 6.

37   Nijō is clearly despondent. "Years have passed without your understanding the situation," Nijō reports him stating, "so I came thinking that at least an occasion like this would [make it clear]. Now people around us have doubtless learned that it has happened. How can you continue being so cold?" "I was amazed," Nijō continues, "to know that I had enough of a mind to think, 'So, that's how it is. This is not even the [sort of] dream that is kept secret, but one known to everyone, a night's dream from which I would have barely awakened before the worries come.' Such were my thoughts, and it was amazing that I still had the mind to think." Go-Fukakusa's poem repeats the central images in the poems exchanged between Nijō and Sanekane, employing the metaphor of sleeves of *sayogoromo* that did not meet, though Nijō's perfume lingers on them. *Amata toshi / sasuga ni nareshi / sayogoromo / kasanenu sode ni / nokoru utsuriga.* Misumi, *Towazugatari*, p. 8.

38   *Shirareji na / omoimidarete /yūkeburi / nabiki mo yaranu / shita no kokoro wa.* Misumi, *Towazugatari*, p. 9.

39   The question of whether or not this expression represents an act of rape is dealt with in Tonomura, "Coercive Sex."

40   *Kokoro yori / hoka ni tokenuru / shitahibo no / ikanaru fushi ni / ukina nagasan.* Misumi, *Towazugatari*, p. 10.

41   Misumi, *Towazugatari*, p. 10.

42   Nijō shows a similar response later after another undesirable and coerced tryst with a high-ranking courtier which we will address below in "Episode Three: Nijō in Kamakura."

43   Tonomura, "Coercive Sex," p. 294. Yokoo Yutaka, *Kamakura jidai no kōkyū seikatsu*, pp. 6–8, 94, 119–120, 206.

44   Misumi, *Towazugatari*, p. 13.

45   Misumi, *Towazugatari*, p. 17.

46   The reference here is to the so-called Disturbance of the Second Month (*Nigatsu sōdō*). Tokisuke had fallen out with the bakufu leader Hōjō Tokimune, his brother, over personal and policy differences, and Tokimune then ordered Yoshimune to kill Tokisuke and raze his house.

47   Misumi, *Towazugatari*, pp. 18, 20.

48   The creation of a false chronology allows Nijō to construct an alternative narrative unity that helps to highlight certain experiences and meanings in relationship to other episodes. One pertinent example is the birth of Higashi-Nijō-in's daughter in 1270, which, according to Nijō's memoir, takes place in 1272, after Nijō's reentry into the court as Go-Fukakusa's companion. The effect of the alteration of events is to contrast Nijō's own humble birth-giving circumstance in 1273 against Higashi-Nijō-in's lavish and celebrated experience, which in fact took place before Nijō's memoir begins. Misumi, *Towazugatari*, pp. 13–15, 44–45. This technique also allows Nijō to include the daughter of Higashi-Nijō-in as one of the important characters to appear at the end of her memoir, thus creating one axis of narrative unity.

49   This section is taken from Tonomura, "Coercive Sex," pp. 318–319.

50   Go-Fukakusa sends a poem in 1273.12 to Nijō, who is staying away from the palace and having an affair with Sanekane. This poem states that he has had a dream in which Nijō's sleeves of *sayogoromo* were touching those of another. In describing this poem, Nijō carefully prefaces it with a statement that it came amid many other words of unusual kindness, and although it pained her to do so, she deceived him with a poem in response that depicted her solitary sleeves graced only by the moonlight. Nijō's guilt consciousness begins to take shape. Misumi, *Towazugatari*, pp. 45–46.

51   Misumi, *Towazugatari*, pp. 49–50.

52   This daughter's identity is debated but may be either Eifukumon-in (1271–1352), the adopting mother of Go-Fushimi and a famous poet, or Shōkunmon-in (1273–1336). Misumi, *Towazugatari*, p. 417.

53   Nijō's strategy to heighten the significance of Sanekane's involvement in her birth is made abundantly clear by comparing her short description of giving birth in 1281, the result of an affair with Ariake, another lover who likewise attended the birth of their child. Regarding this birthing experience, Nijō merely states that "as the morning bell chimed, a child was born and it was a boy." Misumi, *Towazugatari*, p. 139.

54   Misumi 1994, pp. 47–50.

55   Similar to the type of travel experienced by Saigyō (1118–1190), whose pictorial work Nijō saw when she was nine. Saigyō was known for his itinerant and ascetic practices. Misumi, *Towazugatari*, p. 52.

56   *Shiryō sōran*, vol. 5, p. 209; entry for Kenji 1 (1275).4.9.

57   *Shiryō sōran*, vol. 5, p. 212; entry for Kenji 1 (1275).11.5.

58   Matsumoto, *Towazugatari no kenkyū*, p. 114.

59   *Kokushi daijiten,* vol. 6, p. 127. This entry on Sanekane is by Matsumoto Yasushi. Also see Matsumoto, *Towazugatari no kenkyū*, p. 114.

60   Takagi Yōko,"Go-Fukakusa insei no seiritsu katei (I)"; Kanpaku Takatsukasa Kanehira, "Daijōdaijin Takatsukasa Mototada no rinin to sono kiketsu," p. 14.

61   Takagi Yōko, "Go-Fukakusa insei no seiritsu katei (II)," p. 54.

62   Misumi, *Towazugatari*, p. 107; Brazell, *The Confessions of Lady Nijō*, p. 112.

63   Mori, *Kamakura jidai no chōbaku kankei*, p. 52.

64   Misumi, *Towazugatari*, pp. 109–113.

65   Matsumoto, *Towazugatari no kenkyū*, pp. 132–134.

66   Hongō Kazuto, "Kameyama'in to Takatsukasa Kanehira," pp. 50–52.

67 Misumi, *Towazugatari*, p. 109. This translation follows Brazell, *The Confessions of Lady Nijō*, p. 114.

68 Cormorant fishermen occupied a position in the chains of patron-client relationships extending from the imperial family and shrines. According to Amino Yoshihiko, they were "providers" (*kugonin* or *jinin*) and had privileges such as protection from taxation, until the mid-fourteenth century. See Amino Yoshihiko, "Ukai to katsurame" in his *Nihon chūsei hinōgyōmin to tennō*, esp. pp. 392–410.

69 Misumi, *Towazugatari*, p. 113–114.

70 Misumi, *Towazugatari*, p. 135.

71 Misumi, *Towazugatari*, pp. 151–152.

72 Misumi, *Towazugatari*, pp. 155–168.

73 Go-Fushimi's biological mother was Fujiwara Keishi (?–1324). The fate of the Saionji was closely intertwined with that of the imperial family, but took different turns in the new century. In 1315, following the untimely death of his son, Kinhira, the Kantō liaison, the now sixty-seven-year-old Sanekane returned to the liaison position and immediately shifted from his long-standing posture of supporting Go-Fukakusa's line (and Go-Fukakusa's son, Fushimi, in particular) to attacking it and supporting Kameyama's camp. This change was marked first by a strike against the retired emperor Fushimi's ally, Kyogoku Tamekane (1254–1332). Kyogoku, who had wielded power under Fushimi's patronage, was now charged with involvement in alleged anti-bakufu activities. Fushimi, with a wife from the Tōin line, had earlier been promoted by Sanekane, and even served by him as chamberlain of the crown prince's household; but now, he came perilously close himself to being implicated in anti-bakufu plotting with Kyogoku. Meanwhile, Sanekane placed one of his daughters in Kameyama's court and engineered the appointment of Go-Uda's son (later Go-Nijo) as crown prince. Sanekane's policies effectively initiated a pattern of alternating succession between the two lines that would lead ultimately to Go-Daigo's efforts to alter the national policy itself. In the midst of this multi-directional animosity, the throne bounced from Kameyama's line to Go-Fukakusa's line twice, then to Kameyama's, again to Go-Fukakusa's, and then finally, with Go-Daigo, to the Kameyama side once more. Mori, *Kamakura jidai no chōbaku kankei*, p. 53; Takagi, "Go-Fukakusa insei no seiritsu katei (I)," pp.

14–18; *Kokushi daijiten*, vol. 6, p. 127. For treatment of the various complexities of this long process and the impact on the Saionji family and those in their orbit, see Robert N. Huey, *Kyōgoku Tamekane: Poetry and Politics in Late Kamakura Japan*, esp. pp. 12–15, 41–62; Goble, *Kenmu*, pp. 3–20, 55–63, 73–79, 86–89. On the later fate of one Saionji and his wife, Hino Meishi, see Hitomi Tonomura, "Re-envisioning Women in the Post-Kamakura Age."

74   Tonomura, "Coercive Sex," pp. 328–329. That Nijō lacks an identity of her own is reflected in an entry in a modern guide to classical Japanese literature, published in 1985, which lists her work under "Gofukakusa In [Retired Emperor] Nijō." Earl Miner, Hiroko Odagiri, and Robert E. Morrell, eds., *The Princeton Companion to Classical Japanese Literature*, p. 157.

75   "Yatsuhashi," for example. Misumi, *Towazugatari*, p. 170.

76   Misumi, *Towazugatari*, p. 171.

77   The ritual is "something that is called Ten Thousand on the Beach (*Hama no ichiman tokayate*)," the meaning of which is unclear. Misumi, *Towazugatari*, p. 172.

78   Misumi, *Towazugatari*, p 174.

79   Misumi, *Towazugatari*, pp. 174–175. Her father's Minamoto line traces its origin to Emperor Murakami (926–967).

80   The shogun was Koreyasu (1264–1326). For the identity of Lady Komachi, see Misumi, *Towazugatari*, p. 176, notes 37–39.

81   For this episode see Karen Brazell, "The Changing of the Shogun 1289: An Excerpt from *Towazugatari*"; and Brazell, *The Confessions of Lady Nijō*, pp. 189–195.

82   Misumi, *Towazugatari*, pp. 176–177.

83   Misumi, *Towazugatari*, pp. 177–178.

84   Misumi, *Towazugatari*, p. 178.

85   Misumi, *Towazugatari*, p. 179.

86   Misumi, *Towazugatari*, p. 179.

87   Although Nijō is entirely silent on this matter, when she was in Kamakura, the bakufu was still recovering from psychological and economic damages inflicted upon warrior society by the Mongol invasions of 1274 and 1281. Although they caused relatively little

devastation in Japan—compared to China and Korea, and many other parts of the world—the invasions compounded the preexisting fiscal problems and lowered the morale of the entire military community. Historical records indicate that Go-Fukakusa ordered prayers against the alien enemy in 1289. Three years before Nijō's arrival in Kamakura, the bakufu had sought to ameliorate warriors' mounting discontent by granting some rewards for fighting against the invaders. And, as we know, the bakufu was also involved from a distance in the succession disputes that continued to plague the imperial family. This was the condition of the bakufu that Nijō found when she visited.

88   Fusako was the daughter of Sanjō Kinchika (c. 1220–1291). Identified by Nijō as Mikushigedono, she appears in her memoir, for example, seated at the low seat in a palanquin with Ōmiya-in and Higashi-Nijō-in as they travel to Go-Saga's place in 1272. In other words, she was Nijō's co-worker. Misumi, *Towazugatari*, p. 16.

89   Brazell, *The Confessions of Lady Nijō*, p. 194.

90   Misumi, *Towazugatari*, pp. 181–183. See the translation of types of clothes and colors in Brazell, *The Confessions of Lady Nijō*, p. 194.

91   Descriptions of these last days may be found in Tonomura, "Coercive Sex," pp. 322–329.

Outcasts before the Law: Pollution and Purification in Medieval Japan
Thomas Keirstead

Notions of Discrimination in Early Modern Japan

"While passing through the village of Utsunoya [in 1706]," the Japanese philosopher Ogyū Sorai recalled, "I felt a great urge to smoke. But refined emissaries should not break customs. I could not ask for a light."[1] Sorai was stymied because Utsunoya was a community of *kawata*, that is, a community of people whom the Tokugawa regime deemed so impure as to fall altogether outside of the category of human. *Kawata*—the term means "leather workers"—were more often known then by the far more pejorative term *eta*, which means "plentifully defiled." Together with a group known as *hinin* (literally, the "nonhuman"), *kawata* occupied the lowest position in the status system of early modern Japan.

The circular designation of *kawata* reflects, first, the kind of occupation that the regime regarded as fitting for people it sought to ostracize, and, second, the fact that the regime attributed their ostracism to an intrinsic quality of the *kawata* themselves. Indeed, *kawata* were seen as defiled because they engaged in defiling occupations, and they engaged in defiling occupations because they were already defiled.

Sorai's remark constituted a passing moment in the history of discrimination against *kawata* and *hinin*, a history already replete with such humiliations by Sorai's time. Beginning in the 1660s, for example, *kawata* were segregated into special hamlets (sometimes by means of a wall literally bifurcating sections of existing villages).[2] Successive measures made the social status of both *hinin* and *kawata* hereditary.[3] Both groups also faced economic restrictions. By the early eighteenth century, they were barred from ordinary trades. *Kawata* could engage only in the leather trade and certain distasteful official duties, such as attending at executions. *Hinin* were restricted to licensed begging, street cleaning (including disposal of dead horses and cattle), and other "janitorial" services (such as cleaning the jails). The Tokugawa regime also sought to render *kawata/hinin* status visible. Racially, linguistically, and in all other outward respects indistinguishable from ordinary Japanese, *kawata* and *hinin* were forced from the beginning of the eighteenth century to display visible signs of their status. Small squares of fur or leather served to identify *kawata*, while wooden tags marked *hinin*. Worried that *hinin* were coming to look too much like "regular people" (*tsune no mono*), authorities in Edo rounded up 3,659 *hinin* in 1723 and cropped their hair. Sumptuary laws meanwhile dictated that they wear "coarse clothes," and that women not blacken their teeth like commoners. *Hinin* were also prohibited from wearing hats.[4]

Sorai's further remarks in his memoir are notable not only because they register the fact of discrimination, but also because they tell us about the means employed to legitimize the discrimination. His quip about the residents of Utsunoya—"They are all butchers (*toke*),"—identifies one "explanation" regularly adduced at the time to suggest that *kawata* were less than human. Although the scores of directives issued to confine *kawata* to the leather trade suggest that they had not previously been so confined, and likely lived much like other peasants, contemporary scholars repeated ad nauseum the conventional wisdom that *kawata* were all "polluted" because they were butchers and ate meat. Invoking a handful of medieval texts that identified *eta* as people who made a living dealing in animal hides, and citing as well Buddhist commandments against the taking of life and Shinto strictures surrounding death, Edo scholars argued that ancient notions of pollution justified the current restrictions against outcasts.

About two decades after the journey that took him past Utsunoya, Sorai returned to the question of *kawata* and *hinin*. In his "Political Discourses" (c. 1725), he provides us with a comparatively early example of the second pillar in the intellectual armature of oppression: the idea that *kawata/eta* were not Japanese. "Not sharing fire with *eta*," he wrote, "is the custom of this divine land and a necessity," because *kawata* "are of different stock," and a polluted stock (or seed) as well. "In both China and Japan, now and in the past, [*kawata*] are despised," he noted. When commoners mixed with *kawata* (i.e., when the different races mixed) the result was an "undeniable deterioration in morals," the only remedy for which was to "follow the ancient laws, segregate the races ... and strictly forbid [*kawata*] from mixing with commoners."[5] Others followed Sorai's intellectual lead. Roughly half a century later, Kaiho Seiryō, Confucian scholar and mercantilist, wrote that "in the set of their eyes and the shape of their faces, *eta* are utterly unlike the people of this country." They are, he averred, "barbarians from a foreign land ... and like beasts nothing is too degrading for them."[6] Still other commentators, perhaps with an eye to developing the new northern frontier, were more specific: they identified *kawata* and *hinin* as descendants of the original inhabitants of Hokkaido and proposed that they be shipped back en masse. Thus, as the social stigma and webs of legal and economic regulations governing *kawata* and *hinin* grew more restrictive, Tokugawa intellectuals worked to justify the official oppression. Citing the ancient customs of "this divine land" or declaring that *kawata* were "foreign arrivals," the Tokugawa intelligentsia invented a history for *kawata* and *hinin* proclaiming the Edo outcast order as part of the deep structure of Japanese society. In so doing they displaced the origins of the discrimination against *kawata* and *hinin* from contemporary legislation and the political and economic expediencies it catered to, and relocated them in custom and antiquity.

Seeking Precedents in Medieval Practices

The complex of political/legal restrictions and intellectual justifications cobbled together during the Tokugawa period has left two important legacies for the study of outcast groups. First, the system devised by Tokugawa authorities provided the framework for subsequent discrimination. Even after the laws that targeted *kawata* and *hinin* were abolished in 1871, the informal discrimination continued; to this day their descendants remain subject to practices and thinking akin to those the Tokugawa system encouraged. Second, it is the contemporary discrimination and the hope of redressing it that motivates our interest in the history of outcast groups in earlier times. We who write about outcasts have, by and large, followed the lead of Tokugawa intellectuals in attempting to write the history of early modern and modern discrimination back into the premodern past. Perhaps because the terminology used in early modern Japan to identify outcasts is medieval in origin, there is a strong temptation to extrapolate backwards from Tokugawa practices and write about medieval practices as if they constituted the prehistory of later discrimination. Nagahara Keiji thus begins his well-known investigation of the origins of *eta* and *hinin* with today's *burakumin* movement and works back from there:

> If we are to examine the origins of the [present-day] *burakumin,* we must begin our study from the ancient and medieval periods. Thus, the goals of this essay are to examine how and why ... the discrimination originating in the medieval period was then transformed into the *eta-hinin* system of the Tokugawa period.[7]

On this premise Nagahara constructs a continuous history of discrimination that begins in the middle ages and carries on into the Tokugawa period and beyond. The *eta* and *hinin* that one encounters in medieval sources are, he asserts, the same groups one meets with in the Tokugawa period, and their descendants are the *burakumin* of today. In presuming the continuity of discrimination, this history naturalizes the Tokugawa legislation, which institutionalized a body politic founded on status.

It is important, however, to challenge the idea that Tokugawa-era legislation simply regularized a system of discrimination already existing in the medieval era. To assume, as Nagahara and many other commentators have, that Tokugawa practices must have had earlier precedents, that there is a history of discrimination and of those discriminated against that begins in the middle ages (if not earlier) and reaches fruition in early modern times, is both to misunderstand the operation of the law and to subscribe to its fictions. Herman Ooms has demonstrated how Tokugawa regulations brought the *eta/hinin* into existence as subjects before the law, yet at the same time hid the law's performativity behind a screen:

> The *ought* of the law slides under the *is* of an imaginary order structured according to symbolic categories such as nature, descent, purity, and pollution, which are presented as direct readings of reality but are in fact nothing but political values or social norms.[8]

In order to effect that slide, to pretend that it merely represents and regulates what in fact it has instituted, the law calls on ancillary discourses such as history, philosophy, and science. Thus, while it is tempting to answer the question, "Where did the Tokugawa-period *eta/hinin* come from?" with a history that pushes back to the medieval appearances of the terms, we must resist that impulse. Yielding to it would be to summon the precedent that Tokugawa-era legislation mobilized (and that contemporary discrimination against the *burakumin* continues to mobilize) to naturalize its prescriptions.

To be sure, there is a history to be told here, and this essay is an attempt to do just that. But it is not necessarily a history that connects directly to later discriminatory practices or prejudices; the significance of medieval practices surrounding *hinin* and *kawata* does not, I think, have primarily to do with intolerance or bigotry or discrimination against down-and-out social groups. This essay will attempt to examine medieval practices without prejudging their significance, without assuming, that is, that their interest lies in the legacy they left for subsequent eras. While as designators of social phenomena the terms *hinin* and *kawata* (and a host of others used to identify lowly or outcast groups) are medieval in origin, it is by no means certain that the Tokugawa *hinin* and *kawata* or present-day *burakumin* are their direct heirs. While the middle ages bequeathed to Tokugawa and later times a vocabulary and a grabbag of notions about pollution, despised trades, defiling occupations and acts, it did not present them with a ready-made subject for discrimination, an *eta* or a *hinin* to be exploited. It requires a particular kind of history to deal with these subjects "before the law": one that acknowledges that medieval practices may have supplied important elements to the Tokugawa formulation of *eta* and *hinin*, but that also sees that formulation as unprecedented. If there is a logic (that is, a "law") to medieval practices regarding outcast groups, it will be a logic peculiar to that time and to its power structures and symbolic constructs; it may well not form part of a general history of discriminatory practices in Japan.

An inquiry into the ideas and practices surrounding *eta*, *hinin*, and other outcasts in the middle ages offers instead insights into the character of the medieval polity and into the ways in which kingship was understood and operated. Medieval Japan was marked by the coexistence of two very different political and symbolic economies. One, the dominant, was anchored in agriculture and articulated through the hierarchies of offices that delivered rents and taxes from the provinces to the central elite; its titular and symbolic head was the emperor. The other encompassed a multiplicity of non-agrarian activities—from hunting and fishing to a variety of manufactures and trades. Characterized by movement and exchange, this economy created connections between disparate groups singled out for their "special talents" (*shokunō*). Marginal to the first order, outcasts are almost archetypal carriers of the second. Therefore, their place in the medieval order of things cannot be reduced to a single category; they had a place in both economies.

Fluidity of Outcasts in Medieval Japan

Any discussion of outcasts in medieval Japan must begin by recognizing the sheer variety of groups and people who might fall under that heading. In addition to *hinin, kawata,* and *eta,* the most common names by which outcasts were known were *kawaramono* (riverbank people), *toji/tosha* (people who kill), *saka no mono* (people of the slope), *katai* ("lepers," a catchall term for those suffering from a variety of disfiguring diseases), *inujinin* ("dog" shrine attendants), *kojiki* (beggars), and *kiyome* (purifiers). Collectively, these terms reflect a bewildering range of occupations and types of people. A conservative list of occupations would include gardeners and garden designers; roof thatchers; makers of straw sandals; leather workers; plasterers; professional mourners and those who handled the dead; policemen and executioners; hunters, fishers, as well as traders in meat, poultry, and seafood products; diggers of wells; makers of armor and weaponry; various kinds of monks and shrine attendants; drovers, teamsters, and boatmen; ditch diggers; people afflicted with certain diseases, notably skin diseases such as leprosy (*rai*), those who cleaned and purified temple and shrine precincts; as well as artists and entertainers of various sorts. Amino Yoshihiko's compelling argument that the taint of defilement extended to some degree to anyone who was not a farmer, aristocrat, certain kind of monk, or warrior (after the late twelfth century), expands the range of the potentially or partially defiled even further.[9] If we add in the many peasants who were also at times craftsmen or traders, then we must conclude that most of the commoner population quite possibly belonged among the defiled. Of course, there is no need to stop there. According to Buddhist thought, women were afflicted with "seven grave vices," beginning with having "no compunction about arousing sexual desire in men" on through their "bodies [being] forever unclean," that rendered them polluted.[10] Throughout the medieval period, aristocrats and monks observed complex rules defining pollution and prescribing the defilement that accompanied any contact with a polluting body or practice; at any given time a good number of the elite must have been in some respect "defiled."

One is left therefore with a "defiled" group that might encompass all of society at one time or another. In this light, it is difficult to conjure up a single principle or set of principles or law that might allow us to distinguish one group from the other and place each group securely in its proper place. As we have already noted, a concept of pollution, assisted by a concept of foreignness, supplied the logic in early modern Japan that separated *kawata/eta* from the rest of society and allowed intellectuals and lawmakers to place them on the margins of the realm. They could be so placed because pollution was understood as an attribute inherent to *kawata* alone. In the middle ages, however, pollution extended throughout society. To be sure, in some cases, such as with the diseased or those who disposed of corpses or conducted funerals, a notion of pollution (through contact with physically or spiritually endangering substances) came close to operating, as it did in the Tokugawa period, to mark certain people as different and especially defiled. But the medieval understanding of pollution was not in fact one that permitted hard and fast distinctions. If our desire is to find a medieval rule that will allow us to declare conclusively that one group was defiled while another group was not, to construct a map of society in which center and margin are clearly demarcated, then we are bound to find the middle ages exasperating.

The few medieval texts that do comment on the question of outcasts are, unfortunately, not very enlightening on the subject. They offer a frustratingly circular definition of outcast status: to be an outcast was to be set apart from the rest of society. The late thirteenth-century compendium of useful knowledge, *Chiribukuro* (Bag of Dust), informs us that "*hinin,* lepers (*raija*), *eta,* etc., are alike in that they are shunned by human society" (*hinin, katai, eta nado, hitomajiroi mo senu onajisama no mono*).[11] *Zōtanshū* (Collection of Miscellaneous Remarks), a similar collection from 1308, likewise makes no distinction among beggars, lepers, *hinin*, and *eta*, defining the lot as the Japanese equivalent of "the lowest caste [*sendara*; Sanskrit, *candala*] in India; that is, the butchers." [12] When it comes to specifying what causes defilement or how someone becomes an outcast, the sources again offer only a few suggestions. *Chiribukuro* indicates that *eta* derives from *etori*, a term that referred to the office of falconer described in the seventh-century *ritsuryō* law codes. The tenth-century *Book of Japanese Words* (*Wamyōshō*) glosses *etori* as "someone who kills and skins horses and cattle and sells their meat or takes their meat as feed for hawks,[13] so perhaps the connection is to be found in the act of killing animals and eating or using their meat and skins. The most detailed attempt at definition, found in the early seventeenth-century *Dictionary of Japanese* compiled by the Portuguese (*Vocabvlario da Lingoa de Iapam*; *Nippo jisho*) reiterates the connection between outcast groups and disease and the butchering of horses and cattle. *Kawaramono,* for example, are defined as "those who take the skins of dead animals; also those who supervise lepers." It also, however, defines *hinin* as simply "poor people." [14] So, while there is a certain regularity in the way these texts keep returning to the idea that outcasts are butchers or otherwise involved in the killing of animals, they are silent on the question of how this restricted range of activities could be parlayed into the much wider assortment of occupations mentioned earlier.

If it is difficult to account for the variety of outcast groups and to distinguish one from another, it is also extremely challenging to specify exactly what defilement meant. For the aristocracy the annual cycle of court rites and laws like the tenth-century *Engi shiki* established a complex system of abstinence for a variety of defiling situations. During the month of the Ise Virgin's procession to Ise Shrine, for example, no burials or rites of mourning were to be held in the capital. An abstinence of thirty days was prescribed for the death of a person and six days for the death of an animal (excluding chickens). Women of the palace had to withdraw when they became pregnant and during menstruation, and a miscarriage entailed absenting oneself from court and court observances for thirty days.[15]

For the rest of society, however, there were no such prescriptions, and this makes it extremely difficult to say exactly what defilement meant more generally. Standards presently used to measure the consequences of "outcast" status, such as discrimination in education, low wages and high unemployment, difficulty finding marriage partners, and substandard housing, are of limited value in an era before widespread wage labor, systematic education, and the like. While certain tasks performed by outcasts in the medieval era (such as ditch digging or executing criminals and collecting corpses for burial) are quite clearly the kinds of "dirty work" that carry stigma and have regularly been reserved for lower class or lower status groups, it is less obvious but true that similar stigma attached as well to other elevated tasks performed by outcasts: garden design, drama, and weapons-making patronized by shoguns or powerful temples; or hunting and tanning to supply dried meat, deerskins, and antlers for the Great Purification (Ōharae) rituals performed by the imperial court.

One twelfth-century source suggests that for many, being a *hinin* or *kawaramono* may simply have meant a life spent "wandering the roads, without food and without a home, begging for a living and making illness a profession."[16] But it is also clear that outcast status was not necessarily an obstacle to wealth, and that outcasts owned and cultivated land.[17] Likewise, outcasts suffered no disadvantage in the judicial system: *hinin* and *kawaramono* were not subjected to different, more severe punishments simply because of their status, nor did their status limit access to the courts. Similarly, although *kawaramono* and *hinin* may have been shunned by society at large, they were not necessarily estranged from society in all ways. Large, well-organized groups of *hinin* served powerful temples and shrines in Kyoto and Nara, and sources from throughout the middle ages show these groups acting forcefully to defend their customary rights to monopolize funerary observances, or to supervise the sick and regulate the activity of beggars.[18]

Perhaps the only modern measure that has an obvious medieval parallel is that some sort of stigma attached to the members of outcast groups. Certain sources indicate, for instance, that *hinin* were not deemed fit to swear oaths; as already impure beings, they could not suffer further divine punishment, and any oath they swore would therefore be worthless.[19] This was not a rigid rule, though, as suggested by a number of surviving oaths sworn by outcasts.[20] Occasionally, especially later in the medieval period (from the fifteenth century on), evidence suggests that *hinin* and *kawaramono* were regarded with contempt. In a well-known lament, Matashirō, the grandson of a famous garden designer (and favorite of the Shogun Yoshimasa), turns some of the scorn upon himself: he mourns the fact that he was "born a butcher [*toke*; i.e., an *eta*]" and pledges "therefore never to take the life of any being." Some of the sting goes out of these words of self-reproach, however, when we read on to find that the monk who records Matashirō's lament in fact sees him as something of an exemplar. He uses Matashirō's uprightness and humility to upbraid his fellow ecclesiastics, who, he says, "can't even match the standard of a butcher."[21] In another well-known example, Madenokōji Tokifusa, whose diary spanned some forty years of court life, observed in 1428, "Some *kawaramono* (that is, *eta*) came to the imperial palace in order to work in the gardens. This cannot be allowed; they are impure beings. It was decided last year that they should not [perform such work]."[22] Exactly how Tokifusa could claim that *kawaramono* had been banned from working in the palace is unclear; what is clear, however, is that he was wrong. There is ample evidence that *kawaramono* and *eta* continued to work as gardeners and garden designers at the palace and for other members of the aristocracy.

In short, we do not know how outcast status was regulated and maintained in medieval Japan. Crucial questions remain unanswered, including how and why these people came to dwell on the riverbanks and become categorized as *kawaramono*, or, once they came to such places, how they were kept there (if indeed they were). There are indications that people diagnosed with "leprosy" may, as a matter of course, have been removed from their families and sent to live at a *hinin* shelter.[23] But other sources suggest that the decision to enter a shelter was left to the individual; one intriguing document intimates that people might come and go from shelters.[24] As with so many other aspects of outcast life in medieval Japan, there seem to have been few general rules. Save in the case of the organized bodies of *hinin* attached to temples and to shrines, outcast status seems fairly piecemeal. Even for the most famous groups of outcasts in medieval Japan, the *hinin* attached to Kiyomizu temple in Kyoto and to Kōfukuji in Nara, we have only sketchy ideas about how "members" were recruited. Did one become a *hinin* by chance, as a result of disease or economic distress, and was it therefore environment that produced and reproduced *eta*, *kawaramono*, and other outcasts? Or, did these names designate true status groups, ones called into being and populated by legal or ideological pronouncements?

The Medieval Social Topography

There is yet another way of construing the information we have on outcasts in the middle ages. Perhaps medieval practices seem mysterious or piecemeal as an artifact of our framework of analysis, rather than as a consequence of deficiencies in the documentary record. Efforts to identify exactly what distinguished *eta* from *hinin*, or to establish their precise relationship to "proper" society, have been largely unproductive.[25] Perhaps this is so because we remain engaged in the Tokugawa project of categorizing and classifying *eta* and *hinin* as a status. Tokugawa intellectuals repeatedly proclaimed that such "nonhumans" could not be Japanese; their constructions of *kawata/eta* sought to displace such people from the polity altogether, to make them truly outcasts (i.e., separated from the rest of the status system). By contrast, the heterogeneous nature of the groups who lived on medieval Japan's margins suggests that we are dealing with a system that produced and reproduced outcasts, not an unchanging outcast order. Medieval *eta* and *hinin* were much more integral a part of the social fabric than their later namesakes. Instead of looking to the medieval era for the origins of social classification that produced the Tokugawa status system we might look to the middle ages for signs of a very different social topography.

Part of the difficulty we have had in understanding the medieval social practices that produced *kawaramono* and *hinin* may arise from the fact that concepts we typically rely on to think about outcasts, terms such as status and center and margin, do not in the end prove very helpful. Center and margin are spatial terms, which compel us to think of society as an arrangement of distinct, if complementary, spaces. Such a conception of the social order may be appropriate for a place like Tokugawa Japan, where society was conceived of in just such spatial terms, as the isolation of *kawata* into special hamlets suggests.[26] In the medieval period, by contrast, the spaces belonging to outcasts and to "normal" society were not well differentiated. Status, too, is a notion unhelpful in charting the slippery and shifting terrain in which medieval outcasts were constituted. However imperfectly they may work in practice, status systems are premised on the idea that society can be mapped, that each status group can be situated in its own space. The effort expended by Tokugawa intellectuals to locate for *kawata* a place outside the polity seems typical of the work required to maintain status systems, the primary task of which is to categorize and differentiate.

Of course, the reality was far more complicated than any simple dichotomy between the "slippery and shifting" middle ages and the status-obsessed early modern period. The logic of center and margin and of status is, in fact, useful for understanding certain aspects of the medieval polity. For example, medieval Japan was dominated by an agrarian order. Built around the system of private estates and public lands (the *shōen-kokugaryō* system) that provided the main economic support for the central elites, this order propounded a spatial and static vision of the polity.[27] The great landholders laid out society in the same way they mapped their estates. They conceived of their lands as social and economic units and stressed that social categories like peasant and proprietor could likewise be fixed. The monarch served in this conception as the ultimate guarantor of the stability of the land and of the social order. In this imagining, the polity had a clear center at court, distinct margins, and an unambiguous status hierarchy as well. The rent-paying peasant served as the normative commoner, while the structure of offices within the landholding system provided a template for the status system as a whole.

In a variety of ways, *eta, hinin,* and *kawaramono* were marginal to the agrarian order. The very name of the *kawaramono,* riverbank people, gives evidence of this fact. The banks of the Kamo and Katsura rivers, the rivers that marked, literally, the margins of medieval Kyoto, were metaphorically marginal as well. They were burial grounds and execution sites; like the liberties of early modern London, they were places of exile and asylum, home to a motley assortment of the diseased and dying, entertainers and prostitutes, and those engaged in a variety of trades—beggars, tanners, butchers, boatmen, and cloth dyers. Above all, riverbanks and the people who inhabited them had no part in the production and consumption of rents, the sine qua non of status within the agrarian order. Buddhist thought, moreover, supplied an ideology that understood disease, particularly disfiguring diseases like leprosy, to be punishment for misdeeds in former lives. Likewise, the regularity with which medieval texts offer either "*eta*" or "butcher" as a gloss for *kawaramono,* while ignoring all the other trades that were plied along the riverbanks, highlights the desire to replace the disorderly congregations gathered on the riverbanks with a single, fixed, identifiable category. Tokifusa's insistence in 1428 that the palace gardeners were *eta* and that their pollution precluded entry within the sacred precincts of the emperor's palace, seems symptomatic. His observation proposes a simple equation, of the sort that laws defining status are eager to make: outcast = *eta* = polluted.

That Tokifusa was wrong also seems symptomatic. In medieval Japan, attempts to fix outcasts securely in one social location could be only partially successful. There was another economy in which medieval monarchs were also enrolled, this one based in non-agrarian trades and marked by motion (itinerant peddlers, wandering monks, all the hustle and bustle one met on the riverbanks of the capital), and it is to this alternative construction of the polity that outcasts belong. The key spaces for this aspect of the economy are roads, rivers, riverbanks, and cities, precisely the places where one finds outcasts, and the spaces themselves are not as important as the fact that they are conduits along which goods, services, and information flow. Tellingly, the emperor was closely tied to the business of this portion of the realm. Merchants traveled under privileges guaranteed by imperial writ, and a startling variety of tradesmen and women were shielded from interference by warriors and others because they were designated purveyors to the imperial household. Moreover, certain merchants and outcasts provided a military force under the direct control of the emperor. To make sense of the world in which outcasts and merchants circulated, the medieval realm must be viewed through the lens provided by an alternative mode of social description, one more sensitive to linkages and exchange than to oppositions such as margin and center. We need to consider as well the odd equivalences such a system creates between entities that might at first seem to be polar opposite.

Outcasts as Evidence of Medieval Social Ambiguities

Outcasts embody these ambivalences in the medieval polity. In certain respects, they look very much like the typical subjects of discrimination. In other important respects, however, outcasts were intimately connected with the body politic and its operations. In 1183, warriors pursuing Retired Emperor Go-Shirakawa were met, it is said, by a motley force composed of "rock-throwing" *hinin, kawaramono*, and Horikawa lumber merchants who turned out to defend the monarch. In other words, a representative subsection of the non-agrarian strand of the medieval order has here identified itself directly with the emperor.[28] In a more organized (if somewhat less personal) manner, "riverbank people" figured prominently throughout the medieval era as the policemen of the capital,[29] with a relationship to the state's policing apparatus dating back to the eleventh century. Picture scrolls depicting scenes of punishment invariably show *kawaramono* in attendance.[30] A few examples from later in the medieval era also illustrate the relationship. In 1433, a detail of riverbank people was mobilized to drive off some marauders; they remained on guard under the command of a daimyo for several days to prevent further disturbances.[31] Similarly, in 1441, one thousand armed "riverbank people" stood guard as the head of Akamatsu Mitsusuke (assassin of the Shogun Yoshinori) was paraded through the streets of the capital to be displayed on the gates of the jail.[32]

Additional insights into the nature of the affiliation networks joining outcasts with the central institutions of state may be gleaned from a court case between two groups of outcasts, heard by the bakufu court convened at Rokuhara in 1243–1244. The case came at the culmination of twenty or more years of rancor and occasional warfare between one group linked to Kōfukuji in Nara, and another from Kiyomizu temple in Kyoto.[33] At stake were the rights to control burial services, begging, and other activities in the central provinces. The particulars of the affair involved sneak attacks and revenge killings, arson, murder, and betrayals on both sides. Even some of the more mundane details are interesting. For instance, the suit allows a glimpse into the network of *hinin* shelters throughout Japan. Located at major crossroads or along important thoroughfares, at the nodes of commercial relations, the network of shelters traces, in effect, the sinews of the non-agrarian realm.

Moreover, in their connections with temples, the shelters reveal an affinity with core institutions that belied their inhabitants' marginal status. Indeed, the temples and the shelters seem to describe parallel networks, each the inverted image of the other: sites of concentrated disease and "uncleanliness" stand entwined with holy or sanctified sites. Each seems to have fed off the other; the *hinin* shelters were supported by fees from burial and other services they performed for temples, while the temples relied on *hinin* not only for these services, but also as objects for the good works and spiritual exercises that comprised their spiritual practices.

It should be noted that the links between outcasts and key parts of the state apparatus were not simply institutional. Pairing shelters and temples recalls the ways divinity and disease were frequently coupled in the medieval Japanese imagination. Many of the so-called new Buddhist sects popularizing the faith in the twelfth and thirteenth centuries explicitly addressed themselves to the sick and destitute.[34] The monk Eison (1201–1290), for example, held that lepers and *hinin* were incarnations of the Bodhisattva Monju. Accordingly, he devoted much of the latter half of his life to ceremonies in which he distributed food and clothing and preached to *hinin* at numerous shelters.[35] The practice of distributing alms to *hinin* was far from limited to Eison and his sect. Commonplace from the twelfth century on, such rituals capitalized on the aura of the sacred invested in outcasts, to the credit of the alms-givers. In Eison's work with *hinin*, we can see in operation the peculiarly medieval idea that a special (albeit negative) divinity adhered to outcasts. Perhaps because of the diseases they suffered or the trades they followed or simply by virtue of being wretched and impoverished, they seemed marked by divine selection, making them particularly apposite subjects for good works and religious ritual.[36]

The court case mentioned above featured *hinin* named Echizen, Iga, Kawachi, Inaba, Tanba, Yamato, and Wakasa. These, of course, are the names of provinces. As other sources attest, it was general practice for the heads of *hinin* shelters to bear such names, sobriquets that openly identified *hinin* with the state. Indeed, the names seem to suggest that *hinin* were meant to personify the state in some way.[37] Such a practice would be incomprehensible if outcasts were nothing more than marginal outsiders. Instead, the convention points to a symbolic affiliation between outcasts and the very institutions of the polity. Amino Yoshihiko, who more than any other historian has detailed the multifarious connections between the central institutions of the medieval state and the realm of non-agrarian practices, argues that people in the middle ages attributed a special power (he calls it "the power of the strange" [*igyō no chikara*]) to those who fell outside the agrarian mainstream, and that nowhere was this power more concentrated than in outcasts and emperors.[38] The names that these *hinin* leaders bore seem to affirm this bond, and they suggest that, at least in part, the state articulated itself by means of affiliations that mobilized the power of "strange" beings.

The belief that certain people possessed special abilities emerged during the eleventh century to become one of the structuring principles of the medieval social imagination. Cutting across what we think of as class and status boundaries, it linked the very heights of society with its lowest depths. The ways this belief might influence social structure may be seen in an undated (late fifteenth century?) tax record.[39] The document is a list of groups to be exempted from a tax on dwellings, and it presents us with a hierarchy of the tax-exempt in seven ranks, beginning with shrines and temples, then the imperial family, the military and civil aristocracy, and concluding with "beggars, riverbank people, and the like." This tax roll is exceptional for the orderliness of its survey, but the practice it records was commonplace. Groups acknowledged to possess special talents—from the monks and aristocrats, to craftsmen such as carpenters, smiths, and tatami-makers, on down to entertainers, beggars, and other denizens of the riverbanks—were typically exempted from taxes and other levies. At times they were provided with special stipends and trading privileges.[40] What is notable about such tax policies is the view of the polity that underlies it. In effect, it establishes a table of equivalences underwritten by the idea that certain people possess special abilities. The list includes temples and shrines as well as the emperor because the sacred authority wielded by emperors and priests was the prototype for all "special abilities," from those embodied by craftsmen who could turn chunks of ore into razor-sharp blades, to those possessed by riverbank people. While this tax roll certainly does not suggest that beggars were the equal of the imperial family, it does indicate that there was reason for singling them out and according them special privilege.

Within this order of things, outcasts were recognized as the possessors of a singular, indeed, at times, quasi-sacred talent: the power to cleanse sites that had become polluted. In the court case mentioned earlier, for example, the Nara *hinin* describe themselves as "*kiyome*" and stress that as such they "perform a vital task for the temple." This assertion is the linchpin of their argument to the court; indeed, it is the key to their claim of social standing in general. The word *kiyome* derives from *kiyomu*, to cleanse or to purify, and it refers to people charged with the task of "purifying" sites, e.g., sweeping temple and shrine grounds, performing functions related to funerals, disposing of dead horses and cattle, and, as we know from a picture scroll depicting the Gion festival, cleansing the path the image of the shrine's deity was to follow.[41] This cleansing or purification was one of the most important functions performed by medieval outcasts. Outcasts appear repeatedly in the sources as *kiyome*. As we have seen, they referred to themselves as such, and, on occasion, competing groups of outcasts went to court to argue the question of who had the right to perform *kiyome* functions.[42]

Purifying, like policing, naturally necessitated performing "impure" tasks, such as the removal of dead bodies and the execution of criminals. But more seems at stake than the question of who should do the dirty work. *Eta* and *hinin* were also *kiyome*, the instrument by which society was returned to purity. This notion presumes a social imagination in which the power to purify lay with the impure, a social imagination, in other words, that posited a complicity between defilement and purity. This imagination outlined a social order in which butchers, beggars, tanners, and the like were "deprived of human contact," but were necessarily called upon by those who ostensibly excluded them. Society needed the special abilities that butchers, tanners, and undertakers, for instance, possessed; they knew what to do with the carcasses of horses, cattle, and equally the bodies that piled up after human skirmishes. The "special ability" attributed to outcasts also carried with it an aura; *kiyome* was not simply janitorial work.

Symbols of outcast status could be usefully deployed by those who were not outcasts. At the beginning of the fourteenth century, a band of brigands called the Terada terrorized Harima province. According to *Mineaiki* (*Hōsōki*), a record of the province written in 1348 by a local monk, these brigands presented an "aberrant and freakish appearance" (*irui igyō*); they were "not at all like [normal] human beings." The intent of this account is, of course, to make the Terada something worthy of the label "evil brigands" (*akutō*); what is interesting is how the author achieves this end. He begins by describing their clothing: "They wore unlined persimmon-colored robes (*kaki katabira*) and ladies' head coverings (*roppō gasa*), not proper hats and trousers. They hid their faces from everyone and lurked about in a stealthy manner."[43] From a variety of sources, we can verify that persimmon-colored robes and a cloth wrapped about the head so as to cover the face were badges of leprosy.[44] The orange brown robes were, then, a device intended to identify and exclude; they are signs of an effort to single out the diseased and graphically signal their estrangement from normal society. With the bandits and rebels, though, this sign takes on a different meaning. The costume of otherness figures here as a badge of rebellion; reworking the sign by which society proper marked and contained its others, the rebels turn the motif of exclusion to account. They recast the symbol of enforced exile into an emblem of self-estrangement, emphasizing thereby their place outside of society and its strictures, and magnifying their threat.

It is interesting to note that orange brown robes and a white cloth wrapped around the head to cover the lower half of the face was also the uniform of the bosses (*chōri*) of the *hinin* shelters.[45] Here again, a sign of outcast status assumes a different meaning; it turns abjection into a kind of power—in the case of the Kiyomizu shelter the economic and political might possessed by the leader of a one thousand-strong band of *hinin* who monopolized vital functions in the capital.

Purification and Purifiers

Uses of the symbols of outcast status would be unthinkable unless that status were acknowledged to possess some sort of power. The special ability that outcasts possessed as purifiers was imbued with a very particular aura: the ability to deal with the most polluting, and therefore in some respects the most dangerous, objects. Outcasts were in many ways thought to resemble the objects they handled. They were filthy, polluted, and dangerous. Yet they also possessed a unique ability to purify. In his essay on "Plato's Pharmacy," Jacques Derrida speaks of the *pharmakon*, the medicine that is also a poison, the remedy that can both cure and kill.[46] Simultaneously polluted and purifying, outcasts seem to be the *pharmakon* of the medieval Japanese imagination. Moreover, just as the double nature of the *pharmakon* resists classification, so, too, do outcasts. Defilement in medieval Japan was never exclusively the property of one party. Therefore, rather than trying to determine the logic that definitively identified only certain people as polluted or defiled, we might instead think of purification, a process touching all members of society.[47] Pure and impure do not appear in medieval sources primarily as ontological conditions, but as stages in a never-completed process. Whereas the law of early modern Japan produced the *eta/kawata* as the very epitome of impurity, medieval *eta* and *hinin* lived in much more fluid states of being. Just about anyone or anything could be rendered impure. *Konjaku monogatari* tells the story of a hapless monk who almost by accident finds himself married to the daughter of a *hinin* boss and, as a result, becomes a *hinin* himself.[48] A dog carried a corpse's foot into a major shrine, thereby obliging the shrine to undergo a seven-day purification. According to rules for the Gion Shrine, anyone who ate garlic was polluted for fifty days. The death of a shogun rendered the entire realm impure.[49]

Thus, medieval Japanese peopled their realm and ordered their society as if they were themselves ambivalent about what made a state and what its relationship to purity/virtue/the good might be. From about the eleventh century, legal and political treatises began to offer one elaboration of the polity when, in a manner that recalls medieval Europe's "three orders," they divided power among three great blocs or "houses" (*ke*), the aristocracy (*kuge*), warriors (*buke*), and religious establishments (*jike*). At the same time a system of land rents and labor services developed that offered a complementary vision of the social order, dividing the commoner population into peasants ("those who tilled the fields" and paid rents), and craftsmen, tradespeople, and others with special skills (who did not owe rents). These articulations of the social order gave medieval Japan a character divided between agrarian and non-agrarian practices.

Both segments of the polity participated in the logic of purity and defilement. The dominant, agrarian order staged in imperial and ecclesiastical rituals emphasized the sacred person of the monarch. A paragon of purity, to be shielded from defilement at all costs, the emperor stood at the sanctified center of a polity that conceived of itself as a realm of "agrarian purity." Two of the emperor's most important duties were to perform the Great Purification ceremonies and to offer the first fruits of the harvest to his divine ancestors. In powerful ways prestige and status in the medieval era were constructed in terms of proximity to this sanctified center. What constituted aristocrats, temples and shrines, even warriors (at least at the upper levels), as privileged elites was never articulated in terms of superior force or wealth, but rather in terms of refinement, in terms of the distance of these elites from defiling practices. What might be termed a "structure of purity" gave order to medieval society in the capital, and the emperor, the embodiment of purity, anchored this conception of social order. Thus, as state ceremonial made apparent and imperial law stressed, the emperor was a pure being who guaranteed the purity of the realm.

Maintaining this structure of purity meant, however, that the monarch had to function as purifier. As a purifier, the monarch was allied with the non-agrarian portion of the polity, which emphasized the special talent of craftsmen, traders, entertainers, and the like. This articulation of the social, as we have seen, produced an emphasis on the process of purification rather than on states of purity or defilement. The medieval world turned on the fundamental irony that the effort to secure the agrarian order necessarily involved embracing people excluded from that order.

The moment of the production of this ambivalence is the eleventh century, marking the beginnings of the development of a distinctively medieval polity. One sees here a fascinating double movement transforming the monarchic functions. On the one hand, it became imperative for the emperor to be shielded from pollution. The foundation and growth of Kyoto as the imperial capital involved the successive displacement of impure sites (such as burial grounds) and polluting practices (tanning, etc.) to the margins, so as to create a sanctified zone about the palace and the person of the emperor. Where the seventh-century *ritsuryō* codes dictated that executions take place in the centrally located markets, the eleventh century saw their removal to the riverbank areas (home to the *kawaramono*, who from this period forward come to play a crucial role in the exercise of justice in the capital).[50] Burial grounds and institutions charged with caring for the sick and dying (the *hiden'in*) were likewise pushed to the outskirts of the capital. These developments seem completely consistent with the ideas that underwrote the agrarian order. Here, the relationship between emperor and outcast is very much one of center and margin. The emperor stands at the fixed center of the polity, and around him are arrayed the successive ranks, with status falling in order from those nearest at hand to those on the edges of the capital.

At the same time, paradoxically, the state and the emperor came over the course of the eleventh century to play an increasingly intimate role in dispelling pollution. The state, for example, took action to assert its monopoly over certain important kinds of purification rituals. From the end of the tenth century, a series of edicts were issued that forbade private ceremonies to dispel angry ghosts and demons (goryōe). The court began to appropriate certain of these observances (notably those associated with the Gion Shrine) and make them the province of the state.[51] Reflecting the growing emphasis on pollution and the growing importance of the monarch in dispelling pollution, the Great Purification ceremony in the course of the eleventh century ceased to be a regular semiannual observance and became instead a ritual invoked more frequently, whenever pollution was encountered.[52] An official who came to court despite the death of a relative, a fire that left hundreds dead, even a dead dog discovered in the palace, all became reasons for performing the Great Purification. Thus, although concern with pollution can be traced back to the earliest Japanese polities and given a religious gloss that makes it seem an inevitable part of the Japanese order of things, pollution emerged as a special, political principle as the medieval court defined itself. The renewed concern for pollution and the central role played by the emperor in dispelling pollution, must be counted among the distinguishing features of kingship in medieval Japan.

This medieval articulation of defilement established the monarch in an anomalous position. First, structuring society about a sanctified center rather effectively removes that center from the very society it supposedly anchors. In order to work as purifier, it would appear, the monarch had to be removed, cordoned off, from any possibility of pollution; he could not be fully part of the society structured about him. At once center of the social and exterior to it, the emperor bears a perilously close resemblance to the eta and others who ostensibly marked society's edge. Second, in his role as purifier, as one who (increasingly from the eleventh century onward) "touches defilement" (shokue) in order to dispel it, the monarch shares with outcasts certain essential traits. The "filthy rites" performed by outcasts had a clear affinity to the state and religious rituals that purportedly defined society's core. And though the one is conjured as central and pure and the other as excluded and defiled, emperors and outcasts were essentially purifiers; their primary charge was to cleanse society and maintain its sanctity. In emperors and *eta* we have the twin poles of a circuit of purification.

In medieval usage, *kegare*—pollution—always called forth *kiyome*; there seems to have been no such thing as a completely impure being. A basic ambivalence pervades the definitions and symbols of exclusion. From the perspective of the agrarian core, orange robes or the names *eta* and *hinin* or the rhetoric of defilement were devices meant to contain and exclude; they put forward a claim to power over the others whom these codes marked. Yet if impurity is the proof of purity, then we must recognize that the very same codes that sought to divide and exclude could be the basis for a claim of equivalence. The process of purification, the process that linked emperors and outcasts, speaks to the basic ambivalence of the medieval order of things, to the ways in which the agrarian order and its grid-like spaces and secure social categories depended on people who did not fit in those spaces. Judged by purity, by the standards of the "agrarian realm," a vast gulf separated emperors from outcasts, but the act of purification established equivalences between them and linked both to the world of non-agrarian practices. As a result, the achievement of a structure of full and settled meanings (in which, for example, the place of every person was fixed and self-evident) was continually deferred; and this realization suggests that we need to recognize in medieval society not only an "order" or "structure," with those terms' implications of fixity and stasis, but also a ceaseless production. By practicing a mode of social description attentive to such production and reproduction, and by elaborating a historiography less preoccupied with continuity, we may, at last, be able to recognize outcasts not simply as a denigrated status group, but as the very emblem of the ambivalence fundamental to the medieval polity.

NOTES

1   Ogyū Sorai, *Fūryūshishaki,* cited in Herman Ooms, *Tokugawa Village Practice: Class, Status, Power, Law*, pp. 300–301. In this and the following paragraphs, I draw on the discussions of *kawata* ("leather workers") and *hinin* ("nonhumans") in Ooms, *Tokugawa Village Practice*, pp. 286–311, and Gerald Groemer, "Creation of the Edo Outcaste Order."

2   See, e.g., the order calling for a bamboo fence to be built around Kōike village in 1695. In Buraku mondai kenkyūjo, ed., *Burakushi shiryō senshū* (hereafter *BSS*), 2:61–62.

3   See, for example, the undated (though probably early nineteenth century) report from Danzaemon, in which he declares, "It has generally been forbidden by ancient custom for *hinin*-by-birth to acquire the status of common persons," in John Henry Wigmore, *Law and Justice in Tokugawa Japan*, 8B, pp. 176–177.

4   See Groemer, "Creation of the Edo Outcaste Order," p. 282.

5   Ogyū Sorai, "Seidan," in *BSS*, 3:111.

6   Kaiho Seiryō, *Zenchūdan*, in *BSS*, 3:115–118.

7   Nagahara Keiji, "The Medieval Origins of the *Eta-Hinin*." This is a partial translation of Nagahara's "Chūsei shakai no tenkai to hisabetsu mibunsei."

8   Ooms, *Tokugawa Village Practice*, p. 310.

9   These arguments may be found in many of Amino's works. The most detailed explanation appears in Amino Yoshihiko, *Nihon chūsei no hinōgyōmin to tennō,* but useful discussions can be found in *Muen, kugai, raku: Nihon chūsei no jiyū to heiwa* and, more recently, *Nihon chūsei no hyakushō to shokunōmin.*

10   Mujū Ichien, "Mirror for Women *Tsuma Kagami*," trans. Robert Morrell, pp. 78–79. See also Morrell's introduction to the

translation pp. 45–50. For a more detailed discussion of gender in medieval Japan, see Hitomi Tonomura's examination of tales from the *Konjaku monogatari*, in "Black Hair and Red Trousers: Gendering the Flesh in Medieval Japan."

11   Masamune Atsuo, ed., *Chiribukuro*, 11:366–367.

12   Cited in Yokoi Kiyoshi, *Chūsei minshū no seikatsu bunka*, p. 267.

13   *BSS*, 1:401.

14   *BSS*, 1:404–405.

15   These examples come from *Engi shiki*, book 3. In *Engi-Shiki: Procedures of the Engi Era*, 1:116–118.

16   Eiryaku 2 (1161) Tachibana Tsunemoto kishōmon (*HI*, 7:3144). The text reads: "*yamai o motte, waza to shi, kojiki o motte, eko to su. Ya mo naku, shoku mo nakushite, dōro ni mayou mi to naran.*"

17   For evidence of wealthy *hinin, see* Nagahara Keiji, "Fuyū na kojiki," in his, *Nihon chūsei shakai kōzō no kenkyū*, pp. 280–283. Land registers and rent records from the 1370s and 1380s for Tōji holdings on the outskirts of Kyoto refer to land held by one Kawara Saburōjirō. *Tōzai kujō nyogoden nengu nayosechō narabi ni mishin chōfu.*

18   The largest group, some one thousand strong, was associated with Kiyomizu temple. They held an exclusive right to conduct burials within Kyoto (and frequently, it seems, extorted money from bereaved families to pay for extra mourners or more elaborate funerals). They also controlled the activities of all beggars and supervised the ill within a certain area surrounding the temple (collecting a fee for doing so). See Umata Ayako, "Chūsei Kyoto ni okeru jiin to minshū."

19   See Chijiwa Itaru, "Kishōmon kenkyū nōto," and Niunoya Tetsuichi, *Nihon chūsei no mibun to shakai*, pp. 505–507.

20   For examples of *hinin* oaths, see Kenji 1 (1275).8 Hinin shuku chōri ige shichinin renpan no kishōmon (*KI*, 16:11993). For a discussion of outcasts and oaths, see Niunoya Tetsuichi, *Nihon chūsei no mibun to shakai*, pp. 503–514.

21   *Rokuon nichiroku* Entoku 1 (1489).6.5 (*BSS*, 1:314).

22   Madenokōji Tokifusa, *Kennaiki*, entry for Shōchō 1 (1428).6.10 (in *BSS*, 1:210). For more about outcasts as gardeners, see Kawashima Masao, *Chūsei Kyoto bunka no shūen*, pp. 133–154 and 238–253.

23   In 1472, for example, a group of *hinin* came to fetch a Kōfukuji retainer (*rikisha*) who had contracted leprosy. (The retainer had, however, already slipped out of Nara for Mt. Kōya). See Harada Tomohiko, *Hennen sabetsushi shiryō shūsei* (hereafter *HSS*), 4:554. An agreement between Eison and leaders of the Kiyomizuzaka *hinin* shelter in Kyoto specifies that the shelter's jurisdiction covers only the "severely ill" (*jūbyō*); they must consult with the family before removing someone to the shelter who is simply "ill." What distinguishes "severely ill" from "ill" is unclear. See *BSS*, 1:231.

24   *BSS*, 1:236. The document is a fragment (the very end) of a defense statement responding to a suit by one Keiu (Keiyū), who is suing to recover unspecified damages from someone named Rendō, who is said to have entered a *hinin* shelter at the Higo kokubunji on the "reappearance of his leprosy" (*raibyō kōhatsu ni yori*). Rendō's ever-so-convenient flight raises the possibility that he was using the shelter as a sanctuary.

25   Much debate, for example, has focused on how many types of outcasts there might have been. Kuroda Toshio argues that *hinin* comprise the basic model for medieval outcasts, while Hosokawa Ryōichi and Niunoya Tetsuichi follow the Tokugawa-period division of outcasts into two ideal types, *kawaramono* and *hinin*. Wakita Haruko adds a third type, *sanjo*. There has also been a good deal of contention over the question of whether or not outcasts are truly outcaste. Kuroda proposed in 1975 that *hinin* were indeed a "status beyond status" (*mibungai no mibun*). Ōyama Kyōhei, by contrast, insists that outcasts, though discriminated against, were seen as part of the overall status hierarchy. Amino Yoshihiko sides with Ōyama in viewing outcasts as fully part of medieval society; he argues that *kawaramono* in particular should be considered one of the social groups possessing a special talent. See Kuroda, "Chūsei no mibunsei to hisen kannen," in his *Nihon chūsei no kokka to shūkyō*, pp. 351–398; Ōyama, "Chūsei no mibunsei to kokka," in his *Nihon chūsei nōsonshi no kenkyū*, pp. 373–427; and Amino, "Chūsei mibunsei no ichi kōsatsu: chūsei zenki no hinin o chūshin ni." Hosokawa offers a good overview of the debates in "Chūsei hininron no genjō to kadai" in his *Chūsei no mibunsei to hinin*, pp. 3–51.

26   An important aspect of the sixteenth-century social, economic, and military revolution that underlay the Tokugawa regime involved precisely this spatialization of the social groupings. Samurai were

brought into castle towns, so that rural areas became purely peasant space. Castle towns were divided according to occupation and status, with metalworkers here, weavers there, and *kawata* removed to the outskirts.

27   See Thomas Keirstead, "Gardens and Estates: Medievality and Space," and *The Geography of Power in Medieval Japan*, esp. chap. 3.

28   This is reported in both *Genpei Jōsuiki* and the *Tale of Heike*. See Amino Yoshihiko, *Chūseiteki sekai to wa nandarō ka*, pp. 103–104.

29   See Niunoya Tetsuichi, *Kebiishi: chūsei no kegare to kenryoku*.

30   E.g., *Hōnen Shōnin eden*.

31   *HSS*, 4:366–367.

32   *HSS*, 4:389–390.

33   A detailed examination of this suit may be found in Ōyama, *Nihon chūsei nōsonshi no kenkyū*, pp. 428–439. The documents in the case are in *BSS*, 1:117–141.

34   Shinran spoke of *eta* as "one of us" (*warera*) and held that they could be saved, just like any one else. Nichiren repeatedly claimed—for rhetorical effect, it would seem—that he came from "*senmin*" or "*sendara*" stock, while Myōe referred to himself as a "*hinin*." The Ippen scroll contains many scenes depicting lepers or showing Ippen dispensing alms to *hinin*. For Shinran and Nichiren, see *BSS*, 1:181–185.

35   For a discussion of Eison's life and work, see Janet Goodwin, *Alms and Vagabonds: Buddhist Temples and Popular Patronage in Medieval Japan*, pp. 117–127. The main source of information about Eison is *Kongō busshi Eison kanshingaku shōki*, in Nara kokuritsu bunkazai kenkyūjo, ed., *Saidaiji Eison denki shūsei*.

36   Eison's views were in contrast to those of earlier Buddhist thinkers, who dismissed out of hand the possibility that outcasts were suitable subjects. For example, Kūkai declared that "*sendara* ... were the great enemies of the dharma and the state."

37   The naming convention is discussed in Hosokawa, *Chūsei no mibunsei to hinin*, pp. 120–122, and in Matsuo Kenji, *Chūsei no toshi to hinin*, pp. 140–152. For other examples, see Shōka 2 (1258) Shaka

nenbutsu kechie kyōmyō (*KI*, 11:8235). *Hosshinshū* relates a tale about a *hinin* named Ōmi. See Kamo no Chōmei, *Hōjōki, Hosshinshū*, pp. 230–231.

38   See Amino Yoshihiko, *Igyō no ōken*, pp. 96–116 and 160–212. Followers of non-agrarian pursuits were often described as "freakish and aberrant." For example, in the following passage from the Ippen scroll: "Among the people who gathered [in Anō to hear Ippen preach] were those of freakish and aberrant appearance. These were hunters and fishermen, whose livelihood involved killing living beings." See *Ippen shōnin eden*, pp. 203–204. Amino points out that Emperor Go-Daigo's rule was characterized in the same way.

39   The document is reproduced in Niunoya, *Nihon Chūsei no mibun to shakai*, p. 615.

40   For examples of the tax exemptions afforded craftsmen—as well as *kawaramono* and *hinin*—see Amino Yoshihiko, *Chūsei no hinin to yūjo*, pp. 65–69.

41   Nonetheless, not all observers were comfortable with this scene. Nakahara Moromori criticized the use of *eta* (which he glossed as "*enta*") to carry one of the *mikoshi* (shrines) used during the Gion festival. *Moromoroki*, entry for Jōji 4 (1365).6.14.

42   Both *kawaramono* and *hinin* were *kiyome*. The earliest record of *kawaramono* acting as *kiyome* is from the mid-twelfth century; see Niunoya, *Kebiishi*, p. 29. Evidence that *hinin* referred to themselves as *kiyome* is available in the Narazaka *hinin* statement (*BSS*, 1:123–124). The immediate cause of struggles between competing groups of outcasts was almost certainly the money and other goods *kiyome* were paid to perform their services. But the same motive cannot be ascribed to the man who styles himself an "*onkiyome*" (honorable *kiyome*) in defending himself from the charge that he had stolen a fellow *kiyome*'s wife. Something more intangible was at stake when outcasts declared themselves *kiyome*. The defendant's statement is quoted in full by Miura Keiichi, *Nihon chūsei senminshi no kenkyū*, p. 343. For the struggle between *kawaramono* and *inujinin* over the right to perform as *kiyome*, see *HSS*, 4:236. Kawashima Masao produces a chart of the fees outcasts received for various functions. *Kiyome* and gardening were by far the most highly rewarded of their various activities. Kawashima Masao, *Chūsei Kyoto bunka no shūen*, p. 97.

43   *Hōsōki*, pp. 248-249.

44   For instance, *Konjaku monogatari*, a collection of moralizing tales written in the twelfth century, contains a story about a young woman who is found to have leprosy. Upon learning of this condition, her father presents her with orange robes and casts her out of the house and the village. See Mabuchi Kazuo and Kunisaki Fumimaro, eds., *Konjaku monogatari shū*, 38:10. Likewise, among the beggars and others who crowd the gates of temples in medieval picture scrolls, there are invariably some who are dressed in orange brown robes; these, as Yokoi Kiyoshi has painstakingly established, are lepers. See Yokoi Kiyoshi, "Chūsei minshū shi ni okeru 'raija' to 'fugu' no mondai," in his *Chūsei minshū no seikatsu bunka*, pp. 295–334.

45   Kuroda Hideo, *Sugata to shigusa no chūsei shi* and *Kyōkai no chūsei, shōchō no chūsei*.

46   Jacques Derrida, "Plato's Pharmacy," trans. Barbara Johnson, *Dissemination,* pp. 63–119.

47   Jean-Claude Schmitt warns against the "ill-considered uses of the notion of 'belief.' We must be careful not to reify belief, to turn it into something established once and for all, something that individuals and societies need only express and pass on to each other. It is appropriate to substitute a more active notion for the term 'belief': the verb 'to believe.' In this way belief is a never-completed activity, one that is precarious, always questioned, and inseparable from recurrences of doubt." Jean-Claude Schmitt, *Ghosts in the Middle Ages: The Living and the Dead in Medieval Society*, p. 9.

48   Mabuchi Kazuo and Kunisaki Fumimaro, eds., *Konjaku monogatari shū*, 36:279–282.

49   For the dog, see *Gion shigyō nikki* Shōhei 7 (1352).12.25 (*BSS*, 1:263, and *HSS*, 4:128). On garlic, see *Yasaka jinja monjo*, Entoku 1 (1489).12.8 Gionsha monoimi rei (*HSS*, 5:637–38). For the death of the shogun Ashikaga Yoshimasa, see *Kitano shake nichiroku*, entry for Entoku 2 (1490).1 (*HSS*, 5:638).

50   On these changes, see Niunoya Tetsuichi, "Hinin, kawaramono, sanjo"; also Itō Kiyoshi, "Chūsei ni okeru tennō no jujutsuteki ken'i to wa nani ka."

51   Neil McMullin, "The Enryaku-ji and the Gion Shrine-Temple Complex in the Mid-Heian Period."

52   Yamamoto Kōji, *Kegare to ōharae.*

LIQUID ASSETS

An Open and Shut Case? Thoughts on Late Heian Foreign Trade

Bruce L. Batten

Preface: Historiographical Context

It is no exaggeration to say that views of the Japanese past have undergone a revolution in recent decades.[1] Not too long ago, most works on Japan, both popular and scholarly, emphasized the country's supposed isolation during premodern times.[2] Of course, all authors agreed that Japan had developed under the tutelage of the older and more "advanced" civilizations on the Asian continent, particularly China. But, it was argued, this influence took the form of conscious imitation by the Japanese, not the result of direct, day-to-day interaction. Japan was close enough to the continent to borrow what it wanted, when it wanted, but far enough not to have to worry about invasion or other forms of uncontrolled cross-border traffic. Isolation gave Japan the luxury of developing at its own pace, along its own lines, resulting in the formation of the distinctive and homogeneous culture about which so much has been written.

While this view of Japanese history remains current at the textbook level,[3] many active scholars no longer endorse it. For one thing, recent works tend to emphasize social and regional diversity, rather than homogeneity.[4] Further, they portray the country as fundamentally open to foreign contacts, rather than isolated. Revision of thoughts of isolation began with relatively recent periods of history and then moved backward in time toward the more distant past. Ronald Toby and other scholars during the 1980s concluded that, contrary to prevalent views, early modern Japan (seventeenth–early nineteenth centuries) was

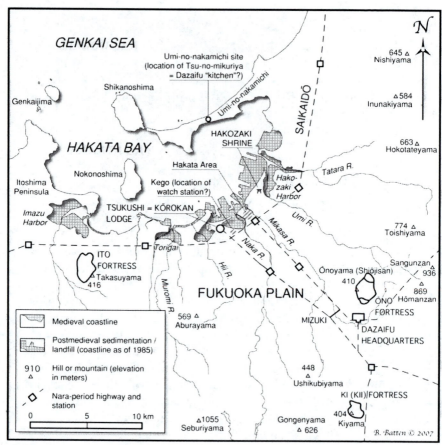

Map 1. Hakata and Vicinity
Sources: (1) modern coastline based on 1:200,000 Chiseizu N1-52-10 Fukuoka, by Kokudochiriin (1986); (2) medieval coastline from Kawazoe Shōji, *et al.*, *Fukuoka ken no rekishi*, map on p. 123; (3) ancient roads/stations from Kinoshita Ryō, ed., *Kodai o kangaeru: kodai dōro*, map on pp. 274–75

not really a "closed country" (*sakoku*) at all.[5] During the 1990s, Murai Shōsuke and other scholars in Japan produced a number of works on medieval foreign relations, all of which argued that Japan was essentially "borderless" from the thirteenth through sixteenth centuries.[6]

No scholarly consensus has been reached on the "isolation" issue for the ancient era prior to the thirteenth century. This essay is intended to contribute to the dialogue on "isolation" versus "openness" in ancient Japan through a detailed case study.[7] Specifically, I will be examining visits by Chinese merchants to the northern Kyushu port of Hakata in the tenth through twelfth centuries, that is, during the second half of the Heian period (794–1185). A close examination of the relevant historical and archaeological sources will suggest that for much of this period, the old stereotype of an "isolated" Japan was perhaps not so far off the mark after all. Central controls over cross-border traffic, instituted during a time of foreign crisis in the late seventh century, remained relatively effective through at least 1100.

Background

A familiarity with the geography and early history of the Hakata region is important backdrop to an understanding of the material under consideration here.[8] The port of Hakata was located at the conjunction of various sea routes connecting Kyushu with Honshu to the east, the Korean peninsula and China to the west, and the Ryukyu Islands to the south. From very early times, political authorities in west-central Honshu (the core area of the ancient Japanese state) attempted to assert control over these routes, partly to prevent unwanted negative influences from abroad, and partly to gain monopolistic access to foreign prestige goods, information, and diplomatic recognition.

These efforts achieved success in the late seventh century, during a period of intense intraregional competition in East Asia caused by the emergence of the Tang dynasty (618–907) in China. Japanese leaders adroitly exploited the resulting crisis atmosphere to create a centralized state (the so-called *ritsuryō* polity) and monopolize cross-border exchanges through the creation of a command post near Hakata. Contemporary documents make clear that this outpost, known as Dazaifu, was conceived as a "barrier-gate" (*kanmon*) that both separated Japan from, and connected it to, the outside world. Viewed in this way, the establishment of Dazaifu represents nothing less than an attempt by the central authorities to create Japan's first real political border. While Hakata was blessed by its location, the emergence of the border was by no means "natural." It resulted from purely political decisions taken in the general context of interstate rivalry and domestic centralization.

In general, Dazaifu functioned effectively during the Nara period (710–784). The military forces (especially *sakimori*, or border guards) under its supervision served as a barrier against unwanted foreign visitors (although in reality there were very few). For the several categories of visitors who were welcomed by the court, Dazaifu operated as a gateway for the supervision of arrivals and (when necessary) departures. For example, arriving diplomats from continental kingdoms such as Silla were initially processed by Dazaifu and stayed at a facility called the Tsukushi Lodge (Tsukushi-no-murotsumi; later renamed Kōrokan) on the shores of Hakata Bay until they were summoned to court to meet the emperor. On their return journey, the visitors also passed through Hakata and spent time at the same lodge under Dazaifu supervision.

During the first part of the subsequent Heian period, the court managed to maintain the spirit, if not the letter, of its system of border controls in Kyushu. Externally, the level of military interactions gradually rose as pirates (originally from the Korean state of Silla but later from other regions as well) began to infest the East China Sea. Foreign diplomats ceased to visit Japan, but private merchants, initially from Silla but later primarily from China, replaced them. Internally, the state's ability to influence directly events at the local level (both in the interior and in frontier regions) gradually declined during the same period. As a result of these two intersecting trends (increased external demands and decreased internal capacities), a state of crisis emerged around 900. It was resolved by what might be termed a lowering of expectations. Central officials, while retaining veto power over important decisions, yielded day-to-day authority over boundary functions to officials at Dazaifu. As a result, effective control over cross-border traffic was maintained until at least the late eleventh century. As I have argued elsewhere, this system seems to have worked well for a time because the field agents, who were court aristocrats temporarily stationed in Kyushu, had a vested interest in maintaining the status quo.[9]

Studies hitherto have presented several conflicting views on border control during the later Heian period. Historiographical orthodoxy in Japan has been represented for more than six decades by the work of Mori Katsumi, whose voluminous publications are not easily summarized.[10] Generally, he seems to argue that central controls on cross-border traffic failed in the late Heian period. Mori gives many examples of Dazaifu officials abusing their powers in the interest of private gain, and also describes many foreign merchants who purportedly avoided Dazaifu in order to conduct private trade with coastal estates (*shōen*) in Kyushu and western Honshu. Mori's view forms the basis of recent English-language work by Mimi Yiengpruksawan, although Yiengpruksawan emphasizes the positive, cosmopolitan aspects of the trade, rather than loss of control by the center.[11] Recent authors in Japan have tended to challenge Mori's interpretations (and, by implication, those of Yiengpruksawan). The most important contemporary researcher in this field is Yamauchi Shinji, who has devoted much effort to debunking Mori's pronouncements about the state's inability to regulate unauthorized trade at Kyushu estates in late Heian times.[12] In other words, current historiography on this particular era runs counter to the larger trend (noted at the beginning of this chapter) toward emphasizing the "openness" of premodern Japan.

An empirical investigation demonstrates that the volume of foreign trade was in fact extremely low through most of the Heian period, but increased rapidly during the twelfth century.[13] A parallel picture may be painted for government controls over trade, which were surprisingly robust through most of the period, beginning to fail only in the twelfth century.

Volume of Trade

Data relating to Heian foreign trade are of two types: historical and archaeological. The historical narrative is drawn from primary source materials such as administrative documents and courtier diaries, most of which have been thoroughly mined by generations of historians. The archaeological record, by contrast, has become clear only in the last few decades as the result of new site-based investigations. Let us explore in turn what each of these data sets can tell us about foreign trade in the Heian period.

Although the relevant historical sources have long been known, two recent publications have made their content much more accessible: the detailed chronology of foreign relations compiled by Tajima Isao and that assembled by Tanaka Takeo and his students. The Tajima chronology[14] summarizes all known records of exchanges between Japan and the continent from 702 to 1185. While appearing first in print as an appendix to a 1993 coffee-table volume on imported porcelain, a Tajima pre-print was circulated privately in 1991. The Tanaka chronology,[15] published in book form in 1999, contains less information about individual events, but is much broader than Tajima's in geographical and chronological coverage. Tanaka's work covers foreign relations not just with China and the Korean peninsula, but also with areas such as Hokkaido and Okinawa, which were inside the archipelago but outside Japan "proper." Chronologically, the volume covers external relations from the beginning of history until 1879.

The more detailed Tajima chronology offers to generate much statistical information about foreign trade during the Heian era. Graph 1 shows the number of officially recorded arrivals by all categories of peaceful visitors from China and the Korean peninsula during successive twenty-year periods between 820 and 1179.[16] (The 820s represent the presumed beginnings of maritime commerce between Japan and the Asian mainland.[17]) While the figures for the ninth and early tenth centuries include a number of diplomatic missions from Parhae (698–926) and other states, most of the reported visits from the tenth century on probably represent private merchants (although in many cases the sources refer merely to "men from Tang" or "men from Song"). Twenty-year periods illustrate general historical trends well, because the total number of arrivals is so small that graphing them on a finer scale would give undue prominence to random, short-term fluctuations.

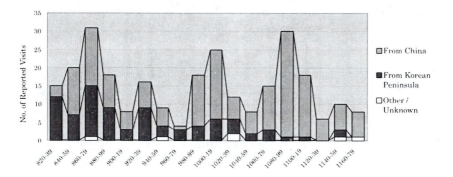

Graph 1. Frequency of Recorded Peaceful Visits from Abroad
Source: Compiled from data in Tajima Isao, "Nihon, Chūgoku, Chōsen taigai kōryū shi nenpyō: Taihō gannen—Bunji gannen."

Before drawing any conclusions from Graph 1, it is necessary to consider the reliability of the data, specifically, to what extent the records accurately reflect the total number of arrivals within each twenty-year period. At first glance, it appears that the trends evident in the graph reflect real changes in the number of foreign visitors over time.[18] However, further inquiry reveals that such is not the case.

Many or most of the original records on which Graph 1 is based consist of entries in diaries kept by courtiers living in the capital. However, the degree of coverage provided by such diaries is by no means constant over time. If one counts the number of extant diaries with entries for each month of the period 880–1184 and then averages these monthly tallies over five-year periods, a surprising trend emerges. As an example, the bar in Graph 2 for the period 1005–1009 measures 3.07, meaning that for any given month during this five-year period, an average of just over three courtier diaries survive (in this case, generally *Shōyūki*, *Gonki*, and *Midō kanpakuki*).

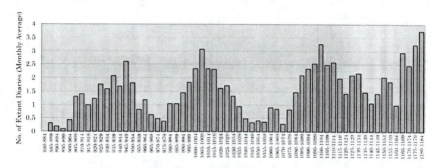

Graph 2. Coverage of Events in Courtier Diaries
Source: Compiled from data in chart appended to Hashimoto Yoshihiko, "Kiroku."

The results of comparing Graph 2 with Graph 1 are presented in Graph 3, showing trends in both recorded arrivals and diary coverage. The two curves are strikingly similar in shape. Both peak in the 930s and 940s, dip through the 960s and 970s, peak again at the beginning of the eleventh century and continue in close conformity until the late twelfth century. These findings suggest that the chronological "trends" evident in Graph 1 are not "real" at all; they are simply the result of stochastic fluctuations in the quantity of surviving source materials.

Fortunately, the data in Graph 1 retain some utility for our inquiry. The number of recorded arrivals shown in periods of *good* diary coverage actually seems fairly close to the true number. In periods of poor coverage, most arrivals are known from only one source, inevitably leading to the assumption that others occurred but records of these have not survived. However, in periods of good coverage (particularly during the peaks around the beginnings of the eleventh and twelfth centuries), most arrivals are mentioned in several independent sources. This type of mutual corroboration suggests that court diarists shared a common pool of information that (for these periods) has survived largely intact. Of course, it might be argued that the information diarists shared was limited to only a fraction of the total number of arrivals. A close reading of the sources, however, suggests that this was probably not the case. Because their jobs depended on it, local officials in Kyushu and other coastal areas were literally obsessed with discovering and reporting the presence of foreign vessels in their jurisdictions. As a result, courtiers in Kyoto were surprisingly well informed about events on the periphery, as illustrated below in case studies.[19]

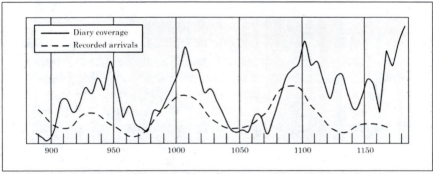

Graph 3. Comparison of Trends in Diary Coverage and Recorded Arrivals
Source: Curves interpolated from data in Graphs 1 and 2.

This argument suggests that if we trust the figures in Graph 1 for the peaks and ignore the troughs as unknowable, we may still obtain an excellent approximation of the actual trends in the arrival of foreign ships. As is obvious from an examination of the graph, the result for the ninth through eleventh centuries shows a relatively constant rate of arrivals (between fifteen and thirty per twenty-year period, or just over one ship per year on average).[20] The actual rate of recorded arrivals declines markedly in the twelfth century.

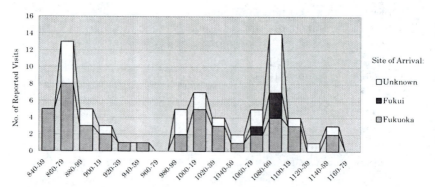

Graph 4. Reported or Inferred Points of Entry by Chinese Merchants
Source: Compiled from data in Tajima Isao, "Nihon, Chūgoku, Chōsen taigai kōryū shi nenpyō: Taihō gannen—Bunji gannen."

From the information in the Tajima chronology, it seems that almost all visits involved single vessels, each carrying roughly between thirty and one hundred individuals.[21] Since, as argued above, an average of perhaps one such ship visited Japan each year, the average annual number of Chinese and/ or Korean visitors to Japan during the ninth through eleventh centuries would have been about fifty-five. Japan's population at this time was about six-and-a-half million people,[22] so this figure is remarkably miniscule. Of course, the numbers cited for the Heian period here are likely underestimated somewhat. But in any event, Heian Japan was extraordinarily isolated by almost any standard.

Next, let us see what the sources have to say about the ports of entry used by foreign ships. Graph 4 shows the reported or inferred point of entry for visitors specifically labeled as "merchants" (*shōnin* or *shōkyaku*, etc.) from China (Tang, Song, etc.) between 920–1179.[23] The total number of such arrivals reported by Tajima is seventy-nine, and of these forty-two clearly took place at Hakata (given in the graph as "Fukuoka" for purposes of comparison with the archaeological data presented below).[24] However, in the late eleventh and early twelfth centuries, Tsuruga (given in the graph as "Fukui"), a coastal port on the Sea of Japan, was another important point of arrival for merchants (ten recorded cases). Tsuruga was also the port of entry for diplomatic envoys from Parhae during the eighth through early tenth centuries. It was also the site of a guesthouse called the Matsubara Guest Lodge (Matsubara kyakkan), which functioned like, and was presumably modeled upon, the Hakata Kōrokan.[25] Surviving records show that some merchants arriving in Tsuruga during the late Heian period were deported or advised to go to Hakata, but it is also clear that in most cases the court tacitly approved their use of this second port of entry.[26]

The point of entry in the remaining twenty-seven cases is unknown, but it is likely that most of these merchants came to Hakata but that fact was not recorded. One such case, involving a merchant from Song whose goods were seized by Dazaifu authorities in 1133, has been traditionally cited as evidence that Chinese merchants docked at Kanzaki estate in Hizen, but the source material is ambiguous and recent authorities tend to argue in favor of a Hakata arrival.[27] Similarly, one can find examples of Kyushu estates sending "Chinese goods" to court as tribute.[28] These goods, too, might have been obtained directly

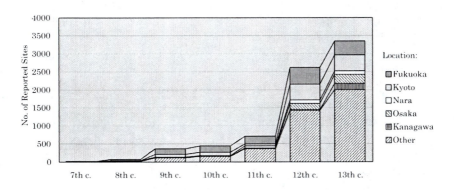

Graph 5. Number and Location of Archaeological Sites Yielding Imported Porcelain
Source: Compiled from data in Tsuchihashi Riko. "Nissō bōeki no shosō," p. 73 (Table 2)

from merchants or smugglers trying to avoid Hakata, but they might equally have been purchased at the Kōrokan as part of the official trade. There is simply no way to know.

The archaeological evidence in this context is quite revealing. Chinese porcelain was one of the most significant imports during Heian times, and because porcelain tends to be well preserved in archaeological contexts, it is possible to obtain statistically valid evidence about the volume of imports. The data in Graph 5, taken from a recent study by Tsuchihashi Riko,[29] represents a breakdown by century of the number of sites yielding imported porcelain in different parts of the country. This calculation is not the same as an actual count of recovered vessels or fragments thereof; a site that has produced a single fragment of porcelain gets the same weight as one that has produced tons of archaeological material.

In any case, some significant insights may be derived from this graph. First, the distribution of imported porcelain is relatively limited until the twelfth century, when the number of sites begins to increase rapidly. Second, the single largest group of sites is in Fukuoka prefecture, where the Kōrokan and Dazaifu were located, and where most (or, in some periods, all) of the actual trade was conducted. Third, significant quantities of porcelain are also found in contemporary capitals such as Nara, Kyoto, and later, Kanagawa prefecture (where Kamakura is located). These represent the consumption centers of the elite. Fourth, porcelain has also been recovered at many sites in other parts of the country, particularly from the twelfth century on. Tsuchihashi's original data (not reflected in my graph) shows significant numbers of sites in Shiga prefecture (the site of Ōtsu, a town on Lake Biwa that functioned as a port for Kyoto), Osaka and Okayama prefectures on the Honshu coast of the Inland Sea (along which trade goods were transported from Kyushu to the capital region), and Saga prefecture in Kyushu (the site of Kanzaki estate). The archaeological material from Saga (and other areas in coastal Kyushu) is particularly interesting when considered together with the historical record from 1133: the archeological finds may reflect either direct trade between local residents and Chinese "smugglers" or redistribution within Kyushu of goods imported through the official trade in Hakata.[30]

In fact, there is no real contradiction between archaeological data and the historical record until the twelfth century. Both types of data seem to agree on two points, namely, that the volume of foreign trade remained quite low until around 1100, and that most (or in some periods all) of this trade was channeled through Hakata. The divergence between archeological and archival data occurs only in the early twelfth century, when historical sources show an apparent drop in the number of visits by merchants, while the archaeological record shows a dramatic leap in imports of ceramics. We can account for this disparity by questioning either the archaeological or the historical records.

On the archaeological side, it is possible that the data cited above do not adequately reflect actual trends in the volume of trade. Perhaps, for example, there was a major change in the composition of imports, so that the percentage of ceramics went up substantially even though the overall level of trade declined. This seems unlikely; if anything, the percentage of ceramics actually went *down* as merchants began to import more Chinese coins.[31] Alternatively, trade goods at older sites still undiscovered might, when found, add to estimates of earlier trade, thereby reducing calculations of the extent of later growth. However, while the sample may be skewed geographically (excavations tend to take place in more populated areas), a chronological skewing seems unlikely because of the sheer number of sites that have been investigated.

The real source of the divergence, most likely, is to be found in the historical record. It is not a matter of poor survival of sources; as evident in Graphs 3 and 4, the historical record reflected in court diaries actually improves dramatically in the twelfth century. It appears, however, that these sources for the first time now under-report rather consistently the actual volume of foreign trade.

Changes in the nature of the trade itself likely made it less "newsworthy" to courtiers in the twelfth century, resulting in a significant decline in arrivals recorded. It is not simply a case where the longer foreign merchants came to Japan, the more "ordinary" their activities would have seemed. The effect in that case would have been gradual, not comparatively sudden. Something much more important is suggested here, namely, a fundamental change in the way the trade was organized. As noted, the trade was originally dependent upon visits by foreign merchants, but as Kamei Meitoku and others have shown,[32] some of the merchants eventually settled along the bay in the Hakata and Hakozaki areas east of the Kōrokan. By the twelfth century, much of Japan's foreign trade was conducted not by transient visitors from China, but by "guild heads" (*kōshu*) resident in this diaspora community. Although these individuals were still viewed as "Chinese" (specifically, as "men from Song" or *Sōjin*) by Japanese authorities, their comings and goings were presumably far less newsworthy than those of truly alien visitors. It stands to reason that the return of a local ship, even one manned by resident Chinese, would have attracted far less comment on the part of court diarists and administrators than the arrival of a completely unknown vessel filled with visitors from abroad. This hypothesis explains, at least in part, how the actual volume of foreign trade could have increased without leaving much trace in the historical record.

An additional reason for the low number of records may be related to the government's declining ability to supervise commercial activity. The emergence of the Chinese diaspora community in Hakata coincides more or less precisely with the final disappearance of the Kōrokan from both historical and archaeological records.[33] The eclipse of this hitherto key facility symbolizes the shift from a period in which central authorities maintained relatively effective control over cross-border traffic (through Dazaifu), to one in which such traffic began to have a life of its own, largely (or at least, partially) free from central controls. Ironically, the court had little trouble convincing authentic visitors from overseas to observe its rules and regulations, but was completely impotent when the driving force behind trade shifted to merchants—even Chinese merchants—living in Japan itself. In short, courtiers' failure to record the arrival of merchants stems not just from a lack of interest but also, and perhaps more importantly, from a lack of knowledge.

To summarize, both the "old" and "new" views of Heian foreign trade have something to recommend them, if we apply them to different chronological periods. It is true, as Mori Katsumi and others argued, that the government eventually lost control of trade, but not until the twelfth century, near the very end of the Heian period. Until around 1100, it would seem, the government did a rather good job of managing the comings and goings of merchants through its agents at Dazaifu, much as Yamauchi Shinji and other recent Japanese scholars emphasize.

Three Cases

Since so few good descriptions of the mechanics of trade supervision exist in the English-language literature, an examination of several documents from the late eleventh and very early twelfth centuries may prove illuminating. Our source in this instance is the twelfth-century compilation known as *Chōya gunsai*, which was originally assembled to provide mid- to low-ranking bureaucrats with representative examples of document formats they might expect to encounter in the course of their official duties. Three selections follow, each relating to the arrival of Chinese merchant ships in Hakata. These examples provide support for the above contentions regarding the volume and nature of foreign trade in late Heian Japan.

The first selection is a verbatim transcript of a "cabinet meeting" (*jin no sadame* session), held at court in late 1070. It concerns a Chinese merchant named Pan Huaiqing, and the ministers in attendance are trying to decide whether he should be deported or "accommodated" (a euphemism for being permitted to stay in Hakata at the Kōrakan for the purpose of trade). The arguments for deporting him are compelling: his documents are not in order and, more fundamentally, he has failed to observe the legal minimum of two years between visits, a requirement dating from the early 900s.[34] Arguments for letting him stay are based on special pleading: that sending him away might give other merchants the idea that their gifts were not wanted, that his failure to observe the legal interval between visits should be excused because it reflects his great love for Japan, that it would be cruel to send him back across the sea in the cold winter months, and that making an exception in this case would in any event cause no real harm. In the end, the special pleaders seem to have won out over the legal sticklers, and Pan Huaiqing was allowed to stay.

SELECTION NO. 1[35]

Concerning whether or not to accommodate the merchant Pan Huaiqing of Fuzhou, Great Country of Song, whose arrival was reported by Dazaifu:

Palace minister and Master of the Crown Prince's Household Fujiwara *no ason* [and four others] said: "The matter is much as major controller of the right Minamoto *no ason* says [i.e., Pan has violated the minimum two-year interval between visits]. However, the freight declaration mentions presents of Buddhist icons and writings. If he is deported, it may be thought that such Buddhist icons and writings are not used here, and merchants arriving in the future may no longer bring them as presents. So what harm would there be in letting him stay and receiving the gifts?"

Provisional Middle Counsellor Minamoto *no ason* and Major Controller of the Right Minamoto *no ason* said: "This Huaiqing came during the Jiryaku era [1065–1069], but because he was in violation of the term [between visits], he received an order of deportation, and returned home last year. Nonetheless, he has come again this year, as if he has forgotten the laws of the land. Also, he has presented only a copy of his sailing papers; is it not customary to present the original? It was most inappropriate of Dazaifu not to ask him the reason for this. However, according to the interrogation record, despite his [earlier] deportation, he has come again from far across the sea out of yearning for the Imperial Virtue. Regarding this, we feel that while he has truly erred in violating the term, one can certainly sympathize with his yearning from afar for the Great Virtue. Moreover, it is the last month of the year, and the cold is at its most fearsome. Therefore, what special harm would there be in issuing an order to [this] effect and accommodating him? Since a term was [first] established for merchants, there have been cases where they have been accommodated without strictly following the stipulated term. This is because they serve the court and cause no special problems. At any rate, if he is to be accommodated, let the goods that have been sent up be inspected and received."

2nd year of Enkyū [1070], 12th month, 7th day

The second selection is the transcript of a similar meeting, held in 1085. Here, two cases have come up for review. The first involves a group of merchants requesting permission to stay in Hakata long enough to repair their ship while waiting for favorable winds. The lords in attendance decry the recent tendency of foreign merchants to come and go as they please, and the failure of Dazaifu to adequately enforce the laws. In the end, however, they agree that these particular merchants have a good excuse for staying in Hakata, and decide to grant their request, pending imperial approval. The second case involves another ship docked at Hakata at the same time. Here, the lords find no extenuating circumstances, and decide to issue an order of deportation to be carried out by Dazaifu, which again is roundly denounced for its failure to carry out similar orders in the past.

SELECTION NO. 2[36]

Concerning the arrival of the merchants Wang Duan, Liu Cong, and Ding Zai, from the Great Country of Song, reported by Dazaifu:

Master of the crown prince's household Fujiwara *no ason* [and four others] said: "Since a term was first established for the arrival of foreign guests, those who have not followed the term have sometimes been accommodated and sometimes been deported. However, in recent years [Dazaifu] Headquarters officials have been especially lenient to foreign guests, making decisions on the basis of personal feelings, even if they have seen a State Council order of deportation. It is as though the orders issued are [never] carried out. According to rumor, in ancient times these merchant guests waited for the seasonal winds of the second and eighth months before leaving, but in recent years they come and go as they please, without regard for the season. They should be notified to leave and speedily deported. However, if they are repairing their vessels while waiting for the seasonal winds, those circumstances should be taken into account when making the decision. Henceforth, if it is reported that [merchants] have been allowed to tarry for other reasons, an order should be issued to give them a clear rebuke. Otherwise, so long as they cause no real trouble, what harm is there in accommodating them for the time being? Nonetheless, imperial permission should be secured. At any rate, it is said that in recent years foreign guests arrive in the various provinces, carrying out trade and setting up fairs, filling the cities up and overflowing the wards. Even if there is no particular cause for suspicion, this is still in violation of the old laws."

Concerning the arrival of merchant guests Sun Zhong and Lin Gao, also reported by Dazaifu:

The same lords said, "We have previously reached a decision on the arrival of merchant guests. In particular, this Sun Zhong and company have used the sailing [winds] as an excuse [for not returning home]. Why should the wishes of our court fail to be carried out for the sake of foreign guests? Send an order to Dazaifu that they should be deported. Furthermore, in recent years things are not always carried out smoothly. A ship is said to have turned stern, while in fact its bow does not move. The failure of merchants to observe propriety is the fault of Dazaifu officials for not providing [adequate] surveillance. Promptly issue an order for them to be rebuked.

2nd year of Ōtoku [1085], 10th month, 29th day

The third and final selection, dating from 1105, is not a transcript of a cabinet meeting per se but a set of the actual documents upon which such discussions were based. We have three items, all sent to the capital by Dazaifu. The first is a report by the Hakata Watch Station, or Keigosho, informing Dazaifu of the arrival of a Chinese ship in the waters off Shikanoshima.[37] The second is a transcript of an interrogation of the captain by officials at Dazaifu, conducted with the aid of an interpreter. The captain is asked, among other things, to state his reasons for coming, to declare his freight and the tonnage of his vessel, show his official sailing papers, and list the names of his crew members. The report is signed not only by interrogators from Dazaifu, but also by the captain, indicating that he has been given an opportunity to review its content for accuracy. The third document in the set consists of a copy of the sailing papers submitted by the captain. These were issued by the port authorities in Mingzhou (modern Ningbo) and, among other things, list the names of the captain, his two mates, and the sixty-six members of his crew, together with the nature of his cargo, which consisted principally of Chinese textiles and porcelain. Dazaifu forwarded all of these documents to Kyoto, where they were presumably used to decide the fate of the vessel in a cabinet meeting such as those just described. The end result in this case is unfortunately not known.

SELECTION NO. 3[38]

The Watch Station petitions concerning a report:
Reporting on details of the newly arrived Chinese ship:
This ship arrived this afternoon between 5 and 7 pm in the waters of Shikanoshima, Hakata Bay, Naka district,

Chikuzen province. Following precedent, the details are reported as above, whereby this petition.

2nd year of Chōji [1105], 8th month, 20th day

Latchkeeper [*kagitori*] Taguchi Yoshitō
Head of Office/Deputy Executive Secretary Kudara Koresuke

———

Interrogation record of same:

A record of the interrogation of the visitor from the Great Country of Song in the 2nd year of Chōji [1105], 8th month, 22nd day:

The visitor was asked: "According to the Watch Station's report of the 20th day, 'Between 5 and 7 pm today, one ship from the Great Country of Song arrived in the waters of Shikanoshima, Hakata Bay, Naka district, Chikuzen province. The report is as above.' According to precedent, officials from the Headquarters have been sent to conduct the interrogation. State clearly the name of your captain and your reason for coming."

The visitor replied: "I come from the Great Country of Song. I am Li Chong, a resident of Quanzhou. I came to your country in the 4th month of Kōwa [1102], last, as a crew member of Zhuang Yan. Last year, Zhuang Yan received a State Council order of deportation, and I returned home with him. At that time, I had a small amount of freight with me. Some people of this country borrowed it, but when I solicited the debtors, they fled and would not return it. Therefore, I arranged another ship and, consulting with my crew members, made the journey here in order to appeal to the court [*kuge*] about the matter and retrieve [my goods]."

He was asked again: "If there were people who did not return the goods they had borrowed when you came here last time, this fact should have been reported. However at that time no report was made. It is difficult to believe that your journey was planned in order to retrieve borrowed goods. There are clear precedents for the practice of bringing presents on arrival. Promptly declare, according to custom, the freight you have with you, the sailing papers from your place of origin, a list of your crew members' names, and the capacity of your ship."

The visitor said: "I present [separately] the sailing papers from my place of origin and the list of my crew members' names. The capacity of my ship is one hundred-plus *koku* [i.e., about twenty-five tons]. It is by no means a fabrication that my goods were borrowed by people of this country. I will present a list of the debtors. If they are summoned and questioned about the truth of the matter, the greed of [these] merchants will be laid bare. If the lost goods cannot be retrieved I shall lament greatly. Therefore I came to petition the court. As you say, I should have reported the matter when I returned home last time. However, because Captain Zhuang Yan was censured by the authorities and took sail in great haste, I was unable to report it. My grief did not pass, so I have come this time in order to petition the court. The matter should be reported promptly and the judgment carried out."

He was asked again: "The list of the debtors that you have presented deserves inspection by the headquarters. At any rate, declare a list of the freight you have with you this time."

Li Chong said: "A list is contained in the sailing papers that I have presented. There is no need to make a second declaration. The quantity of freight I have with me is extremely small. I intend to sell it for provisions for the return journey. Can goods of such poor quality be fit to present to the court? Beforehand, however, the report should be made and the judgment carried out."

The man from Song:
Li Chong (seal)
Headquarters officials:
Headquarters Administrator [*fuzai*] Atai Tamesue
Interpreter Kose Tomotaka
Scribe [*bunden*] Munakata Narihiro
Office Head [*chōtō*] Ōnakatomi *no ason* Sukeyoshi
Foreman [*kanshu*] Takahashi Munesada

Headquarters Elder [*furō*] Ki *no ason* Tomozane

Sailing papers:

Submitted to the Liangzhe[39] Office of Shipping:
According to the petition of Quanzhou merchant Li Chong,
"I am now in charge of my own ship and am assembling
sailors. I wish to go to the country of Japan to conduct
trade for their wages, by way of Mingzhou. I beg the
Shipping Commissioner to issue a permit and allow me
to proceed."

Items: crew, ship, and freight
One private ship
Captain Li Chong, Helmsman Lin Yang, Purser Zhuang
Quan
Mercenaries [*bingdu*] under their command:
    First deck: [list of twenty-three names omitted]
    Second deck: [list of twenty-five names omitted]
    Third deck: [list of eighteen names omitted]
Freight:
    Damask, 10 bolts
    Raw silk, 10 bolts
    White twill, 20 bolts
    Porcelain bowls, 200 crates
    Porcelain plates, 100 crates

[Remainder of document omitted]

Conclusions

One way to read these documents is as an account of an
era wherein there was a lot of trade, and it was not very well
supervised. One of the participants in the 1085 cabinet meeting,
for example, claims that "in recent years foreign guests arrive
in the various provinces, carrying out trade and setting up fairs,
filling up the cities and overflowing the wards." (Perhaps this
is an oblique reference to the trade at Tsuruga, which was at its
most active during this general period.) There is also much talk
about the inadequate supervision provided by Dazaifu. In 1070,

officials at Dazaifu are censured for failing to question Pan Huaiqing about some of the documents he has submitted, while in 1085, the opinion is voiced that "in recent years headquarters officials have been especially lenient to foreign guests, making their decisions on the basis of personal feelings, even if they have seen a State Council order of deportation." It is also worth noting that in both 1070 and 1085 the court itself felt little compunction about approving exceptions to its own rule that merchants could visit Japan only once every two years. Although various reasons are given, the determining factor may well have been simply a desire for continued access to foreign luxury goods.

While this viewpoint emphasizes a decline in, or loss of, central control over foreign trade, there is a rather different picture to be drawn from these records as well. First, it is clear that, at least until 1105, the authorities were able to limit "official" entrance to Japan to merchants coming through Hakata. Traders did on occasion stop at other ports, but such transgressions were tolerated rather than encouraged. Second, officials at Dazaifu were fully capable, at least in some cases, of noting the arrival of individual merchant ships, interrogating their captains, and inspecting their cargo.[40] Third, final authority over the disposition of individual merchants was retained, and in fact actively exercised, by the central government. Details of each case were heatedly discussed at the highest levels of state. Fourth, and following from the first three points, the actual volume of cross-border traffic must have remained relatively low, for otherwise such a top-heavy system would have rapidly become too cumbersome to maintain. Needless to say, all of these observations fit in rather well with the conclusions reached earlier on the basis of statistical evidence, both documentary and archaeological.

But the conditions in which foreign trade took place, and the volume of that commerce were already changing. Indeed, the documents from *Chōya gunsai* offer a brief glimpse of what was to come. The selections from 1070 and 1085 contain repeated references to the official act of "accommodation" of foreign merchants, while there is no such reference in the set of documents from 1105. Possibly we lack a transcript of the relevant cabinet meeting (assuming that one actually took place). More likely, however, the Kōrokan itself had simply ceased to function.[41] Judging from the documents in question, inspectors at Dazaifu simply went out to Shikanoshima, where the ship in question lay at anchor. There is no mention of moving the ship to an anchorage near the Kōrokan, as would inevitably have been the case in earlier times.[42]

This, in fact, marked the beginning of the end of effective central controls. Not long after the events of 1105, Dazaifu itself ceased to pay close attention to the arrival of merchant ships. At any rate, there is no evidence of such attention in the historical records. As has already been suggested, this change is very likely related to the emergence of an active (and perhaps relatively autonomous) Chinese diaspora community in the Hakata/Hakozaki area. Undoubtedly, however, it also relates to ongoing changes in the central-local balance of power in Japan.

For example, after around 1120 ranking Dazaifu officials generally ceased traveling to Kyushu, and chose instead to oversee the affairs of their office from their Kyoto mansions with the help of private "deputies," or *mokudai,* based in Kyushu.[43] Of course, there were exceptions, such as when acting governor-general Taira Yorimori astounded his peers at court by actually journeying to Dazaifu in 1166. Further, absenteeism in and of itself did not automatically equate to a loss of control over the local merchant community. Some local "deputies" could wield considerable power, as in 1151, when five hundred mounted troops under the command of Dazaifu deputy Muneyori conducted a raid of immigrant households in Hakata.[44] On the whole, however, there is no denying that the level of direct government control over cross-border traffic atrophied over the course of the twelfth century.

Perhaps a better way of describing this same phenomenon is to say that local actors—residents of Hakata's "Chinatown," estate administrators, and other notables with access to docking facilities in Kyushu—became much more independent of central controls on trade during the twelfth century.[45] Put this way, the increasing "porosity" of Japan's borders and growing volume of foreign trade become part and parcel of the much more general shift in the balance of central-local power relations in the twelfth century. It is perhaps no coincidence that whatever substantial "opening" of the country took place, it occurred only a few decades before the dramatic reorganization of power at the center itself during the civil wars of the 1180s.

NOTES

1   I am grateful to Ethan Segal for reading and commenting on an earlier version of this essay.

2   Good examples are John W. Hall, *Japan: From Prehistory to Modern Times*, and Edwin O. Reischauer, *The Japanese Today*.

3   See, for example, W. G. Beasley, *The Japanese Experience: A Short History of Japan*.

4   See, for example, the various essays in Donald Denoon et al., eds., *Multicultural Japan: Paleolithic to Postmodern*, especially the chapter by Amino Yoshihiko, the "founding father" of the recent trend to emphasize diversity in Japanese history.

5   Ronald Toby, *State and Diplomacy in Early Modern Japan: Asia in the Development of the Tokugawa Bakufu*.

6   See, for example, Murai Shōsuke, *Chūsei wajin den*; *Umi kara mita sengoku Nihon*; *Chūsei Nihon no uchi to soto*.

7   For a more comprehensive analysis, see Bruce Batten, *To the Ends of Japan: Premodern Frontiers, Boundaries and Interactions*.

8   Much of the material in this section is summarized from Batten, "Cross-border Traffic on the Kyushu Coast, 794–1086." Also see my recent book, *Gateway to Japan: Hakata in War and Peace, 500-1300*.

9   Batten, "Cross-border Traffic."

10   In Japanese, Mori's most important work is *Shintei Nissō bōeki no kenkyū*. In English, see his "The Beginning of Overseas Advance of Japanese Merchant Ships."

11   Mimi Yiengpruksawan, "Chinese Traders, Kyoto Aristocrats, and the Transmarine Factor in the Formation of Medieval Japanese Culture."

12   See Yamauchi Shinji, *Nara Heian ki no Nihon to Ajia*, esp. pp. 128–166.

13   This finding echoes the results of some recent English-language publications by Charlotte von Verschuer. (Von Verschuer earlier published some of this same material in French.) See note 20, below.

14   Tajima Isao, "Nihon, Chūgoku, Chōsen taigai kōryū shi nenpyō: Taihō gannen Bunji gannen."

15   Taigai kankei shi sōgō nenpyō henshū iinkai, ed., *Taigai kankei shi sōgō nenpyō*.

16   Specifically, I counted the number of arrivals listed by Tajima in the fourth and final column of his chart, which gives information on "point of departure, point(s) of transit, and point of arrival." It would be possible to quibble with some of these entries because of problems in interpreting the original source materials. For example, many Chinese merchants visited Japan on more than one occasion, and it is not always possible to determine whether two references in the historical sources pertain to a single extended visit or to separate, closely spaced visits. In almost all such cases I have deferred to Tajima's judgment, which reflects a superb knowledge of the primary sources.

17   For background, see Batten, "Cross-border Traffic."

18   I initially made attempts to link these apparent trends with socio-political changes in Japan and/or other countries, hypothesizing, for example, that the trough at the beginning of the tenth century resulted from the imposition of stricter Japanese trade controls (in 911 the court ruled that foreign merchant vessels had to observe a minimum two-year interval between visits to Japan, ibid.) while that around the middle of the same century had to do with political instability on the continent during the Tang-Song transition.

19   For evidence to substantiate these claims, see the material presented below under the section, "Three Cases."

20   For a similar estimate, see von Verschuer, "Across the Sea: Intercourse of People, Know-How, and Goods in East Asia," chart on p. 19.

21   The following figures for number of crewmen per vessel may be found in the Tajima chronology: 33 (862), 63 (865), 41 (866) 36 (874), 31 (876), 63 (877), 60 (893), 100 (945), 69 (1105). In a rare mistake, Tajima claims that the 945 visit involved three ships as opposed

to one (the correct number). For a detailed study of this incident, see Batten, *Gateway to Japan*, pp. 105–111.

22   Nihon jinkō gakkai, ed., *Jinkō daijiten*, pp. 91–92.

23   As in Graph 1, data on points of arrival come from the fourth column of Tajima's chart. I have included a few cases where the visitor is simply described as (for example) a "man from Song" but where he is clearly involved in buying and selling goods and/or is referred to as a "merchant" in other historical sources. Note that another reading for the term *shōnin* is *akindo*.

24   This figure includes a few cases where merchants first weighed anchor elsewhere in Kyushu but were immediately redirected to Hakata.

25   Little has been written on the Matsubara Guest Lodge. One good but elusive source is Kōjiya Yoshiaki, ed., *Matsubara kyakkan no nazo ni semaru: kodai Tsuruga to higashi Ajia.* For relations with Parhae in general, see Sakayori Masashi, *Bokkai to kodai no Nihon,* and Ishii Masatoshi, *Nihon Bokkai kankei shi no kenkyū.*

26   Note, however, a record from 1119 that mentions that merchants were no longer coming regularly to this area because they were afraid of being mistreated by Japanese provincial authorities. See entries for this year in either of the chronologies cited in notes 14 and 15. For original sources, see [Gen'ei 2? (1119)] Bō shojō (HI, 9:4673, 4674).

27   For details of this episode, see entries for this year in either of the cited chronologies; the original source is *Chōshūki* Chōjō 2 (1133).8.13. The "traditional" view is represented by Mori Katsumi, *Shintei Nissō bōeki no kenkyū.* A good recent study is Ishii Masatoshi, "Hizen no kuni Kanzaki no shō to Nissō bōeki."

28   See, for example, the entries for 934 (Satsuma), 1147 (various Kyushu estates), and 1148 (Kishima estate, Hizen) in either of the two cited chronologies.

29   Tsuchihashi Riko, "Nissō bōeki no shosō." For much more detailed (but also older and somewhat less convenient) information on archaeological sites yielding imported porcelain, see the volume in which Tajima's chronology was published: Nara kenritsu Kashihara kōkogaku kenkyūjo fuzoku hakubutsukan, ed., *Bōeki tōji: Nara Heian no Chūgoku tōji.*

30 Interestingly, very few relevant archaeological sites are known from Tsuruga in Fukui, despite clear documentary evidence, cited above, that Chinese merchants were active in this region during the late eleventh and early twelfth centuries.

31 See the essay by Ethan Segal in this volume.

32 E.g., Kamei Meitoku, *Nihon bōeki tōjishi no kenkyū*; "Nissō bōeki kankei no tenkai"; Saeki Kōji, "Hakata."

33 Kamei Meitoku, "Kōrokan bōeki"; Tajima Isao, "Dazaifu Kōrokan no shūen: 8 seiki – 11 seiki no taigai kōeki shisutemu no kaimei."

34 See note 18, above.

35 *Chōya gunsai* Enkyū 2 (1070).12.7 *jin no sadame*, pp. 130–131.

36 Ibid., Ōtoku 2 (1085).10.29 *jin no sadame* (both documents), pp. 131–132.

37 Many works in English refer to this location as "Shiga Island" or the equivalent. Although the characters in question are indeed usually read as "Shiga," the correct reading is as given here. Also, note that this "island" is in fact connected to the mainland (on the east side of Hakata Bay) by a narrow sand spit (and now by a very heavily used road as well). See Map 1.

38 *Chōya gunsai* Chōji 2 (1105).8.5 keigosho *ge*, pp. 450–451; *Chōya gunsai* Chōji 2 (1105).8.22 *zonmonki*, pp. 451–452; *Chōya gunsai* Chōji 2 (1105).6 *kōhyō*, pp. 452–455.

39 A Song Dynasty "route" in the Lower Yangzi region that contained Mingzhou, Hangzhou, and other ports.

40 That said, I must also note that border controls were hardly perfect. We know, for example, of at least two Heian-period monks who managed to evade Dazaifu inspectors and "sneak" out of the country on Chinese vessels. See Borgen, "Jōjin's Travels from Center to Center," pp. 388–399.

41 See sources cited in note 33, above.

42 For a clear example, see the entries for 945 in either of the Tajima or Tanaka chronologies. These involve a ship from Wu Yue (907–978) which first arrived in Hizen but was then redirected to the

"Kōrosho" (Kōrokan) under Dazaifu supervision. The original source is *Honchō seiki* Tengyō 8 (945).7.26.

43   Batten, "Documentary Evidence for Institutional Change at the Dazaifu, 1000–1185." Provincial governors ceased to travel to their provinces of appointment around this time as well; see Tomita Masahiro, "Kokumu monjo." Much of the existing English-language literature seems to assume that governors were absentee figures through much of the Heian period. As Tomita shows, absenteeism did not become the norm until the twelfth century.

44   These events have been described countless times; for a recent summary (with full references to original sources), see my *Kokkyō no tanjō: Dazaifu kara mita Nihon no genkai*, pp. 216–219.

45   For a case study relating to ports in southern Kyushu, see Yanagihara Toshiaki, "Chūsei zenki minami Kyushu no minato to Sōjin kyoryūchi."

Awash with Coins: The Spread of Money in Early Medieval Japan
Ethan Segal

By the mid-thirteenth century, the warrior government known as the Kamakura bakufu had established itself as a strong, stable institution. It had secured the right to appoint its retainers over most of the country, developed an effective judicial system to minimize disputes, and survived an attempt at its destruction by an emperor. Yet some of the bakufu's retainers (*gokenin*), even those located in the home region of the eastern provinces, found themselves in severe financial straits. One warrior writes of being repeatedly ordered to travel to Kyushu and trying to cover the expenses by borrowing money. "Every time (I borrow), they take interest (*rizeni*) from me," he writes. The identity of the "they" is not specified, but clearly moneylenders are involved. Another provincial figure writes of the urgent need to repay a creditor and tells his subordinate that if funds cannot be raised he may be forced to sell off land holdings.[1]

That bakufu-affiliated warriors such as these men should have had to struggle with monetary problems might strike modern readers as incongruous. After all, the late twelfth-century establishment of the Kamakura bakufu has frequently been described as the triumph of warriors over older imperial institutions.[2] Jeffrey Mass quite correctly revised that characterization by showing how warrior dominance emerged more gradually and how older civilian institutions retained some authority well into the thirteenth century. The legal documents that Mass used to prove his case, however, still suggest warriors were generally successful in appropriating ever more rights to income from civilian land proprietors over the course of the Kamakura period. Even so, many retainers found that their financial troubles only worsened during the thirteenth century, leading some like the retainers quoted above to use their land rights as collateral against loans from moneylenders.

Bakufu officials knew of the difficult financial position that some warriors found themselves in and tried to use legal proclamations to prevent Kamakura's retainers from losing their lands. At various times it attempted to forbid gambling or the use of land as collateral for loans. Most famous was the virtuous government edict (*tokuseirei*) of 1297, which, among other things, proclaimed that warriors' debts were forgiven and that they could reclaim lands lost to debt default even if they could not repay their creditors.[3] Efforts at fixing economic problems with political decrees proved unsuccessful, though, and the growing money economy of early medieval Japan not only proved to be the undoing of more than one warrior house, but also contributed to the general discontent that led warriors to overthrow the bakufu in 1333.

Money itself was nothing new in Japan. The imperial court had minted its own coins during the eighth, ninth, and tenth centuries. Rice, silk, and other kinds of cloth had all served as units of exchange and stores of wealth—two of the essential functions of money—into the twelfth century and beyond. But the money that came to dominate the medieval economy was quite different from those earlier forms of currency. Starting in the last decades of the Heian period, imported Chinese cash—copper-alloy coins with a square hole in the middle, bearing a four-character inscription on one face—started to enter Japan from Song China. Described in contemporary documents as "money of the times," "copper coins," and "cash from the Song," the use of this form of currency so alarmed the late twelfth-century nobility that they referred to it as an epidemic and repeatedly tried to ban it.[4] Even so, foreign coins proliferated and became the major instrument of exchange in Japan from the thirteenth to sixteenth centuries.

In fact, we might see the use of foreign coins as one characteristic that defined Japan's medieval age.

Where did this new money come from and what function(s) did it serve in early medieval society? What were the relationships among money, the imperial court, and the Kamakura bakufu? How were warriors affected by the influx of cash into the economy? These and other questions have not received much scholarly treatment in English. Although there are several excellent monographs addressing different aspects of the pre-1600 Japanese economy, money and monetization have not been the focus of a major study in over fifty years.[5] In fact, many historians have tended to overlook the impact of money on medieval institutions. At least one early twentieth-century scholar failed to acknowledge the presence of money in pre-1600 Japan at all; others confidently date the rise of a commercial, monetary economy only from the advent of Edo period (1600–1868).[6] Undoubtedly, the level of commercialization in the seventeenth century under Tokugawa rule was far greater than what occurred in earlier centuries, but it is misleading to ignore the significant role that metallic money began to play in Japan's thirteenth and fourteenth centuries.

Even among specialists of the medieval period, much of the English language scholarship tends to highlight issues of land rather than money when describing the economy.[7] This stems in part from the types of documents that survive. Landowners held onto deeds (needed to prove claim if a property dispute arose) much more dearly than to cash receipts or records, which frequently held little value to later generations. They retained such land records with good reason, for medieval primary sources reveal that judicial battles and inheritance disputes over land rights were common. But there were also times when the bakufu made payments in precious metals and cases in which parents provided for their children by leaving them monetary legacies.[8] Legal disputes over cash income were frequently and bitterly contested. Proprietors kept careful records of how much their provincial estates paid them—and of how much remained outstanding. Substituting money (*daisennō*) for rice or cloth in tax payments became common by the late thirteenth-century, and spread hand-in-hand with provincial markets. Cash was the primary medium of exchange in those markets, and coins had penetrated provincial society sufficiently by the late thirteenth century that, on some estates, household taxes (*munabechisen*) could be levied in cash.[9] Clearly money played a significant role in the medieval Japanese economy.

This essay highlights the need to re-evaluate the place of money in medieval Japan and its impact on late Heian and Kamakura society. The early medieval adoption of copper cash is particularly interesting because the use of foreign coins during those years became widespread in defiance of elite control. In the earlier Nara and Heian periods, described briefly below, coins were creatures and instruments of the state. Government mints produced the currency, imperial ministers established policies to encourage its use, and the state played a significant role in collecting taxes, redistributing goods, and paying salaries. In contrast, Japan's medieval age lacked a strong central authority capable of regulating the economy or backing its own currency. As a result, noncentral elites were able to import coins, trade in regional markets, and otherwise bypass older forms of elite-controlled exchange. In addition, the demand for cash led samurai retainers to defy Kamakura bakufu policymakers by borrowing against their land holdings and thereby endangering the retainer system that underpinned the bakufu. In these ways, the increasingly monetized economy of the twelfth to sixteenth centuries directly contributed to the breakdown of traditional political authority that became endemic during Japan's later medieval age.

Money and Economic Policies in the Nara and Early Heian Periods

Japan's early monetary history was closely tied to state development. The late seventh-century Japanese court undertook major reforms over several decades as it strengthened central government power, seeking to refashion itself on the model of Tang China.[10] These reforms included plans for the issuance of Chinese-style copper coins. In the partially monetized Tang economy, cash and cloth were the primary forms of currency. Cash was used in the payment of taxes and was a significant component of state salaries.[11] Chinese officials saw coins as a manifestation of state power, and they took care to monitor and regulate the money supply. The Japanese knew of the Chinese use of money, both from their travels to the continent and from references in the Chinese *lüling*, the Tang legal codes that became the basis of similar Japanese *ritsuryō* codes. Consequently, the Japanese created a mint and appointed officials for the mint in the 690s.[12] The oldest coins found and thought to have been produced in Japan, known as *fuhonsen*, have been dated to approximately the same period. Much remains unknown about these coins, including who made them and whether they actually served an economic function. There is no evidence to suggest that they were used either for exchange or to store wealth, and some scholars believe that they may have served as good luck or religious tokens rather than as money.[13]

The availability of precious metals played a major part in the government's ability to produce coins at this time. The discovery of silver on the island of Tsushima in 674 was considered a find of great import, and reports of gold on Tsushima in 701 and of copper in Musashi province in 708 were each considered so auspicious that the reign names were changed (to *Taihō*, "great treasure," and to *Wadō*, "native copper," respectively). All three metals were coined during the Nara period, but silver and gold issues were extremely limited and probably did not circulate. Of course, the greater availability of copper was not the only reason that the court favored it for coinage over other precious metals. Gold and silver were valuable for use in trade with the continent, surely leading the nobles to promote the use of copper coins domestically. Starting with the *Wadō kaichin* coins of 708, the imperial court minted twelve different copper-alloy issues, as well as a much more limited number of silver and gold coins, over the next 250 years.[14] The *Wadō kaichin* remain the oldest native specimens known to have been produced by the government for the purpose of serving as money. They bear a striking resemblance to the primary Tang coin, the *Kaiyuan tongbao*, on which they were based.[15]

The eighth-century Japanese court took active steps to promote the circulation of its coins and maintain their value. Although it briefly promoted silver coins as well, for the most part the court forbade the domestic use of non-copper metal currency. It also attempted to educate people on the benefits of using coins, encouraging travelers to carry cash rather than bulkier goods to use during their journeys, and it paid part of the official salaries (*roku*) given to rank and office holders in cash.[16] The court also attempted to raise the value of its money by allowing individuals to purchase rank with coins. Those without rank could acquire entry-level rank for five thousand coins, and those already holding ranks could advance for ten thousand. This may have proven counterproductive, however, leading people to hoard coins and thereby take them out of circulation. The ability to purchase rank with coins was eliminated in the year 800.[17]

The court also issued strict regulations against the private minting of coins (i.e., counterfeiting), which was listed as one of the "great crimes" to be punished severely under the *ritsuryō* codes. Those caught producing counterfeit coins faced two hundred lashes with a cane and the prospect of having all of their assets confiscated and given to informants who reported on them. Of course, the need for skilled coin producers sometimes prevented the government from carrying out its threatened punishment, as seen in a case from the year 765 in which counterfeiters were put to work in the minting bureau.[18] However, the fact that counterfeiters sought to produce coins and risked punishment to do so shows that coins had value in eighth-century Japan.

Yet to what degree did coins penetrate the economy? While for some time there were doubts among scholars whether the imperial twelve coins enjoyed much acceptance outside of the capital region,[19] recent archaeological evidence suggests that they circulated more widely than was once believed. Excavations over the last thirty years have unearthed *Wadō kaichin* in all but ten of modern Japan's forty-seven prefectures, and other coins from the imperial twelve series have been unearthed in every part of the country. In addition, eighth-century sources such as the *Shoku Nihongi* list various provinces as paying taxes (*chō*) in cash.[20] We cannot escape the fact that the largest numbers of coins have been found in the centrally located Kinai area, suggesting that they enjoyed greatest acceptance in areas under close government control. But during the Nara and very early Heian periods, there appears to have been a notable degree of circulation outside of the capital region as well.

The Disappearance of Coins in the Mid- and Late Heian Period

The various government policies listed above helped coins enjoy some degree of circulation during the Nara and early Heian periods. But rice, silk, and other forms of cloth remained in use as instruments of exchange, and the government had difficulty maintaining the value of its metallic currency over time. One reason for this difficulty may have been that overproduction led to inflation. As Wayne Farris has argued, government officials found that issuing coins could be quite profitable and attempted to put increasing numbers of coins into circulation to compensate for declining tax revenues in the mid-eighth century.[21] Another related problem was that the government had an inadequate supply of copper. Reports from one of the mints in 821 indicated that little more than half of its four-year coin production quota could be met due to a lack of copper.[22] This copper shortage not only led to reduced output; it also forced the mint to begin debasing its new issues. Simple visual comparison of the different imperial twelve coins shows that their size and copper content steadily declined over time. Moreover, X-ray fluorescence (XRF) analysis performed by the Nara Cultural

Properties Research Institute confirms increased levels of lead content in coins minted during the ninth and tenth centuries.[23]

The court took a number of steps to compensate for the inadequate coin supply, including melting old coins for recasting and declaring newly issued coins to be worth more than older issues. For example, in 907, as the court produced its new *Engi tsūhō* coins, it proclaimed them to be worth ten coins of the older currency.[24] Although it is possible that these policies may have met with limited short-term success, over the long term, government decreed values were ignored and all coins circulated with the same value. Lacking any true basis (such as increased copper content) for the higher value, the government's policies only contributed to the further depreciation of its currency.

Other actions taken by the Heian court included issuing "price laws" (*kokahō*) in an effort to stop the depreciation of its currency. These were legal proclamations that attempted to fix the cash value of various commodities such as rice, salt, or even raw copper. The court also attempted to require that the Imperial Police Agency (*kebiishichō*), responsible for both criminal and public administrative matters within the capital area, enforce regulations mandating coin use. And in at least one instance, the government ordered temples to pray for the use of coins by the populace.[25] In spite of these and other efforts, written references to copper money become increasingly scarce over the course of the tenth century. The last of the imperial twelve, the *Kengen taihō* coin, was issued in 958. No Japanese government would officially mint a coin again until the sixteenth century.

Why did government economic policies fail to stimulate coin use in the Heian period? Did the court give up on its own currency? To answer these questions, let us examine the price law policy in greater detail. Originally, price laws appear to have been based on actual marketplace information. According to the eighth-century *ritsuryō* codes, officials were to use marketplace prices as their guide in fixing price laws, and the ninth-century legal commentary *Ryō no gige* indicates that officials were expected to learn market prices by visiting the market itself.[26] But while earlier price laws were tied to actual market conditions, later Heian price laws were issued with little regard for the market. Instead, idealized exchange rates, such as one *koku* of rice to one *kanmon* of coins, became commonplace.[27] The court had not given up on its coinage, but rather had come to view price laws as a ritual means of asserting authority.

The timing of price laws seems to confirm the change described above. When were *kokahō* issued? If the nobles promulgated a price law at the same time that they issued a new coin, then we might conclude that they sought to set the value of various goods vis-à-vis the new currency. Yet as the court stopped minting in the second half of the tenth century but continued promulgating price laws into the Kamakura period, this explanation is difficult to sustain. Rather, as Hotate Michihisa has shown, price laws correlate most strongly with the issuance of the first set of official proclamations (*shinsei*) of a new emperor.[28] Rather than responding to changing prices or to problems with the availability of money or goods, Heian elites issued price laws as a way of establishing political legitimacy.

Kokahō had not always been exclusively political tools, but this pattern of issuing price laws as part of an emperor's "new proclamations" became a process that "defined and limited" Heian economic policies, and thus became a powerful institution in the sense that economists use the term.[29] This concern with asserting political authority rather than addressing changing economic conditions would later limit the ability of the nobles to handle the large influx of Chinese coins in the twelfth century.

Twelfth-Century Coins and the Late Heian Elite

Coins are rarely mentioned in the surviving documents for the final two hundred years of the Heian period, and only then at the very end of that time span. They first appear in a document from the year 1150, which notes that twenty-seven strings of cash were the medium of exchange used in the sale of a private land holding and villa.[30] Citing this document, Mori Katsumi contends that Japanese began importing Chinese copper currency from the middle of the twelfth century and that they valued it because they could use it in trade to acquire Chinese goods.[31] However, other documentary evidence suggests that both of Mori's contentions require further consideration.

First, coins must have started to find purchase in Japan even earlier, if only by a few decades. The land sale from 1150 is for a large sum of cash and surely involved rather well-to-do parties. But a religious fund-raising register dated 1151—just one year later—lists the names and amounts given by supporters to the Hōrakuji temple in Tosa province.[32] These parishioners reflect a more diverse section of society, and their donations were in small thirty- and fifty-coin sums, suggesting that Tosa residents already had easy access to and familiarity with cash by the mid-twelfth century. Such evidence might be all the more surprising because Tosa was quite distant from the economically advanced capital region and the main trade routes of the Inland Sea. Further evidence can be found in a ban by Chinese authorities on the export of copper currency from coastal regions in 1155, suggesting that monetary outflow was already a serious problem by that date.[33] Although the 1155 document does not name the exporting culprits, the Korean economy was not monetized at this time, and similar bans issued only decades later quite clearly specify the Japanese. Southeast Asian states also had an interest in Chinese coins, but no other group is known to have imported more Song coins by sea than the Japanese.

Second is the issue of why the Japanese came to favor Chinese coins at this time. Of course, Mori is correct in highlighting the attractiveness of the Chinese goods and trade for Heian elites. The China of their day was an economic powerhouse. Northern (960–1127) and Southern (1127–1279) Song experienced unprecedented levels of economic growth and commercialization that are widely recognized by scholars as having transformed Chinese society.[34] These changes included the full-fledged monetization of the economy. Although the Tang had used coins for many types of transactions, it was only during the Northern Song that coins became the exclusive form of money. The newly developing Song commercial economy had a voracious appetite for copper cash. Chinese mints produced between one and two billion coins per year during the first half of the eleventh century, yet could not keep up with the twin demands of the military budget and expanding trade. Wang Anshi's reforms stimulated even greater levels of coin production, with a peak of almost six billion coins reached in the year 1073. The government could not maintain this extraordinary level of production, but annual coin production remained at between two and three billion for much of the early twelfth century.[35] This rapid economic growth accompanied similar expansions in productivity, commerce, and trade. Chinese merchants exported a wide range of goods including porcelain ware, medicines, and perfumes, and Song coins came to travel far beyond state borders. Among the leading importers of both goods and coins were the Japanese.

But did the Japanese acquire cash in order to pay for the Chinese goods that they sought? Mori's proposition is difficult to defend on this point. As noted above, coins appearing in twelfth-century Japanese documents were used for domestic purposes ranging from land sales to temple fund-raising, but there is no evidence that they were used to pay for products from abroad. When trading in the international arena, gold was the primary medium of exchange. Chinese and Korean traders came to Japan seeking gold, and Japanese elites readily paid in gold in order to obtain Chinese goods. Some Japanese finished goods were exported as well, such as lacquerware and items incorporating animal hides or mother-of-pearl.[36] Copper cash does not appear to have been used by Japanese traders as a significant means of international trade payments until the Muromachi period. This view is consistent not only with the fact that gold was the preferred means of payment for Japan-China trade in the Heian period, but also with the fact that the late Heian nobility—the very group most likely to engage in trade with the Chinese—opposed the importation of Chinese coins.

In order to understand the twelfth-century elite's opposition to imported cash, let us look at the text *Gyokuyō* to see how the nobles regarded money. *Gyokuyō* was the diary of Kujō Kanezane (1149–1207), a member of the northern Fujiwara with strong ties to the Kamakura bakufu who served as regent (*sesshō*) and later chancellor (*kanpaku*). Kanezane's diary, spanning the years 1164 to 1203, offers a first-hand account of important events, such as the debates of late twelfth-century elite lawmakers on a wide range of issues, including money.

The first detailed discussion in *Gyokuyō* of Chinese coins comes in the year 1179. In the excerpt below, Kanezane listens to the opinion of Nakahara Motohiro, a top adviser from the Imperial Police Agency:

> Motohiro spoke with me about transactions using coins, stating "Recently, it is reported that coins from the land of the Tang [i.e., China] come into our court and are used greedily in buying and selling. The private minting of coins [i.e., counterfeiting] is one of the eight high crimes [under the *ritsuryō* legal codes]. Although the coins currently being imported are not counterfeit, using them is the same [as using counterfeit coins]. Truly the use of these coins should be banned. Although letters of instruction (*migyōsho*) to this effect have been issued by the Chamberlain in the past, the ban has not been carried out. There is no justification for this!"[37]

Kanezane goes on to express his agreement with Motohiro and his support for a prohibition against foreign currency. His diary entry reveals much about the state of the nobles' thinking about coinage. Of particular interest is Motohiro's claim that the imported coins should be banned because they are the equivalent of counterfeit money. Although Motohiro recognizes that the coins in question are the legal product of a state mint, the state in question is a foreign power (Song China). Not surprisingly, Motohiro was concerned about the political implications of allowing foreign currency to circulate. In most of premodern East Asia, the right to mint and set the value of currency was regarded as an imperial prerogative and a statement of official authority. Economic historian Richard von Glahn describes this thinking as follows: "In China, as elsewhere, the authority to issue money remained a closely-guarded sovereign privilege. The state exercised greater direct control over money than over virtually any other facet of the economy."[38] This high regard for the control of money led the rival Chinese kingdoms of the tenth century to each issue their own currencies as part of their efforts to assert sovereign independence. It also influenced thinking on money in Japan, as seen in the Japanese decision to mint coins based on Chinese models.

Thus, for the nobles of the Heian court, coins produced by a foreign power were the same as coins minted by counterfeiters within Japan—in either case, the minter did not hold the right to produce coins within the Japanese realm. Perceiving Chinese cash to be a threat to Japanese authority, Kanezane and Motohiro viewed this matter as a political issue rather than an economic one. Later debates in *Gyokuyō* over the fate of coinage confirm this interpretation. For example, Chinese coins were the topic of a *sengi*, the highest administrative meeting of nobles, during the third month of 1192. Kanezane recorded the discussion in *Gyokuyō* as follows:

> Next, there was a *sengi* to determine whether or not to ban the use of currency. Although a final decision was not written out, the nobles were of one mind in declaring that the use of coins should be forbidden. Only the Palace Minister spoke up [recommending a different course of action], saying "It is inexcusable that the Imperial Police have not enforced the price laws! First, we should order the Imperial Police to carry out the previous edicts that already address this problem. If this matter falls outside the existing laws, then I agree that we should ban coin use." The Minister of the Left replied, saying "Coins should be banned, but if we do not issue a new edict that includes a price law, then in the end, the problems will not stop with a halt in the use of coins."[39]

This excerpt offers valuable insight into elite thinking on money and authority in late Heian Japan. First of all, the entry indicates that the nobles were united in their opposition to coin use. Not a single high official saw any advantage to defending copper currency, suggesting that elites had little personal investment in the importation or use of cash. Second, the *Gyokuyō* passage shows that the nobles were confident that their legislative proclamations could solve the problem. If they issued the appropriate commands, and the Imperial Police Agency did its job, then all would be made proper (or so they thought). The nobles never questioned whether or not the agency could actually enforce their commands or whether there were economic factors that would have made banning coins difficult or perhaps even impossible.

Third and most important, the entry confirms that the officials' primary concern was for maintaining their political authority. Although the Palace Minister suggested a policy that differed from the majority, his proposal to require stricter enforcement of previous coin regulations still reflected concern for authority rather than the marketplace. The Minister of the Left disagreed only in approach, maintaining that new edicts containing price laws were necessary even if they replicated earlier pronouncements because the merchants' disregard for the law must be stopped. Both the Palace Minister and the Minister of the Left aimed to ensure that the will of the court be followed.

Of course, inflation might also explain the elite opposition to coins. Inflation likely occurred as the large influx of imported coins increased the money supply, thereby reducing the value of coins and causing higher prices. Economist Kozo Yamamura favors this interpretation, emphasizing the importance of inflation and dismissing the nobles' concern over the foreign nature of the coins.[40] Although it is logical to conclude that there was inflation at this time, I find it difficult to accept that inflation was the sole motivation behind the nobility's opposition to coins. First of all, it seems unlikely that the nobles would have been cognizant of a rise in prices. In the strictly hierarchical society of late Heian Japan, such men and women of elite status would have had little direct knowledge of prices or market transactions, and warriors had not yet gained the independence to safely interfere with proprietors' income. Second, we must consider the other points that are deemed problematic by Motohiro and Kanezane, such as that previous letters of instruction issued by the court were not heeded, and that the coins are symbols of a foreign state power. These reflect concern over political authority, not rising prices, and suggest that the primary motivation for the ban on Chinese coins lay in protecting the imperial right to mint coinage and set its value.

The nobles' views, seen in these *Gyokuyō* entries, eventually led to action. According to an 1193 entry in the legal compendium *Hossō shiyōshō*, a price law making coins illegal was promulgated in the eighth month of the previous year. Yet the use of coins continued unabated, for the same entry notes that "Of its own accord, the exchange of coins has not stopped. How can this be since a price law has been fixed in the marketplace?"[41] The ban was reissued in 1193, but repeated court efforts at regulating the use of copper cash failed. Coins began to replace cloth and silk as the major unit of exchange by the early thirteenth century and went on to supplant rice by the early fourteenth century.

There were numerous incentives for those who were not Kyoto high elites to use imported coins. Cash presented obvious advantages over silk, cloth, and even rice. Unlike those alternative currencies, coins did not spoil and could be transported without concern for the weather. Coins also had the advantage of being of relatively uniform quality; even when the government attempted to declare some coins to be worth more than others, people appear to have used coins as if they were of identical value. Surely these were important factors that led individuals to import and use coins. Yet these advantages are always present when comparing metal currency to agricultural goods for use as money. Why did coins become so popular in the late twelfth century?

To begin with, the twelfth century was unique for the Japanese in that there was a ready supply of Chinese cash available due to the massive scale of Northern Song minting. Although the Song officially prohibited the export of copper currency, it was not difficult to find merchants quite willing to sell cash, and enough bureaucrats failed to prevent its sale that Chinese copper money came to be widely used outside Song borders—not only in Japan, but in Southeast Asia as well.[42] The vast majority of medieval coins found in Japan are Northern Song issues.[43] Even considering that only a fraction of the total Song coin production made it to Japan, the supply of coins was far superior to what the Japanese court had been able to produce in earlier centuries. Thus the timing of China's boom in money production was a key factor in the widespread adoption of coins in Japan.

In addition, merchants were likely able to enjoy large profits from the importation of copper coins. Yamamura and Kamiki have analyzed the relative values of gold, silver, and copper in China and Japan during Japan's medieval period. Although incomplete data sets make precise conclusions difficult, they contend that the value of gold to copper was significantly higher in China than in Japan. As they explain, "During the twelfth and thirteenth centuries, the differential was large: one *ryō* of gold in China could be exchanged for nearly five to six times the amount of copper coins that could be obtained in Japan."[44] This meant that someone from the Japanese islands could obtain more copper coins in China than at home for the same amount of gold. The potential for profit from importing coins must have been enormous.

Unfortunately, we do not know who brought Chinese cash to Japan or whether they did in fact realize a profit from their actions. No merchant or shipping records survive from the late Heian or Kamakura periods. It is also not clear how many coins were brought to Japan in the twelfth century. But the few indirect documentary references to coins that survive reveal a good deal of information. First, there must have been enough coins circulating in the economy to support both large-scale transactions (such as a land purchase for twenty-seven strings of cash) and smaller transactions (such as the temple fund-raising in Tosa province). Second, the level of coin importation must have been significant since it attracted the attention of the nobility. Third and finally, the nobility's opposition to the use of coins, as well as the fact that the importers are not mentioned in elite diaries or government records, suggest that those who were trading in cash did not have central elite connections.

Money in the Kamakura Era Economy

Although we can only speculate about the twelfth century, there is more information available for the thirteenth and later centuries. Documentary evidence suggests that increasingly large amounts of cash were brought to Japan from the middle of the Kamakura period. To cite just two examples, an entry in the diary *Minkeiki* reveals that the courtier Saionji Kintsune sponsored a ship that brought one hundred thousand strings of cash to Japan in the 1240s, while Hōjō Tokimune (who later became shogunal regent) is reported to have sent an envoy to China to purchase copper coins with gold in the 1260s.[45] By this time, the widespread use of coins in medieval society had led elite families such as the Hōjō and Saionji to take an interest in imported cash.

Archaeological evidence confirms that coins were quite popular in the early medieval period. Caches of coins that were buried in the thirteenth or early fourteenth centuries have been uncovered all over Japan. According to Suzuki Kimio, caches containing at least one thousand coins have been unearthed in twenty-five different locations, ranging from Aomori and Iwate prefectures in the north to Kagawa and Fukuoka prefectures in the south.[46] The volume of importation, however, may be best suggested by the trove of coins found in the remains of a sunken merchant ship found off the coast of Korea. The ship, believed to have been heading to Hakata from the Chinese port of Ningbo sometime around the year 1323, contained over eighteen tons of copper currency in its hold, including coins of the Tang, Northern Song, Southern Song, Jin, Yuan, and other dynasties.[47] Ships such as this one evidently brought Chinese cash to Japan in massive quantities.

As the Kamakura period progressed, the imported cash came to be used in a wide range of transactions. Most notable was the use of coins in large transactions such as land sales and tax payments. Land sale deeds, known as *baiken*, were prepared whenever property was sold, and buyers carefully maintained their deeds because the documents were needed to prove rightful ownership in case of a later dispute. Analysis of *baiken* by Tamaizumi Tairyō has shown that whereas coins were used in just under 40 percent of land sales during the first quarter of the Kamakura period, they came to be used in over 80 percent of transactions during the last third of the period.[48] Coins also were increasingly used to pay rents and taxes. Provincial estate managers were pushing to pay taxes in cash as early as the 1220s, and disputes persisted between central elites and those based in the countryside over whether or not coins could be used (and if so, at what rate) over the remainder of the Kamakura period.[49]

Copper currency appeared in smaller transactions as well, such as the temple fund-raising document of 1151 mentioned above, that lists people making donations in thirty- and fifty-coin sums. Kamakura period documents show that cash levies in small denominations could be imposed on individuals. For example, the family rules left behind in the testament of one Shibuya Jōshin hold that one hundred- and two hundred-coin sums should be collected whenever a great hunt is held.[50] Peasants sometimes found these taxes onerous. One of the most famous cases is recorded in the 1275 petition of the cultivators of Ategawa estate.[51] Along with complaints about horrific physical abuse suffered at the hands of their local *jitō*, the peasants protested over being forced to pay an extraordinary land tax. Yet the Ategawa peasants complained not because they were being taxed in cash but rather because the local warrior was forcing them to pay a tax that they had already paid to the proprietor. Clearly access to copper coins was not a problem for these rural estate residents.

Unfortunately, there are few surviving records that speak to the use of money for the purchase of daily necessities. The paucity of historical records presumably reflects that there was no need to preserve such documents rather than a lack of coin use. Kamakura period warriors frequently tried to force peasants to provide them with cash to cover various living expenses when they were summoned for guard duty in the capital, and bakufu price decrees reflect that cash was used to purchase daily goods in the thirteenth century. More complete information can be found in later documentary records such as the early fifteenth-century papers of the temple Shōmyōji, which reveal the local prices of daily goods such as chestnuts, beans, radishes, salt, oil, and more, all of which were small purchases paid for with coins.[52]

Money and the Bakufu-Retainer Relationship

The increased use of money did not merely facilitate exchange; it appears to have also placed a great deal of stress on Kamakura warrior society. The origins of the Kamakura bakufu lay in Yoritomo's guarantee of land rights to provincial warriors. By offering to secure their positions irrespective of the imperial government, Yoritomo found something to unite warrior families under his leadership.[53] In exchange for confirming those rights, samurai retainers were expected to provide service to the bakufu. They were tested repeatedly, and those who failed to fight—during the Genpei war, the Ōshū campaign of 1189, or on other occasions—were deprived of their positions. Of course, warriors were expected to use their landed income to equip themselves and cover the costs of participating in battle, serving on guard duty, or performing other functions.

Although the bakufu was a "warrior government," one of its primary functions was judicial arbitration; in disputes between warriors and civilian proprietors, the bakufu often forced warriors to follow precedents and thereby limited its retainers' ability to grow their incomes.[54] Warriors appointed to estates following the 1221 Jōkyū insurrection were further hampered by the bakufu's decree that such warriors could not use precedent but instead must limit themselves to one-eleventh of an estate's rice production. Consequently, with only limited land-derived income, many warriors turned to moneylenders when they sought additional cash, using their land holdings as collateral. Those who failed to repay their debts had their lands confiscated and given to nonwarriors who were not affiliated

with the bakufu and had no obligation to render service to it.
Thus, the use of money held dire consequences for the bakufu
and its relationship to its retainers.

The seriousness of the issue is reflected in Kamakura
bakufu efforts to stop money lending and the loss of retainers'
lands. Bans on gambling and money lending can be found in
the bakufu's official chronicle, the *Azuma kagami*, as early
as 1226. A proclamation from that year calls for the names of
retainers who violate the ban to be forwarded to Kamakura for
punishment.[55] The fact that such bans were frequently reissued,
however, suggests that they had little effect. As warriors fell
into debt, they took drastic measures to improve their financial
situations. In some cases, retainers appointed their creditors
as deputy *jitō* in order to allow them to collect directly from
provincial holdings. The bakufu condemned the practice, noting
in a 1239 proclamation that moneylenders "think only of profits,
without considering the financial consequences for the future";
and in 1255 it went as far as to compare moneylenders to
thieves.[56] Robbers or not, some combination of greed and need
led warriors to continue turning to those with cash, often at the
risk of losing their hereditary holdings. The loss of warrior lands
to nonretainers led the bakufu to interfere in inheritance law,
limiting the ability of individuals to pass on property. It also led
the bakufu to issue "virtuous government edicts" (*tokuseirei*),
essentially debt abrogation decrees that arbitrarily erased the
outstanding loans of retainers without compensation to lenders.

Yet at the same time that the bakufu attempted to rescue
warriors from moneylenders, it added to warriors' financial
difficulties by placing its own monetary demands upon them.
For example, in the eleventh month of 1240 Kamakura extracted
money from retainers on matters related to the performance of
guard duty in the city of Kyoto. Expenses for the construction
of watchhouses in Kyoto were levied on *jitō* appointed after the
Jōkyū war (the *shinpo jitō*) at the rate of fifty *kanmon* per fifty
chō of land that they held. In addition, *gokenin* who reported one
month late for guard duty faced a fine of ten *kanmon*.[57] And only
a few weeks later, in the twelfth month, an entry in the *Azuma*

kagami cites a special tax on retainers to pay for the shogun's prayer services (*onritsugan*). The entry notes that an enormous sum of money (*bakudai yōto*) is required, and that the levy is a source of anxiety for the *gokenin*. As a result of that concern, the amount insisted upon was reduced, but this did not alter the fact that the bakufu was imposing a new financial requirement on retainers that had to be paid in cash. Later in the same entry, there is reference to "thank you money" (*kōsen*), cash that *gokenin* paid to bakufu officials in order to secure appointments.[58]

Local documents, such as those cited at the start of this chapter, reflect warriors' desperation to raise funds to meet their obligations. For example, the *jitō* of Sasakibe estate imposed a monetary tax to fund his upcoming trip to the capital, which was severe enough to lead the estate's manager to file a lawsuit in 1238.[59] Disputes such as this one were all too frequent during the thirteenth century, for while some *gokenin* successfully took advantage of their posts to increase their incomes, others found their financial positions either unsatisfactory or untenable. And for warriors who lost their rights to income, conditions became even more severe. This was precisely the situation that the warrior Takezaki Suenaga found himself in at the time of the Mongol invasions. He had lost his family holding in an earlier dispute, and by 1274, when the Mongols invaded, Takezaki was desperate to secure a reward and/or income for his service. As he describes in his narrative picture scroll, he had to borrow cash (*yōto*) to cover his travel expenses as he journeyed to Kamakura to petition the government.[60] For warriors such as Takezaki, functioning with limited land-derived income in an expanding monetary economy proved to be a significant challenge.

Conclusions

By the mid-thirteenth century, Chinese cash had attained a secure position in the Japanese economy. It had displaced silk and cloth as a primary means of payment and exchange, and over the course of the next hundred years, transactions formerly carried out in rice would come to be conducted more and more frequently in coin. Examination of the processes by which coins achieved this status, and the impact of early monetization, illuminates different aspects of late Heian and Kamakura society than those highlighted in the study of struggles for control of land.

First of all, the twelfth-century importation of Chinese coins represented a major shift in the Japan-China trade. Earlier traders catered to the needs of central elites. They exchanged Japanese gold, raw materials including sulphur, or in some cases finished goods such as lacquerware, for imported porcelain, incense, medicines, and other luxury goods. Central elites were not only the primary beneficiaries of that trade, they also maintained a relatively secure monopoly on exchange with the continent, effectively directing most continental merchants to the government-controlled port of Dazaifu. Some of that trade continued into the medieval period, but the government's ability to regulate and monopolize such trade greatly diminished. Instead, from the twelfth century onward, Dazaifu's importance in foreign trade began to wane.[61] At the same time, the most important object of trade gradually shifted to imported coins that were used by a much larger segment of society than just Kyoto-based elites. By the Muromachi period, Japanese boats were interested first and foremost in bringing coins back to Japan.

Second, coins played a key role in the creation of the new medieval economy by facilitating exchange. For merchants and traders, coins could be obtained cheaply in China and imported for significant profit. For those selling goods or agricultural products in local and regional markets, the relatively uniform quality and long-term stability of coins made them more desirable than rice or silk. By the early fourteenth century, institutions of credit began to develop around coin use.[62] Provincial managers could sell their produce to traveling merchants in exchange for paper certificates (*kawase* bills of exchange), which could then be forwarded to central proprietors who redeemed them for cash. In this way, regional markets and trade networks became important institutions that helped redefine the relationship between center and periphery in early medieval Japan.

Third, and perhaps most significantly, there was a transformation in the relationship between the government and money. Nara and early Heian coins were produced by elites and sponsored by the government. Their value was determined (with limited success) by officials of the highest rank. Late Heian and early Kamakura coins, however, were quite independent of the government and of high elites. They were produced overseas and defied efforts by high officials to fix their value. Members of the nobility, who primarily saw coins as an extension of their political authority, found themselves increasingly unable to influence the expanding medieval economy. Within decades, demand for cash among samurai affiliated with the Kamakura bakufu led to the loss of retainers' lands and interfered with bakufu-retainer relations. Interestingly, these developments seem to have parallels with economic growth in medieval Europe, where rulers found themselves unable to control markets and knights found themselves falling into debt in the emerging monetary economy.[63]

These conclusions challenge the view that was dominant in much of the modern scholarship through the 1980s—a view that portrayed the pre-1600 Japanese economy as exclusively rice-based, with provincial estates supplying rice (or, in some cases, other agricultural goods) to central elites. That literature also depicted warriors as primarily concerned with appropriating land from civilians. Only within the last fifteen years or so have scholars both inside and outside Japan begun to rethink that view. In its place, recent research (including that found in this essay) calls attention both to estate managers who sold agricultural produce in local or regional markets and sent cash to their proprietors as well as samurai who were as concerned about cash as they were about land. The changes that the evolving medieval economy brought about proved a difficult challenge for both court and bakufu in twelfth- and thirteenth-century Japan. Unresolved, these problems contributed to the popular resentment against the Kamakura bakufu that led to its destruction in the 1330s.

NOTES

This chapter draws upon material from my forthcoming book, with a working title of "Coins, Trade, and the State: Economic Growth in Early Medieval Japan." The research would not have been possible without the support of the IIE Fulbright, a Geballe Fellowship at the Stanford Humanities Center, and the MSU History Department Sesquicentennial Fund. I also gratefully acknowledge my colleagues at Michigan State University and other institutions, the two anonymous reviewers for the press, and the editors, especially Andrew Goble, for their valuable suggestions and criticisms.

1   For the first document see undated Bō shojō (*KI*, 10:7180); for the second see undated Bō shojō (*KI*, 10:7289). These documents, concatenated with other undated material in *Kamakura ibun*, are found also in *Chiba ken no rekishi: shiryōhen chūsei 2*, document 14, Bō shojō, on pp. 1028–1029; and document 19, Saishin (?) shojō, on pp. 1090–1091.

2   For example, Sir George Sansom, in a section entitled "The Taira Ascendancy," describes the last half of the twelfth century as a transfer of power from the court and nobility to the emerging warrior class, and Mikiso Hane subtitles his chapter on the Kamakura period "The Triumph of the Warriors." Sansom, *A History of Japan to 1334*, p. 255; Mikiso Hane, *Premodern Japan: A Historical Survey*.

3   An early treatment in English is Delmer Brown, "The Japanese *Tokusei* of 1297."

4   The terms listed in the text that refer to coins are *kinsen*, *dōsen*, and *sōchō no zeni*. The court nobles described the sudden rise in coin use as *zeni no yamai* ("the money disease" or "cash fever"). *Hyakurenshō* Jijō 3 (1179).6.

5   Among several recent works important to any broader understanding of the medieval Japanese economy are Kozo Yamamura, "The Growth of Commerce in Medieval Japan"; Hitomi Tonomura, *Community and Commerce in Late Medieval Japan: The Corporate Villages of Tokuchin-ho*; Suzanne Gay, *The Moneylenders of Late Medieval Kyoto*; Bruce Batten, *To the Ends of Japan: Premodern Frontiers, Boundaries, and Interactions*; and William Wayne Farris, *Japan's Medieval Population: Famine, Fertility, and Warfare in a Transformative Age*. For an English language study that is primarily focused on money, however, one must turn to Delmer Brown, *Money Economy in Medieval Japan*, though this work favors the fifteenth and sixteenth centuries over earlier periods. Recently there has been renewed interested in medieval economic history among Japanese scholars as well; important works include Sakurai Eiji, *Nihon chūsei no keizai kōzō*, and Usami Takayuki, *Nihon chūsei no ryūtsū to shōgyō*.

6   Takizawa Matsuyo attempts to correct a misperception that money entered Japan only in the nineteenth century by dating its appearance to the early Edo period, which is also incorrect. See Takizawa, *The Penetration of Money Economy in Japan and Its Effects upon Social and Political Institutions*. Subsequent scholarship, though not focused primarily on money, perpetuates the notion of Edo being the period of monetization. See Thomas Smith, "The Growth of the Market," in *The Agrarian Origins of Modern Japan*; Yokota Fuyuhiko, "Imagining Working Women in Early Modern Japan," p. 167; and Sone Hiromi, "Prostitution and Public Authority in Early Modern Japan," p. 183. These articles are correct in highlighting a major shift in the level and degree of monetization during the early modern period, but it is important to make clear that money began appearing and having an impact in rural communities centuries earlier.

7   For example, in the volume *Medieval Japan: Essays in Institutional History*, ed. John W. Hall and Jeffrey P. Mass, the articles by Sato, Kiley, Mass, Hori, and Wintersteen each address issues of rights to income from land in Heian, Kamakura, and Muromachi Japan, but there is no article devoted primarily to the monetary economy.

8   Officials of the early bakufu presented gold to the imperial court and paid workers with precious metals. See *Azuma kagami* Kenkyū 5 (1194).3.22 and 5.10, *Azuma kagami* Kenkyū 6 (1195).3.13. For a father leaving money rather than land to his children, see Fujiwara

Tametoki's bequest in1265: Bun'ei 2 (1265) Iren [Fujiwara Tametoki] yuzurijō (*KI*, 13:9354).

9   For an example of a legal decision handed down concerning money and the rate for converting tax payments from goods to cash, see Karoku 3 (1227).8.16 Kantō gechijō an (*KI*, 6:3649). For a translation into English of a legal settlement concerning arrears on cash payments, see Jeffrey P. Mass, *The Kamakura Bakufu: A Study in Documents*, doc. 125, pp. 147–148. English translations of documents concerning the household tax can also be found in the same volume; see docs. 176–177, pp. 185–186.

10   On these reforms, see Bruce Batten, "Foreign Threat and Domestic Reform: The Emergence of the *Ritsuryō* State," and Joan Piggott, *The Emergence of Japanese Kingship*.

11   Alongside cash and cloth, other items such as grain and salt functioned as forms of money in certain instances. Peng Xinwei, *A Monetary History of China*, pp. 246–247.

12   The *Nihon shoki* lists mint officials being appointed on Jitō 8 (694).3.2 and Monmu 3 (699).12.20. As the appointment of these minters preceded the production of the *Wadō kaichin* coin by over ten years, scholars disagree on the function and significance of these appointments.

13   Tōno Haruyuki, *Kahei no Nihonshi*, pp. 5–15. Might the mint officials appointed in the 690s have supervised production of *fuhonsen*? See also Sakaehara Towao, "Kahei no hassei."

14   The first of the imperial twelve coins, the *Wadō kaichin* of 708, was initially issued in both silver and copper, but by 710 the government prohibited the use of silver coins. *Shoku Nihongi* Wadō 2 (708).5.11, *Shoku Nihongi* Wadō 2 (708).8.10, *Shoku Nihongi* Wadō 3 (709).3.27, *Shoku Nihongi* Wadō 4 (710).9.18. In 760, the court produced small quantities of gold *Kaiki shōhō* and silver *Taihei genpō* coins, but there is no evidence that they circulated widely or were used in ordinary transactions.

15   Both types are approximately the same size (between 2.4 and 2.5 mm in diameter) and they share a four-character inscription on the obverse face as well as a similar calligraphic style.

16   *Shoku Nihongi* Wadō 4 (711).10.23 and *Shoku Nihongi* Wadō 5 (712).10.29.

17   On purchasing rank, see *Shoku Nihongi* Wadō 4 (711).10.23.
For the end of this practice, see *Ruijū sandai kyaku* Enryaku 19
(800).2.4 and *Ruijū sandai kyaku* Jōgan 9 (867).5.10.

18   Penalties for counterfeiting are listed in *Shoku Nihongi* Wadō
2 (709).3.27. The counterfeiters of 765 are discussed in Tōno, *Kahei
no Nihonshi*, p. 70. For more on problems of counterfeit currency
during the Nara period, see William Wayne Farris, "Trade, Money, and
Merchants in Nara Japan," p. 316.

19   A strong argument that the imperial twelve did not circulate
outside of the Kinai region can be found in Kobata Atsushi, *Nihon kahei
ryūtsūshi*. Farris also holds that the coins primarily found purchase in
the provinces around the capital (Farris, "Trade, Money, and Merchants
in Nara Japan," p. 315).

20   For a detailed breakdown of where coins of the imperial
twelve lines have been unearthed, see the appendix to Sakaehara
Towao, *Nihon kodai senka ryūtsūshi no kenkyū*.

21   Farris, "Trade, Money, and Merchants," pp. 314–318.

22   Kobata Atsushi, *Nihon no kahei*, p. 20.

23   Nara kokuritsu bunkazai kenkyūjo, *Heijōkyū hakkutsu chōsa
hōkoku* VI, pp. 97-103.

24   *Nihon kiryaku* Engi 7 (907).11.3.

25   Price laws are discussed in detail in Hotate Michihisa, "Chūsei
zenki no shinsei to kokahō: toshi ōken no hō, ichiba, kahei, zaisei";
Nakajima Keiichi, "Nihon no chūsei senka to kokka"; and Ihara Kesao,
"Sōsen yu'nyū no rekishiteki ishiki." Orders to the *kebiishichō* and to
temples can be found in the *Nihon kiryaku* Eikan 2 (984).11.27, *Nihon
kiryaku* Eien 1 (987).11.2 and 11.27.

26   Ihara, "Sōsen yu'nyū no rekishiteki ishiki," p. 67. For a
description of early official markets and the functions of market police,
see Farris, "Trade, Money, and Merchants," pp. 304–308.

27   One *kanmon* and one *koku* were both standard unit terms for
large amounts. The *kanmon* was approximately one thousand coins,
though as was the case in China, strings of 980 or 970 coins frequently
circulated as if they contained one thousand. One *koku* was a common
measure of volume for grains such as rice. In the Meiji period, one *koku*
was fixed at roughly 180 liters, but there was tremendous variation in

the size of medieval *koku*. Even among estates all held by the same proprietor (Tōji), one *koku* seems to have ranged from as little as 63 percent to as much as 118 percent of the Meiji *koku*, depending on the region. See Nagahara Keiji et al., *Chūseishi handobukku*, p. 465.

28   Hotate, "Chūsei zenki no shinsei to kokahō," p. 2.

29   Avner Greif defines institutions as "the non-technological constraints on human interactions," while Douglass North explains institutions as "the rules of the game in a society... the humanly devised constraints that ... define and limit the set of choices of individuals." Greif, as cited in Masahiko Aoki, *Toward a Comparative Institutional Analysis*, p. 8; North, *Institutions, Institutional Change, and Economic Performance*, pp. 3–4.

30   Kyūan 6 (1150).8.25 Tachibana Yukinaga kachi baiken (*HI*, 6:2707).

31   Mori Katsumi, "Sōdōsen no wagakuni ryūnyū no tansho," in *Zoku zoku Nissō bōeki no kenkyū*.

32   Ninpei 1 (1151).8.4 Tosa no kuni Hōrakuji zōzō Chishiki zeni chūmon (*HI*, 6:2736).

33   This is mentioned in the Chinese compendium *Jianyan yilai xi nian yao lu*, as cited in the 1155 entry of the *Taigai kankeishi sōgō nenpyō*, p. 144.

34   Mark Elvin famously referred to urbanization, improvements in farming and water transport, and the increased availability of money and credit as having created a medieval economic revolution. Elvin, *The Pattern of the Chinese Past*, pp. 113–178.

35   Jacques Gernet, *A History of Chinese Civilization*, pp. 324–325. Gernet estimates that total coin production in Northern Song equaled approximately two hundred million strings of cash (i.e., two hundred billion coins!). For additional details on northern Song coin production, see the tables in Peng Xinwei, *A Monetary History of China*, pp. 387–388.

36   For specific examples of Chinese traders seeking gold in Japan, see Ethan Segal, "Economic Growth and Changes in Elite Power Structures in Medieval Japan, 1150–1500," esp. pp. 41–44. Heian trade with Chinese merchants is also discussed in Charlotte von Verschuer, *Across the Perilous Sea: Japanese Trade with China and Korea from the Seventh to the Sixteenth Centuries;* and Batten's two works, *To*

the Ends of Japan and *Gateway to Japan: Hakata in War and Peace, 500–1300.*

37 *Gyokuyō* Jishō 3 (1179).7.27.

38 Richard von Glahn, *Fountain of Fortune: Money and Monetary Policy in China, 1000–1700*, p. 1. See also pp. 24–26.

39 *Gyokuyō* Kenkyū 3 (1192).10.1.

40 According to Yamamura, the late twelfth-century court justified banning coins by citing "such inconsistent facts as that imported coins were no more legal than the prohibited, privately minted coins and that the use of coins caused undesirable price fluctuations." Yamamura, "The Growth of Commerce," p. 359.

41 *Hossō shiyōshō* Kenkyū 4 (1193).7.4.

42 Kenneth Hall notes that some areas of the Southeast Asian mainland and of Java used Chinese currency by the thirteenth century. Hall, "Coinage, Trade and Economy in South India and Its Bay of Bengal Neighbors," pp. 448, 457. See also Robert Hartwell, "The Evolution of the Early Sung Monetary System, A.D. 960–1025."

43 Yamamura and Kamiki assembled a table combining the analyses of unearthed coins performed by Irita Seizo and Kobata Atushi, concluding that of the Chinese copper coins found in Japan, eighty-five percent were minted by the Northern Song. Kozo Yamamura and Tetsuo Kamiki, "Silver Mines and Sung Coins—A Monetary History of Medieval and Modern Japan in International Perspective," p. 338.

44 Yamamura and Kamiki, "Silver Mines and Sung Coins," p. 343.

45 *Minkeiki* Ninji 3 (1242).7.4, cited in Ōyama Kyōhei, *Kamakura Bakufu*, pp. 379–380. The reference to Tokimune appears in Delmer Brown, *Money Economy in Medieval Japan*, p. 11.

46 Suzuki Kimio, *Shutsudo senka no kenkyū*, pp. 18–26.

47 Tokyo National Museum et al., *The Sunken Treasures Off the Sinan Coast*, p. 82.

48 Tamaizumi found that only 39.7 percent of land transactions were carried out in coin between 1186 and 1219, but that 84.2 percent were conducted in coin between 1284 and 1333. Tamaizumi Tairyō, *Muromachi jidai no denso*.

49   See, for example, the dispute between Sōma mikuriya of Shimōsa province and its proprietor temple, Toyouke Daijingū, over the payment of dues in cash. See Karoku 3 (1227).8.16 Kantō gechijō an (*KI*, 6:3649), and Antei 2 (1228).8.23 Kantō mikyōsho (*KI*, 6:3777).

50   Kangen 3 (1245).5.21 Shibuya Jōshin okibumi (*KI*, 9:6485).

51   Kenji 1 (1275).10.28 Kii no kuni Ategawa no shō Kamimura hyakushō ra gonjō jō (*KI*, 16:12076).

52   For example, in 1269 the warrior Tadakiyo demanded that the peasants of Tara estate supply him with cash for the purchase of charcoal, rice bran, vegetables, fodder for his horses, and other items during his upcoming term of guard duty in the capital. See Bun'ei 6 (1269).4 Kyoto ōban'yaku zōji chūmon an (*KI*, 14:10432), and Bun'ei 6 (1269).5.28 Wakasa Tara no shō zasshō mōshibumi an (*KI*, 14:10443). Bakufu price laws set in cash include that promulgated on Kenchō 5 (1253).10.11: *CHSS*, 1, *tsuikahō* nos. 296 and 297 (also see *KI*, 10:7623). The prices of daily goods purchased by Shōmyōji can be found throughout the *Kanazawa bunko monjo*, such as document 5989, dated Ōei 26 (1419).11.15.

53   Jeffrey P. Mass, "The Kamakura Bakufu," p. 53.

54   Jeffrey P. Mass's pioneering work on bakufu institutions remains the best available. See, for example, *The Development of Kamakura Rule, 1180–1250*, and *Yoritomo and the Founding of the First Bakufu: The Origins of Dual Government in Japan*.

55   *Azuma kagami* Karoku 2 (1226).1.26.

56   *CHSS*, 1, *tsuikahō* no. 120, dated En'ō 1 (1239).9.17 (*KI*, 8:5475), and *CHSS*, 1, *tsuikahō* no. 305, dated Kenchō 7 (1255).8.12 (*KI*, 11:7892).

57   Respectively, *CHSS*, 1, *tsuikahō* no. 152, dated Ninji 1 (1240).11.23 (*KI*, 8:5674); *CHSS*, 1, *tsuikahō* no. 153, dated Ninji 1 (1240).11.28 (*KI*, 8:5679). Both of these regulations are also noted in the *Azuma kagami*.

58   *Azuma kagami* Ninji 1 (1240).12.16.

59   Katei 4 (1238).10.19 Rokuhara gechijō (*KI*, 7:5315).

60   For the Mongol invasions and Takezaki Suenaga's tale in English, see Thomas Conlan, *In Little Need of Divine Intervention:*

Takezaki Suenaga's Scrolls of the Mongol Invasions of Japan. The original Japanese scroll refers to cash as both *zeni* and *yōto.*

61   On Dazaifu, see Batten, *Gateway to Japan,* as well as his essay in this volume.

62   For the early development of bills of exchange (*kawase*), see Segal, "Economic Growth and Changes," esp. pp. 162–177.

63   Joel Kaye describes thirteenth-century markets for precious metals that "survived every governmental attempt at control and essentially came to dictate the price of gold and silver to the royal mints." Kaye, *Economy and Nature in the Fourteenth Century,* pp. 21–25. Georges Duby, in *The Chivalrous Society,* writes of the plight of nobles in late medieval Europe.

The Matsura Pirate-Warriors of Northwestern Kyushu in the Kamakura Age
Hyungsub Moon

Introduction. The Matsura-tō (Matsura League)

The Matsura-tō, a group of coastal warriors who controlled northwestern Kyushu from the twelfth through the fifteenth centuries,[1] would seem to be marginal figures. They resided in a remote area of northwestern Hizen consisting of the Higashi Matsura and Nishi Matsura peninsulas, as well as several islands including the Gotō chain and Hirado.

This Matsura[2] region consisted primarily of secluded islands of various sizes and sprawling peninsulas with deeply indented coasts. It included bays, inlets, coves, straits, and smaller regions of sea, broadly encompassed by the East China Sea. The islands and peninsulas were mountainous and not easily traversed. The soil was not of high quality, the fields were small, and their yields were inadequate to support a large population.

While the land may have been restrictive, the sea was not. The population clustered about ports, harbors, havens, anchorages, and landings. Egress, ingress, transit through, and communication within and without, all depended upon boats. Lives were oriented toward the sea and to a seasonal cycle quite different from those involved in agricultural production. In short, residents of the Matsura region relied greatly upon the sea for their existence; indeed, property rights and deeds of ownership explicitly record tenure of the sea. For example, the "four boundaries" of the *jitō shiki* for the Urabeshima portion of Ojika island were described as "in the north the Toraku Strait; in the east Hitao; in the west in the sea the "Korea Door" (*umi no Kōrai no to*), in the south Cape Sao."[3] Understanding that Matsura "property" stretched into the sea, possibly up to fifty miles or more,[4] is crucial because those areas of sea which were regarded as integral to the Matsura domain happened to lie astride and adjacent to the most important international sea routes of northeast Asia. In this sense, the Matsura maritime sphere was anything but peripheral, despite its distance from Kyoto or Kamakura.

The Matsura-tō developed into two groups during the fourteenth century. The "upper Matsura-tō" was located in the Higashi Matsura peninsula while the "lower Matsura-tō" spread over the Nishi Matsura peninsula and the nearby islands. Their activities—fishing, piracy, family disputes, property conflicts, and participation in military activity—have produced a significant documentary legacy. Over one thousand documents (ranging from 1088 through the mid-seventeenth century) relating to Matsura-tō families have survived,[5] of which at least eight hundred cover the period up through the end of the fourteenth century.[6]

The documents include family genealogies, charts of property ownership, inventories of lands, bills of sale, testaments and wills, and litigation. They reveal in impressive detail the dynamics of families and family groups, patterns of inheritance and consociation, and naming practices. We also see the Matsura families as both bakufu housemen (*gokenin*) and estate managers (*jitō*). Some bakufu documents (for example, judicial settlement edicts and edicts related to the Mongol invasions) demonstrate that the bakufu had considerable influence on the Matsura-tō's local development. However, reflecting the common symbiotic pattern of "central-local relationships," Matsura-tō families employed the bakufu's authority to their own local advantage. While our focus here will be on the Kamakura era, it is worth noting that during the fourteenth century Matsura-tō families were active as both land and naval forces in the struggle between the Muromachi bakufu and Go-Daigo's Southern Court (which had a particularly strong presence in Kyushu). Such activity prepared Matsura-tō families for drawing up a series of *ikki* (alliance)[7] contracts (nine from 1373 to 1436) designed to ensure group solidarity. These *ikki*-related documents are of great value in creating typologies in the study of warrior *ikki* organizations of the early Muromachi period.

The activities of the Matsura warriors are also recounted in a number of narrative and chronicle sources that shed light in a way that documents do not on the broader activities of the Matsura-tō over an extended period of time and an extensive geographic area. The Matsura appear in Japanese sources covering major political developments in the twelfth century (*Heiji monogatari*, *Genpei jōsuiki*, *Heike monogatari*), the thirteenth-century Mongol invasions (*Hachiman gudōkin*),[8] and the fourteenth-century civil war (*Taiheiki* and *Baishōron*). Overseas pirate activity which we know involved the Matsura-tō is attested in the Kamakura bakufu chronicle *Azuma kagami*, *Hyakurenshō*, and courtier diaries such as *Meigetsuki* and *Minkeiki*. Moreover, the Matsura-tō appears in Korean souces as well. Works from the Koryŏ and Chosŏn periods such as the *Koryŏsa*, *Koryŏsa choryo*, *Tongguk t'onggam*, *Haedong chegukki*, and records of some of the royal eras contained in the *Chosŏn wangjo sillok*, provide valuable information unavailable in Japanese sources.[9] It is certainly remarkable that a group not belonging to court or warrior elites had its activities recorded in such detail by both domestic and foreign documentary and narrative sources.

This essay will reveal some elements and rhythms that shaped the Matsura-tō and its families through the early fourteenth century, and will also provide us with new insight into the multiplicity of factors that might enter into central-local relationships. We will also see clearly that "the local Matsura" were anything but "peripheral," and in fact, are most usefully seen as liminally central. We will first explore the Matsura as they appear in some Japanese and Korean sources (narratives, chronicles, and the like), and then analyze them as plunderers and pirates around the coasts of the East China Sea, focusing on them as precursors of *wakō*, or Japanese pirates. Then, after

Narrative sources about the Matsura must be used with care. The two passages from the *Heike monogatari* and the *Azuma kagami* cited above list the numbers of Taira vessels in an exaggerated manner, particularly in the case of the one thousand ships noted in the *Heike monogatari*. Scholars generally believe the *Azuma kagami* account is also exaggerated.[12] Moreover, the *Heike monogatari* and the *Azuma kagami* were not compiled contemporaneously with the events they present. The former is the product of narrative evolution, the latter of editorial compilation and selection of original sources that are largely no longer extant.[13] At times the compilers of the *Azuma kagami*, no doubt wishing for uniform nomenclature and institutional history, provide anachronistic information, even with respect to the institutions of the bakufu itself.[14] Nevertheless, given the lack of contemporary written documents which would be more reliable accounts of the maritime behavior of the Matsura-tō, we have no options except utilizing such narrative sources, albeit warily.

In general, maritime activity by the Matsura-tō is reported in Japanese and Korean narrative materials dating from after the Genpei era. From the early thirteenth century on, the Matsura-tō appears as a notorious band of pirates dominating the Straits of Korea between Kyushu and Pusan. Japanese piracy itself was well-known by the Kamakura era,[15] but according to official Korean histories, Japanese piracy against Korea broke out only in the early 1220s. The *Koryŏsa*, the standard history for the Koryŏ period, records that "Fifth month, 22nd day, 1223 year, Japanese [*wa*] raided [*kō*] Kumju [modern Kimhae]."[16] Seven additional Japanese raids on Korea are listed during the remainder of the thirteenth century.[17] The source materials that pertain to the Japanese raiders are not as complete as we might like, but they do provide a degree of cross-referencing with hitherto underutilized sources, such as the official Korean compilations *Koryŏsa* and the *Chosŏn wangjo sillok*.

In the case of the Japanese raid in 1226, the *Koryŏsa* supports Japanese sources. This chronicle laconically states: "sixth month, Japanese raided Kumju."[18] This brief entry provides little material for conjecture, but the raid came to the attention of Japanese courtiers such as Fujiwara Teika (1162–1241). Two entries from his diary, *Meigetsuki*, in the eleventh month of 1226, provide some information about this encounter.

> Sixteenth day. High Priest [*hōgen*] Onshin reported a rumor that Tsushima had clashed with Koryŏ.
> Seventeenth day. At noon, High Priest [Onshin] visited for a talk.... [According to Onshin] the other day, High Priest Teiki had entered the capital as a diplomatic envoy of the Kantō. During his talk with the Senior High Priest [Teiki] informed him that ... "beyond doubt there had been a battle with Koryŏ." A band of villains in Chinzei [Kyushu] called the Matsura-tō organized several tens of warships, made for some islands off the coast of that country and did battle. The villains destroyed people and houses and looted valuables and property. It is reported that on their way home, almost half of them were killed, but the remainder stole silver articles and other loot. Obviously this is a serious matter to the court! In this affair, soldiers from throughout Koryŏ rose in arms. When ships from our country are heading west for China they land as a matter of course in Koryŏ. When they return from China, they are often blown off course and drift to Koryŏ. If this country were to become a hostile enemy, passage to and from China would be impossible. It is said that just recently one China ship hove into Koryŏ, was set afire, and every last person [on board] was burned to death.[19]

Clearly the consequences of the attack were substantial, and the entry provides us much valuable information about the apparent identity of the Japanese raiders. The Matsura-tō, with "several tens of warships," appears to have been a main offender in the raid. The first *Meigetsuki* entry, based on the type of information that commonly circulated orally in court society, simply touches on the fighting between Tsushima and Koryŏ. While the second entry is also based on orally transmitted information, it draws upon the detailed report by an official bakufu envoy about extensive plundering by the Matsura-tō. Considering the fact that "in this affair, soldiers from throughout the country [Koryŏ] rose in arms," the Matsura-tō's raid proved so substantial, it devolved into open war with Korean soldiers. In fact, the 1226 raid may even have led to diplomatic complications between Japan and Korea. The following year, the Koryŏ government dispatched a mission to Mutō Sukeyori at Dazaifu to complain of the raid, and also transmitted a letter of protest to both the bakufu and the court.[20] This letter, preserved in its entirety in the *Azuma kagami*, offers a fuller account of the raid from the viewpoint of the Korean government. It states as follows:

> Fifth month, fourteenth day [of 1227]... Governor of Cholla province, country of Koryŏ sent a letter to Official of Dazaifu, General Supervisor, country of Japan. The Tsushima islanders of your country have long come here annually, presenting tribute in Japanese products, and cultivating harmonious intercourse with us. For our part, in an effort to offer convenience to them, our court not only had a special residence constructed but also bestowed its grace and trust [upon them]... [However] according to the report from the magistracy of Kimhae [Kumju], while people coming from Tsushima stayed at the residence reserved for them, one night in the sixth month of 1226, they came through an opening in the castle under cover of darkness, and sacked the main buildings. Then, [the situation] worsened, as looting occurred outside the town in [several] coastal villages. Then those inside joined the looters outside in pillaging even innocent commoners [*hyakushō*].[21]

The letter clearly focuses on men from Tsushima who had hitherto been engaged in tribute trade now repaying the customary hospitality of the Koryŏ government by pillaging the main buildings of Kumju. The protest makes no explicit reference to the Matsura-tō.[22] Nevertheless, we may conjecture that those who joined the Tsushima raiders from "outside" were Matsura-tō marauders. Indeed, Benjamin Hazard, an expert on Japanese piracy in medieval Korea, hypothesizes that the Matsura-tō played the leading role in this action, and that it was they who suggested to the men of Tsushima that they join together in the raid. From the earliest times, according to Hazard, Tsushima had been closely associated with Matsura economically and militarily. The Tsushima men were essential as guides, for they alone had firsthand knowledge of the Korean coast and knew intimately the area to be raided.[23]

A later Korean complaint about another thirteenth-century raid reveals the enduring bonds between the Matsura and residents of Tsushima when it came to attacking Korea. According to the *Koryŏsa*, a mission was dispatched in 1263 from the Koryŏ government to protest a Japanese incursion. This complaint pointed out that:

> On the 22nd day of the second month of this year a ship of your honorable country came without reason to the island of Mul within the boundaries of Ungsin-hyon. They carried away 120 *sok* of grain and rice and 43 *p'il* [bolts] of pongee [from] the tax ships anchored off that island. They also entered Yondo and carried away all the food, clothing and articles essential people needed for their daily lives.[24]

Japanese officials, presumably at Dazaifu, appeared responsive to the Korean protest mission. After thorough investigation, they handed over information showing that it was natives of Tsushima who had raided the tax ships off Mul. The *Koryŏsa* notes (of the mission):

> Hong Cho, Kwak Wang-bu and others returned from Japan and reported that the pirates in question were Japanese from the island of Tsushima. [The mission] came back having obtained [in restitution] twenty *sok* of rice, thirty *sok* of barley, and seventy oxhides.[25]

Other sources suggest that collaboration between Tsushima and Matsura persisted in this case as well. A Matsura-tō document suggests that men from the Matsura regions were either directly or indirectly involved in the 1263 raid. This document not only contains a list of the locals presumed responsible for that raid, but also substantiates, in part, the record of the *Koryŏsa*.

> In the ninth month of the previous year, a Korean mission arrived with a letter which contends that twenty-third day, second month last year, one ship of Japan without reason came to Koryo and carried away 123 *sok* of grains and rice and 43 *p'il* [bolts] of pongee. These pirates should be [following characters missing].[26]

In light of these historical sources, one can surmise that Matsura men commonly participated in, and perhaps led, Japanese raids on Korea in the thirteenth century. This has led some scholars to conclude that the Matsura-tō constituted the core members of the *wakō* who plundered Korean and Chinese coastal areas from the fourteenth to the fifteenth centuries.[27]

Piracy and Plunder

The historical impact of *wakō* activity against other countries bounding the East China Sea has long been considered significant. When the *wakō* began to pillage overseas in the middle of the fourteenth century,[28] they did so in large numbers, with great frequency, and over a vast area. They struck Korea, and after dealing repeated blows to that country for more than fifty years, they passed on to China and lands to the south of Japan.[29] There is little reliable material available on the early developments of the *wakō*, and most scholars extrapolate from information found in the writings of Korean envoys who had travelled to Japan in the fifteenth century. Those envoys note that the first major locations where the *wakō* operated were Matsura, Tsushima, and the island of Iki.[30]

Another envoy, evidently well acquainted with western Japan, highlighted the geographical and economic factors that influenced Matsura piracy:

> The Japanese communities in the area from Hakata to Ōuchi territory are crowded. The soil is fertile, and the people are honest. There is no need to fear invasion or piracy from these districts. [In contrast] Tsushima, Iki, and Matsura are more sparsely populated but arable land is limited. Since people there are not self-sufficient, starvation is inevitable at times. Consequently, they are temperamentally inclined to thievery, and very cunning and violent by nature.[31]

This account challenges the standard view which asserts that, while organized *wakō* appeared sporadically in thirteenth-century raids, they emerged as a dynamic and fearsome force only in the fourteenth century. This report, by contrast, held that the nucleus of the *wakō* was comprised of pirate bands from Tsushima (and Iki) and Matsura that had already preyed on Korea during the thirteenth century.[32]

Examining the basic conditions that stimulated the initiation of raids in the early thirteenth century, some scholars have pointed to Japan-Korea commercial relations at the time.[33] Aoyama Kōryō, for instance, saw provocation for the raids emanating from the frustration of northern Kyushu merchants and officials who hoped to expand trade with Koryŏ. According to Aoyama, Japan-Korea relations from the eleventh to the thirteenth century worsened as the Koryŏ government, beset with internal difficulties, sought to curtail the official "tribute trade" with Japan.[34] The restrictions placed by the Koreans on Japanese merchants coming to make "presentations" of "local products" impoverished some of the merchants, leading to their raids and pillaging of Korea.

Contemporary historical evidence indicates, however, that responsible Japanese in Kyushu, far from showing any hostile intentions, were favorably disposed toward Koryŏ, acted to suppress the early raids, and deprived raiders of their booty. For instance, in 1227 *Dazai shōni* Mutō Sukeyori seized ninety of the raiders and decapitated them in the presence of the Korean envoy.[35] Five years later, in 1232, the Mutō were still attempting to suppress piracy. In that year a group of raiders from upper Matsura conducted a night attack in Koryŏ, and carried away much plunder. The local constable (*shugonin*; presumably Mutō Sukeyoshi) secured bakufu approval to investigate the matter and apprehend those involved, but the estate manager (*azukaridokoro*) where the individuals were resident sought to prevent this by arguing that there should be no "overlapping" of the constable's jurisdiction. The matter was decided by the bakufu, supporting the constable's jurisdiction. Kamakura ordered that the designated miscreants be called in, and that disposition of their boats and the valuables be at the discretion of the constable.[36]

Whatever the originating factors may have been, piracy became endemic in coastal waters dominated by the Matsura-tō. Chinese and Korean ships bound for Hakata normally passed close to the Matsura peninsula, as did outbound traffic from Hakata sailing for China, Korea, or Tsushima. The bulk of the goods carried on these ships, as well as goods coming around the northwest corner from the west coast of Kyushu, could easily be picked off by the Matsura-tō before they reached port. No doubt some goods destined for Chinese ports or for Kyoto or Kamakura were lost before being recorded at Hakata, and consequently the causes of their loss would have remained something of a mystery. On other occasions, however, loss of goods, and the fact that a ship had been plundered, did not go unnoticed, as we learn from an incident in 1298.[37] On this occasion, a Chinese ship carrying Japanese trade goods bound for China suffered some unspecified damage and ended up drifting in the open seas close to the coast of Hinoshima in the Gotō chain. A bakufu emissary, the Chinese Zen priest Presider (*shusho*) Yi, recorded the following:

> On the twenty-fourth of the fourth month a Chinese ship
> was on the Uminomata open seas, and had sustained some

damage. It drifted damaged for about one *ri* or so. Since it
now fell within the bounds of Hinoshima, harbor people
and villagers resident on Hinoshima launched seven boats,
and carried off various goods, including gold and textiles.
They made repeated trips back and forth, in full view on the
open seas. Boat groups from the inlets and islands likewise
came and carried goods away. This scene was replayed on
the twenty-fifth, and (again) on the twenty-sixth.[38]

Obviously, word of the ship helplessly floating adrift had spread
very quickly.

Some detail on the goods thus plundered comes from four
inventory lists drawn up by parties in Kamakura who owned
at least some of the cargo. Presider Yi's composite inventory
listed a total of 337 "cuts" of gold, mercury, silver swords, and
white cloth. Three other inventories, which provided the basis
for Presider Yi's composite inventory, offer still greater detail. In
one inventory: 240 *ryō* of gold dust worth forty *monme*, a total of
113 *tan* of thin cloth in four different sizes, 2 barrels of mercury,
1 *ryō* of *kanatō* torso armor with purple leather binding, 1 *ryō*
of *haraate* vest armor with "ark shell binding," 1 large sword
with gold and pearl decoration, 2 cutting knives with some
gilding, a stand for a teacup, a small half-size ablution basin
with pear-skin gold-dust background design, 8 tin boxes with
pear-skin gold-dust background design, deep purple night duty
clothing with a specified weave on the outer side, a stand for
things used with tea decorated with gold-dust branches sprinkled
on a "pear-skin background design" which you would know on
sight, a gold-flecked inkstone, and 4 white *kosode* kimono, 2 of
which are of cotton and 2 of mixed weave.[39] A second inventory
lists 124 "cuts" and 5 *ryō* combined of round gold and gold dust
in all worth thirty *monme*, 10 silver swords with silver-worked
designs, 1 sack of pearls containing 5 bags each of large and
small ones, and 40 *kan* (about 320 pounds) of mercury.[40] The
third and final inventory counts 128 "cuts" of gold of which 35
were round gold and 93 were gold dust, 17 tubes of mercury, 5

silver swords, 28 bolts of white cloth, 2 white curtain dividers, and a Chinese-style monk's surplice.[41]

At least two of the plunderers were ultimately identified, including Shisa Iwau, a member of the Matsura-tō, but the goods were slow to return to their rightful owners. An order sent to a certain Aokata Takaie by high-ranking Kyushu warriors conveyed the directive of the bakufu's new governor-general for Kyushu (*Chinzei tandai*), Kanezawa Sanemasa, and noted that it was in fact a repeat directive, that the original deadline for returning the items had passed, and that there was to be no delay in getting them back by the middle of the current eighth month.[42] It is somewhat ironic that the order was sent to Aokata Takaie. Only four years earlier Takaie had been successfully sued in bakufu court by a local resident for the return of two ships and cargo that Takaie claimed to have simply "borrowed."[43] His precise role in the Hinoshima affair, and the final outcome of the efforts to reclaim the stolen cargo, are both unknown but it is in any event easy to see why Matsura area inhabitants valued the sea and its bounty.

In the final analysis, it seems quite likely that for the Matsura-tō domestic piracy prepared the ground, as it were, for the transition to overseas ventures. Their earlier experience seems to have served to establish the habit and develop the techniques of organized pillaging and piracy. For the Matsura-tō, the thirteenth to fifteenth centuries represented a period where large-scale raiding became an enterprise and looting became an end in itself, rather than a means for raiders to tide themselves over temporarily during periods of food shortage or famine.

The Matsura-tō as a Fishing Organization

While members of the Matsura-tō held rights to land and farmed barley and other crops, their daily economic activity was heavily dependent upon the sea. The Matsura documents provide us with some sense of how fishing activity, a regular and daily affair, was organized in medieval times. We might also assume that this same organization was deployed when the Matsura-tō engaged in piracy and raiding expeditions.

Judging from extant documents, members of the Matsura-tō fell into three categories: the *kaifu* (seamen), *shitanosata* (subauthority), and the *ryōshū* (local lord). However, in order to gain a sense of the broader workings of the Matsura-tō as a collective entity we will attempt to delineate two types of governing relationships. The first consists of vertical relations among the *kaifu*, *shitanosata*, and *ryōshū*, while the second is the horizontal relationships among Matsura-tō members of the same status.

The word *kaifu* first appears in Matsura-related documents early in the thirteenth century.[44] According to a 1218 testamentary document, Mine Hiraku transferred to his son Noboru several net-groups (*tō*) of seamen—including those in the Gotō Islands—along with fishing territories.[45] Later, in Noboru's 1246 letter of release to his grandson Tomuru, we are informed that those net-groups are identified as the Ohira-tō and the Imatomi-tō in the Gotō Islands, and the Oura-tō of the main estate.[46] Each net-group was made up of several subgroups called *ichirui* (one type), each *ichirui* comprising three vessels.[47] We infer from the term *ichirui* that many of the crews on the vessels were based on (real or presumed) consanguinous relations.[48] Amino Yoshihiko, an authority on medieval society, assumes that those seamen were basically unfree people, counted among the movable assets belonging to proprietary lords. They were to be sold, pawned, or transferred either individually or collectively.[49] However, seamen also had special privileges owing to their skills as fishermen or pirates. In a way, they enjoyed freewheeling lives guaranteed by exemptions from normal taxation, which were granted by the powerful elite in exchange for particular service.[50]

The seamen were collectively under the leadership of the *shitanosata*, the headman or small-scale warrior in a fishing village. He apparently enjoyed significant power over the net-groups, in some cases possessing not only fishing nets and boats but also a large quantity of weapons, including armor, helmets, spears, bows, and arrows.[51] The ultimate masters of the net-groups, however, were the *ryōshū*. It was they who, working through the *shitanosata*, could arbitrarily recruit or dismiss the seamen working in their net-groups.

The most important factor in enabling certain Matsura families to claim the dominant role of *ryōshū* was their connection to central authority. During the Kamakura era the new and privileged title of *jitō* boosted certain families to positions of recognized leadership in each village which had exclusive fishing territories. As housemen of the Kamakura regime and managers of property,[52] Matsura *jitō* families were able to utilize local law-enforcement posts to control seamen within their jurisdiction.[53] Through the offices of the *kebiishi*[54] and *kaifu honshi*,[55] for instance, these families could actively extend their policing and tax-collecting rights to the fishing grounds.[56]

As noted at the beginning of this essay, the "four boundaries" of a *jitō* post might extend into and over portions of the sea. Coastal areas of the sea, in other words, were considered to be alienable parcels of property. They were quite literally liquid assets. Fishing villages received access to the sea only through payment of rents or taxes to the lords. Usufruct of these territories was established; trespassers would be either punished or forced to pay parts of their catch to the owners of the asset. In reality, the sea became closed territory; only seamen who lived in a village which held a territory as an estate had access to the sea and its resources.[57]

The status of *ryōshū* involved a set of rights and obligations toward the net-groups. The *ryōshū* could control the fishing villages by monopolizing the resources necessary for maritime activities. Matsura familes supplied the net-groups with equipment for fishing and piracy[58] and received a substantial percentage of the catch and the plunder in return.[59] From their earliest times, Matsura families kept under their control nearby "ship wood" mountains (*funakiyama*), where trees such as camphor were raised as ship-building materials.[60] Apparently, Matsura families, using their local appointment rights, attempted to place the *shitanosata* into the *shōen* hierarchy. In this case, the hierarchy of the *ryōshū-shitanosata* was converted into that of the *jitō* and deputy *jitō* (*jitōdai*). Mass explains "the *jitō* deputy was a creation and vassal of the *jitō*; under normal circumstances he was not subject to direction or discipline from either the bakufu or a proprietor. This meant, among other things, that the *jitō* had complete freedom on the question of electing a deputy *jitō*."[61]

An instructive illustration of this phenomenon may be seen in the relationship between the Mine family (of the Lower Matsura lineage) and one of its subordinates, the Aokata family. The Aokata family had once controlled the fishing village of Urabeshima within the Ojika Islands, claiming its ancestry from Jinkaku, who had been involved in a dispute over the islands with Matsura families. The Mine, having been granted a *jitō* post on the Ojika Islands in a 1228 bakufu settlement,[62] solidified their control over the Aokata in compromise agreements dating from 1238, that allowed them to assume the status of the *shitanosata* of Urabeshima.[63] This same compromise document reveals that the term *shitanosata* corresponds to the deputy of the *jitō* (*jitōdai*).

From one extraordinarily rich document, containing a series of petitions from the Aokata to the Mine, we see that the *jitōdai* was indeed totally subordinate to the *jitō*. From time to time, the Mine threatened the Aokata with divestment of title on the pretext that they had disobeyed orders. On at least one occasion, to secure complete submission from the deputy *jitō*, the Mine even ordered the Aokata to send sons as hostages to the residence of the *jitō*.[64] The Mine could call on the service of the Aokata at almost any time. On special occasions (such as the obligation for palace guard duty in Kyoto), the Mine forcibly demanded from the Aokata extra services or dues paid by labor, tribute goods, or money. The Aokata, in turn, brought pressure to bear on their seamen by passing on to them the cost of the sea products as well as the labor-based dues.[65] As the *ryōshū* emerged as a dominant power in the fishing villages, the *shitanosata* acted on behalf of the *ryōshū*, trying to establish close personal ties with his seamen. He extended economic aid to his men in time of need, and served as mediator when his men raised a disturbance.[66]

The *shitanosata* thus appears to have lacked a great deal of independent resources, and was subject to pressures from two sides. On the one hand, he was responsible to the *ryōshū*, and on the other he needed to take account of the basic dynamic between his office and the seamen. He needed corvee labor and they needed a place to work. Thus, the *shitanosata* needed to combine the skills of a labor organizer, a labor negotiator, and a subordinate manager. Some of the challenges involved in the role are highlighted in one case where the seamen united to complain strongly about the extortionary duties demanded by the Aokata.[67] In another case the seamen complained about the burden of dues levied on them and refused to follow Aokata orders, thus necessitating that the Aokata attempt to recruit labor from outside the Ojika island area.[68] The most stable seamen relationships seemed to be obtained when there were clear distinctions on the boat in terms of status and the resources that various personnel possessed. When the seamen perceived a vertical structure—with the head of the fishing village (*shitanosata*) at the top—they would scarcely challenge this authority. The relationship between the *shitanosata* and his men seems to have extended beyond that of formal contract, often resembling an *oyabun-kobun* (boss-follower) relationship. Apparently, the dyads between the *shitanosata* and the seamen were more intimate and personal than ones between the *ryōshū* and the seamen.

In sum, the Matsura-tō was a vertical group characterized by a set of dyads linking the leader and his subordinates. It was important to knit the members in vertical relationships, and to ensure that one member always held the position of leader. This was achieved through a rigid ranking system, where one's peers were regarded as potential enemies.

By institutionalizing succession, many potential problems in local leadership could be avoided. Testaments of the Mine and the Aokata families reveal that both made their important

offices hereditary; the former as the *ryōshū* inherited as a part of
the household property the title of *jitō*, *kebiishi*, or *kaifu honshi*,
whereas the latter as the *shitanosata* inherited the title *jitōdai*.[69]

In addition to these leadership ties, horizontal associations
also existed, most notably on the level of the *shitanosata*.
As an intermediary between the *ryōshū* and the seamen, the
shitanosata helped forge the maritime confederation. Through
their association, the *shitanosata* facilitated both fishing and
piracy, sometimes on quite a large scale. It appears that the
cooperation of the net-groups depended on strong personal ties
among those who actually managed the fishing villages. During
the mid-thirteenth century, for instance, the Aokata intermarried
with at least three other local families within the Gotō Islands,
the Uku, the Arikawa, and the Ayukawa,[70] bringing them almost
equal to the Matsura families.[71] Indeed, by the late Kamakura
era, the Aokata family had become ascendant in Matsura, as it
could use its riches to influence the fishing community, even
managing to buy land rights within the *shōen*. The Mongol
wars gave Aokata family members opportunities to distinguish
themselves as *gokenin*.[72] As the family members continued to
develop their power within the Matsura-tō organization, the
horizontal principles of cooperation and equality contributed in
no small part to their success.

After the fall of Kamakura, and during the onset of the wars
of the fourteenth and fifteenth centuries, the Matsura alliance (*tō*)
brought together not only Matsura families but also neighbors
who wished to live and work with them.[73] Some of its members
claimed a single common ancestor and common blood, but it
was primarily a political and military association whereby those
in geographical proximity and with overlapping social and
economic interests might provide for collective self-defense, or
alleviate conflicts among its membership.[74]

The Matsura-tō asserted itself most often as a collective
organization, in accordance with the articles of sworn contracts
(*ikki*). At times of civil war, its members were grouped into *ikki* at
first temporarily, on the occasion of a battle, and later more or less

permanently. Through the *ikki*, the Matsura-tō institutionalized rotational leadership, managing not to differentiate status among its major members. The earlier Matsura-tō also presumably had some regional alliances based on the horizontal principle. Apparently, the Matsura-tō as a maritime group frequently constituted a confraternity that embraced all of the "profession" regardless of their origins. The group appears to have been organized according to tacit agreements that are difficult to find or to document. Only later, during the turbulent fourteenth century, when Matsura families urgently sensed the necessity of mutual cooperation, did both kindred and nonkindred group leaders think to draw up contracts for signature.[75]

Early Familial Structure: The Matsura and the *Sōryō* System

When we turn to an examination of the internal structures of the individual Matsura families, we discover a different set of social dynamics at work, which ultimately benefited the Matsura-tō as a whole. During most of the Kamakura period, the horizontal principle would give way to a more vertical one where siblings were regarded as actual or potential competitors. By looking at some of the dynamics involved we are able to draw broader lessons about the structure of warrior society, most particularly with respect to the position of *sōryō*, or clan head.

During the middle decades of the Kamakura period, Matsura-tō families reached an extreme point of fragmentation. Gradually, as the principle of partible inheritance became the norm, there was proliferation within each new generation, and the distance among brothers and sisters increased. Within this tide of disintegration, sibling quarrels could not always be avoided, in many cases involving litigation over an inheritance. In one sense, we might regard disintegration and confrontation within the Matsura-tō as particular, unique features that occurred within their own family conditions. However, given that the families acted as local prominent warriors under the bakufu rule, we need to understand their experiences in the larger context of contemporary warrior society.

Scholars generally agree that Kamakura warrior society was organized on the basis of the *sōryō* system,[76] but there is less agreement on how to define that system.[77] It is often argued that the essence of the system lay in the contradiction between unitary headship and multiple inheritance. While social custom demanded the division of family property upon inheritance, a kinship mechanism centering on the clan head (*sōryō*) became the norm to hold together the clan property. The authority of the *sōryō* was increasingly emphasized as he retained general leadership over other clan members and their holdings.

The *sōryō* system also had social and political dimensions in Kamakura history since the bakufu took advantage of the practices to guarantee tax collections and guard-duty calls. The *sōryō* was entrusted by the bakufu with the allocation of dues (*onkuji*) among his family members, and he led his men in the performance of guard duty and in war. Even though there were some cases in which branch families received confirmation of holdings directly from the bakufu, their position was not equal to that of the *sōryō*.

Many scholars argue that the origins of the *sōryō* system have their roots in the late twelfth-century Kantō region, the birthplace of the Kamakura bakufu. They believe that the system was created by Minamoto Yoritomo, the founder of the bakufu, as the basis for his *gokenin* (vassal) system. According to their hypotheses, Yoritomo succeeded in rallying local support by forming feudal relations with each clan, that is, by actively granting the head of the clan the status of *gokenin* and giving him benefice in the form of land. In return for these rewards, the *sōryō* pledged continued military duty as well as tax obligations.

As the authority of the bakufu expanded beyond the boundaries of the Kantō region, the *sōryō* system was established in the new areas. After the Jōkyū war in 1221, in particular, eastern *gokenin* were given new estates in western Japan that had been confiscated from supporters of Go-Toba. Because many eastern families sent younger sons (*shoshi*) to administer, on the clan's behalf, new holdings in central and western parts of the country,[78] the *sōryō* system became more universal than locally confined to eastern Japan. This account of the development of the *sōryō* system is echoed in Western scholarship. For instance, Kyotsu Hori defines the *sōryō* sytem as a feudal practice of eastern warrior society which worked best in the comparatively small Kantō region where there were strong personal ties between members of a clan and their clan head. However, with the expansion of the Kamakura regime, the system began to suffer. As the authority of the clan head became weakened, the Kamakura vassal system gradually became ineffective.[79] According to Hitomi Tonomura, the *sōryō* system originated from informal family and inheritance practices prior to Kamakura. However, after the establishment of the bakufu, the *sōryō* system took on a new political role and was incorporated into a more formal legal and political structure. As the bakufu extended its power and influence on a national basis, the system was disseminated with the more formalized bakufu vassal system.[80]

On the other hand, some scholars do not locate the origin of the *sōryō* system in late twelfth-century Kantō society. For instance, Jeffrey Mass argues that the *sōryō* system, like key Kamakura institutions such as *gokenin*, *shugo* and *jitō*, did not acquire its historic meaning until after Yoritomo's lifetime.[81] It was the successors of Yoritomo, not the founder himself, who actually promoted the system as an apparatus for controlling bakufu vassals. For Mass, the term *sōryō*, with its meaning of house head, assumed its historical usage in the aftermath of the Jōkyū war, when the bakufu tightened its own links with house heads, as it intended to make them serve as the instruments for vassal dues and recruitment calls. Despite this development, however, the bakufu did not depend exclusively on house heads; other clan members had equal access to the bakufu court so long as they received proper confirmations from Kamakura. According to Mass, "the designation [*sōryō*] itself was not a title that the regime distributed. House heads may have been recognized as *sōryō*, but they received their status from a parent, not from Kamakura. The bakufu neither selected *sōryō* nor terminated them."[82] In this regard, it is no coincidence that the *sōryō* title, and the *sōryō* system in general, is best documented and studied in individual family and inheritance documents, rather than in bakufu law codes such as the *Goseibai shikimoku*.

During the Heian period the house head was called *katoku* (literally, a person who controls the house), an occasional equivalent for *chakushi* (literally, legitimate son). Unlike *sōryō*, however, *katoku* in the meaning of titular blood-line headship was lacking in elements of property control.[83] That usage continued into the Kamakura period, most notably and prominently in the case of the Hōjō family of bakufu regents. By contrast, in Heian times the term *sōryō*, literally meaning "the whole land," had a long association with land and land possession. Ultimately, however, and allowing for exceptions, from the early Kamakura period the term *sōryō* came to supersede the term *katoku*, and came to embrace the meaning of a larger descent group's designated head.

Mass has presciently argued that the earliest clear historical use of the term *sōryō* in the sense of a house head appears first not in the Kantō, but in Kyushu. That early usage occurs in a Matsura-tō family document from the year 1222, and deals with an inheritance dispute between two brothers of the Ishishi family, one of the influential Upper Matsura-tō families.[84] This dispute occurred when the elder brother named Ken protested his younger brother Kiramu's inheritance from their late father, Kasan.[85] Against Ken's infringement, Kiramu lodged a lawsuit and eventually the two brothers were summoned to trial at Dazaifu by the *shugo* of Hizen province. In his petition Kiramu noted that:

> during his lifetime, the father Kasan made the written promise that the holdings Ishishi, Ōsogi, and Tomo were to have been transferred to Kiramu (whose childhood name had been Kumaichi). In fact, on the tenth day of

the intercalary fourth month of the second year of Jōgen [1208], Kiramu as principal heir (*chakushi*) was granted the various paddy and uplands of the holding by a bakufu edict (*onkudashibumi*), accompanied by the sequence of hereditary proof records. Shortly thereafter, in the first month of this year, when Kasan became seriously ill, small parcels of his holdings were allocated to his sons and daughters. At that moment, Yamamoto Shirō Ken was conveyed ten *chō* of paddy field, three orchards, and one *chō* of exempt paddy field as the *shōen* officer's stipend (*kumon kyū*). Now although possessing that conveyance, he has seized the wheat harvest from the Kikushi-no-hara within Kiramu's holding, also making a small parcel of *myō* land from the original Fukunaga *myō* to be converted into a separate *myō* called Tokumoto. [Kiramu] petitions that such attempts by Ken do not stand to reason at all.[86]

According to Kiramu's accusation, Kasan designated his younger son, Kiramu himself, as the principal heir (*chakushi*), transferring the main inheritance to him. The father's transfer was duly approved by the bakufu's edict, along with the hereditary documents accorded to Kiramu. Later, the father divided and left the remaining property to the rest of his children—including his elder son Ken. After Kasan's death Ken unlawfully seized the shares belonging to the principal heir. Ken, however, defended his position, offering the following rebuttal:

Our real father Kasan *nyūdō* had three sons and three daughters. However, ever since the principal heir (*chakushi*) Genta Nanoru died many years ago, Ken has been known as the principal heir [of the Ishishi house] by Matsura clan members. Thus, in the case of palace guard duty in Kyoto last winter, [Ken] went up to the capital in his capacity as deputy for his father. However, on the sixth day of the past first month of this year while dispatched to Imazu, Ken was informed that his father's illness had been serious, and on the fourteenth he returned to Matsura. On the eighteenth day the father Kasan entered the priesthood, and that evening Kiramu argued that he had had the

so-called testamentary document written by the priest
himself. [Kiramu] expected [Ken] to cosign it, but [Ken]
had no intention to do it....After all, even though Ken
himself had been principal heir (*chakushi*), his younger
brother Kiramu tried to be house head (*sōryō*). [His act]
neither corresponded to the father's plan nor would follow
a principle of law. Considering the falsified document,
how could [Kiramu] argue about unlawful seizure of land?
In fact the paddy field and valuable belongings, large or
small, should have been equally distributed.[87]

Ken ultimately attempted to base his claim on the rationale
that Kiramu as the younger brother should naturally not be the
principal heir. Among the Matsura-tō family members, Ken, as
the eldest son, was recognized as the successor to his father,
Kasan; Ken had also once acted as his father's deputy at the time
of palace guard duty in the capital. Thus, Ken suggested that he,
and not Kiramu, should assume the rights of the *sōryō* over his
family's holdings. In the bakufu's court, however, it was Kiramu
who was in a stronger position. Not only had he received his
father's conveyance which stated that he was to be the principal
heir[88] but the conveyance had also been duly authorized by the
bakufu itself.[89] After all, the bakufu verdict had stated:

In general, the parents' disposal of property during their
lifetime does not depend on the distinction between
older and younger; rather, the possessors [as parents] can
dispose of the property at will. Then, why should Ken, after
having received [his own] bequest from Kasan, pursue an
argument calling himself the elder brother? Forthwith, Ken
is to terminate his false suit.[90]

The 1222 document marks a new era in the history of the
sōryō system, for it represents, as Mass has shown, the first
articulation of the equivalency of main heir (*chakushi*) and *sōryō*.
And when the bakufu rejected Ken's presumption, it was really
"expanding the usage of *chakushi* and paving the way for *sōryō*."
As the term *chakushi* was to be freely applied to a younger son,

the term *sōryō* could now take the greater significance in the shape of family organization and inheritance.[91] In fact, during the Kamakura period it seems not to have been uncommon for parents to bypass the elder son (or others for that matter) because of lack of talent or unfilial behavior, and we find such cases within the Matsura-tō.[92] The father's choice of a younger son (or in some cases, daughter) instead of the elder son resulted in fierce competition among heirs. Fathers (and mothers) enjoyed arbitrary freedom not only in naming of house heads but also in disposing of property. Convinced that their testaments would be approved by the bakufu,[93] fathers freely gave and withheld property from their children. The 1222 bakufu verdict reveals that Kamakura law and tribunal did not interfere with the prerogatives of the father, virtually giving him carte blanche authority with respect to the transmission of property.

Thus, by the 1220s, the essential components of the *sōryō* system were fully in place: partible inheritance among heirs, unitary headship by the principal heir, and the *sōryō*'s performance of the vassal dues. As demonstrated by the episode of 1222, this triangle of contradictory, separate duties and privileges created tension between the principal heir and junior heir, a tension that became one of the main characteristics of the *sōryō* system. These forces exerted a powerful influence on the Matsura and its development during the remainder of the medieval era, a long and fascinating story which we shall leave for another occasion.[94]

Conclusion

The social taxonomy of the Matsura-tō presents us with an exceptionally informative window into medieval Japanese history. It is clear that this population does not fit neatly into social categories, even as it is clear that it was inhabited by a number of obvious social groups. It is also clear, most particularly with respect to the *sōryō* model for understanding the medieval warrior family, that the Matsura present us with strong evidence that while descriptors and terms may have been common to the era, the content of those descriptors might vary from region to region. Though literally "on the margin" of Japan and its history, the Matsura call into question the relevance of too strong an adherence to the notions of center and periphery, and they make clear that those "on the margin" are by no means marginal.

At the same time, what is perhaps most striking about the Matsura is that they actively shaped their own existence. They interacted with larger elements that came within their orbit, including the Korean peninsula, maritime trade, and political entities located in distant central and eastern Japan. They straddled boundaries and negotiated economic, political and social change with a fluid engagement that reflected not the regularities of land, but the constant yet shifting movement of tides and currents. Their experience truly helps us broaden our horizons as we view the medieval era.

NOTES

I would like to thank Andrew Goble, as well as Thomas Conlan and Kenneth R. Robinson, for their feedback and comments on this essay.

1   The literature on the Matsura-tō has grown in recent years. For an introduction, see Seno Seiichirō, *Chinzei gokenin no kenkyū*, esp. pp. 424–530; Shirōzu Satoshi, "Nishi no umi no bushidan Matsura tō–Aokata monjo ni mieru sōkoku no yōsō"; Hyungsub Moon, "Matsura-tō: Pirate Warriors in Northwestern Kyushu, Japan, 1150–1350."

2   It is generally accepted that "Matsura" is the pre-Meiji pronunciation, and that in modern times "Matsuura" is standard. However, as Thomas Conlan's essay in this volume points out, proper nouns admitted of a range of readings and pronunciations in the premodern era. Thus, we even find "Matsuura" spelled out phonetically in a document from the fourteenth century. For "Matsuura no hingashi shima" (the eastern island[s] of Matsuura, with east as "hingashi" rather than "higashi"), see Jōwa 6 (1350).3.24 Yamashiro Hiromu yuzurijō (*Matsuratō kankei shiryōshū*, vol. 2, doc. 600; *Nanbokuchō ibun Kyushu hen*, vol. 3, doc. 2718; hereafter, *MKS*, 2:600; *NBI-Ky*, 3:2718). As a separate point, we note that Higashi Matsura was also referred to as Kami Matsura, and Nishi Matsura as Shimo Matsura.

3   Kōan 10 (1287).1.15 Aokata Kakushin yuzurijō an (*MKS*, 1:161; *KI*, 21:16153, as Kakushin Aokata Yoshitaka yuzurijō an).

4   The key here is the reference to "*umi no Kōrai to*" (the Korea Door in the sea). The phrase is written in phonetic script, and the word "*to*" has been interpreted by the editor as meaning "door." However, it is quite possible that the reference is to the spot in the sea later referred to as "Korea Island" (*Kōrai tō*). On this latter, see Tatehira Susumu,

"Gotō rettō to saikai chiiki no seikatsu gijutsu shi," pp. 329–333, and the map on p. 330.

5   The two major collections are the *Aokata monjo* (about 430 documents) and the *Ariura monjo* (more than 300 documents). The *Aokata monjo* contains 234 documents from the Kamakura era and 200 from Muromachi. The documents included in the *Matsuratō Ariura monjo* cover mainly the Muromachi era. Apart from these two, most of the documents have also appeared earlier in three other printed editions of primary sources: *Hirado Matsurake shiryō*, which includes documents relating to the Matsura, Imari, Ishishi, and Yoshinaga families; *Saga ken shiryō shūsei*, vol. 4 (Tsurata family), vol. 14 (Arita family), vol. 15 (Matsura Yamashiro family), vol. 19 (Ariura, Madarashima, and Shirai families), vol. 21 (Tsuruta family), vol. 27 (Ishishi and Imari families); and *Matsuratō shoke monjo*, which includes documents from the Nakamura, Matsura Yamashiro, Kurushima, and Sōda families.

6   The recent *Matsuratō kankei shiryōshū* contains 907 items, most of which are primary-source documents, but also includes some references to the Matsura that appear in diaries and chronicles. I have used the materials appearing in this three-volume collection as the definitive version of the primary documents, and references are to this collection.

7   For an introduction to *ikki*, see David L. Davis, "*Ikki* in Late Medieval Japan."

8   The relevant sections are excerpted in *MKS*, 1:115, 118, 120. For treatment of Matsura involvement in resisting the Mongol invasions, and the impact on them of the invasions, see Hyungsub Moon, "Matsura-tō: Pirate-Warriors in Northwestern Kyushu, Japan, 1150–1350," chap. 5. For more on the contributions of the *Hachiman Gudōkin* to post-Mongol perspectives, see Haruko Wakabayashi, "The Mongol Invasions and the Making of the Iconography of Foreign Enemies: The Case of *Shikaumi Jinja Engi*."

9   Although not cited further here, published renditions are readily available for the *Koryŏsa choryo* or *Tongguk t'onggam*. For reference, their bibliographical information is: *Koryŏsa choryo* (Seoul: Asea Munhwasa, 1973), and *(Kugyok) Tongguk t'onggam* (Seoul: T'amgudang, 1990).

10   *Azuma kagami* Bunji 1 (1185).3.24 (also in *MKS*, doc. no. 19, p. 32). For a slightly different rendering of the passage, see Minoru Shinoda, *The Founding of the Kamakura Shogunate, 1180–1185*, p. 300.

11   *Heike monogatari*, "Kake ai Dannoura kassen," excerpted in *MKS*, 1:20. See also Helen Craig McCullough, *The Tale of the Heike*, p. 374.

12   See William Wayne Farris, *Heavenly Warriors: The Evolution of Japan's Military, 500–1300*, especially pp. 300–302, 318–319, 324–325.

13   On the former, see Kenneth Butler, "The Textual Evolution of the *Heike Monogatari*." For recent study of the *Azuma kagami*, see Gomi Fumihiko, *Zōho Azuma kagami no hōhō: jijitsu to shinwa ni miru chūsei*; and Ichikawa Hiroshi, *Azuma kagami no shisōshi*.

14   For instance, the *Azuma kagami* dates the rise of *gokenin* (bakufu vassals) and *shugo* (provincial constables) to 1180, but contemporaneous documents attest that the first *gokenin* and *shugo* actually appeared only after 1190. See details in Jeffrey P. Mass, *Antiquity and Anachronism in Japanese History*, chap. 3.

15   For other recent work on Japanese piracy, see Peter D. Shapinsky: "With the Sea as Their Domain: Pirates and Maritime Lordship in Medieval Japan"; and "Lords of the Sea: Pirates, Violence, and Exchange in Medieval Japan."

16   *Koryōsa* 22:23b [1223.5.22]. As denoted in the *Koryōsa*, "*wakō*" in the thirteenth century represented two semantic units, "Japanese" (*wa*) and "raided" (*kō*). According to Tanaka Takeo, it was only after 1350, when Japanese attacks became more regular and violent, that "*wakō*" become a fixed concept meaning "Japanese pirates/raiders." See Tanaka, *Wakō—umi no rekishi*, pp. 12–16; and Tanaka, "Japan's Relations with Overseas Countries," p. 161.

17   Tamura Hiroyuki, *Chūsei Nitchō bōeki no kenkyū*, p. 4.

18   *Koryōsa* 22:29b [1226.6.1].

19   See Imagawa Fumio, ed., *Kundoku Meigetsuki* Karoku 2 (1226).11.16, 11.17 (see also *MKS*, 1:40). In fact, the *Koryōsa* records two Japanese raids in 1226, one in January, and one in June. (*Koryōsa* 22:29a [1226.1.27], 22:29b [1226.6.1].) The *Meigetsuki* entry of the eleventh month most likely refers to the raid of the sixth month.

20   See Aoyama Kōryō, *Nichi-Rai kōshōshi no kenkyū*, p. 27; *Minkeiki* Antei 1 (1227).5.1.

21   See *Azuma kagami* Karoku 3 (Antei 1, 1227).5.14.

22   Tsushima, only thirty-five miles from the nearest point on the Korean peninsula, is closer to Korea than to Kyushu. Its inhabitants traditionally enjoyed extensive unofficial contacts with Korea, and played a particularly important intermediary role in contacts between Japan and Korea. See Saeki Kōji, "Kokkyō no chūsei kōshōshi."

23   Benjamin H. Hazard, "The Formative Years of the Wakō, 1223–63," pp. 262–63.

24   *Koryŏsa* 25:31a-b [1263.4.5].

25   *Koryŏsa* 25:32a [1263.8.1].

26   Undated [1264?] dankan monjo an (*MKS*, 1:211; *KI*, 26:19725, as Hizen no kuni zaichō (?) ge an).

27   The most frequent rendering of *wakō* is "Japanese pirates" or "Japanese raiders," implying that the pirate bands of the fourteenth and fifteenth centuries were composed of Japanese. In the past decade, however, Japanese historians such as Tanaka Takeo and Murai Shōsuke have challenged that view, and argued that during the fourteenth and fifteenth centuries the *wakō* consisted mainly of Korean outcasts and bandits. See details in Tanaka Takeo, "Wakō to higashi Ajia tsūkōken"; Murai Shōsuke, *Ajia no naka no chūsei Nihon*, chap. 8.

28   Many scholars date the beginning of the *wakō* to 1350, following the entry in the *Koryŏsa* which states that: "the *wakō* incursions began with this [raid] in the second month of 1350." (*Koryŏsa* 37:21b–22a [1350.2].)

29   For a detailed account on the fourteenth century *wakō* forays into Korea, see Benjamin Hazard, *Japanese Marauding in Medieval Korea: The Wako Impact on Late Koryo*. For the impact on the Ming, see Kwan-wai So, *Japanese Piracy in Ming China During the 16th Century*.

30   Located between Tsushima and Matsura, the island of Iki was Tsushima's link with Matsura. Concerning the earlier history of Iki, see Naganuma Kenkai, *Matsura tō no kenkyū-kita Kyushu kaizoku-shi*, pp. 199–227. For examples of statements by Korean envoys, see *Chongjong sillok* 1:13a-b [1399.5.16] and *Haedong chegukki*, p. 95.

31   *Sejong sillok* 104:7b–9a [1444.4.29].

32   To these hard-core raiders were soon added the various Japanese pirate groups from the rest of the entire coast of Kyushu, as well as the islands and inlets of the Inland Sea. Saeki Kōji, "Kaizoku ron," pp. 47–48.

33   For example, Aoyama Kōryō, *Nichi-Rai kōshōshi no kenkyū*, pp. 25–32; Mori Katsumi, "International Relations Between the 10th and the 16th Century and the Development of the Japanese International Consciousness," p. 90; Tamura Hiroyuki, *Chūsei nitchō bōeki no kenkyū*, p. 13; Kawazoe Shōji, "Japan and East Asia," p. 406.

34   Aoyama's argument presupposes that there existed during the twelfth century an imbalance in the levels of the productive capacities between Japan and Korea. While Japan enjoyed a rapid growth of agricultural production and market activities, Koryō suffered from the low level of productivity and a lack of commercial development.

35   See *Hyakurenshō*, entry for Antei 1 (1227).7.21.

36   See *Azuma kagami* Jōei 1 (1232).intercalary 9.17.

37   For a brief study of this incident, see Seno Seiichirō, "Kamakura ni okeru totōsen no sōnan ni miru tokusōke bōeki dokusen no ichi keitai."

38   Einin 6 (1298).6.29 Kantō shisha Gi [Yi] shusho chūshinjō an (*MKS*, 1:206; *KI*, 26:19724).

39   Einin 6 (1298).5.20 Junshō onmotsu ika chūshinjō an (*MKS*, 1:202; *KI*, 26:19692).

40   Einin 6 (1298).6.23 Bō onmotsu insū chūshinjō an (*MKS*, 1:204; *KI*, 26:19721).

41   Einin 6 (1298).6.27 Ezai onmotsu ika chūshinjō an (*MKS*, 1:205; *KI*, 26:19722).

42   Einin 6 (1298).8.18 Tsushima no kami bō, Shōni Morisuke renshō shigyōjō an (*MKS*, 1:208; *KI*, 26:19770).

43   See Einin 2 (1294).8 Aokata Takaie chinjō an (*MKS*, 1:195; *KI*, 24:18658, as Aokata Takaie chinjō toshiro); Einin 2 (1294).12.23 Hizen no kuni shugo Hōjō Sadamune kakikudashi an (*MKS*, 1:196; *KI*, 24:18715, as Hizen shugosho bugyōnin hōsho an).

44   In fact, the earliest existence of *kaifu* in Matsura regions is located in literary works of the late tenth century. See Kawazoe Shōji,

"Kurushima monjo to Hizen Ōshima shi—Kamakura jidai made," pp. 19–20.

45   Kenpō 6 (1218).8 Minamoto Hiraku yuzurijō an (*MKS*, 1:33; *KI*, 4:2395).

46   Kangen 4 (1246).8.13 Shami Sainen yuzurijō an (*MKS*, 1:76; *KI*, 9:6727, as Sainen yuzurijō an). Throughout the Kamakura period, these groups of seamen, along with fishing territories, were handed down to later generations of the Mine family. See Bun'ei 6 (1269).7.20 Minamoto Tomuru yuzurijō an (*MKS*, 1:103; *KI*, 14:10459); Shōchū 3 (1326).3.7 Imari Myōsei yuzurijō an (*MKS*, 2:385; *KI*, 38:29375, as Minamoto Masaru yuzurijō an).

47   In total, in one instance, a *tō* named Genroku was composed of ten vessels. See Kenchō 6 (1254).4.16 Madarashima Todomu shoryō chūmon (*MKS*, 1:82; *KI*, 11:7734, as Minamoto Todomu shoryō chūmon).

48   Amino, "Nihon chūsei ni okeru kaimin no sonzai keitai," p. 21.

49   Written documents concerning such real estate assets as paddies, dry fields, and residences have been comparatively well preserved. In contrast, documents concerning seamen as movable assets, because of their merely temporary legal effect, were customarily discarded; therefore, we cannot expect to come upon any great number of them.

50   Amino Yoshihiko, "Kodai, chūsei, kinsei shoki no gyogyō to kaisanbutsu no ryūtsū," pp. 254–257.

51   See details in Kagen 3 (1305).3 Mine Sadashi chinjō an (*MKS*, 1:251; *KI*, 29:22156).

52   For an informative introduction to the *jitō*, see Jeffrey P. Mass, "*Jitō* Land Possession in the Thirteenth Century: The Case of *Shitaji Chūbun*."

53   In their testaments, some Matsura fathers conveyed the *jitō* post, together with those of the *kebiishi* and the *kaifu honshi*. In a Jōō 3 (1224).4.14 Kantō gechijō utsushi (*MKS*, 1:38; *KI*, hoi 2:ho 847) we find that only the four *jitō* shiki involved are noted; whereas when the *shiki* to one of these was conveyed in a later generation the *kebiishi*, *kaifu*, and other *honshi shiki* were specified: see Bun'ei 7 (1270).9.15 Shami Ikkei shojō (*MKS*, 1:104; *KI*, 14:10693, as Ikkei hōsho).

54   According to Friday, the *kebiishi* was originally appointed by the capital to deal with provincial outlaws, but during the Kamakura period, the post was completely absorbed by the provincial government and became a department, staffed by locally appointed functionaries. Karl Friday, *Hired Swords*, pp. 136–139.

55   Yasuda Motohisa suggests that the word *honshi* in *kaifu honshi* (*honshi* for the seamen) should be understood as another term for estate manager (*gesu*). During the Kamakura era, the *gesu* was often replaced by Kamakura-appointed *jitō*. Yasuda Motohisa, *Jitō oyobi jitō ryōshūsei no kenkyū*, p. 207.

56   See details in Kagen 3 (1305).3 Mine Sadashi chinjō an (*MKS*, 1:251; *KI*, 29:22156).

57   According to Hotate Michihisa, sea tenure based on exclusive fishing territories had developed prior to the Kamakura period. See Hotate Michihisa, "Chūsei zenki no gyogyō to shōen sei." Obviously, his argument makes a revision of earlier theory (represented by Amino Yoshihiko) that the exclusive fishing territories were formed in the later Kamakura period. Concerning the scholarly debates on the issue, see Haruta Naoki, "Suimen ryōyū no chūsei teki tenkai: amiba gyogyō no seiritsu o megutte"; Shirōzu Satoshi, "Chūsei kaison no hyakushō to ryōshū."

58   See, for instance, Kagen 3 (1305).3 Mine Sadashi chinjō an (*MKS*, 1:251; *KI*, 29:22156).

59   This was paid partly in kind, such as fish, salt, and other sea products. In one case, the *ryōshū* collected several vessels of sea products under the guise of labor-based dues (*kuji*). See Kenchō 6 (1254).4.16 Madarashima Todomu shoryō chūmon (*MKS*, 1:82; *KI*, 11:7734, as Minamoto Todomu shoryō chūmon); Kagen 3 (1305).3 Mine Sadashi chinjō an (*MKS*, 1:251; *KI*, 29:22156).

60   In fact, Minamoto Hisashi, the putative founder of the Matsura clan, transferred to his sons the *funakiyama*, along with ports and islands, as inheritances. See Kōwa 4 (1102).8.29 Minamoto Hisashi yuzurijō an (*MKS*, 1:7; *HI*, 4:1496, as Hizen no kuni Uno Onmikuriya kengō Minamoto Hisashi yuzurijō an), and Kōwa 4 (1102).9.23 Minamoto Hisashi yuzurijō an (*MKS*, 1:8; *HI*, 4:1500, as Hizen no kuni Minamoto Hisashi shobunjō an). *Funakiyama* appear in a number of testamentary records, such as Kangen 4 (1246).8.13 Shami Sainen yuzurijō an (*MKS*,

1:76; *KI*, 9:6727); Kōan 2 (1279).10.8 Kantō saikyōjō an (*MKS*, 1:130; *KI*, 18:13730, as Kantō gechijō an); and Genkō 2 (1322).6.22 Aokata Takatsugu yuzurijō an (*MKS*, 2:353; *KI*, 36:28066).

61   See Mass, *Warrior Government in Early Medieval Japan*, pp. 182–183. Also, the precarious and subordinate positions of the *jitōdai* vis-à-vis the *jitō* are convincingly demonstrated in Seno Seiichirō, "*Jitōdai* yori *jitō* e no shojō," in Seno, *Rekishi no kansei*.

62   Antei 2 (1228).3.13 Kantō saikyōjō an (*MKS*, 1:41; *KI*, 6:3732, as Kantō gechijō an). See also Hyungsub Moon, "Matsura-tō: Pirate-Warriors in Northwestern Kyushu, Japan, 1150–1350," chap. 2.

63   See Ryakunin 1 (1238).12.25 Mine Tamotsu, Minamoto Kanau wayojō an (*MKS*, 1:50; *KI*, 8:5359, as Minamoto Tamotsu, Minamoto Kanau wayōjō an).

64   Kagen 3 (1305).3 Mine Sadashi chinjō an (*MKS*, 1:251; *KI*, 29:22156).

65   Kagen 3 (1305).3 Mine Sadashi chinjō an (*MKS*, 1:251; *KI*, 29:22156).

66   In one letter, the Aokata begged the Mine to set free the seamen who had committed a murder and then been taken away by the provincial police officer. See Kagen 3 (1305).3 Mine Sadashi chinjō an (*MKS*, 1:251; *KI*, 29:22156).

67   Kōan 3 (1280).11.25 Hyakushō ra rensho kishōmon an (*MKS*, 1:134~136; *KI*, 19:14186~14189, as Hizen Urabeshima hyakushō ra renshō kishōmon an).

68   Kagen 3 (1305).3 Mine Sadashi chinjō an (*MKS*, 1:251; *KI*, 29:22156).

69   Kagen 3 (1305).3 Mine Sadashi chinjō an (*MKS*, 1:251; *KI*, 29:22156).

70   Concerning the kinship relations among the four families, see Gen'ō 2 (1320).8 Aokata Takamitsu moshijō an (*MKS*, 2:343; *KI*, 36:27559).

71   After the Mongol wars, the Aokata came to challege the authority of the Mine, becoming entangled in the land disputes over the Urabeshima. See Kagen 3 (1305).3 Mine Sadashi chinjō an (*MKS*, 1:251; *KI*, 29:22156).

72   This is discussed further in Hyungsub Moon, "Matsura-tō: Pirate-Warriors in Northwestern Kyushu, Japan, 1150–1350," chap. 4.

73   Scholars generally agree that territory became a stronger basis of links than kinship in the warrior *ikki* of the time. See Miyagawa Mitsuru, "From Shōen to Chigyō: Proprietary Lordship and the Structure of Local Power," pp. 97–100.

74   Naganuma, *Matsura tō no kenkyū—kita Kyushu no kaizokushi*.

75   The elaboration of detailed *ikki* marked a second phase of the history of the Matsura-tō; this phase was less spontaneous and more institutionalized. While the *ikki* and *ikki* contracts remained the basis of political life, numerous other *ikki*-related documents remain, such as documents of confirmation, administrative directives, and certificates for military loyalty.

76   For brief introductions to scholarly debates on the *sōryō* system, see Seki Yukihiko, "Sōryōsei o meguru shogakusetsu"; Jeffrey P. Mass, *Lordship and Inheritance in Early Medieval Japan*, chap. 3.

77   A lack of consensus on the definition of the *sōryō* system lies behind studies of its origins, parameters, periodization, and eventual collapse. Among Japanese historians, there are two different approaches. The historical approach focuses on legal and institutional practices associated with bakufu policy and law: see Satō Shin'ichi, "Bakufu ron"; Uwayokote Masataka, "Sōryō sei josetsu"; Suzuki Hideo, "Katoku to sōryō ni kansuru oboegaki." The socio-economic approach looks primarily at issues of family structure and inheritance practices: see Matsumoto Shinpachirō, *Chūsei shakai no kenkyū*, chaps. 3, 5; Nagahara Keiji, "Tōgoku ni okeru sōryō sei no kaitai katei no kenkyū"; Toyoda Takeshi, *Bushidan to sonraku*, chap. 3.

78   For example, nearly 130 eastern *gokenin* came to Kyushu after receiving land rights there. Seno Seiichirō, *Chinzei gokenin no kenkyū*, pp. 215–314.

79   See, for example, Hori Kyotsu, *The Mongol Invasions and the Kamakura Bakufu*, pp. 19–26; and "The Economic and Political Effects of the Mongol Wars," pp. 191–193.

80   Hitomi Tonomura, "Women and Inheritance in Japan's Early Warrior Society."

81   According to Mass, one problem with earlier scholarship on the *sōryō* system was its reliance on the *Azuma kagami*, which had read

back later key institutional terms into the beginning of the Yoritomo era. See Mass, *Antiquity and Anachronism in Japanese History*, chap. 2.

82   Jeffrey P. Mass, *Lordship and Inheritance in Early Medieval Japan*, p. 58.

83   Concerning scholarly debate on the *katoku/sōryō* distinction, see Suzuki Hideo, "Katoku to sōryō ni kansuru oboegaki," pp. 283–298.

84   Jōō 1 (1222).12.23 Hizen no kuni shugosho kudashibumi an (*MKS*, 1:37; in *KI*, 5:3032, as Dazaifu shugosho kudashibumi an). In fact, the 1222 document addresses two inheritance disputes in the Ishishi family. The second dispute is between the uncle and his cousin.

85   For discussion of this dispute, see Seno Seiichirō, *Chinzei gokenin no kenkyū*, pp. 476–478; Jeffrey Mass, *Lordship and Inheritance in Early Medieval Japan*, pp. 64–65.

86   Jōō 1 (1222).12.23 Hizen no kuni shugosho kudashibumi an (*MKS*, 1:37; in *KI*, 5:3032, as Dazaifu shugosho kudashibumi an).

87   Jōō 1 (1222).12.23 Hizen no kuni shugosho kudashibumi an (*MKS*, 1:37; in *KI*, 5:3032, as Dazaifu shugosho kudashibumi an).

88   In fact, two of the father's releases survive in Matsura-tō documents. See Kaō 1 (1169).12.4 Minamoto Kasan yuzurijō an (*MKS*, 1:12; *HI*, 7:3525, as Minamoto bō yuzurijō an); Jōgen 2 (1208).intercalary 4.10 Minamoto Kasan yuzurijō an (*MKS*, 1:29, *KI*, 3:1738).

89   To possess duly authorized, public records (*shōmon*) was more advantageous than to possess private, essentially hearsay records (*kishōmon*) in the Kamakura judicial system. To some scholars, *shōmon* are records of property transactions such as bills of sale (*baiken*) or final testaments (*yuzurijō*). See, for instance, Satō Shin'ichi, *Komonjogaku nyūmon*, chap. 3, pt. 5. However, many scholars regard *shōmon* as much broader official records, including not only *baiken* and *yuzurijō* but also decrees of the court, the bakufu, and *shōen* owners. On the other hand, *kishōmon* include private affidavits such as the testimony of witness and the sworn oaths of disputants.

90   Jōō 1 (1222).12.23 Hizen no kuni shugosho kudashibumi an (*MKS*, 1:37; in *KI*, 5:3032, as Dazaifu shugosho kudashibumi an).

91   Mass, *Lordship and Inheritance in Early Medieval Japan*, p. 65.

92   See, for example, Aokata Yoshitaka's redirection of a bequest from his elder son, Takaie, to a younger sibling, Chikahira, on the grounds of Takaie's lack of talent: Shōō 2 (1289).3.4 Aokata Kakujin yuzurijō an (*MKS*, 1:175; *KI*, 22:16912); or the disowning of a son for contravening his father's decision: Kōan 9 (1286).9.10 Seimyō shoryō daikanjō (*MKS*, 1:157; *KI*, 21:15980).

93   Parallel to the ascending power of the fathers was the rapid privatization of the *jitō shiki*, the most prestigious and lucrative property right among bakufu vassals. Under Yoritomo, the *jitō shiki* was a conditional indivisible lifetime title, subject to the bakufu interference. After a *jitō*'s death, the *shiki* came to be regarded as heritable family property, frequently parceled in vassals' conveyances. See details in Mass, *Lordship and Inheritance in Early Medieval Japan*, chap. 2.

94   For more extended discussion of these matters, see Hyungsub Moon, "Matsura-tō: Pirate-Warriors in Northwestern Kyushu, Japan, 1150–1350," chaps. 4, 5, and 6.

REVISITING INTERPRETIVE STREAMS

Navigating Kamakura History: Perspectives on the Last Work of Jeffrey P. Mass
Joan R. Piggott

Few scholars have the chance to rewrite their first book, and perhaps few would wish to do so. In his final monograph prior to his unexpected early death in 2001, Jeffrey P. Mass published a masterful rethinking of his first monograph, *Warrior Government in Early Medieval Japan* (1974), on the basis of a quarter century of additional research, writing, and teaching.[1] Over the interim his thinking evolved and matured, notably with respect to issues of the character, historical development, and significance of the Kamakura bakufu. His final monograph, *Yoritomo and the Founding of the First Bakufu: The Origins of Dual Government in Japan* (1999), thus articulates a number of important new insights and perspectives, while challenging the reader to think both forward and backward, Janus-like, from where Mass began his study of Minamoto Yoritomo's bakufu in the 1970s to where he left it at the dawn of the twenty-first century. The purpose of this essay is to highlight some of those changes, while considering how two decades of research and writing brought them about.

Mass's published work, comprising translated documentary collections, conference volumes, and monographs, can be classified into two groups. Early on, he focused on the birth and early development of what he called "Japan's first warrior government." Then, in later publications, Mass looked at issues concerning the Kamakura government across a longer time span and in broader, more thematic terms. The analysis of political structures remained his core concern, but he also spent time studying social and economic aspects of Kamakura's institutions.

During the late 1970s, Mass's distinctive "history through documents" collections provided readers with the foundation for his approach to Kamakura-period history. Therein, he gave abundant insights into his favored mode of research: teasing out the stuff of history through careful reading and analysis of individual documents (*monjo*).[2] As he stated in the introduction to these collections, "I hope to offer through documents a more direct representation of the institutions of this emerging medieval society."[3] First, in *The Kamakura Bakufu: A Study in Documents* (1976) and later in *The Development of Kamakura Rule: A History with Documents* (1979), Mass introduced readers to the rich archive of primary sources upon which the writing of Kamakura's history—the history of both the age and its "warrior government"—depends. In the first of these two volumes, Mass not only presented carefully annotated and contextualized translations of more than 300 primary sources through which the development of the government in Kamakura up to the mid-thirteenth century can be traced; he also provided a guide to 584 printed titles where original sources can be found. At the time of publication, this was a more extensively annotated guide to such sources than existed even in Japan. In the second work, a groundbreaking study of the development of legal institutions and procedures in Kamakura, he likewise provided an extensive set of annotated translations, while using them to bring to light judicial processes, and the underlying social problems with which they contended. Such documents, he demonstrated, are more than dry chronicles of institutions, as some have pronounced them. When adequately contextualized, they become critical and exciting sources of social history. Given that Mass was one of a very few pioneering historians of the Kamakura age outside of Japan, his English translations of these documentary materials were especially beneficial for launching a new field of historical scholarship in the English-reading world.

Mass wanted readers to concentrate on primary sources, but he also understood that close reading of such documents required a scaffolding of historical narrative within which individual records or sets of sources could be contextualized and interpreted. To this end, he labored not only to write his own monographs and articles but also to provide opportunities for a growing number of fellow researchers to interact, collaborate, and expand the range of topics and sources available for study. Mass soon revealed himself to be a skilled organizer, and the end result of his efforts was the appearance of four edited collections. Three were the results of conferences, and comprised papers revised subsequent to the conference. The fourth was a collection of papers solicited around a theme. These four volumes, for which Mass made a conscious effort to include a mix of scholars at various stages of their careers, lay open key themes and issues in Japan's history from Heian (794–1180) through Tokugawa (1600–1868) times.

In the first of his conference volumes, *Medieval Japan, Essays in Institutional History* (1974), which Mass co-edited with his mentor John Whitney Hall, we find essays on the Kyoto capital, the organization of the Heian court and both Kamakura and Ashikaga warrior governments, the nature and development of the retired monarch system of court leadership (*insei*), the estate (*shōen*) system, the Mongol invasions, and popular uprisings (*ikki*). Essays in the subsequent *Court and Bakufu in Japan* (1982) provided the first sustained articulation of the "dual-polity" (*kōbu*) concept that now shapes so much of our thinking about politics and society in medieval Japan, notably published at a time when Kyoto seemed forgotten by most researchers in Kamakura studies.

A third volume of essays, *The Bakufu in Japanese History* (1985), demonstrated the broadening of Mass's interest to warrior government beyond Kamakura times. Co-edited with William Hauser, it traced the longer trajectory of the dual polity from 1180 to 1868. In his contribution therein, Mass encouraged researchers to focus on "the great divide in Japan's warrior history," whereby warriors became overlords (*daimyō*) and shoguns became hegemons during the transition from medieval to early modern times. It was also in that volume that Mass cautioned readers against the tendency to think anachronistically about bakufu history. For instance, he pointed out that neither courtiers nor warriors had used the term "bakufu" in extant sources dating from Kamakura times. At the time, contemporaries thought rather in geographic terms, differentiating the centers of courtier and warrior power as "Kyoto" and "Kamakura" (or "Kantō") respectively."[4]

Causes and the significance of the Genpei fighting between 1180 and 1185 remained a key issue for Mass throughout his career. His talent for writing compelling analytical prose on the subject is particularly visible in his contribution to the third volume of *The Cambridge History of Japan* (1990), wherein he summarized the complex story of how Kyoto and Kamakura came to share power in the resulting *kōbu* diarchy.[5] Whereas in Heian times warriors had served as the court's mercenaries, Yoritomo's establishment of a Kamakura headquarters during and after the Genpei war was seen to have resulted in significant historical change because the bakufu represented an "initial breakthrough to power on the part of elite fighting men." It was furthermore Japan's "first non-central locus of authority overseen by men not of the most exalted social ranks." Mass pointed out too that Kamakura's clients (*gokenin*, literally, the shogun's "housemen")[6] were for the most part provincial magnates who had served as officers (*zaichō kanjin*) at provincial headquarters. In later Heian times their fortunes were increasingly enhanced by courtiers willing to exchange dominance over the public realm for proprietorship over estates in which the magnates also participated.[7] As for the important question of how courtiers managed to hold onto their power until the 1180s, Mass agreed with G. Cameron Hurst that central and local remained closely joined throughout Heian times because of a deeply shared respect for ascriptive status (*kishu*) among courtiers and warriors.[8] Mass noted, however, that once Yoritomo succeeded in establishing his regional security system in eastern Honshu in the 1180s, thereby bypassing Kyoto and guaranteeing client-warriors' landed interests, such respect weakened substantially. From that time forward, Yoritomo's role as adjudicator became increasingly important, since "Kamakura's objective [was] to bottle up potentially explosive situations in litigation."[9] If warrior government was to control its clients and keep them from feuding over land holdings, then law, investigation, and adjudication would be crucial. For Mass, such functions were the vectors of Kamakura's development, especially after the Kyoto court was further weakened by the retired monarch Go-Toba's futile revolt in the brief Jōkyū war of 1221.

This grasp of the importance of Kamakura's judicial role led Mass to focus more attention on the exercise of shogunal lordship over houseman families. Specifically, in *Lordship and Inheritance in Early Medieval Japan* (1989), he augmented his translation of 150 documents with a substantial analysis of inheritance practices within warrior houses.[10] The story here spanned the entire thirteenth century and led to new questions beyond the institutional and political spheres. How had warriors' inheritance practices taken form from Heian times on, and why did Kamakura's newly instituted courts find themselves mediating among aggrieved warrior clients? Mass's conclusion here was that since membership in Kamakura's clientage band was kin-based (patriarchs who had been designated military stewards (*jitō*) were recognized with their progeny as shogunal clients), Kamakura was forced to resolve clients' inheritance struggles when kin structures failed to unify house members under their paterfamilias. "Though the [Jōkyū] war (of 1221) has always been depicted as a bloodletting between the two power centers," Mass argued, "the dominant divisions were actually among fighting men. One of the principal axes on which participants separated was the splits that existed within their own families."[11] Without efficacious results at judicious peaceful settlement—which settlement also had the benefit of shoring up shogunal authority—housemen would have decimated each other and set the countryside aflame with armed conflicts. So did "Kamakura justice" emerge dynamically in the 1210s and 1220s, even as Go-Toba was trying to entice disgruntled Kamakura housemen to deploy against Yoritomo's successors in Kamakura, his Hōjō affines.

Strengthening the command structure of warrior families that could be leveraged by the paterfamilias as house head (sōryō) thus became a critical objective for shogunal administration. Policies included confirming their religious, military, and policing authority, as well as their prerogatives of homeland possession, agricultural supervision, and control of females. But such tactics enjoyed limited success. The documentary record excavated by Mass in *Lordship and Inheritance* demonstrates how kinship continued to fail in binding warrior kin, seriously compromising Kamakura's authority by the mid-thirteenth century. Still later, the defense strategy engineered by Kamakura in response to the Mongol invasions in the 1270s compounded a worsening economic crisis among housemen, even as warrior mobilization weakened age-old practices such as partible inheritance and a female's birthright to a share in a father's estate.[12] Meanwhile, cultivators were adopting many of the inheritance practices followed in warrior households, as *shiki* rights in land became more alienable in a marketplace where coinage facilitated exchange as never before. Given such profound social and economic shifts, the moorings of Kamakura houseman warriors were seriously shaken.

In a collection of historiographical essays, *Antiquity and Anachronism in Japanese History* (1992), Mass gave readers additional insights into some of the methodological puzzles that most interested him.[13] As the title suggests, he was especially concerned with how history-telling in narrative form mixes the present and the past, thus introducing serious anachronism into the story.[14] For Mass, the way to avoid such skewing was to attend carefully to the language of contemporary documents, as opposed to reliance on narrative sources such as tales and chronicles, including the *Heike monogatari* and the *Azuma kagami*. In an essay entitled "Yoritomo and Feudalism," he also shared his views on a particularly contentious issue for medieval historians across the globe: the difficulties of applying the vocabulary of feudalism in specific historical contexts.

In fact, Mass was generally reticent in using the term "feudal" in his work, given his awareness of its various meanings and their frequent conflation in what Susan Reynolds has termed a "mega-paradigm."[15] Instead, he employed what might be termed the language of lordship, utilizing such terms as lord, chieftain, vassal, and follower. Although these can be seen to have ultimately derived from the feudal parlance of F. L. Ganshof and Max Weber's ideas of patrimonial authority, Mass avoided the term "fief" and was careful to translate distinctively Japanese terms such as *kenin* and *jitō* as "houseman" and "military steward" respectively.[16]

Given Mass's rare usage of "feudal," his choice of the title, "Yoritomo and Feudalism," in *Anachronism* is particularly notable. Here, Mass signaled that while the feudal paradigm might still hold a place in his analysis of the development of warrior institutions in Japan, his view of periodization and the historical trajectory of feudalism in Kamakura times was quite different from that of other historians. He rejected the idea that Shogun Yoritomo represented a high mark in the development of feudal institutions, or that the trajectory in Japan was similar to that in Europe. Quite the contrary:

> The [feudal] chieftainship withered away as the shogunal title became institutionalized. The chieftain became a figurehead as the Kamakura regime grew stronger. In Europe, there were always weak or incompetent feudal kings. The difference was that, sooner or later, such weakness was reflected in the debility of their regimes. In Japan, conditions were exactly the opposite. The full flowering of military government emerged with the disappearance of feudal leadership. The office of shogun—itself necessary—transcended its occupants.[17]

That is to say, as the institutions of warrior government took regular form during the thirteenth century, feudal leadership gave way to more routinized, bureaucratized processes and bonds. Moreover, lord-houseman relations during Kamakura times were cross-cut by the diarchy that linked Kamakura and Kyoto. So were the *jitō shiki* of warrior clients created from the same land tenure system—the *shōen* system—as that in which generations of the court's clients had participated. That meant that the organization of courtier and warrior clientage pyramids was more similar than different. Meanwhile, he wrote, Yoritomo and his shogunal successors performed for two groups of spectators. One comprised warriors who served Yoritomo as Kamakura Lord; the other comprised the court in Kyoto, which appointed Yoritomo its supreme commander of the right (*utaishō*). In sum, while he occasionally used "feudalism," perhaps largely to invoke the European familiar, Mass remained concerned that its use glossed over variant conditions of great significance. Again, his bent was toward careful study and analysis of legions of contemporary documents that would avoid such glossing.

In the 1990s, as Mass worked on what would be his final conference volume, *The Origins of Japan's Medieval World: Courtiers, Clerics, Warriors, and Peasants in the Fourteenth Century*, his vision of Kamakura warrior government in a longer-term context led him to question his own earlier notions about the emergence of the medieval age in Japan. For *Origins,* he assembled research by colleagues and graduate students from both Oxford and Stanford to consider a wide range of developments from Kamakura into Muromachi times, including the emergence of a second warrior government, that of the Ashikaga shoguns. While his earlier work had emphasized the formation of the Kyoto-Kamakura diarchy through the mid-thirteenth century, he was now looking closely at the demise of the Kamakura regime in the later thirteenth and early fourteenth centuries. As he and other members of the *Origins* group did that, they collectively came to the conclusion that a new periodization was needed for Japan's medieval epoch. Looking back from Muromachi times, Kamakura's warrior government seemed considerably less revolutionary and even more classical than medieval. As Mass explained in *Origins* in his introduction and the first chapter, he had come to see the Kenmu era of the 1330s as the dawn of a new age, and as a definitive moment of historical rupture. He now held that it was Go-Daigo in the early fourteenth century, rather than the retired Go-Shirakawa at the end of the twelfth century, who should be viewed as Japan's first medieval monarch.[18] Moreover, the failure of Go-Daigo's revolt against warrior government in the 1330s resulted in the breaking of "the spell cast by courtiers." Then and only then could hegemonic national lordship by shoguns be replaced by the territorial lordship of warlords as more mature feudal rulers. Mass summed it up this way:

> The start of the medieval, then, involved a merging of the worlds of the courtiers and the warriors, followed by an inversion of their relative positions, and a decline in the momentarily enhanced status of the center itself. The age of Kamakura had witnessed none of these conditions and had been an era best characterized by the separation in jurisdictional spheres. Japan's bold experiment with two authority systems ended in the 1330s.[19]

Therefore, by the time Mass undertook to rewrite his revised history of the beginnings of the Kamakura government, his frame of reference, once bounded by the mid-thirteenth century, had changed appreciably. His later vantage point on Yoritomo as warrior lord and institution builder now afforded better understanding of the conditions that led to the fall of the Kamakura regime in the 1330s and its subsequent replacement by the chieftaincy of another, but very different, warrior leader, Ashikaga Takauji (1305–1358). Overall, Mass's view of premodern Japanese warrior and bakufu history had evolved significantly from what it had been in the early 1970s.

His new view of periodization was clear in a changed title. Where the earlier book had been entitled *Warrior Government in Early Medieval Japan*, the new one was called *Yoritomo and the Founding of the First Bakufu*. And Mass brought another revision to the rewriting process. He had decided that the Kamakura dual-polity arrangement, rather than weakening the court, had actually strengthened it. The new argument could be summarized in three points:

1) Establishment of the Kamakura government represented an epochal moment in Japanese history, [because]

2) Its founding in the 1180s led to a very different sharing of power, a "dual polity," comprised of court and bakufu, [but]

3) Rather than weakening the power of the Kyoto court, establishment of the regime in Kamakura extended the court's authority and the classical polity by at least a century.

This formulation amounted to a major recasting of earlier common wisdom—including Mass's own original views—concerning the historical significance of the Kamakura bakufu. By this time he and others had come to see that Kamakura's warrior government initiated not the "medieval age" but rather the final epoch of Japan's classical "charter" polity, which gave way to the "secondary" or medieval polity only in the early fourteenth century.[20]

Despite the new periodization, in *Yoritomo and the Founding* Mass continued exploring many of the same themes as he had done earlier, especially "Kamakura justice" and "dual polity." And yet the book is still a "must read" because its recasting and re-articulation of key issues significantly sharpen our understanding of the epoch.

The book is divided into eight chapters grouped into four mostly chronological sections: Japan before 1180, the Genpei War, the Dual Polity, and Constables and Managers.

In the first chapter devoted to "The Taira Moment," Mass re-entered the debate as to whether it was Minamoto Yoritomo or Taira Kiyomori who should be credited with founding Japan's first warrior government. With incisive strokes he painted Kiyomori as nothing more than the junior partner of the retired Go-Shirakawa, who was the actual hegemon of court politics in the 1160s and 1170s.[21] In contrast to William Wayne Farris, who sees Kiyomori as a regime organizer, Mass saw Kiyomori as a royal client, whose "career of service built around a sequence of governorships did not provide the necessary springboard for an independent base of power."[22] Kiyomori's lordship—his authority over land and men—was no different from that of other military aristocrats of his time. It was based on Kiyomori's role near (but not at) the top of a three-tiered hierarchy of estate relations wherein the power of the Taira chieftain was legitimated by Go-Shirakawa as court leader.[23] Only for a few brief months after the eleventh month of 1179, when Kiyomori staged a coup and confined Go-Shirakawa under house arrest, did he function independently; and that was precisely the moment when his position was challenged by rivals from all sides, resulting in the Genpei civil war. For Mass, then, there was a significant historical gap between Kiyomori and Yoritomo as warrior commanders, a distinction confirmed by the lack of extant written documents from Kiyomori's own household chancellery (*mandokoro*). Were they to have existed, such documents might have proven that Kiyomori recruited followers for his own warrior headquarters. But that no such records are extant indicated to Mass that there was never a Taira-led warrior organization serving as predecessor of the Kamakura bakufu.

As to the character and condition of the late twelfth-century polity over which Go-Shirakawa and his martial lieutenant Kiyomori held sway, Mass also disagreed with the notion of a decline of court government that resulted in a power vacuum in the late Heian countryside.[24] He argued instead for the health and vibrancy of court government into Kamakura times. Although linkages between capital and provinces were no longer like those prescribed initially in the earlier *ritsuryō* codes, the late Heian realm was nonetheless successfully integrated by vertical factions, including those structured around estates and warrior bands.[25] Synthesizing recent research in both Japanese and English, Mass presented a useful list of characteristics for the post-*ritsuryō* "transitional polity" of mid-to-late Heian times—what some scholars have called *ōchō kokka*, or the "court-centered polity"—as including an ascriptive status society; continued involvement in governance by the senior courtiers (*kugyō*) of the Council of State; a mixed tenurial regime of public and private landholdings (*shōen-kokugaryō*); ongoing provincial administration by provincial governors and their staffs at provincial headquarters; competing vertical factions functioning as patronage blocs; essentially hereditary (and thus privatized) office-holding; commended estates whose management was merged into great blocs by faction leaders at court who enjoyed considerable legal immunities; and proprietary provinces (*chigyōkoku*), taxes from which supported court leaders such as the retired monarch and regent.[26] "Fundamentally," explained Mass, "a bureaucratic monolith came to be absorbed and distributed among its leading officials, who used their offices much like poker chips to bid for private wealth," while eroding "the public essence of imperial government without weakening its grip."[27] Mass deftly provided here a more complete and nuanced overview of conditions in the late Heian polity than had ever before been articulated in English.

In "The Missing Minamoto," Mass went on to build his case to prove the innovative and epochal character of Yoritomo's warrior regime. He argued that since Yoritomo's ancestors had never constructed a regional base in eastern Japan before 1180, Yoritomo personally could be credited with successful innovation in establishing the Kamakura regime as a realm-wide entity.[28] At the same time, he rejected the views of "regionalists," who contend that conditions in eastern and western Japan were fundamentally different, and that Yoritomo's reach outside of eastern Honshū was attenuated. For Mass, the same hierarchy of offices and tenurial regime were in place across the archipelago.[29] Meanwhile, patriarchs of military lineages—"chieftains" in Mass's parlance—in all regions were undercut in their ability to recruit and maintain followers by the dominant family structures of the time, one of segmenting conical clans and partible inheritance. Both Taira and Minamoto chieftains participated in a multiplicity of competing factions and patronage networks, and centripetal tendencies made it exceedingly difficult for would-be commanders to gain and maintain loyal followers. To be sure, only the exercise of provincial policing authority (*kendanken*) associated with the provincial governor's office (*kokufu*) had enabled a warrior commander like Yoritomo's father, Minamoto Yoshitomo (1123–1160), to gain followers. But since judicial decisions at the Kyoto court could deprive both military governors and provincial magnates of their proprietary rights, those seeking protection necessarily resorted to commending land upwards to powerful courtier patrons while also assembling military forces to defend their interests. Such conditions empowered Yoritomo, a "creative bandit," in fashioning autonomous structures of lordship at Kamakura, far away from Kyoto.[30] Indeed, Mass noted how it was beneficial for Yoritomo to be a man outside the court's law, one who had the temerity to issue unprecedented patents of confirmation to followers.

In Part 2 of *Yoritomo and the Founding* Mass focused on the Genpei war, with chapters devoted to "The East on the Move" and "*Shugo* and *Jitō* Imagined." He categorized the Genpei war as a civil conflict fought mostly in small engagements that nonetheless represented an epochal development in Japan's history. It provided, after all, the jolt that led to Yoritomo's founding of the bakufu as his eastern regional military system, and therefore it inaugurated the structure of the bakufu that would be central to Japan's governance for the next seven hundred years.[31] Mass reiterated how the outlawed Yoritomo successfully recruited provincial magnates with his anti-Taira strategy and "governor-like documents," portraying himself as successor to the court's authority in eastern Japan while contemporaneously forging "the Minamoto" as his private clientage network.[32] But here again Mass revised the common wisdom. Based upon his unparalleled grasp of the documentary record—including archives from warrior lineages, temples, and Kamakura's own *Azuma kagami* chronicle—Mass teased out the strands of varying strategies employed by Yoritomo and his lieutenants in different provinces, as well as local responses to those strategies. Only quite gradually did such titles as "honorable houseman" and "land steward" come to define membership in the Minamoto network. Despite Mass's view that regionalism was not an important issue at the turn of the thirteenth century, he nonetheless showed in this section of the book how much needed to be learned through regional, provincial, and local case studies focused on the rich archive of Kamakura sources.

In "*Shugo* and *Jitō* Imagined," Mass sketched out in broad strokes how the new warrior authority came to fit within older practices of court authority, resulting in two vertical faction-like entities comprising the new "dual polity" as national order. Kamakura's institutions developed to include the houseman system, provincial constableships (*shugo*), and land stewardships (*jitō shiki*), all to be assigned, defined, and adjudicated by the Kamakura headquarters of warrior government. Between 1180 and 1185 Yoritomo's quite aggressive policies of confirming land stewardships succeeded in breaching the sovereignty of the Kyoto court in unprecedented fashion. Subsequently, however, when Yoritomo was working quite consciously to routinize his legacy between 1186 and 1199, compromise and integration became his preferred strategies. As a result, he could serve as "a conduit between classes and bulwark of the old order," not unlike military aristocrats (*miyako no musha*) in Heian times.[33] That, Mass said, was why Yoritomo was no "conservative revolutionary." Ultimately he was more conservative than revolutionary.[34]

In this same chapter Mass added new facets to our understanding of how land stewardships frequently functioned as two-tiered, vertical *jitō* postings: a military steward often appointed a local deputy (*jitōdai*), while the steward himself resided extra-locally. There were also supra-*jitō* (*sōjitō*) appointments—"vertically arranged *jitō*"—like those recorded for Kyushu. This means that stewards were not just local land openers (*zaichō ryōshū, kaihatsu ryōshū*) as older research frequently painted them. Moreover, the vertical bonds such arrangements solidified contributed substantially to center-periphery ties in the new dual-polity arrangement. Through such bonds, two national hegemonic centers, symbolized by their capstone figures of monarch and shogun, were able to stabilize the realm in a way that neither center could have done alone. It was this enlightenment that was behind Mass's surprising statement in the book's introduction: "It is the central contention of this book that, thanks to the policies fashioned by Yoritomo in the period before 1200, the traditional order in Japan was extended for another century."[35]

In Part 3, entitled "The Dual Polity," Mass rethought the process involved in the development of the *jitō* network and explained the "dual polity" concept with still greater clarity. Moving beyond a general recognition of the fact that there co-existed two power centers within a single polity, Mass seems to have envisioned Kyoto and Kamakura as two separate if closely linked judicial regimes.[36] Building on ideas he and others articulated in the earlier *Court and Bakufu in Japan*, Mass called for increased study of the Kyoto court—comprising throne, retired monarch, nobility, officialdom, elite religious structures, and their ties to local elites and places across the archipelago—to better understand Kamakura politics and society.

In "The Four Corners" Mass elucidated key moments in the process by which Yoritomo constructed "the Minamoto" houseman network as his realm-wide clientage bloc. Clients, many of whom had been provincial magnates in late Heian times, had to be identified and organized in every part of the realm. Yoritomo's strategies to strengthen bonds between himself and these clients included the Northern Campaign of 1189, purges of rivals in the middle Tōkai and Tōsan provinces in 1190, and selection and promotion of clients in the west. The death of Go-Shirakawa in 1192 made Yoritomo senior statesman in the realm, but when the death of Yoritomo's daughter in 1195 marked the failure of "court and bakufu united" (*kōbu gattai*) as advocated by leading courtiers like Abbot Jien of Mount Hiei, other means of co-existence for the two power centers in

Kamakura and Kyoto were needed. Yoritomo's death in 1199 further complicated the situation, and resulted in a power struggle that left Yoritomo's Hōjō affines in control of the Kamakura headquarters. A further outcome was the 1221 Jōkyū war.

In "A Place in the Sun," Mass assumed the task of demonstrating how the institutions of *gesu* (the proprietor's resident manager) and *jitō* reflected the power of the diarchy at the most local levels of administration, in estates, townships and villages.[37] A key problem for Yoritomo and his Hōjō successors as bakufu administrators proved to be finding the means to "deny local men everywhere a pretext for abuses," or incursions into local landholdings.[38] Mass found that one surprising strategy pursued by Kamakura was to urge the retired sovereign in Kyoto to revive his own Records Office (*Kirokujo*), so that it could adjudicate tenurial and other suits. Another strategy was to elaborate Kamakura's own policies vis-à-vis *jitō*. Adding to the documents he translated in earlier documentary collections, Mass reported here on an array of materials from both Kamakura and other locales that demonstrate the substance and outcome of such measures, which also served to institutionalize Kamakura's own houseman system.

In Part 4, concerning "Constables and Managers," Mass took a hard look back at earlier Kamakura history from a later vantage point in the 1270s, the time when the Mongols invaded Japan and challenged Kamakura's long prized mandate to defend throne and realm. In "A *Shugo* in Every Province," Mass—hitherto interested primarily in the stewards and their roles—provided his most complete diachronic analysis of provincial constableship, beginning with what he called "the emergence of pre-*shugo*" in the 1190s. In joining this long-running debate in Japanese scholarship concerning the chronology and origins of the *shugo* post, Mass looked back to find possible precedents in the supraprovincial warrant officers (*sōtsuibushi*) of the Heian period and to province-wide *kuni jitō* appointments of the early Kamakura age. He demonstrated that although references to a "protection headquarters" (*shugosho*) at the Kyushu Dazaifu appear from 1197 onward, full-bodied *shugo*—all of whom were easterners and clearly Kamakura's emissaries in the same way that provincial governors had long represented Kyoto—do not emerge in the extant record before 1215. And it was still later, between 1222 and 1232, when the post-Jōkyū settlement led to the further elaboration of the *shugo*'s responsibilities as articulated in the formulary for suits, the *Goseibai shikimoku* (of 1232). Mass attributed this very slow development of provincial constableship to its profoundly revolutionary nature, and to the troubled relations between *shugo* and the court's provincial governors.[39]

In a final chapter entitled "The Indiscipline of *Jitō*," Mass took up a question that in many ways capped his career as a historian of the Kamakura bakufu. He considered the long-term development of warrior stewardship from the vantage point of the late thirteenth century. Ever true to his "history through documents" methodology, he began by opining that only specific case studies can tell us what any given *jitō* achieved over time; but he also confirmed that the extant record demonstrates how *jitō* constantly tested the limits of their prerogatives—they consistenty squeezed both proprietors and cultivators.[40] The result was ongoing contention among *jitō*, estate proprietors' agents, and farmers.[41] Meanwhile, authorities in Kamakura encouraged negotiated settlements (*wayō*) whenever disputes broke out, largely because warrior government lacked both the resources and will to move against its own housemen.[42] At the same time, however, Mass appreciated how such continuing disputation signaled success not by warriors but rather by the authorities in Kyoto, especially religious institutions. It was on that basis that he elaborated his final evaluation of Kamakura-period stewardship, which he finally came to see as representing only an early stage in the very long process whereby local elites gained increasing autonomy from both Kyoto and Kamakura. Yoritomo shepherded Japan's polity into a new phase, but it was only the "first stage of the shift from a hitherto hegemonic court to a countryside that began to apply pressure in new ways."[43] The historical trajectory had become clear for Mass only when he could gain a vantage point from the late Kamakura and post-Kamakura eras.

At various points in *Yoritomo and the Founding*, Mass turned his thoughts to a curious paradox that has taxed many scholars over the years. Why, he wondered, should the story of Kamakura warrior government involve more stories of judicial encounters and judgments than stories of battle and warfare? His answer, as suggested earlier in this essay, was that the administration of justice addressed the warrior government's awareness that the danger to its own stability posed by unmediated disputes within kinship groups was greater than any military threat from without. Mass was certainly not alone in stressing the centrality of the judicial function in Japan's charter polity. Cornelius Kiley has argued that in pre-Kamakura times the Heian monarch presided over what was primarily a "judicial state," and historians of the classical polity have shown how Heian courtiers regarded governance (*matsurigoto*) as synonymous with decision-making (*sadame*) in response to petitions, suits, or claims. In this respect, the Heian *tennō* was both apical ordinator and adjudicator.[44] Just as the *tennō*'s court made decisions as requested by its supplicants—whether courtiers, government offices, or religious institutions—so did the shogun's apparatus make decisions as requested by its clients, the houseman-stewards.

At this juncture, a word on where the final work of Jeffrey Mass leaves Western-language historical studies on the Kamakura era seems appropriate. Together with the essays of the *Origins* collection that prepared the way, *Yoritomo and the Founding of the First Bakufu* helps us rethink the character and historical significance of Yoritomo's warrior government and the possibility of a new periodization for "classical" and "medieval" in Japan. Combined, these two works provided the energy for other scholars—many of whom were Mass's students—to "re-locate" Kamakura with regard to medieval studies. Mass's re-examination of his initial postulates on Kamakura and medieval studies has thus had an impact far beyond that of the typical monograph.

The work Jeffrey Mass helped all of us begin has since led us in directions unanticipated by both mentor and mentee. But again, the foundations of technique and analysis he provided have proven essential to our paths, wherever they have led us. I know this fact from my own experience, which, since beginning with studies on Nara religious institutions and kingship, has moved in the direction of embracing new and diverse topics and research approaches in Heian studies—political, cultural, intellectual, and archaeological.

There is always more to do, as Mass himself indicated in this last monograph. By giving us this last book—his first one rewritten—he gave us both a rich retrospective laced with important revisions that formed the capstone of his unique perspective, and also a springboard for navigating Kamakura history, and indeed, medieval history as well, in new directions. This forward-thinking orientation, accompanied by his enthusiasm for such scholarly collaboration as this volume represents, has already proven to be a major part of the life work and legacy of Jeffrey Mass.

NOTES

1   Mass's other monographs include *Warrior Government in Early Medieval Japan*; *The Kamakura Bakufu: A Study in Documents*; *The Development of Kamakura Rule, 1180–1250*; and *Lordship and Inheritance in Early Medieval Japan: A Study of the Kamakura Sōryō System*. He also compiled a collection of his own essays, *Antiquity and Anachronism in Japanese History*. Beyond these, he was editor or co-editor of a number of essay collections: *Medieval Japan: Essays in Institutional History* (with John W. Hall); *Court and Bakufu: Essays in Kamakura History*; *The Bakufu in Japanese History* (with William B. Hauser); and *The Origins of Japan's Medieval World: Courtiers, Clerics, Warriors, and Peasants in the Fourteenth Century*. Mass also published prolifically in journals and conference volumes, those essays being: "The Emergence of the Kamakura Bakufu"; "Jitō Land Possession in the Thirteenth Century: The Case of *Shitaji Chūbun*"; "The Origins of Kamakura Justice"; "Kamakura bakufu shoki no soshō seido: monchūjo to mandokoro o chūshin ni"; "Translation and Pre-1600 History"; "The Early Bakufu and Feudalism"; "Patterns of Provincial Inheritance in Late Heian Japan"; "What Can We Not Know About the Kamakura Bakufu"; "The Kamakura Bakufu"; "The Missing Minamoto in the Twelfth-century Kantō"; and "Of Hierarchy and Authority at the End of the Kamakura." His last work to be published was "Family, Law, and Property in Japan, 1200–1350," the text of a talk given at Harvard University's Edwin O. Reischauer Institute of Japanese Studies in 2000.

2   Mass defined such documents as follows: they "deal with specific subjects (or groups of subjects) and are authored on single occasions." Conveyance, he thought, was also a defining feature. He contrasted them "with chronicles and diaries, which treat long periods and divide material by calendar entries." For the Kamakura era, there are about thirty thousand documents extant. See *The Kamakura*

Bakufu, p. 9. On Mass's "history through documents" methodology, see also his own discussion "Documents, Translation, and History," in *Antiquity and Anachronism in Japanese History*, pp. 128–156.

3   *The Kamakura Bakufu*, p. 3.

4   The latter was an idea Mass would explicate further in later work. See "Black Holes in Japanese History: The Case of Kamakura," in *Antiquity and Anachronism*, pp. 157–177.

5   The essay was entitled "The Kamakura Bakufu," pp. 46–88. It was later republished in Marius Jansen's *Warrior Rule in Japan*.

6   On my use of "client" rather than "vassal" here, in the interest of both transparency and historical comparison, I prefer the language of patronage rather than that of feudalism. The latter has been increasingly problematized by European medievalists as well (see note 15 below). Mass himself increasingly used the parlance of patronage in *Yoritomo*.

7   "The Kamakura Bakufu," p. 47.

8   See G. Cameron Hurst III, "The Kōbu Polity: Court-Bakufu Relations in Kamakura Japan," p. 7.

9   "The Kamakura Bakufu," p. 78.

10   Mass established the foundation for this study of warrior inheritance practices in an early article, "Patterns of Provincial Inheritance in Late Heian Japan." It focused particularly on the historical development of house headship ("chieftaincy" in Mass's parlance) and property transmission among provincial elites.

11   *Lordship and Inheritance*, p. 55.

12   *Lordship and Inheritance*, pp. 102–103.

13   For an excellent evaluation of its contents, see Carl Steenstrup's review in the *Journal of Japanese Studies* 20.1 (1994), pp. 239–245.

14   As an example, see Mass's discussion of how the *Azuma kagami* leads to a skewed view of the emergence of *shugo* in "The Kamakura Bakufu," p. 62.

15   Among its many usages, the term "feudal" has been drawn from its European origins to serve as the translation of a very old East Asian political concept (Ch. *fengjian*, Ja. *hōken*) denoting a decentralized political authority that results when a monarch delegates authority to a powerful military subordinate. In addition, "feudalism"

has also long been used by European medievalists such as F. L. Ganshof and Marc Bloch to denote the exercise of territorial lordship by military professionals who utilize such practices as vassalage and the assignment of landed fiefs to attract and maintain followers. See Bloch's formulation in his *Feudal Society*, p. 446; and for Ganshof's usage, see his *Feudalism*. This use of "feudal" has been employed by historians of Japan both in Japan and in the West from at least the 1950s onward. Third, there is also the Marxist use of feudalism, wherein an agrarian economy is dominated by a "feudal mode of production." Thereby, a ruling class of landlords and serf cultivators are bound by rent and other relations of dependence. Historians of medieval Japan, especially those working in Japan, have used "feudal" in the Marxist sense since the 1930s. Finally, Max Weber defined feudalism as a subtype of patrimonial authority. By that definition, feudal authority is exercised by a chieftain over dependents whose swearing of fealty and vassalage is generally contractual. According to Weber, such relations could augment rather than diminish a dependent's status. This usage of feudalism has been common among Western historians studying Japan since the 1930s. Widely read historians of Japan such as Kan'ichi Asakawa and John Whitney Hall have frequently merged the meanings of "feudal" as used by Ganshof, Bloch, and Weber. For Hall's definition, see his "The Feudal Age," in *Japan From Prehistory to Modern Times*, p. 77. The result is, that what Susan Reynolds has portrayed as a problematic "mega-paradigm" for studying European history, is even more problematic in its application to Japanese history. See Susan Reynolds, *Fiefs and Vassals*; and also, Frederic Cheyette on feudalism as a "concept-theory" in *Lordship and Community in Medieval Europe*.

16   For a sense of Mass's vocabulary, see "The Kamakura Bakufu," esp. p. 61; and his exploration of the topic, "The Early Bakufu and Feudalism."

17   See "Yoritomo and Feudalism," in *Antiquity and Anachronism in Japanese History*, p. 78. Earlier, however, Mass had written somewhat less surely, "Feudalism at the end of the twelfth century registered only modest beginnings: Yoritomo's reach remained strictly limited, and more importantly, the bequests he made were over lands neither owned nor controlled by him. At all events, the chieftain in Kamakura did come to exercise a type of authority that was new to

Japan. Its precise limits and nature are bound up with the office of *jitō.*"
See *Kamakura Bakufu*, p. 60.

18   See *The Origins of Japan's Medieval World*, esp. pp. 1–4
and pp. 17–38. For more on Go-Daigo and his revolution, see Andrew
Edmund Goble, *Kenmu: Go-Daigo's Revolution.*

19   *The Origins*, p. 3.

20   The term "charter polity," meaning the earliest polity in
a given region and one from which later polities derive, is used
by state-formation theorists. For instance see Victor Lieberman's
introduction in *Beyond Binary Histories: Re-imagining Southeast Asia
to c. 1830.*

21   Mass rejected (see *Yoritomo*, p. 28) William Wayne Farris's
belief that it was Kiyomori, not Yoritomo, who should be credited with
fashioning the first warrior government. For Farris' overall treatment
of the late Heian system, see his *Heavenly Warriors: The Evolution of
Japan's Military, 500-1300*, esp. pp. 273–310.

22   See *Yoritomo*, p. 17.

23   Mass defined the three tiers as those of the proprietary lord
(*ryōke*), the custodial agent (*azukaridokoro*), and lower managers
(*gesu*). See *Yoritomo*, p. 24.

24   See, for example, the well-known description of these
developments in John Whitney Hall, *Government and Local Power in
Japan 500-1700: A Study Based on Bizen Province*, p. 122.

25   See *Yoritomo*, pp. 5, 16. For the concept of vertical factions,
see Cornelius Kiley, "Estate and Property in the Late Heian Period,"
esp. pp. 110–112.

26   See *Yoritomo*, pp. 2–3.

27   See *Yoritomo*, p. 2.

28   This chapter resulted from the re-thinking of a journal article,
"The Missing Minamoto in the Twelfth-century Kantō."

29   See *Yoritomo*, p. 38.

30   See *Yoritomo*, p. 41.

31   Not all historians agree—the Genpei War was mentioned
almost in passing in the first edition of Conrad Totman's *A History of
Japan*. See chap. 5 passim. The second edition makes rather more of
it.

32   See *Yoritomo*, p. 71.

33   See *Yoritomo*, pp. 252, 255; and Karl Friday's *Hired Swords: The Rise of Private Warrior Power in Early Japan*, pp. 88–93.

34   The term "conservative revolutionary" was coined by G. Cameron Hurst, who offers the contrary view. See his "Kōbu Polity," in Jeffrey P. Mass, *Court and Bakufu*, p. 7.

35   See *Yoritomo*, p. 10.

36   See *Yoritomo*, p. 174.

37   For further on this, see Jeffrey P. Mass, "The Kamakura Bakufu," p. 62.

38   See *Yoritomo*, p. 172.

39   See *Yoritomo*, p. 210.

40   See *Yoritomo*, p. 252.

41   Mass describes the situation in detail in his "Jitō Land Possession in the Thirteenth Century: The Case of *Shitaji Chūbun*."

42   See *Yoritomo*, p. 252.

43   See *Yoritomo*, p. 7.

44   Cornelius J. Kiley, "Estate and Property in the Late Heian Period," p. 114. As for how the new role of the *tennō* as adjudicator developed in Heian times, in tandem with growing competition for access to the wealth of the countryside by various power centers comprising the Heian court, see Joan R. Piggott, "Court and Provinces Under Fujiwara no Tadahira"; and Joan R. Piggott and Yoshida Sanae, eds., Teishinkōki: *What Did a Heian Regent Do? (The Year 939 in the Journal of Regent Fujiwara no Tadahira)*, esp. pp. 65–68.

BIBLIOGRAPHY

Primary Sources

Aokata monjo 青方文書. Compiled by Seno Seiichirō 瀬野精一郎. *Shiryō sanshū, komonjo hen* 史料参集古文書編. 2 vols. Tokyo: Zoku gunsho ruijū kanseikai 続群書類従完成会, 1975–76.

Azuma kagami 吾妻鏡. Vols. 32–33 of *Shintei zōho kokushi taikei* 新訂増補国史大系. Tokyo: Yoshikawa kōbunkan 吉川弘文館, 1968.

Azuma kagami 吾妻鏡. Edited by Ryō Susumu 龍粛. Vol. 4 of *Iwanami bunko* 岩波文庫. Tokyo: Iwanami shoten 岩波書店, 1941.

Baishōron 梅松論. Edited by Yashiro Kazuo 矢代和夫 and Kami Hiroshi 加美広. In *Shinsen Nihon koten bunko* 新選日本古典文庫. Tokyo: Gendai shichōsha 現代思潮社, 1975.

Bungo no kuni Ōno no shō shiryō 豊後国大野荘史料. Edited by Watanabe Sumio 渡辺澄夫. Tokyo: Yoshikawa kōbunkan 吉川弘文館, 1979.

Burakushi shiryō senshū 部落史史料選集. Edited by Buraku mondai kenkyūjo 部落問題研究所. Kyoto 京都: Buraku mondai kenkyūjo 部落問題研究所, 1988–1989.

Chiba ken no rekishi shiryōhen chūsei 2 (kennai monjo 1) 千葉県の歴史, 資料編, 中世 2 (県内文書 1). Compiled by Chibaken shiryō kenkyū zaidan 千葉県史料研究財団. Chiba shi 千葉市, 1997.

Chiribukuro 塵袋. Edited by Masamune Atsuo 正宗敦夫. Tokyo: Nihon koten zenshū kankōkai 日本古典全集刊行会, 1977.

Chŏngjong sillok 定宗實錄. In *Chosŏn wangjo sillok* (CWS) 朝鮮王朝實錄. Seoul: Kuksa p'yŏnch'an wiwŏnhoe 国史編纂委員会, 1969–1972.

Chōshūki 長秋記. Vols. 16–17 of *Zōho shiryō taisei* 増補史料大成. Kyoto 京都: Rinsen shoten 臨川書店, 1965.

Chosŏn wangjo sillok 朝鮮王朝實錄. Seoul: Kuksa p'yŏnch'an wiwŏnhoe 国史編纂委員会, 1969–1972.

Chōya gunsai 朝野群載. Vol. 29.1 of *Shintei zōho kokushi taikei* 新訂増補国史大系. Tokyo: Yoshikawa kōbunkan 吉川弘文館, 1964.

Chūsei hōsei shiryōshū 中世法制史料集. Vol 1. Edited by Satō Shin'ichi 佐藤進一 and Ikeuchi Yoshisuke 池内義資. Tokyo: Iwanami Shoten 岩波書店, 1963.

Chūsei seiji shakai shisō 中世政治社会思想. 2 vols. Edited by Satō Shin'ichi 佐藤進一 et al. Tokyo: Iwanami shoten 岩波書店, 1972.

Chūyūki 中右記. By Fujiwara Munetada 藤原宗忠. Vols. 9–13 of *Zōho shiryō taisei* 増補史料大成. Kyoto 京都: Rinsen shoten 臨川書店, 1965.

Dai Nihon komonjo, hennen monjo 大日本古文書編年文書. 25 vols. Tokyo: Tōkyō daigaku shiryō hensanjo 東京大学史料編纂所, 1901–40.

Dai Nihon komonjo Yamanouchi Sudō ke monjo 大日本古文書山内首藤家文書. Tokyo: Tōkyō daigaku shiryō hensanjo 東京大学史料編纂所, 1940.

Daigoji monjo mokuroku 醍醐寺文書目録. 3 vols. Tokyo: Bunkachō bunkazai hogobu jutsu kōgeibu 文化庁文化財保護部術工芸部, 1989.

Denreki 殿暦. By Fujiwara Tadazane 藤原忠実. 5 vols. In *Dai Nihon kokiroku* 大日本古記録. Tokyo: Iwanami shoten 岩波書店, 1956.

Eisei hiyō shō 衛生秘用抄. By Tanba Yukinaga 丹波行長. In *Zatsu bu* 雑部, vol. 31.1 of *Zoku gunsho ruijū* 続群書類従, 205–218. Tokyo: Zoku gunsho ruijū kansei kai 続群書類従完成会, 1924.

Fūchinroku 風塵録. Vol. 7 of *Murata Masashi chosakushū* 村田正志 著作集, edited by Murata Masashi. Kyoto 京都: Shibunkaku shuppan 思文閣出版, 1986.

Fukudenpō 福田方. By Yūrin 有林. Tokyo: Kagaku shoin 科学書 院, 1988.

Fukutomi sōshi 福富草紙. Edited by Komatsu Shigemi 小松茂実. Vol. 25 of *Nihon emaki taisei* 日本絵巻大成. Tokyo: Chūō kōronsha 中央公論者, 1979.

Fukutomi sōshi 福富草紙. Edited by Umezu Jirō 梅津次郎 and Okami Masao 岡見正雄. Vol. 18 of *Nihon emakimono zenshū* 日本絵巻物全集. Tokyo: Kadokawa shoten 角川書 店, 1968.

Fusō ryakki 扶桑略記. Vol. 12 of *Shintei zōho kokushi taikei* 新訂 増補国史大系. Tokyo: Yoshikawa kōbunkan 吉川弘文館, 1965.

Gaun nikkenroku batsuyū 臥雲口件録跋尤. By Zuikei Shūhō 瑞溪 周鳳. Vol. 13 of *Dainihon kokiroku* 大日本古記録, edited by Tōkyō daigaku shiryō hensanjo 東京大学史料編纂所. Tokyo: Iwanami shoten 岩波書店, 1961.

Genpei jōsuiki 源平盛衰記. 6 vols. Edited by Matsuo Ashie 松尾葦 江, et al. Tokyo: Miyai shoten 三弥井書店, 1991.

Gōdanshō, Chūgaishō, Fukego 江談抄. 中外抄. 富家語. In *Shin Nihon koten bungaku taikei* 新日本古典文学大系. Edited by Gotō Akio 後藤昭雄 et al. Tokyo: Iwanami shoten 岩波 書店, 1997.

Gyokuyō 玉葉. By Kujō Kanezane 九条兼実. 3 vols. Edited by Kokusho sōsho kankōkai 国書叢書刊行会. Tokyo: Meicho kankōkai 名著刊行会, 1993.

Go-Nijō Moromichi ki 後二条師通記. By Fujiwara Moromichi 藤原 師通. Vol. 5 of *Dainihon kokiroku* 大日本古記録. Tokyo: Iwanami shoten 岩波書店, 1956.

Goseibai shikimoku 御成敗式目. In 1. *Buke bu* 武家部 (1), vol. 17 of *Shinkō gunsho ruijū* 新校群書類, edited by Hanawa Hokinoichi 塙保己一. Tokyo: Meicho fukyūkai 名著普及 会, 1930; 2. *Chūsei hōsei shiryōshū* 中世法制史料集, vol. 1, 3–31; 3. *Chūsei seiji shakai shisō* 中世政治社会思想, vol. 1, 8–41.

Gotai shinbun shū 五体身分集. Microfilm hard copy of text belonging to the library of Keiō University; held in the Department of the History of Medicine of the Oriental Medicine Research Center of the Kitasato Research Institute 北里研究所東洋医学総合研究所医史学研究部.

Gumaiki 愚昧記. By Sanjō Sanefusa 三条実房. Unpublished facsimile at the Historiographical Institute, University of Tokyo.

Haedong chegukki 海東諸国記. By Sin Sukchu 申淑舟. Translated by Yi Ŭlho 李乙浩. Seoul: Taeyang Sōjŏk 大洋書籍, 1982.

Haseo sōshi, Eshi zōshi 長谷雄草紙，絵師草紙. Vol. 11 of *Nihon no emaki* 日本の絵巻, edited by Komatsu Shigemi 小松茂実. Tokyo: Chūō kōronsha 中央公論社, 1983.

Heian ibun 平安遺文. Edited by Takeuchi Rizō 竹内理三. 15 vols. Tokyo: Tōkyōdō shuppan 東京堂出版, 1963–1992.

Heihanki 兵範記. By Taira Nobunori 平信範. *Zōho shiryō taisei* 増補史料大成. Kyoto 京都: Rinsen shoten 臨川書店, 1965.

Heikoki 平戸記. By Taira Tsunetaka 平經高. 2 vols. *Shiryō taisei* 史料大成. Kyoto 京都: Rinsen shoten 臨川書店, 1965.

Hennen Ōtomo shiryō 編年大友資料. 2 vols. Edited by Takita Manabu 田北學. Tokyo: Fuzanbō 風山房, 1942–1946.

Hennen sabetsushi shiryō shūsei 編年差別史資料集成. Edited by Harada Tomohiko 原田伴彦. Tokyo: San'ichi shobō 三一書房, 1983.

Hirado Matsura ke shiryō 平戸松浦家史料. Edited and published by Kyoto daigaku bungakubu kokushi kenkyūshitsu 京都大学文学部国史研究室. Kyoto 京都, 1951.

Hirasan kojin reitaku 比良山古人霊託. In *Hōbutsushū, Kankyo no tomo, Hirasan kojin reitaku* 宝仏集・閑居友・比良山古人霊託. Edited by Koizumi Hiroshi 小泉弘. Vol. 40 of *Shin Nihon koten bungaku taikei* 新日本古典文学大系. Tokyo: Iwanami shoten 岩波書店, 1993.

Hōgen monogatari 保元物語. Vol. 31 of *Nihon koten bungaku taikei* 日本古典文学体系. Tokyo: Iwanami shoten 岩波書店, 1961.

Hōgen monogatari 保元物語. In *Hōgen monogatari, Heiji monogatari, Jōkyūki* 保元物語・平治物語・承久記. Vol. 43 of *Shin Nihon koten bungaku taikei* 新日本古典文学体系, edited by Tochigi Yoshitada 栃木孝惟, Kusaka Tsutomu 口下力, Masuda Takashi 益田宗, and Kubota Jun 久保田淳. Tokyo: Iwanami shoten 岩波書店, 1992.

Hōgen monogatari (Nakaraibon) to kenkyū 半井本保元物語と研究. Edited by Yamagishi Tokuhei 山岸徳平 and Takahashi Teiichi 高橋貞. Toyohashi 豊橋: Mikan kokubun shiryō kankokai 未刊国文資料刊行会, 1959.

Hōjōki, Hosshinshū 方丈記, 発心集. By Kamo no Chōmei 鴨長明. In *Shin Nihon koten zenshū* 新日本古典全集, edited by Miki Sumito 三木紀人. Tokyo: Shinchōsha 新潮社, 1976.

Honchō seiki 本朝世紀. Vol. 9 of *Shintei zōho kokushi taikei* 新訂増補国史大系. Tokyo: Yoshikawa kōbunkan 吉川弘文館, 1935.

Hōnen Shōnin eden 法然上人絵伝. Vols. 1–3 of *Zoku Nihon no emaki* 続日本の絵巻, edited by Komatsu Shigemi 小松茂美. Tokyo: Chūō kōronsha 中央公論社, 1990.

Hōryūji bettō ki 法隆寺別当記. In *Honin bu* 補任部, vol. 4.2 of *Zoku gunsho ruijū* 続群書類従, 789–835. Tokyo: Zoku gunsho ruijū kanseikai 続群書類従完成会, 1958.

Hōsōki 峰相記. In *Sekke bu* 釈家部. Vol. 28.1 of *Zoku gunsho ruijū* 続群書類従, 217–253. Tokyo: Zoku gunsho ruijū kanseikai 続群書類従完成会, 1959.

Hossō shiyōshō 法曹至要抄. In *Kanshiki bu, Ritsuryō bu, Kuji bu* 官職部 律令部 公事部 (1), vol. 4 of *Shinkō gunsho ruijū* 新校群書類従, 164–211. Tokyo: Naigai shoseki kabushiki kaisha 経済雑誌社, 1928–1937.

Hyakurenshō 百練抄. Vol. 11 of *Shintei zōho kokushi taikei* 新訂増補国史大系. Tokyo: Yoshikawa kōbunkan 吉川弘文館, 1965.

Idanshō 医談抄. By Koremune Tomotoshi 惟宗具俊. In *Idanshō* 医談抄. Edited by Minobe Shigekatsu 美濃部重克. Vol 22 of *Denjō bungaku shiryō shūsei* 伝承文学資料集成. Tokyo: Miyai shoten 三弥井書店, 2006.

Ihon yamai no sōshi 異本病草紙. In *Zuroku Nihon iji bunka shiryō shūsei* 図録日本医事文化資料集成, 1: 105–142. Edited by Nihon ishi gakkai 日本医史学会. Tokyo: San'ichi shobō 三一書房, 1978.

Ihon yamai no sōshi 異本病草紙. As *Kishitsu emaki* 奇疾絵巻 in *Tan'yū Shukuzu* 探幽縮図, edited by Kyoto kokuritsu habutsukan 京都国立博物館, 79–93. Kyoto 京都: Dōmeisha 同朋社, 1980.

Ilbon haengnok 日本行録. Translated by Murai Shōsuke 村井章. In *Rōshōdō Nihon gyōroku* 老松堂日本行録. Tokyo: Iwanami shoten 岩波書店, 1987.

Iken jūnikajō 意見十二箇条. In *Zatsubu* 雑部, vol. 17 of *Gunsho ruijū* 群書類従, 115–128. Tokyo: Keizai zasshisha 経済雑誌社, 1893–1894.

Ippen hijiri e 一遍聖絵. Edited by Mochizuki Nobunari 望月信成. Vol. 10 of *Nihon emakimono zenshū* 日本巻物全集. Tokyo: Kadokawa shoten, 角川書店, 1960.

Ippen shōnin eden 一遍聖人絵伝. Vol. 27 of *Nihon emaki taisei* 日本絵巻大成, edited by Komatsu Shigemi 小松茂実. Tokyo: Chūō kōronsha 中央公論社, 1978.

Ippen shōnin eden 一遍上人絵伝. Vol. 20 of *Nihon no emaki* 日本の絵巻, edited by Komatsu Shigemi 小松茂美. Tokyo: Chūō kōronsha 中央公論社, 1988.

Ishinpō 医心方. By Tanba Yasuyori. In C. H. Hsia, Ilza Veith, and Robert H. Geertsma, *The Essentials of Medicine in Ancient China and Japan, Yasuyori Tamba's Ishimpo*. Leiden: E. J. Brill, 1986.

Ishinpō 医心方. By Tanba Yasuyori. In *The Tao of Sex: An Annotated Translation of the Twenty–Eighth Section of the Essence of Medical Prescriptions* (*Ishinpo*), translated by Howard Levy and Akira Ishihara. Yokohama 横浜: Shibundō 至文堂, 1968.

Jie daisōjō den 慈恵大僧正伝. In *Honin bu* 補任部. Vol. 4 of *Gunsho ruijū* 群書類従. Tokyo: Keizai zasshisha 経済雑誌社, 1898.

Jigoku zōshi 地獄草子. In *Gaki zōshi, Jigoku zōshi, Yamai no sōshi, Kuzōshi emaki* 餓鬼草紙, 地獄草子, 病草紙, 九相紙絵

巻. Vol. 7 of *Nihon emaki taisei* 日本絵巻大成, edited by Komatsu Shigemi 小松茂実. Tokyo: Chūō kōronsha 中央公論社, 1976.

Jigoku zōshi 地獄草子. In *Jigoku zōshi, Gaki zōshi, Yamai no sōshi* 餓鬼草紙, 地獄草子, 病草紙. Vol. 7 of *Nihon emakimono zenshū* 日本絵巻全集, edited by Ienaga Saburō 家永三郎. Tokyo: Kadokawa shoten 角川書店, 1958.

Kamakura ibun 鎌倉遺文. Edited by Takeuchi Rizō 竹内理三. 52 vols. Tokyo: Tōkyōdō shuppan 東京堂出版, 1971–1997.

Kamakura nendaiki, buke nendaiki, Kamakura dai nikki 鎌倉年代記、武家年代記、鎌倉大日記. Vol. 51 of *Zōho zoku shiryō taisei* 増補続史料大成, edited by Takeuchi Rizō 竹内理三. Kyoto 京都: Rinsen shoten 臨川書店, 1979.

Kanazawa bunko monjo 金沢文庫文書, Vol. 2. Yokohama: Kanazawa bunko 金沢文庫, 1937.

Kanchūki 勘仲記. By Kadenokōji Kanenaka 勘解由小路兼仲. Vols. 34–36 of *Shiryō taisei* 史料大成. Kyoto 京都: Rinsen shoten 臨川書店, 1965.

Kanemi kyōki 兼見卿記. By Yoshida Kanemi 吉田兼見. *Shiryō sanshū* 史料纂集 edition. Tokyo: Zoku gunsho ruijū kanseikai 続群書類従完成会, 1971.

Kanmon gyoki 看聞御記. By Fushimi no Miya Sadafusa 伏見宮貞成. 2 vols. In *Hoi 2* 補遺 2, *Zoku gunsho ruijū* 続群書類従. 3rd corrected edition. Tokyo: Zoku gunsho ruijū kanseikai 続群書類従完成会, 1958 and 1959.

Kansai hikki 閑際筆記. Vol. 17 of *Nihon zuihitsu taisei* 日本随筆大成. Tokyo: Yoshikawa kōbunkan 吉川弘文館, 1975.

Kasuga gongen genki e 春日権現験記絵. Vol. 15 of *Nihon emakimono zenshū* 日本絵巻物全集, edited by Noma Seiroku 野間清六. Tokyo: Kadokawa shoten 角川書店, 1963.

Kebiishi bunin 検非違使補任. Edited by Miyazaki Yasumitsu 宮崎康充. 2 vols. Tokyo: Zoku gunsho ruijū kanseikai 続群書類従完成会, 1999.

Kemmu shikimoku 建武式目. In *Buke bu* 1 武家部, vol. 17 of *Shinkō gunsho ruijū* 新校群書類従, 380–382. Tokyo: Meisho fukyūkai 名著普及会, 1930.

Kōfukuji bettō sangō keizu 興福寺別当三綱系図. Unpublished facsimile at the Historiographical Institute, University of Tokyo.

Kōfukuji bettō shidai 興福寺別当次第. In *Dai Nihon bukkyō zensho: Kōfukuji sōsho* 大日本仏教全書興福寺叢書, pt. 2: 1–59. Tokyo: Bussho kankōkai 仏書刊行会, 1917.

Kōfukuji ryaku nendaiki 興福寺略年代記. In *Zatsu bu* 雑部, vol. 29.2 of *Zoku gunsho ruijū* 続群書類従, 107–205. Tokyo: Zoku gunsho ruijū kanseikai 続群書類従完成会, 1959.

Kōfukuji sangō bunin 興福寺三綱補任. In *Honin bu* 補任部, vol. 4.2 of *Zoku gunsho ruijū* 続群書類従, 701–788. Tokyo: Zoku gunsho ruijū kanseikai 続群書類従完成会, 1958.

Kokawadera engi 粉河寺縁起. Vol. 5 of *Nihon no emaki* 日本の絵巻, edited by Komatsu Shigemi 小松茂. Tokyo: Chūō kōronsha 中央公論社, 1977.

Kokawadera engi shū 粉河寺縁起集. In *Kokawa chō shi* 粉河町史, 3: 155–230. Tokyo: Kokawa chō shi hensan iinkai 粉川町史編纂委員会, 1988.

Kokon chomonjū 古今著聞集. 3 vols. *Shinchō Nihon koten shūsei* 新潮日本古典集成. Tokyo: Yoshikawa kōbunkan 吉川弘文館, 1985.

Kokon chomonjū 古今著聞集. Vol. 84 of *Nihon koten bungaku taikei* 日本古典文学大系. Tokyo: Iwanami shoten 岩波書店, 1966.

Kokushi bunin 国司補任. 5 vols. Tokyo: Zoku gunsho ruijū kanseikai 続群書類従完成会, 1990.

Kongō busshi Eison kanshingaku shōki 金剛仏子叡尊感心学正気. In *Saidaiji Eison denki shūsei* 西大寺叡尊伝記修正, edited by Nara kokuritsu bunkazai kenkyūjo 奈良国立文化財研究所. Kyoto 京都: Hōzōkan 宝蔵館, 1977.

Konjaku monogatari shū 今昔物語集. Vols. 21–24 of *Nihon koten bungaku zenshū* 日本古典文学全集. Tokyo: Shōgakkan 小学館, 1971.

Konjaku monogatari shū 今昔物語集. Vols. 35–38 of *Nihon koten bungaku zenshū* 日本古典文学全集, edited by Mabuchi

Kazuo 馬淵和夫 and Kunisaki Fumimaro 国東文麿. Tokyo: Shōgakkan 小学館, 1999.

Koryŏsa 高麗史. 3 vols. Seoul: Asea Munhwasa 細亞文化社, 1972.

Koshibagaki zōshi 小柴垣草子. In *Higa emaki Koshibagaki zōshi* 秘画絵巻小柴垣草子. Edited by Hayashi Yoshikazu 林美一 and Richard Lane リチャード・レイン. Tokyo: Kawade shobō shinsha 河出書房新社, 1997.

Maeda hon "Gyokudaku hōten" shihai monjo to sono kenkyū 前田本「玉燭宝典」紙背文書とその研究. Edited by Imae Hiromichi 今江廣道. Tokyo: Zoku gunsho ruijū kanseikai 続群書類従完成会, 2002.

Masukagami 増鏡. Compiled and edited by Tokieda Motoki 時枝誠記 and Kidō Saizō 木藤才蔵. In *Jinnō shōtōki, Masukagami* 神皇正統記 増鏡. Vol. 87 of *Nihon koten bungaku taikei* 日本古典文学体系. Tokyo: Iwanami shoten 岩波書店, 1961.

Mataga ke monjo 俣賀家文書. Kyoto: Hanazono University Media and Information Center 1995.

Matsuratō Ariura monjo 松浦党有浦文書. Edited by Fukuda Ikuo 福田郁夫 and Murai Shōsuke 村井章介. Osaka 大阪: Seibundō 清文堂出版, 2001.

Matsuratō kankei shiryōshū 松浦黨關係資料集. 3 vols. Edited by Seno Seiichirō 瀬野精一郎. Tokyo: Zoku gunsho ruijū kanseikai 続群書類従完成会, 1996–2004.

Matsuratō shoke monjo 松浦党諸家文書. Edited by Seno Seiichirō 瀬野精一郎. Fukuoka 福岡: Kyūshū shiryō kankōkai 九州史料刊行会, 1958.

Meigetsuki 明月記. By Fujiwara Sadaie 藤原低定家. Tokyo: Kokusho kanko kai 国書刊行会, 1911–1912.

Meigetsuki 明月記. In *Kundoku meigetsuki* 訓読明月記. Edited by Imagawa Fumio 今川文雄. Tokyo: Kawade shobō shinsha 河出書房新社, 1978.

Mineaiki 峰相記. In *Hyōgo kenshi shiryōhen chūsei* 4 兵庫県史史料編中世 4. Edited by Hyōgo kenshi henshū senmon iinkai 兵庫県史編集専門委員会, 36–68. Kobe 神戸: Hyōgo ken 兵庫県, 1991.

Minkeiki 民経記. By Hirohashi Tsunemitsu 廣橋經光. 9 vols. to date. *Dai Nihon kokiroku* 大日本古記録. Tokyo: Iwanami shoten 岩波書店, 1975–.

Moromori ki 師守記. By Nakahara Moromori 中原師守. Vol 8. Tokyo: Zoku gunsho ruijū kanseikai 続群書類従完成会, 1968–1982.

Mutsuwaki 陸奥話記. In *Kassen bu 1* 合戦部, vol. 20 of *Shinkō gunsho ruijū* 新校群書類従, 33–48. Tokyo: Zoku gunsho ruijū kanseikai 続群書類従完成会, 1941.

Nanbokuchō ibun Chūgoku Shikoku hen (NBI-Ch) 南北朝遺文中国四国編. 6 vols. Edited by Matsuoka Hisato 松岡久人. Tokyo: Tōkyōdō shuppan 東京堂出版, 1987–1995.

Nanbokuchō ibun Kantō hen (NBI-Ka) 南北朝遺文関東編. 3 vols. to date. Edited by Satō Kazuhiko 佐藤和彦, Itō Kazuhiko 伊東和彦, Yamada Kuniaki 山田邦明, Tsunoda Tomohiko 角田朋彦, Shimizu Ryō 清水亮. Tokyo: Tōkyōdō shuppan 東京堂出版, 2007–.

Nanbokuchō ibun Kyūshū hen (NBI-Ky) 南北朝遺文九州編. 7 vols. Edited by Seno Seiichirō 瀬野精一郎. Tokyo: Tōkyōdō shuppan 東京堂出版, 1985–1992.

Nanbokuchō ibun Tōhoku hen (NBI-To) 南北朝遺文東北編. 1 vol. to date. Edited by Ōishi Naomasa 大石直正 and Nanami Masato 七海雅人. Tokyo: Tōkyōdō shuppan 東京堂出版, 2008–.

Nanto daishū jurakuki 南都大衆入洛記. In *Zatsu bu* 雑部, vol. 29.2 of *Zoku gunsho ruijū* 続群書類従, 325–329. Tokyo: Zoku gunsho ruijū kanseikai 続群書類従完成会, 1959.

Nenchū gyōji emaki 年中行事絵巻. Vol. 24 of *Nihon emakimono zenshū* 日本絵巻全集, edited by Fukayama Toshio 福山敏男. Tokyo: Kadokawa shoten 角川書店, 1968.

Nihon kiryaku 日本記略. Vols. 10–11 of *Shintei zōho kokushi taikei* 新訂増補国史大系. Tokyo: Yoshikawa kōbunkan 吉川弘文館, 1968.

Nihon kōki 日本後記. Vol. 3 of *Shintei zōho kokushi taikei* 新訂増補国史大系. Tokyo: Yoshikawa kōbunkan 吉川弘文館, 1984.

Nihon sandai jitsuroku 日本三代実録. Vol. 4 of *Shintei zōho kokushi taikei* 新訂増補国史大系. Tokyo: Yoshikawa kōbunkan 吉川弘文館, 1986.

Nihon shoki 日本書紀. Vol. 1 of *Shintei zōho kokushi taikei* 新訂増補国史大系. Tokyo: Yoshikawa kōbunkan 吉川弘文館, 1985.

Obusuma Saburō ekotoba 男衾三郎絵詞. In *Obusuma Saburō ekotoba—Ise shinmeisho eutaawase* 男衾三郎絵詞・伊勢新名所絵歌合. Vol. 18 of *Zoku Nihon no emaki* 続日本の絵巻, edited by Komatsu Shigemi 小松茂美. Tokyo: Chūō kōronsha 中央公論社, 1992.

Ōkagami 大鏡. Vol. 21 of *Nihon koten bungaku taikei* 日本古典文学大系, edited by Matsumura Hiroji 松村博司. Tokyo: Iwanami shoten, 1960.

Ruijū kokushi 類聚国史. Vols. 5–6 of *Shintei zōho kokushi taikei* 新訂増補国史大系. Tokyo: Yoshikawa kōbunkan 吉川弘文館, 1986.

Ruijū mojishō 類集文字抄. In *Zatsu bu* 雑部, vol. 30.2 of *Zoku gunsho ruijū* 続群書類従, 316–334. Tokyo: Zoku gunsho ruijū kanseikai 続群書類従完成会, 1959.

Ruijū sandai kyaku 類聚三代格. Vol. 25 of *Shintei zōho kokushi taikei* 新訂増補国史大系. Tokyo: Yoshikawa kōbunkan 吉川弘文館, 1968.

Saga ken shiryō shūsei 佐賀県史料集成. Saga 佐賀: Saga kenshi hensan iinkai 佐賀県史編纂委員会, 1955.

Sanetaka kyōki 實隆卿記. By Sanjōnishi Sanetaka 三条西實隆. 9 vols. plus 4 vols. Tokyo: Zoku gunsho ruijū kanseikai 続群書類従完成会, 1931–1963.

Sangō shiiki, Shōryōshū 三教指歸・性靈集. By Kūkai 空海. Vol. 71 of *Nihon koten bungaku taikei* 日本古典文学大系, edited by Watanabe Shōkō 渡邊照宏 and Miyasaka Yūshō 宮坂宥勝. Tokyo: Iwanami shoten 岩波書店, 1965.

Sanemi kyōki 實躬卿記. By Sanjō Sanemi 三条實躬. 5 vols. to date. *Dai Nihon kokiroku* 大日本古記録. Tokyo: Iwanami shoten 岩波書店, 1991–.

Satsujōshū 撮壤集. By Inoo Tametomo 飯尾為相. In *Zatsu bu* 雑
　　部, vol. 30.2 of *Zoku gunsho ruijū* 続群書類従, 286–315.
　　Tokyo: Zoku gunsho ruijū kansei kai 続群書類従完成会,
　　1959.

Sejong sillok 世宗實錄. In *Chosŏn wangjo sillok* 朝鮮王朝實錄.
　　Seoul: Kuksa p'yŏnch'an wiwŏnhoe 国史編纂委員会,
　　1969–1972.

Shasekishū 沙石集. By Mujū Ichien 無住一円. Vol. 85 of *Nihon
　　koten bungaku taikei* 日本古典文学大系, edited by
　　Watanabe Tsunaya 渡辺綱也. Tokyo: Iwanami shoten 岩波
　　書店, 1960.

Shigisan engi 信貴山縁起. Vol. 4 of *Nihon emaki taisei* 日本絵巻
　　大成, edited by Komatsu Shigemi 小松茂実. Tokyo: Chūō
　　kōronsha 中央公論社, 1977.

Shinsarugaku ki 新猿楽記. By Fujiwara Akihira 藤原明衡. In *Kodai
　　seiji shakai shisō* 古代政治社会思想. Vol. 8 of *Nihon shisō
　　taikei* 日本思想体系. Tokyo: Iwanami shoten 岩波書店,
　　1986.

Shinsen Yamai no sōshi 新選病草紙. In *Zuroku Nihon iji bunka
　　shiryō shūsei* 図録日本医事文化資料集成, vol. 1. Edited
　　by Nihon ishi gakkai 日本医史学会, 177–193. Tokyo:
　　San'ichi shobō 三一書房, 1978.

Shinsen Yamai no sōshi 新選病草紙. In *Kyōrin sōsho* 杏林叢書, vol.
　　1. Edited by Fujikawa Yū 富士川遊 et al., 161–198. Tokyo:
　　Tohōdō shoten 吐鳳堂書店, 1922.

Shinsen Yamai no sōshi 新選病草紙. Online, http://www.library.
　　tohoku.ac.jp/med/d-lib/zoushi/ks-1/flowers.html.

Shoku Nihongi 続日本紀. Vol. 2 of *Shintei zōho kokushi taikei* 新訂
　　増補国史大系. Tokyo: Yoshikawa kōbunkan 吉川弘文館,
　　1986.

Shōmonki 将門記. Edited by Hayashi Rokurō 林陸朗. Vol. 2 of
　　Shinsen Nihon koten bunko 新撰日本古典文庫. Tokyo:
　　Gendai shichōsha 現代思潮社, 1975.

Shunki 春記. By Fujiwara Sukefusa 藤原資房. *Zōho shiryō taisei* 増
　　補史料大成. Kyoto 京都: Rinsen shoten 臨川書店, 1965.

Sochiki 帥記. By Minamoto Tsunenobu 源経信. Vol. 5 of Zōho
　　shiryō taisei 増補史料大成. Kyoto 京都: Rinsen shoten 臨
　　川書店, 1965.

Sōgō bunin 僧綱補任. In *Dai Nihon bukkyō zensho: Kōfukuji sōsho* 大日本仏教全書興福寺叢書, 1:61–288. Tokyo: Bussho kankōkai 仏書刊行会, 1915.

Sonpi bunmyaku 尊卑文脈. Vols. 58–60 of *Shintei zōho kokushi taikei* 新訂増補国史大系. Tokyo: Yoshikawa kōbunkan 吉川弘文館, 1983.

Suisaki 水左紀. By Minamoto Toshifusa 源俊房. Vol. 12 of *Zōho shiryō taisei* 増補史料大成. Kyoto 京都: Rinsen shoten 臨川書店, 1965.

Taiheiki 太平記. In *Jingū chōkokanbon* 神宮微古館本. Edited by Hasegawa Tadashi 長谷川端 et al. Osaka 大阪: Izumi shoin 和泉書院, 1994.

Taiki 台記. By Fujiwara Yorinaga 藤原頼長. Vols. 23–25 of *Zōho shiryō taisei* 増補史料大成. Kyoto 京都: Rinsen shoten 臨川書店, 1965.

Tamefusa kyōki 為房卿記. By Fujiwara Tamefusa 藤原為房. Edited by Komazawa daigaku daigakuin shigakkai kodaishi bukai 駒沢大学大学院史学会古代史部会. *Shishū* 史聚 10 (1979): 67–130.

Tamon'in nikki 多聞院日記. By Eishun 英俊. 6 vols. Edited by Tsuji Zennosuke 辻善之助. Tokyo: Kadokawa shoten 角川書店, 1967.

Tendai zasuki 天台座主記. Edited by Shibuya Jigai 渋谷慈鎧. Tokyo: Daiichi shobō 第一書房, 1973.

Tengu zōshi 天狗草紙. Vol. 19 of *Zoku Nihon emakimono taisei* 続日本絵巻物大成, edited by Komatsu Shigemi 小松茂実. Tokyo: Chūō kōronsha 中央公論社, 1984.

Tettsui den 鐵槌傳. By Fujiwara Akihira 藤原明衡 [Ratai 羅泰]. In Vol. 69 of *Nihon koten bungaku taikei* 日本古典文学大系 *Kaifūsō* 懐風藻, *Bunka shūreishū* 文華秀麗集, *Honchō monzui* 本朝文粋. Edited by Kojima Noriyuki 小島憲之, 429–436. Tokyo: Iwanami shoten 岩波書店, 1960.

Tokitsugu kyōki 言継卿記. By Yamashina Tokitsugu 山科言継. 6 vols. Tokyo: Zoku gunsho ruijū kanseikai 続群書類従完成会, 1998.

Tokitsune kyōki 言経卿記. By Yamashina Tokitsune 山科言経. 14 vols. *Dai Nihon kokiroku* 大日本古記録. Tokyo: Iwanami shoten 岩波書店, 1959–1991.

Ton'ishō 頓医抄. By Kajiwara Shōzen 梶原性全. Tokyo: Kagaku shoin 科学書院, 1986.

Ton'ishō 頓医抄. By Kajiwara Shōzen 梶原性全. Naikaku bunko 内閣文庫 text. Microfilm hard copy held in the Department of the History of Medicine, Oriental Medicine Research Center of the Kitasato Institute 北里研究所東洋医学総合研究所医史学研究部.

Towazugatari とはずがたり. Edited by Misumi Yōichi 三角洋一. In *Towazugatari, Tamakiharu* とはずがたり　たまきはる. Vol 50 of *Shin Nihon koten bungaku taikei* 新日本古典文学大系. Tokyo: Iwanami shoten 岩波書店, 1994.

Towazugatari とはずがたり. Vol. 4 of *Chūsei nikki kikō bungaku zenhyōshaku shūsei* 中世日記紀行文学全評釈集成, edited by Nishizawa Masashi 西沢正史 and Shimegi Miyako 標宮子. Tokyo: Bensei shuppan 勉誠出版, 2000.

Uji shūi monogatari 宇治拾遺物語. Vol. 27 of *Nihon koten bungaku taikei* 日本古典文学大系, edited by Watanabe Tsunaya 渡辺綱也 and Nishio Kōichi 西尾光一. Tokyo: Iwanami shoten 岩波書店, 1960.

Ukiyoburo 浮世風呂. Vol. 63 of *Nihon koten bungaku taikei* 日本古典文学大系, edited by Nakamura Michio 中村通夫. Tokyo: Iwanami shoten 岩波書店, 1960.

Unshū shōsoku 雲洲消息 (alt. *Meigō ōrai* 明衡往来). By Fujiwara Akihira 藤原明衡. In *Shōzoku bu 2, Bunpitsu bu, Shōsoku bu* 装束部　2, 文筆部, 消息部, vol. 6 of *Shinkō gunsho ruijū* 新校群書類従, 519–555. Tokyo: Naigai shoseki kabushiki kaisha 内外書籍株式会社, 1931.

Wakayama kenshi, chūsei shiryō 2 和歌山県史中世史料二. Edited by Wakayama kenshi hensan iinkai 和歌山県史編さん委員会. Wakayama 和歌山, 1983.

Yamai no sōshi 病の草紙. In *Jigoku zōshi, Gaki zōshi, Yamai no sōshi* 地獄草紙　餓鬼草紙　病草紙. Vol. 6 of *Shinshū Nihon emakimono zenshū* 新集日本絵巻物全集. Edited by Ienaga Saburō 家永三郎. Tokyo: Kadokawa shoten 角川書店, 1976.

Yamai no sōshi 病の草紙. In *Gaki zōshi, Jigoku zōshi, Yamai no sōshi, Kuzōshi emaki*, 餓鬼草紙 地獄草紙 病草紙 九相死絵巻. Vol. 7 of *Nihon emaki taisei* 日本絵巻大成, edited by Komatsu Shigemi 小松茂. Tokyo: Chūō kōronsha 中央公論社, 1977.

Yōkōki 葉黄記 By Hamuro Sadatsugu 葉室定嗣. 2 vols. Edited by Kikuchi Yasuaki 菊地康明 et al. Tokyo: Zoku gunsho ruijū kanseikai 続群書類従完成会, 1971–2004.

Yūgyō shōnin engi e 游行上人縁起絵. Vol. 23 of *Nihon emaki zenshū* 日本絵巻全集, edited by Miya Tsuguo 宮次男. Tokyo: Kadokawa shoten 角川書店, 1968.

Zōho teisei hennen Ōtomo shiryō 増補訂正編年大友資料. 33 vols. Edited by Takita Manabu 田北學. Ōita 大分: Takita Manabu 田北學, 1962–71.

Zoku kojidan 続古事談. In *Zatsubu* 3, vol. 27 of *Shinkō gunsho ruijū* 新校群書類従, 344–392. Tokyo: Naigai shoseki 内外書籍, 1930.

Zōtei Kamakura bakufu saikyojō shū 増訂鎌倉幕府裁許状集. Second edition. 2 vols. Edited by Seno Seiichirō 瀬野精一郎. Tokyo: Yoshikawa kōbunkan 吉川弘文館, 1994.

Secondary Sources

Abe, Ryūichi. "Swords, Words, and Deformity: On Myōe's Eccentricity." In *Discourse and Ideology in Medieval Japanese Buddhism*, edited by Richard K. Payne and Taigen Dan Leighton, 148–159. London: Routledge, 2006.

Adolphson, Mikael S. "Enryakuji: An Old Power in a New Era." In *The Origins of Japan's Medieval World: Courtiers, Clerics, Warriors, and Peasants in the Fourteenth Century*, edited by Jeffrey P. Mass, 237–260. Stanford, CA: Stanford University Press, 1997.

———. *The Gates of Power: Monks, Courtiers and Warriors in Premodern Japan*. Honolulu: University of Hawai'i Press, 2000.

————. *The Teeth and Claws of the Buddha: Monastic Warriors and* Sōhei *in Japanese History*. Honolulu: University of Hawai'i Press, 2007.

Adolphson, Mikael S., Edward Kamens, and Stacie Matsumoto, eds. *Heian Japan, Centers and Peripheries*. Honolulu: University of Hawai'i Press, 2007.

Akutagawa Tetsuo 芥川哲夫. "Nihon ni okeru bakufu tairitsu no seiritsu 日本における幕府対立の成立." In *Ōita kenshi chūsei 1*, 大分県史中世 1, edited by Ōita-ken sōmubu sōmuka 大分県総務部総務課, 1–63. Ōita 大分: Ōita ken 大分県, 1982.

Amino Yoshihiko 網野善彦. "Chūsei mibunsei no ichi kōsatsu: chūsei zenki no hinin o chūshin ni 中世身分制の一考察— 中世前期の非人を中心に." *Rekishi to chiri* 歴史と地理, 289 (1979): 1–19.

————. *Chūsei no hinin to yūjo* 中世の非人と遊女. Tokyo: Akashi shoten 明石書店, 1994.

————. *Chūseiteki sekai to wa nandarō ka* 中世的世界とは何だろうか. Tokyo: Asahi shinbunsha 朝日新聞社 1996.

————. "Commerce and Finance in the Middle Ages: The Beginnings of Capitalism" *Acta Asiatica* 81 (2001): 1–19.

————. "Deconstructing 'Japan.'" *East Asian History* 3 (1992): 121–142.

————. *Igyō no ōken* 異形の王権. Tokyo: Heibonsha 平凡社, 1986.

————. "Kodai, chūsei, kinsei shoki no gyogyō to kaisanbutsu no ryūtsū 古代中世近世初期の漁業と海産物の流通." In *Kōza Nihon gijutsu no shakaishi 2 engyō gyogyō* 講座日本技術の社会史 2 塩業漁業, edited by Nagahara Keiji 長原慶二 and Yamaguchi Keiji 山口啓二, 197–271. Tokyo: Nihon hyōronsha 日本評論者, 1983.

————. "Kodai, chūsei no Hiden'in wo megutte 古代中世の悲田院をめぐって." In *Chūsei shakai to ikkō ikki* 中世社会と一向一揆, edited by Kitanishi Hiromu Sensei kanreki kinenkai 北西弘先生還暦記念会. Tokyo: Yoshikawa kōbunkan吉川弘文館, 1985.

————. "Le Moyen Age Japonaise." *Cipango* 3 (1994): 125–170.

————. *Muen, kugai, raku: Nihon chūsei no jiyū to heiwa* 無縁・公界・楽—日本中世の自由と平和. Tokyo: Heibonsha 平凡社, 1978; expanded edition, 1987.

————. "Nihon chūsei ni okeru kaimin no sonzai keitai 日本中世における海民の存在形態." *Shakai keizai shigaku* 社会経済史学 36, no. 5 (1971): 1–26.

————. *Nihon chūsei no hinōgyōmin to tennō* 日本中世の非農業民と天皇. Tokyo: Iwanami shoten 岩波書店, 1984.

————. *Nihon chūsei no hyakushō to shokunōmin* 日本中世の百姓と職能民. Tokyo: Heibonsha 平凡社, 1998.

————. "Nihon no moji shakai no tokushitsu o megutte 日本の文字社会の特質をめぐって." *Rettō no bunkashi* 列島の文化史 5 (1988): 19–57.

————. "Some Problems Concerning the History of Popular Life in Medieval Japan." *Acta Asiatica* 44 (1983): 77–97.

————. "Ukai to katsurame 鵜飼と桂女." In *Nihon chūsei no hinōgyōmin to tennō* 日本中世の非農業民と天皇, 392–430. Iwanami shoten 岩波書店, 1984.

Aoki, Masahiko. *Toward A Comparative Institutional Analysis.* Cambridge, MA: MIT Press, 2001.

Aoyama Kōryō 青山公亮. *Nichi-Rai kōshōshi no kenkyū* 日麗交渉史の研究. Tokyo: Meiji daigaku bungakubu bungaku kenkyujo 明治大学文学部文学研究所, 1955.

Arnesen, Peter. "The Struggle for Lordship in Late Heian Japan: The Case of Aki." *Journal of Japanese Studies* 10, no. 1 (1984): 101–141.

————. "Suō Province in the Age of Kamakura." In *Court and Bakufu in Japan: Essays in Kamakura History*, edited by Jeffrey P. Mass, 92–120. New Haven, CT: Yale University Press, 1982.

————. *The Medieval Japanese Daimyo: The Ōuchi Family's Rule of Suō and Nagato.* New Haven, CT: Yale University Press, 1979.

Arntzen, Sonja. *Ikkyū and the Crazy Cloud Anthology.* Tokyo: University of Tokyo Press, 1986.

Asakawa, Kan'ichi. *Land and Society in Medieval Japan*. Edited by Committee for the Publication of Dr. K. Asakawa's Works. Tokyo: Japan Society for the Promotion of Science, 1965.

Ashikari Seiji 芦刈政治. "Tōgoku bushidan no tōchaku to hatten 東国武士団の到着と発展." In *Ōita kenshi, chūsei 1*, 大分県史中世, 1, edited by Ōitaken sōmubu sōmuka 大分県総務部総務課, 63–171. Ōita 大分: Ōita ken 大分県, 1982.

Aston, W.G. *Nihongi: Chronicles of Japan from the Earliest Times to 697 AD*. Rutland, VT.: Charles E. Tuttle, 1972.

Bal, Mieke. *Lethal Love: Feminist Literary Readings of Biblical Love Stories*. Bloomington: Indiana University Press, 1987.

Batten, Bruce L. "Cross-Border Traffic on the Kyushu Coast, 794–1086." In *Heian Japan, Centers and Peripheries*, edited by Mikael S. Adolphson, Edward Kamens, and Stacie Matsumoto, 357–383. Honolulu: University of Hawai'i Press, 2007.

———. "Documentary Evidence for Institutional Change at the Dazaifu, 1000–1185." *Kokusai bunka kenkyū (Obirin University)* 国際文化研究 (桜美林大学), no. 113 (1990): 23–60.

———. "Foreign Threat and Domestic Reform: The Emergence of the Ritsuryō State." *Monumenta Nipponica* 41, no. 22 (Summer 1986): 199–219.

———. *Gateway to Japan: Hakata in War and Peace, 500–1300*. Honolulu: University of Hawai'i Press, 2006.

———. *To the Ends of Japan: Premodern Frontiers, Boundaries, and Interactions*. Honolulu: University of Hawai'i Press, 2003.

———. *Kokkyo no tanjō: Dazaifu kara mita Nihon no genkei* 国境の誕生 大宰府から見た日本の原形. Vol. 922. NHK bukkusu NHKブックス. Tokyo: Nihon hōsō shuppan kyōkai 日本放送出版協会, 2001.

Beasley, W. G. *The Japanese Experience: A Short History of Japan*. Berkeley and Los Angeles: University of California Press, 1999.

Bock, Felicia, trans. *Engi–Shiki: Procedures of the Engi Era*. Tokyo: Monumenta Nipponica, 1970.

Borgen, Robert. "Jōjin's Travels from Center to Center (with Some Periphery in Between)." In *Heian Japan, Centers and Peripheries*, edited by Mikael S. Adolphson, Edward Kamens, and Stacie Matsumoto, 384–413. Honolulu: University of Hawai'i Press, 2007.

Brandt, R.B. "Utilitiarianism and the Rules of War." In *War and Moral Responsibility*, edited by Marshall Cohen, Thomas Nagel, and Thomas Scanlon, 25–45. Princeton, NJ: Princeton University Press, 1974.

Brazell. Karen. "The Changing of the Shogun 1289: An Excerpt from *Towazugatari*." *The Journal of the Association of Teachers of Japanese* 8, no.1 (1972): 58–65.

———, trans. *The Confessions of Lady Nijō*. Stanford, CA: Stanford University Press, 1973.

Brown, Delmer. *Money Economy in Medieval Japan*. New Haven, CT: Institute of Far Eastern Languages, 1951.

———. "The Japanese Tokusei of 1297." *Harvard Journal of Asiatic Studies* 12 (June 1949): 188–206.

Brown, R. Allen. *Origins of English Feudalism*. London: George Allen & Unwin, 1973.

Brunner, Otto. *Land and Lordship: Structures of Governance in Medieval Austria*. Translated by Howard Kaminsky and James Van Horn Melton. 4th revised edition. Philadelphia: University of Pennsylvania Press, 1992.

Buraku mondai kenkyūjo 部落問題研究所, ed. *Burakushi shiryō senshū* 部落史料選集. 3 vols. Kyoto 京都: Buraku mondai kenkyūjo 部落問題研究所, 1988–1989.

Butler, Kenneth D. "The Heike Monogatari and the Japanese Warrior Ethic." *Harvard Journal of Asiatic Studies* 29 (1969): 93–108.

———. "The Textual Evolution of the Heike Monogatari." *Harvard Journal of Asiatic Studies* 26 (1966): 5–51.

Butler, Lee. "Washing Off the Dust: Baths and Bathing in Late Medieval Japan." *Monumenta Nipponica* 60, no. 1 (Spring 2005): 1–41.

Caron, François and Joost Schouten. *A True Description of the Mighty Kingdoms of Japan and Siam*. London: Argonaut Press, 1935.

Cheyette, Frederic. *Lordship and Community in Medieval Europe*. Huntington, NY: Robert E. Krieger Publishing Company, 1968. Reprint, 1975.

Chijiwa Itaru 千々和到. "Kishōmon kenkyū nōto 起請文研究ノート." *Jinmin no rekishigaku* 人民の歴史学 78 (1984).

Childs, Margaret. "Didacticism in Medieval Short Stories: *Hatsuse monogatari* and *Akimichi*." *Monumenta Nipponica* 42, no. 3 (Autumn 1987): 253–288.

———. *Rethinking Sorrow*. Ann Arbor: University of Michigan Center for Japanese Studies, 1991.

Chin, Gail. "The Gender of Buddhist Truth: The Female Corpse in a Group of Buddhist Paintings." *Japanese Journal of Religious Studies* 25, nos. 3–4 (1998): 277–317.

Clanchy, M. T. *From Memory to Written Record in England 1066–1307*. 2nd ed. Oxford: Blackwell Publishers, 1993.

Collcutt, Martin. *Five Mountains: The Rinzai Zen Monastic Institution in Medieval Japan*. Cambridge, MA: Harvard University Press, 1981.

Conlan, Thomas D. *In Little Need of Divine Intervention: Takezaki Suenaga's Scrolls of the Mongol Invasions of Japan*. Ithaca, NY: East Asia Program, Cornell University, 2001.

———. "Largesse and the Limits of Loyalty in the Fourteenth Century." In *The Origins of Japan's Medieval World*, edited by Jeffrey P. Mass, 39–64. Stanford, CA: Stanford University Press, 1997.

———. "State of War: The Violent Order of Fourteenth Century Japan." Doctoral dissertation, Stanford University, 1998.

———. *State of War: The Violent Order of Fourteenth Century Japan*. Ann Arbor: University of Michigan Center for Japanese Studies, 2003.

———. "The Nature of Warfare in Fourteenth-Century Japan: The Record of Nomoto Tomoyuki." *Journal of Japanese Studies* 25, no. 2 (1999): 299–330.

————. "Thicker Than Blood: The Social and Political Significance of Wet Nurses in Japan, 950–1330." *Harvard Journal of Asiatic Studies* 65, no. 1 (2005): 159–205.

Cooper, Michael. *They Came to Japan*. Berkeley, CA: University of California Press, 1965.

Coulborn, Rushton, ed. *Feudalism in History*. Princeton, NJ: Princeton University Press, 1956.

Covell, Jon Carter. *Untangling Zen's Red Thread*. New Jersey and Seoul: Hollym International Corporation, 1980.

Denoon, Donald, Mark Hudson, Gavan McCormack, and Tessa Morris Suzuki, eds. *Multicultural Japan: Palaeolithic to Postmodern*. Cambridge: Cambridge University Press, 1996.

Derrida, Jacques. "Plato's Pharmacy." Translated by Barbara Johnson. In *Dissemination*. Chicago: University of Chicago Press, 1981.

Duby, Georges. *The Chivalrous Society*. Translated by Cynthia Postan. Berkeley, CA: University of California Press.

Elshtain, Jean Bethke. *Public Man, Private Woman: Women in Social and Political Thought*. Princeton, NJ: Princeton University Press, 1981.

Elvin, Mark. *The Pattern of the Chinese Past*. Stanford, CA: Stanford University Press, 1973.

Farris, William Wayne. "Diseases of the Premodern Period in Japan, 500–1600." In *The Cambridge History and Geography of Human Disease*, edited by Kenneth Kiple, 376–385. Cambridge: Cambridge University Press, 1993.

————. *Heavenly Warriors: The Evolution of Japan's Military, 500–1300*, Cambridge, MA: Council on East Asian Studies, Harvard University, 1992.

————. *Japan's Medieval Population: Famine, Fertility and Warfare in a Transformative Age*. Honolulu: University of Hawai'i Press, 2006.

————. "Japan to 1300." In *War and Society in the Ancient and Medieval Worlds: Asia, the Mediterranean, Europe, and Mesoamerica*, edited by Kurt Raaflaub and Nathan Rosenstein, 47–70. Cambridge, MA: Center for Hellenic Studies, Harvard University, 1999.

————. *Population, Disease and Land in Japan, 600–900.*
Cambridge, MA: Harvard University Press, 1985.

————. "Trade, Money, and Merchants in Nara Japan." *Monumenta Nipponica* 53, no. 3 (Autumn 1998): 303–334.

Friday, Karl. *Hired Swords: The Rise of Private Warrior Power in Early Japan.* Stanford, CA: Stanford University Press, 1992.

————. "Lordship Interdicted: Taira Tadatsune and the Limited Horizons of Warrior Ambition." In *Heian Japan, Centers and Peripheries*, edited by Mikael Adolphson, Edward Kamens, and Stacie Matsumoto, 329–56. Honolulu: University of Hawai'i Press, 2007.

————. "Mononofu: The Warrior of Heian Japan." MA thesis, University of Kansas, 1983.

————. "Pushing Beyond the Pale: The Yamato Conquest of the Emishi and Northern Japan." *Journal of Japanese Studies* 23, no. 1 (1997): 1–24.

————. *Samurai, Warfare & the State in Early Medieval Japan.* London: Routledge, 2004.

————. "Valorous Butchers: The Art of War During the Golden Age of the Samurai." *Japan Forum* 5, no. 1 (1993): 1–19.

Frois, Luis. "*Nichiō bunka hikaku* 日欧文化比較." In *Taikōkai jidai sōsho* 大航海時代叢書, vol. 11. Translated by Okada Akio 岡田章雄. Tokyo: Iwanami shoten 岩波書店, 1965.

Fujikawa Yū. *Japanese Medicine.* Translated by John Runrah. Reprint, New York: AMS Press, 1978.

Fujiki Hisashi 藤木久志. *Zōhyōtachi no senjō* 雑兵たちの戦場. Tokyo: Asahi shinbunsha 朝日新聞社, 1995.

Fujinami Kōichi 藤浪剛一. "Emakimono shosai no yamai ni kansuru ishigaku teki kōsatsu 絵巻物所載の病に関する医史学的考察 (1)." *Nihon ishigaku zasshi* 日本医史学雑誌, 1275 (1939): 1–19.

————. "Emakimono shosai no yamai ni kansuru ishigaku teki kōsatsu 絵巻物所載の病に関する医史学的考察 (2)." *Nihon ishigaku zasshi* 日本医史学雑誌, 1276 (1939): 69–75.

Fujino Yutaka 藤野豊, ed. *Rekishi no naka no "raija"* 歴史のなかの
「癩病」. Tokyo: Yumiru shuppan ゆみる出版, 1996.

Fujiwara Yoshiaki 藤原良章. "Chūsei zenki no byōja to kyūzai 中世
前期の病者と救済." In his *Chūseiteki shii to sono shakai*
中世的思惟とその社会, 111–143. Tokyo: Yoshikawa
kōbunkan 吉川弘文間, 1997.

Ganshof, Eric. *Feudalism*. New York: Harper, 1961.

Gay, Suzanne. *The Moneylenders of Late Medieval Kyoto.* Honolulu:
University of Hawai'i Press, 2001.

Gernet, Jacques. *A History of Chinese Civilization*. Translated by
J. R. Foster and Charles Hartman. Cambridge: Cambridge
University Press, 1982.

Gill, Robin D., trans. *Topsy-turvy 1585*. Key Biscayne, FL: Paraverse
Press, 2004.

Goble, Andrew Edmund. "Kajiwara Shōzen (1265–1337) and the
Medical Silk Road: Chinese and Arabic Influences on
Medieval Japanese Medicine." In *Tools of Culture: Japan's
Cultural, Intellectual, Medical, and Technological Contacts
in East Asia, 1000s–1500s*, edited by Andrew Edmund
Goble, Kenneth R. Robinson, and Haruko Wakabayashi,
231–257. Ann Arbor: Association for Asian Studies, 2009.

———. *Kenmu: Go-Daigo's Revolution*. Cambridge, MA: Council
on East Asian Studies, Harvard University, 1996.

———. "Medicine and New Knowledge in Medieval Japan:
Kajiwara Shōzen (1266–1337) and the *Man'anpō* (1)."
Nihon ishigaku zasshi 日本医史学雑誌 47, no. 1 (2001):
193–226.

———. "Medicine and New Knowledge in Medieval Japan:
Kajiwara Shōzen (1266–1337) and the *Man'anpō* (2)."
Nihon ishigaku zasshi 日本医史学雑誌 47, no. 2 (2001):
452–432.

———. "Medieval Japan." In *A Companion to Japanese History*,
edited by William M. Tsutsui, 47–66. Oxford: Blackwell
Publications, 2007.

———. "Nichiren Calming Karma: Fear, Sickness and Lotus Unto
Death." In *Deep Hearing in Buddhism and Psychotherapy*,

edited by Richard K. Payne and Mark T. Unno (forthcoming, Boston: Wisdom Publications, 2010).

———. "Visions of an Emperor." In *The Origins of Japan's Medieval World: Courtiers, Clerics, Warriors, and Peasants in the Fourteenth Century*, edited by Jeffrey P. Mass, 113–137. Stanford, CA: Stanford University Press, 1997.

———. "War and Injury: The Emergence of Wound Medicine in Medieval Japan." *Monumenta Nipponica* 60, no. 3 (Autumn 2005): 297–338.

Goble, Andrew Edmund, Kenneth R. Robinson, and Haruko Wakabayashi, eds. *Tools of Culture: Japan's Cultural, Intellectual, Medical, and Technological Contacts in East Asia, 1000s–1500s*. Ann Arbor: Association for Asian Studies, 2009.

Gomi Fumihiko 五味文彦. *Chūsei no kotoba to e* 中世の言葉と絵. Tokyo: Chūkō shinsho 中公新書, 1990.

———. *Zōho Azuma Kagami no hōhō: jijitsu to shinwa ni miru chūsei* 増補吾妻鏡の方法—事実と神話にみる中世. Tokyo: Yoshikawa kōbunkan 吉川弘文館, 2000.

Gomi Katsuo 五味克夫. "Kamakura gokenin no ban'yaku kinshi ni tsuite (1) 鎌倉御家人の番役勤仕について." *Shigaku zasshi* 史学雑誌 63, no. 9 (1954): 28–46.

———. "Kamakura gokenin no ban'yaku kinshi ni tsuite (2) 鎌倉御家人の番役勤仕について." *Shigaku zasshi* 史学雑誌 63, no. 10 (1954): 22–34.

Goodwin, Janet R. *Alms and Vagabonds: Buddhist Temples and Popular Patronage in Medieval Japan*. Honolulu: University of Hawai'i Press, 1994.

———. "The Buddhist Monarch: Go-Shirakawa and the Rebuilding of Tōdaiji." *Japanese Journal of Religious Studies* 17, nos. 2–3 (1990): 219–242.

———. *Selling Songs and Smiles: The Sex Trade in Heian and Kamakura Japan*. Honolulu: University of Hawai'i Press, 2007.

Gosho Translation Committee, ed. *The Writings of Nichiren Daishōnin*. Tokyo: Soka Gakkai, 1999.

Greif, Avner. "Cultural Beliefs and the Organization of Society: A Historical and Theoretical Reflection on Collectivist and Individualist Societies." *Journal of Political Economy* 102, no. 5 (1994): 912–950, as cited in Masahiko Aoki, *Toward a Comparative Institutional Analysis* (Cambridge, MA: MIT Press, 2001).

Groemer, Gerald. "Creation of the Edo Outcaste Order." *Journal of Japanese Studies* 27, no. 2 (2001): 263–293.

Groner, Paul. *Ryōgen and Mt. Hiei: Japanese Tendai in the Tenth Century*. Honolulu: University of Hawai'i Press, 2002.

Grossberg, Kenneth A. *The Laws of the Muromachi Bakufu*. Tokyo: Monumenta Nipponica Monographs, 1981.

Hall, John W. *Government and Local Power in Japan 500–1700: A Study Based on Bizen Province*. Princeton, NJ: Princeton University Press, 1966.

———. *Japan: From Prehistory to Modern Times*. New York: Dell, 1970.

Hall, John W. and Jeffrey P. Mass, eds. *Medieval Japan: Essays in Institutional History*. New Haven, CT: Yale University Press 1974.

Hall, Kenneth. "Coinage, Trade, and Economy in South India and its Bay of Bengal Neighbors." *The Indian Economic and Social History Review* 36, no. 4 (1999): 431–459.

Hanada Yūkichi 花田雄吉. "*Tokitsune kyōki kō* 言経卿記考." In *Takahashi Ryūzō sensei kiju kinen ronshū Kokiroku no kenkyū* 高橋隆三先生喜寿記念論集古記録の研究, edited by Takahashi Ryūzō sensei kiju kinen ronshū hakkōkai 高橋隆三先生喜寿記念論集発行会, 857–893. Tokyo: Yoshikawa kōbunkan 吉川弘文間, 1970.

Hane, Mikiso. *Premodern Japan: A Historical Survey*. Boulder, CO: Westview Press, 1991.

Harada Tomohiko 原田伴彦, ed. *Hennen sabetsushi shiryō shūsei* 編年差別史資料集成. 21 vols. Tokyo: San'ichi shobō 三一書房, 1983–1995.

Hare, R. M. "The Rules of War and Moral Reasoning." In *War and Moral Responsibility*. Edited by Marshall Cohen,

Thomas Nagel, and Thomas Scanlon, 46–61. Princeton, NJ: Princeton University Press, 1974.

Harrington, Lorraine F. "The Regional Outposts of Muromachi Bakufu Rule: The Kantō and Kyushu." In *The Bakufu in Japanese History*, edited by Jeffrey P. Mass and William B. Hauser, 66–98. Stanford, CA: Stanford University Press, 1985.

Hartwell, Robert. "The Evolution of the Early Sung Monetary System, A.D. 960–1025." *Journal of the American Oriental Society* 87 (1967): 280–289.

Haruta Naoki 春田直紀. "Suimen ryōyū no chūsei teki tenkai: amiba gyogyō no seiritsu o megutte 水面領有の中世的展開―網場漁業の成立をめぐって." *Nihonshi kenkyū* 日本史研究 373 (1993): 1–29.

Hashimoto Hatsuko 橋本初子. "Chūsei no kebiishi chō kankei monjo ni tsuite 中世の検非違使庁関係文書について." *Komonjo kenkyū* 古文書研究 16 (1981.7): 1–36.

Hashimoto Yoshihiko 橋本義彦. "Kiroku 記録." In *Kokushi daijiten* 国史大辞典, 4: 459–503. Tokyo: Yoshikawa kōbunkan 吉川弘文館, 1984.

Hattori Toshirō 服部敏郎. *Heian jidai igaku shi no kenkyū* 平安時代医学史の研究. Tokyo: Yoshikawa kōbunkan 吉川弘文館, 1959.

———. *Kamakura jidai igaku shi no kenkyū* 鎌倉時代医学史の研究. Tokyo: Yoshikawa kōbunkan 吉川弘文館, 1964.

———. *Muromachi Azuchi Momoyama jidai igaku shi no kenkyū* 室町安土桃山時代医学史の研究. Tokyo: Yoshikawa kōbunkan 吉川弘文館, 1971.

———. *Nihon igaku shi kenkyū yowa* 日本医学史研究余話. Tokyo: Kagaku shoin 科学書院, 1981.

———. "*Yamai no zōshi* igakuteki kaisetsu 病草紙医学的解説." In *Gaki zōshi, Jigoku zōshi, Yamai no sōshi, kuzōshi emaki*, vol. 7 of *Nihon emakimono taisei* 日本絵巻物大成, edited by Komatsu Shigemi 小松茂実, 61–65. Tokyo: Chūō kōronsha 中央公論, 1977.

Hayakawa Shōhachi 早川庄八. "Kangen ninen no Iwashimizu Hachimangū shinden oai jiken 寛元二年の石清水八幡宮

神殿汚穢事件." *Nagoya daigaku bungakubu kenkyū ronshū shigaku* 名古屋大学文学部研究論集史学 32, no. 95 (1986): 237–303.

Hayashi Yoshikazu 林美一 and Richard Lane リチャード。レイン. *Higa emaki Koshibagaki zōshi* 秘画絵巻小柴垣草子.Tokyo: Kawade shobō shinsha 河出書房新社, 1997.

Hayashi Yoshirō 林美朗. "Ihon *Yamai no sōshi* no denbon ni tsuite 異本病草紙の伝本に就いて." *Nihon ishigaku zasshi* 日本医史学雑誌 48, no. 1 (2002): 67–79.

Hazard, Benjamin H. "The Formative Years of the Wakō, 1223–63." *Monumenta Nipponica* 22, nos. 3/4 (1967): 260–277.

———. "Japanese Marauding in Medieval Korea: The Wakō Impact on Late Koryŏ". Doctoral dissertation, University of California at Berkeley, 1967.

Hioki Shōichi 日置昌一. *Nihon sōhei no kenkyū* 日本僧兵の研究. Tokyo: Heibonsha 平凡社, 1934.

Hiraoka Jōkai 平岡定海. *Nihon jiin shi no kenkyū* 日本寺院史の研究. Tokyo: Yoshikawa kōbunkan 吉川弘文館, 1981.

Hirata Toshiharu 平田俊春. "Nanto hokurei no akusō ni tsuite 南都北嶺の悪僧について." In *Ronshū Nihon bukkyō shi*, vol. 3, *Heian jidai* 論集日本仏教史, 3, 平安時代, edited by Hiraoka Jōkai 平岡定海. Tokyo: Yūzankaku shuppan 雄山閣各出版, 1986.

———. "Yoshida Sadafusa 吉田定房." In *Yoshino jidai no kenkyū* 吉野時代の研究. Tokyo: San'ichi shobō 山一書房, 1943.

———. *Sōhei to bushi* 僧兵と武士. Tokyo: Nihon kyōbunsha 日本教文社, 1965.

Hisano Nobuyoshi 久野修義. "Kakunin kō: Heian makki no Tōdaiji akusō 覚鑁考：平安末期の東大寺悪僧." *Nihon shi kenkyū* 日本史研究 219 (1980): 1–34.

Hongō Kazuto 本郷和人. "Go-Daigo tennō rinji 後醍醐天皇綸旨." *Nihon rekishi* 日本歴史 649 (2002): i–ii.

———. "Kameyama'in to Takatsukasa Kanehira 亀山院と鷹司兼平." *Komonjo kenkyū* 古文書研究 32 (1990): 46–57.

Hori, Kyotsu. "The Economic and Political Effects of the Mongol Wars." In *Medieval Japan: Essays in Institutional History,* edited by John W. Hall and Jeffrey P. Mass, 184–200. New Haven, CT: Yale University Press, 1974.

———. "The Mongol Invasions and the Kamakura Bakufu." Doctoral dissertation, Columbia University, 1967.

Hosokawa Ryôichi 細川涼一. "Chûsei hininron no genjô to kadai 中世非人論の現状と課題." In *Chūsei no mibunsei to hinin* 中世の身分制と非人. Tokyo: Nihon Editā sukūru shuppanbu 日本エヂタースクール出版部, 1994.

———. *Chūsei no mibunsei to hinin* 中世の身分制と非人. Tokyo: Nihon Editā sukūru shuppanbu 日本エディタたースクール出版部, 1994.

———. *Itsudatsu no Nihon chūsei: kyōki, tōsaku, ma no sekai* 逸脱の日本中世—狂気倒錯魔の世界. Tokyo: Shinsensha 新泉社, 1996.

Hotate Michihisa 帆立道久. *Chūsei no ai to jūzoku* 中世の愛と従属. Tokyo: Heibonsha 平凡社, 1986.

———. "Chūsei zenki no gyogyō to shōensei: kakai ryōyū to gyomin mibun o megutte 中世前期の漁業と庄園制-河海領有と漁民身分をめぐって." *Rekishi hyōron* 歴史評論, 376 (1981): 15–43.

———. "Chūsei zenki no shinsei to kokahō: toshi ōken no hō, ichiba, kahei, zaisei 中世前期の新制と沽価法-都市王権の法、市場、貨幣、財政." *Rekishigaku kenkyū* 歴史学研究 687 (1996): 1–17.

———. "Monogusa Tarō kara Sannen Netarō e ものぐさ太郎から三年寝太郎へ." In *Monogatari no chūsei – shinwa, setsuwa, minwa no rekishigaku* 物語の中世—神話、説話、民話の歴史学, 259–287. Tokyo: Tōkyō daigaku shuppankai 東京大学出版会, 1998.

Hsia, C. H., Ilza Veith, and Robert H. Geertsma. *The Essentials of Medicine in Ancient China and Japan, Yasuyori Tamba's Ishimpō*. Leiden: E. J. Brill, 1986.

Huey, Robert N. *Kyōgoku Tamekane: Poetry and Politics in Late Kamakura Japan*. Stanford, CA: Stanford University Press, 1989.

———. "*Sakuragawa*, Cherry River." *Monumenta Nipponica* 38, no. 3 (1983): 295–312.

Hurst, G. Cameron, III. *Insei: Abdicated Sovereigns in the Politics of Late Heian Japan, 1086–1185*. New York: Columbia University Press, 1976.

———. "The Kobu Polity: Court-Bakufu Relations in Kamakura Japan." In *Court and Bakufu in Japan*, edited by Jeffrey P. Mass, 3–28. Stanford, CA: Stanford University Press, 1982.

———. "Michinaga's Maladies." *Monumenta Nipponica* 34, no. 1 (Spring 1979): 101–112.

Ichikawa Hiroshi 市川浩史. *Azuma kagami no shisōshi* 吾妻鏡の思想史. Tokyo: Yoshikawa kōbunkan 吉川弘文館, 2002.

Ichizawa Satoshi 市沢哲. "Kamakura kōki kuge shakai no kōzō to 'chiten no kimi' 鎌倉後期公家社会の構造と「治天の君」." *Nihonshi kenkyū* 日本史研究 314 (1988): 23–45.

Ienaga Saburō 家永三郎, ed. *Jigoku zōshi, Gaki zōshi, Yamai no sōshi* 地獄草紙 餓鬼草紙 病草紙. Vol. 6 of *Shinshū Nihon emakimono zenshū* 新集日本絵巻物全集. Tokyo: Kadokawa shoten 角川書店, 1976.

Ihara Kesao 井原今朝男. "Sōsen yu'nyū no rekishiteki igi 宋銭輸入の歴史的意義." In *Senka: zenkindai Nihon no kahei to kokka* 銭貨-前近代日本の貨幣と国家, edited by Ike Susumu 池享, 63–92. Tokyo: Aoki shoten 青木書店, 2001.

Ikegami, Eiko. *The Taming of the Samurai: Honorific Individualism and the Making of Modern Japan*. Cambridge, MA: Harvard University Press, 1995.

Ishii Masatoshi 石井正敏. "Hizen no kuni Kanzaki no shō to Nisso bōeki 肥前国神崎荘と日宋貿易." In *Kodai chūsei shi kagaku kenkyū 2* 古代中世史料学研究（下）, edited by Minagawa Kan'ichi 皆川完一, 175–206. Tokyo: Yoshikawa kōbunkan 吉川弘文館, 1998.

———. *Nihon Bokkai kankei shi no kenkyū* 日本渤海関係史の研究. Tokyo: Yoshikawa kōbunkan 吉川弘文館, 2001.

Ishii Shirō 石井紫郎. "Kassen to tsuibu 合戦と追捕." In *Nihonjin no kokka seikatsu* 日本人の国家生活. Nihon kokuseishi kenkyū II 日本国制史研究 II, 14–24. Tokyo: Tōkyō daigaku shuppankai 東京大学出版会, 1986.

Ishii Susumu 石井進. *Chūsei bushidan* 中世武士団. Tokyo: Shōgakukan 小学館, 1974.

Itō Kiyoshi 伊東喜良. "Chūsei ni okeru tennō no jujutsuteki ken'i to wa nani ka 中世における天皇の呪術的権威とは何か." *Rekishi hyōron* 歴史評論 437 (1986): 34–53.

Iwasa Miyoko 岩佐美代子. *Kyūtei ni ikiru: tennō to nyōbō to* 宮廷に生きる：天皇と女房と. Vol. 8 of *Koten raiburarī* 古典ライブラリー. Tokyo: Kasama shoin 笠間書院, 1997.

———. *Kyūtei joryū bungaku dokkaikō: chūsei hen* 宮廷女流文学読解考：中世編. Tokyo: Kasama shoin 笠間書院, 1999.

Iwasaki Kae 岩崎佳枝. *Shokunin uta awase* 職人歌合. Tokyo: Heibonsha 平凡社, 1987.

Izumiya Yasuo 泉谷康夫. *Kōfukuji* 興福寺. Tokyo: Yoshikawa kōbunkan 吉川弘文館, 1997.

Jannetta, Ann Bowman. "Disease Ecologies in East Asia." In *The Cambridge History and Geography of Human Disease*, edited by Kenneth Kiple, 476–482. Cambridge: Cambridge University Press, 1993.

Jansen, Marius ed. *Warrior Rule in Japan*. New York: Cambridge University Press, 1995.

Johnson, James Turner. *Just War Tradition and the Restraint of War*. Princeton, NJ: Princeton University Press, 1981.

Johnston, William. *The Modern Epidemic: A History of Tuberculosis in Japan*. Cambridge, MA: Council on East Asian Studies, Harvard University, 1995.

Kamei Meitoku 亀井明徳. "Kōrokan bōeki 鴻臚館貿易." In *Shinpan kodai no Nihon 3 Kyūshū, Okinawa hen* 新版 古代の日本3九州・沖縄編, edited by Shimojō Nobuyuki 下條信行, Hirano Hiroyuki 平野博之, Chinen Isamu 知念勇, Takayoshi Kurayoshi 高良倉吉, and Hirano Kunio 平野邦雄, 345–356. Tokyo: Kadokawa shoten 角川書店, 1991.

———. *Nihon bōeki tōjishi no kenkyū* 日本貿易陶磁史の研究. Tokyo: Dōbōsha shuppan 同朋舎出版, 1986.

———. "Nissō bōeki kankei no tenkai 日宋貿易関係の展開." In *Iwanami kōza Nihon tsūshi 6 kodai 5* 岩波講座 日本通史 6 古代 5, edited by Asao Naohiro 朝尾直弘, Amino Yoshihiko 網野善彦, Ishii Susumu 石井進, Shikano Masanao 鹿野政直, Hayakawa Shōhachi 早川庄八, and

Yamamaru Yoshio 安丸良夫, 107–140. Tokyo: Iwanami shoten 岩波書店, 1995.

Kanagawa kenritsu Kanazawa bunko 神奈川県立金沢文庫, ed. *Kanezawa Sadaaki no tegami* 金沢貞顕の手紙. Yokohama 横浜: Kanagawa kenritsu Kanazawa bunko 神奈川県立金沢文庫, 2004.

Kanai Kiyomitsu 金井清光. *Chūsei no raija to sabetsu* 中世の癩者と差別. Tokyo: Iwata shoin 岩田書院, 2003.

Kanazawa Sadaaki no tegami 金沢貞顕の手紙. Kanazawa: Kanazawa bunko 金沢文庫, 2004.

Kanda, Fusae. "Behind the Sensationalism: Images of a Decaying Corpse in Japanese Buddhist Art." *The Art Bulletin*, 87, no. 1 (March 2005): 24–49.

Kasamatsu Hiroshi 笠松宏至. "Bakufu no hō to shugo no hō 幕府の法と守護の法." In *Iwanami kōza Nihon tsūshi*, vol. 8, *chūsei* 2 岩波講座日本通史, 8, 中世, 2, edited by Asao Naohiro 朝尾直弘 et al., 339–355. Tokyo: Iwanami shoten 岩波書店, 1994.

Katsuda Itaru 勝田至. *Shishatachi no chūsei* 死者たちの中世. Tokyo: Yoshikawa kōbunkan 吉川弘文館, 2003.

Katsumata Shizuo 勝俣鎮夫. "Shigai tekitai 死骸敵対." In *Chūsei no tsumi to batsu* 中世の罪と罰, edited by Amino Yoshihiko 網野善彦 et al., 43–58. Tokyo: Tōkyō daigaku shuppankai 東京大学出版会, 1994.

Katsuno Ryūshin 勝野隆信. *Sōhei* 僧兵. Tokyo: Shibundō 至文堂, 1966.

Kawai Yasushi 川合康. "Jishō Jūei no nairan to chiiki shakai 治承・寿永の内乱と地域社会." *Rekishigaku kenkyū* 歴史学研究, no. 730 (1999): 2–13.

Kawashima Masao 川嶋将生. *Chūsei Kyoto bunka no shūen* 中世京都文化の周縁. Kyoto 京都: Shibunkaku shuppan 思文閣出版, 1992.

Kawauchi Masayoshi 河内将芳. "Toyotomi seikenka no toshi Nara ni okotta ichi jiken—*Narakashi, kin shōnin jiken, Nara kashi* 豊臣政権下の都市奈良に起こった一事件―ならかし、金商人事件、奈良借." *Shichō* 史潮 36 (1995): 28–41.

Kawazoe Shoji. "Japan and East Asia." In *The Cambridge History of Japan*, vol. 3, edited by Kozo Yamamura, 396–446. Cambridge: Cambridge University Press, 1990.

―――.川添昭二. "Kurushima monjo to Hizen Ōshima shi-Kamakura jidai made 来島文書と肥前大島氏―鎌倉時代まで." *Matsuratō kenkyū* 松浦党研究 9 (1990): 8–37.

Kawazoe Shōji, Takesue Jun'ichi 武末純一, Okafuji Yoshitaka 岡藤良敬, Nishitani Masahiro 西谷正浩, Kajiwara Yoshinori 梶原良則, and Orita Etsurō 折田悦郎. *Fukuoka ken no rekishi* 福岡県の歴史. Vol. 40 of *Kenshi shiriizu* 県史シリーズ. Tokyo: Yamakawa shuppansha 山川出版社, 1997.

Kaye, Joel. *Economy and Nature in the Fourteenth Century*. Cambridge: Cambridge University Press, 1998.

Keene, Donald. *Seeds in the Heart*. New York: Henry Holt, 1993.

―――, trans. *Dōjōji*. In *Traditional Japanese Theater*, edited by Karen Brazell, 193–206. New York: Columbia University Press, 1998.

―――, trans. *Essays in Idleness: The Tsurezuregusa of Kenkō*. New York: Columbia University Press, 1967.

Keirstead, Thomas. "Gardens and Estates: Medievality and Space." *Positions: East Asia Cultures Critique* 1, no. 2 (1993): 289–320.

―――. *The Geography of Power in Medieval Japan*. Princeton, NJ: Princeton University Press, 1992.

Kidō Saizō 木藤才蔵. "Masukagami no sakusha to seiritsu shita jidai 増鏡の作者と成立した時代." In *Masukagami* 増鏡, edited by Nishizawa Masashi 西沢正史, 1–27. Vol. 6 of *Rekishi monogatari kōza* 歴史物語講座. Tokyo: Kazama shobō 風間書房, 1997.

Kiley, Cornelius J. "Estate and Property in the Late Heian Period." In *Medieval Japan: Essays in Institutional History*, edited by John W. Hall and Jeffrey P. Mass, 109–126. New Haven, CT: Yale University Press, 1974.

―――. "The Imperial Court as a Legal Authority in the Kamakura Age." In *Court and Bakufu in Japan*, edited by Jeffrey P. Mass, 29–44. Stanford, CA: Stanford University Press, 1982.

Kinoshita Ryō 木下良, ed. *Kodai o kangaeru: kodai dōro* 古代を考える　古代道路. Tokyo: Yoshikawa kōbunkan 吉川弘文館, 1996.

Kiple, Kenneth, ed. *The Cambridge History and Geography of Human Disease*. Cambridge: Cambridge University Press, 1993.

Klein, Susan Blakeley. "When the Moon Strikes the Bell: Desire and Enlightenment in the Noh Play *Dōjōji*." *Journal of Japanese Studies* 17, no. 2 (1991): 291–322.

Kobata Atsushi 小葉田淳. *Nihon no kahei* 日本の貨幣. Tokyo: Shibundō 至文堂, 1958.

———. *Nihon kahei ryūtsūshi* 日本貨幣流通史. Tokyo: Tōkō shoin 刀江書院, 1969.

Kodama Kōta 児玉幸多, ed. *Hino shishi tsūshi hen 2 jō* 日野市史通史編二上. Hino shi 日野市, 1994.

Kojiki. Translated by Donald Philippi. Tokyo: University of Tokyo Press, 1968.

Kōjiya Yoshiaki 糀谷好晃, ed. *Matsubara kyakkan no nazo ni semaru: kodai Tsuruga to higashi Ajia* 松原客館の謎にせまる—古代敦賀と東アジア. Tsuruga 敦賀: Kehi shigakukai 気比史学会, 1994.

Kokushi daijiten 国史大辞典. 15 vols. Tokyo: Yoshikawa kōbunkan 吉川弘文館, 1985.

Komatsu Shigemi 小松茂, ed. *Gaki zōshi, Jigoku zōshi, Yamai no sōshi, Kuzōshi emaki*, 餓鬼草紙　地獄草紙　病草紙　九相死絵巻. Vol. 7 of *Nihon emaki taisei* 日本絵巻大成. Tokyo: Chūō kōronsha 中央公論社, 1977.

———, ed. *Kokawadera engi* 粉河寺縁起. Vol. 5 of *Nihon no emaki* 日本の絵巻. Tokyo: Chūō kōronsha 中央公論社, 1987.

———, ed. *Shigisan engi* 信貴山縁起. Vol. 4 of *Nihon emaki taisei* 日本絵巻大成. Tokyo: Chūō kōronsha 中央公論社, 1977.

Kōno Katsuyuki 河野勝行. *Shōgaisha no chūsei* 障害者の中世. Kyoto 京都: Bunrikaku 文理閣, 1987.

Koyama Satoko 小山聡子. "*Yamai no sōshi* seisaku to Go-Shirakawa hōkō no shisō 病草紙製作と後白河法皇の思想." *Nihon ishigaku zasshi* 日本医史学雑誌 51, no. 4 (2005): 593–614.

Koyama Yasunori. "East and West in the Late Classical Age." Translated by Bruce L. Batten. In *Capital & Countryside in Japan, 300–1180: Japanese Historians Interpreted in English*, edited by Joan R. Piggott, 366–401. Ithaca, NY: Cornell University East Asia Series, 2006.

Kuroda Hideo 黒田日出男. "Chūsei minshū no hifu kankaku to kyōfu 中世民衆皮膚感覚と恐怖." In his *Kyōkai no chūsei, shōchō no chūsei* 境界の中世，象徴の中世, 233–258. Tokyo: Tōkyō daigaku shuppankai 東京大学出版会, 1986.

———. *Kyōkai no chūsei, shōchō no chūsei* 境界の中世象徴の中世. Tokyo: Tōkyō daigaku shuppankai 東京大学出版会, 1986.

———. *Sugata to shigusa no chūsei shi: ezu to emaki no fūkei kara* 姿としぐさの中世史絵図と絵巻の風景から. Tokyo: Heibonsha 平凡社, 1986.

———. "*Tengu zōshi ni okeru Ippen* 天狗草紙における一遍." In his *Sugata to shigusa no chūseishi* 姿としぐさの中世史, 15–29. Tokyo: Heibonsha, 1986.

Kuroda Toshio 黒田俊雄. "Chūsei no mibunsei to hisen kannen 中世の身分制と卑賤観念." In *Nihon chūsei no kokka to shūkyō* 日本中世の国家と宗教, 351–410. Tokyo: Iwanami shoten 岩波書店, 1975.

———. *Jisha seiryoku* 寺社勢力. Tokyo: Iwanami shoten, 岩波書店, 1980.

———. *Nihon chūsei no kokka to shūkyō* 日本中世の国家と宗教. Tokyo: Iwanami shoten 岩波書店, 1975.

Kyoto kokuritsu hakubutsukan 京都国立博物館, ed. *Tan'yū shukuzu* 探幽縮図. Kyoto 京都: Dōmeisha 同朋社, 1980.

LaFleur, William. "Hungry Ghosts and Hungry People: Somaticity and Rationality in Medieval Japan." In *Fragments for a History of the Human Body, Part One*, edited by Michael Feher, 270–303. New York: Zone Publications, 1989.

Leupp, Gary. *Male Colors*. Berkeley, CA: University of California Press, 1995.

Levy, Howard and Akira Ishihara, trans. *The Tao of Sex: An Annotated Translation of the Twenty-Eighth Section of the*

*Essence of Medical Prescriptions (Ishinpō).*Yokohama: Shibundō, 1968.

Lewis, Archibald. *Knights and Samurai: Feudalism in Northern France and Japan.* London: Temple Smith, 1979.

Lieberman, Victor. *Beyond Binary Histories: Re-imagining Southeast Asia to c.1830.* Ann Arbor: University of Michigan Press, 1999.

Lieteau, Haruyo. "The Yasutoki-Myōe Discussion: A Translation From Togano-o Myōe Shōnin Denki." *Monumenta Nipponica* 30, no. 2 (Summer 1975): 203–210.

Marra, Michele. *Representations of Power.* Honolulu: University of Hawai'i Press, 1993.

———. *The Aesthetics of Discontent: Politics and Reclusion in Medieval Japanese Literature.* Honolulu: University of Hawai'i Press, 1991.

Maruyama Yumiko 丸山裕美子. *Nihon kodai no iryō seido* 日本古代医療制度. Tokyo: Meicho shuppankai 名著出版会, 1998.

Masamune Atsuo 正宗敦夫, ed. *Chiribukuro* 塵袋. Tokyo: Nihon koten zenshū kankōkai 日本古典全集刊行会, 1977.

Mass, Jeffrey P. *Antiquity and Anachronism in Japanese History.* Stanford, CA: Stanford University Press, 1992.

———. "Black Holes in Japanese History: The Case of Kamakura." In his *Antiquity and Anachronism in Japanese History*, 157–177. Stanford, CA: Stanford University Press, 1992.

———, ed. *Court and Bakufu in Japan: Essays in Kamakura History.* New Haven, CT: Yale University Press, 1982.

———. *The Development of Kamakura Rule 1180–1250: A History with Documents.* Stanford, CA: Stanford University Press, 1979.

———. "Documents, Translation, and History." In his *Antiquity and Anachronism in Japanese History*, 157–177. Stanford, CA: Stanford University Press, 1992.

———. "The Early Bakufu and Feudalism." In *Court and Bakufu in Japan: Essays in Kamakura History*, edited by Jeffrey P. Mass, 123–142. New Haven, CT: Yale University Press, 1982.

————. "The Emergence of the Kamakura Bakufu." In *Medieval Japan: Essays in Institutional History*, edited by John W. Hall and Jeffrey P. Mass, 127–156. New Haven, CT: Yale University Press, 1974.

————. "Family, Law, and Property in Japan, 1200–1350." In *Occasional Papers in Japanese Studies*. Boston: Edwin O. Reischauer Institute of Japanese Studies, Harvard University, 2000.

————. "*Jitō* Land Possession in the 13th Century: The Case of *Shitaji Chūbun*." In *Medieval Japan: Essays in Institutional History*, edited by John W. Hall and Jeffrey P. Mass, 157–183. New Haven, CT: Yale University Press, 1974.

————. *The Kamakura Bakufu: A Study in Documents*. Stanford, CA: Stanford University Press, 1976.

————. "The Kamakura Bakufu." In *Medieval Japan*, vol. 3 of *The Cambridge History of Japan*, edited by Kozo Yamamura, 46–88. New York: Cambridge University Press, 1990.

————. "Kamakura bakufu shoki no soshō seido: monchūjo to mandokoro o chūshin ni 鎌倉幕府初期の訴訟制度、問注所と政所を中心に." *Komonjo kenkyū* 古文書研究 12 (1979): 96–114.

————. *Lordship and Inheritance in Early Medieval Japan: A Study of the Kamakura Sōryō System*. Stanford, CA: Stanford University Press, 1989.

————. "The Missing Minamoto in the Twelfth-Century Kantō." *Journal of Japanese Studies* 19, no.1 (1993): 121–145.

————. "Of Hierarchy and Authority at the End of the Kamakura." In *The Origins of Japan's Medieval World: Courtiers, Clerics, Warriors, and Peasants in the Fourteenth Century*, edited by Jeffrey P. Mass, 17–38. Stanford, CA: Stanford University Press, 1997.

————, ed. *The Origins of Japan's Medieval World: Courtiers, Clerics, Warriors, and Peasants in the Fourteenth Century*. Stanford, CA: Stanford University Press, 1997.

————. "The Origins of Kamakura Justice." *Journal of Japanese Studies* 3, no. 2 (1977): 299–322.

———. "Patterns of Provincial Inheritance in Late Heian Japan." *Journal of Japanese Studies* 9, no. 1 (1983): 67–96.

———. "Translation and Pre-1600 History." *Journal of Japanese Studies* 6, no. 1 (1980): 61–88.

———. *Warrior Government in Early Medieval Japan: A Study of the Kamakura Bakufu, Shugo and Jitō.* New Haven, CT: Yale University Press, 1974.

———. "What Can We Not Know About the Kamakura Bakufu?" In *The Bakufu in Japanese History*, edited by Jeffrey P. Mass and William B. Hauser, 13–31. Stanford, CA: Stanford University Press, 1985.

———. "Yoritomo and Feudalism." In his *Antiquity and Anachronism in Japanese History*, 70–90. Stanford, CA: Stanford University Press, 1992.

———. *Yoritomo and the Founding of the First Bakufu.* Stanford, CA: Stanford University Press, 1999.

Mass, Jeffrey P., and William B. Hauser, eds. *The Bakufu in Japanese History.* Stanford, CA: Stanford University Press, 1985.

Matisoff, Susan. "Holy Horrors." In *Flowing Traces*, edited by William LaFleur, 234–261. Princeton, NJ: Princeton University Press, 1993.

Matsumoto Shinpachirō 松本新八郎. *Chūsei shakai no kenkyū* 中世社会の研究. Tokyo: Tōkyō daigaku shuppankai 東京大学出版会, 1956.

Matsumoto Yasushi 松本寧至. *Towazugatari no kenkyū* とはずがたりの研究. Tokyo: Ōfūsha 桜楓社, 1971.

Matsuo Kenji 松尾剛次. *Chūsei no toshi to hinin* 中世の都市と非人. Kyoto 京都: Hōzōkan 宝蔵館, 1998.

McCullough, Helen Craig, trans. *Ōkagami, The Great Mirror: Fujiwara Michinaga (966–1027) and His Times: A Study and Translation.* Princeton, NJ: Princeton University Press and University of Tokyo Press, 1980.

———. *The Taiheiki: A Chronicle of Medieval Japan.* New York: Columbia University Press, 1959.

———. *The Tale of the Heike.* Stanford, CA: Stanford University Press, 1988.

McCullough, William H. "The Capital and Its Society." In *Heian Japan*, vol. 2 of *The Cambridge History of Japan*, edited by Donald H. Shively and William H. McCullough, 97–182. Cambridge: Cambridge University Press, 1999.

———, trans. "The *Azuma Kagami* Account of the Shōkyū War." *Monumenta Nipponica* 23, nos. 1–2 (1968): 102–155.

———, trans. "*Shōkyūki*: An Account of the Shōkyū War of 1221." *Monumenta Nipponica* 19 (1964): 163–215 and 21 (1966): 420–453.

McCullough, William H. and Helen Craig McCullough, trans. *A Tale of Flowering Fortunes: Annals of Japanese Aristocratic Life in the Heian Period*. 2 vols. Stanford, CA: Stanford University Press, 1980.

McMullin, Neil. "The Enryaku-ji and the Gion-Shrine Temple Complex in the Mid-Heian Period." *Japanese Journal of Religious Studies* 14, nos. 2–3 (1987): 161–184.

Mills, D. E. *A Collection of Tales From Uji*. Cambridge: Cambridge University Press, 1970.

Minegishi Sumio 峰岸純夫. "Tainai monjo to inbutsu 胎内文書と印仏." In *Hino shishi shiryōshū Takahata fudō tainai monjo hen* 日野市史史料集高幡不動胎内文書編. Hino shi 日野市, 1994.

Miner, Earl, Hiroko Odagiri, and Robert E. Morrell, eds. *The Princeton Companion to Classical Japanese Literature*. Princeton, NJ: Princeton University Press, 1985.

Misumi Yōichi 三角洋一, ed. *Towazugatari* とはずがたり. In *Towazugatari, Tamakiharu* とはずがたり　たまきはる. Vol. 50 of *Shin Nihon koten bungaku taikei* 新日本古典文学大系, 3–250. Tokyo: Iwanami shoten 岩波書店, 1994.

Miura Keiichi 三浦圭一. *Nihon chūsei senminshi no kenkyū* 日本中世賎民史の研究. Kyoto 京都: Buraku mondai kenkyūjo shuppanbu 部落問題研究所出版部, 1990.

Miyagawa Mitsuru. "From Shōen to Chigyō: Proprietary Lordship and the Structure of Local Power." In *Japan in the Muromachi Age*, edited by John W. Hall and Toyoda Takeshi, 89–105. Berkeley, CA: University of California Press, 1977.

Mizutani Isaku 水谷惟紗久. "Kokiroku ni mietaru Muromachi jidai no kanja to iryō (2)—*Tokitsugu kyōki* Eiroku kyūnen Minami Mukai tōbyō kiroku kara 古記録にみえたる室町時代の患者と医療（二）—言継卿記永禄九年南向闘病記録から—." *Nihon ishigaku zasshi* 日本医史学雑誌 43, no. 2 (1997): 187–209.

Moon, Hyungsub. "Matsura-tō: Pirate-Warriors in Northwestern Kyushu, Japan, 1150–1350." Doctoral dissertation, Stanford University, 2005.

Mori Katsumi. "The Beginning of Overseas Advance of Japanese Merchant Ships." *Acta Asiatica* 23 (1972): 1–24.

———. "International Relations Between the 10th and the 16th Century and the Development of the Japanese International Consciousness." *Acta Asiatica* 2 (1961): 69–93.

——— 森 克己. *Nissō bōeki no kenkyū* 日宋貿易の研究. Tokyo: Kokuritsu shoin 国立書院, 1948.

———. *Shintei Nissō bōeki no kenkyū* 新訂日宋貿易の研究. Vol. 1 of *Mori Katsumi chosakushū* 森克己著作集. Tokyo: Kokusho kankōkai 国書刊行会, 1975.

———. "Sōdōsen no wagakuni ryūnyū no tansho 宋銅銭の我が国流入の端緒." In *Zoku zoku Nissō bōeki no kenkyū* 続々日宋貿易の研究, vol. 3 of *Mori Katsumi chosakushū* 森克己著作集, 177–201. Tokyo: Kokusho kankōkai 国書刊行会, 1975.

Mori Shigeaki 森茂暁. *Kamakura jidai no chōbaku kankei* 鎌倉時代の朝幕関係. Kyoto 京都: Shibunkaku shuppan 思文閣出版, 1991.

Morino Muneaki 森野宗明. *Ōchō kizoku shakai no josei to gengo* 王朝貴族社会の女性と言語. Yūseidō shuppan 有精堂出版, 1975.

Morrell, Robert E. *Sand and Pebbles* (Shasekishū)*: The Tales of Mujū Ichien, A Voice for Pluralism in Kamakura Buddhism*. Albany, NY: State University of New York Press, 1985.

———, trans. "Mirror for Women: *Tsuma Kagami*." *Monumenta Nipponica* 35, no. 1 (Spring 1980): 45–75.

Morris, Ivan, trans. *The Pillow Book of Sei Shōnagon*. Harmondsworth, Middlesex: Penguin Books, 1967.

Murai Shōsuke 村井章介. *Ajia no naka no chūsei nihon* アジアのな
　かの中世日本. Tokyo: Azekura shobō 校倉書房, 1988.

———. "The Boundaries of Medieval Japan." *Acta Asiatica* 81
　(2001): 72–91.

———. *Chūsei Nihon no uchi to soto* 中世日本の内と外. Vol. 128
　of Chikuma purimā bukkusu ちくまプリマーブックス.
　Tokyo: Chikuma shobō 筑摩書房, 1999.

———. *Chūsei Wajin den* 中世倭人伝. Vol. 274 of *Iwanami shinsho*
　岩波新書. Tokyo: Iwanami shoten 岩波書店, 1993.

———. *Umi kara mita sengoku Nihon: rettōshi kara sekaishi e* 海
　から見た戦国日本―列島史から世界史へ. Vol. 127 of
　Chikuma shinsho ちくま新書. Tokyo: Chikuma shobō 筑摩
　書房, 1997.

———. "Yoshida Sadafusa sōjō wa itsu kakareta ka 吉田定房奏状
　はいつ書かれたか." *Nihon rekishi* 日本歴史 587 (1997):
　92–96.

Murayama Shūichi 村山修一. *Hieizan shi: tatakai to inori no seichi*
　比叡山史戦いと祈りの聖地. Tokyo: Tōkyō bijutsu 東京美
　術, 1994.

Nagahara Keiji 永原慶二. "Chūsei shakai no tenkai to hisabetsu
　mibunsei 中世社会の展開と被差別身分制." In *Burakushi
　no kenkyū: zenkindai hen* 部落史の研究―前近代篇, edited
　by Buraku mondai kenkyūjo 部落問題研究所. Kyoto 京都:
　Buraku mondai kenkyūjo 部落問題研究所, 1979.

———. "The Medieval Origins of the *Eta-Hinin*." *Journal of
　Japanese Studies* 5, no. 2 (1979): 385–403.

———. *Nihon chūsei shakai kōzō no kenkyū* 日本中世社会構造の
　研究. Tokyo: Iwanami shoten 岩波書店, 1973.

———. "Tōgoku ni okeru sōryō sei no kaitai katei no kenkyū 東
　国における惣領制の解体過程の研究." In *Nihon hōken
　sei seiritsu katei no kenkyū* 日本封建制成立過程の研究.
　Tokyo: Iwanami shoten 岩波書店, 1961.

——— et al. *Chūseishi handobukku* 中世史ハンドブック. Tokyo:
　Kondō shuppansha 近藤出版社, 1973.

Naganuma Kenkai 長沼賢海. *Matsura tō no kenkyū: kita Kyūshū no
　kaizokushi* 松浦党の研究―北九州の海賊史. Fukuoka:

Kyūshū daigaku bungakubu kokushi kenkyū shitsu 福岡：
九州大学文学部国史研究室, 1957.

———. *Nihon no kaizoku* 日本の海賊. Tokyo: Shibundō 至文堂,
1957.

Nagel, Thomas. "War and Massacre." In *War and Moral
Responsibility*, edited by Marshall Cohen, Thomas Nagel,
and Thomas Scanlon, 3–24. Princeton, NJ: Princeton
University Press, 1974.

Nakajima Keiichi 中島圭一. "Nihon no chūsei kahei to kokka 日本
の中世貨幣と国家." In *Ekkyō suru kahei* 越境する貨幣,
edited by Rekishigaku kenkyūkai 歴史学研究会, 109–139.
Tokyo: Aoki shoten 青木書店, 1999.

Nakamura Naokatsu 中村直勝. "Yoshida Sadafusa 吉田定房."
Nakamura Naokatsu chosakushū 村直勝著作集, vol. 3,
Nanchō no kenkyū 南朝の研究. Kyoto 京都: Tankōsha 淡交
社, 1978.

Nakazawa Katsuaki 中沢克昭. *Chūsei no buryoku to jōkaku* 中世
の武力と城廓. Tokyo: Yoshikawa kōbunkan 吉川弘文館,
1999.

Nam Ki-hak 南基鶴. *Mōko shūrai to Kamakura bakufu* 蒙古襲来と
鎌倉幕府. Kyoto 京都: Rinsen shoten 臨川書店, 1996.

Nara kenritsu Kashihara kōkogaku kenkyūjo fuzoku hakubutsukan 奈
良県立橿原考古学研究所付属博物館, ed. *Bōeki tōji: Nara
Heian no Chūgoku tōji* 貿易陶磁　奈良平安の中国陶磁.
Kyoto: Rinsen shoten 臨川書店, 1993.

Nara kokuritsu bunkazai kenkyūjo 奈良国立文化財研究所.
Heijōkyū hakkutsu chōsa hōkoku VI 平城宮発掘調査報告
VI. Nara 奈良: Nara meishinsha 奈良明新社, 1974.

Nelson, Thomas. "Bakufu and Shugo Under the Early Ashikaga." In
The Origins of Japan's Medieval World, edited by Jeffrey P.
Mass, 78–90. Stanford, CA: Stanford University Press, 1997.

———. "The Early Shugo to 1390: The Ōtomo Lords of Northern
Kyushu." Doctoral dissertation, University of Oxford, 1998.

———. "Slavery in Medieval Japan." *Monumenta Nipponica* 59, no.
4 (Winter 2004): 463–492.

Newman, John. *Bushido: The Way of the Warrior*. Wigston, Leicester:
Magna Books, 1989.

Nihon ishi gakkai 日本医史学会, ed. *Zuroku Nihon iji bunka shiryō shūsei* 図録日本医事文化資料集成. Tokyo: San'ichi shobō 三一書房, 1978.

Nihon jinkō gakkai 日本人口学会, ed. *Jinkō daijiten* 人口大事典. Tokyo: Baifūkan 培風館, 2002.

Nihon kokugo daijiten 日本国語大辞典. 10 vols. Tokyo: Shōgakkan 小学館, 1982.

Nishi Nobito 西野人. "Sōhei, koto shinzei hōkisu 僧兵、古都新税蜂起す." *Chūō kōron* 中央公論 100, no. 5 (1985): 256–262.

Nishimata Fusō 西股総生. "Kassen no rūru to manā 合戦のルールとマナー." In *Gempei no sōran* 源平の争乱, vol. 3 of *Senran no Nihonshi: kassen to jinbutsu* 戦乱の日本史：合戦と人物, edited by Yasuda Motohisa 安田元久, 146–147. Tokyo: Daiichi hōki shuppan 第一法規出版, 1988.

Nishiyama Ryōhei 西山良平. "*Yamai no sōshi* no rekishigaku 病草紙の歴史学." *Kyōu* 杏雨 9 (2006): 3–22.

Nishizawa Masashi 西沢正史 and Shimegi Miyako 標宮子. *Towazugatari* とはずがたり. Vol. 4 of *Chūsei nikki kikō bungaku zenhyōshaku shūsei* 中世日記紀行文学全評釈集成. Tokyo: Bensei shuppan 勉誠出版, 2000.

Nitta Ichirō 新田一郎. "Taibon sankajō isetsu – jōshiki no saikentō 大犯三ヶ条異説—常識の再検討." In *Haruka naru chūsei* 遥かなる中世 14 (1995): 67–76.

Niunoya Tetsuichi 丹生谷哲一. "Hinin, kawaramono, sanjo 非人・河原者・散所." In *Iwanami kōza Nihon tsūshi 8, chūsei 2* 岩波講座日本通史 8, 中世 2, 217–254. Tokyo: Iwanami shoten 岩波書店, 1994.

———. *Kebiishi: chūsei no kegare to kenryoku* 検非違使—中世の穢れと権力. Tokyo: Heibonsha 平凡社, 1986.

———. *Nihon chūsei no mibun to shakai* 日本中世の身分と社会. Tokyo: Hanawa shobō 塙書房, 1993.

Noguchi Minoru 野蛍実. *Buke no tōryō no jōken: chūsei bushi o minaosu* 武家の棟梁の条件：中世武士を見直す. Tokyo: Chūō kōronsha 中央公論社, 1994.

Nomura Ikuyo 野村育世. "Nyōin kenkyū no genjō 女院研究の現状." *Rekishi hyōron* 歴史評論 525 (1994): 44–55.

North, Douglass. *Institutions, Institutional Change, and Economic Performance*. New York: Cambridge University Press, 1990.

Ōae Akira 大饗亮. *Hōkenteki shujūsei seiritsushi kenkyū* 封建的主従制成立史研究. Tokyo: Kazama shobō 風間書房, 1967.

Ober, Joseph. "Classical Greek Times." In *The Laws of War: Constraints on Warfare in the Western World*, edited by Michael Howard, George J. Andreopoulos, and Mark R. Shulman, 12–26. New Haven, CT: Yale University Press, 1994.

Okada Seiichi 岡田清一. "Kassen to girei 合戦と儀礼." In *Ikusa* いくさ, edited by Fukuda Toyohiko 福田豊彦, 154–181. Tokyo: Yoshikawa kōbunkan 吉川弘文館, 1993.

Okuno Tetsuji 奥野哲士. "Sōhei no ran imada owarazu 僧兵の乱いまだ終らず." *Chūō kōron* 中央公論 101, no. 10 (1986): 308–328.

Ong, Walter. *Orality and Literacy: The Technologizing of the Word*. London: Routledge, 1982.

Ooms, Herman. *Tokugawa Village Practice: Class, Status, Power, Law*. Berkeley and Los Angeles: University of California Press, 1996.

Ōshima Yukio 大島幸雄. "Sōhei no hassei ki ni kansuru isshiki ron 僧兵の発生期に関する一式論." In *Nihon kodai shigaku ronshū* 日本古代史学論集. Tokyo: Komazawa daigakuin shigakkai kodai shi bukai 駒沢大学院史学会古代史部会, 1979.

Ōyama Kyōhei 大山喬平. "Chūsei no mibunsei to kokka 中世の身分制と国家." In his *Nihon chūsei nōsonshi no kenkyū* 日本中世農村史の研究. Tokyo: Iwanami shoten 岩波書店, 1978.

———. *Kamakura bakufu* 鎌倉幕府. Tokyo: Shōgakkan 小学館, 1974.

———. *Nihon chūsei nōsonshi no kenkyū* 日本中世農村史の研究. Tokyo: Iwanami shoten 岩波書店, 1978.

Pandey, Rajyashree. "Women, Sexuality and Enlightenment: *Kankyō no tomo*." *Monumenta Nipponica* 50, no. 3 (Autumn 1995): 325–356.

Peng Xinwei. *A Monetary History of China*. Translated by Edward H. Kaplan. Bellingham, WA: Western Washington University, 1993.

Perkins, George W. *The Clear Mirror: A Chronicle of the Japanese Court During the Kamakura Period (1185–1333)*. Stanford, CA: Stanford University Press, 1998.

Piggott, Joan R. "Hierarchy and Economics in Early Medieval Tōdaiji." In *Court and Bakufu in Japan: Essays in Kamakura History*, edited by Jeffrey P. Mass, 45–91. New Haven, CT: Yale University Press, 1982.

———. "Court and Provinces under Regent Fujiwara no Tadahira." In *Heian Japan, Centers and Peripheries*, edited by Mikael Adolphson, Edward Kamens, and Stacie Matsumoto, 35–65. Honolulu: University of Hawai'i Press, 2007.

———. *The Emergence of Japanese Kingship*. Stanford, CA: Stanford University Press, 1997.

——— and Yoshida Sanae, eds. *Teishinkōki: What Did a Heian Regent Do? (The Year 939 in the Journal of Regent Fujiwara no Tadahira)*. Ithaca, NY: Cornell East Asia Series, 2008.

Putzar, Edward. "Inu Makura: The Dog Pillow." *Harvard Journal of Asiatic Studies* 28 (1968): 98–113.

Quinter, David Ralph. "The Shingon Ritsu School and the Mañjuśrī Cult in the Kamakura Period: From Eison to Monkan." Doctoral dissertation, Stanford University, 2006.

Reischauer, Edwin O. *The Japanese Today: Change and Continuity*. Cambridge, MA.: Belknap Press of Harvard University Press, 1980.

Reynolds, Susan. *Fiefs and Vassals*. Oxford: Oxford University Press, 1994.

Ryō Susumu 龍肅. *Kamakura jidai, jō, Kantō* 鎌倉時代, 上, 関東. Tokyo: Shunjūsha 春秋社, 1957.

Saeki Kōji 佐伯弘次. "Hakata 博多." In *Iwanami kōza Nihon tsūshi* 10 *chūsei* 4 岩波講座二本通史 10 中世 4, edited by Asao Naohiro 朝尾直弘 et al., 283–300. Tokyo: Iwanami shoten 岩波書店, 1994.

——. "Kaizoku ron 海賊論." In *Ajia no naka no Nihon shi* アジア
のなかの日本史, vol. 3, edited by Arai Yasunori 荒井泰
典, Ishii Masatoshi 石井正敏, and Murai Shōsuke 村井章
介, 35–61. Tokyo: Tōkyō daigaku shuppankai 東京大学出
版会, 1992.

——. "Kokkyō no chūsei kōshōshi 国境の中世交渉史." In *Umi to
rettō bunka 3, Genkai nada no shimajima* 海と列島文化 3
玄界灘の島々, edited by Miyata Noboru 宮田登, 243–278.
Tokyo: Shōgakkan 小学館, 1992.

Sakaehara Towao 栄原永遠男. "Kahei no hassei 貨幣の発生." In
Ryūtsū keizaishi 流通経済史, edited by Sakurai Eiji 桜井英
治 and Nakanishi Satoru 中西聡, 5–41. Tokyo: Yamakawa
shuppansha 山川出版社, 2002.

——. *Nihon kodai senka ryūtsūshi no kenkyū* 日本古代銭貨流通
史の研究. Tokyo: Hanawa shobō 塙書房, 1993.

Sakai Shizu. "A History of Opthalmology Before the Opening of
Japan." *Nihon ishigaku zasshi* 日本医史学雑誌 23, no. 1
(1977): 19–43.

——. 酒井シズ. *Nihon no iryōshi* 日本の医療史. Tokyo: Tōkyō
shoseki kabushiki kaisha 東京書籍株式会社, 1982.

Sakayori Masashi 酒寄雅志. *Bokkai to kodai no Nihon* 渤海と古代
の日本. Tokyo: Azekura shobō 校倉書房, 2001.

Sakurai Eiji 桜井英治. *Nihon chūsei no keizai kōzō* 日本中世の経済
構造. Tokyo: Iwanami shoten 岩波書店, 1996.

Sano Midori 佐野みどり. "Monogatari-e dankan nizu 物語絵断簡二
図." *Kokka* 國華, 1271 (2001): 18–25.

——. "*Yamai no sōshi* kenkyū 病草紙研究 (1)." *Kokka* 國華, 1039
(1981): 7–28.

——. "*Yamai no sōshi* kenkyū 病草紙研究 (2)." *Kokka* 國華, 1040
(1981): 7–23.

——. "*Yamai no sōshi* kenkyū 病草紙研究". In her *Fūryū, zōkei,
monogatari: Nihon bijutsu no kōzō to yōtai* 風流・造形・
物語: 日本美術の構造と様態, 519–602. Tokyo: Sukaidoa
スカイドア, 1999.

Sansom, George. *A History of Japan to 1334.* Reprint, Kent, England:
Wm Dawson & Sons Ltd, 1978.

Satō Shin'ichi 佐藤進一. "Bakufu ron 幕府論." In *Nihon chūseishi ronshū* 日本中世史論集, 1–42. Tokyo: Iwanami shoten 岩波書店, 1990.

———. *Komonjogaku nyūmon* 古文書学入門. Tokyo: Hōsei daigaku shuppankyoku 法制大学出版局, 1967.

Schmitt, Jean-Claude. *Ghosts in the Middle Ages: The Living and the Dead in Medieval Society.* Translated by Teresa Lavender Fagan. Chicago and London: University of Chicago Press, 1998.

Screech, Timothy. *Sex and the Floating World.* Honolulu: University of Hawai'i Press, 2000.

Segal, Ethan. "Economic Growth and Changes in Elite Power Structures in Medieval Japan, 1150–1500." Doctoral dissertation, Stanford University, 2003.

Seki Yukihiko 関幸彦. "'Bu' no kōgen: kachū to yumiya 「武」の光源：甲冑と弓矢." In *Ikusa* いくさ, edited by Fukuda Toyohiko 福田豊彦, 1–38. Tokyo: Yoshikawa kōbunkan 吉川弘文館, 1993.

———. "Sōryōsei o meguru shogakusetsu 惣領制をめぐる諸学説." In *Bushidan kenkyū no ayumi* 武士団研究の歩み. Tokyo: Shinjinbutsu ōraisha 新人物往来社, 1988.

Seno Seiichirō 瀬野精一郎. *Chinzei gokenin no kenkyū* 鎮西御家人の研究. Tokyo: Yoshikawa kōbunkan 吉川弘文館, 1975.

———. "*Jitōdai* yori *jitō* e no shojō 地頭代より地頭への書状." In his *Rekishi no kansei* 歴史の陥穽, 268–281. Tokyo: Yoshikawa kōbunkan 吉川弘文館, 1985.

———. "Kaiji shiryō toshite no Aokata monjo 海事史料としての青方文書." *Kaijishi kenkyū* 海事史研究 25 (1975): 1–14.

———. "Kamakura ni okeru totōsen no sōnan ni miru tokusō ke bōeki dokusen no ichi keitai 鎌倉に於ける渡唐船の遭難に見る得宗家貿易独占の一形態." In *Nihon komonjo gaku ronshū 5, Chūsei 1* 日本の古文書学論集 5 中世 1, edited by Seno Seiichirō 瀬野精一郎 and Murai Shōsuke 村井章介, 372–383. Tokyo: Yoshikawa kōbunkan 吉川弘文館, 1988.

———. *Rekishi no kansei* 歴史の陥穽. Tokyo: Yoshikawa kōbunkan 吉川弘文館, 1985.

Seta Katsuya 瀬田勝哉. *Rakuchū rakugai no gunzō—ushinawareta chūsei Kyoto e* 洛中洛外の群像―失われた中世京都へ. Tokyo: Heibonsha 平凡社, 1994.

Shapinsky, Peter D. "Lords of the Sea: Pirates, Violence, and Exchange in Medieval Japan." Doctoral dissertation, University of Michigan, 2005.

———. "With the Sea as Their Domain: Pirates and Maritime Lordship in Medieval Japan." In *Seascapes: Maritime Histories, Littoral Cultures, and Trans-Oceanic Exchanges*, edited by Jerry Bentley, Kären Wigen, and Renate Bridenthal, 221–238. Honolulu: University of Hawai'i Press, 2007.

Shibata Shôji 柴田承二, ed. *Hōryūji shozō Iyaku chōzai koshō – hakken sareta 14 seiki no kusuri* 法隆寺所蔵医薬調剤古抄 ― 発見された 14 世紀の薬. Tokyo: Hirokawa shoten 廣川書店, 1997.

Shimomukai Tatsuhiko 下向井龍彦. "Ōchō kokka gunsei kenkyū no kihon shikaku 王朝国家群生研究の基本視角." In *Ōchō kokka kokuseishi no kenkyū* 王朝国家国政史の研究, edited by Sakamoto Shōzō 坂本賞三, 285–347. Tokyo: Yoshikawa kōbunkan 吉川弘文館, 1987.

Shinmura Taku 新村拓. "Hiden'in to Seyakuin 悲田院と施薬院." In his *Nihon iryō shakaishi no kenkyū* 日本医療社会史の研究, 1–46. Tokyo: Hōsei daigaku shuppan kyoku 法政大学出版局, 1985.

———. *Kodai iryō kanjin sei no kenkyū* 古代医療官人制の研究. Tokyo: Hōsei daigaku shuppan kyoku 法政大学出版局, 1983.

———. *Nihon iryō shakaishi no kenkyū* 日本医療社会史の研究. Tokyo: Hōsei daigaku shuppan kyoku 法政大学出版局, 1985.

———. *Oi to kantori no shakaishi* 老いと看取りの社会史. Tokyo: Hōsei daigaku shuppan kyoku 法政大学出版局, 1991.

———. *Shi to yamai to kango no shakaishi* 死と病と看護の社会史. Tokyo: Hōsei daigaku shuppan kyoku 法政大学出版局, 1989.

———. *Shussan to seishokukan no rekishi* 出産と生殖観の歴史. Tokyo: Hōsei daigaku shuppan kyoku 法制大学出版局, 1996.

———. "Yamai no zuzō hyōgen 病の図像表現." In *Ippen hijiri o yomitoku* 一遍聖を読み解く, edited by Takeda Sachiko 武田佐知子, 162–180. Tokyo: Yoshikawa kōbunkan 吉川弘文館, 1999.

Shinoda, Minoru. *The Founding of the Kamakura Shogunate, 1180–1185*. New York: Columbia University Press, 1960.

Shirai Katsuhiro 白井克浩. "Kamakura-ki kuge seiji kikō no keisei to tenkai: 'Chiten no kimi' no taiseika o megutte 鎌倉期公家政治機構の形成と展開：「治天の君」の体制化をめぐって." *Hisutoria* ヒストリア 158 (1997): 27–52.

Shiroyama Yoshitarō 白山芳太郎. *Shokugenshō no kisoteki kenkyū* 職原鈔の基礎的研究. Kyoto 京都: Rinsen shoten 臨川書店, 1980.

Shirōzu Satoshi 白水智. "Chūsei kaison no hyakushō to ryōshū 中世海村の百姓と領主." In *Rettō no bunkashi* 9 列島の文化史 9 (1994): 109–142.

———. "Nishi no umi no bushidan Matsuratō–Aokata monjo ni miru sōkoku no yōsō 西の海の武士団松浦党青方文書に見る相克の様相." In *Umi to retto bunka,* 4, *Higashi Shina kai to Saikai bunka* 海と列島文化，4，東シナ海と西海文化, edited by Amino Yoshihiko 網野善彦, 206–248. Tokyo: Shōgakkan 小学館, 1992.

Shiryō sōran 史料綜覧. 17 vols. Tokyo: Chōyōkai 朝陽会, 1923.

Shunroan Shujin 舜露庵主人 (Watanabe Shin'ichirō 渡辺信一郎). *Edo no seiai bunka–Hiyaku higu jiten* 江戸の性愛文化−秘薬秘具事典. Tokyo: Miki shobō 三樹書房, 2003.

Skord, Virginia. *Tales of Tears and Laughter*. Honolulu: University of Hawai'i Press, 1991.

Smith, Henry. "Japaneseness and the History of the Book." *Monumenta Nipponica* 53, no. 4 (Winter 1998): 495–515.

Smith, Thomas. The Agrarian Origins of Modern Japan. Stanford CA: Stanford University Press, 1959.

Smits, Ivo. "The Way of the Literati: Chinese Learning and Literary Practice in Mid-Heian Japan." In *Heian Japan, Centers and*

Peripheries, edited by Mikael Adolphson, Edward Kamens, and Stacie Matsumoto, 105–128. Honolulu: University of Hawai'i Press, 2007.

So, Kwan-wai. *Japanese Piracy in Ming China During the 16th Century.* Lansing, MI: Michigan State University Press, 1975.

Sone Hiromi. "Prostitution and Public Authority in Early Modern Japan." In *Women and Class in Japanese History*, edited by Hitomi Tonomura, Anne Walthall, and Wakita Haruko, 169–186. Ann Arbor, MI: University of Michigan Center for Japanese Studies, 1999.

Souyri, Pierre François. *The World Turned Upside Down: Medieval Japanese Society*. New York: Columbia University Press, 2001.

Stacey, Robert C. "The Age of Chivalry." In *The Laws of War: Constraints on Warfare in the Western World*, edited by Michael Howard, George J. Andreopoulos, and Mark R. Shulman, 27–39. New Haven, CT: Yale University Press, 1994.

Standlee, Mary. *The Great Pulse*. Rutland, VT: Charles E. Tuttle, 1959.

Steenstrup, Carl. *Hōjō Shigetoki [1198-1261] and his Role in the History of Political and Ethical Ideals In Japan*. London: Curzon Press, 1979.

———. Review of *Antiquity and Anachronism in Japanese History*. In *Journal of Japanese Studies* 20, no.1 (1994): 239–245.

Stone, Jacqueline. "By the Power of One's Nembutsu: Deathbed Practices in Early Medieval Japan." In *Approaching the Land of Pure Bliss*, edited by Richard K. Payne and Kenneth K. Tanaka, 77–119. Honolulu: University of Hawai'i Press, 2004.

Strickland, Matthew. *War & Chivalry: The Conduct and Perception of War in England and Normandy, 1066–1217*. New York and London: Cambridge University Press, 1996.

Suitō Makoto 水藤真. *Chūsei no sōsō, bosei: sekitō o zōritsu suru koto* 中世の葬送，墓制：石塔を造立すること. Tokyo: Yoshikawa kōbunkan 吉川弘文館, 1991.

Sunagawa Hiroshi 砂川博. "Ishō toshite no Ippen 医聖としての一
　　遍." In *Ippen Hijiri-e no sōgō teki kenkyū* 一遍聖絵の総
　　合的研究, edited by Sunagawa Hiroshi 砂川博, 171–181.
　　Tokyo: Iwata shoin 岩田書院, 2002.

Suzuki Hideo 鈴木英雄. "Katoku to sōryō ni kansuru oboegaki 家
　　督と総領に関する覚書." In *Shoki hōkensei no kenkyū*
　　期封建制の研究, edited by Yasuda Motohisa 安田元久,
　　281–310. Tokyo: Yoshikawa kōbunkan 吉川弘文館, 1964.

Suzuki Kimio 鈴木公雄. *Shutsudo senka no kenkyū* 出土銭貨の研
　　究. Tokyo: Tōkyō daigaku shuppankai 東京大学出版会,
　　1999.

Suzuki Noriko 鈴木則子. "Shodai Manase Dōsan no rai igaku 初代
　　曲直瀬道三の癩医学." *Nihon ishigaku zasshi* 日本医史学
　　雑誌 41, no. 3 (1995): 349–368.

Taigai kankei shi sōgō nenpyō henshū iinkai 対外関係史総合年表編
　　集委員会, ed. *Taigai kankei shi sōgō nenpyō* 対外関係史総
　　合年表. Tokyo: Yoshikawa kōbunkan 吉川弘文館, 1999.

Tajima Isao 田島公. "Dazaifu Kōrokan no shūen: 8 seiki—11 seiki
　　no taigai kōeki shisutemu no kaimei 大宰府鴻臚館の終
　　焉 八世紀〜十一世紀の対外交易システムの解明."
　　Nihonshi kenkyū 日本史研究 389 (1995): 1–29.

———. "Nihon, Chūgoku, Chōsen taigai kōryū shi nenpyō: Taihō
　　gannen—Bunji gannen 日本・中国・朝鮮対外交流史
　　年表 大宝元年〜文治元年." In *Bōeki tōji: Nara Heian
　　no Chūgoku tōji* 貿易陶磁 奈良平安の中国陶磁, edited
　　by Nara kenritsu Kashihara kōkogaku kenkyūjo fuzoku
　　hakubutsukan 奈良県立橿原考古学研究所付属博物館,
　　417–540. Kyoto 京都: Rinsen shoten 臨川書店, 1993.

Takagi Yōko 高木葉子. "Go-Fukakusa insei no seiritsu katei 後深草
　　院政の成立過程 (I)." *Seiji keizai shigaku* 政治経済史学
　　268 (1988): 1–13.

———. "Go-Fukakusa insei no seiritsu katei 後深草院政の成立
　　過程 (II)." *Seiji keizai shigaku* 政治経済史学 269 (1988):
　　48–65.

Takahashi Masaaki 高橋昌明. *Bushi no seiritsu: bushizō no sōshutsu*
　　武士の成立：武士象の創出. Tokyo: Tōkyō daigaku
　　shuppankai 東京大学出版会, 1999.

———. "Nihon chūsei no sentō: yasen no kijōsha o chūshin ni 日本中世の戦闘： 野戦の騎乗者を中心 に." In *Tatakai no shisutemu to taigai senryaku* 戦いのシステムと対外戦略, vol. 2 of *Jinrui ni totte tatakai to wa* 人類にとって戦いとは, edited by Matsugi Takehiko 松木武彦 and Udakawa Takehisa 宇田川武久, 193–224. Tokyo: Tōyō shorin 東洋書林, 1999.

Takamatsu Momoka 高松百香. "Nyōin no seiritsu: sono yōin to chii o megutte 女院の成立： その要因と地位をめぐって." *Sōgō joseishi kenkyū* 総合女性史研究 15 (1998): 1–14.

Takeoka Masao 竹岡正夫. *Ise monogatari zenhyōshaku* 伊勢物語全評釈. Yūbun shoin 右文書院, 1988.

Takizawa Matsuyo. *The Penetration of Money Economy in Japan and Its Effects upon Social and Political Institutions*. New York: Columbia University Press, 1927.

Tamaizumi Tairyō 玉泉大梁 et al. *Muromachi jidai no denso* 室町時代の田租. Tokyo: Yoshikawa kōbunkan 吉川弘文館, 1969.

Tamura Hiroyuki 田村洋幸. *Chūsei Nitchō bōeki no kenkyū* 中世日朝貿易の研究. Tokyo: Sanwa shobō 三和書房, 1967.

Tanaka, Takeo. "Japan's Relations with Overseas Countries." In *Japan in the Muromachi Age*, edited by John W. Hall and Toyoda Takeshi, 159–178. Berkeley, CA: University of California Press, 1977.

———. 田中健夫. "Wakō to higashi Ajia tsūkōken 倭寇と東アジア通行圏." In *Nihon no shakaishi,* vol. 1, *Rettō naigai no kōtsū to kokka* 日本の社会史, 1, 列島内外の交通と国家, edited by Amino Yoshihiko 網野善彦, 139–181. Tokyo: Iwanami shoten 岩波書店, 1986.

———. *Wakō—umi no rekishi* 倭寇海の歴史. Tokyo: Kyōikusha 教育社, 1982.

Tatehira Susumu 立平進. "Gotō rettō to saikai chiiki no seikatsu gijutsushi, 五島列島と西海地域の生活技術史." In *Umi to rettō bunka 4, Higashi Shinakai to saikai bunka* 海と列島文化４東シナ海と西海文化, edited by Amino Yoshihiko 網野喜彦, 329–368. Tokyo: Shōgakkan 小学館, 1992.

Tatsukawa Shōji. "Diseases of Antiquity in Japan." In *The Cambridge History and Geography of Human Disease,* edited by Kenneth Kiple, 373–375. Cambridge: Cambridge University Press, 1993.

———. 立川昭二. *Nihonjin no byōreki* 日本人の病歴. Tokyo: Chūō kōronsha 中央公論社, 1976.

———."Shishatachi no chūsei 死者たちの中世." In *Chūseishi kōza, 9, chūsei no seikatsu to gijutsu* 中世史講座, 9, 中世の生活と技術, 209–224. Tokyo: Gakuseisha 学生社, 1991.

Teramoto, John Tadao. "The *Yamai no Sōshi*: A Critical Reevaluation of Its Importance to Japanese Secular Painting of the Twelfth Century." Doctoral dissertation, University of Michigan, 1994.

Toby, Ronald P. *State and Diplomacy in Early Modern Japan: Asia in the Development of the Tokugawa Bakufu.* Princeton, NJ: Princeton University Press, 1983.

Tokyo National Museum et al. *The Sunken Treasures Off the Sinan Coast.* Nagoya: Chūnichi shinbunsha, 1983.

Tomita Masahiro 富田正弘. "Chūsei kuge seiji monjo no saikentō 中世公家政治文書の再検討. *Rekishi kōron* 歴史公論 4, nos. 11–12 (1978): 154–162.

———. "Kokumu monjo 国務文書." In *Nihon komonjogaku kōza 3 kodai hen 2* 日本古文書学講座 3 古代編 2, edited by Akamatsu Toshihide 赤松俊秀 et al., 102–136. Tokyo: Yūzankaku 雄山閣, 1979.

Tōno Haruyuki 東野治之. *Kahei no Nihon shi* 貨幣の日本史. Tokyo: Asahi shinbunsha 朝日新聞社, 1997.

Tonomura, Hitomi. "Black Hair and Red Trousers: Gendering the Flesh in Medieval Japan." *American Historical Review* 99, no. 1 (1994): 129–154.

———. "Coercive Sex in the Medieval Japanese Court: Lady Nijō's Memoir." *Monumenta Nipponica* 61, no. 3 (Autumn 2006): 283–338.

———. *Community and Commerce in Late Medieval Japan: The Corporate Villages of Tokuchin-ho.* Stanford, CA: Stanford University Press, 1992.

———. "Women and Inheritance in Japan's Early Warrior Society." *Comparative Studies in Society and History* 32, no. 3 (1990): 592–621.

———. "Re-envisioning Women in the Post-Kamakura Age." In *The Origins of Japan's Medieval World: Courtiers, Clerics, Warriors, and Peasants in the Fourteenth Century*, edited by Jeffrey P. Mass, 138–169. Stanford, CA: Stanford University Press, 1997.

Totman, Conrad. *A History of Japan*. Oxford: Blackwell Publishers, 2000.

Toyama Mikio 外山幹夫. *Chūsei Kyūshū shakai shi no kenkyū* 中世九州社会史の研究. Tokyo: Yoshikawa kōbunkan 吉川弘文館, 1986.

———. *Daimyō ryōkoku keisei katei no kenkyū* 大名領国形成過程の研究. Tokyo: Yūzankaku 雄山閣, 1983.

———. "Ōtomo shi to Zenshū 大友氏と禅宗." *Kyūshū shigaku* 九州史学 20 (December 1965): 1–14.

Toyoda Takeshi 豊田武. *Bushidan to sonraku* 武士団と村落. Tokyo: Yoshikawa kōbunkan 吉川弘文館, 1963.

Tsuchida, Bruce, and Hiroshi Kitagawa, trans. *The Tale of the Heike*. Tokyo: University of Tokyo Press, 1975.

Tsuchihashi Riko 土橋理子. "Nissō bōeki no shosō 日宋貿易の諸相." In *Kōkogaku ni yoru Nihon rekishi 10 taigai kōshō* 考古学による日本歴史 10 対外交渉, edited by Ōtsuka Hatsushige 大塚初重, Shiraishi Taiichirō 白石太一郎, Nishitani Shō 西谷正, and Machida Shō 町田章, 61–76. Tokyo: Yūzankaku 雄山閣, 1997.

Tsuda Daisuke 津田大輔. "'Kazuginu' seido no seiritsu: Shashi kinsei to yūsoku kojitsu 「数衣」制度の成立: 奢侈禁制と有職故実." *Minato* 水門 20 (2002): 45–71.

Tsuji Zennosuke 辻善之助. *Nihon bukkyō shi: jōsei hen* 日本仏教史: 上世篇. Tokyo: Iwanami shoten 岩波書店, 1944.

Tsunoda Bun'ei 角田文英. *Ōchō no eizō: Heian jidai shi no kenkyū* 王朝の映像: 平安時代史の研究. Tokyo: Tōkyōdō shuppan 東京堂出版, 1970.

———. *Ōchō no meian: Heian jidai shi no kenkyū* 王朝の明暗：平安時代史の研究. Vol. 2. Tokyo: Tōkyōdō shuppan 東京堂出版, 1977.

Turnbull, Stephen R. *The Book of the Samurai: The Warrior Class of Japan*. New York: Gallery Books, 1982.

———. *The Lone Samurai and the Martial Arts*. London: Arms and Armour Press, 1990.

Tyler, Royall. *Japanese Tales*. New York: Pantheon Books, 1987.

Ulak, James. "Fukutomi zōshi: The Genesis and Transmutations of a Medieval Scatological Tale." Doctoral dissertation, Case Western Reserve University, 1994.

Umata Ayako 馬田綾子. "Chūsei Kyoto ni okeru jiin to minshū 中世京都における寺院と民衆." *Nihonshi kenkyū* 日本史研究 235 (1982): 28–48.

Ury, Marian, trans. *Tales of Times Now Past*. Berkeley and Los Angeles: University of California Press, 1979.

Usami Takayuki 宇佐見隆之. *Nihon chūsei no ryūtsū to shōgyō* 日本中世の流通と商業. Tokyo: Yoshikawa kōbunkan 吉川弘文館, 1999.

Uwayokote Masataka 上横手雅敬. "Kamakura Muromachi bakufu to chōtei" 鎌倉室町幕府と朝廷. In *Ken'i to shihai* 権威と支配. Vol. 3 of *Nihon no shakaishi* 日本の社会史, edited by Asao Naohiro 朝尾直弘, Amino Yoshihiko 網野善彦, Yamaguchi Keiji 山口啓二, and Yoshida Takashi 吉田孝, 83–118. Tokyo: Iwanami shoten 岩波書店, 1987.

———. "Sōryō sei josetsu 惣領制序説." In *Nihon chūsei kokka shi ronkō* 日本中世国家史論考, 179–201. Tokyo: Hanawa shobō 塙書房, 1994.

Uyenaka Shuzo. "A Study of Baishoron: A Source for the Ideology of Imperial Loyalism." Doctoral dissertation, University of Toronto, 1979.

Varley, H. Paul. *Imperial Restoration in Medieval Japan*. New York: Columbia University Press, 1971.

———. *The Ōnin War: History of Its Origins and Background: With a Selective Translation of* The Chronicle of Ōnin. New York: Columbia University Press, 1967.

————. *Warriors of Japan as Portrayed in the War Tales*. Honolulu: University of Hawai'i Press, 1994.

von Glahn, Richard. *Fountain of Fortune: Money and Monetary Policy in China, 1000–1700*. Berkeley, CA: University of California Press, 1996.

von Verschuer, Charlotte. *Across the Perilous Sea: Japanese Trade with China and Korea from the Seventh to the Sixteenth Centuries*. Translated by Kristen Lee Hunter. Cornell East Asia Series, vol. 133. Ithaca, NY: Cornell University East Asia Program, 2006.

————. "Across the Sea: Intercourse of People, Know-How, and Goods in East Asia." In *8–17 seiki no Higashi Ajia chiiki ni okeru hito, mono, jōhō no kōryū: kaiiki to kōshi no keisei, minzoku, chiiki kan no sōgo ninshiki o chūshin ni* 8～17世紀 の東アジア地域における人・物 ・情報の交流―海域と港市の形成, 民族 地域間の相互認識を中心に, edited by Murai Shōsuke 村井章介, 13–28. Tokyo: Tōkyō daigaku daigakuin jinbun shakai kei kenkyūka 東京大学大学院人文社会系研究科, 2004.

————. "Life of Commoners in the Provinces: The *Owari no gebumi* of 988." In *Heian Japan: Centers and Peripheries*, edited by Mikael Adolphson, Edward Kamens, and Stacie Matsumoto, 305–328. Honolulu: University of Hawai'i Press, 2007.

————. "Looking from Within and Without: Ancient and Medieval External Relations." *Monumenta Nipponica* 55, no. 4 (Winter 2000): 537–566.

Wakabayashi, Haruko. "The Mongol Invasions and the Making of the Iconography of Foreign Enemies: The Case of *Shikaumi Jinja Engi*." In *Tools of Culture: Japan's Cultural, Intellectual, Medical, and Technological Contacts in East Asia, 1000s–1500s*, edited by Andrew Edmund Goble, Kenneth R. Robinson, and Haruko Wakabayashi, 105–133. Ann Arbor: Association for Asian Studies, 2009.

Walzer, Michael. *Just and Unjust Wars: A Moral Argument with Historical Illustrations*. New York: Basic Books, 1977.

————. "Political Action: The Problem of Dirty Hands." In *War and Moral Responsibility*, edited by Marshall Cohen,

Thomas Nagel, and Thomas Scanlon, 62–84. Princeton, NJ: Princeton University Press, 1974.

Watanabe Eshin 渡辺恵進. *Gansan jie daishi no kenkyū* 元三慈恵大師の研究. Ōtsu 大津: Dōbōsha shuppan 同朋舎出版, 1984.

Watanabe Morimichi 渡辺盛道. *Sōhei seisuiki* 僧兵盛衰記. Tokyo: Sanseidō 三省堂, 1984.

Watanabe Sumio 渡辺澄夫. *Bungo Ōtomo shi no kenkyū* 豊後大友氏の研究. Tokyo: Daiichi hōki shuppan 第一法規出版, 1982.

Weik, John F. "Majima Seigan and the Myōgen-in Tradition: The Origins of Opthalmology in Japan." In *A Northern Prospect*, edited by Harold Bolitho and Alan Rix, 1–9. Sydney: Japanese Studies Association of Australia, 1981.

Wigmore, John Henry. *Law and Justice in Tokugawa Japan: Part 8B, Persons: Legal Precedents*. Tokyo: University of Tokyo Press, 1983.

Wilson, William R. "The Way of the Bow and Arrow: The Japanese Warrior in the Konjaku Monogatari." *Monumenta Nipponica* 28, no. 2 (Summer 1973): 177–233.

Yamagishi Tokuhei 山岸徳平 and Takahashi Teiichi 高橋貞一, eds. *Hōgen monogatari (Nakaraibon) to kenkyū* 半井本保元物語と研究. Toyohashi 豊橋: Mikan kokubun shiryō kankokai, 未刊国文資料刊行会, 1959.

Yamamoto Hiroya 山本博也. "Kantō mōshitsugi to Kamakura bakufu 関東申次と鎌倉幕府." *Shigaku zasshi* 史学雑誌 86, no. 8 (1977): 1–38.

Yamamoto Kōji 山本幸司. *Kegare to ōharae* 穢と大祓. Tokyo: Heibonsha 平凡社, 1992.

Yamamura, Kozo. "The Growth of Commerce in Medieval Japan." In *The Cambridge History of Japan*, vol. 3, edited by Kozo Yamamura, 344–395. Cambridge: Cambridge University Press, 1990.

Yamamura, Kozo, and Tetsuo Kamiki, "Silver Mines and Sung Coins—A Monetary History of Medieval and Modern Japan in International Perspective." In *Precious Metals in the Later Medieval and Early Modern Worlds*, edited by J. F.

Richards, 329–362. Durham, NC: Carolina Academic Press, 1983.

Yamauchi Shinji 山内晋治. *Nara Heian ki no Nihon to Ajia* 奈良平安期の日本とアジア. Tokyo: Yoshikawa kōbunkan 吉川弘文館, 2003.

———. "Nissō no shōen nai mitsubōeki setsu ni kansuru gimon jūisseki o chūshin ni 日宋の荘園内密貿易説に関する疑問11世紀を中心に." *Rekishi kagaku* 歴史科学 117 (1989): 11–24.

Yanagihara Toshiaki 柳原敏昭. "Chūsei zenki minami Kyushu no minato to Sōjin kyoryūchi 中世前期南九州の港と宋人居留地." *Nihonshi kenkyū* 日本史研究 448 (1999): 102–134.

Yasuda Motohisa 安田元久. *Jitō oyobi jitō ryōshūsei no kenkyū* 地頭及び地頭領主制の研究. Tokyo: Yamakawa shuppansha, 山川出版社, 1961.

Yiengpruksawan, Mimi. "Chinese Traders, Kyoto Aristocrats, and the Transmarine Factor in the Formation of Medieval Japanese Culture." Paper presented at *Centers and Peripheries in Heian Japan* conference, Harvard University, June 12, 2002.

Yokoi Kiyoshi 横井清. "Chūsei hito to *yamai* 中世人とやまい." In *Nihon no shakai shi, 8, seikatsu kankaku to shakai* 日本の社会史，8，生活感覚と社会, 208–231. Tokyo: Iwanami shoten 岩波書店, 1987.

———. *Chūsei minshū no seikatsu bunka* 中世民衆の生活文化. Tokyo: Tōkyō daigaku shuppankai 東京大学出版会, 1975.

———. "Chūsei minshū shi ni okeru 'raija' to 'fugu' no mondai 中世民衆史における「癩者」と「不具」の問題." In *Chūsei minshū no seikatsu bunka* 中世民衆の生活文化, 295–334. Tokyo: Tōkyō daigaku shuppankai 東京大学出版会, 1975.

———. *Mato to ena* 的と胞衣. Tokyo: Heibonsha 平凡社, 1988.

Yokoo Yutaka 横尾豊. *Kamakura jidai no kōkyū seikatsu* 鎌倉時代の後宮生活. Tokyo: Kashiwa shobō 柏書房, 1976.

Yokota Fuyuhiko. "Imagining Working Women in Early Modern Japan." In *Women and Class in Japanese History*. Edited by Hitomi Tonomura, Anne Walthall, and Wakita Haruko,

153–168. Ann Arbor, MI: University of Michigan Center for Japanese Studies, 1999.

Yokota Noriko 横田則子. "Kinsei toshi shakai to shōgaisha — misemono o megutte 近世都市社会と障害者―見世物をめぐって." In *Mibun teki shūen* 身分的周縁, edited by Tsukada Takashi 塚田孝, Yoshida Nobuyuki 吉田伸之, and Wakita Osamu 脇田修, 529–562. Tokyo: Buraku mondai kenkyūjo 部落問題研究所, 1994.

———. "*Monoyoshi* kō - kinsei Kyōto no raija ni tsuite 物吉考―近世京都の癩者に就いて," *Nihonshi kenkyū* 日本史研究 352 (1991): 1–29.

Yoshikawa Shinji 吉川真司. "Shinbun shibun kō 申文剌文考." *Nihonshi kenkyū* 日本史研究 382, no. 4 (1994): 1–35.

Zen'yaku Azuma kagami 全訳吾妻鏡. 5 vols., plus a supplementary vol. Edited by Nagahara Keiji 永原慶二 and Kishi Shōzō 貴志正造. Tokyo: Shinjinbutsu ōraisha 新人物往来社, 1976–1979.

INDEX

Page numbers in boldface type refer to illustrations.